FIFTH EDITION

STUDY GUIDE AND SELF-EXAMINATION REVIEW

FOR

KAPLAN & SADOCK'S
SYNOPSIS OF
PSYCHIATRY

SENIOR CONTRIBUTING EDITOR

ROBERT CANCRO, M.D., MED.D.Sc.

Professor and Chairman, Department of Psychiatry,
New York University School of Medicine;
Director, Department of Psychiatry, Tisch Hospital,
the University Hospital of the New York University Medical Center, New York, New York;
Director, Nathan S. Kline Institute for Psychiatric Research, Orangeburg, New York

CONTRIBUTING EDITORS

CAROLY S. PATAKI, M.D.

Assistant Director of Training and Education
of Child Psychiatry Fellowship Program,
New York University Medical Center;
Clinical Assistant Professor of Psychiatry,
New York University School of Medicine;
Chief of Child and Adolescent Psychiatry,
Lenox Hill Hospital, New York, New York

REBECCA M. JONES, M.D.

Acting Assistant Professor of Psychiatry
and Behavioral Sciences, University of Washington
School of Medicine, Seattle, Washington

FIFTH EDITION

STUDY GUIDE AND SELF-EXAMINATION REVIEW

FOR

KAPLAN & SADOCK'S
SYNOPSIS OF

PSYCHIATRY

HAROLD I. KAPLAN, M.D.

Professor of Psychiatry, New York University School of Medicine;
Attending Psychiatrist, Tisch Hospital, the University Hospital of
the New York University Medical Center;
Attending Psychiatrist, Bellevue Hospital;
Consultant Psychiatrist, Lenox Hill Hospital, New York, New York

BENJAMIN J. SADOCK, M.D.

Professor and Vice Chairman, Department of Psychiatry,
New York University School of Medicine;
Attending Psychiatrist, Tisch Hospital, the University Hospital of
the New York University Medical Center;
Attending Psychiatrist, Bellevue Hospital;
Consultant Psychiatrist, Lenox Hill Hospital, New York, New York

Williams & Wilkins

BALTIMORE • PHILADELPHIA • HONG KONG
LONDON • MUNICH • SYDNEY • TOKYO

A WAVERLY COMPANY

Editor: David C. Retford
Managing Editor: Molly L. Mullen
Designer: Norman W. Och
Illustration Planner: Lorraine Wrzosek
Production Coordinator: Barbara J. Felton

Copyright © 1994
Williams & Wilkins
428 East Preston Street
Baltimore, Maryland 21202, USA

Accurate indications, adverse reactions, and dosage schedules for drugs are provided in this book, but it is possible that they may change. The reader is urged to review the package information data of the manufacturers of the medications mentioned.

Printed in the United States of America

First edition 1983 Second edition 1985 Third edition 1989 Fourth edition 1991

Library of Congress Cataloging-in-Publication Data

Kaplan, Harold I.
    Study guide and self-examination review for Kaplan and Sadock's synopsis of psychiatry / Harold I. Kaplan, Benjamin J. Sadock ; [senior contributing editor, Robert Cancro ; contributing editors, Caroly Pataki, Rebecca Jones].—5th ed.
        p.   cm.
    Includes index.
    Rev. ed. of: Study guide and self-examination review for Synopsis of psychiatry and Comprehensive textbook of psychiatry.
    Study guide to: Kaplan and Sadock's synopsis of psychiatry / Harold I. Kaplan, Benjamin J. Sadock, Jack A. Grebb. 7th ed. © 1994.
    ISBN 0-683-04541-5
    1. Mental illness—Examinations, questions, etc.   2. Psychiatry—Examinations, questions, etc.   I. Sadock, Benjamin J.
II. Kaplan, Harold I. Study guide and self-examination review for Synopsis of psychiatry and Comprehensive textbook of psychiatry.   III. Kaplan, Harold I.   Kaplan and Sadock's synopsis of psychiatry.   IV. Title.
    [DNLM: 1. Mental Disorders—examination questions.   2. Psychiatry—examination questions. WM 100 K172s 1994 Suppl.]
RC454.K35   1994 Suppl.
616.89'0076—dc20
DNLM/DLC   94-13269
for Library of Congress   CIP

                                                        96 97 98
                                    3   4   5   6   7   8   9   10

Dedicated to our wives
Nancy Barrett Kaplan
and
Virginia Alcott Sadock
without whose help and sacrifice
this textbook would not have been possible

Preface

This is the fifth edition of *Study Guide and Self-Examination Review for Kaplan and Sadock's Synopsis of Psychiatry*. The book is keyed to the seventh edition of *Kaplan and Sadock's Synopsis of Psychiatry*.

Significant changes have been made to improve this text so that it meets the needs of medical students, psychiatrists, neurologists, and others who require a review of the behavioral sciences and clinical psychiatry.

Among the unique aspects of this edition are the following: All nosology terms follow the fourth edition of the American Psychiatric Association's *Diagnostic and Statistical Manual of Mental Disorders* (DSM-IV), published in 1994. The authors have added many new questions and have modified the questions and answers from earlier editions. The answers have been carefully researched and defined, and certain phrases have been italicized to emphasize the main idea encompassed by the question. In addition, the authors have added extensive case material derived from the *DSM-III Case Book* and the *DSM-III-R Case Book*, updated to reflect the changes in DSM-IV, published by the American Psychiatric Association and used with permission.

Because this book is a study guide, each chapter begins with an introduction that can be used as an outline and that directs students to areas of special significance used in their studying. The authors have prepared lists of helpful hints that present key terms and concepts essential to a basic knowledge of psychiatry. Students should be able to define and discuss each of the terms in depth as preparation for examinations. In their review, students should emphasize each term. We also included a new chapter, "Objective Examinations in Psychiatry." A careful reading will provide the student with helpful hints on how to take those examinations.

Study Guide forms one part of a comprehensive system developed by the authors to facilitate the teaching of psychiatry and the behavioral sciences. At the head of the system is *Comprehensive Textbook of Psychiatry*, which is global in depth and scope; it is designed for and used by psychiatrists, behavioral scientists, and all other workers in the mental health field. *Kaplan and Sadock's Synopsis* is a relatively brief, highly modified, original, and current version useful for medical students, psychiatric residents, practicing psychiatrists, and other mental health professionals. Other parts of the system are the pocket handbooks: *Pocket Handbook of Clinical Psychiatry*, *Pocket Handbook of Psychiatric Drug Treatment*, and *Pocket Handbook of Emergency Psychiatric Medicine*. Those books cover the diagnosis and the treatment of mental disorders, psychopharmacology, and psychiatric emergencies, respectively, and are compactly designed and concisely written to be carried in the pocket by clinical clerks and practicing physicians, whatever their specialty, to provide a quick reference. Finally, *Comprehensive Glossary of Psychiatry and Psychology* provides simply written definitions for psychiatrists and other physicians, psychologists, students, other mental health professionals, and the general public. Taken together, these books create a multipronged approach to the teaching, study, and learning of psychiatry.

Study Guide is especially useful for students preparing for certification examinations, such as the United States Medical Licensing Examination of the National Board of Medical Examiners and the Federation of State Medical Boards and the American Board of Psychiatry and Neurology. The questions are modeled after and are consistent with the new format used in the United States Medical Licensing Examination. It is also useful for physicians who wish to update their general psychiatric knowledge or to identify areas of weakness and of strength. The allocation of questions has been carefully weighted, with subjects of both clinical and theoretical importance taken into account.

To use this book most effectively, the student should attempt to answer all the questions in a particular chapter. By allowing about one minute for each answer, the student can approximate the time constraints of an actual examination. The answers should then be verified by referring to the corresponding answer section in each chapter. The page numbers printed in dark type indicate a major discussion of the topic in *Synopsis of Psychiatry*. The student can then refer to the appropriate pages of that book for an extensive and definitive discussion of the material.

We wish to thank Robert J. Campbell, M.D., and his publisher, Oxford University Press, for giving us permission to derive some of the definitions used in this text from his book, the sixth edition of *Psychiatric Dictionary*.

In the preparation of this edition, we have been most fortunate to enlist the assistance of our contributing editors, Rebecca Jones, M.D., Acting Assistant Professor of Psychiatry and Behavioral Sciences at the University of Washington School of Medicine, and Caroly Pataki, M.D., Assistant Director of Training and Education of the Child Psychiatry Fellowship Program and Clinical Assistant Professor of Psychiatry at New York University School of Medicine and Chief of Child and Adolescent Psychiatry at Lenox Hill Hospital. They assumed major key roles in the revision of this book and contributed immensely to its present form. Their dedication, enthusiasm, and academic and clinical skills were invaluable. The authors thank both for their incalculable contributions.

We also thank Norman Sussman, M.D., Clifford Feldman, M.D., and Jeff Landau, M.D. We especially thank Jack Grebb, M.D., who has joined us as a coauthor of *Synopsis of Psychiatry*. A distinguished clinician and scholar, Dr. Grebb helped in the conceptualization, the writing, and the implementation of every aspect of that book. We express our appreciation to Jay E. Kantor, Ph.D., Research Associate Professor of Humanities at New York University School of Medicine, for his help in the ethics section of *Kaplan and Sadock's Synopsis of Psychiatry*. We also thank our close friend Joan Welsh for her valuable help in editing this textbook. Virginia A. Sadock, M.D., Clinical Professor of Psychiatry and Director of Graduate Education in Human Sexuality at the New York University School of Medicine, also played an important role in planning and implementation. We also thank Nancy B. Kaplan, James Sadock, Victoria Sadock, Jennifer Kaplan, Peter Kaplan, M.D., and Phillip Kaplan, M.D., for their help. Justin Hollingsworth and Laura Marino played key roles in assisting us in all aspects of our work. Their prodigious efforts were extremely important.

Robert Cancro, M.D., Professor and Chairman of the Department of Psychiatry at New York University Medical Center, participated as senior contributing editor of this edition. He is also senior contributing editor of both *Synopsis of Psychiatry* and *Comprehensive Textbook of Psychiatry*. Dr. Cancro's support, encouragement, and inspiration have been of inestimable value. He is a personal friend and colleague whose collaboration has contributed immeasurably to the new ideas and directions shaping these books. He is one of America's leading psychiatrists, and it is our privilege to be associated with this outstanding clinician, researcher, and educator.

We thank Barbara Felton, Amy Evans, and our psychiatry editor, David Retford, at Williams & Wilkins for their cooperation in every aspect of this textbook. Finally, we extend our best wishes and heartfelt thanks to Sara Finnegan, who retired from Williams & Wilkins in 1994, and we welcome George Stamathis, who has replaced her as the President of the Book Division.

New York University Medical Center
New York, New York
March 1994

Harold I. Kaplan, M.D.
Benjamin J. Sadock, M.D.

Contents

The Doctor-Patient Relationship and Interviewing Techniques

Nothing is more basic than the relationship between doctor and patient in the practice of medicine, yet that relationship is often the most underemphasized aspect of medical training. Deep and long-lasting dissatisfactions about the perceived nature of the relationship have led to cynicism and frustration on the part of both patients and physicians. A rigorous, organized, and focused study of the factors that shape both productive and nonproductive relationships between physicians and patients is possible and necessary. Such a study involves the process of making concrete and teachable what has long been described as the art of medicine. To some degree, the ability to establish rapport with any patient and to manage particularly difficult patients is a product of the physician's ability to establish empathic and responsive relationships with people in general; and to some degree that ability is based on the physician's innate capacity for self-knowledge and interpersonal sensitivity.

Physicians with that innate capacity, it has been argued, are always the best and most effective caretakers, regardless of their specific training in the doctor-patient relationship. Still, basically intelligent, thoughtful students, given the rudimentary building blocks of crucial interpersonal skills, can learn to integrate specific techniques and ways of thinking that will inevitably enhance the practice of medicine. To that end, this chapter discusses in some detail the nuances of such topics as transference, countertransference, compliance, interviewing techniques, and the management of difficult patients. Students should review Chapter 1 in *Kaplan and Sadock's Synopsis VII* and then test their knowledge of the subject by studying the questions and answers provided below.

HELPFUL HINTS

The key terms listed below should be known by the student as they apply to the doctor-patient relationship and to interviewing techniques.

personality	unresolved conflicts	humor
therapeutic limitations	individual experience	listening
psychodynamics	cultural attitudes	distortion
rapport	socioeconomic background	emotionally charged statements
transference	"good patients"	misrepresentation
countertransference	aggression and counteraggression	misperception
identification	sublimation	early social pressures
empathy	unconscious guilt	emotional reactions
authority figures	defensive attitudes	biopsychosocial model
active versus passive patients	belligerent patient	illness behavior
mutual participation	overcompensatory anger	sick role
compliance versus noncompliance		

QUESTIONS

DIRECTIONS: Each of the incomplete statements below is followed by five suggested completions. Select the *one* that is *best* in each case.

1.1. The skills of active listening, which are the cornerstones of communication within the doctor-patient relationship, are the abilities of the physician to
A. comprehend the underlying meaning of the patient's spoken words while not overlooking the literal interpretation
B. formulate a differential diagnosis while taking the patient's history
C. understand both what the patient and the physician are saying and the undercurrents of unspoken feelings between the two
D. clarify what the patient relates without being paternalistic
E. evaluate the effect that transference is having on the doctor-patient relationship

1.2. At the beginning of her appointment, a patient wants to discuss her perception of why she fell ill, but the physician wants to know the chronology of her symptoms. The physician should
A. allow the patient to finish her discussion
B. politely interrupt the patient and continue with closed-ended questions
C. inform her that time is of the essence
D. inform her that an extra charge will be made if more time is needed for the appointment
E. immediately discuss how compliance will be affected by her perceptions

DIRECTIONS: Each set of lettered headings below is followed by a list of numbered statements. For each numbered statement, select the *best* lettered heading. Each heading can be used once, more than once, or not at all.

Questions 1.3–1.7
A. Active-passive model
B. Teacher-student model
C. Mutual participation model
D. Friendship model

1.3. A patient is admitted to the hospital with a sudden onset of altered mental status when he is found thrashing about in his bed. After a workup, a physician restrains him to perform a lumbar puncture.

1.4. A 64-year-old woman with diabetes mellitus visits her physician after repeatedly drawing high blood glucose levels during home monitoring.

1.5. After a patient's recovery from her illness, her physician continues to phone and visit her and declares his love for her.

1.6. Three days after abdominal surgery, a 32-year-old man has mild basal rales by auscultation. His surgeon tells him to ambulate.

1.7. The doctor of a 16-year-old girl with persistent lower abdominal complaints tells her that she must go for a lower gastrointestinal (GI) series.

Questions 1.8–1.11
A. Transference
B. Countertransference

1.8. "That patient is the worst patient I've had in years; he keeps going for second opinions."

1.9. "Doc, I've been lying here for three days; aren't you going to give me some medicine or something to make me feel better?"

1.10. "No doctor ever listens to what I have to say, and you're no exception."

1.11. "As your surgeon, just listen to me: have the operation, and I'll make you all better."

Questions 1.12–1.13
A. Content of the interview
B. Process of the interview

1.12. "Doc, I've had a sore throat for the past three days"

1.13. The patient clenches his fists each time the physician mentions heart disease

Questions 1.14–1.18
A. Sick role
B. Illness behavior

1.14. A patient's reactions to the experience of being sick

1.15. The societal attribute conveyed to a sick person

1.16. A person receives worker's compensation for pneumoconiosis

1.17. A defendant is declared incompetent to stand trial

1.18. A person with influenza stays in bed all day

Questions 1.19–1.23
A. Reflection
B. Summation
C. Compliance
D. Facilitation
E. Confrontation

1.19. The physician says, "Let me go over what you've told me so far"

1.20. The degree to which the patient carries out the physician's clinical recommendations

1.21. An empathetic response meant to reassure the patient to know that the physician is listening to the patient's concerns and understands them

1.22. Verbal and nonverbal cues that encourage the patient to keep talking

1.23. Meant to point out to a patient something that the physician thinks the patient is not paying attention to, is missing, or is in some way denying

Questions 1.24–1.28
A. Histrionic patients
B. Impulsive patients
C. Narcissistic patients
D. Malingering patients
E. Hypervigilant patients

1.24. Behave as if superior to everyone around them

1.25. Are often seductive and flirtatious

1.26. Consciously feign illness for some clear secondary gain

1.27. Have a difficult time delaying gratification

1.28. Are critical, evasive, and suspicious

DIRECTIONS: The lettered headings in the questions below are followed by a list of numbered phrases. For each numbered phrase, select

  A. if the item is associated with *A only*
  B. if the item is associated with *B only*
  C. if the item is associated with *both A and B*
  D. if the item is associated with *neither A nor B*

Questions 1.29–1.32
  A. Surgical interview
  B. Psychiatric interview
  C. Both
  D. Neither

1.29. Characterized by desire to communicate information to the patient and to implement the treatment plan

1.30. Adaptive and maladaptive coping mechanisms are seen

1.31. Physician is able to release medical records to patient's siblings

1.32. Multiple brief interventions are used

ANSWERS

The Doctor-Patient Relationship and Interviewing Techniques

1.1.   The answer is C (*Synopsis VII*, page 1).

All the responses are partially correct, but only C covers both essential parts of active listening in the doctor-patient relationship.

One of the supreme tasks of any medical training center is to help the physician acquire skills of *active listening both to what the patient and the physician are saying and to the undercurrents of unspoken feelings between the two.* A physician who is continually monitoring not only the content of the interaction (what the patient and the physician say) but also the process (what the patient or the physician may not say but conveys in a variety of other ways) is a physician who realizes that communication between two people occurs on several levels at once. A physician who is sensitive to the effects that history, culture, environment, and psychology have on the doctor-patient relationship is a physician who is working with a multifaceted patient, not a disease syndrome. When the art and the technique of active listening are not emphasized, respected, and conveyed, physicians fail to be trained in the rudiments of establishing a relationship with their patients, and patient care is the inevitable loser.

The other responses contain only part of the equation needed for active listening. The doctor needs to comprehend and interpret what the patient is saying but that is not the major first task. A *differential diagnosis* is important, but the patient should not be looked on solely as a disease entity, nor should a differential diagnosis be formulated before a complete history is taken.

Clarification is an important technique used in the interviewing process. Through clarification the physician attempts to get details from the patient about what the patient has already said. For example, the physician may say: "You're feeling depressed. When is it that you feel most depressed?" But clarification is not the physician's major task.

Transference is defined as the set of expectations, beliefs, and emotional responses that a patient brings to the doctor-patient relationship. This, too, is not the physician's major initial task, although it is an important part of understanding the patient.

1.2.   The answer is A (*Synopsis VII*, page 9).

The early part of the interview is generally the most open-ended, in that the physician allows patients to speak as much as possible in their own words by asking open-ended questions and allows them to *finish*. An example of an open-ended question is, "Can you tell me more about that?"

That type of questioning is important to establish rapport, which is the first step in an interview. In one survey of 700 patients, the patients substantially agreed that physicians do not have the time or the inclination to listen and to consider the patient's feelings, that physicians do not have enough knowledge of the emotional problems and socioeconomic background of the patient's family, and that physicians increase the patient's fear by giving explanations in technical language. Psychosocial and economic factors exert a profound influence on human relationships, so the physician should have as much understanding as possible of the patient's subculture.

Ekkehard Othmer and Sieglind Othmer defined the development of rapport as encompassing six strategies: (1) putting the patient and the interviewer at ease, (2) finding the pain and expressing compassion, (3) evaluating the patient's insight and becoming an ally, (4) showing expertise, (5) establishing authority as a physician and a therapist, and (6) balancing the roles of empathic listener, expert, and authority.

Interviewing any patient involves a fine balance between allowing the patient's story to unfold at will and obtaining the necessary data for diagnosis and treatment. Most experts on interviewing agree that the ideal interview is one in which the interviewer begins with broad open-ended questions, continues by becoming specific, and closes with detailed direct questions.

Although closed-ended questions are valuable during the interview, they are generally not used at the start of the interview. A *closed-ended* or directive question is one that asks for specific information and that does not allow the patient many options in answering. Too many closed-ended questions, especially in the early part of the interview, can lead to a restriction of the patient's responses.

If the patient states that he or she has been feeling depressed, a closed-ended question might be, "Your mother died recently, didn't she?" That question can be answered only by a "yes" or a "no," and the mother's death may or may not be the reason the patient is depressed. More information is likely to be obtained if the physician responds with, "Can you tell me more about what you're feeling and what you think may be causing your depression?" That is an open-ended question. Sometimes directive questions are necessary to obtain important data, but, if they are used too often, the patient may think that information is to be given only in response to direct questioning by the physician.

As for *time* and *charges*, physicians should inform patients about their fee policies but should not interrupt patients to state such policies. Instead, those areas of business should ideally be dealt with before the initial visit, so that an ongoing relationship with a patient can be established. The matter of fees must be openly discussed from the beginning: the physician's charges, whether the physician is willing to accept insurance company payments directly (known as assignments), the policy concerning payment for missed appointments, and whether the physician uses a sliding scale based on the patient's ability to pay. Discussing those questions and any other questions about fees at the beginning of the relationship between the physician and the patient can minimize misunderstandings later.

A discussion of compliance with a medical plan is important, but it is premature to discuss compliance early in the interview. Furthermore, *compliance*, which is the degree to which the patient carries out clinical recommendations by the treating physician, is a two-way street. Studies have shown that noncompliance is associated with physicians who are perceived as rejecting and unfriendly. Noncompliance is also associated with asking a patient for information without giving any feedback and with failing to explain a diagnosis or the cause of the presenting symptoms. A physician who is aware of the patient's belief system, feelings, and habits and who enlists the patient in establishing a treatment regimen increases compliant behavior.

1.3–1.7

1.3. The answer is A. (*Synopsis VII*, page 2).

1.4. The answer is C (*Synopsis VII*, page 2).

1.5. The answer is D (*Synopsis VII*, page 2).

1.6. The answer is B (*Synopsis VII*, page 2).

1.7. The answer is B (*Synopsis VII*, page 2).

The doctor-patient relationship has a number of potential models. Often, neither the physician nor the patient is fully conscious of choosing one or another model. The models most often derive from the personalities, expectations, and needs of both the physician and the patient. The fact that their personalities, expectations, and needs are largely unspoken and may be different for the physician and the patient may lead to miscommunication and disappointment for both participants in the relationship. The physician must be consciously aware of which model is operating with which patient and must be able to shift models, depending on the particular needs of specific patients and on the treatment requirements of specific clinical situations.

Models of the doctor-patient relationship include the active-passive model, the teacher-student (or parent-child or guidance-cooperation) model, the mutual participation model, and the friendship (or socially intimate) model.

The *active-passive model* implies the complete passivity of the patient and the taking over by the physician that necessarily results. In that model, patients assume virtually no responsibility for their own care and take no part in treatment. The model is appropriate when a patient is unconscious, immobilized, or delirious.

The sudden onset of the patient's altered mental status can be a potentially life-threatening situation. Possible causes of the suddenly altered mental status are trauma, vascular disorders, brain tumors, meningitis, encephalitis, and toxicological, metabolic, endocrine, and psychiatric disorders. For some patients with an altered mental status, a *lumbar puncture* is necessary and should be performed, as long as increased intracranial pressure, which can cause brainstem herniation, is not suspected. A computed tomographic (CT) scan or an eye examination that checks for papilledema may aid in the assessment before a lumbar puncture is performed.

The *mutual participation model* implies equality between the physician and the patient; both participants in the relationship require and depend on each other's input. The need for a doctor-patient relationship based on a model of mutual, active participation is most obvious in the treatment of such chronic illnesses as renal failure and *diabetes*, in which a patient's knowledge and acceptance of treatment procedures are critical to the success of the treatment. The model may also be effective in subtle situations—for example, in pneumonia.

The *friendship model* of the doctor-patient relationship is generally considered dysfunctional if not unethical. It is most often prompted by an underlying psychological problem in the physician, who may have an emotional need to turn the care of the patient into a relationship of mutual sharing of personal information and *love*. The model often involves a blurring of boundaries between professionalism and intimacy and an indeterminate perpetuation of the relationship, rather than an appropriate ending.

In the *teacher-student model* the physician's dominance is assumed and emphasized. The physician is paternalistic and controlling; the patient is essentially dependent and accepting. That model is often observed *after surgery* and before such diagnostic tests as a *GI series*.

1.8–1.11

1.8. The answer is B (*Synopsis VII*, page 7).

1.9. The answer is A (*Synopsis VII*, pages 6–7).

1.10. The answer is A (*Synopsis VII*, pages 6–7).

1.11. The answer is B (*Synopsis VII*, page 7).

Transference is generally defined as the set of expectations, beliefs, and emotional responses that a patient brings to the doctor-patient relationship. They are not necessarily based on who the physician is or how the physician acts in reality; rather, they are based on persistent experiences the patient has had with other important figures throughout life.

Patients' attitudes toward a physician are apt to be repetitions of their attitudes toward authority figures. A patient's attitude may range from one of realistic basic trust, with the expectation that the physician will have the patient's best interest at heart, through one of overidealization and even eroticized fantasy to one of basic mistrust, with the expectation that the physician will be contemptuous and potentially abusive. A patient may expect the physician to do something—for example, prescribe *medicine* or perform surgery—and can accept the physician's care as sufficient and competent only if those actions occur. Inherent in that attitude is the patient's role as a passive recipient in relation to the physician's role as an active bestower of help. A patient in whom those expectations are established feels uncomfortable if the physician has different expectations. Another patient may be active and expect to participate fully in treatment and, correspondingly, feels at odds with a physician who does not want patient participation and does not *listen*.

Just as patients bring transferential attitudes to the doctor-patient relationship, physicians often have countertransferential reactions to their patients. *Countertransference* may take the form of negative feelings that are disruptive to the doctor-patient relationship, but it may also encompass disproportionately positive, idealizing, or even eroticized reactions. Just as patients have expectations of physicians—for example, competence, lack of exploitation, objectivity, comfort, and relief—physicians often have unconscious or unspoken expectations of patients. Most commonly, patients are thought of as good patients if their expressed severity of symptoms correlates with an overtly diagnosable biological disorder, if they do not seek *second opinions*, if they *listen* and are generally nonchallenging about the treatment, if they are emotionally controlled, and if they are grateful. If those expectations are not met, the patient may be blamed and experienced as unlikable, unworkable, or bad.

The physician must understand such complex interpersonal factors as transference and countertransference in order to establish a genuine rapport with a patient. The failure of the physician to establish good rapport with the patient accounts for much of the ineffectiveness in care. The presence of rapport implies that understanding and trust between the physician and the patient are present. Differences in social, intellectual, and educational status can interfere seriously with rapport. Understanding or not understanding the patient's beliefs, use of language, and attitudes toward illness influences the character of the physician's examination and treatment.

1.12–1.13

1.12. The answer is A (*Synopsis VII*, pages 8–9).

1.13. The answer is B (*Synopsis VII*, pages 8–9).

The *content of an interview* is literally what is said between the physician and the patient: the topics discussed—for example, a *sore throat*. The *process of the interview* is what occurs nonverbally between the physician and the patient: what is happening in the interview beneath the verbal surface. Process involves feelings and reactions that are unacknowledged or unconscious. For example, patients may use body language to express feelings they cannot express verbally—*clenched fists* or nervous tearing at a paper tissue in the face of an apparently calm outward demeanor. Patients may shift the interview away from the anxiety-provoking subject onto a neutral topic without realizing that they are doing so. A patient may return again and again to a particular topic, regardless of what direction the interview appeared to be taking. Trivial remarks and apparently casual asides may reveal serious underlying concerns—for example, "Oh, by the way, a neighbor of mine tells me that he knows someone with the same symptoms as my son, and that person has cancer."

1.14–1.18

1.14. The answer is B (*Synopsis VII*, pages 1–2).

1.15. The answer is A (*Synopsis VII*, pages 1–2).

1.16. The answer is A (*Synopsis VII*, pages 1–2).

1.17. The answer is A (*Synopsis VII*, pages 1–2).

1.18. The answer is B (*Synopsis VII*, pages 1–2).

Illness behavior is the term used to describe a *patient's reactions to the experience of being sick*. Patients react to illness in various ways, depending on their habitual modes of thinking, feeling, and behaving. For example, one *patient with influenza may stay in bed all day*; another person with influenza may insist on going to work or may sit in a chair in front of the television set all day. Influenza is caused by a virus that annually results in significant mortality. Its symptoms are the abrupt onset of headaches, fever, chills, and myalgia accompanied by respiratory tract symptoms, particularly a cough and a sore throat.

Edward Suchman described five stages of illness behavior: (1) the symptom-experience stage, in which a decision is made that something is wrong; (2) the assumption-of-the-sick-role stage, in which a decision is made that one is sick and needs professional care; (3) the medical-care-contact stage, in which a decision is made to seek professional care; (4) the dependent-patient-role stage, in which a decision is made to transfer control to the physician and to follow the prescribed treatment; and (5) the recovery or rehabilitation stage, in which a decision is made to give up the patient role.

The *sick role* is the role that *society attributes* to sick persons because they are ill. The characteristics of the sick role include such factors as being excused from certain responsibilities and being expected to want to obtain help to get well.

Being excused from certain responsibilities is the essence of *worker's compensation*. Some patients who worked in coal mines developed black lung or pneumoconiosis. At times, that condition prevented them from working and made them eligible for compensation. Pneumoconiosis is caused by the deposition of coal dust around the bronchioles. Another example of the sick role is the declaration that a defendant is *incompetent to stand trial*. The Supreme Court of the United States has stated that the prohibition against trying someone who is mentally incompetent is fundamental to the United States system of justice. Accordingly, in *Dusky v. United States* the Court approved a test of competence that seeks to ascertain whether a criminal defendant has sufficient present ability to consult with his lawyer with a reasonable degree of rational understanding—and whether he has a rational as well as factual understanding of the proceedings against him.

1.19–1.23

1.19. The answer is B (*Synopsis VII*, page 10).

1.20. The answer is C (*Synopsis VII*, pages 11–12).

1.21. The answer is A (*Synopsis VII*, page 9).

1.22. The answer is D (*Synopsis VII*, page 9).

1.23. The answer is E (*Synopsis VII*, pages 9–10).

Many techniques are used during the interviewing process. In *summation*, the physician periodically takes a moment to briefly summarize what the patient has said thus far. Doing so assures both the patient and the physician that the information the physician has heard is the same as what the patient has actually said. For example, the physician may say, "*Let me go over what you've told me so far.*"

Compliance, also known as adherence, is *the degree to which a patient carries out the physician's clinical recommendations.* Examples of compliance include keeping appointments, entering into and completing a treatment program, taking medications correctly, and following recommended changes in behavior or diet. Compliance behavior depends on the specific clinical situation, the nature of the illness, and the treatment program. In general, about one third of all patients comply with the treatment regimen, one third sometimes comply with certain aspects of treatment, and one third never comply with the treatment regimen. An overall figure assessed from a number of studies indicates that 54 percent of patients comply with the treatment regimen at any given time. One study found that up to 50 percent of hypertensive patients do not follow up at all with the treatment regimen and that 50 percent of those who do follow the regimen leave treatment within one year.

In the technique of *reflection*, the physician repeats to the patient in a supportive manner something that the patient has said. The purpose of reflection is twofold: to make sure that the physician has correctly understood what the patient is trying to say and to let the patient know that the physician is listening to what is being said. It is *an empathic response meant to reassure the patient that the physician is listening to the patient's concerns and understands them.* For example, if the patient is speaking about fears of dying and the effects of talking about those fears with the family, the physician may say, "It seems that you're concerned about becoming a burden to your family." That reflection is not an exact repetition of what the patient said but, rather, a paraphrase that indicates that the physician has perceived what the patient was trying to say.

In *facilitation* the physician helps the patient continue by providing both *verbal and nonverbal cues that encourage the patient to keep talking.* Nodding one's head, leaning forward in one's seat and saying, "Yes, and then . . ." or "Uh-huh, go on" are all examples of facilitation.

The technique of *confrontation* is meant to point out to a patient something that the physician thinks the patient is not paying attention to, is missing, or is in some way denying. Confrontation must be done in a skillful way, so that the patient is not forced to become hostile and defensive. The confrontation is meant to help the patient face whatever needs to be faced in a direct but respectful way. For example, the physician may confront the patient with the need to lose weight. Or a patient who has just made a suicidal gesture but is telling the physician that it was not serious may be confronted with the statement, "What you have done may not have killed you, but it's telling me that you are in serious trouble right now and that you need help so that you don't try suicide again."

1.24–1.28

1.24. The answer is C (*Synopsis VII*, pages 13–14).

1.25. The answer is A (*Synopsis VII*, page 13).

1.26. The answer is D (*Synopsis VII*, page 14).

1.27. The answer is B (*Synopsis VII*, page 13).

1.28. The answer is E (*Synopsis VII*, page 14).

Some patients create undue stress if they are not treated effectively. Inherent in the treatment of all such patients is the physician's understanding of the covert emotions, fears, and conflicts that the patient's overt behavior represents. An appropriate understanding of what is hidden behind a particular patient's difficult behavior can lead the physician away from responding with anger, contempt, or anxiety and toward responding with helpful interventions.

Narcissistic patients act as though they were *superior to everyone around them*, including the physician. They have a tremendous need to appear perfect and are contemptuous of others, whom they perceive to be imperfect. They may be rude, abrupt, arrogant, or demeaning. They may initially overidealize the physician in their need to have their physician be as perfect as they are, but the overidealization may quickly turn to disdain when they discover that the physician is human. Underneath their surface arrogance, narcissistic patients often feel inadequate, helpless, and empty, and they fear that others will see through them.

Histrionic patients are often *seductive and flirtatious* with physicians out of an unconscious need for reassurance that they are still attractive, even if ill, and out of fear that they will not be taken seriously unless they are found to be sexually desirable. They often appear overly emotional and intimate in their interactions with physicians. The physician needs to be calm, reassuring, firm, and nonflirtatious. The patients do not really want to seduce the physician, but they may not know any other way to get what they feel they need.

Sociopathic patients are often *malingering patients*. They *consciously feign illness for some clear secondary gain* (for example, to obtain drugs, to get a bed for the night, or to hide out from people pursuing them). Obviously, they sometimes do get sick, just as nonsociopathic people do; when they are sick, they need to be cared for in the same ways that others are cared for. The physician must treat them with respect but with a heightened sense of vigilance.

Sociopathic patients are those described in psychiatric terminology as having antisocial personality disorder; they do not appear to experience appropriate guilt and, in fact, may not even be consciously aware of what it means to be guilty. On the surface they may appear charming, socially adept, and intelligent, but they have over many years perfected the behavior they know to be appropriate, and they perform almost as an actor would. They often have histories of criminal acts, and they get by in the world through lying and manipulation. They are often self-destructive, harming not only others but themselves, in perhaps an unacknowledged expression of self-punishment.

Impulsive patients have a difficult time delaying gratification and may demand that their discomfort be eliminated immediately. They are easily frustrated and may become petulant or even angry and aggressive if they do not get what they want as soon as they want it. The patients may impulsively do something self-destructive if they feel thwarted by their physician and may appear manipulative and attention seeking. They may fear that they will never get what they need from others and, thus, must act in an inappropriately aggressive way. They can be particularly difficult patients for any physician to treat; the physician must set firm, nonangry limits at the outset, defining clearly acceptable and unac-

ceptable behavior. The patients must be treated with respect and care but must be held responsible for their actions.

Hypervigilant patients are often paranoid patients who fear that people want to hurt them and are out to do them harm. The patients may misperceive cues in their environment to the degree that they see conspiracies in neutral events. They *are critical, evasive, and suspicious*. They are often called grievance seekers, because they tend to blame others for everything bad that happens in their lives. They are extremely mistrustful and may question everything that the physician says needs to be done. The physician must remain somewhat formal, albeit always respectful and courteous, as expressions of warmth and empathy are often viewed with suspicion ("what does he want from me?"). As with obsessive patients, the physician should be prepared to explain in detail every decision and planned procedure and should react nondefensively to the patients' suspicions.

1.29–1.32

1.29. **The answer is C** (*Synopsis VII*, page 4).

1.30. **The answer is C** (*Synopsis VII*, page 4).

1.31. **The answer is D** (*Synopsis VII*, page 4).

1.32. **The answer is B** (*Synopsis VII*, page 4).

A *psychiatric interview* and a *surgical interview* have many similarities and a few differences. Mack Lipkin, Jr., described three functions of the medical interview: (1) to assess the nature of the problem, (2) to develop and maintain a therapeutic relationship, and (3) to *communicate information and implement a treatment plan*. Those functions are exactly the same in *both* psychiatric and surgical interviews. Also found in *both* interviews are the predominant *coping mechanisms, both adaptive and maladaptive*. Those mechanisms include such reactions as anxiety, depression, regression, denial, anger, and dependence. Those reactions must be anticipated, recognized, and addressed by every physician if any treatment or intervention is to be effective. Many psychiatric problems present as medical illnesses; conversely, many medical and surgical problems present with psychiatric symptoms. For that reason alone, all physicians must recognize the importance of obtaining a comprehensive biopsychosocial history for each patient.

As for *releasing medical records, neither* a psychiatrist nor any other physician may ever release a patient's records to other family members unless the patient gives explicit permission. However, as much as one must legally and ethically respect a patient's confidentiality, in some situations confidentiality may be either partially or wholly broken. For instance, if a patient makes clear that he or she intends to violently harm another person, the physician has a legal responsibility to warn the intended victim.

One difference between a psychiatric interview and a surgical interview is that the psychiatric patient may not be able to tolerate a traditional interview format, especially in the acute stages of a disorder. For instance, a psychiatric patient suffering from increased agitation, paranoia, or depression may not be able to sit for 30 to 45 minutes of discussion or questioning. In that case the physician must be prepared to conduct *multiple brief interventions* over a period of time—sitting or standing with the patient for as long as the patient is able, then stopping and returning when the patient appears to be able to tolerate more.

Other differences include the fact that a psychiatric patient must often contend with stresses and pressures different from those suffered by the patient who does not have a psychiatric disorder. Those stresses include the stigma attached to being a psychiatric patient (it is more acceptable to have a medical or surgical problem than to have a mental problem), difficulties in communicating because of a disorder in thinking (for example, delusions, hallucinations, or a disorganized thought process), oddities of behavior, and impairments of insight and judgment that make compliance with treatment particularly difficult. Because psychiatric patients often find it difficult to describe what is going on, the physician must be prepared to obtain information from other sources. Family members, friends, and the patient's spouse can provide critical pieces of information—such as the patient's past psychiatric history, responses to medication, and precipitating stresses—that the patient may not be able to provide.

Human Development Throughout the Life Cycle

A map to an understanding of a person's current functioning is embedded in that person's developmental history. If one believes, as do virtually all developmental theorists, that each successive development phase in a person's life is built on the foundation of the preceding phase, one can begin to understand the effects of a solid and stable foundation on the shaping of adult character and behavior.

Human development can be viewed from many perspectives; when combined, they provide an intricate, three-dimensional overview of physical, intellectual, and psychological evolution. The theorists presented in Chapter 2 in *Synopsis VII* described development from varying perspectives. Arnold Gesell and Stella Chess focused on the relation of the child's developing motor-sensory capacities to the associated personal-social behavior. Jean Piaget emphasized the evolution of intellectual functioning; each gain in cognitive ability translates into a developmental step forward in the child's ability to think and reason clearly. Margaret Mahler emphasized the development of the capacity for stable relationships with other people; she based her concept on the necessary steps involved in the integration of object constancy and the resolution of a process of separation and individuation. Sigmund Freud devoted his investigation of development to that of psychosexual maturation and its effects on

fantasy, conflict, and self-esteem. Erik Erikson focused on the psychosocial aspects of development; he correlated his observations of the characteristic crises generated by the confrontation with social expectations and influences with Freud's underlying concepts of psychosexual maturational crises occurring at the same times. Many recent developmental theorists have elaborated on and enriched the seminal understanding of development provided by those pioneering theorists.

Understanding developmental theory is essential to the full understanding of both normal and pathological functioning. Investigating how development proceeds along a relatively uneventful path and the ways in which it can go awry provides clinically useful information about patients' current behavior and relationships. Physicians equipped with a solid developmental understanding of their patients are most likely to have a firm, effective grasp of difficult, apparently irrational behavior (for example, the personality disorders). An appreciation of early structural deficits in any dimension of development (motor-neurological, cognitive, sexual, social, relational) provides an appreciation of deficits in the patient's current functioning.

Reviewing Chapter 2 in *Kaplan and Sadock's Synopsis VII* and then studying the questions and answers below will provide useful knowledge of the subject.

HELPFUL HINTS

The student should be aware of the following theories, theorists, and developmental stages as they relate to human development throughout the life cycle.

life cycle
epigenetic principle
oral, anal, phallic, and latency
    phases
Karl Abraham
Melanie Klein
Carl Jung
Jean Piaget
characteristics of thought
    sensorimotor phase (object
        permanence)
    preoperational phase
    concrete operations
    formal operations
Daniel Levinson
George Vaillant
concepts of normality as health,
    utopia, average, and process;
    psychoanalytic concepts
Heinz Hartmann
autonomous ego functions
Anna Freud
Daniel Offer
Thomas Szasz
social and community psychiatry
Alexander Leighton
Roy Grinker
pregnancy and childbirth
postpartum mood disorders and
    psychosis
pregnancy and marriage
Madonna complex
family size
inborn errors of metabolism
fetal development
genetic counseling: principles and
    conditions
prenatal diagnosis
drug effects and hazards
perinatal complications
maternal behavior
feeding and infant care
maternal neglect
failure to thrive
neural organization of infancy
ethology
imprinting
Harry Harlow
surrogate mother
John Bowlby
bonding
attachment
René Spitz
social deprivation syndromes
    (anaclitic depression-hospitalism)

fathers and attachment
temperament
parental fit
spacing of children
birth order
Arnold Gesell
developmental landmarks
Harry Stack Sullivan
Erik Erikson: eight psychosocial
    stages
Margaret Mahler: infant-
    developmental stages
normal autistic and normal
    symbiotic phases
smiling
negativism
toilet training
anal personality
gender identity
sibling rivalry
play and pretend
imaginary companions
egocentrism
Oedipus complex
castration anxiety
Electra complex
superego
ego ideal
penis envy
identification
school adjustment, behavior,
    refusal
learning problems
psychosexual moratorium
socially decisive stage
dreams in children
language development
imagery and drawings
somnambulism
effects of divorce
stepparents and siblings
foster parents
adoption
puberty
primary and secondary sex
    characteristics
Masters and Johnson
masturbation
cults
peer group
formal operations and morality
menarche
body image
crushes
adolescent homosexuality

dependence
identity
religious behavior
normative crisis
reactions to authority
intimacy
generativity
integrity
gender expectations
dual-career families
vocation and unemployment
core identity
racism, prejudice
mutuality
separation-individuation process
    differentiation
    practicing
    rapprochement
    consolidation (object constancy)
stranger and separation anxiety
oppositionalism
age 30 transition
parenthood
middle age
mid-life crisis
climacterium
vasomotor instability
empty-nest syndrome
marriage
divorce
remarriage
separation
alimony
spouse and child abuse
single-parent home
parental-right doctrine
custody
adultery
geriatric period
biological landmarks of aging
average life expectancy
sex in the aged
age-related cell changes
retirement
senility
cognitive decline
handicaps
pseudodementia
suicide in the aged
thanatology
Elisabeth Kübler-Ross
pain management
DNR
living wills
brain dead

death and children	John Bowlby's stages of	self-blame, worthlessness
sibling and parental death	bereavement	*Mourning and Melancholia*
grief	affectional bond	uncomplicated bereavement
mourning	bereavement in children	hospice
bereavement	delayed, inhibited, and denied grief	Dame Cicely Saunders
survivor guilt	anticipatory grief	burnout
linkage objects	grief versus depression	

QUESTIONS

DIRECTIONS: Each of the statements or questions below is followed by five suggested responses or completions. Select the *one* that is *best* in each case.

2.1. Infancy is said to end when a child is able to
A. creep
B. stand without assistance
C. control his or her anal sphincter completely
D. climb stairs
E. speak

2.2. In an infant, social smiling is elicited preferentially by the mother at age
A. under 4 weeks
B. 4 to 8 weeks
C. 8 to 12 weeks
D. 3 to 4 months
E. more than 4 months

2.3. The main characteristic of Margaret Mahler's differentiation subphase is
A. separation anxiety
B. stranger anxiety
C. rapprochement
D. castration anxiety
E. none of the above

2.4. During pregnancy, sexual behavior may change because of
A. physiological changes in the woman
B. psychological factors in the woman
C. psychological factors in the man
D. fear, on the part of either partner, of harming the developing fetus
E. all the above

2.5. During pregnancy
A. maternal deaths have resulted from forcibly blowing air into the vagina during cunnilingus.
B. sexual intercourse is prohibited by most obstetricians
C. if the husband has an extramarital affair, it is usually in the first trimester of his wife's pregnancy
D. psychological attachment to the fetus in utero rarely develops
E. 75 percent of Native American mothers do not receive prenatal care during their first trimester

2.6. Pseudocyesis
A. is a presumptive sign of pregnancy seen in the first trimester
B. is a synonym for couvade
C. is a condition in which the patient has signs and symptoms of pregnancy but in reality is not pregnant
D. is associated with chronic, persistent, and frequent vomiting that leads to ketoacidosis, weight loss, and dehydration
E. is the repeated ingestion of nonnutritious substances

2.7. Statistics show that
A. 80 percent of all medical expenses incurred by the aged are covered by Medicare
B. of those persons who voluntarily retire, very few reenter the work force within the next two years
C. most nursing home care costs are covered by Medicare
D. 75 percent of the aged have incomes below $10,000
E. fewer than 40 percent of men over 60 are still sexually active

2.8. A person who is dying
A. should rarely have narcotics liberally dispensed
B. is legally allowed in some states to request a physician-assisted death
C. may have hospice care covered by Medicare if the patient's physician states that the patient has a life expectancy of six months or less
D. follows a fixed sequence of responses toward the impending death
E. may have a major depressive disorder, which is considered a normal reaction under the circumstances

2.9. Infants are born with
A. the Moro reflex
B. the Rooting reflex
C. the Babinski reflex
D. Endogenous smiling
E. all the above

2.10. An infant can differentiate
A. sweet-tasting sugar
B. the sour taste of lemon
C. the smell of bananas
D. the smell of rotten eggs
E. all the above

2.11. Normal adolescence is marked by
A. episodes of depression
B. occasional delinquent acts
C. the dissolution of intense ties to parents
D. vulnerability to crisis
E. all the above

2.12. The defense mechanisms used by the average 50-year-old man or woman include all the following *except*
A. dissociation
B. repression
C. sublimation
D. altruism
E. splitting

2.13. The percentage of people between the ages of 65 and 85 living in nursing homes is
A. 5 percent
B. 10 percent
C. 15 percent
D. 20 percent
E. more than 25 percent

2.14. A child is generally able to conceptualize the true meaning of death by age
A. 3 years
B. 5 years
C. 7 years
D. 10 years
E. 13 years

2.15. Patients, on being told that they have a fatal illness, may respond with
A. denial
B. anger
C. bargaining
D. depression
E. all the above

DIRECTIONS: Each group of questions below consists of five lettered headings followed by a list of numbered words or statements. For each numbered word or statement, select the *one* lettered heading that is most closely associated with it. Each lettered heading may be selected once, more than once, or not at all.

Questions 2.16–2.20
A. 4 weeks
B. 16 weeks
C. 28 weeks
D. 40 weeks
E. 12 months

2.16. Grasping and manipulation

2.17. Ocular control

2.18. Verbalization of two or more words

2.19. Standing with slight support

2.20. Sitting alone

Questions 2.21–2.25
A. Sigmund Freud
B. Carl Gustav Jung
C. Harry Stack Sullivan
D. Jean Piaget
E. George Vaillant

2.21. Human development is largely shaped by social interactions, the quality of which influences the personality

2.22. Cognitive development in childhood occurs in successive stages

2.23. Childhood phases of development correspond to successive shifts in the investment of sexual energy to specific areas of the body

2.24. Individuation is the growth and the expansion of personality that occur through realizing and learning what one intrinsically is

2.25. Defense mechanisms mature over the years, and maturation depends more on development from within than on changes in the interpersonal environment

Questions 2.26–2.30
    A. Distress
    B. Shame
    C. Anger
    D. Sadness
    E. Guilt

2.26. Birth

2.27. 3 to 4 months

2.28. 8 to 9 months

2.29. 12 to 18 months

2.30. 3 to 4 years

Questions 2.31–2.35
    A. 18 months
    B. 2 years
    C. 3 years
    D. 4 years
    E. 6 years

2.31. Copies a triangle

2.32. Copies a cross

2.33. Walks up stairs with one hand held

2.34. Puts on shoes

2.35. Refers to self by name

Questions 2.36–2.40
    A. Birth to 6 months
    B. 7 to 11 months
    C. 12 to 18 months
    D. 54 months on
    E. None of the above

2.36. Plays at making sounds and babbles

2.37. Plays language games (pat-a-cake, peekaboo)

2.38. Understands up to 150 words and uses up to 20 words

2.39. Speech is 100 percent intelligible

2.40. Uses language to tell stories and share ideas

DIRECTIONS: The lettered headings below are followed by a list of numbered phrases. For each numbered phrase, select

    A. if the item is associated with *A only*
    B. if the item is associated with *B only*
    C. if the item is associated with *both A and B*
    D. if the item is associated with *neither A nor B*

Questions 2.41–2.44
    A. Normal grief
    B. Major depressive disorder
    C. Both
    D. Neither

2.41. Marked preoccupation with worthlessness

2.42. Psychomotor retardation or agitation

2.43. Weight loss

2.44. Suicide attempts

ANSWERS

Human Development Throughout the Life Cycle

2.1. The answer is D (*Synopsis VII*, pages 40–45).

Infancy is considered to end when the child is able to *speak*. It is the period from birth until about 18 months of age. During the first month of life, the infant is termed a neonate or newborn. The child *creeps* at 40 weeks, *stands without assistance* at 52 weeks, develops meaningful speech and language at 15 months, *climbs stairs* at 2 years, and *controls his or her anal sphincter completely* at 3 years. There are variations in these figures among children.

2.2. The answer is B (*Synopsis VII*, pages 37–38).

Arnold Gesell, a developmental psychologist and physician, described developmental schedules that outline the qualitative sequence of motor, adaptive, language, and personal-social behavior of the child from the age of 4 weeks to 6 years. Gesell's approach is normative; he viewed development as the unfolding of a genetically determined sequence. According to his schedules, at birth, all infants have a repertoire of reflex behaviors—breathing, crying, and swallowing. By 1 to 2 weeks of age, the infant smiles. The response is endogenously determined, as evidenced by smiling in blind infants. By 2 to 4 weeks of age, visual fixation and following are evident. By *4 to 8 weeks*, social smiling is elicited preferentially by the face or the voice of the caretaker.

2.3. The answer is B (*Synopsis VII*, pages 20–24 and 43–44).

Margaret S. Mahler (1897–1985) was a Hungarian-born psychoanalyst who practiced in the United States and who studied early childhood object relations. She described the separation-individuation process, resulting in a person's subjective sense of separateness and the development of an inner object constancy. The separation-individuation phase of development begins in the fourth or fifth month of life and is completed by the age of 3 years.

As described by Mahler, the characteristic anxiety during the differentiation subphase of separation-individuation is *stranger anxiety*. The infant has begun to develop an alert sensorium and has begun to compare what is and what is not mother. The subphase occurs between 5 and 10 months of age. A fear of strangers is first noted in infants at 26 weeks of age but does not fully develop until about 8 months. Unlike babies exposed to a variety of caretakers, babies who have only one caretaker are likely to have stranger anxiety. But, unlike stranger anxiety, which can occur even when the infant is in its mother's arms, *separation anxiety*—which is seen between 10 and 16 months, during the practicing subphase—is precipitated by the separation from the person to whom the infant is attached. The practicing subphase marks the beginning of upright locomotion, which gives the child a new perspective and a mood of elation, the "love affair with the world." The infant learns to separate as it begins to crawl and to move away from its mother but continues to look back and to return frequently to its mother as home base. Between the ages of 16 and 24 months, the *rapprochement* subphase occurs, with the characteristic event being the rapprochement crisis, during which the infant's struggle becomes one between wanting to be soothed by its mother and not wanting to accept her help. The symbol of rapprochement is the child standing on the threshold of a door in helpless frustration, not knowing which way to turn. *Castration anxiety*, as described by Sigmund Freud, is a characteristic anxiety that arises during the oedipal phase of development, ages 3 to 5 years, concerning a fantasized loss or an injury to the genitalia.

2.4. The answer is E (all) (*Synopsis VII*, pages 25–26).

During pregnancy, a couple's sexual activity may increase or decrease. *Physiological changes in the woman*, including pelvic vasocongestion, help some women become more sexually responsive than before pregnancy, but symptoms such as nausea, vomiting, and fatigue lead some women to less frequent sexual activity.

Psychological factors in the woman and *psychological factors in the man* may affect sexual behavior. Women may exhibit increased interest in sex because of the resolution of their ambivalent feelings regarding birth control or because of their subjective sense of being attractive while pregnant. Alternatively, a woman may associate pregnancy as an asexual period, or she may feel unattractive because of the changes in her body proportions.

Psychological factors similarly affect men. Some men find their pregnant partners attractive; others find their partners ugly or become fearful of defiling a pregnant woman. The Madonna complex is exhibited by some men who view the pregnant woman as sacred.

Fear, on the part of either partner, of harming the developing fetus is common and may be due to misinformation. The physician can reassure the couple that most obstetricians advise the couple to abstain from sex only in the last four to six weeks of pregnancy.

2.5.   The answer is A (*Synopsis VII*, page 26).

During pregnancy, *maternal deaths have resulting from forcibly blowing air into the vagina during cunnilingus*. Presumably, air emboli entered the placental-maternal circulation. Cunnilingus should be interdicted during pregnancy.

However, *sexual intercourse is not prohibited by most obstetricians*. Some suggest that sexual intercourse cease four to five weeks antepartum. If bleeding occurs early in pregnancy, it is usually, although not invariably, followed by a spontaneous abortion. In those cases the obstetrician prohibits coitus on a temporary basis as a therapeutic measure.

Some couples, on their own, stop having sexual intercourse during pregnancy. Either the man or the woman may erroneously regard intercourse as potentially harmful to the developing fetus and as something to be avoided for that reason.

If *the husband has an extramarital affair, it usually occurs during the last trimester, not the first* trimester, of his wife's pregnancy.

Psychological attachment to the fetus begins in utero; by the beginning of the second trimester, most women have a mental picture of the infant. The fetus is viewed as a separate being, even before being born, and is endowed with a prenatal personality. According to psychoanalytic theorists, the child-to-be is a blank screen on which the mother projects her hopes and fears. In rare instances those projections account for postpartum pathological states, such as the mother's wanting to harm the infant, who is viewed as a hated part of herself. Normally, however, giving birth to a child fulfills a woman's basic need to create and nurture life.

Prenatal care should begin before conception, so that the prospective mother's health can be assessed. The mother can be examined to ensure fetal health and survival, and information about the use of substances (including the interdiction of alcohol, tobacco, and coffee), exercise, and diet can be provided. Mothers who are under stress have a greater than usual risk of miscarriage, premature birth, and other complications. The risk of postpartum depression is increased if there is a history of depression in the mother or her family or if the mother had a previous postpartum psychiatric illness.

According to the U.S. Department of Health and Human Services, 21 percent of white mothers, 39.6 percent of black mothers, 40.5 percent of Hispanic mothers, and *42.1 percent, not 75 percent, of Native American mothers, receive no prenatal care during the first trimester*. Mexican Americans, Native Americans, Alaskan natives, and African Americans are the four ethnic groups who are least likely to receive prenatal care.

2.6.   The answer is C (*Synopsis VII*, page 27).

Pseudocyesis is a rare condition in which a patient *who is not pregnant has the signs and symptoms of pregnancy*—such as abdominal distention, breast enlargement, pigmentation, cessation of menses, and morning sickness. Pseudocyesis was first reported by Hippocrates; Mary Tudor, queen of England (1516–1558), allegedly had two episodes of pseudocyesis; and Sigmund Freud's patient Anna O. also suffered from pseudocyesis.

Pseudocyesis can occur at any age, and it has been reported in men, as well as in women. Male pseudocyesis is different from *couvade*, which occurs in some primitive cultures; in couvade, the father takes to his bed during or shortly after the birth of his child, as though he himself had given birth to the child.

The incidence of pseudocyesis has decreased over the past 50 years. It may be viewed as a somatoform disorder related to conversion disorder. Unconscious mechanisms may include the restitution of a lost object or conflicts over gender role and generativity. The term "somatic compliance" is used to indicate that the body undergoes genuine physiological changes in response to unconscious needs and conflicts.

Thus, pseudocyesis is not *a presumptive sign of pregnancy seen in the first trimester*, although patients with pseudocyesis may have presumptive signs of pregnancy. The first presumptive sign of pregnancy is the absence of menses for one week. Other presumptive signs are breast engorgement and tenderness, changes in breast size and shape, nausea with or without vomiting (morning sickness), frequent urination, and fatigue.

Some patients during pregnancy may exhibit hyperemesis gravidarum, *vomiting that is chronic, persistent, and frequent and that leads to ketoacidosis, weight loss, and dehydration*. Maternal or fetal death may ensue. The cause is unknown. Preexisting hepatorenal disease may predispose to the condition. Women with a history of anorexia nervosa or bulimia nervosa may be at risk.

In some subcultures, most notably among African-American women in the rural South, pica is seen in many pregnant women. Pica *is the repeated ingestion of nonnutritious substances*, such as dirt, clay, starch, sand, and feces.

2.7.   The answer is D (*Synopsis VII*, page 72).

The economics of old age is of paramount importance to the aged themselves and to the society at large. In the United States about *75 percent of the aged have incomes below $10,000*, and only about 10 percent have incomes above $20,000. About 3.5 million persons over age 65 live below the poverty line. Those over age 85 have the lowest incomes. Women make up the largest single group of the elderly poor and are twice as likely as men to be poor. Black elderly women over 65 are five times more likely to be poor than are white elderly women.

Medicare (Title 18) provides both hospital and medical insurance for those over age 65. About 150 million bills are reimbursed under the Medicare program each year, but only about *40 (not 80) percent of all medical expenses incurred by the aged are covered by Medicare.* The rest is paid by private insurance, state insurance, or personal funds. Some services—such as outpatient psychiatric treatment, skilled nursing care, physical rehabilitation, and preventive physical examinations—are covered minimally or not at all.

Many aged patients who are infirm require institutional care. Although only 5 percent of the aged are institutionalized in nursing homes at any one time, about 35 percent of the aged require care in a long-term facility at some time during their lives. Elderly nursing home residents are mainly widowed women, and about 50 percent are over age 85. *Nursing home care costs are not covered by Medicare,* and they range from $20,000 to $40,000 a year. About 20,000 long-term nursing care institutions are available in the United States—not enough to meet the need.

As for retirement, many elderly persons view it as a time for the pursuit of leisure and for freedom from the responsibility of previous working commitments. For others, it is a time of stress, especially if retirement results in economic problems or a loss of self-esteem. Ideally, employment after age 65 should be a matter of choice. With the passage of the Age Discrimination in Employment Act of 1967 and its amendments, forced retirement at age 70 has been virtually eliminated in the private sector, and it is not legal in federal employment. *Of those persons who voluntarily retire, a majority, not very few, reenter the work force within two years.* They do so for a variety of reasons—negative reactions to being retired, feelings of being unproductive, economic hardship, and loneliness.

Far more than 40 percent of men over 60 are still sexually active. In fact, an estimated 70 percent of men and 20 percent of women over age 60 are sexually active. Sexual activity is usually limited by the absence of an available partner. Longitudinal studies have found that the sex drive does not decrease as men and women age; some report an increase in sex drive. William Masters and Virginia Johnson reported sexual functioning of persons in their 80s.

2.8. The answer is C (*Synopsis VII*, page 85).

A person who is dying *may have hospice care covered by Medicare* if the patient's physician states that the patient has a life expectancy of six months or less. In one study by C. M. Parkes, however, predictions concerning the length of survival for patients referred to a hospice did not correlate with the actual length of survival. Physicians were able to state only that patients with incurable cancer would die within a relatively short time and could not be more precise than that. Unfortunately, current federal regulations do not provide for financing hospital care once federally sponsored hospice care has begun; thus, a patient who enters a hospice will not be insured on reentry to a hospital if the need arises.

Other factors need to be considered in caring for the dying patient. Pain management should be vigorous in the terminally ill. A dying patient needs to function as effectively as possible. Doing so is made relatively easy when the patient is free of pain. The physician should use *narcotics as liberally as they are needed and tolerated,* so that the patient can attend to any business with a minimum of discomfort. The risk of dependence on narcotics used for pain management is minimal.

Currently, *no laws in any state explicitly allow physician-assisted death.* Some states, such as Michigan, have passed laws strictly forbidding euthanasia in response to the actions of Jack Kevorkian, a doctor who has openly participated in euthanasia. The ethical and legal issues surrounding active and passive deprivation of life in severely ill patients are controversial. *Euthanasia,* the act of killing a hopelessly ill or injured person for reasons of mercy, may take one of two forms, either direct (active) or indirect (passive). Either form may be voluntary or nonvoluntary. In view of the technological advances that prolong life, coupled with limitations on resources required to sustain human life of acceptable quality, society will probably move increasingly in the direction of designing a legal framework within which euthanasia can be clarified.

A number of researchers have studied reactions to death. One of the earliest and most useful organizations of reactions to impending death came from the psychiatrist and thanatologist Elisabeth Kübler-Ross. Seldom does any dying patient *follow a fixed sequence of responses* that can be clearly identified; no established sequence is applicable to all patients. However, the following five stages proposed by Kübler-Ross are widely encountered: stage 1, shock and denial; stage 2, anger; stage 3, bargaining; stage 4, depression; and stage 5, acceptance.

In the fourth stage, patients show clinical signs of depression—withdrawal, psychomotor retardation, sleep disturbances, hopelessness, and, possibly, suicidal ideation. The depression may be a reaction to the effects of the illness on their lives (for example, the loss of jobs, economic hardship, helplessness, hopelessness, and isolation from friends and family), or it may be in anticipation of the loss of life that will eventually occur. If a major depressive disorder with vegetative signs and suicidal ideation develops, treatment with antidepressant medication or electroconvulsive therapy (ECT) may be indicated. All persons feel some degree of sadness at the prospect of their own deaths, and normal sadness does not require biological intervention. However, *major depressive disorder is not a normal reaction* to impending death. A person who suffers from major depressive disorder may be unable to sustain hope. Hope can alter longevity and can enhance the dignity and the quality of the patient's life.

2.9. The answer is E (all) (*Synopsis VII*, pages 38 and 40).

Infants are born with a number of reflexes, many of which were once needed for survival. Experts assume that the genes carry messages for those reflexes. Among the reflexes are the *Moro reflex*, flexion of the extremities when startled; the *rooting reflex*, turning toward the touch when the cheek is stroked; and the *Babinski reflex*, spreading of the toes with an upgoing big toe when the sole of the foot is stroked.

Infants are also born with the innate reflex pattern, *endogenous smiling*, which is unintentional and is unrelated to outside stimuli.

2.10. The answer is E (all) (*Synopsis VII*, pages 40–43).

Infants are able to differentiate among various sensations. Babies as young as 12 hours old gurgle with satisfaction when *sweet-tasting sugar* water is placed on the tongue, and they grimace at *the sour taste of lemon* juice. Infants smile at *the smell of bananas* and protest at *the smell of rotten eggs*. At 8 weeks of age, they can differentiate between the shapes of objects and colors. Stereoscopic vision begins to develop at 3 months of age.

2.11. The answer is E (all) (*Synopsis VII*, pages 53–56).

Early adolescence (12 to 15 years) is marked by increased anxiety and *episodes of depression*, acting-out behavior, and *occasional delinquent acts*. Teenagers, for example, obtain about 300,000 legal abortions and give birth to about 600,000 babies each year. They have a diminution in sustained interest and creativity; there is also *a dissolution of intense ties* to siblings, parents, and parental surrogates. Middle adolescence (14 to 18 years) is marked by efforts to master simple issues concerned with object relationships. The late adolescent phase (17 to 21 years), which is marked by the resolution of the separation-individuation tasks of adolescence, is characterized by *vulnerability to crisis*, particularly with respect to personal identity.

If adolescence does not proceed normally, the teenager may have an identity problem, which is characterized by a chaotic sense of self and a loss of the sense of personal sameness, usually involving a social role conflict as perceived by the person. Such conflict occurs when adolescents feel unwilling or unable to accept or adopt the roles they believe are expected of them by society. The identity problem is often manifested by isolation, withdrawal, rebelliousness, negativism, and extremism.

2.12. The answer is E (*Synopsis VII*, pages 70–72).

According to Melanie Klein, *splitting* is not a defense mechanism but an ego mechanism in which the object is perceived as either all good or all bad; it is a mechanism used against ambivalent feelings toward the object. It is also used by children and by patients in borderline states.

A 50-year-old person is in mid-life, which is marked by the use of certain defense mechanisms.

The defenses that dominate during those years are dissociation, repression, sublimation, and altruism.

Dissociation is an unconscious defense mechanisms involving the segregation of any group of mental or behavioral processes from the rest of the person's psychic activity. It may entail the separation of an idea from its accompanying emotional tone, as seen in dissociative disorders.

Repression is an unconscious defense mechanism in which unacceptable mental contents are banished or kept out of consciousness. A term introduced by Sigmund Freud, it is important in both normal psychological development and in neurotic and psychotic symptom formation.

Sublimation is an unconscious defense mechanism in which the energy associated with unacceptable impulses or drives is diverted into personally and socially acceptable channels. Unlike other defense mechanisms, sublimation offers some minimal gratification of the instinctual drive or impulse.

Altruism is a regard for and dedication to the welfare of others. In psychiatry the term is closely linked with ethics and morals. Freud recognized altruism as the only basis for the development of community interest; Eugen Bleuler equated it with morality.

2.13. The answer is A (*Synopsis VII*, pages 75 and 212–213).

More than 25 million Americans are over age 65, and, although a myth persists that most elderly people live in nursing homes, only *5 percent* of persons between the ages of 65 and 85 are so institutionalized. With increasing age, however, the rate of institutionalization does increase. Over the age of 85, about 20 percent of people live in nursing homes.

2.14. The answer is D (*Synopsis VII*, pages 83–84).

By the age of *10 years*, a child is able to conceptualize the true meaning of death—something that may happen to the child, as well as to the parent. At that time, the child shows a great tendency for logical exploration to dominate fantasy and shows an increased understanding of feelings and interactions in relationships. The child has well-developed capacities for empathy, love, and compassion, as well as emerging capacities for sadness and love in the context of concrete rules. As opposed to parents in some other parts of the world, middle-class adults in the United States tend to shield children from a knowledge of death. The air of mystery with which death is surrounded in such instances may unintentionally create irrational fears in children. Attending funerals is recommended for children if the adults present are trustworthy and reasonably composed. A funeral may act as an introduction to the adult world of crises and tribulations, on the way to a full transition to other phases of development.

The preschool child under age 5 years is beginning to be aware of death not in the abstract sense but as a separation similar to sleep. Between the ages of 5 and 10 years, the child shows a developing sense of inevitable human mortality; the child first fears that the parents may die and that the child will be abandoned.

Discussing death with an inquiring child requires simplicity and candor. Adults are cautioned not to invent answers when they have none. Basically, death must be conveyed as a natural event that cannot be avoided but that causes pain because it separates people who love each other.

2.15. The answer is E (all) (*Synopsis VII*, pages 76–77).

Elisabeth Kübler-Ross described five psychological stages that a dying person may experience on being told of the prognosis. Although Kübler-Ross presented the five stages in the sequential order of denial, anger, bargaining, depression, and acceptance, she did not intend that order to be taken literally. From her work with dying patients, she recognized that the experience of those stages was fluid and individual; one person may initially react with anger, then denial, then depression, then anger again; another person may respond with immediate acceptance, whereas another may never experience the acceptance stage.

Kübler-Ross's description of those stages has been important to the understanding of the emotional life of a dying person. *Denial* is the first stage, when a patient may first appear dazed and then refuse to believe the diagnosis. *Anger* is often characterized by the response "Why me?" The *bargaining* stage occurs when the patient attempts to negotiate with the physician, friends, or even God by promising to fulfill certain bargains in return for a cure. *Depression* may result as a reaction to the reality of impending death or to the debilitating effects of illness. Acceptance is the stage when a patient is able to come to terms with the inevitability of death and with the losses associated with death. In that stage a patient may be able to talk about death and to face the unknown.

2.16–2.20

2.16. The answer is C (*Synopsis VII*, page 37).

2.17. The answer is A (*Synopsis VII*, page 37).

2.18. The answer is E (*Synopsis VII*, pages 41–42).

2.19. The answer is E (*Synopsis VII*, page 37).

2.20. The answer is D (*Synopsis VII*, page 37).

Most of the developmental landmarks are readily observed. Growth is so rapid during infancy that developmental landmarks are measured in terms of weeks. Examples of some major developmental events and their approximate time of appearance are *ocular control, 4 weeks*; balance, 16 weeks; *grasping and manipulation, 28 weeks*; *sitting alone*, creeping, poking, and ability to say one word, *40 weeks*; stand-

ing with slight support, cooperation in dressing, and *verbalization of two or more words, 12 months*; and the use of words in phrases, 18 months.

2.21–2.25

2.21. The answer is C (*Synopsis VII*, page 17).

2.22. The answer is D (*Synopsis VII*, pages 24, 44–47, and 158–159).

2.23. The answer is A (*Synopsis VII*, pages 16–17).

2.24. The answer is B (*Synopsis VII*, page 17).

2.25. The answer is E (*Synopsis VII*, page 18).

Work on the human life cycle has been shaped by a handful of highly influential sources; however, the dominant work on the subject is the developmental scheme introduced by *Sigmund Freud* in 1905 in *Three Essays on the Theory of Sexuality*. Freud's theory, which focused on the childhood period, was organized around his libido theory. According to Freud, *childhood phases of development correspond to successive shifts in the investment of sexual energy to specific areas of the body* usually associated with eroticism: the mouth, the anus, and the genitalia. He discerned developmental periods that were accordingly classified as follows: oral phase, birth to 1 year; anal phase, ages 1 to 3 years; and phallic phase, ages 3 to 5 years. Freud also described a fourth period, latency, which extends from age 5 years until puberty. Latency is marked by a diminution of sexual interest, which is reactivated at puberty. The basic outlook expressed by Freud was that the successful resolution of the childhood phases is essential to normal adult functioning. By comparison, what happens in adulthood is of relatively little consequence.

Carl Gustav Jung viewed external factors as playing an important role in personal growth and adaptation. According to Jung, *individuation is the growth and the expansion of personality that occur through realizing and learning what one intrinsically is.* Libido is every possible manifestation of psychic energy; it is not limited to sexuality or to aggression but includes the religious or spiritual urges and the drive to seek a clear or deep understanding of the meaning of life.

Harry Stack Sullivan approached the issue of the life cycle by stating that *human development is largely shaped by external events, specifically by social interaction.* His influential model of the life cycle states that each phase of development is marked by a need for interaction with certain other people. The quality of that interaction influences the personality.

Another major model is *Jean Piaget's* theory of cognitive (intellectual) development. By conducting intensive studies of the way children think and behave, Piaget theorized that *cognitive development in childhood occurs in successive stages*—sensorimotor, preoperational thought, concrete operations, and formal operations.

George Vaillant noted that a hierarchy of ego mechanisms is constructed as people advance in age. Defenses are organized along a continuum that reflect two aspects of the personality: immaturity versus maturity and psychopathology versus mental health. Vaillant found that the maturity of the defenses is related to both psychopathology and objective adaptation to the external environment. Moreover, defensive style shifts as a person matures. Vaillant concluded that *defense mechanisms mature over the years, and maturation depends more on development from within than on changes in the interpersonal environment.*

2.26–2.30

2.26. **The answer is A** (*Synopsis VII*, pages 42–43).

2.27. **The answer is C** (*Synopsis VII*, pages 42–43).

2.28. **The answer is D** (*Synopsis VII*, pages 42–43).

2.29. **The answer is B** (*Synopsis VII*, pages 42–43).

2.30. **The answer is E** (*Synopsis VII*, pages 42–43).

Mood or general emotional tone is an internal judgment based on the way children look and behave, as well as on their content of speech. During the first 12 months, mood is highly variable and is intimately related to internal states, such as hunger. Toward the second third of the first year, mood is also related to external social cues. When the child is internally comfortable, a sense of interest and pleasure in the world and in the primary caretakers should prevail. From 3 to 5 years, Sigmund Freud's oedipal phase and Erik Erikson's psychosocial crisis of initiative versus guilt prevail; thus, the child is capable of experiencing the complex emotions of jealousy and envy, as well as a growing sense of separation and security. At *birth*, the infant can experience *distress*; at *3 to 4 months*, *anger*; at *8 to 9 months*, fear and *sadness*; at *12 to 18 months*, *shame*; and at *3 to 4 years*, *guilt.*

2.31–2.35

2.31. **The answer is E** (*Synopsis VII*, pages 37–38).

2.32. **The answer is D** (*Synopsis VII*, pages 37–38).

2.33. **The answer is A** (*Synopsis VII*, pages 37–38).

2.34. **The answer is C** (*Synopsis VII*, pages 37–38).

2.35. **The answer is B** (*Synopsis VII*, pages 37–38).

To understand normal development, one must take a comprehensive approach and have an internal map of the age-expected norms for various aspects of human development. The areas of neuromotor, cognitive, and language milestones have many empirical normative data. The normal child is able to accomplish specific tasks at certain ages. For example, a *cross* can be copied at *4 years*, a square can be copied at 5 years, and a *triangle* can be copied at *6 years*. At *18 months*, children can *walk up the stairs with one hand held*, at *2 years*, they can *refer to themselves by name*, and at *3 years* they can *put on their shoes*. Some children may be able to perform a task at an earlier or later age and still fall within the normal range. Other landmarks of normal behavioral development are listed in Table 2.1.

2.36–2.40

2.36. **The answer is A** (*Synopsis VII*, pages 40–42).

2.37. **The answer is B** (*Synopsis VII*, pages 40–42).

2.38. **The answer is C** (*Synopsis VII*, pages 40–42).

2.39. **The answer is D** (*Synopsis VII*, pages 40–42).

2.40. **The answer is D** (*Synopsis VII*, pages 40–42).

Language development occurs in well-delineated stages. At *birth to 6 months*, the child *plays at making sounds and babbles*; at *7 to 11 months*, the child *plays language games (pat-a-cake and peekaboo)*; at *12 to 18 months*, the child *uses up to 20 words and understands up to 150 words*; and from *54 months on*, the child's *speech is 100 percent intelligible*, and the child *uses language to tell stories and share ideas.*

2.41–2.44

2.41. **The answer is B** (*Synopsis VII*, page 83).

2.42. **The answer is C** (*Synopsis VII*, pages 80–85).

2.43. **The answer is C** (*Synopsis VII*, pages 80–85).

2.44. **The answer is B** (*Synopsis VII*, page 83).

Although depression as a symptom may occur as a prominent feature of normal bereavement, as well as of a depressive disorder, and although both conditions may be precipitated by a loss, some features differentiate grief from major depressive disorder. The full depressive syndrome may occur in complicated bereavement, although *marked preoccupation with worthlessness*, extended functional impairment,

Table 2.1
Landmarks of Normal Behavioral Development

Age	Motor and Sensory Behavior	Adaptive Behavior	Personal and Social Behavior
Under 4 weeks	Makes alternating crawling movements Moves head laterally when placed in prone position	Responds to sound of rattle and bell Regards moving objects momentarily	Quiets when picked up Impassive face
16 weeks	Symmetrical postures predominate Holds head balanced Head lifted 90 degrees when prone on forearm Visual accommodation	Follows a slowly moving object well Arms activate on sight of dangling object	Spontaneous social smile (exogenous) Aware of strange situations
28 weeks	Sits steadily, leaning forward on hands Bounces actively when placed in standing position	One-hand approach and grasp of toy Bangs and shakes rattle Transfers toys	Takes feet to mouth Pats mirror image Starts to imitate mother's sounds and actions
40 weeks	Sits alone with good coordination Creeps Pulls self to standing position Points with index finger	Matches two objects at midline Attempts to imitate scribble	Separation anxiety manifest when taken away from mother Responds to social play, such as pat-a-cake and peekaboo Feeds self cracker and holds own bottle
52 weeks	Walks with one hand held Stands alone briefly	Seeks novelty	Cooperates in dressing

Table adapted from Arnold Gesell, M.D., and Stella Chess, M.D.

and marked psychomotor retardation are more often observed in *major depressive disorder*. Sadness, crying, and tension expressed as *psychomotor retardation or agitation* may be seen in *both* normal grief and major depressive disorder. Decreased appetite with *weight loss*, decreased libido, and withdrawal may be found in *both* conditions. The grief-stricken person, however, shows shifts of mood from sadness to a normal state within a reasonably short time and increasingly finds enjoyment in life as the loss recedes. A key aspect of the distinction between major depressive disorder and *normal grief* is similar to Sigmund Freud's original distinction between mourning and melancholy; that is, in normal grief a person does not show the marked lowering of self-esteem and the sense of personal badness that may be of delusional proportions in major depressive disorder, which may also give rise to *suicide attempts*.

3

The Brain and Behavior

Many branches of neuroscience—neuroanatomy, neurophysiology, neurochemistry, molecular neurobiology, and brain imaging—have made major contributions to the understanding of how the normal brain functions, how abnormal brain functioning may differ from normal brain functioning, and how the drugs that are used to treat neurological and mental disorders exert their effects. The student of psychiatry must know and understand the basic concepts of neuroanatomy, the mechanisms of neurotransmission and signal transduction, and the related fields of neuroendocrinology, neuroimmunology, chronobiology, neurogenetics, and brain imaging. An understanding of those areas can help the student understand the relations of the environment, the psychology of human interactions, and the biology of the brain.

To understand neuroanatomy, the student must be familiar with the structural building blocks of the brain—neurons and glia. Of primary importance is a knowledge of the major structural divisions of the brain that are most relevant to psychiatry—the cerebral cortex, the limbic system, the basal ganglia, and the brainstem. Both normal functioning and abnormal functioning of each of the cerebral lobes (frontal, parietal, temporal, and occipital) have clinical relevance for psychiatrists. The student should also know the structural components of the limbic system and the basal ganglia. The student should particularly understand how neurological and psychiatric symptoms can result from pathology in each of those brain regions. For example, the aphasias and the apraxias are seen in patients with cerebral cortical injuries, emotional and memory disturbances are seen in patients with injuries to the limbic system, and motor system and mood effects are associated with lesions of the basal ganglia. The student should also be familiar with the nuclei of the brainstem that contain

many of the biogenic amine-containing neurons of the brain (for example, the norepinephrine-containing neurons of the locus ceruleus), since the biogenic amine-containing neurons are most commonly affected by currently used psychiatric drugs.

The neuroanatomical study of the brain in specific mental disorders has found some data that relate specific brain regions to specific mental disorders, and the student should understand the data supporting those associations. Specifically, schizophrenia is associated with pathology in the basal ganglia, the limbic system, and the frontal cortex; mood disorders are associated with pathology in the limbic system; and anxiety disorders are associated with dysfunction of the noradrenergic nuclei of the brainstem. However, the potential areas of neuropathology are not limited to those areas in each of the disorders.

The current data and hypotheses regarding particular brain regions and psychopathology often derive from studies using brain-imaging technologies, such as computed tomography (CT), magnetic resonance imaging (MRI), magnetic resonance spectroscopy (MRS), single photon emission computed tomography (SPECT), and positron emission tomography (PET). Although CT and MRI, along with electroencephalography (EEG) and evoked potentials (EPs), are used clinically, those techniques—along with MRS, SPECT, and PET—are also used in research settings. Because so many published research studies now use brain-imaging technologies, the student must understand the bases of those approaches and the implications of their findings for mental disorders. The differences among the various brain-imaging technologies and an understanding of how the findings complement one another are useful for students of psychiatry.

Because all currently used psychiatric drugs

have neurotransmitter systems as their primary sites of action, the student of psychiatry must know the major classes of neurotransmitters (biogenic amines, peptides, and amino acids) and understand how members of each class act in significant detail. For the biogenic amine neurotransmitters, the student should know where the neurons are located in the brain, the distribution of their neuronal projections, the characteristics of the receptor subtypes, and how the neurotransmitter system may be affected by diseases and psychiatric drugs. The student should also understand how the adverse effects of psychotherapeutic drugs are mediated by their neurotransmitter effects.

The student of psychiatry should have at least an introductory level of understanding regarding three other areas of brain function and regulation—psychoendocrinology, psychoimmunology, and chronobiology. *Psychoendocrinology* is the study of the interactions of the brain, the neurotransmitters, and the hormonal axes, most of which originate in the hypothalamus. The most frequently studied of the hormonal axes are the thyroid and adrenal axes; those and other hormonal axes have been found to be abnormally regulated in specific mental disorders. Primary dysregulations of those hormonal axes, moreover, can themselves lead to the development of psychiatric symptoms. *Psychoimmunology* is the study of the interactions of the brain, the neurotransmitters,

and the immune system, which may have the hypothalamus as a key center for its regulation. As researchers gain increased understanding of those relations, a mechanism for psychosomatic disorders may eventually be elucidated. The third area, *chronobiology*, is the study of the various naturally occurring rhythms in the human body. The most obvious rhythms are those of the sleep-wake cycle and of hormonal regulation. Some research data indicate that abnormal relations in bodily rhythms can result in the signs and symptoms of mental disorders, and the student must be able to explain the bases for those theories.

Perhaps the final frontier for psychiatry and even medicine as a whole is the study of the molecular genetics of disease and the effects of treatment on genetic expression. The student should have a thorough knowledge of the principles of population genetics and of how various types of studies (for example, adoption studies) have shed light on mental disorders. In addition to understanding the relevant basic principles, the student should understand how to evaluate modern genetics studies, such as those utilizing restriction fragment length polymorphism (RFLP) markers.

Students should review Chapter 3 in *Kaplan and Sadock's Synopsis VII* and then test their knowledge of the subject by studying the questions and answers below.

HELPFUL HINTS

The following items, including their structure and function and their relations with mental disorders and drugs, should be known by the student.

neuroanatomical structures and associated syndromes	Klüver-Bucy syndrome; Wernicke-Korsakoff syndrome	neuromodulators neuromessengers, second messengers
neurons and glia	basal ganglia and associated clinical syndromes	neurohormones
cerebral, frontal, temporal, parietal, and occipital lobes; Broca's area; laterality	hypothalamus, pituitary, thalamus	receptors tuning and grading aplysia experiment
epilepsy; complex partial seizures, kindling, anticonvulsant medications, *déjà vu*	brain-imaging techniques (CT, MRI, EP, PET, CBF) electroencephalography and wave forms	dopaminergic system and associated clinical syndromes; dopamine hypothesis of schizophrenia and mood disorders
aphasia: fluent, receptive, expressive, productive, anomic, thalamic, global	neurochemical and neurophysiological concepts	noradrenergic system and associated clinical syndromes (VMA, MHPG)
amygdala, hippocampus, and limbic system; Papez circuit	CNS location neurotransmission	

serotonergic system and
associated clinical syndromes
(5-HIAA, L-tryptophan)
cholinergic system and
associated clinical syndromes
(tardive dyskinesia)
amino acid neurotransmitters
(GABA)
peptide neurotransmitters
(endorphins)
psychoendocrinology
adrenal axis
vasopressin, oxytocin
LHRH
melatonin
pineal gland
estrogen
endocrine assessment
pituitary challenge
third ventricle enlargement in
schizophrenia
psychoneuroimmunology
neurotoxic virus (AIDS)
neural regulation of immunity
β-endorphin
stress and T-cell proliferation
immunoglobulin
chronobiology
ultradian
circadian
zeitgebers
phase advance and phase delay
seasonal affective disorder
genetics
family risk
twin studies (MZ, DZ)
adoption studies
genome
DNA, tRNA
RFLPs
cellular and physiological
neuroanatomy
neurons
glia
blood-brain barrier
neuronal migration
brain structures
meninges
ventricular system and
cerebrospinal fluid
cerebral cortex
lobes: frontal, temporal,
parietal, occipital
cytoarchitecture, modality,
laterality
thalamus

limbic system: nucleus
accumbens, hippocampus,
amygdala, Papez circuit
hypothalamus and pituitary
basal ganglia: striatum, globus
pallidus, substantia nigra
cerebellum
brainstem
reticular activating system
neuropsychiatric disorders
normal pressure hydrocephalus
epilepsy
aphasias: Broca's, Wernicke's,
fluent, receptive, expressive,
productive
apraxias
agnosias
alexias
agraphias
Klüver-Bucy syndrome
Korsakoff's syndrome
Parkinson's disease
Huntington's disease
Wilson's disease
brain-imaging techniques, clinical
applications, research findings
structural versus functional
brain imaging
computed tomography (CT)
magnetic resonance imaging
(MRI)
comparisons of CT and MRI
magnetic resonance spectroscopy
(MRS)
single photon emission computed
tomography (SPECT)
positron emission tomography
(PET)
comparisons of SPECT and PET
electroencephalography (EEG)
and evoked potentials (EPs)
polysomnography
computed topographic EEGs and
EPs
basic electrophysiology
polarization of neuronal
membrane
action potential
ion channels
basic concepts of
neurotransmission and signal
transduction
synapse
receptor
G proteins

second-messenger systems
(cAMP, cGMP, phosphoinositol
metabolites)
protein phosphorylation
aplysia experiment
neurotransmitter types: biogenic
amines, peptides, amino acids,
nitric oxide
specific neurotransmitters:
neuroanatomical distribution,
pathways, neurophysiology,
receptor subtypes, metabolites,
relation to illnesses and drugs
biogenic amines: dopamine,
norepinephrine, epinephrine,
serotonin, acetylcholine,
histamine
amino acids: GABA and
glutamate
peptides: endogenous opioids,
substance P, neurotensin
psychoneuroendocrinology
hormonal axes: thyroid, adrenal,
growth hormone, prolactin,
melatonin
endocrine assessment
endocrine dysregulation in
mental disorders
psychoimmunology
neural regulation of immunity
chronobiology
phase advance and phase delay
zeitgebers
seasonal pattern
behavioral genetics
genetic models
genetic susceptibility
gene therapy
heterogeneity
family-risk studies
assortative mating
DNA and RNA
genes and chromosomes
transcription and translation
introns and exons
initiation, promotor, and
enhancer regions
immediate early genes
family studies
twin studies
adoption studies
meiotic recombinations
LOD scores
restriction fragment length
polymorphisms (RFLPs)

QUESTIONS

DIRECTIONS: Each of the questions or incomplete statements below is followed by five suggested responses or completions. Select the *one* that is *best* in each case.

3.1. Which of the following statements regarding the neurotransmitters is accurate?
A. Glutamate is an inhibitory amino acid
B. Phencyclidine (PCP) acts at the level of the GABA receptors
C. Peptide neurotransmitters are made in the cell body of the neuron
D. Serotonin is synthesized from the amino acid precursor tyrosine
E. The nigrostriatal tract is a serotonergic tract

3.2. The advantage of computed tomography (CT) over magnetic resonance imaging (MRI) in psychiatric clinical practice is that
A. CT has superior resolution
B. CT can distinguish between white matter and gray matter
C. CT has the ability to take thinner slices through the brain than does MRI
D. CT is superior in detecting calcified brain lesions
E. CT avoids exposing the patient to radiation

3.3. The image-resolution level of both positron emission tomography (PET) and single photon emission computed tomography (SPECT) is affected by
A. Compton effect
B. signal attenuation
C. anatomical resolution
D. partial volume effect
E. all the above

3.4. The pedigree chart shown in Figure 3.1 shows a particular type of genetic inheritance known as
A. dominant
B. Y-linked
C. X-linked
D. recessive
E. none of the above

3.5. The dietary amino acid precursor of serotonin is
A. neurotensin
B. phenylalanine
C. glycine
D. tryptophan
E. tyramine

3.6. Enkephalins are
A. opiatelike peptides
B. cholinergic agents
C. dopamine blocking agents
D. monoamine oxidase inhibitors (MAOIs)
E. tricyclic drugs

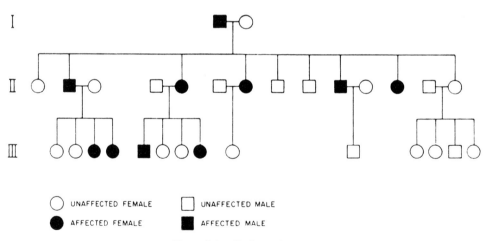

Figure 3.1. Pedigree chart.

DIRECTIONS: Each set of lettered headings below is followed by a list of numbered words or statements. For each numbered word or statement, select the *one* lettered heading that is most closely associated with it. Each lettered heading may be selected once, more than once, or not at all.

Questions 3.7–3.11
    A. Frontal lobe
    B. Temporal lobe
    C. Parietal lobe
    D. Occipital lobe

3.7. Alexia

3.8. Ideomotor apraxia

3.9. Broca's aphasia

3.10. Klüver-Bucy syndrome

3.11. Wernicke's aphasia

Questions 3.12–3.14
    A. Gerstmann syndrome
    B. Anton's syndrome
    C. Balint's syndrome

3.12. Cortical blindness and the denial of blindness

3.13. Optic ataxia, loss of panoramic vision, and supranuclear gaze palsy

3.14. Agraphia, acalculia, right-left disorientation, and finger agnosia

Questions 3.15–3.19
    A. Major depressive disorder
    B. Schizophrenia
    C. Seizure disorders
    D. Sleep apnea
    E. Cognitive disorders

3.15. Positron emission tomography (PET)

3.16. Computed tomography (CT)

3.17. Electroencephalography (EEG)

3.18. Polysomnography (PSG)

3.19. Dexamethasone-suppression test (DST)

DIRECTIONS: The lettered headings below are followed by a list of numbered phrases. For each numbered phrase, select

    A. if the item is associated with *A only*
    B. if the item is associated with *B only*
    C. if the item is associated with *both A and B*
    D. if the item is associated with *neither A nor B*

Questions 3.20–3.23
    A. Computed tomography (CT)
    B. Magnetic resonance imaging (MRI)
    C. Both
    D. Neither

3.20. Uses x-ray photons

3.21. Differs attenuation by the density of the structure

3.22. Is able to discriminate gray matter and white matter

3.23. Differs attenuation by proton density

ANSWERS

The Brain and Behavior

3.1. The answer is C (*Synopsis VII*, pages 130–131).

The three major types of neurotransmitters in the brain are the amino acids, the biogenic amines, and the peptides. Peptides differ from the other two major types of neurotransmitters in that only *peptides are made in the cell body*, where the genetic information for making them resides. Peptide neurotransmitters are usually first synthesized as long forms called preprohormones and are further processed during their transport to the axon terminals. First, the preprohormones are cleaved to make prohormones; then the prohormones are cleaved to make the final hormones.

The two major amino acid neurotransmitters are γ-aminobutyric acid (GABA) and glutamate. GABA is an inhibitory amino acid, and *glutamate is an excitatory amino acid*. An important drug of abuse, *phencyclidine (PCP) acts at the level of the glutamate receptors, not the GABA receptors.*

The six biogenic amine neurotransmitters are dopamine, norepinephrine, epinephrine, serotonin, acetylcholine, and histamine (Figure. 3.2). Dopamine, epinephrine, and norepinephrine are all synthesized from the same amino acid precursor, tyrosine, and are classified as a group as the catecholamines. *Serotonin is not synthesized from the amino acid precursor tyrosine*. Serotonin is synthesized from the amino acid precursor tryptophan and is the only indolamine in the group. Serotonin is also known as 5-hydroxytryptamine (5-HT); therefore, the abbreviation for serotonin is often written as 5-HT. A common feature of all the biogenic amine neurotransmitters is that they are synthesized in the axon terminal. *The nigrostriatal tract*, the mesolimbic-mesocortical tract, and the tuberoinfundibular tract are *dopaminergic tracts, not serotonergic tracts*. The nigrostriatal tract projects from its cell bodies in the substantia nigra to the corpus striatum. When the dopamine receptors at the end of that tract are blocked by classic antipsychotic drugs, the parkinsonian side effects of those drugs are the result. In Parkinson's disease the nigrostriatal tract degenerates, resulting in the motor symptoms of the disease. Because of the significant association between Parkinson's disease and depression, the nigrostriatal tract may somehow be involved with the control of mood, in addition to its classic role in motor control.

The mesolimbic-mesocortical tract projects from its cell bodies in the ventral tegmental area (which lies adjacent to the substantia nigra) to most areas of the cerebral cortex and the limbic system. Because the tract projects to the limbic system and the neocortex, the tract may be involved in mediating the antipsychotic effects of antipsychotic drugs.

The cell bodies of the tuberoinfundibular tract are in the arcuate nucleus and the periventricular area of the hypothalamus and project to the infundibulum and the anterior pituitary. Dopamine acts as a release-inhibiting factor in the tract by inhibiting the release of prolactin from the anterior pituitary. Patients who take antipsychotic drugs have elevated prolactin levels because the blockade of dopamine receptors in the tract eliminates the inhibitory effect of dopamine.

3.2. The answer is D (*Synopsis VII*, pages 113–116).

One reason to order a computed tomographic (CT) scan in preference to a magnetic resonance imaging (MRI) scan is that CT is superior in detecting calcified brain lesions. Whether to order a CT or a more expensive MRI is one of the common clinical questions in psychiatric practice. The resolution of both techniques is under 1mm, but *MRI has the capability of taking thinner slices through the brain, does have superior resolution*, and *can distinguish between white matter and gray matter*. CT is based on X-ray technology, while MRI utilizes magnetic fields. Therefore, *MRI, not CT, avoids exposing patients to radiation*.

3.3. The answer is E (all) (*Synopsis VII*, page 119).

Four major factors affect the resolution level of both PET and SPECT: Compton effect, signal attenuation, anatomical resolution, and partial volume effect.

The emitted photons in both positron emission tomography (PET) and single photon emission computed tomography (SPECT) are deviated from a straight path by the tissues through which they pass. That effect of the tissue is called the *Compton effect*; it limits the anatomical resolution of both PET and SPECT.

Not only are the photons deviated from their straight path by the tissue, but also the energy of the photons is dissipated by bone, air, fluid, and brain tissue. In fact, the most carefully done PET and

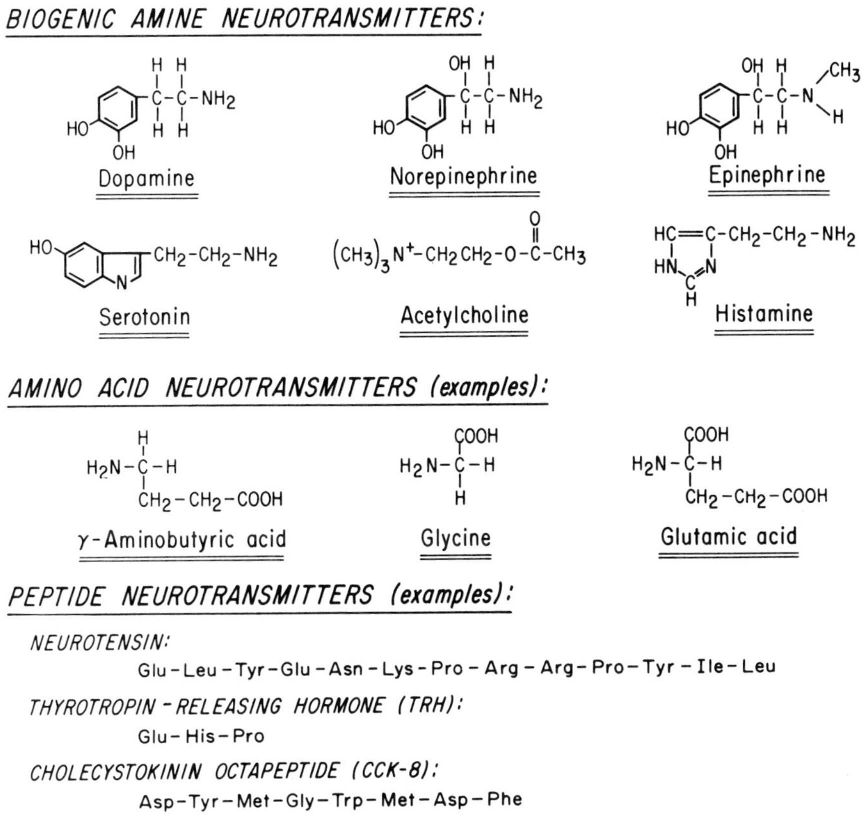

BIOGENIC AMINE NEUROTRANSMITTERS:

Dopamine   **Norepinephrine**   **Epinephrine**

Serotonin   **Acetylcholine**   **Histamine**

AMINO ACID NEUROTRANSMITTERS (examples):

γ-Aminobutyric acid   **Glycine**   **Glutamic acid**

PEPTIDE NEUROTRANSMITTERS (examples):

NEUROTENSIN:

Glu–Leu–Tyr–Glu–Asn–Lys–Pro–Arg–Arg–Pro–Tyr–Ile–Leu

THYROTROPIN-RELEASING HORMONE (TRH):

Glu–His–Pro

CHOLECYSTOKININ OCTAPEPTIDE (CCK-8):

Asp–Tyr–Met–Gly–Trp–Met–Asp–Phe

Figure 3.2. The three classes of neurotransmitters.

SPECT studies use prestudy CT examinations to correct for variable *signal attenuations* caused by differences in patients' head sizes.

A common term used in describing the *anatomical resolution* for both PET and SPECT is "full width at half maximum" (FWHM), which refers to the width of the curve of distribution for the signal at 50 percent of the maximal signal. In PET studies, FWHM is about 5 to 6 mm; in SPECT studies, FWHM is about 8 to 9 mm, reflecting the better resolution of the PET technique compared with the SPECT technique.

In both PET and SPECT, areas of interest within the slice are selected. However, the signal from each area of interest also has an effect on the neighboring areas of interest, called *partial-volume effect*. In some studies of SPECT and PET, the investigators use various computer modeling programs to subtract the energy contribution of neighboring areas from the areas of interest.

3.4.   The answer is A (*Synopsis VII*, pages 148–150).

The *dominant* mode of inheritance, in which each child of an affected parent has a 50 percent chance of receiving a particular gene, is shown in Figure 3.1. The pedigree chart shown is of a family affected by Huntington's disease.

In sex-linked inheritance, a gene is located on a sex chromosome. It is *Y-linked* if it is located on the Y (male) chromosome and *X-linked* if it is located on the X chromosome. In *recessive* inheritance, both genes of a pair must be of one type (homozygosity) for a trait to be apparent. If the genes are different and one of the pair is dominant, the recessive gene's effect is not apparent.

3.5.   The answer is D (*Synopsis VII*, page 139).

Tryptophan is the dietary amino acid precursor of serotonin. It is hydroxylated by the enzyme tryptophan hydroxylase to form 5-hydroxytryptophan; 5-hydroxytryptophan is decarboxylated to serotonin. Serotonin is destroyed by reuptake into the presynaptic terminal and subsequent metabolism by monoamine oxidase (MAO), which oxidatively deaminates it to 5-hydroxyindoleacetic acid (5-HIAA).

Neurotensin is a neurotransmitter and an amino acid peptide that can lower blood pressure; it acts as an analgesic when injected directly into the brain. *Phenylalanine* is an amino acid in proteins that, when not present in infants, causes mental retardation. *Glycine*, an amino acid, functions as an inhibitory neurotransmitter within the spinal cord.

Tyramine is a sympathomimetic amine that has an action similar to that of epinephrine. It is present in ripe cheese, herring, and other foods. Tyramine-containing substances must be avoided by patients on monoamine oxidase inhibitors (MAOIs), because of the danger of adrenergic potentiation.

3.6. The answer is A (*Synopsis VII*, page 144).

Enkephalins are *opiatelike peptides* that are found in many parts of the brain and that bind to specific receptor sites. They are opiatelike because they decrease pain perception. They also serve as neurotransmitters.

Cholinergic agents are drugs that cause the liberation of acetylcholine. *Dopamine blocking agents* are drugs, such as the antipsychotic haloperidol (Haldol), that block dopamine receptors on postsynaptic neurons, thus effectively decreasing the functional levels of the neurotransmitter dopamine. Dopamine blockers are most often used to treat psychotic patients whose psychosis is related to a hyperdopaminergic state.

The two major classes of antidepressant drugs are the *monoamine oxidase inhibitors (MAOIs)* and the *tricyclic drugs*. MAOIs are a group of agents with widely varying chemical structures that have in common the ability to inhibit monoamine oxidase (MAO). Inhibition of MAO results in a functional increase of the monoamines norepinephrine (NE), dopamine, and serotonin within nerve terminals. When these amines start leaking out into the synaptic cleft, facilitation of the actions of all monoamines occurs. The tricyclic drugs are potent inhibitors of the reuptake inactivation mechanism of catecholamine and serotonin neurons. The ability of tricyclic drugs to inhibit the reuptake process results in a functional increase of such neurotransmitters as NE and serotonin, leading to the medication's antidepressant activity.

3.7–3.11

3.7. The answer is D (*Synopsis VII*, page 104).

3.8. The answer is C (*Synopsis VII*, page 103).

3.9. The answer is A (*Synopsis VII*, page 102).

3.10. The answer is B (*Synopsis VII*, pages 106–107).

3.11. The answer is B (*Synopsis VII*, page 102).

The human brain is the common denominator for all schools of thought regarding human behavior. With the innovative techniques of contemporary basic and clinical psychiatric research, science is rapidly revealing the functional organization of the human brain. The major functions of the frontal cortex involve motor activation, intellect, conceptual planning, aspects of personality, and aspects of language production; lesions of the frontal cortex produce abnormalities in those functional areas.

Alexia is loss of the ability to read. Reading comprehension and reading out loud can be independently impaired. Alexia should be distinguished from

dyslexia, which is a developmental problem in reading. *Alexia* is due to an *occipital lobe* lesion.

Ideomotor apraxia is loss of the ability to perform simple tasks (for example, hitting a nail with a hammer) on request by the examiner. However, the patient may be able to perform the identical task in its usual context (for example, hanging a picture on a wall). *Ideomotor apraxia* can be produced by lesions in the dominant *parietal lobe*. The association cortices for auditory input are contained within the parietal lobes, and in ideomotor apraxia those receptive language areas are disconnected from the motor execution areas.

Broca's aphasia is due to a lesion in the *frontal lobe*. Aphasia is an acquired disorder of language (comprehension, word choice, expression, syntax) that is not due to dysarthria (a dysfunction of the muscles necessary for speech production). Broca's aphasia is produced by a lesion in Broca's area (Brodmann's area 44 in the frontal lobe), which is involved in the motor production of speech. Broca's aphasia is called anterior aphasia, motor aphasia, and expressive aphasia. Comprehension is unimpaired, but the patient's speech is telegraphic and agrammatical.

Klüver-Bucy syndrome is produced by a bilateral *temporal lobe* lesion. It affects the part of the limbic system that is located in the temporal lobes. The limbic system was originally proposed as an anatomical substrate for the emotions. Subsequently, it has become clear that memory is a major function of the limbic system. The symptoms of Klüver-Bucy syndrome include placidity, apathy, hypersexuality, and visual and auditory agnosia. Amnesia, aphasia, dementia, and seizures may also be seen in people with the syndrome.

Wernicke's aphasia is due to a lesion in the *temporal lobe*. Wernicke's area (Brodmann's area 22 in the superior temporal gyrus) is involved in the comprehension of speech. Wernicke's aphasia is also called posterior aphasia, fluent aphasia, and receptive aphasia. The speech of patients with Wernicke's aphasia is characterized by a fluent but incoherent speech because the patients are unable to comprehend their own language or that of others.

3.12–3.14

3.12. The answer is B (*Synopsis VII*, page 101).

3.13. The answer is A (*Synopsis VII*, page 101).

3.14. The answer is C (*Synopsis VII*, pages 101–102).

The occipital lobe is the primary sensory cortex for visual input, and lesions of the lobe result in various visual symptoms. *Anton's syndrome* is associated with bilateral occlusion of the posterior cerebral arteries, resulting in *cortical blindness and the denial of blindness*. The most common causes are hypoxic injury, encephalitis, leukodystrophy, and trauma. *Balint's syndrome* is caused by bilateral occipital lesions and is characterized by *optic ataxia* (abnormal visual guidance of limb movements, *loss of panoramic vision, and supranuclear gaze paralysis.*

Gerstmann syndrome has been attributed to lesions of the dominant parietal lobe; the syndrome includes *agraphia*, calculation difficulties *(acalculia), right-left disorientation, and finger agnosia.*

3.15–31.9

3.15. **The answer is B** (*Synopsis VII*, page 119).

3.16. **The answer is E** (*Synopsis VII*, pages 112–113).

3.17. **The answer is C** (*Synopsis VII*, pages 119–123).

3.18. **The answer is D** (*Synopsis VII*, page 123).

3.19. **The answer is A** (*Synopsis VII*, pages 107 and 282–283).

Positron emission tomography (PET) scans measure cerebral oxygen and glucose metabolism and have demonstrated differences in regional glucose uptake and oxygen consumption in persons with *schizophrenia* compared with persons without schizophrenia; the schizophrenic patients tend to show relatively diminished function in specific areas. Differences among persons with schizophrenia have also been found. In catatonic schizophrenia, a decrease is seen in the volume of blood flow and in oxygen consumption in the precentral regions of the cerebrum, whereas hallucinating patients and patients with thought disorders have relatively high activity in the postcentral, temporal, and latero-occipital regions of the cerebral cortex.

A *computed tomography (CT)* scan of the head is a sophisticated X-ray in which relative tissue densities of thousands of areas within one plane are processed and represented photographically. The cerebral cortex can be visualized, as well as ventricular size and displacement and many lesions. A CT scan is useful in the diagnosis of *cognitive disorders*, as it reveals intracerebral space-occupying lesions and degenerative changes that may be creating the clinical picture.

Electroencephalography (EEG) measures voltages between electrodes placed in the scalp and provides a description of the electrical activity of the brain and its neurons. It is most helpful in the diagnosis of specific *seizure disorders* and is also useful in diagnosing space-occupying lesions, vascular lesions, and encephalopathies. Characteristic EEG changes are caused by specific drugs.

Polysomnography (PSG) is a battery of tests that include an EEG, an electrocardiogram (ECG), and an electromyogram (EMG). It is often given with tests for penile tumescence, blood oxygen saturation, body movement, and body temperature. It is the diagnostic procedure for *sleep apnea*, which consists of transient cessations of breathing during sleep. The battery of tests is also useful in the assessment of insomnia, enuresis, impotence, and seizure disorders.

The *dexamethasone-suppression test (DST)* is useful in making the diagnosis of *major depressive disorder* with melancholic features. The administration of dexamethasone, an exogenous corticosteroid, leads to a suppression of the endogenous production of cortisol in nondepressed people. An abnormal finding on a DST is one in which the patient's cortisol level, generally tested 12 hours after the administration of dexamethasone, has not been suppressed (above 5 mg/dL). Suppression of endogenous cortisol indicates that the hypothalamic-adrenal-pituitary axis is functioning properly.

3.20–3.23

3.20. **The answer is A** (*Synopsis VII*, page 113).

3.21. **The answer is A** (*Synopsis VII*, page 113).

3.22. **The answer is B** (*Synopsis VII*, pages 113–114).

3.23. **The answer is B** (*Synopsis VII*, pages 113–115).

Computed tomography (CT) is based on the same physical principles as a skull X-ray—that is, the measurement of the attenuation of *X-ray photons* that have been passed through the brain. The *attenuation differs according to the density of the structure.* X-ray photons are attenuated less by low-density tissues, such as cerebrospinal fluid (CSF), than by high-density tissues, such as bone. The image of low-density tissues appears black, and the image of high-density tissues appears white. The major differences between CT and a skull X-ray are CT's application of X-ray photon detectors and computers in lieu of X-ray film. The CT image can be enhanced by the use of iodinated contrast materials that are injected into the blood circulation and that cause a high attenuation of the X-ray photons and thus appear white in the image. The use of contrast materials can help the radiologist detect certain types of tumors, infections, and cerebrovascular diseases.

Magnetic resonance imaging (MRI) produces images of the brain that look much like CT scans but that have an increased in-focus appearance and are *able to discriminate gray matter and white matter.* The ability to discriminate gray matter and white matter and other subtle differences within the brain tissue makes MRI good for such lesions as those seen in multiple sclerosis. Multiple sclerosis is characterized by diffuse multifocal lesions in the white matter of the central nervous system and by a course characterized by exacerbations and remissions. MRI is performed by placing the patient in a long tubelike structure that contains powerful magnets. MRI *differs attenuation by proton density.* Once the patient is in the magnetic field, all the patient's hydrogen-containing molecules (especially water) line up in parallel and antiparallel arrays and move in a symmetrical fashion around their axes in a movement called precession. That orderly arrangement and movement are interrupted by radiofrequency pulses from the MR device. The radiofrequency pulses cause the molecules to flip 90° or 180° from their axes; then the magnetic field results in the release of electromagnetic energy that is detected by the MR equipment. Those data, which are essentially measurements of hydrogen nuclei densities, are then relayed into the computer, which processes the information into images of the brain.

Contributions of the Psychosocial Sciences to Human Behavior

The influence of research in the fields of psychology, anthropology, ethology, epidemiology, and sociology on the understanding of human behavior has been huge. In conjunction with the rapidly expanding universe of biological research, the contributions of the social sciences have provided a multidimensional overview of human functioning. Among the vast array of theorists and researchers from that realm of investigation, several persons and foci of study stand out.

Jean Piaget (1896–1980), a Swiss psychologist, investigated and described a theory of cognitive development that has greatly influenced the understanding of the evolution of human thought. Although a number of legitimate criticisms have been directed at some of the tenets of Piaget's work, it nonetheless continues to serve as a useful paradigm of how persons probably learn to think, reason, and communicate verbally.

John Bowlby (1907–1990), a British psychoanalyst, developed theories of attachment and human relationships that have influenced the understanding of normal and abnormal child development. Bowlby's theories have been further bolstered by the work of such ethologists as Harry Harlow in his work with primates and Konrad Lorenz in his work with ducklings. Ethology, the study of animal behavior, has shed clinically useful light on such human symptoms as depression and anxiety and on such factors in development as critical periods, isolation, and maternal deprivation.

Learning theory, as developed by research psychologists, has provided the theoretical basis for the clinical application of behavior therapy. Aspects of both operant and clinical conditioning, the basic tenets of learning theory, are incorporated into specific techniques of behavior therapy.

Various other areas of study from the social sciences contribute to an understanding of behavior. Research into the nature of aggression and the biological, social, and psychological determinants of aggressive behavior contribute data to those workers involved in the treatment of aggressive patients. Anthropological research has expanded the recognition and the understanding of cross-cultural issues involved in human behavior and development. Epidemiological research has contributed to the understanding of human behavior by helping to specify and define the distribution, incidence, prevalence, and duration of various mental disorders. The emergence of community psychiatry and the socioeconomics of health care spring directly from the traditions of social sciences and will play a critical role in the development and the evaluation of a redesigned health care system in this country.

The student should study Chapter 4 in *Kaplan and Sadock's Synopsis VII*. The questions and answers in this chapter will help students test their knowledge of the subject.

HELPFUL HINTS

The student should know the following terms, theoreticians, and concepts.

aversive stimuli
Joseph Wolpe
reciprocal inhibition
anxiety hierarchy
systematic desensitization
frustration-aggression hypothesis
tension-reduction theory
learned helplessness
cognitive triad
social learning
reciprocal determinism
Eric Kandel
set
motivation
cognitive dissonance
aggression
Konrad Lorenz
catharsis
ethology
Nickolaas Tinbergen
H. S. Liddell
experimental neurosis
behavior disorders
social isolation and separation
Jean Piaget
genetic epistemology
epigenesis
adaptation
assimilation
accommodation
organization
sensorimotor stage
preoperational stage
concrete operations
formal operations
scheme
object permanence
symbolization
egocentric
phenomenalistic causality
syllogistic reasoning
abstract thinking
John Bowlby
attachment

monotropic
bonding
preattachment stage
René Spitz
deviation, significance
lifetime expectancy
variation, average
risk factors
cash registers
indirect surveys
reliability
validity
Type I and Type II errors
bias
double-blind method
use of controls
randomization
basic study design
Faris and Dunham
drift hypothesis
segregation hypothesis
social class and mental disorders
social causation and selection
  theory
Monroe County Study
Midtown Manhattan Study
New Haven Study
Hollingshead and Redlich
hospitalism
anaclitic depression
protest-despair-detachment
imprinting
Mary Ainsworth
learning theory
operant and classical conditioning
Ivan Petrovich Pavlov
extinction
John B. Watson
B. F. Skinner
primary and secondary reward
  conditioning
escape and avoidance conditioning
respondent behavior
operant behavior

positive and negative
  reinforcement
fixed and variable ratios
punishment
Harry Harlow
contact comfort
surrogate mother
therapist monkeys
sensory deprivation
Ruth Benedict
Margaret Mead
Alexander Leighton
family types, studies
roles of women
national character
acculturation
therapeutic community
illness behavior
culture-bound syndromes
epidemiology
normative
frequency
prevalence
incidence
Stirling County Study
NIMH ECA
DIS
Holmes and Rahe
vulnerability theory
cross-cultural studies and
  syndromes: amok, latah windigo,
  plibokto, curandero, esperitismo,
  voodoo
Hans Selye
CMHC
primary, secondary, and tertiary
  prevention
deinstitutionalization
hospitals: beds, admissions, length
  of stay
mortality trends
insurance
health care providers

QUESTIONS

DIRECTIONS: Each of the questions or incomplete statements below is followed by five suggested responses or completions. Select the *one* that is *best* in each case.

4.1. Jean Piaget's theory of cognitive development states that
A. children are egocentric during the stage of concrete operations
B. immanent justice is the belief that punishment for bad deeds is inevitable
C. object permanence is developed during the stage of preoperational thought
D. symbolization is the endowing of physical events and objects with lifelike psychological attributes
E. the most important sign that children have proceeded from the stage of preoperational thought to the stage of formal operations is the acheivement of conservation and reversibility

4.2. Attachment theory states that
A. infants are generally polytropic in their attachments
B. attachment occurs instantaneously between the mother and the child
C. attachment is synonymous with bonding
D. attachment disorders may lead to a failure to thrive
E. separation anxiety is most common when an infant is 5 months old

4.3. In operant conditioning
A. continuous reinforcement is the reinforcement schedule least susceptible to extinction
B. negative reinforcement is a type of punishment
C. the process is related to trial-and-error learning
D. shaping occurs when responses are coincidentally paired to a reinforcer
E. respondent behavior is independent of a stimulus

4.4. Cross-cultural studies
A. are free from experimental bias
B. show that depression is not a universally expressed symptom
C. show that incest is not a universal taboo
D. show that schizophrenic persons are universally stigmatized as social outcasts
E. show that the nuclear family of mother, father, and children is a universal unit

4.5. According to Piaget, an important process that develops during the stage of concrete operations is the
A. ability to reason about reasoning or thinking
B. ability to make and follow rules
C. ability to distinguish between the ideal self and the real self
D. use of phenomenological causality as a mode of thinking
E. attainment of object permanence

4.6. John Bowlby's stages of bereavement include
A. protest
B. yearning
C. despair
D. reorganization
E. all the above

4.7. The final stage in Piaget's theory of cognitive development is
A. formal operations
B. sensorimotor
C. preoperational thought
D. concrete operations
E. epigenesis

4.8. The development of object permanence is associated with the
A. latency stage
B. sensorimotor stage
C. preattachment stage
D. stage of concrete operations
E. stage of formal operations

4.9. Children in Piaget's stage of preoperational thought characteristically display
A. intuitive thinking
B. egocentric thinking
C. magical thinking
D. animistic thinking
E. all the above

4.10. Attachment to a mothering figure is
A. a reciprocal affectionate relationship
B. developed during the first year of life
C. dependent on the intensity, the quality, and the amount of the time spent together
D. an instinctive behavior pattern
E. all the above

4.11. Predictive validity is
A. the extent to which knowledge that a person has a particular mental disorder is useful in predicting the future course of the illness
B. related to management and treatment
C. relevant to the specificity with which patients with bipolar I disorder improve when treated with lithium
D. the basis on which Emil Kraepelin differentiated manic-depressive psychosis from dementia precox
E. all the above

4.12. The increased frequency of aggressive behavior in abnormal children has been correlated with all the following *except*
A. brain injury
B. faulty identification models
C. cultural environment
D. violence in movies
E. curiosity

4.13. Which of the following statements best describes the long-term effects of six months of total social isolation in monkeys?
A. They rarely exhibit aggression against age-mates who are more physically adept than they are
B. They are able to make a remarkable social adjustment through the development of play
C. They are totally unresponsive to the new physical and social world with which they are presented
D. They are both abnormally aggressive and abnormally fearful
E. They assume postures that are bizarre and schizoid

4.14. Figure 4.1 depicts an experiment that interferes with normal social interactions among monkeys. *A* and *B* represent the two sequential stages that occur when the infant is separated from its mother. The stages are protest and
A. yearning
B. resolution
C. despair
D. acceptance
E. none of the above

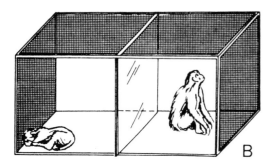

Figure 4.1. Two stages that occur when the infant is separated from its mother.

4.15. In a study of induced anaclitic depression in monkeys, Harry Harlow found
A. at initial separation, the rhesus infants exhibited a protest stage
B. the protest stage changed to despair
C. play was almost abolished during a three-week period of maternal separation, but resumed rapidly after maternal reunion
D. monkeys tested showed a nearly complete picture of anaclitic depression
E. all the above

4.16. To provide information regarding a planned modification of circumstances designed to lower the incidence of disease in a given population, experimenters most often use
A. preventive trials
B. community prevention
C. primary prevention
D. secondary prevention
E. tertiary prevention

4.17. Prevalence is the
A. proportion of a population that has a condition at one moment in time
B. ratio of persons who acquire a disorder during a year's time
C. risk of acquiring a condition at some time
D. standard deviation
E. rate of first admissions to a hospital for a disorder

4.18. In the Stirling County study by Alexander Leighton, all the following were found *except*
A. only about 20 percent of the population were free of psychiatric symptoms
B. men showed more mental disorders than did women
C. psychophysiological symptoms were found in more than 50 percent of the population
D. mental disorders increased with age
E. mental health was related to economic status

4.19. Which of the following statements apply to the ways in which hospitals are organized in the United States?
A. The state mental hospital system has about 140,000 beds
B. Investor-owned hospitals are increasing in importance nationally
C. Veterans Affairs (VA) hospitals are usually affiliated with medical schools
D. In special hospitals, 70 percent of the facility must be designated for the treatment of a single condition
E. All the above

DIRECTIONS: Each set of lettered headings below is followed by a list of numbered phrases. For each numbered phrase, select

    A. if the item is associated with *A only*
    B. if the item is associated with *B only*
    C. if the item is associated with *both A and B*
    D. if the item is associated with *neither A nor B*

Questions 4.20–4.23
    A. Health maintenance organization (HMO)
    B. Preferred provider organization (PPO)
    C. Both
    D. Neither

4.20. Members pay a prepayment or capitation fee to cover health care services.

4.21. Uses a prospective payment system

4.22. Is equivalent to a health systems agency

4.23. Arranges health services at lower than usual rates for its members

Questions 4.24–4.28
    A. Lower class
    B. Upper middle class
    C. Both
    D. Neither

4.24. More able to delay gratification

4.25. Seek health care earlier

4.26. See pregnancy as a time of crisis

4.27. Longer hospital stays

4.28. Low contraceptive use

DIRECTIONS: Each set of lettered headings below is followed by a list of numbered words or phrases. For each numbered word or phrase, select the *one* lettered heading that is most closely associated with it. Each lettered heading may be selected once, more than once, or not at all.

Questions 4.29–4.32
    A. Ivan Petrovich Pavlov
    B. Eric Kandel
    C. Konrad Lorenz
    D. Harry Harlow

4.29. Imprinting

4.30. Surrogate mother

4.31. Experimental neurosis

4.32. Aplysia

Questions 4.33–4.37
    A. Magical thinking
    B. Thinking about thoughts
    C. Object permanence
    D. Symbolic thought
    E. Cause and effect

4.33. 9 to 12 months

4.34. 18 to 24 months

4.35. 2 to 7 years

4.36. 7 to 11 years

4.37. 11 years through adolescence

ANSWERS

Contributions of the Psychosocial Sciences to Human Behavior

4.1. The answer is B (*Synopsis VII*, pages 157–161).

Jean Piaget described four major stages leading to the capacity for adult thought. Each stage is a prerequisite for the one that follows. However, the rate at which children move through the stages varies with each child's native endowment and environmental circumstances. The four stages are (1) the sensorimotor stage, (2) the stage of preoperational thought, (3) the stage of concrete operations, and (4) the stage of formal operations.

Children in the preoperational stage of thought (2 to 7 years of age) have a sense of *immanent justice, the belief that punishment for bad deeds is inevitable.* However, children in the preoperational stage are unable to deal with moral dilemmas, even though they have a sense of what is good and what is bad. For example, when asked, "Who is more guilty: the person who breaks one dish on purpose or the person who breaks 10 dishes by accident?" the young child usually answers that the person who breaks 10 dishes by accident is more guilty because more dishes are broken.

Children are egocentric during the stage of preoperational thought, *not the stage of concrete operations.* They see themselves as the center of the universe, they have a limited point of view, and they are unable to take the role of another person. The children are unable to modify their behavior for someone else. For example, children are not being negativistic when they do not listen to commands to be quiet because their brother has to study. Their egocentric thinking prevents an understanding of their brother's point of view.

Object permanence is developed during the sensorimotor stage (birth to 2 years), *not during the preoperational stage.* Object permanence is the critical achievement in the sensorimotor stage. It tends to develop between 18 months and 2 years of age, and it marks the transition from the sensorimotor stage to the stage of preoperational thought. Through object permanence the child can understand that objects have an existence independent of the child's involvement with them. Infants learn to differentiate themselves from the world and are able to maintain a mental image of an object, even though it is not present and visible. If an object is dropped in front of infants, they learn to look down to the ground to search for the object; that is, they behave as though the object has a reality outside themselves.

Object permanence is achieved through the process of symbolization. At about 18 months, infants begin to develop mental symbols and to use words. Symbolization is the ability of an infant to create a visual image of a ball or a mental symbol of the word "ball" to stand for the real object. Such mental representations allow children to operate on new conceptual levels. Thus, *symbolization is not the endowing of physical events and objects with lifelike psychological attributes.* Such animistic thinking is seen in children already in the stage of preoperational thought.

During the stage of concrete operations (7 to 11 years), the child operates and acts on the concrete, real, and perceivable world of objects and events. Egocentric thought is replaced by operational thought, which involves attending to and dealing with a wide array of information outside the child. A child in the stage of concrete operations can see things from someone else's perspective. *The most important sign that children have proceeded from the stage of preoperational thought to the stage of concrete operations, not formal operations, is the achievement of conservation and reversibility.* Conservation is the ability to recognize that, even though the shape and the form of objects change, the objects maintain other characteristics that enable them to be recognized as the same. For example, if a ball of clay is rolled into a long and thin sausage shape, the child in the stage of concrete operations recognizes that the same amount of clay is in the two forms. In the stage of preoperational thought, the child declares that more clay is in the sausage-shaped form because it is longer. Reversibility is the capacity to understand the relation between things, to understand that one thing can turn into another and back again—for example, ice and water.

The most important sign that children are in the stage of formal operations (11 years through the end of adolescence) is that they have the ability to think abstractly, to reason deductively, and to define concepts. The stage of formal operations is so named because the person's thinking operates in a formal, logical, systematic, and symbolic manner. The stage is also characterized by skills in dealing with permutations and combinations; the young person can grasp the concept of probabilities. The adolescent attempts to deal with all possible relations and hypotheses to explain data and events. During the stage of formal operations, language use is complex, follows formal rules of logic, and is grammatically correct. Abstract thinking is shown by the adolescent's interest in a variety of issues: philosophy, religion, ethics, and politics.

4.2. The answer is D (*Synopsis VII*, pages 161–164).

Attachment disorders are characterized by biopsychosocial pathology that results from maternal deprivation, a lack of care by and interaction with the infant's mother or caretaker. Psychosocial dwarfism, separation anxiety disorder, avoidant personality disorder, depressive disorders, delinquency, learning disorders, borderline intelligence, and *failure to thrive* have been traced to negative attachment experiences. Failure to thrive results in the infant's being unable to maintain viability outside a hospital setting. When maternal care is deficient because the mother is mentally ill, because the child is institutionalized for a long time, or because the primary object of attachment dies, the child suffers emotional damage.

John Bowlby formulated a theory that normal attachment is crucial to healthy development. According to Bowlby, attachment occurs when the infant has a warm, intimate, and continuous relationship with its mother and both mother and infant find satisfaction and enjoyment. *Infants are generally monotropic, not polytropic, in their attachments*, but multiple attachments may also occur; attachment may be directed toward the father or a surrogate. *Attachment does not occur spontaneously between the mother and the child*; it is a gradually developing phenomenon. Attachment results in one person's wanting to be with a preferred person, who is perceived as stronger, wiser, and able to reduce anxiety or distress. Attachment produces a feeling of security in the infant. It is a process that is facilitated by interaction between the mother and the infant. The amount of time together is less important than the amount of activity between the two.

Attachment is not synonymous with bonding; they are different phenomena. Bonding concerns the mother's feelings for her infant and differs from attachment because a mother does not normally rely on her infant as a source of security, a requirement of attachment behavior. A great deal of research on the bonding of a mother to her infant reveals that it occurs when they have skin-to-skin contact or other types of contact, such as voice and eye contact.

Separation from the attachment person may or may not produce intense anxiety, depending on the child's developmental level and the current phase of attachment. Separation anxiety is an anxiety response, expressed as tearfulness or irritability, in a child who is isolated or separated from its mother or caretaker. *Separation anxiety is most common when an infant is 10 to 18 months of age (not 5 months)*, and it disappears generally by the end of the third year.

4.3. The answer is C (*Synopsis VII*, pages 165 and 168–169).

B. F. Skinner (1904–1990) proposed a theory of learning and behavior known as operant or instrumental conditioning. In operant conditioning the subject is active and behaves in a way that produces a reward—that is, learning occurs as a consequence of action.

The process is related to trial-and-error learning, as described by the American psychologist Edward L. Thorndike (1874–1949). In trial-and-error learning, one attempts to solve a problem by trying out a variety of actions until one action proves successful; a freely moving organism behaves in a way that is instrumental in producing a reward. For example, a cat in a Thorndike puzzle box must learn to lift a latch to escape from the box. Operant conditioning is sometimes called instrumental conditioning for that reason. Thorndike's law of effect states that certain responses are reinforced by reward, and the organism learns from those experiences.

In operant conditioning, the experimenter can vary the schedule of reward or reinforcement given to a behavioral pattern—a process known as programming. The intervals between reinforcements may be fixed (for example, every third response is rewarded) or variable (for example, sometimes the third response is rewarded; at other times, the sixth response is rewarded). A continuous reinforcement (also known as contingency reinforcement or management) schedule, in which every response is reinforced, leads to the most rapid acquisition of a behavior. However, *continuous reinforcement is the reinforcement schedule most susceptible to extinction*. Extinction occurs when a desired response no longer occurs.

Negative reinforcement is not punishment. Punishment is an aversive stimulus (for example, a slap) that is presented specifically to weaken or suppress an undesired response. Punishment reduces the probability that a response will recur. In learning theory, the punishment delivered is always contingent on performance, and its use reduces the frequency of the behavior being punished. Negative reinforcement is the process by which a response that leads to the removal of an aversive event increases that response. For example, a teenager mows the lawn to avoid parental complaints, and an animal jumps off a grid to escape a painful shock. Any behavior that enables one to avoid or escape a punishing consequence is strengthened.

Shaping involves changing behavior in a deliberate and predetermined way. By reinforcing those responses that are in the desired direction, the experimenter shapes the subject's behavior. If the experimenter wants to train a seal to ring a bell with its nose, the experimenter can give a food reinforcement as the animal's random behavior brings its nose near the bell. *Shaping does not occur when responses are coincidentally paired to a reinforcer*. When that occurs, it is called adventitious reinforcement. Adventitious reinforcement may have clinical implications on the development of phobias and other behaviors.

In formulating his theory of operant conditioning, Skinner described two types of behavior: (1) respondent behavior, which results from known stimuli (for example, the knee jerk reflex to patellar stimulation) and (2) operant behavior, which is independent of a stimulus (for example, the random movements of an infant or the aimless movements of a laboratory rat in a cage). Thus, *operant behavior, not respondent behavior, is independent of a stimulus.*

4.4. The answer is E (*Synopsis VII*, pages 186–187).

Cross-cultural studies examine and compare various cultures along a number of parameters: attitudes, beliefs, expectations, memories, opinions, roles, stereotypes, prejudices, and values. Usually, the cultures studied use differing languages and have differing political organizations.

The nuclear family of mother, father, and children is a universal unit in all cultures. The extended family—in which grandparents, parents, children, and other relatives all live under the same roof—is no longer common in the United States, but it is still prevalent in less industrialized cultures. In the United States, more than 85 percent of the men and women between the ages 35 and 45 are husbands or wives in a nuclear family.

Cross-cultural studies *are not free from experimental bias*; in fact, they are subject to extreme bias because of problems in translation and other areas of information gathering. Questions have to be asked in ways that are clearly understood by the group under study. One of the best known cross-cultural studies, *Psychiatric Disorder among the Yoruba* by Alexander Leighton, was his attempt to replicate in Nigeria the Stirling County study he had conducted in Canada. The study was criticized because not only did it fail to distinguish psychophysiological symptoms from those associated with infections, parasites, and nutritional diseases but also it assumed that the indicators of sociocultural disintegration in Stirling County could be used among the Yoruba. All cultures are relative; that is, each must be examined within the context of its own language, customs, and beliefs.

Nevertheless, some generalizations can be made about cross-cultural or comparative psychiatry. Certain symptoms exist in all societies; anxiety, mania, thought disorder, suicidal ideation, somatization, paranoia (persecutory delusions), and *depression are universally expressed symptoms.* Although various labels may be applied in various cultures, recognition of deviant behavior and agreement that conditions are treatable (whether by the psychiatrist in one culture or the shaman in another) are universal.

Some universals are observed in various cultures: (1) Smiling is a social greeting exhibited by all normal members of every known society. (2) Homicide and *incest are universal taboos.* (3) Gender role differences go beyond reproduction. (4) Males are more aggressive than females. (5) Strong attachments and fear of separation and of strangers appear in the second half of the first year of life.

Cross-cultural studies have also found that schizophrenia exists among all groups and is constant across cultures. The differences occur in the perception and the treatment of schizophrenia cross-culturally. *Schizophrenic persons are not universally stigmatized as social outcasts*; in some cultures, they are integrated into the society.

4.5. The answer is B (*Synopsis VII*, page 159).

The *ability to make and follow rules* occurs during the stage of concrete operations. At that time, syllogistic or deductive reasoning occurs, and children learn to engage in a form of deductive reasoning that allows them to begin to acquire and abide by rules.

The *ability to reason about reasoning or thinking* occurs during the stage of formal operations, as does the *ability to distinguish between the ideal self and the real self.* The *use of phenomenological causality as a mode of thinking* is seen during the stage of preoperational thought. The *attainment of object permanence* occurs during the sensorimotor stage.

An overview of the major developmental stages of the life cycle is presented in Table 4.1.

4.6. The answer is E (all) (*Synopsis VII*, pages 161–164).

John Bowlby is best known for his theory of attachment, which has influenced the understanding of normal and abnormal child development. Bowlby identified specific stages that occur in children who are separated from their mothers, comparing those phases to mourning and bereavement in adults.

Stage 1, called *protest*, is characterized by outbursts of distress, fear, or anger. Stage 2 is characterized by *yearning* and searching for the lost figure. That stage may last for several months or even years and is marked by preoccupation with the lost person to the point that the griever actually believes that the person is present. Stage 3 occurs as a result of a gradual recognition and integration of the reality of the loss, leading to a sense of disorganization and *despair*. In that stage, the person may be restless and aimless and make only ineffective and inefficient efforts to resume normal patterns of living. Stage 4 is the final stage, in which, ideally, the person begins to resolve grief and to *reorganize*, with a gradual recession of the grief and a replacement with cherished memories. Those stages are not discrete, and persons show tremendous variability. In general, normal grief resolves within one or two years as the person experiences the calendar year at least once without the lost person.

4.7. The answer is A (*Synopsis VII*, pages 159–161).

The final developmental stage that Piaget defined is the period of *formal operations* (from about 11 to

Table 4.1
Life Cycle in Development Stages

Age (yr)	Epigenetic Stages of Erikson	Psychosexual Stages of Freud	Stages of Cognitive Development of Piaget	Major Emotional and Developmental Disorders
0–1	Trust vs. mistrust: Basic feelings of being cared for by outer-providers	Oral (merges into oral sadistic)	Sensorimotor: Infant moves from an indifferent stage to awareness of self and the outside world. Object permanence developed (birth to 2 yr).	Rumination, pylorospasm. Stranger anxiety at 8 months, infantile autism, failure to thrive
1–3	Autonomy vs. shame, doubt (begins at 18 mo): Rebellion, clean-dirty issues, compulsive behavior	Anal (divided into anal-explusive and anal-retentive)		Sleep disturbances, pica, negativism, temper tantrums, toilet-training problems. Night terrors, separation anxiety, phobias
3–7	Initiative vs. guilt: Competitiveness develops, self-confidence emerges	Phallic (includes urethral eroticism and Oedipal-Electra complex)	Preoperational thought: A prelogical period in which thinking is based on what child wants, not what is (3–7 yr)	Somnambulism. School phobias, encopresis, enuresis, reading disorder, gender identity disorders. Tic disorders
7–13	Industry vs. inferiority: Peer relations important, risk-taking behavior begins	Latency	Concrete operations: Child appears rational and able to conceptualize shapes and sizes of observed objects (7–13 yr)	Psychosomatic disorders, personality disorders, neurotic disorders, antisocial behavioral patterns, anorexia nervosa, bulimia nervosa
13–18	Identity vs. role diffusion: Develops sense of self, role model important	Genital phase	Formal operations: Person is able to abstract and can deal with external reality. Can conceptualize in adult manner and evaluate logically. Ideals develop (12 or 13 yr through adulthood)	Suicidal peak in adolescents, schizophrenia, identity crisis.
Early adulthood	Intimacy vs. isolation: Love relationships, group affiliations important	Genital phase consolidation		Anxiety states. Bipolar I disorder
Middle adulthood	Generativity vs. self-absorption or stagnation: Contributing to future generations, acceptance of accomplishments	Maturity		Mid-life crisis. Dysthymic disorder
Late adulthood	Integrity vs. despair: Learning to accept death, maintaining personal values			Highest suicide rates, cognitive disorders

about 15 years of age). The child develops true abstract thought during that time and is able to make hypotheses and test them logically.

The critical achievement of the *sensorimotor* stage (birth to 2 years) is the construction of object concepts. Objects and one's sense of their permanence are constructed during the first year or so of life by the progressive coordination of sensorimotor schemata—elementary concepts—that result from the infant's actions on the world and from its growing mental abilities and motor skills.

During the stage of *preoperational thought* (2 to 5 years), children begin to give evidence of having attained a new level of mental functioning. The evidence is shown not only in the child's language but also in its play, dreams, and imitative behavior. Those behaviors are symbolic. They are processes by which the child re-presents objects and activities in their absence. The attainment of object permanence, which involves representation by means of visual images, marks the transition from sensorimotor to preoperational or intuitive intelligence.

Toward the age of 5 or 6, children give evidence of having attained another level of mental structures that Piaget called *concrete operations.* Those operations enable children to engage in syllogistic reasoning, which permits them to acquire and to follow rules. In addition, concrete operations enable young people to construct unit concepts (a unit, such as a number, is both like and different from every other number) and thus to quantify their experience. That period of development is characterized by the construction of the lawful world.

Epigenesis is a term introduced by Erik Erikson to refer to the stages of ego and social development during the various stages of the life cycle.

4.8.   The answer is B (*Synopsis VII*, page 158).

The critical cognitive achievement of *Piaget's sensorimotor stage* of development (birth to 2 years) is the construction of object concepts. The most important of those concepts is object permanence, and its attainment heralds the end of the sensorimotor period. To adults, objects have an existence independent of their immediate experience; a person or an object continues to exist even when it is not immediately present. That capacity is not innate, nor is it simply learned. A sense of object permanence is constructed during the first year or so of life, as the infant becomes progressively more coordinated—visually, motorically, and mentally.

The *latency stage* was described by Sigmund Freud as a stage of relative quiescence of the sexual drive; the latency stage occurs after the resolution of the Oedipus complex and extends until pubescence. The *preattachment stage* is a concept of John Bowlby's; it refers to the period during the first two to three months of life. Piaget's *stage of concrete operations* is characterized by deductive or syllogistic reasoning and encompasses the years between 7 and 11. The *stage of formal operations* is characterized by

the attainment of abstract thought and extends from the age of 11 through the end of adolescence.

4.9.   The answer is E (all) (*Synopsis VII*, pages 158–159).

Piaget's stage of preoperational thought coincides in time with Sigmund Freud's oedipal phase and Erik Erikson's phase of initiative versus guilt. It is characterized by *intuitive,* as opposed to logical, *thinking* and transductive reasoning. Preoperational children display *egocentric thinking,* believing themselves to be the center of the universe, and they assume that whatever they are thinking or talking about is automatically—in fact, *magically*—understood by the other. The children are also observed to engage in thinking that is *animistic* and phenomenalistic. Animistic thinking is characterized by the endowment of inanimate objects with lifelike attributes (for example, "The chair hates me," "The moon is running"). Phenomenalistic causality is the belief that events that occur in close temporal proximity cause one another (for example, thinking bad thoughts about the mother caused the mother to get sick) and is another term for magical thinking. When adults regress under stress, they can return to the stage of preoperational thought.

4.10.   The answer is E (all) (*Synopsis VII*, pages 161–164).

John Bowlby was concerned with the concept of attachment, its development, and the consequences of its disruption. Bowlby defined attachment as the *reciprocal affectionate relationship* between the infant and the primary caretaker that is gradually *developed during the first year of life.* The development of attachment between the infant and the caretaker is *dependent on the intensity, the quality, and the amount of time spent together.*

Bowlby believed that early separation and disruption of attachment have persistent and irreversible effects on personality and intelligence. He pointed to the overt and dynamic similarities between withdrawn, depressed behavior in infants and young children separated from the primary caretaker and mourning behavior in adults. He viewed attachment to a mothering figure as *an instinctive behavior pattern* and hypothesized that smiling increases the infant's chances of survival, as it makes the infant more appealing to the mother. He further suggested that smiling has been favorably selected in evolutionary terms and that infants without a strong smiling response have a higher than usual mortality rate.

4.11.   The answer is E (all) (*Synopsis VII*, page 195).

Validity is the degree to which a test measures what it claims to measure and the degree to which an experimental design yields data truly applicable to the phenomenon under investigation. Predictive validity is one type of validity used to judge the classification of a mental disorder. The validity of mental disorder classification is the extent to which the entire classification and each of its specific diagnostic categories achieve the purposes of communication, control, and comprehension. Predictive validity is also *the extent to which knowledge that a person has a particular mental disorder is useful in predicting the future course of the illness*, complications, and response to treatment. Predictive validity is directly *related to management and treatment; thus, it is relevant to the specificity with which patients with bipolar I disorder improve when treated with lithium* whereas (Eskalios) patients with depressive disorders do not. Predictive validity is *the basis on which Emil Kraepelin differentiated manic-depressive psychosis from dementia precox* because, in dementia precox deterioration occurred, whereas in manic-depressive psychosis the patient did not deteriorate.

4.12. The answer is E (*Synopsis VII*, pages 171–172).

Curiosity and aggression show no correlation. In the normal child, aggression can be effectively understood in terms of the motives—for example, defense and mastery—for which aggressiveness is a suitable mediator. Its increased frequency in abnormal children can be correlated with defects in the organism, as in the case of *brain injury*, or with distortions in the child's environment, as in the case of *faulty identification models*. Moreover, the frequency of the display of aggressive behavior is a function of the child's *cultural environment*. Aggressive fantasy materials—*violence in movies*, crime comics, and television—rather than affording catharsis for instinctual aggressiveness, generate the very tensions they profess to release.

A central issue is the meaning to be ascribed to the term "aggression." If a boy is observed taking apart a watch, that behavior may be aggressive—if, for example, the watch belongs to the child's father, and the father has just punished him. However, if the watch is an old one in his stock of toys, the boy's motive may be curiosity about its mechanism, especially if he takes delight in reassembling it. If he strikes another child, that act may be motivated by aggression if the victim is the baby sister his parents have just embraced. Or the blow may be defensive if the victim has made a threatening gesture or has tried to seize the boy's favorite toy. Homely anecdotes make the point, but documented experimental examples of aggressive children are also available: children emulating adult models, children systematically subjected to frustration, and children watching films or television of aggressive behavior—all of whom show predictable increases in aggressiveness.

4.13. The answer is D (*Synopsis VII*, pages 181–184).

The long-term effects of six months of total social isolation produce adolescent monkeys that *are both abnormally aggressive and abnormally fearful*. The isolates *exhibit aggression against agemates who are more physically adept than they*.

Infant monkeys that survive a three-month, rather than a six-month, total social isolation can *make a remarkable social adjustment through the development of play*. When allowed to interact with equal-age normally reared monkeys, the isolates play effectively within a week.

Monkeys totally isolated for a 12-month period *are totally unresponsive to the new physical and social world with which they are presented*. Those isolates are devoid of social play and strong emotion. Totally isolated monkeys exhibit a depressive-type posture, including self-clutch, rocking, and depressive huddling. Partially isolated monkeys assume, with increasing frequency, *postures that are bizarre and schizoid*, such as extreme stereotypy and sitting at the front of the cage and staring vacantly into space.

4.14. The answer is C (*Synopsis VII*, pages 181–184).

The initial reaction of the infant monkey to separation from mother is the strongly emotional protest stage, which is characterized by upset and continuous agitation on the part of the infant. When the separation is prolonged beyond two or three weeks, the infant's behavior changes to reflect the onset of the *despair* stage, in which the deprived monkey engages in less than usual activity, little or no play, and occasional crying. There is a parallel here to separation among humans and the occurrence of grief that is sometimes reflected in initial protest and later in despair.

Yearning is an urgent longing that is sometimes felt toward the deceased. *Resolution* is similar to C. M. Parkes' stage of reorganization in which a person comes to accept the loss of a loved one. *Acceptance* is the final stage to impending death described by Elisabeth Kübler-Ross and is the recognition that death is universal.

4.15. The answer is E (all) (*Synopsis VII*, pages 181–184).

Harlow's study showed that, *at initial separation, the rhesus infants exhibited a protest stage* which included aggressive attempts to regain maternal contact, plaintive vocalization, and a persistent pattern of nondirected behavior. *The protest stage changed to despair* during the subsequent 48 hours. The most dramatic indicator of the despair stage was the almost total suppression of play. Associated with the suppression was a marked decrease in vocalization and movement. *Play was almost abolished during the three-week period of maternal separation, but resumed rapidly after maternal reunion.* The separated monkey infants typically reattached to the monkey mother vigorously and rapidly when the separation phase ended. In contrast, John Bowlby noted that, when many human children are reunited with their mothers, their responses are often those of rejection, termed by Bowlby the detachment stage.

In Harlow's study of monkeys, the age chosen to begin experimental maternal deprivation was 6 months, which was the age at which play appeared to be maximally matured. The separation was obtained by physically preventing the infant monkeys from being able to touch their mothers or to return from their play area into the home area, where their mothers could be seen. All *monkeys tested showed a nearly complete picture of human anaclitic depression.* Anaclitic depression is the term used by René Spitz for the syndrome shown by infants who are separated from their mothers for long periods of time. In Spitz's series, the reaction occurred in children who were 6 to 8 months old at the time of the separation, which continued for a practically unbroken period of three months.

4.16. The answer is A (*Synopsis VII*, page 203).

Planned *preventive trials* determine whether a planned modification of circumstances actually lowers the incidence of disease. The trials provide more information than any other method about the causes of disease.

A form of preventive trial occurs when a major reform is introduced with the intent of preventing a specific form of disorder. The trial cannot be designed to include a control group because the reform involves the reorganization of all the mental health services of a community to effect *community prevention.*

Encompassed within the scope of prevention in psychiatry are measures to prevent mental disorders *(primary prevention)*; measures to limit the severity of illness, as through early case finding and treatment *(secondary prevention)*; and measures to reduce disability after a patient has a disorder *(tertiary prevention)*. An example of primary prevention is prenatal parent training groups, an example of secondary prevention is psychotherapy, and an example of tertiary prevention is social skills rehabilitation training of schizophrenic patients.

4.17. The answer is A (*Synopsis VII*, pages 149 and 198).

Prevalence is the *proportion of a population that has a condition at one moment in time.* The *ratio of persons who acquire a disorder during a year's time* (new cases) is called the annual incidence. In a stable situation, the prevalence is approximately equal to the annual incidence times the average duration, measured in years, of the condition. The *risk of acquiring a condition at some time* in the future is the accumulation of age-specific annual incidence rates over a period of time.

Standard deviation (SD) is a statistical measure of variability within a set of values so defined that, for a normal distribution, about 68 percent of the values fall within one SD of the mean, and about 95

percent lie within two SDs of the mean. It is sometimes represented by σ, the Greek letter sigma.

The *rate of first admissions to a hospital for a disorder* is the ratio of all first admissions to an average general hospital during a particular year.

4.18. The answer is B (*Synopsis VII*, page 194).

Alexander Leighton headed a psychiatric epidemiological study of Stirling County in Canada. The Stirling County study found that *women showed more mental disorders than did men* and that *only about 20 percent of the population were free of psychiatric symptoms.* In terms of symptom categories, *psychophysiological symptoms were found in 66 percent* of the men and 71 percent of the women. Neurosis was found in 44 percent of the men and 64 percent of the women. Age was found to be a factor; *mental disorders increased with age.* The study also disclosed that *mental health was related to economic status.*

4.19. The answer is E (all) (*Synopsis VII*, pages 212 and 214)

Hospitals are organized in a variety of ways in the United States. *The state mental hospital system has about 119,000 beds.* State psychiatric hospitals have been markedly reduced in population since the 1960s and the 1970s, when deinstitutionalization and effective somatic therapies combined to focus on the outpatient treatment of mentally ill persons. *Investor-owned hospitals* are for-profit hospitals and *are increasing in importance. Veterans Affairs (VA) hospitals are usually affiliated with medical schools* and with the U.S. Department of Defense, Public Health Service, and other entities. In *special hospitals, 70 percent of the facility must be designated for the treatment of a single condition* (not including substance-abuse or other mental disorders). Table 4.2 summarizes some aspects of hospital organization.

4.20–4.23

4.20. The answer is A (*Synopsis VII*, pages 213–215).

4.21. The answer is C (*Synopsis VII*, pages 213–215).

4.22. The answer is D (*Synopsis VII*, pages 213–215).

4.23. The answer is B (*Synopsis VII*, page 215).

A *health maintenance organization (HMO)* is an organized system providing comprehensive (both inpatient and outpatient) health care in all specialties, including psychiatry. *Members* voluntarily *pay a prepayment or capitation fee to cover all health care services* for a fixed period of time (a month or a year). There are currently 553 HMOs in the United States—down from 647 in 1987—despite an increase in enrollment to about 34 million people. By using a capitation or prospective payment method, the HMO

Table 4.2
Some Aspects of Hospital Organization

Criteria	Investor-Owned Hospitals	State Mental Hospital System	Federal Hospital System	Special Hospitals*
Patient population	All illnesses, although hospital may specialize	Mental illness	All illnesses	70 percent of facility must be for single diagnosis
Number of hospitals	834	285 (119,000 beds nationally)	342	150
Profit orientation	For profit	Nonprofit	Nonprofit	For profit or nonprofit
Ownership	Private corporation: may be owned by MDs	State	Federal government	Private or public
Affiliation	May be owned by large chains, such as Humana Corporation	Free-standing or affiliated with various medical schools	Department of Defense (190); Public Health Service, Coast Guard, Prison, Merchant Marine, Indian Health Service; Veterans Affairs (139)	Optional affiliation with medical schools
Other	Increasing in importance nationally	Deinstitutionalization number of patients has been reduced	VA hospitals usually have affiliations with medical schools	Less regulated than other types of hospitals

*Special hospitals include obstetrics and gynecology; eye, ear, nose, and throat; etc. They do not include psychiatric hospitals or substance-abuse hospitals.

is assuming a dominant role in United States health care. The HMO is popular because it decreases health care costs by limiting the number of new hospitalizations and by discharging patients from the hospital earlier than usual. The emphasis on prevention and health promotion and on performing as much diagnosis and therapy as possible on an outpatient basis also helps control expenses.

Both the HMO and the preferred provider organization (PPO) use a prospective payment system. In the PPO, however, a corporation or an insurance company makes an agreement with a particular group of community hospitals and doctors to *supply health services at a lower than usual rate for its members.* Patients who enroll in a PPO select their physicians from among the list of participating doctors, which includes both specialists and primary care physicians. Inpatient care is provided at the designated hospital that the patient chooses. There are about 1,000 PPOs in the United States at this time.

Neither the HMO nor the PPO is equivalent to a health systems agency. Health systems agencies (HSAs) are nonprofit organizations mandated by the federal government and set up on a statewide basis. HSAs promote or limit the development of health services and facilities, depending on the needs of a particular locality or state. They are made up of consumers and have considerable power in medicine. HSAs control capital expenditures and, therefore, the availability of health resources. In each state, HSAs develop both long-term and short-term goals and plans, approve health care proposals requesting federal funding, review existing facilities and services, and suggest future construction and renovation projects on the basis of their findings.

4.24–4.28

4.24. The answer is B (*Synopsis VII*, pages 193–194, 199, and 207).

4.25. The answer is B (*Synopsis VII*, pages 193–194, 199, and 207).

4.26. The answer is A (*Synopsis VII*, pages 193–194, 199, and 207).

4.27. The answer is A (*Synopsis VII*, pages 193–194, 199, and 207).

4.28. The answer is A (*Synopsis VII*, pages 193–194, 199, and 207).

A person's socioeconomic status is not based solely on income but includes such factors as education, occupation, and life-style. The socioeconomic status of the patient influences attitudes toward physical and mental health, as listed in Table 4.3. For example, *upper middle class* persons are *more able to delay gratification* than lower class persons and *seek health care earlier* than lower class persons. Lower class persons often *see pregnancy as a time of crisis*, have *longer hospital stays* than upper middle class persons, and have *low contraceptive use.*

Table 4.3
Attitudes toward Health Issues

Lower Class	Upper Middle Class
Look for immediate solutions	More able to delay gratification
Negative view on life	More positive view of life
Low contraceptive use	High contraceptive use
Seek health care later	Seek health care earlier
Longer hospital stays	Shorter hospital stays
See pregnancy as a time of crisis	See pregnancy as a normal event

4.29–4.32

4.29. **The answer is C** (*Synopsis VII*, page 179).

4.30. **The answer is D** (*Synopsis VII*, page 182).

4.31. **The answer is A** (*Synopsis VII*, page 181).

4.32. **The answer is B** (*Synopsis VII*, page 170).

Imprinting has been described as the process by which certain stimuli become capable of eliciting certain innate behavior patterns during a critical period of an animal's behavioral development. The phenomenon is associated with *Konrad Lorenz*, who in 1935 demonstrated that the first moving object (in that case, Lorenz himself) a duckling sees during a critical period shortly after hatching is thereafter regarded and reacted to as the mother duck.

Harry Harlow is associated with the concept of the *surrogate mother* from his experiments in the 1950s with rhesus monkeys. Harlow designed a series of experiments in which infant monkeys were separated from their mothers during the earliest weeks of life. He found that the infant monkeys, if given the choice between a wire surrogate mother and a cloth-covered surrogate mother, chose the cloth-covered surrogates even if the wire surrogates provided food.

Ivan Petrovich Pavlov coined the term *"experimental neurosis"* to describe disorganized behavior that appears in the experimental subject (in Pavlov's case, dogs) in response to an inability to master the experimental situation. Pavlov described extremely agitated behavior in his dogs when they were unable to discriminate between sounds of similar pitch or test objects of similar shapes.

Eric Kandel contributed to the knowledge of the neurophysiology of learning. He demonstrated in the study of the snail *aplysia* that synaptic connections are altered as a result of learning.

4.33–4.37

4.33. **The answer is C** (*Synopsis VII*, page 158).

4.34. **The answer is D** (*Synopsis VII*, page 158).

4.35. **The answer is A** (*Synopsis VII*, pages 158–159).

4.36. **The answer is E** (*Synopsis VII*, page 159).

4.37. **The answer is B** (*Synopsis VII*, pages 159–161).

During Piaget's sensorimotor stage of development, the child develops *object permanence*. By *9 to 12 months*, the child has the ability to retain an object in its mind when the object is no longer in view. At that time, peekaboo becomes a game joyfully played with the child.

The end of the sensorimotor stage is marked by the attainment of *symbolic thought* by the child of *18 to 24 months* of age. With the acquisition of symbolic thought, the whole world of symbolic play is open to the child.

Ages *2 through 7 years* mark the years of preoperational thought, the stage of prelogical thinking. The child believes in immanent justice—that a bad deed will inevitably be punished. The child also believes in *magical thinking*, the idea that thoughts or wishes—good or bad—can come true. Magical thinking has positive and negative repercussions. After some ill has befallen a loved one, for example, the child may blame himself or herself because of "bad" wishes. Happily, some children believe they are gaining a new sibling because they have wished for it, and they can view a new baby as a present.

Ages *7 to 11 years* are the years of concrete operations. The child is able to understand classifications and *cause and effect*. At that time the child is also able to take another's point of view, and in games children can take turns and follow rules.

The stage of formal operations is entered at about age *11 years through adolescence*. It is the time of the acquisition of abstract logic. In addition to being able to hypothesize and make deductions, the young person can comprehend probabilities and can now *think about thoughts*.

Psychology and Psychiatry: Psychometric and Neuropsychological Testing

Psychometric and neuropsychological testing are essential and widely used investigative tools in the workup and the treatment of many patients. Psychometric testing provides a valuable evaluation of cognitive functioning, intelligence, and personality that can help clarify the diagnosis, the prognosis, and the treatment. The tests vary from objective to projective and from individual to group. Neuropsychological tests evaluate cognitive and behavioral disturbances produced by injury or abnormal development of the brain. A number of tests together constitute a battery that can provide a wide and diverse evaluation of various areas of functioning—memory, visual-spatial orientation, abstract reasoning, and mood. Psychiatrists rely on clinical psychologists to perform the tests, but psychiatrists must be knowledgeable about which tests are available, what each test evaluates, the implications of the test results, and each test's validity and reliability. A number of factors can interfere with the validity of neu-

ropsychological test results, including anxiety, depression, medications, language barriers, and formal educational deficits.

One aspect of neuropsychological testing that is becoming increasingly sophisticated and thus increasingly relevant to both clinical practice and research is neuroanatomical localization of deficits. For instance, many mental status cognitive tests, from spelling words backward to writing a sentence, help direct the clinician's or the researcher's attention to a specific area of the brain from which the ability to perform those tasks is thought to emanate. As knowledge about neuroanatomical localization becomes increasingly specific, neuropsychiatric testing will become even more critically useful than it is at present.

Chapter 5 in *Kaplan and Sadock's Synopsis VII* covers both psychological and neuropsychiatric testing. Students should review that chapter and then study the questions and answers below.

HELPFUL HINTS

The psychological terms and tests listed here should be defined and memorized.

psychodynamic formulations	WAIS	Henry Murray and Christiana Morgan
standardization	verbal subtests	Morgan
validity	performance subtests	Raven's Progressive Matrices
reliability	full-scale I.Q.	representational
objective tests	bell-shaped curve	motivational aspects of behavior
projective tests	scatter pattern	SCT
individual and group tests	WISC	word-association technique
battery tests	WPPSI	stimulus words
Alfred Binet	classification of intelligence	reaction times
mental age	personality testing	clang association
intelligence quotient (I.Q.)	Rorschach test	perseveration
average I.Q.	TAT	MMPI

accurate profile	neuropsychiatric tests	dysgraphia
Bender Visual-Motor Gestalt test	Shipley Abstraction test	attention
maturational levels	dementia	catastrophic reaction
Gestalt psychology	abstract reasoning	attention-deficit/hyperactivity
coping phase	behavioral flexibility	disorder
recall phase	memory—left versus right	Stanford-Binet
organic dysfunction	hemisphere disease	learning disability
DAPT	orientation	EEG abnormalities
interrogation procedure	temporal orientation	manual dexterity
House-Tree-Person test	visual-object agnosia	Luria-Nebraska
test behavior	dressing apraxia	Neuropsychological Battery
personality functioning	DSS	(LNNB)
inferred diagnosis	prosody	Halstead-Reitan
prognosis	fluency	mental status cognitive tasks
primary assets and weaknesses	dyslexia	

QUESTIONS

DIRECTIONS: Each of the incomplete statements below is followed by five suggested completions. Select the *one* that is *best* in each case.

5.1. The patient was an 82-year-old widow who, over the previous five years, had been hospitalized for three minor strokes, from which she had recovered except for some slurred speech and right-side weakness. Over the past year, her friends had noticed an apathetic attitude toward her previously meticulously maintained apartment. She had some loss of memory about such things as whether she had gone shopping or had bathed, and she showed some lapses in judgment. Her long-term memory was relatively good. When visited by a medical team in her home, the patient was cooperative and cheerful and denied any problems but showed evidence of recent memory loss, disorientation to time, and concrete interpretations of proverbs.

The most likely diagnosis, based on those findings, is
A. amnestic disorder
B. normal aging
C. vascular dementia
D. dementia of the Alzheimer's type
E. major depressive disorder

5.2. In the assessment of personality
A. the Thematic Apperception Test (TAT) requires the patient to construct or create stories about pictures
B. in the Rorschach test, lack of attention to detail is common in paranoid and obsessive subjects
C. tests using a projective approach are interpreted against a set of normative data
D. the word-association technique is no longer used
E. the Minnesota Multiphasic Personality Inventory (MMPI) uses a projective approach

5.3. In the field of memory
A. a nonverbal visual task is a poor assessor of immediate memory
B. recent memory can be tested by digit-span tasks
C. episodic memory is memory for knowledge and facts
D. the Wechsler Memory Scale yields a memory quotient
E. semantic memory and implicit memory decline with age

5.4. An intelligence quotient (I.Q.) of 100 corresponds to intellectual ability for the general population in the
A. 20th percentile
B. 25th percentile
C. 40th percentile
D. 50th percentile
E. 65th percentile

5.5. The first sign of beginning cerebral disease is often impairment in
A. remote memory
B. long-term memory
C. immediate memory
D. recent memory
E. none of the above

Figure 5.1. Drawing done on the Draw-a-Person Test (DAPT).

5.6. The most likely diagnosis for a 43-year-old college professor who drew Figure 5.1 on the Draw-a-Person Test (DAPT) is
A. obsessive-compulsive personality disorder
B. dysthymic disorder
C. brain damage
D. conversion disorder
E. bipolar I disorder, most recent episode manic

5.7. In the assessment of intelligence
A. the highest divisor is the intelligence quotient (I.Q.) formula is 25
B. the I.Q. is a measure of future potential
C. the Stanford-Binet test is the most widely used intelligence test
D. the average or normal range of I.Q. is 70 to 100
E. intelligence levels are based on the assumption that intellectual abilities are normally distributed

5.8. The Bender Visual-Motor Gestalt test is administered to test
A. maturation levels in children
B. organic dysfunction
C. loss of function
D. visual and motor coordination
E. all the above

5.9. In interpreting the Thematic Apperception Test (TAT), the examiner considers
A. many areas of the patient's functioning
B. with whom the patient identifies
C. all the figures
D. motivational aspects of behavior
E. all the above

DIRECTIONS: Each group of questions below consists of lettered headings followed by a list of numbered statements. For each numbered statement, select the *one* lettered heading that is most closely associated with it. Each lettered heading may be selected once, more than once, or not at all.

Questions 5.10–5.12
A. Bender Visual-Motor Gestalt test
B. Shipley Abstraction test
C. Raven's Progressive Matrices

5.10. A test of visuomotor coordination

5.11. A multiple-choice pictorial display

5.12. Impaired performance is associated with poor visuoconstructive ability

Questions 5.13–5.16
A. Wechsler Adult Intelligence Scale (WAIS)
B. Minnesota Multiphasic Personality Inventory (MMPI)
C. Thematic Apperception Test (TAT)
D. None of the above

5.13. The patient is asked to construct stories

5.14. Eleven subtests, six verbal and five performance, yielding a verbal I.Q., a performance I.Q., and a full-scale I.Q.

5.15. The self-report inventory consists of 550 statements to which the person has to respond with "True," "False," or "Cannot say"

5.16. A series of sentence stems, such as "I like . . . ," that patients are asked to complete in their own words

Questions 5.17–5.21

A. Rorschach test
B. Luria-Nebraska Neuropsychological Battery
C. Halstead-Reitan Battery of Neurological Tests
D. Stanford-Binet
E. None of the above

5.17. Consists of 10 tests, including the trail making test and the critical flicker frequency test

5.18. Is extremely sensitive in identifying discrete forms of brain damage, such as dyslexia

5.19. Consists of 120 items, plus several alternative tests, applicable to the ages between 2 years and adulthood

5.20. Furnishes a description of the dynamic forces of personality through an analysis of the person's responses

5.21. A test of diffuse cerebral dysfunction to which normal children by the age of 7 years respond negatively

Questions 5.22–5.26

A. Frontal lobes
B. Dominant temporal lobe
C. Nondominant parietal lobe
D. Dominant parietal lobe
E. Occipital lobes

5.22. The loss of gestalt, the loss of symmetry, and the distortion of figures

5.23. Patient cannot name a camouflaged object but can name it when it is not camouflaged

5.24. Two or more errors or two or more seven-second delays in carrying out tasks of right-left orientation

5.25. Any improper letter sequence in spelling "earth" backward

5.26. Patients cannot name common objects

Questions 5.27–5.30

A. Wechsler Adult Intelligence Scale (WAIS)
B. Wechsler Intelligence Scale for Children (WISC)
C. Wechsler Preschool and Primary Scale of Intelligence (WPPSI)
D. All the above
E. None of the above

5.27. A scale for children ages 6 through 16 years

5.28. A scale for children ages 4 to 6½ years

5.29. Educational background affects the information and vocabulary segments

5.30. Assesses children from 8 weeks to 2½ years of age

Questions 5.31–5.34

A. Beck Depression Inventory
B. Hamilton Depression Rating Scale
C. Brief Psychiatric Rating Scale

5.31. Self-administered

5.32. Emphasizes subjective mood and thoughts

5.33. Emphasizes neurovegetative symptoms

5.34. Provides a global pathology index

ANSWERS

Psychology and Psychiatry: Psychometric and Neuropsychological Testing

5.1. **The answer is C** (*Synopsis VII*, pages 230–236).

The most likely diagnosis for the patient described is *vascular dementia* because of her stepwise deterioration associated with focal neurological signs, suggesting that the patient's strokes contributed to the dementia. The salient features of the case are the patient's loss of intellectual abilities of sufficient severity to interfere with functioning (no longer able to maintain apartment or personal hygiene), loss of memory, impaired abstract thinking (concrete interpretation of proverbs), personality change (apathetic attitude), and impaired judgment—all occurring in a clear state of consciousness.

Although memory disturbance is prominent, it is not an *amnestic disorder*, an impairment of short-term and long-term memory attributed to a specific organic factor. The diagnosis is not made if it is associated with impairment in abstract thinking, impaired judgment, other disturbances of high cortical function, or personality change. *Normal aging* does not involve a global deterioration in intellectual abilities; in the absence of evidence for a cause other than those associated with aging (for example, a neoplasm or an endocrine disturbance), the differential diagnosis is between *dementia of the Alzheimer's type* and vascular dementia. In the elderly, apathy, loss of interest, and apparent memory loss may indicate a *major depressive disorder*. However, in this case the patient's cheerful mood rules that out.

5.2. **The answer is A** (*Synopsis VII*, pages 229–230).

The Thematic Apperception Test (TAT) requires the patient to construct or create stories about pictures. It is a projective personality test that consists of 30 pictures and one blank card. Although most of the pictures depict people and all are representational, each picture is ambiguous. Generally, the TAT is more useful as a technique for inferring motivational aspects of behavior than as a basis for making a diagnosis.

The Rorschach test, another projective personality test, consists of standard set of 10 inkblots that serve as stimuli for associations. The cards are shown to the patient in a particular order. The examiner keeps a record of the patient's verbatim response, initial reaction time, and total time spent on each card. After the completion of the free-association phase, the examiner conducts an inquiry phase to determine important aspects of each response that are crucial to its scoring. An overattention to detail, not a *lack of attention to detail, is common in paranoid and obsessive subjects.*

Projective tests are essentially idiographic. *Tests using a projective approach are not interpreted against a set of normative data.* Typically, the interpretation is based on a theory of human behavior and personality; each person is assumed to have certain needs, characteristics, defenses, and other qualities that become apparent through the testing process.

The word-association technique is still used, primarily by psychodynamically oriented psychiatrists. In the technique, devised by Carl Gustav Jung, stimulus words are presented to patients, who respond to them with the first word that comes to mind. After the initial administration of the list, some clinicians repeat the list, asking the patient to respond with the same words used previously. Discrepancies between the two administrations of the list may reveal association difficulties.

The Minnesota Multiphasic Personality Inventory (MMPI), uses an objective approach, not a projective approach, to personality assessment. The objective approach is characterized by reliance on structured, standardized measurement devices—that is, straightforward test stimuli, such as direct questions regarding the subjects' opinions of themselves, and unambiguous instructions regarding the completion of the test. The MMPI is a self-report inventory that is the most widely used and most thoroughly researched of the objective personality assessment instruments. The test consists of more than 500 statements—such as, "I worry about sex matters," "I sometimes tease animals," and "I believe I am being plotted against"—to which the subject must respond with "true," "false," or "cannot say." The MMPI gives scores on 10 standard clinical scales, each of which was derived empirically (that is, homogeneous criterion groups of psychiatric patients were used in developing the scales). The items for each scale were selected for their ability to separate medical and psychiatric patients from normal controls. Various researchers have identified numerous personality correlates of various MMPI scales as the basis for core interpretive statements.

5.3. **The answer is D** (*Synopsis VII*, page 231).

Memory is a comprehensive term that covers the retention of all types of material over various periods of time and that involves diverse forms of response. The Wechsler Memory Scale (WMS) is the most widely used memory test battery for adults. It is a composite of verbal paired-associate retention, paragraph retention, visual memory for designs, orientation, digit span, rote recall of the alphabet, and counting backward. *The Wechsler Memory Scale yields a memory quotient* (M.Q.), which is corrected for age and generally approximates the Wechsler Adult Intelligence Scale (WAIS) I.Q.

Immediate (or short-term) memory is the reproduction, recognition, or recall of perceived material within 30 seconds of presentation. It is most often assessed by digit repetition and reversal (auditory) tests and memory-for-designs (visual) tests. Both an auditory-verbal task, such as digit span or memory for words or sentences, and a nonverbal visual task, such as memory for designs or for objects or faces, are good assessors of the patient's immediate memory. Patients can also be asked to listen to a standardized story and to repeat the story as they heard it. Patients with lesions of the right hemisphere of the brain are likely to show more severe defects on visual nonverbal tasks than on auditory verbal tasks. Conversely, patients with left hemisphere lesions, including patients who are not aphasic, are likely to show severe deficits on the auditory verbal tests, with variable performance on the visual nonverbal tasks.

Recent memory cannot be tested by digit-span tasks, as can immediate memory. Recent memory concerns events over the past few hours or days; it can be tested by asking patients what they had for breakfast and who visited them in the hospital.

Other types of memory that theorists have described include episodic memory, semantic memory, and implicit memory. Episodic memory is memory for specific events, such as a telephone message. *Episodic memory is not memory for knowledge and facts*; that is semantic memory. An example of semantic memory is knowing who was the first President of the United States. *Semantic memory and implicit memory do not decline with age*; persons continue to accumulate information over a lifetime. Episodic memory shows a minimal decline with aging that may relate to impaired frontal lobe functioning.

5.4. The answer is D (*Synopsis VII*, page 222).

An intelligence quotient (I.Q.) of 100 corresponds to the *50th percentile* in intellectual ability for the general population. Modern psychological testing began in the first decade of the 20th century when Alfred Binet (1857–1911), a French psychologist, developed the first intelligence scale to separate the mentally defective (who were to be given special education) from the rest of the children (whose school progress was to be accelerated).

5.5. The answer is D (*Synopsis VII*, page 231).

Impairment in *recent memory*, the inability to recall the past several hours or days, is a prominent

behavioral deficit in brain-damaged patients and is often the first sign of beginning cerebral disease. Recent memory is also known as short-term memory. *Remote memory*, also known as *long-term memory*, consists of childhood data or important events known to have occurred when the patient was young or free of illness. *Immediate memory* is memory after five seconds and is the ability to repeat four to seven digits forward and backward. Patients with unimpaired memory can usually recall six or seven digits backward.

Memory is based on three essential processes: (1) registration, the ability to establish a record of an experience; (2) retention, the persistence or permanence of a registered experience; and (3) recall, the ability to arouse and repeat in consciousness a previously registered experience. A good memory involves the capacity to register swiftly and accurately, to retain for long periods of time, and to recall promptly. Memory is usually evaluated from the view of recent memory and remote memory.

5.6. The answer is C (*Synopsis VII*, page 229).

The most likely diagnosis for the 43-year-old college professor who drew Figure 5.1 on the Draw-a-Person Test (DAPT) is *brain damage*. Brain-damaged patients often have a great deal of trouble projecting their images of the body into a figure drawing. Experience with the drawing technique allows for recognition of differences in drawings by brain-damaged patients from drawings by patients with other disorders. The DAPT should be used with other psychological tests to confirm the diagnosis. Deficiencies that accompany brain malfunctioning are frequently highlighted by means of psychological tests. Occasionally they are most apparent in areas ordinarily conceptualized as intellectual—in memory ability, arithmetical skills, and the analysis of visual designs. At other times they are most apparent in graphomotor productions, such as the DAPT, in which such distortions as difficulties in spatial orientation, fragmentation, and oversimplification of the figures can occur.

Obsessive-compulsive personality disorder patients in general pay attention to details of anatomy and clothing and show long, continuous lines; *dysthymic disorder* patients may draw small sizes, heavy lines, few details, and dejected facial expressions; patients with *conversion disorder* may show exaggeration, emphasis, or, conversely, negligence of body parts involved in the conversion symptom; persons with *bipolar I disorder, most recent episode manic*, may draw large, colorful figures with exaggerated features, sometimes filling the whole page.

5.7. The answer is E (*Synopsis VII*, pages 221–222).

Intelligence levels are based on the assumption that intellectual abilities are normally distributed (in a bell-shaped curve) throughout the population. Intelligence can be defined as a person's ability to assimilate factual knowledge, recall either recent or remote events, reason logically, manipulate concepts (either numbers or words), translate the abstract to the literal and the literal to the abstract, analyze and synthesize forms, and deal meaningfully and accurately with problems and priorities deemed important in a particular setting. In 1905 Alfred Binet introduced the concept of the mental age (M.A), which is the average intellectual level at a particular age. The intelligence quotient (I.Q.) is the ratio of M.A. over C.A. (chronological age) multiplied by 100 to do away with the decimal point; it is represented by the following equation:

$$I.Q. = \frac{M.A.}{C.A.} \times 100$$

When the chronological age and the mental age are equal, the I.Q. is 100—that is, average. Since it is impossible to measure increments of intellectual power past the age of 15 by available intelligence tests, *the highest divisor in the I.Q. formula is 15, not 25.*

As measured by most intelligence tests, I.Q. is an interpretation or a classification of a total test score in relation to norms established by a group. *I.Q. is a measure of present functioning ability, not of future potential.* Under ordinary circumstances the I.Q. is stable throughout life, but there is no certainty about its predictive properties.

The Wechsler Adult Intelligence Scale (WAIS), not the *Stanford-Binet test, is the most widely used intelligence test* in clinical practice today. The WAIS was constructed by David Wechsler at New York University Medical Center and Bellevue Psychiatric Hospital. It comprises 11 subtests—six verbal subtests and five performance subtests—yielding a verbal I.Q., a performance I.Q., and a combined or full-scale I.Q. The verbal I.Q., the performance I.Q., and the full-scale I.Q. are determined by the use of separate tables for each of the seven age groups (from 16 to 64 years) on which the test was standardized.

The average or normal range of I.Q. is 90 to 110, not 70 to 100. I.Q. scores of 120 and higher are considered superior. According to the American Association of Mental Deficiency (AAMD) and the fourth edition of *Diagnostic and Statistical Manual of Mental Disorders* (DSM-IV), mental retardation is defined as an I.Q. of 70 or below, which is found in the lowest 2.2 percent of the population. Consequently, 2 out of every 100 persons have I.Q. scores consistent with mental retardation, which can range from mild to profound.

Table 5.1 presents the DSM-IV classification of intelligence by I.Q. range.

5.8. The answer is E (all) (*Synopsis VII*, pages 232–233).

The Bender Visual-Motor Gestalt test, devised by the American neuropsychiatrist Lauretta Bender in 1938, is a technique that consists of nine figures that are copied by the subject (Figure 5.2). It is adminis-

Table 5.1
Classification of Intelligence by I.Q. Range

Classification	I.Q. Range
Profound mental retardation (MR)*	Below 20 or 25
Severe MR*	20–25 to 35–40
Moderate MR*	35–40 to 50–55
Mild MR*	50–55 to about 70
Borderline	70–79
Dull normal	80 to 90
Normal	90 to 110
Bright normal	110 to 120
Superior	120 to 130
Very superior	130 and above

*According to the fourth edition of *Diagnostic and Statistical Manual of Mental Disorders* (DSM-IV).

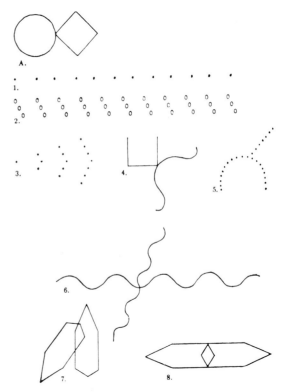

Figure 5.2. Test figures from the Bender Visual-Motor Gestalt test, adapted from Max Wertheimer. (Figure from Bender: *A Visual Motor Gestalt Test and Its Clinical Use.* American Orthopsychiatric Association, New York, 1938.)

tered as a means of evaluating *maturation levels in children* and *organic dysfunction.* Its chief applications are to determine retardation, *loss of function,* and organic brain defects in children and adults. The designs are presented one at a time to the subject, who is asked to copy them onto a sheet of paper. The subject then is asked to copy the designs from memory (Figure 5.3 and Figure 5.4); thus, the Bender designs can be used as a test of both *visual-motor coordination* and immediate visual memory.

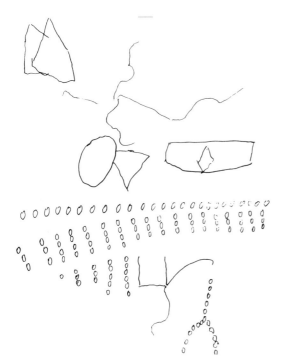

Figure 5.3. Bender Visual-Motor Gestalt drawings of a 57-year-old brain-damaged woman.

Figure 5.4. Bender Visual-Motor Gestalt recall by the 57-year-old brain-damaged patient who drew Figure 5.3.

5.9.   The answer is E (all) (*Synopsis VII*, page 229).

The Thematic Apperception Test (TAT) was introduced by Henry A. Murray in 1943 as a new way of interpreting stories made up by the patient about pictures representing human beings of both sexes and varying ages, alone or in a group, and in a variety of surroundings and interactions. Originally, the test's chief usefulness was seen as revealing drives of which the patient was unaware. However, the test revealed conscious tendencies, as well as unconscious tendencies. Its aim expanded to include the study of *many areas of the patient's functioning*, including personality traits, emotions, neurotic defenses, conflicts, intellectual level, ambitions, attitudes toward parental figures, and psychopathology. The patient is shown one picture at a time and is asked to tell a complete story, including the interactions occurring, the events leading up to those interactions, the thoughts and feelings of the figures,

and the outcome. In interpreting the TAT, the examiner, among other factors, notes *with whom the patient identifies* and assumes that *all the figures* may represent varying aspects of the patient being projected onto the ambiguous scenes and interactions; drives or attitudes that the patient considers as negative may, for instance, be projected onto the figures that are apparently most unlike the patient. The TAT appears to be most useful in helping the examiner infer *motivational aspects of behavior*, as opposed to providing a clear-cut and definitive diagnosis. As with all projective tests, there are disagreements about the value of the TAT; for example, investigators have failed to duplicate exactly the studies they set out to check, and a sufficiently comprehensive, clear, and formalized basis for the interpretations of TAT results are still lacking. Psychologists and other workers who believe that projective tests are useful maintain that any measure of potential behavior is valuable. Experienced clinical psychologists (who are most likely to administer and interpret a useful TAT) generally agree about the difficulty in acquiring sufficient skill and experience for satisfactory interpretations of TAT results. It is easy to learn how to administer the test but hard to interpret it well.

5.10–5.12

5.10.   The answer is A (*Synopsis VII*, pages 232–233).

5.11.   The answer is C (*Synopsis VII*, page 233).

5.12.   The answer is C (*Synopsis VII*, page 233).

The Bender Visual-Motor Gestalt test is a test of visuomotor coordination that is useful for both children and adults. The test material consists of nine designs adapted from those used by Max Wertheimer in his studies in Gestalt psychology. Each design is printed against a white background on a separate card. Patients are given unlined paper and asked to copy each design with the card in front of them. There is no time limit. That phase of the test is highly structured and does not investigate memory function, since the cards remain in front of the patients. Many clinicians then remove the cards and, after an interval of 45 to 60 seconds, ask the patients to reproduce as many of the designs as they can from memory. That recall phase not only investigates visual memory but also presents a less structured situation, since patients must rely essentially on their own resources. Comparing the patient's functioning under the two conditions is often helpful. The Bender Visual-Motor Gestalt test is probably used most frequently with adults as a screening device for signs of organic dysfunction. Evaluation of the protocol depends on the form of the reproduced figures and on their relation to one another and to the whole spatial background.

Raven's Progressive Matrices requires the patient to select from *a multiple-choice pictorial display* the stimulus that completes a design in which a part is omitted. The difficulty of the discrimination increases over trials in the lengthy test. A briefer, less difficult version (Color Matrices) is especially useful for patients who are unable to complete the standard test, which can require 30 to 45 minutes. *Impaired performance is associated with poor visuoconstructive ability* and with posterior lesions of either cerebral hemisphere, but receptive language deficit may contribute to poor performance in patients with dominant-hemisphere damage.

The Shipley Abstraction test requires the patient to complete logical sequences; it assesses the patient's capacity to think abstractly. Because performance on a test of that type is related to educational background, an accompanying vocabulary test is also given to the patient, and a comparison is made between the patient's performances on the two tests. A low abstraction score in relation to vocabulary level is interpreted as reflecting an impairment in conceptual thinking.

5.13–5.16

5.13. The answer is C (*Synopsis VII*, pages 221 and 229).

5.14. The answer is A (*Synopsis VII*, pages 222–223).

5.15. The answer is B (*Synopsis VII*, pages 223–226).

5.16. The answer is D (*Synopsis VII*, pages 221 and 229).

The *Thematic Apperception Test (TAT)* consists of a series of 20 pictures of ambiguous figures and events and one blank card. Most patients are shown 10 pictures, the choice of pictures generally depending on the examiner's wish to clarify specific conflict areas. *The patient is asked to construct stories* based on the pictures. With the blank card, the patient has to imagine a scene first and then tell a story about it. The patient is asked to relate the story with a beginning, a middle, and an end. That projective test elicits information regarding a broad spectrum of psychological functioning, including needs, attitudes, and motives. Scoring of the TAT is not standardized. Although scoring systems exist, test interpretation is typically impressionistic and informal. The patient's stories are examined for recurrent themes to provide evidence of mood, conflict, interpersonal relationships, and areas of strengths and weaknesses.

The *Wechsler Adult Intelligence Scale (WAIS)* is an intelligence test designed for persons 16 years old or older. It is the best standardized and most widely used intelligence test in clinical practice today. The scale is designed for individual administration and consists of *11 subtests, six verbal and five performance, yielding a verbal I.Q., a performance I.Q., and a full-scale I.Q.*. Norms are provided for each of the tests, thus eliciting an I.Q. for the verbal test group, for the nonverbal performance test group, and for the entire scale. The subtests are information, comprehension, arithmetic, similarities, digit span, vocabulary, picture completion, block design, picture arrangement, object assembly, and digit symbol. A person's I.Q. score indicates the degree of deviation of the person's intellectual capacity from the average.

The *Minnesota Multiphasic Personality Inventory (MMPI)*, introduced in 1943 and revised (MMPI-2) in 1990, is the most widely used and most thoroughly researched of the objective personality assessment instruments. The inventory is easy to administer and requires little time or effort on the part of the examiner, as the persons evaluate themselves. *The self-report inventory consists of 550 statements to which the person has to respond with "True," "False," or "Cannot say."* The statements pertain to many personality aspects, such as physiological functions, habits, attitudes, and psychopathology, and the persons are asked to report whether the statements apply to them. The MMPI gives scores on 10 standard clinical scales, each of which was derived from homogeneous-criteria groups of psychiatric patients. Each scale was validated by studying various diagnostic groups to determine whether the scale items truly differentiated between normal controls and medical or psychiatric patients.

The Sentence Completion Test (SCT) is composed of *a series of sentence stems, such as "I like . . . ," that patients are asked to complete in their own words* with the first words that come to mind. The test is designed to tap a patient's conscious associations to areas of functioning in which the examiner may be interested—for instance, responses that are highly emotional, repetitive, humorous, bland, or only factually informative.

5.17–5.21

5.17. The answer is C (*Synopsis VII*, page 236).

5.18. The answer is B (*Synopsis VII*, page 234).

5.19. The answer is D (*Synopsis VII*, pages 223 and 234).

5.20. The answer is A (*Synopsis VII*, pages 227–229).

5.21. The answer is E (*Synopsis VII*, pages 232–233).

Various neuropsychiatric tests, including the Halstead-Reitan and the Luria-Nebraska batteries, are sometimes useful in bringing to light subtle organic dysfunctions that are undetected in standard psychiatric, psychological, and even neurological assessments. The *Halstead-Reitan Battery of Neuropsychological Tests consists of 10 tests, including the trail making test and the critical flicker frequency test*. It was developed in an attempt to improve the reliability of the criteria used to diagnose brain damage. Assessment data were gathered on a group of patients with left-hemisphere injury, right-hemisphere injury, and global involvement. The trail making test is a test of visuomotor perception and motor speed, and the critical flicker frequency test (noting when a flickering light becomes steady) tests visual perception.

The *Luria-Nebraska Neuropsychological Battery (LLNB) is extremely sensitive in identifying discrete forms of brain damage, such as dyslexia* (an impairment in the ability to read) and dyscalculia (an inability to perform arithmetical operations), rather than more global forms.

The *Stanford-Binet* Intelligence Scale is the test most frequently used in the individual examination of children. It *consists of 120 items, plus several alternative tests, applicable to the ages between 2 years and adulthood.* The tests have a variety of graded difficulties, both verbal and performance, designed to assess such functions as memory, free association, orientation, language comprehension, knowledge of common objects, abstract thinking, and the use of judgment and reasoning.

The *Rorschach test* is a psychological test consisting of 10 inkblots that the person is asked to look at and interpret. It *furnishes a description of the dynamic forces of personality through an analysis of the person's responses.*

The face-hand test, devised by Lauretta Bender, is *a test of diffuse cerebral dysfunction to which normal children by the age of 7 years respond negatively.* The person, whose eyes are closed, is touched simultaneously on the cheek and the hand; retesting is done with the person's eyes open. The results are considered positive if the person fails consistently to identify both stimuli within 10 trials.

5.22–5.26

5.22. The answer is C (*Synopsis VII*, page 235).

5.23. The answer is E (*Synopsis VII*, page 235).

5.24. The answer is D (*Synopsis VII*, page 235).

5.25. The answer is A (*Synopsis VII*, page 235).

5.26. The answer is B (*Synopsis VII*, page 235).

Numerous mental status cognitive tasks are available to test and localize various brain dysfunctions. Construction apraxia—*the loss of gestalt, the loss of symmetry, and the distortion of figures*—seen in the task of copying the outline of simple objects, is localized to the *nondominant parietal lobe.* Dysfunction of the *occipital lobes* is suggested when a *patient cannot name a camouflaged object but can name it when it is not camouflaged. Two or more errors or two or more seven-second delays in carrying out tasks of right-left orientation* (for example, place left hand to right ear, right elbow to right knee) are localized to dysfunction of the *dominant parietal*

lobe. A dysfunction in concentration is thought to be localized to the *frontal lobes* and can be tested by eliciting *any improper letter sequence in spelling "earth" backward.* In anomia the *patient cannot name common objects* (for example, watch, key); the impairment is localized to the *dominant temporal lobe.*

5.27–5.30

5.27. The answer is B (*Synopsis VII*, page 222).

5.28. The answer is C (*Synopsis VII*, page 222).

5.29. The answer is D (*Synopsis VII*, pages 222–223).

5.30. The answer is E (*Synopsis VII*, pages 222 and 1020–1021).

The *Wechsler Adult Intelligence Scale (WAIS)* was originally designed in 1939; it has gone through several revisions since then. It is the test most often used to determine I.Q. in the average adult. *A scale for children ages 6 through 16 years has been devised—the Wechsler Intelligence Scale for Children (WISC)—and a scale for children ages 4 to 6½ years—the Wechsler Preschool and Primary Scale of Intelligence (WPPSI).* The WISC is an individual test that, like the WAIS, provides separate verbal and performance I.Q.s, based on separate sets of tests, and a full-scale I.Q.; it requires a highly trained examiner. The WPPSI, devised in 1967, an individual test, extended the range of assessment downward in age. In practice, the WAIS, the WISC, or the WPPSI is used as part of a battery of psychological tests.

Educational background affects the information and vocabulary segments of the scales and must be taken into account when evaluating a subject's scores on *all the tests.*

The Bayley Infant Scale of Development *assesses children from 8 weeks to 2½ years of age.* The test examines both motor and social functioning. The developmental quotient (D.Q.) obtained is based on standardized norms for the child's age.

5.31–5.34

5.31. The answer is A (*Synopsis VII*, page 224).

5.32. The answer is A (*Synopsis VII*, page 224).

5.33. The answer is B (*Synopsis VII*, pages 332 and 534).

5.34. The answer is C (*Synopsis VII*, page 330).

The *Beck Depression Inventory* is a *self-administered* scale. It *emphasizes subjective mood and thoughts* within the framework of Aaron Beck's cognitive theory of depression. The scale has been criticized because it puts little emphasis on the neurovegetative symptoms of depression.

The *Hamilton Depression Rating Scale* is administered by the examiner. The patient is rated on signs and symptoms of depression, including psychomotor retardation, changes in sleep and appetite, and weight loss. The scale *emphasizes neurovegetative symptoms* and has been criticized for giving little attention to the affective and cognitive changes that may occur in patients with major depressive disorder.

The *Brief Psychiatric Rating Scale provides a global pathology index*. The scale, filled out by the examiner after the interview, screens for a wide range of psychiatric symptoms, including somatic concerns, anxiety, disorganization, guilt, tension, grandiosity, hostility, and suspiciousness. Because the scale covers many symptoms, it is best used as a barometer of a patient's global pathology and improvement during treatment.

6

Theories of Personality and Psychopathology

The question of what forces contribute to the development of normal and abnormal personality structures has attracted influential, creative, and intellectually sophisticated thinkers. Sigmund Freud's revolutionary concepts of infantile sexuality, a dynamic unconscious psychic determinism, and unconscious conflict continue to stimulate debate. Many personality theorists have taken Freud's theories as their basis but have elaborated and refined his ideas with their own ideas. Other theorists have rejected Freud's concepts and have formulated developmental scenarios based on ideas that challenge psychoanalytic thinking.

Classic ego psychology, object relations theory, self psychology, the interpersonal school—the range of personality theory is a map of psychological intellectual history. Each theorist has usually emphasized a particular psychological perspective of personality development

and, with it, an associated belief about psychotherapeutic techniques. Carl Gustav Jung, Alfred Adler, Karen Horney, Harry Stack Sullivan, Melanie Klein, Otto Kernberg, Heinz Kohut, Wilhelm Reich, Jacques Lacan, Frederick S. Perls, Erik Erikson, and Carl Rogers have grappled with personality structure, development, and treatment. Many therapeutic techniques, such as Freud's use of free association and transference interpretation, have evolved directly from the underlying core beliefs about personality structure. An understanding of the various theoretical approaches to personality is essential to an understanding of the techniques used to treat pathological manifestations of personality functioning.

Students should review Chapter 6 in *Kaplan and Sadock's Synopsis VII* and should study the questions and answers below.

HELPFUL HINTS

The student should know the various theorists, their schools of thought, and their theories.

psychoanalytic theory	regression	latent dream
libido and instinct theories	behaviorism	nocturnal sensory stimuli
free association	psychodynamic thinking	*The Ego and the Id*
fundamental rule	ego psychology	ego ideal
hysterical phenomena	psychic determinism	reality testing
psychoneurosis	symbolism	object relations
psychosexual development	Joseph Breuer	object constancy
reality principle	hypnosis	synthetic functions of the ego
The Interpretation of Dreams	*Studies on Hysteria*	primary autonomous functions
conscious	abreaction	Anna Freud
secondary process	resistance	unconscious motivation
manifest dream	narcissism	conflict
dream work	Eros and Thanatos	repression
day's residue	topographic theory	talking cure
structural model	preconscious	narcissistic, immature, neurotic,
instinctual drives	primary process	and mature defenses
ego functions	wish fulfillment	signal anxiety

infantile sexuality	Sandor Ferenczi	interpretation
primary and secondary gains	Kurt Goldstein	Karl Abraham
working through	Carl Gustav Jung	Franz Alexander
transference	Kurt Lewin	Gordon Allport
repetition compulsion	Adolph Meyer	Ronald Fairbairn
Alfred Adler	Henry Murray	Donald Winnicott
Eric Berne	Sandor Rado	Erich Fromm
Raymond Cattell	Wilhelm Reich	Karen Horney
Michael Balint	Heinz Kohut	Melanie Klein
Wilfred Bion	Heinz Hartmann	Abraham Maslow
behaviorism	defense mechanisms	Gardner Murphy
multiple self-organizations	pregenital	Frederick S. Perls
The Trauma of the Birth	character traits	Otto Rank
Søren Kierkegaard	acting out	Harry Stack Sullivan
Erik Erikson	analytical process	

QUESTIONS

DIRECTIONS: Each of the questions or incomplete statements below is followed by five suggested responses or completions. Select the *one* that is *best* in each case.

6.1. In the structural theory of the mind
A. the superego controls the delay and the modulation of drive expression
B. the superego is the executive organ of the psyche
C. the superego's activities occur unconsciously to a large extent
D. the reality principle and the pleasure principle are aspects of id functioning
E. the id operates under the domination of secondary process

6.2. In Carl Gustav Jung's psychoanalytic school
A. the collective unconscious is a collection of impulses of the id and the ego
B. archetypes contribute to complexes
C. the male part of the self is called the persona
D. individuation is a process that is completed in childhood
E. an emphasis is placed on infantile sexuality

6.3. In Erik Erikson's descriptions of the stages of the life cycle
A. the stage of industry versus inferiority corresponds to Freud's phallic-oedipal stage
B. the stage of identity versus role diffusion corresponds to Freud's latency stage
C. the stage of autonomy versus shame and doubt corresponds to Freud's anal stage
D. generativity can occur only if a person has or raises a child
E. the stage of integrity versus despair occurs from late adolescence through the early middle years

6.4. Which of the following statements applies to the unconscious?
A. Its elements are inaccessible to consciousness
B. It is characterized by primary process thinking
C. It is closely related to the pleasure principle
D. It is closely related to the instincts
E. All the above

6.5. According to Carl Gustav Jung, archetypes are
A. instinctual patterns
B. expressed in representational images
C. expressed in mythological images
D. organizational units of the personality
E. all the above

6.6. According to Alfred Adler, the helplessness of the infant accounts for
A. feelings of inferiority
B. a need to strive for superiority
C. fantasied organic or psychological deficits
D. compensatory strivings
E. all the above

6.7. Masculine protest is
A. a universal human tendency
B. a move from a female or passive role
C. a concept introduced by Alfred Adler
D. an extension of Adler's ideas about organ inferiority
E. all the above

6.8. According to Harry Stack Sullivan, anxiety is characterized by
A. feelings of disapproval from a significant adult
B. an interpersonal context
C. somatic symptoms
D. restriction of functioning
E. all the above

6.9. The fundamental rule of psychoanalysis is
A. resistance and repression
B. psychic determinism
C. abreaction
D. free association
E. the concept of the unconscious

6.10. Which of the following statements about dreams is true as described by Freud?
A. Dreams are the conscious expression of an unconscious fantasy
B. Dreams represent wish-fulfillment activity
C. Latent dream content derives from the repressed part of the id
D. Sensory impressions may play a role in initiating a dream
E. All the above

6.11. Autonomous functions of the ego include all the following *except*
A. perception
B. language
C. motor development
D. repression
E. intelligence

6.12. A male office worker steals supplies from the office and, when confronted with the evidence, states: "Well, everybody does it, and you can't fire me. I quit." Which of the following defense mechanisms is he using?
A. Denial and rationalization
B. Rationalization and identification with the aggressor
C. Identification and undoing
D. Projection and identification with the aggressor
E. Intellectualization and denial

6.13. Which of the following statements about dreams is *not* true?
A. Dreams have a definite but disguised meaning
B. Dreams are considered a normal manifestation of unconscious activity
C. Dreams represent unconscious wishes
D. The core meaning of the dream is expressed by its manifest content
E. Nocturnal sensory stimuli may be incorporated into the dream

6.14. The major defense mechanism used in phobia is
A. projection
B. identification
C. displacement
D. undoing
E. reaction formation

6.15. Mature defenses, according to George Vaillant, include
A. altruism
B. controlling
C. intellectualization
D. rationalization
E. all the above

6.16. Isolation, the defense mechanism involving the separation of an idea or memory from its attached feeling tone, is found most clearly in
A. obsessive-compulsive disorder
B. anxiety disorders
C. pain disorder
D. dissociative disorders
E. dysthymic disorder

6.17. Psychobiology is best characterized by which of the following concepts?
A. Analysis of the ego through the interpretation of defense mechanisms
B. Biographical study and common-sense understanding of patients
C. Primary understanding of the biological and biochemical origins and treatment of mental illness
D. Emphasis on genetic factors in mental illness and the use of drugs in psychiatry
E. Psychological factors affecting physical illness

6.18. Alienation from the self is a concept developed by
A. Sigmund Freud
B. Harry Stack Sullivan
C. Eric Berne
D. Karen Horney
E. Alfred Adler

6.19. The term "habit training" was coined by
A. Adolf Meyer
B. Carl Gustav Jung
C. Otto Rank
D. B.F. Skinner
E. Joseph Wolpe

6.20. The self-system concerns Harry Stack Sullivan's concept of the
A. unconscious
B. personality
C. libido
D. defense mechanisms
E. Oedipus complex

6.21. Erik Erikson used the term "generativity versus stagnation" to describe the conflict occurring in
A. childhood
B. adolescence
C. young adulthood
D. middle adulthood
E. late adulthood

6.22. Consistent and affectionate maternal behavior during infancy provides the child with a continuing sense of
A. trust
B. autonomy
C. initiative
D. industry
E. identity

6.23. The stage of industry versus inferiority is characterized by
A. eagerness and curiosity
B. self-indulgence
C. expanded desires
D. confidence in one's ability to use adult materials
E. preoccupation with one's appearance

6.24. Erik Erikson's stage of generativity versus stagnation is characterized by
A. interests outside the home
B. establishing and guiding the next generation
C. self-absorption
D. bettering society
E. all the above

6.25. According to Sigmund Freud's structural theory of the mind, the psychic apparatus is divided into
A. id, ego, and superego
B. ego, unconscious, and id
C. superego, ego, and unconscious
D. unconscious, conscious, and preconscious
E. none of the above

6.26. According to Sigmund Freud, which of the following does *not* explain why a man falls in love with a particular type of woman?
A. She resembles the man's idealized self-image
B. She resembles someone who took care of him when he was a boy
C. She provides him with narcissistic gratification
D. There is a sexual resemblance between them
E. All the above

DIRECTIONS: Each group of questions below consists of lettered headings followed by a list of numbered words or statements. For each numbered word or statement, select the *one* lettered heading that is most closely associated with it. Each lettered heading may be selected once, more than once, or not at all.

Questions 6.27–6.30
A. Alfred Adler
B. Carl Rogers
C. Adolf Meyer
D. Karen Horney

6.27. Psychobiology

6.28. Person-centered theory of personality

6.29. Inferiority complex

6.30. Holistic psychology

Questions 6.31–6.35
A. Rationalization
B. Projection
C. Denial
D. Reaction formation
E. Sublimation

6.31. A 45-year-old man who is having problems at work begins to complain that his boss "has it in for me."

6.32. A 34-year-old married woman who finds herself strongly attracted to a friend of her husband's is nasty to that friend.

6.33. A 35-year-old gambler loses $500 at the race track but says that he is not upset because "I would have spent the money on something else anyway."

6.34. A 42-year-old man is discharged from a cardiac intensive care unit after suffering a severe myocardial infarction, but he continues to smoke two packs of cigarettes a day.

6.35. A 30-year-old man finds his greatest source of relaxation by going to watch football games.

Questions 6.36–6.40
A. Franz Alexander
B. Donald Winnicott
C. Karen Horney
D. Melanie Klein
E. Heinz Kohut

6.36. Introduced the concept of the transitional object.

6.37. Believed that oedipal strivings are experienced during the first year of life and that, during the first year, gratifying experiences with the good breast reinforce basic trust

6.38. Emphasized cultural factors and disturbances in interpersonal and intrapsychic development

6.39. Introduced the concept of the corrective emotional experience

6.40. Expanded Sigmund Freud's concept of narcissism; theories are known as self psychology

Questions 6.41–6.45
A. Shadow
B. Anima
C. Animus
D. Persona
E. Collective unconscious

6.41. Face presented to the outside world

6.42. Another person of the same sex as the dreamer

6.43. A man's undeveloped femininity

6.44. A woman's undeveloped masculinity

6.45. Mythological ideas and primitive projections

Questions 6.46–6.50
A. Harry Stack Sullivan
B. Abraham Maslow
C. Wilhelm Reich
D. Kurt Lewin
E. Frederick S. Perls

6.46. "Group dynamics"

6.47. Peak experience

6.48. Participant observer

6.49. Character formation and character types

6.50. Gestalt therapy

Questions 6.51–6.55
A. Basic trust versus basic mistrust
B. Integrity versus despair
C. Initiative versus guilt
D. Intimacy versus isolation
E. Identity versus role diffusion

6.51. Infancy

6.52. Early childhood

6.53. Puberty and adolescence

6.54. Early adulthood

6.55. Late adulthood

DIRECTIONS: Each set of lettered headings below is followed by a list of numbered words or phrases. For each numbered word or phrase select

    A. if the item is associated with *A only*
    B. if the item is associated with *B only*
    C. if the item is associated with *both A and B*
    D. if the item is associated with *neither A nor B*

Questions 6.56–6.60
    A. Topographic theory
    B. Structural theory
    C. Both
    D. Neither

6.56. Set forth by Sigmund Freud in *The Interpretation of Dreams* in 1900

6.57. Presented in *The Ego and the Id* in 1923

6.58. Unconscious, preconscious, and conscious

6.59. Id, ego, and superego

6.60. First systematic and comprehensive study of the defenses used by the ego

Questions 6.61–6.65.
    A. Primary process
    B. Secondary process
    C. Both
    D. Neither

6.61. Characteristic of very young children

6.62. The unconscious

6.63. The id

6.64. The preconscious

6.65. The ego

ANSWERS

Theories of Personality and Psychopathology

6.1. The answer is C (*Synopsis VII*, pages 247–248).

In *The Ego and the Id*, published in 1923, Sigmund Freud developed the tripartite structural model of ego, id, and superego. That model of the psychic apparatus, which is the cornerstone of ego psychology, represented a transition for Freud from his topographical model of the mind (conscious, preconscious, and unconscious). The three provinces of id, ego, and superego are distinguished by their varying functions.

The superego's activities occur unconsciously to a large extent. It establishes and maintains the person's moral conscience in the complex system of ideals and values internalized from one's parents. Freud viewed the superego as the heir to the Oedipus complex. In other words, the child internalizes the parental values and standards around the age of 5 or 6 years. The superego then serves as an agency that provides ongoing scrutiny of the person's behavior, thoughts, and feelings. It makes comparisons with expected standards of behavior and offers approval or disapproval.

The superego does not control the delay and the modulation of drive expression. The delay and the modulation of drive expression is achieved by the ego. *The ego, not the superego, is the executive organ of the psyche*, through the mechanisms of defense available to it and through mobility, perception, and contact with reality. According to Freud, the ego spans all three topographical dimension of conscious, preconscious, and unconscious. Logical and abstract thinking and verbal expression are associated with its conscious and preconscious functions. Defense mechanisms reside in its unconscious domain.

Freud also believed that the ego brings influences from the external world to bear on the id, and the ego simultaneously substitutes the reality principle for the pleasure principle. Thus, in Freud's view, both *the reality principle and the pleasure principle are aspects of ego functioning, not id functioning.* The id, according to Freud, harbors the innate, biological, instinctual drives; it is the source of libido and follows the pleasure principle. Secondary process is the form of thinking that is logical, organized and reality-oriented.

6.2. The answer is B (*Synopsis VII*, page 256).

According to Carl Gustav Jung's psychoanalytic school, known as analytical psychology, *archetypes contribute to complexes.* That occurs because complexes, which are feeling-toned ideas, develop as a result of personal experiences interacting with archetypal imagery. Archetypes are representational images and confirmations that have universal meanings. Archetypal figures exist for the mother, the father, the child, and the hero, among others. Thus, a mother complex is determined not only by the mother-child interaction but also by the conflict between archetypal expectations and actual experiences with the real woman who functions in a motherly role.

Archetypes are a part of Jung's concept of the collective unconscious, which consists of all humankind's common and shared mythological and symbolic past. *The collective unconscious is not a collection of the impulses of the id and the ego.*

The persona is the mask covering the personality; it is what the person presents to the outside world. The persona may become fixed, so that the real person is hidden even from the person. *The male part of the self is called the animus, not the persona.*

The aim of Jungian treatment is to bring about an adequate adaptation to reality, which involves fulfilling one's creative potentialities. The ultimate goal is to achieve *individuation, a process that continues throughout life* in which persons develop unique senses of their own identities. That developmental process may lead persons down new paths that may differ from their previous directions in life.

In analytical psychology *an emphasis is not placed on infantile sexuality.*

6.3. The answer is C (*Synopsis VII*, pages 243 and 264).

Erik Erikson described eight stages of the life cycle (Table 6.1). The stages are marked by one or more internal crises, which are defined as turning points—periods when the person is in a state of increased vulnerability. Ideally, the crisis is mastered successfully, and the person gains strength and is able to move on to the next stage.

In Erikson's stage of autonomy versus shame and doubt (about 1 to 3 years), autonomy concerns children's sense of mastery over themselves and over their drives and impulses. Toddlers gain a sense of their separateness from others. "I," "you," "me," and "mine" are common words used by children during that period. Children have a choice of holding on or letting go, of being cooperative or stubborn. *The stage of autonomy versus shame and doubt corresponds with Freud's anal stage* of development. For Erikson, it is the time for the child either to retain feces (hold-

Table 6.1
Erik Erikson's Stages of the Life Cycle

Stage 1. Basic Trust versus Basic Mistrust
(birth to about 1 year)
    Corresponds to the oral psychosexual stage
    Trust is shown by ease of feeding, depth of sleep, bowel
      relaxation
    Depends on consistency and sameness of experiences
      provided by caretaker or outerprovider
    Second six months: teething and biting move the infant from
      getting to taking
    Weaning leads to nostalgia for the lost paradise
    If basic trust is strong, the child maintains a hopeful attitude
      and develops self-confidence
    Oral zone is associated with the mode of being satisfied

Stage 2. Autonomy versus Shame and Doubt
(about 1 to 3 years)
    Corresponds to the muscular-anal stage
    Biologically includes learning to walk, feed self, talk
    Need for outer control and firmness of caretaker before
      development of autonomy
    Shame occurs when the child is overtly self-conscious
      through negative exposure and punishment
    Self-doubt can evolve if the parents overtly shame the child,
      e.g., about elimination
    Anal zone is associated with the mode of holding on and
      letting go

Stage 3. Initiative versus Guilt
(3 to 5 years)
    Corresponds to the phallic psychosexual stage
    Initiative arises in relation to tasks for the sake of activity,
      both motor and intellectual
    Guilt may arise over goals contemplated (especially
      aggressive goals)
    Desire to mimic adult world; involvement in oedipal struggle
      leads to resolution through social role identification
    Sibling rivalry is frequent
    Phallic zone is associated with the mode of competition and
      aggression

Stage 4. Industry versus Inferiority
(6 to 11 years)
    Corresponds to the latency psychosexual stage
    Child is busy building, creating, accomplishing
    Child receives systematic instruction and fundamentals of
      technology

Danger of a sense of inadequacy and inferiority if the child
    despairs of tools, skills, and status among peers
Socially decisive age
No dominant zone or mode

Stage 5. Identity versus Role Diffusion
(11 years through the end of adolescence)
    Struggle to develop ego identity (sense of inner sameness
      and continuity)
    Preoccupation with appearance, hero worship, ideology
    Group identity (with peers) develops
    Danger of role confusion, doubts about sexual and
      vocational identity
    Psychosexual moratorium, stage between morality learned
      by the child and the ethics developed by the adult
    No dominant zone or mode

Stage 6. Intimacy versus Isolation
(21 to 40 years)
    Tasks are to love and to work
    Intimacy is characterized by self-abandonment, mutuality of
      sexual orgasm, intense friendship, attachments that are
      lifelong
    Isolation is marked by separation from others and by the
      view that others are dangerous
    General sense of productivity
    No dominant zone or mode

Stage 7. Generativity versus Stagnation
(40 to 65 years)
    Generativity includes raising children, guiding new
      generation, creativity, altruism
    Stagnation is not prevented by having a child; the parent
      must provide nurturance and love
    Self-concern, isolation, and the absence of intimacy are
      characteristic of stagnation
    No dominant zone or mode

Stage 8. Integrity versus Despair
(over 65 years)
    Integrity is a sense of satisfaction that life has been
      productive and worthwhile
    Despair is a loss of hope that produces misanthropy and
      disgust
    Persons in the state of despair are fearful of death
    An acceptance of one's place in the life cycle is
      characteristic of integrity

---

ing in) or to eliminate feces (letting go); both behaviors have an effect on the mother.

The stage of initiative versus guilt (3 to 5 years), not *the stage of industry versus inferiority, corresponds to Freud's phallic-oedipal stage*. The stage of industry versus inferiority (6 to 11 years) corresponds to Freud's latency period. Industry, the ability to work and acquire adult skills, is the keynote of the stage. Children learn that they are able to make things and, most important, able to master and complete a task. A sense of inadequacy and inferiority, the potential negative outcome of the stage, results from several sources: children may be discriminated against in school; children may be told that they are inferior; children may be overprotected at home or excessively dependent on the emotional support of

their families; children may compare themselves unfavorably with the same-sex parent. Good teachers and good parents who encourage children to value diligence and productivity and to persevere in difficult enterprises are bulwarks against a sense of inferiority.

The stage of identity versus role diffusion (11 years through the end of adolescence) *corresponds to Freud's phallic stage, not the latency stage*. According to Erikson, developing a sense of identity is the main task of the period, which coincides with puberty and adolescence. Identity is defined as the characteristics that establish who persons are and where they are going. Healthy identity is built on success in passing through the earlier stages. How successful the adolescents have been in attaining trust, autonomy, initiative, and industry has much to do with developing a sense of identity. Identifying with either healthy parents or parent surrogates facilitates the process. Failure to negotiate the stage leaves the adolescent without a solid identity; the person suffers from role diffusion or identity confusion, characterized by not having a sense of self and by confusion about one's place in the world.

The stage of intimacy versus isolation (21 to 40 years) extends from late adolescence through early middle age. Erikson pointed out that an important psychosocial conflict can arise during the stage; as in previous stages, success or failure depends on how well the groundwork has been laid in earlier periods and on how the young adult interacts with the environment. Erikson quoted Freud's view that a normal person must be able to love and work *(lieben und arbeiten)*. Similarly, Erikson believes that meaningful work, procreation, and recreation within a loving relationship represents utopia.

The stage of generativity versus stagnation (40 to 65 years) occurs during the decades that span the middle years of life. *Generativity can occur even if a person has not had or raised a child.* Generativity also includes a vital interest outside the home in establishing and guiding the oncoming generation or in improving society. Childless people can be generative if they develop a sense of altruism and creativity. But most persons, if able, want to continue their personalities and energies in the production and care of offspring. Wanting or having children, however, does not ensure generativity. Parents need to have achieved successful identities themselves to be truly generative. Stagnation is a barren state. The inability to transcend the lack of creativity is dangerous because the person is not able to accept the eventuality of not being and the idea that death is inescapably a part of life.

The stage of integrity versus despair occurs in old age—not in late adolescence through the early middle years. It is Erikson's eighth stage of the life cycle. The stage (over 65 years) is described as the conflict between the sense of satisfaction that one feels in reflecting on a life productively lived and the sense that life has had little purpose or meaning. Integrity allows for an acceptance of one's place in the life cycle and of the knowledge that one's life is one's own responsibility. There is an acceptance of who one's parents are or were and an understanding of how they lived their lives.

Without the conviction that one's life has been meaningful and that one has made a contribution, either by producing happy children or by giving to the next generation, the elderly person fears death and has a sense of despair or disgust.

6.4. The answer is E (all) (*Synopsis VII*, page 242).

Ordinarily, the repressed ideas and affects of the unconscious *are inaccessible to consciousness* because of the censorship or repression imposed by the preconscious. Those repressed elements may attain the level of consciousness when the censor is overpowered (as in neurotic symptom formation), relaxes (as in dream states), or is fooled (as by jokes).

The unconscious is associated with the form of mental activity that Freud called the primary process or *primary process thinking.* Characteristically seen in infancy and dreams, the primary process is marked by primitive, prelogical thinking and by the tendency to seek immediate discharge and gratification of instinctual demands. Consequently, the unconscious is also *closely related to the pleasure principle*, the principle by which the id seeks immediate tension reduction by direct or fantasied gratification. Similarly, the id also contains the mental representatives and derivatives of the *instinctual drives*, particularly those of the sexual instinct.

6.5. The answer is E (all) (*Synopsis VII*, page 256).

Carl Gustav Jung believed archetypes to be *instinctual patterns*. All psychic energy is transmitted in forms of experience, behavior, and emotion, which are *expressed in representational* or *expressed in mythological images.* Thus, the archetypes represent the basic motivations and drives that become *organizational units of the personality.*

6.6. The answer is E (all) (*Synopsis VII*, page 254).

According to Alfred Adler, infants are born with certain *feelings of inferiority.* As a result, they have *a need to strive for superiority*, perfection, and totality. Adler classified those strivings under the heading of the inferiority complex, which comprises the newborns' feelings secondary to their real or *fantasied organic or psychological deficits. Compensatory strivings* are the person's attempts to overcome feelings of inferiority.

6.7. The answer is E (all) (*Synopsis VII*, page 254).

Masculine protest, the *universal human tendency* to *move from a female or passive role* to a masculine or active role, *is a concept introduced by Alfred Adler.* The doctrine is *an extension of Adler's ideas about organ inferiority.* Adler regarded that concept as the main force in neuroticism. It represents the distorted perception of sex differences caused by the striving for superiority. If it takes an active force in women, they attempt from an early age to usurp the male position. They become aggressive in manner, adopt masculine habits, and endeavor to domineer everyone about them. The masculine protest in a male indicates that he never fully recovered from an infantile doubt about his masculinity. He strives for an ideal masculinity, invariably perceived as the self-possession of freedom and power.

6.8. The answer is E (all) (*Synopsis VII*, page 259).

As with other concepts developed by Harry Stack Sullivan, he saw anxiety as an interpersonal phenomenon that is defined as the response to *feelings of disapproval from a significant adult*. Therefore, it occurs only in *an interpersonal context*, even if the other person is not real but only a fantasied image.

Feelings of disapproval can be communicated and interpreted by the person in a variety of ways, sometimes false. A distressing feeling, such as anxiety, is accompanied by *somatic symptoms* and psychological feelings of doom, which the person cannot tolerate for long.

Sullivan viewed the development of personality as a process of learning to cope with anxiety by using adaptive maneuvers and defense techniques designed to gain approval from significant people in one's life. When a person feels that the anxiety is becoming too widespread, they try to limit opportunities for the further development of such anxiety. Such limitation results in *restriction of functioning* that includes only those patterns of activity that are familiar and well-established.

6.9.   The answer is D (*Synopsis VII*, pages 240 and 253).

Free association is known as the fundamental rule of psychoanalysis. The use of free association in psychoanalysis evolved gradually from 1892 to 1895. Sigmund Freud began to encourage his patients to verbalize, without reservation or censorship, the passing thoughts in their minds. The conflicts that emerge while fulfilling the task of free association constitute *resistance* which was first defined by Freud as the reluctance of his patients to recount significant memories. Later, Freud realized that resistance was often the result of an unconscious *repression* of conflictual material; the repression led to an active exclusion of painful or anxiety-producing feelings from consciousness. Freud thought that repression was at the core of all symptom formation.

Psychic determinism is the concept that actions as adults can be understood as the end result of a chain of psychological events that have a well-defined cause and effect.

Abreaction is a process in which a memory of a traumatic experience is released from repression and brought into consciousness. As the patient is able to express the affect associated with the memory, the affect is discharged, and the symptoms disappear.

The concept of the unconscious was one of Freud's most important contributions—first used to define mental material not in the field of awareness and, later, to designate a topographic area of the mind where psychic material is not readily accessible to conscious awareness.

6.10.   The answer is E (all) (*Synopsis VII*, pages 240–241).

The Interpretation of Dreams, published in 1900, is generally considered to be one of Sigmund Freud's most important contributions to the field. The book includes much of the data derived from his clinical experience with patients and the insights gained from his self-analysis and free association to his own dreams. On the basis of that evidence, Freud concluded that *dreams are the conscious expression of an unconscious fantasy* or wish. Freud maintained that *dreams represent wish-fulfillment activities*, albeit disguised and distorted through such mechanisms as symbolism, displacement, and condensation. Dream analysis yields material that has been repressed by the ego's defensive activities. The dream, as it is consciously recalled and experienced, is termed the manifest dream, and its various elements are termed the manifest dream content; the unconscious thoughts and wishes that make up the core meaning of the dream are described as the latent dream content. *Latent dream content derives from the repressed part of the id* and includes such categories as nocturnal sensory stimuli and the day's residue. Nocturnal sensory stimuli, such as pain or thirst, are *sensory impressions that may play a role in initiating a dream*. Repressed id impulses are wishes that have their origin in oedipal and preoedipal phases of development. The day's residue comprises thoughts and ideas connected with the activities of the dreamer's waking life.

6.11.   The answer is D (*Synopsis VII*, pages 248–251).

Repression is a mechanism of defense employed by the ego to help mediate conflict between the ego, superego, and the id. It is not considered an autonomous ego function. Repression is defined as an unconscious defense mechanism in which unacceptable mental contents are banished or kept out of consciousness.

Autonomous ego functions are based on rudimentary apparatuses that are present at birth. They develop outside the conflict with the id. Heinz Hartmann included *perception*, intuition, comprehension, thinking, *language*, some phases of *motor development*, learning, and *intelligence* among the functions of that conflict-free sphere.

6.12.   The answer is B (*Synopsis VII*, pages 249–252).

The office worker is controlling guilt feelings by *rationalization*, a process that involves justifying unacceptable and irrational behavior by a plausible but invalid excuse. By turning from the victim role (the one who is fired) to the active role (firing himself), the worker is identifying with his boss, whom he views as an aggressor. *Identification with the aggressor is* a process by which persons incorporate the mental image of someone who is a source of frustration. A primitive defense, it operates in the interest and service of the developing ego.

Denial is a defense mechanism in which the existence of unpleasant realities is disavowed. The person keeps out of conscious awareness any aspects of either internal or external reality that, if acknowledged, would produce anxiety.

Identification is a defense mechanism by which

persons pattern themselves after another person; in the process, the self is permanently altered. *Undoing* is a defense mechanism by which a person symbolically acts out in reverse something unacceptable that has already been done or against which the ego must defend itself. A primitive defense mechanism, undoing is a form of magical expiatory action. Repetitive in nature, it is commonly observed in obsessive-compulsive disorder.

Projection is an unconscious defense mechanism in which a person attributes to another those generally unconscious ideas, thoughts, feelings, and impulses that are personally undesirable or unacceptable. Projection protects the person from anxiety arising from an inner conflict. By externalizing whatever is unacceptable, persons deal with it as a situation apart from themselves.

Intellectualization is a defense mechanism in which reasoning or logic is used in an attempt to avoid confrontation with an objectionable impulse and to defend against anxiety. It is also known as brooding compulsion and thinking compulsion.

The most common defense mechanisms are listed and defined in Table 6.2.

6.13. The answer is D (*Synopsis VII*, pages 240–241).

According to Sigmund Freud, the manifest dream is the dream itself as reported by the dreamer. *The core meaning of the dream is not expressed by its manifest content.* However, in the process of analyzing the manifest dream, the psychoanalyst obtains information concerning the patient that would otherwise be inaccessible. That information behind the dream is termed the latent dream-thoughts. The technique by which the latent dream-thoughts are derived from the manifest dream is called dream interpretation. The process by which the latent dream-thoughts become the manifest dream in the dreamer's mental life is called the dream work.

Freud first became aware of the significance of dreams in therapy when he realized that, in the process of free association, his patients frequently described their dreams of the night before or of years past. He then discovered that the *dreams have a definite but disguised meaning.* He also found that encouraging his patients to free-associate to dream fragments was more productive than their associations to real-life events; free-associating to dreams facilitated the disclosure of the patients' unconscious memories and fantasies.

In *The Interpretation of Dreams* Freud concluded that a dream, like a neurotic symptom, is the conscious expression of an unconscious fantasy or wish that is not readily accessible in waking life. Although *dreams are considered a normal manifestation of unconscious activity*, they also bear some resemblance to the pathological thoughts of psychotic patients in the waking state. *Dreams represent unconscious wishes* or thoughts disguised through symbolization and other distorting mechanisms.

Nocturnal sensory stimuli may be incorporated into the dream and can be interpreted through free association.

6.14. The answer is C (*Synopsis VII*, pages 248–251).

A phobia is an abnormal fear reaction caused by a paralyzing conflict resulting from an increase of sexual excitation attached to an unconscious object. The fear is avoided by *displacement*; the conflict is displaced onto an object or situation outside the ego system. Displacement transfers an emotion from the original idea to which it was attached to another idea or object.

Projection is a defense mechanism in which thoughts, feelings, and impulses that are undesirable are transferred to another person. *Identification* is a defense mechanism by which persons pattern themselves after another person. *Undoing* is an unconscious defense mechanism by which a person symbolically acts out in reverse something unacceptable. *Reaction formation* is an unconscious defense mechanism in which a person develops a socialized attitude or interest that is the direct antithesis of some infantile wish.

6.15. The answer is A (*Synopsis VII*, pages 248–251).

George Vaillant's mature defenses include *altruism*, anticipation, asceticism, humor, sublimation, and suppression. In the 1970s he published his 30-year follow-up study of people who had gone to Harvard in the 1930s. He delineated the psychological characteristics he considered essential to mental health in this group, including descriptions of defense mechanisms he thought to be healthy and those he thought to be more psychopathological. Vaillant classified four types of defenses: (1) narcissistic defenses, which are characteristic of young children and psychotic adults; (2) immature defenses, which are characteristic of adolescents and are also seen in psychopathological states, such as depression; (3) neurotic defenses, which may be seen in adults under stress; and (4) mature defenses, which are characteristic of adult functioning. At times, some of the defensive categories overlap; for instance, neurotic defenses may be seen in normally healthy, mature adults. *Controlling, intellectualization*, and *rationalization* are characterized by Vaillant as among the neurotic defenses.

Altruism is a regard for the intents and needs of others. Controlling is the excessive attempt to manage or regulate events or objects in the environment in the interest of minimizing anxiety and solving internal conflicts. Intellectualization represents the attempt to avoid unacceptable feelings by escaping from emotions into a world of intellectual concepts and words. Rationalization is justification, making a thing appear reasonable that otherwise would be regarded as irrational.

Table 6.2
Defense Mechanisms

Acting out. An action rather than a verbal response to an unconscious instinctual drive or impulse that brings about the temporary partial relief of inner tension. Relief is attained by reacting to a present situation as if it were the situation that originally gave rise to the drive or impulse. An immature defense.

Altruism. Regard for and dedication to the welfare of others. The term was originated by Auguste Comte (1798–1857), a French philosopher. In psychiatry the term is closely linked with ethics and morals. Sigmund Freud recognized altruism as the only basis for the development of community interest. Eugen Bleuler equated it with morality. A mature defense.

Anticipation. The act of dealing with, doing, foreseeing, or experiencing beforehand. Anticipation is characteristic of the ego and is necessary for the judgment and planning of suitable later action. Anticipation depends on reality testing—by trying in an active manner and in small doses what may happen to one passively and in unknown doses. The testing affords the possibility of judging reality and is an important factor in the development of the ability to tolerate tensions. A mature defense.

Asceticism. A mode of life characterized by rigor, self-denial, and mortification of the flesh. Asceticism is seen typically as a phase in puberty, when it indicates a fear of sexuality and a simultaneous defense against sexuality. Asceticism is also seen as an extreme type of masochistic character disorder, in which almost all activity is forbidden because it represents intolerable instinctual demands. In such cases the very act of mortifying may become a distorted expression of the blocked sexuality and may produce masochistic pleasure. Examples are eccentrics who devote their lives to the combating of some particular evil that unconsciously may represent their own instinctual demands. A mature defense.

Blocking. The involuntary cessation of thought processes or speech because of unconscious emotional factors. It is also known as thought deprivation. An immature defense.

Controlling. The excessive attempt to manage or regulate events or objects in the environment in the interest of minimizing anxiety and solving internal conflicts. A neurotic defense.

Denial. A mechanism in which the existence of unpleasant realities is disavowed. The mechanism keeps out of conscious awareness any aspects of external reality that, if acknowledged, would produce anxiety. A narcissistic defense.

Displacement. A mechanism by which the emotional component of an unacceptable idea or object is transferred to a more acceptable one. A neurotic defense.

Dissociation. A mechanism involving the segregation of any group of mental or behavioral processes from the rest of the person's psychic activity. It may entail the separation of an idea from its accompanying emotional tone, as seen in dissociative disorders. A neurotic defense.

Distortion. A misrepresentation of reality. It is based on unconsciously determined motives. A narcissistic defense.

Externalization. A general term, correlative to internalization, for the tendency to perceive in the external world and in external objects components of one's own personality, including instinctual impulses, conflicts, moods, attitudes, and styles of thinking. It is a more general term than projection, which is defined by its derivation, form, and correlation with specific introjects. A neurotic defense.

Humor. The overt expression of feelings without personal discomfort or immobilization and without unpleasant effects on others. Humor allows one to bear, yet focus on, what is too terrible to be borne, in contrast to wit, which always involves distraction or displacement away from the affective issue. A mature defense.

Hypochondriasis. An exaggerated concern about one's physical health. The concern is not based on real organic pathology. An immature defense.

Identification. A mechanism by which one patterns oneself after another person. In the process, the self may be permanently altered. An immature defense.

Identification with the aggressor. A process by which one incorporates within oneself the mental image of a person who represents a source of frustration. The classic example of the defense occurs toward the end of the oedipal stage, when a boy, whose main source of love and gratification is his mother, identifies with his father. The father represents the source of frustration, being the powerful rival for the mother; the child cannot master or run away from his father, so he is obliged to identify with his father. An immature defense.

Incorporation. A mechanism in which the psychic representation of another person or aspects of another person are assimilated into oneself through a figurative process of symbolic oral ingestion. It represents a special form of introjection and is the earliest mechanism of identification.

Inhibition. The depression or arrest of a function; suppression or diminution of outgoing influences from a reflex center. The sexual impulse, for example, may be inhibited because of psychological repression. A neurotic defense.

Intellectualization. A mechanism in which reasoning or logic is used in an attempt to avoid confrontation with an objectionable impulse and thus defends against anxiety. It is also known as brooding compulsion and thinking compulsion. A neurotic defense.

Introjection. The unconscious, symbolic internalization of a psychic representation of a hated or loved external object with the goal of establishing closeness to the object and its constant presence. In the case of a loved object, anxiety consequent to separation or tension arising out of ambivalence toward the object is diminished; in the case of a feared or hated object, internalization of its malicious or aggressive characteristics serves to avoid anxiety by symbolically putting those characteristics under one's own control. An immature defense.

Isolation. In psychoanalysis a mechanism involving the separation of an idea or memory from its attached feeling tone. Unacceptable ideational content is thereby rendered free of its disturbing or unpleasant emotional charge. A neurotic defense.

Passive-aggressive behavior. The showing of aggressive feelings in passive ways, such as through obstructionism, pouting, and stubbornness. An immature defense.

Primitive idealization. Viewing external objects as either all good or all bad and as unrealistically endowed with great power. Most commonly, the all-good object is seen as omnipotent or ideal, and the badness in the all-bad object is greatly inflated. A narcissistic defense.

Continued

Table 6.2
Continued

Projection. An unconscious mechanism in which one attributes to another the ideas, thoughts, feelings, and impulses that are unacceptable to oneself. Projection protects a person from anxiety arising from an inner conflict. By externalizing whatever is unacceptable, one deals with it as a situation apart from oneself. A narcissistic and immature defense.

Projective identification. Depositing unwanted aspects of the self into another person and feeling at one with the object of the projection. The extruded aspects are modified by and recovered from the recipient. The defense allows one to distance and make oneself understood by exerting pressure on another person to experience feelings similar to one's own. A narcissistic defense.

Rationalization. A mechanism in which irrational or unacceptable behavior, motives, or feelings are logically justified or made consciously tolerable by plausible means. A neurotic defense.

Reaction formation. An unconscious defense mechanism in which a person develops a socialized attitude or interest that is the direct antithesis of some infantile wish or impulse in the unconscious. One of the earliest and most stable defense mechanisms, it is closely related to repression; both are defenses against impulses or urges that are unacceptable to the ego. A neurotic defense.

Regression. A mechanism in which a person undergoes a partial or total return to early patterns of adaptation. Regression is observed in many psychiatric conditions, particularly schizophrenia. An immature defense.

Repression. A mechanism in which unacceptable mental contents are banished or kept out of consciousness. A term introduced by Sigmund Freud, it is important in both normal psychological development and in neurotic and psychotic symptom formation. Freud recognized two kinds of repression: (1) repression proper—the repressed material was once in the conscious domain, (2) primal repression—the repressed material was never in the conscious realm. A neurotic defense.

Schizoid fantasy. The tendency to use fantasy and to indulge in autistic retreat for the purpose of conflict resolution and gratification. An immature defense.

Sexualization. The endowing of an object or function with sexual significance that it did not previously have or that it possesses to a small degree; it is used to ward off anxieties connected with prohibitive impulses. A neurotic defense.

Somatization. The defensive conversion of psychic derivatives into bodily symptoms; a tendency to react with somatic rather than psychic manifestations. Infantile somatic responses are replaced by thought and affect during development (desomatization); regression to early somatic forms of response (resomatization) may result from unresolved conflicts and may play an important role in psychological reactions. An immature defense.

Splitting. Dividing external objects into all good and all bad, accompanied by the abrupt shifting of an object from one extreme category to the other. Sudden and complete reversals of feelings and conceptualizations about a person may occur. The extreme repetitive oscillation between contradictory self-concepts is another manifestation of the mechanism. A narcissistic defense.

Sublimation. A mechanism in which the energy associated with unacceptable impulses or drives is diverted into personally and socially acceptable channels. Unlike other defense mechanisms, sublimation offers some minimal gratification of the instinctual drive or impulse. A mature defense.

Substitution. A mechanism in which a person replaces an unacceptable wish, drive, emotion, or goal with one that is acceptable. A neurotic defense.

Suppression. A conscious act of controlling and inhibiting an unacceptable impulse, emotion, or idea. Suppression is differentiated from repression in that repression is an unconscious process. A mature defense.

Symbolization. A mechanism by which one idea or object comes to stand for another because of some common aspect or quality in both. Symbolization is based on similarity and association. The symbols formed protect the person from the anxiety that may be attached to the original idea or object. A mature defense.

Turning against the self. Changing an unacceptable impulse aimed at others by redirecting it against oneself. An immature defense.

Undoing. A mechanism by which a person symbolically acts out in reverse something unacceptable that has already been done or against which the ego must defend itself. A primitive defense mechanism, undoing is a form of magical action. Repetitive in nature, it is commonly observed in persons with obsessive-compulsive disorder. A neurotic defense.

Table compiled from Sigmund Freud, Anna Freud, E. Semrad, W. W. Meissner, and George Vaillant. Narcissistic defenses: used by children and psychotics; immature defenses: used by adolescents and in depressive disorders and obsessive-compulsive disorder; neurotic defenses: used by adults under stress and in obsessive-compulsive disorder and somatoform disorders; mature defenses: used by normal adults.

6.16. The answer is A (*Synopsis VII*, pages 251 and 600).

Obsessive-compulsive disorder comes about as a result of the separation of affects from ideas or behavior by the defense mechanisms of undoing and isolation, by regression to the anal-sadistic level, or by turning the impulses against the self. To defend against a painful idea in the unconscious, the person displaces the affect onto some other indirectly associated idea, one more tolerable that, in turn, becomes invested with an inordinate quantity of affect.

Anxiety disorders are disorders in which anxiety is the most prominent disturbance or in which the patients experience anxiety if they resist giving in to their symptoms. The anxiety disorders include phobias, obsessive-compulsive disorder, posttraumatic stress disorder, and panic disorder.

Pain disorder is a disorder characterized by the

complaint of pain. The pain may vary with intensity and duration and may range from a slight disturbance of the patient's social or occupational functioning to total incapacity and the need for hospitalization.

Dissociative disorders are characterized by a sudden, temporary alteration in consciousness, identity, or motor behavior. The dissociative disorders include dissociative amnesia, dissociative fugue, dissociative identity disorder, and depersonalization disorder.

Dysthymic disorder is a mood disorder characterized by depression.

6.17.   The answer is B (*Synopsis VII*, pages 258–259).

Psychobiology, a term introduced by Adolf Meyer, emphasizes the importance of *biographical study and common-sense understanding of patients*. The immediate goal is to identify motives or indications for the psychiatric examination. In identifying important details of the patient's life history through a biographical study, the clinician records the most obvious related personality items, factors, and reactions. In addition, the clinician should study the patient's physical, neurological, genetic, and social status variables and the correlations between those variables and personality factors. The clinician should also formulate a differential diagnosis and a therapeutic schedule for each case.

Analysis of the ego through the interpretation of defense mechanisms is a concept used in psychoanalysis. A *primary understanding of the biological and biochemical origins and treatment of mental illness*, the *emphasis on genetic factors in mental illness, and the use of drugs in psychiatry* are concepts used in psychopharmacology. *Psychological factors affecting physical illness* are concerns in psychosomatic medicine.

6.18.   The answer is D (*Synopsis VII*, pages 255–256).

Alienation from the self is a concept developed by *Karen Horney* to describe the various neurotic mechanisms—such as distorted self-image, self-hatred, and estrangement of one's own feelings—that combine to lead to alienation. Such alienation of one's own feelings is characteristic of obsessive-compulsive disorder. Certain organs and body areas and even the entire body are often perceived as if they did not belong to the person or as if they were different from the usual. Some manifestations are objectively observable; others are subjective and subtle.

Sigmund Freud developed psychoanalysis; *Harry Stack Sullivan* conceptualized the interpersonal theory of psychiatry; *Eric Berne* developed transactional analysis; and *Alfred Adler* is best known for his concept of the inferiority complex.

6.19.   The answer is A (*Synopsis VII*, pages 258–259).

Adolf Meyer used the term "habit training" to explain the process of therapy by which the main goal is to aid patients' adjustment by helping them to modify unhealthy adaptations. In the process of habit trainings, the psychiatrist always emphasizes patients' current life situations by using a variety of techniques, such as guidance, suggestion, reeducation and direction.

Carl Gustav Jung developed the school known as analytic psychology. *Otto Rank* focused on the analytic aspects of what he called the birth trauma. *B. F. Skinner* and *Joseph Wolpe* are known for their work in learning theory and behavior therapy, respectively.

6.20.   The answer is B (*Synopsis VII*, page 259).

Harry Stack Sullivan's self-system concerns the concept of the *personality*. The self-system reflects maternal and paternal attitudes and any accumulated sets of experiences that begin in infancy and continue for a long time.

The *unconscious* is the topographic division of the mind in which the psychic material is not readily accessible to conscious awareness by ordinary means. Its existence may be manifested in symptom formation, in dreams, or under the influence of drugs.

The *libido* is the psychic energy associated with the sexual drive or life instinct. *Defense mechanisms* are unconscious processes acting to relieve conflict and anxiety arising from one's impulses and drives.

The *Oedipus complex* is the constellation of feelings, impulses, and conflicts in the developing child that concern sexual impulses and attraction toward the opposite-sex parent and aggressive, hostile, or envious feelings toward the same-sex parent. Real or fantasied threats from the same-sex parent result in the repression of those feelings. The development of the Oedipus complex coincides with the phallic phase of psychosexual development. One of Freud's most important concepts, the term was originally applied only to boys. The female analogue of the Oedipus complex is called the Electra complex, a term attributed to Carl Jung used to describe unresolved developmental conflicts influencing a woman's relationships with men.

6.21.   The answer is D (*Synopsis VII*, page 265).

Erik Erikson accepted Sigmund Freud's theory of infantile sexuality, but Erikson also saw the developmental potential of all stages of life. In each of Erikson's eight stages, a maturational crisis arises. During *middle adulthood*, each person has the opportunity to become generative, productive through contributions to society, or to become stagnant, preoccupied only with one's own well-being. Erikson used the terms "basic trust versus basic mistrust," "autonomy versus shame and doubt," "initiative versus guilt," and "industry versus inferiority" to describe conflicts occurring in *childhood*; the term "identity versus role diffusion" to describe the conflict occurring during *adolescence*; "intimacy versus isolation" to describe the conflict occurring in *young adulthood*; and "integrity versus despair" to describe the conflict occurring in *late adulthood*. Erikson's stages are outlined in Table 6.1.

6.22.   The answer is A (*Synopsis VII*, page 264).

According to Erik Erikson, the development of what he termed basic *trust* is a result of consistent and affectionate maternal behavior during infancy. The infant is extremely sensitive to the mother; both the overt and the subtle aspects of maternal behavior profoundly affect the infant. The infant's dependence on others is total, a fact that has important psychological effects.

Autonomy is children's ability to control their muscles, their impulses, themselves, and ultimately their environment. *Initiative* provides the freedom and the opportunity for children to begin motor-play gymnastics and intellectual questioning of those around them. During the period of *industry*, children learn to reason deductively; they are concerned with the details of how things are made, how they work, and what they do. *Identity* is a sense of who one is, where one has been, and where one is going.

6.23.   The answer is D (*Synopsis VII*, page 264).

The stage of industry versus inferiority, which runs from ages 6 to 11, is characterized by *confidence in one's ability to use adult materials*. During that period of latency, the child is learning, waiting, and practicing to be a provider.

Eagerness and curiosity are characteristics of the stage of initiative versus guilt. In the stage of intimacy versus isolation, young adults either become *self-indulgent* and self-interested or share themselves in intense, long-term relationships. In the stage of initiative versus guilt, children develop a division between their *expanded desires* and their exuberance at unlimited growth. *Preoccupation with one's appearance* is a characteristic of the stage of identity versus role diffusion.

6.24.   The answer is E (all) (*Synopsis VII*, page 265).

The stage of generativity versus stagnation spans the middle years of life. Generativity is characterized by *interests outside the home*, by *establishing and guiding the oncoming generation*, and by *bettering society*. Even a childless couple or person can be generative. However, when adults live only to satisfy their day-to-day personal needs and to acquire comforts and entertainment for themselves, they become immersed in *self-absorption*.

6.25.   The answer is A (*Synopsis VII*, pages 247–248).

According to Sigmund Freud's structural theory of the mind, the psychic apparatus is divided into three provinces: *id, ego, and superego*. The id is the locus of the instinctual drives. It is under the domination of the primary process; therefore, it operates in accordance with the pleasure principle, without regard for reality. The ego is a more coherent organ-

ization whose task it is to avoid unpleasure and pain by opposing or regulating the discharge of instinctual drives in order to conform with the demands of the external world. In addition, the discharge of id impulses is opposed or regulated by the superego, which contains the internalized moral values and influence of the parental images.

The *unconscious* is the topographical division of the mind in which the psychic material is not readily accessible to conscious awareness by ordinary means. Its existence may be manifested in symptom formation, in dreams, or under the influence of psychoactive substances. The theories about the conscious, preconscious, and unconscious divisions of the psychiatric apparatus predated by many years Freud's structural hypotheses. The conscious, according to Freud, refers to that portion of mental functioning within the realm of awareness at all times. The preconscious includes all mental contents that are not in immediate awareness but that can be consciously recalled with effort.

6.26.   The answer is D (*Synopsis VII*, page 244).

Sigmund Freud's concept of *sexual resemblance* does not explain why a man falls in love with a particular type of woman. Sexual resemblance pertains to homosexual love.

A man may choose a particular type of woman in adult life because *she resembles the man's idealized self-image* or his fantasied self-image or because *she resembles someone who took care of him when he was a boy*. Persons who have an intense degree of self-love, especially certain beautiful women, have, according to Freud, an appeal over and above their esthetic attraction. Such women *provide narcissistic gratification* that their lovers were forced to give up in the process of turning toward object love (love for another).

6.27–6.30

6.27.   The answer is C (*Synopsis VII*, page 255).

6.28.   The answer is B (*Synopsis VII*, page 259).

6.29.   The answer is A (*Synopsis VII*, page 254).

6.30.   The answer is D (*Synopsis VII*, pages 255–256).

Adolf Meyer examined the verifiable and objective aspects of a person's life. His theory of *psychobiology* explains disordered behavior as reactions to genetic, physical, psychological, environmental, and social stresses. Meyer introduced the concept of common sense psychiatry, which focuses on ways in which the patient's current life situation can be realistically improved.

Carl Rogers's name is most clearly associated with the *person-centered theory of personality* and psychotherapy, in which the major concepts are self-actualization and self-direction. Specifically, people are born with a capacity to direct themselves in the healthiest way, toward a level of completeness called self-actualization. From his person-centered approach, Rogers viewed personality not as a static entity composed of traits and patterns but as a dynamic phenomenon involving ever-changing communications, relationships, and self-concepts.

Alfred Adler was one of Freud's prize pupils, but theoretical differences led to their eventual estrangement. Adler felt that Freud overemphasized the sexual theory of neurosis. In Adler's view, aggression is of far more importance, specifically in its manifestation as a striving for power, which he believed to be a masculine trait. Adler coined the term *"inferiority complex"* to refer to a sense of inadequacy and weakness that is universal and inborn. The developing child's self-esteem is compromised by any physical defect, and Adler referred to that phenomenon as organ inferiority. He also thought that a basic inferiority is tied to the child's oedipal longings, which can never be gratified.

Karen Horney was an American psychiatrist who believed that a person's current personality attributes are the result of the interaction between the person and the environment and are not based on infantile libidinal strivings carried over from childhood. Her theory, known as *holistic psychology*, maintains that a person needs to be seen as a unitary whole who influences the environment and is influenced by it. She believed that the Oedipus complex is overvalued in terms of its contribution to adult psychopathology. She believed that rigid parental attitudes regarding sexuality lead to excessive concern with the genitals.

6.31–6.35

6.31. **The answer is B** (*Synopsis VII*, pages 249–251).

6.32. **The answer is D** (*Synopsis VII*, pages 249–251).

6.33. **The answer is A** (*Synopsis VII*, pages 249–251).

6.34. **The answer is C** (*Synopsis VII*, pages 249–251).

6.35. **The answer is E** (*Synopsis VII*, pages 249–251).

Projection is an unconscious defense mechanism in which a person attributes to another those generally unconscious ideas, thoughts, feelings, and impulses that are personally undesirable or unacceptable. Projection protects the person from anxiety arising from an inner conflict. By externalizing whatever is unacceptable, persons deal with it as a situation apart from themselves.

Reaction formation is an unconscious defense mechanism in which a person develops a socialized attitude or interest that is the direct antithesis of some infantile wish or impulse that the person har-

bors either consciously or unconsciously. One of the earliest and most unstable defense mechanisms, it is closely related to repression; both are defenses against impulses or urges that are unacceptable to the ego.

Rationalization is an unconscious defense mechanism in which irrational or unacceptable behavior, motives, or feelings are logically justified or made consciously tolerable by plausible means. Ernest Jones introduced the term.

Denial is a defense mechanism in which the existence of unpleasant realities is disavowed. The term refers to a keeping out of conscious awareness any aspects of either internal or external reality that, if acknowledged, would produce anxiety.

Sublimation is an unconscious defense mechanism in which the energy associated with unacceptable impulses or drives is diverted into personally and socially acceptable channels. Unlike other defense mechanisms, sublimation offers some minimal gratification of the instinctual drive or impulse.

6.36–6.40

6.36. **The answer is B** (*Synopsis VII*, pages 259–260).

6.37. **The answer is D** (*Synopsis VII*, pages 256–257).

6.38. **The answer is C** (*Synopsis VII*, pages 255–256).

6.39. **The answer is A** (*Synopsis VII*, page 254).

6.40. **The answer is E** (*Synopsis VII*, page 257).

Donald Winnicott (1897–1971) was an influential contributor to object relations theory. He focused on the conditions that make it possible for a child to develop awareness as a separate person. One of the conditions is the provision of an environment termed "good-enough mothering." Good-enough mothering enables the child to be nurtured in a nonimpinging environment that permits the emergence of the true self. Winnicott *introduced the concept of the transitional object*, something that helps the child gradually shift from subjectivity to external reality. Such a possession, usually blankets or a soft toy, exists in an intermediate realm as a substitute for the mother and as one of the first objects a child begins to recognize as separate from the self.

Melanie Klein (1882–1960) modified psychoanalytic theory, particularly in its application to infants and very young children. In contrast to orthodox psychoanalytic theory, which postulates the development of the superego during the fourth year of life, Klein's theory maintains that a primitive superego is formed during the first and second years. Klein further believed that aggressive, rather than sexual, drives are preeminent during the earliest stages of development. She deviated most sharply from classic psychoanalytic theory in her formulations concerning the Oedipus complex. She *believed that oedipal strivings are experienced during the first year of life*, as opposed to the classic formulation of its occurring between the ages of 3 and 5. She also believed that, *during the first year, gratifying experiences with the good breast reinforce basic trust* and that frustrating experiences can lead to a depressive position.

Karen Horney (1885–1952) was an American psychiatrist who ascribed great importance to the influence of sociocultural factors on individual development. She raised questions about the existence of immutable instinctual drives and developmental phases or sexual conflict as the root of neurosis while recognizing the importance of sexual drives. Rather than focusing on such concepts as the Oedipus complex, Horney *emphasized cultural factors and disturbances in interpersonal and intrapsychic development* as the cause of neuroses in general.

Franz Alexander (1891–1964) founded the Chicago Institute for Psychoanalysis. He *introduced the concept of the corrective emotional experience*. The therapist, who is supportive, enables the patient to master past traumas and to modify the effects of those traumas. Alexander was also a major influence in the field of psychosomatic medicine.

Heinz Kohut (1913–1981) *expanded Sigmund Freud's concept of narcissism*. In *The Analysis of the Self* (1971), Kohut wrote about a large group of patients suffering from narcissistic personality disorder whom he believed to be analyzable but who did not develop typical transference neuroses in the classic sense. The conflict involves the relation between the self and archaic narcissistic objects. Those objects are the grandiose self and the idealized parent image, the reactivations of which constitute a threat to the patient's sense of integrity. Kohut's *theories are known as self psychology*.

6.41–6.45

6.41. The answer is **D** (*Synopsis VII*, page 256).

6.42. The answer is **A** (*Synopsis VII*, page 256).

6.43. The answer is **B** (*Synopsis VII*, page 256).

6.44. The answer is **C** (*Synopsis VII*, page 256).

6.45. The answer is **E** (*Synopsis VII*, page 256).

With the term *"persona,"* Carl Gustav Jung denoted the disguised or masked attitude assumed by a person, in contrast to the deeply rooted personality components. Such persons put on a mask, corresponding to their conscious intentions, that makes up the *face presented to the outside world*. Through their identification with the persons, they deceive other people and often themselves as to their real character.

The *shadow* appears in dreams as *another person of the same sex as the dreamer*. According to Jung, one sees much in another person that does not belong to one's conscious psychology but that comes out from one's unconscious.

In Jung's terminology, anima and animus are archetypal representations of potentials that have not yet entered conscious awareness or become personalized. *Anima is a man's undeveloped femininity. Animus is a women's undeveloped masculinity.* Those concepts are universal basic human drives from which both conscious and unconscious individual qualities develop. Usually, they appear as unconscious images of persons of the opposite sex.

The *collective unconscious* is defined as the psychic contents outside the realm of awareness that are common to humankind in general. Jung, who introduced the term, believed that the collective unconscious is inherited and derived from the collective experience of the species. It transcends cultural differences and explains the analogy between ancient *mythological ideas and primitive projections* observed in some patients who have never been exposed to those ideas.

6.46–6.50

6.46. The answer is **D** (*Synopsis VII*, page 257).

6.47. The answer is **B** (*Synopsis VII*, pages 257–258).

6.48. The answer is **A** (*Synopsis VII*, page 259).

6.49. The answer is **C** (*Synopsis VII*, pages 258–259).

6.50. The answer is **E** (*Synopsis VII*, page 258).

Kurt Lewin (1890–1947) adapted the field approach from physics into a concept called field theory. A field is the totality of coexisting parts that are mutually interdependent. Applying field theory to groups, Lewin coined the term *"group dynamics"* and believed that a group is greater than the sum of its parts.

Abraham Maslow (1908–1970) was a developer of the self-actualization theory, which focuses on the need to understand the totality of the person. A *peak experience*, according to that school of thought, is an episodic, brief occurrence in which the person suddenly experiences a powerful transcendental state of consciousness. The powerful experience occurs most often in psychologically healthy persons.

Harry Stack Sullivan (1892–1949) made basic contributions to psychodynamic theory with his emphasis on the cultural matrix of personality development. Sullivan defined psychiatry as the study of interpersonal relationships that are manifest in the observable behavior of persons. Those relationships can be observed inside the therapeutic situation; the process is greatly enhanced when the therapist is one of the participants. The transaction is then between the therapist, who is a *participant observer*, and a patient, whose life is disturbed or disordered.

Wilhelm Reich's (1897–1957) major contributions to psychoanalysis were in the areas of *character formation and character types*. Reich placed special emphasis on the influence of social forces in determining character structure, particularly on their repressive and inhibiting effects. Reich's basic concept was that character is a defensive structure, an armoring of the ego against instinctual forces within and the world without. It is the person's characteristic manner of dealing with threats. Reich described four major character types: hysterical, compulsive, narcissistic, and masochistic.

The evolution of *Gestalt therapy* is closely associated with the work of *Frederick S. Perls* (1893–1970), a European émigré trained in the psychoanalytic tradition. Although acknowledging its influences, Perls largely rejected the tenets of psychoanalysis and founded his own school of Gestalt therapy, borrowing the name from Gestalt theory. Gestalt theory proposes that the natural course of the biological and psychological development of the organism entails a full awareness of physical sensations and psychological needs. Perls believed that, as any form of self-control interferes with healthy functioning, modern civilization inevitably produces neurotic people; thus, the task of the therapist is to instruct the patient in discovering and experiencing the feelings and the needs repressed by society's demands.

6.51–6.55.

6.51. **The answer is A** (*Synopsis VII*, pages 261–262).

6.52. **The answer is C** (*Synopsis VII*, pages 261–262).

6.53. **The answer is E** (*Synopsis VII*, pages 261 and 263).

6.54. **The answer is D** (*Synopsis VII*, pages 261 and 263).

6.55. **The answer is B** (*Synopsis VII*, pages 261 and 263–264).

The first of Erik Erikson's developmental stages (*infancy*—birth to 1 year) is characterized by the first psychosocial crisis the infant must face, that of *basic trust versus basis mistrust*. The crisis takes place in the context of the intimate relationship between the infant and its mother. The infant's primary orientation to reality is erotic and centers on the mouth. The successful resolution of the stage includes a disposition to trust others, a basic trust in oneself, a capacity to entrust oneself, and a sense of self-confidence.

During *early childhood* (ages 3 to 5 years) the crisis addressed by the child *is initiative versus guilt*. As the child struggles to resolve the oedipal struggle, guilt may grow because of aggressive thoughts or wishes. Initiative arises as the child begins to desire to mimic the adult world and as the child finds enjoyment in productive activity.

The stage of *puberty and adolescence* (age 11 years through the end of adolescence) is characterized by *identity versus role diffusion*, during which the ado-

lescent must begin to establish a future role in adult society. During that psychosocial crisis the adolescent is peculiarly vulnerable to social and cultural influences.

Early adulthood (21 to 40 years) is characterized by *intimacy versus isolation*. The crisis is characterized by the need to establish the capacity to relate intimately and meaningfully with others in mutually satisfying and productive interactions. The failure to achieve a successful resolution of that crisis results in a sense of personal isolation. *Late adulthood* (65 and older) is characterized by *integrity versus despair*. The crisis implies and depends on the successful resolution of all the preceding crises of psychosocial growth. It entails the acceptance of oneself and of all the aspects of life and the integration of their elements into a stable pattern of living. The failure to achieve ego integration often results in a kind of despair and an unconscious fear of death. The person who fails that crisis lives in basic self-contempt.

A further explanation of Erikson's stages appears in Table 6.1.

6.56–6.60.

6.56. **The answer is A** (*Synopsis VII*, pages 241–242).

6.57. **The answer is B** (*Synopsis VII*, pages 244–248).

6.58. **The answer is A** (*Synopsis VII*, pages 241–242).

6.59. **The answer is B** (*Synopsis VII*, pages 244–248).

6.60. **The answer is D** (*Synopsis VII*, page 249).

The *topographic theory*, as *set forth by Sigmund Freud in* The Interpretation of Dreams *in 1900*, represented an attempt to divide the mind into three regions—*unconscious, preconscious, and conscious*—which were differentiated by their relation to consciousness. In general, all psychic material not in the immediate field of awareness—such as primitive drives, repressed desires, and memories—is in the unconscious. The preconscious includes all mental contents that are not in immediate awareness but can be consciously recalled with effort, in contrast to the unconscious, whose elements are barred from consciousness by some intrapsychic force, such as repression. The conscious is that portion of mental functioning that is within the realm of awareness at all times.

The *structural theory* of the mind was *presented in* The Ego and the Id *in 1923*. It represented a shift from the topographic model. Only when Freud discovered that not all unconscious processes can be relegated to the instincts (for example, that certain aspects of mental functioning associated with the ego and superego are unconscious) did he turn to the study of those structural components. From a structural viewpoint, the psychic apparatus is divided into three provinces—*id, ego and superego*. Each is a particular aspect of human mental functioning and is not an empirically demonstrable phenomenon. The ego controls the apparatus of voluntary movement, perception, and contact with reality; through mechanisms of defense the ego is the inhibitor of primary instinctual drives. Freud conceived of the ego as an organized, problem-solving agent. Freud's concept of the id is as a completely unorganized, primordial reservoir of energy derived from the instincts; it is under the domination of the primary process. The id is not synonymous with the unconscious, as the structural viewpoint demonstrates that certain ego functions (for example; defenses against demands of the id) and aspects of the superego operate unconsciously. The discharge of id impulses is further regulated by the superego, which contains the internalized moral values and influence of the parental images—the conscience. The superego is the last of the structural components to develop; it results from the resolution of the Oedipus complex. Essentially, neurotic conflict can be explained structurally as a conflict between ego forces and id forces. Most often, the superego is involved in the conflict by aligning itself with the ego and imposing demands in the form of guilt. Occasionally, the superego may be allied with the id against the ego.

Sigmund Freud coined the idea of defense functions in 1894 and believed that defense mechanisms serve to keep conflictual ideation out of consciousness. However, the *first systematic and comprehensive study of the defenses used by the ego* was presented in Anna Freud's 1936 book, *The Ego and the*

Mechanisms of Defense, which marked the beginning of ego psychology.

6.61–6.65

6.61. **The answer is A** (*Synopsis VII*, pages 241–242).

6.62. **The answer is A** (*Synopsis VII*, pages 241–242).

6.63. **The answer is A** (*Synopsis VII*, pages 241–242).

6.64. **The answer is B** (*Synopsis VII*, pages 241–242).

6.65. **The answer is B** (*Synopsis VII*, pages 241–242).

Primary process was Sigmund Freud's term for the laws that govern unconscious processes. It is a type of thinking *characteristic of very young children, the unconscious, the id,* and dreams. Primary process is characterized by an absence of negatives, conditionals, and other qualifying conjunctions; by a lack of any sense of time; and by the use of allusion, condensation, and symbols. It is primitive, prelogical thinking marked by the tendency to seek immediate discharge and gratification of instinctual drives.

Secondary process was Freud's term for the laws that regulate events in *the preconscious and the ego*. It is a form of thinking that uses judgment, intelligence, logic, and reality testing; it helps the ego block the tendency of the instincts toward immediate discharge.

Clinical Examination of the Psychiatric Patient

The interview, the assessment, and the treatment of a psychiatric patient is a complex task that takes place on several levels at once. Not only must the clinician be able to listen empathetically and efficiently to people who are often disorganized, but also the clinician must be able to observe significant behavioral manifestations and pay attention to the ongoing subtle and dynamic interpersonal process. A clinician interviewing a psychiatric patient may be dealing not only with bizarre, disturbing psychotic ideas and behavior but also with the patient's fears of and stereotypes about mental illness. With patients who are only moderately disturbed, the psychiatric interview still involves eliciting a history, including material that the patient regards as intimate and private and sometimes shameful or sad.

The clinician must be knowledgeable and skilled in interviewing situations. The interview can take various forms, depending on such factors as where the interview takes place, the purpose of the interview, and the patient's signs. If it is a first interview with a previously unknown patient, the diagnosis may begin to become apparent only in the course of the interview. Skilled interviewers are flexible, approaching different patients differently and changing their interviewing style as diagnostic and clinical impressions change.

To help organize their thinking and to structure the data obtained in the interview, clinicians organize the patient's story and their own observations in certain standard ways. Expertise with the outlines of the patient's psychiatric history and mental status examination is a necessary tool for any clinician. The psychiatric history outline summarizes the patient's story in structured form. The identifying data, chief complaint, history of present and past illnesses, personal history, psychosexual history, and family history are all basic and necessary ingredients in helping the clinician assess, diagnose, and treat the patient.

The psychiatric history provides objective data obtained from the patient and significant others, and the mental status examination provides an organized record of the clinician's observations of the patient's behavior, thought, and cognitive abilities. The mental status examination is a structure for recording observations about such factors as the patient's general appearance, psychomotor activity, mood and affect, speech, perception, thought process and content, level of cognition, impulse control, judgment, insight, and reliability.

The clinician must also use medical and laboratory evaluations of patients to clarify the diagnosis and the needed treatment. A working knowledge of available laboratory procedures and tests is required in today's practice of psychiatry to rule out medical pathology and to monitor treatment. In some cases, laboratory data are essential to make or confirm a diagnosis. Knowledge of basic screening tests, neuroendocrine tests, renal and liver function tests, and plasma blood level tests is now considered standard for any psychiatrist.

Chapter 7 of *Kaplan and Sadock's Synopsis VII* will help the student answer the following questions.

HELPFUL HINTS

The student should know these terms, especially the acronyms and laboratory tests.

rapport	occupational and educational	CT
style	history	rCBF
note taking	social activity	LFT
data	sexuality	antipsychotics
transference	marital and military history	cyclic antidepressants
resistance	judgment and insight	lithium
therapeutic alliance	reliability	carbamazepine
countertransference	psychiatric report	polysomnography
initial interview and greeting	DSM-IV and Axes I-V	EEG
uncovering feelings	prognosis	BEAM
using patient's words	psychodynamic formulation	SSEP
stress interview	treatment plan	family history
patient questions	TFTs	current social situation
subsequent interviews	TSH	dreams, fantasies, and value
psychiatric history	TRH	systems
preliminary and personal	DST	mental status examination
identification	catecholamines	appearance, behavior, attitude, and
chief complaint	BUN	speech
history of present illness; previous	VDRL	mood, feelings, and affect
illnesses	*Treponema pallidum*	appropriateness
medical history	VEP	perception
prenatal history	AER	thought process
early, middle, and late childhood	CSF	sensorium and cognition
history	NMR	consciousness and orientation
psychosexual history	MRI	concentration, memory, and
religious background	PET	intelligence
adulthood		

QUESTIONS

DIRECTIONS: Each of the questions or incomplete statements below is followed by five suggested responses or completions. Select the *one* that is *best* in each case.

7.1. Which of the following substances has been implicated in mood disorders with seasonal pattern?
A. Luteotropic hormone (LTH)
B. Gonadotropin-releasing hormone (GnRH)
C. Testosterone
D. Estrogen
E. Melatonin

7.2. In a psychiatric interview
A. the psychiatrist should not medicate a violent patient before taking a history
B. a violent patient should be interviewed alone to establish a doctor-patient relationship
C. delusions should never be directly challenged
D. the psychiatrist must not ask depressed patients if they have suicidal thoughts
E. the psychiatrist should have a seat higher than the patient's seat

7.3. In the mental status examination
A. the patient's mood can be described as normal, blunted, constricted, or flat
B. hallucinations and illusions are disturbances in the patient's thought process
C. asking a patient to spell the word "world" backward is designed to measure visuospatial ability
D. the highest level of insight is true emotional insight
E. blocking is an attitude assumed by the patient to stop the interview

7.4. In a psychiatric evaluation, a complete medical history may reveal
A. polyuria, polydipsia, and diarrhea, which are signs of lithium toxicity
B. exposure to lead, which can produce anxiety disorders
C. dyspnea and breathlessness, which may occur in manic episodes
D. a hearing impairment, which is commonly associated with impulse control disorders
E. glaucoma, which contraindicates the use of antihistaminic drugs

7.5. Hypothyroidism
A. may present with symptoms of mania
B. may be caused by lithium
C. is found in 40 percent of all patients with depressive disorders
D. does not occur in neonates
E. may be assayed through urinalysis

7.6. Patients receiving
A. benzodiazepines need weekly assessments of their magnesium blood levels
B. clozapine need to be assessed for drug-induced anemia
C. lithium must have their serum drug levels monitored regularly
D. trazodone have reported no serious adverse effects
E. monoamine oxidase inhibitors (MAOIs) need to avoid foods containing glucose

7.7. Each of the following statements is true *except*
A. sodium lactate provokes panic attacks in a majority of patients with panic disorder
B. sodium lactate can trigger flashbacks in patients with posttraumatic stress disorder
C. hyperventilation is as sensitive as lactate provocation in inducing panic attacks
D. panic attacks triggered by sodium lactate are not inhibited by propranolol
E. panic attacks triggered by sodium lactate are inhibited by alprazolam

7.8. If a patient receiving clozapine shows a white blood count (WBC) of 2,000 per cc, the clinician should
A. Increase the dosage of clozapine at once
B. Terminate any antibiotic therapy
C. place the patient in protective isolation in a medical unit
D. monitor the patient's WBC every ten days
E. institute weekly complete blood count (CBC) tests with differential

7.9. An abnormal finding on a dexamethasone-suppression test (DST) means that the patient may have
A. a good response to electroconvulsive therapy (ECT)
B. a good response to cyclic drugs
C. disseminated cancer
D. received high-dosage benzodiazepine treatment
E. all the above

7.10. Thyroid function tests are of use in clinical psychiatric practice because
A. up to 10 percent of patients with depression have thyroid disease
B. hypothyroidism may be a side effect of lithium
C. hypothyroidism may present as mental retardation
D. a blunted thyrotropin-releasing hormone (TRH) stimulation test is associated with depressive disorders
E. all the above

7.11. A 43-year-old woman with progressive systemic lupus erythematosus has been responding poorly to treatment. She appears to be depressed, and her physician is concerned that she may commit suicide. The best treatment strategy is for the physician to
A. avoid further questioning of the patient
B. reassure the patient that she will get well
C. ask directly about any suicidal thoughts
D. request psychiatric hospitalization
E. immediately put the patient on high-dosage antidepressant medication

7.12. The first sign of beginning cerebral disease is impairment of
A. immediate memory
B. recent memory
C. long-term memory
D. remote memory
E. none of the above

7.13. A stress interview is characterized by
A. the use of the Social Readjustment Rating Scale
B. intimidation of the psychiatrist by the patient
C. confrontation of the patient by the psychiatrist
D. the destructive effect it has on the patient's psyche
E. anxiety in both the physician and the patient

7.14. Asking patients what they would do if they received someone else's mail among their own is an example of a test of
A. intelligence
B. abstract thinking
C. insight
D. judgment
E. cognition

7.15. The medication most commonly used in the drug-assisted psychiatric interview is
A. meprobamate
B. diazepam
C. amobarbital
D. chloral hydrate
E. phenothiazine

7.16. The reaction of the patient toward the psychiatrist may be affected by
A. the psychiatrist's attitude
B. previous experiences with physicians
C. the patient's view of authority figures in childhood
D. the patient's cultural background
E. all the above

7.17. Methods to facilitate the development of doctor-patient rapport include all the following *except*
A. conducting a stress interview
B. asking open-ended questions
C. using the patient's own words
D. uncovering feelings
E. understanding the patient

7.18. A 23-year-old heterosexual man, during his first meeting with a female psychiatrist, suddenly states, "All women are whores, and I'm wasting my time talking with you." The patient gives a history of having had long-term sexual relationships with two women over the previous four years, relationships that he says were enjoyable. He describes normal feelings of intimacy toward his present partner. The treating physician's best response is
A. "You are expressing latent homosexual impulses"
B. "Those feelings are oedipal in nature"
C. "Your feelings of hostility toward women will make it impossible for us to work together"
D. "Why do you have those feelings?"
E. "You're bringing on feelings of fear in me"

7.19. A good test for recent memory is to ask patients
A. their date of birth
B. what they had to eat for their last meal
C. the name of the hospital they are in
D. to subtract 7 from 100
E. who is the President of the United States

7.20. A favorable therapeutic window is associated with
A. imipramine
B. nortriptyline
C. desipramine
D. amitriptyline
E. all the above

7.21. Amobarbital (Amytal) interviews
A. are not helpful in the differential diagnosis of muteness
B. often cause a worsening of pseudodementia
C. help recover repressed memories
D. can worsen the symptoms of conversion disorder
E. are not used in the treatment of posttraumatic stress disorder

DIRECTIONS: Each group of questions below consists of lettered headings followed by a list of numbered phrases. For each numbered phrase, select the *best* lettered heading. Each heading may be used once, more than once, or not at all.

Questions 7.22–7.26
A. Serum ammonia
B. Cortisone
C. Copper
D. Creatinine
E. Platelet count

7.22. Increased in hepatic encephalopathy

7.23. Elevated in Wilson's disease

7.24. Decreased by carbamazepine

7.25. Pretreatment workup for lithium therapy

7.26. Increased in response to stress

Questions 7.27–7.31

A. Hyperthyroidism
B. Hypothyroidism
C. Porphyria
D. Hepatolenticular degeneration
E. Pancreatic carcinoma

7.27. Jaundice, sense of imminent doom

7.28. Dry skin, myxedema madness

7.29. Kayser-Fleischer rings, brain damage

7.30. Abdominal crises, mood swings

7.31. Tremor, anxiety, and hyperactivity

Questions 7.32–7.36.

A. Elevated level of 5-HIAA
B. Decreased level of 5-HIAA

7.32. Carcinoid tumors

7.33. Phenothiazine medications

7.34. Aggressive behavior

7.35. High banana intake

7.36. Suicidal patients

ANSWERS

Clinical Examination of the Psychiatric Patient

7.1. The answer is E (*Synopsis VII*, pages 291 and 520).

Melatonin from the pineal gland has been implicated in mood disorders with seasonal pattern. Melatonin's exact mechanism of action is unknown, but its production is stimulated in the dark, and it may affect the sleep-wake cycle. Melatonin is synthesized from serotonin, an active neurotransmitter. Decreased nocturnal secretion of melatonin has been associated with depression. A number of other substances also affect behavior, and some known endocrine diseases (for example, Cushing's disease) have associated psychiatric signs. Symptoms of anxiety or depression may be explained in some patients by changes in endocrine function or homeostasis.

Luteotropic hormone (LTH) is an anterior pituitary hormone whose action maintains the function of the corpus luteum.

Gonadotropin-releasing hormone (GnRH), produced by the hypothalamus, increases the pituitary secretion of luteotropic hormone (LTH) and the follicle-stimulating hormone (FSH). GnRH is secreted in a pulsatile manner that is critical for the control of LTH and FSH from the pituitary. GnRH also acts as a neurotransmitter whose exact function is unknown.

Testosterone is the hormone responsible for the secondary sex characteristics in men. A decreased testosterone level has been associated with erectile dysfunction and depression. Testosterone is formed in greatest quantities by the interstitial cells of the testes, but it is also formed in small amounts by the ovaries and the adrenal cortex.

Estrogen is produced by the granulosa cells in the ovaries, and it is responsible for pubertal changes in girls. Exogenous estrogen replacement therapy has been associated with depression.

7.2. The answer is C (*Synopsis VII*, page 270).

Delusions should never be directly challenged. Delusions are fixed false ideas that may be thought of as a patient's defensive and self-protective, albeit maladaptive, strategy against overwhelming anxiety, low self-esteem, and confusion. Challenging a delusion by insisting that it is not true or possible only increases the patient's anxiety and often leads the patient to defend the belief desperately. However, clinicians should not pretend that they believe the patient's delusion. Often, the best approach is for clinicians to indicate that they understand that the patient believes the delusion to be true but that they do not hold the same belief.

Psychiatrists often encounter violent patients in a hospital setting. Frequently, the police bring a patient into the emergency room in some type of physical restraint (for example, handcuffs). The psychiatrist must establish whether effective verbal contact can be made with the patient or whether the patient's sense of reality is so impaired that effective interviewing is impossible. If impaired reality testing is an issue, *the psychiatrist may have to medicate a violent patient before taking a history.*

With or without restraints, *a violent patient should not be interviewed alone to establish a doctor-patient relationship.* At least one other person should always be present; in some situations that other person should be a security guard or a police officer. Other precautions include leaving the interview room's door open and sitting between the patient and the door, so that the interviewer has unrestricted access to an exit should it become necessary. The psychiatrist must make it clear, in a firm but nonangry manner, that the patient may say or feel anything but is not free to act in a violent way.

Being mindful of the possibility of suicide is imperative when interviewing any depressed patient, even if a suicidal risk is not apparent. *The psychiatrist must ask depressed patients if they have suicidal thoughts.* Doing so does not make patients feel worse. Instead, many patients are relieved to talk about their suicidal ideas. The psychiatrist should ask specifically, "Are you suicidal now?" or "Do you have plans to take your own life?" A suicide note, a family history of suicide, or previous suicidal behavior by the patient increases the risk for suicide. Evidence of impulsivity or of pervasive pessimism about the future also places patients at risk. If the psychiatrist decides that the patient is in imminent risk for suicidal behavior, the patient must be hospitalized or otherwise protected.

The way chairs are arranged in the psychiatrist's office affects the interview. *The psychiatrist should not have a seat higher than the patient's seat.* Both chairs should be about the same height, so that neither person looks down on the other. Most psychiatrists place the chairs without any furniture between the clinician and the patient. If the room contains several chairs, the psychiatrist indicates his or her own chair and then allows patients to choose the chairs in which they feel most comfortable.

7.3. The answer is D (*Synopsis VII*, pages 276–280).

The mental status examination provides the sum total of the examiner's observations and impressions of the psychiatric patient at the time of the interview. Part of the mental status examination includes an assessment of insight. Insight is patients' degree of awareness and understanding that they are ill. *The highest level of insight is true emotional insight*, which occurs when patients' awareness of their own motives and deep feelings leads to changes in their personality or behavior patterns. Other levels of insight include (1) complete denial of illness; (2) slight awareness of being sick and needing help but denying it at the same time; (3) awareness of being sick but blaming it on others, on external factors, or on organic factors; (4) awareness that illness is due to something unknown in the patient; and (5) intellectual insight—that is, admission that the patient is ill and that symptoms or failures in social adjustment are due to the patient's own irrational feelings or disturbances but no application of that knowledge to future experiences.

Mood, affect, thought content, thought process, perception, sensorium, and cognition are also assessed in the mental status examination. *The patient's affect, not mood, can be described as normal, blunted, constricted or flat*. Affect may be defined as the patient's present emotional responsiveness. Affect is what the examiner infers from the patient's facial expression, including the amount and the range of patient's expressive behavior. In the normal range of affect, the patient shows a variation in facial expression, tone of voice, use of the hands, and body movements. When affect is constricted, the patient has a clear reduction in the range and the intensity of expression. In blunted affect, the patient's emotional expression is further reduced. To diagnose flat affect, the clinician should find virtually no signs of affective expression, the patient's voice should be monotonous, and the patient's face should be immobile.

Mood is defined as a pervasive and sustained emotion that colors the person's perception of the world. It is the patient's subjective view of his or her emotional state described as sad, depressed, elated and not as blurred or flat.

Hallucinations and illusions are perceptual disturbances, not disturbances in the patient's thought process. An illusion is a misperception or misinterpretation of real external sensory stimuli. A hallucination is a false sensory perception not associated with real external stimuli; hallucinations indicate a psychotic disturbance only when they are associated with an impairment in reality testing.

Asking a patient to spell the word "world" backward is designed to measure attention, not visuospatial ability. Attention can also be assessed by calculations and by asking the patient to name five things that start with a particular letter. Visuospatial ability is assessed by asking the patient to copy a figure, such as a clock face or interlocking pentagons.

Blocking is not an attitude assumed by the patient to stop the interview. It is a disturbance in thought process, an interruption of the patient's train of thought before an idea has been completed. The patient may indicate an inability to recall what was being said or intended to be said.

7.4. The answer is A (*Synopsis VII*, pages 281 and 284).

The presenting symptoms of some physical illnesses may be psychiatric signs or symptoms, and some symptoms may be caused by medications given to treat mental disorders or by a mental disorder itself. For example, *polyuria, polydipsia, and diarrhea are signs of lithium toxicity*.

Exposure to mercury may result in complaints suggesting a psychosis, and *exposure to lead*, as in smelting, *may produce cognitive disorders, not anxiety disorders*. Imbibing moonshine with a high lead content can also lead to cognitive disorders and brain damage.

Dyspnea and breathlessness may occur in depressive disorders. Those symptoms do not occur in manic episodes.

A hearing impairment is commonly associated with delusional disorders, not impulse control disorders.

A history of *glaucoma contraindicates drugs with anticholinergic adverse effects, not those the use of antihistaminic* drugs (for example, diphenhydramine [Benadryl]).

7.5. The answer is B (*Synopsis VII*, pages 281–284).

Hypothyroidism and, occasionally, hyperthyroidism may be caused by lithium (Eskalith). Patients taking lithium must have their thyroid function monitored.

Hypothyroidism *does not present with symptoms of mania*, but it may present with symptoms of depression. In some studies up to 10 percent of all patients complaining of depression and associated fatigue had incipient hypothyroid disease. Other signs and symptoms common to both depression and hypothyroidism include weakness, stiffness, poor appetite, constipation, menstrual irregularities, slowed speech, apathy, impaired memory, hallucinations, and delusions. *Up to 10 percent, not 40 percent, of all patients with depressive disorders* have some thyroid illness.

Hypothyroidism does occur in neonates. It can lead to cretinism, in which the child suffers from stunted growth and mental retardation. Since the condition is preventable if it is diagnosed at birth, thyroid function tests are included in neonatal screening.

Hypothyroidism *cannot be assessed through urinalysis*. However, a number of thyroid function tests are available, including tests for thyroxine (T4) by competitive protein binding (T4D) and by radioimmunoassay (T4RIA) involving a specific antigen-antibody reaction. More than 90 percent of T4 is bound to serum protein and is responsible for thyroid-stimulating hormone (TSH) secretion and cellular metabolism. Other thyroid measures include the free T4 index (FT4T), triiodothyronine uptake, and total serum triiodothyronine measured by radioimmunoassay (T_3RIA). The thyrotropin-releasing hormone (TRH) stimulation test is indicated in patients who have marginally abnormal thyroid test results with suspected subclinical hypothyroidism, which may account for clinical depression. The test is also used for patients with possible lithium-induced hypothyroidism. The procedure entails an intravenous (IV) injection of 500 mg of TRH, which produces a sharp rise in serum TSH when measured after 15, 30, 60, and 90 minutes. An increase in serum TSH of from 5 to 25 µIU/mL above the baseline is normal. An increase of less than µIU/mL is considered a blunted response, which may correlate with a diagnosis of a depressive disorder.

7.6. The answer is C (*Synopsis VII*, pages 281–284).

Patients receiving *lithium must have their serum drug levels monitored regularly*, since there is a narrow therapeutic range beyond which cardiac, renal, and central nervous system (CNS) problems can occur. Blood is drawn 8 to 12 hours after the last dose of lithium, usually in the morning after the bedtime dose. The serum level should be measured at least twice a week while the patient is being stabilized, and blood may be drawn monthly thereafter.

Patients taking *benzodiazepines do not need weekly assessments of their magnesium blood levels*. However, benzodiazepines metabolized in the liver by oxidation have their half–lives increased by impaired hepatic function. Baseline liver function tests (LFTs) are indicated in patients with suspected liver damage. Urine testing for benzodiazepines is used routinely in cases of substance abuse.

Because of the risk of agranulocytosis (1 to 2 percent), patients who are being treated with the antipsychotic clozapine (Clozaril) must have a baseline white blood count (WBC) and differential count before the initiation of treatment, a WBC every week throughout treatment, and a WBC for four weeks after the discontinuation of clozapine. Clozapine does not affect red blood cells; therefore, patients receiving *clozapine do not need to be assessed for drug-induced anemia*.

Patients receiving trazodone (Desyrel) have reported serious side effects. Trazodone, an antidepressant unrelated to cyclic drugs, has been reported to cause ventricular arrhythmias and priapism (painful, persistent erections), mild leukopenia, and neutropenia.

Patients taking *monoamine oxidase inhibitors (MAOIs) need to avoid foods containing tyramine, not glucose*. Tyramine-containing foods pose the danger of a hypertensive crisis. A baseline normal blood pressure (BP) must be recorded, and the BP must be monitored during treatment. MAOIs may also cause orthostatic hypotension as a direct drug side effect unrelated to the diet. Other than their potential for causing an elevated BP when taken with certain foods, MAOIs are relatively free of other adverse effects.

7.7. The answer is C (*Synopsis VII*, page 287).

Even though hyperventilation can trigger panic attacks in predisposed persons, *hyperventilation is not as sensitive as lactate provocation in inducing panic attacks*. Sodium lactate provokes panic attacks in a majority (up to 72 percent) of patients with panic disorder. Therefore, lactate provocation is used to confirm a diagnosis of panic disorder. *Sodium lactate can also trigger flashbacks in patients with posttraumatic stress disorder.* Carbon dioxide (CO_2) inhalation also precipitates panic attacks in those so predisposed. *Panic attacks triggered by sodium lactate are not inhibited by* peripherally acting β-blockers, such as *propranolol* (Inderal), but are *inhibited by alprazolam* (Xanax) and tricyclic drugs.

7.8. The answer is C (*Synopsis VII*, pages 285–286).

A patient who shows a white blood count of 2,000 while taking clozapine (Clozaril) is at high risk for agranulocytosis. If agranulocytosis develops (that is, if the WBC is less than 1,000) and there is evidence of severe infection (for example, skin ulcerations) the patient should be placed in *protective isolation on a medical unit*. The clinician should *stop the administration of clozapine at once*, not increase the dosage of clozapine. The patient may or may not have clinical symptoms, such as fever and sore throat. *Even if the patient does have such symptoms, antibiotic therapy* may be necessary. Depending on the severity of the condition the physician should *monitor patients' WBC every 2 days, not 10 days* or institute *daily, not weekly, CBC tests* with differential.

Table 7.1 summarizes the treatment of patients with reduced WBCs.

7.9. The answer is E (*Synopsis VII*, pages 282–284).

The dexamethasone-suppression test can be used to confirm a diagnostic impression of major depressive disorder with melancholic features. In such depressions, the test result is abnormal in many cases, meaning that there is nonsuppression of endogenous cortisol production after exogenous steroid ingestion. A positive finding, nonsuppression, indicates a hyperactive hypothalamic-pituitary-adrenal axis. The test is sometimes used to predict which patients will have a *good response to* somatic treatments, such as *electroconvulsive therapy (ECT)* and *cyclic drugs.* The clinician needs to be aware that false-positive findings can result from a number of factors, such as *disseminated cancer.* A false-negative finding can occur in patients who have *received high-dosage benzodiazepine treatment.* In a false-negative result a diseased person has a normal finding. In a false-positive result a nondiseased person has an abnormal finding.

Table 7.1
Treatment of Patients with Reduced White Blood Cell Count, Leukopenia, and Agranulocytosis

Problem Phase	WBC Findings	Clinical Findings	Treatment Plan
Reduced WBC	WBC reveals a significant drop (even if WBC is still in normal range). "Significant drop" = (1) drop of more than 3,000 cells from prior test or (2) three or more consecutive drops in WBC	No symptoms of infection	1. Monitor patient closely 2. Institute twice-weekly CBC tests with differentials if deemed appropriate by attending physician 3. Clozapine therapy may continue
Mild leukopenia	WBC = 3,000–3,500	Patient may or may not show clinical symptoms, such as lethargy, fever, sore throat, weakness	1. Monitor patient closely 2. Institute a minimum of twice-weekly CBC tests with differentials 3. Clozapine therapy may continue
Leukopenia or granulocytopenia	WBC = 2,000–3,000 or granulocytes = 1,000–1,500	Patient may or may not show clinical symptoms, such as fever, sore throat, lethargy, weakness	1. Interrupt clozapine at once 2. Institute daily CBC tests with differentials 3. Increase surveillance, consider hospitalization 4. Clozapine therapy may be reinstituted after normalization of WBC
Agranulocytosis (uncomplicated)	WBC less than 2,000 or granulocytes less than 1,000	The patient may or may not show clinical symptoms, such as fever, sore throat, lethargy, weakness	1. Discontinue clozapine at once 2. Place patient in protective isolation in a medical unit with modern facilities 3. Consider a bone marrow specimen to determine if progenitor cells are being suppressed 4. Monitor patient every 2 days until WBC and differential counts return to normal (about 2 weeks) 5. Avoid use of concomitant medications with bone marrow-suppressing potential
Agranulocytosis (with complications)	WBC less than 2,000 or granulocytes less than 1,000	Definite evidence of infection, such as fever, sore throat, lethargy, weakness, malaise, skin ulcerations	6. Consult with hematologist or other specialist to determine appropriate antibiotic regimen 7. Start appropriate therapy; monitor closely
Recovery	WBC more than 4,000 and granulocytes more than 2,000	No symptoms of infection	1. Once-weekly CBC with differential counts for 4 consecutive normal values 2. Clozapine must not be restarted

Table reprinted with permission of Sandoz Pharmaceuticals Corporation. Table from A MacKinnon, S C Yudofsky: *Principles of Psychiatric Evaluation*. Lippincott, Philadelphia, 1991. Used with permission.

7.10. The answer is E (all) (*Synopsis VII*, pages 281–282 and 293).

Thyroid function tests are of use in clinical psychiatric practice for several reasons. For instance, *up to 10 percent of patients with depression have thyroid disease*, and *hypothyroidism may be a side effect of lithium*; hyperthyroidism may also occur, but less often. In children, *hypothyroidism may present as mental retardation* or as delayed development. Neonatal hypothyroidism can result in mental retardation, which is preventable with early diagnosis and treatment. *A blurred thyrotropin-releasing hormone (TRH) stimulation test is associated with depressive disorders*. The test consists of giving the patient an intravenous injection of 500 mg TRH, which normally produces a rise in plasma thyroid stimulating hormone (TSH).

7.11. The answer is C (*Synopsis VII*, page 269).

Patients with chronic illnesses and deteriorating health often become depressed. The physician must take any suicidal ideation seriously and must carefully evaluate all depressed patients for suicidal risk. Most patients who have suicidal ideation feel better after their physicians *ask directly about any suicidal thoughts*. The risk for suicide does not increase with direct questioning about suicide. *The physician should not avoid further questioning of the patient*. The physician must have a clear picture of the patient's psychiatric status to decide on an appropriate therapeutic plan. *Reassurance, hospitalization*, and *antidepressant medication* should not be used unless indicated.

7.12. **The answer is A** (*Synopsis VII*, pages 278–279).

Memory impairment, most notably *immediate* or short-term *memory*, is usually the first sign of beginning cerebral disease. Memory is a process by which anything that is experienced or learned is established as a record in the central nervous system, where it persists with a variable degree of permanence and can be recollected or retrieved from storage at will. Short-term memory is the reproduction, recognition, or recall of perceived material after a period of 10 seconds or less has elapsed after the initial presentation. *Recent memory* covers a time period from a few hours to a few weeks after the initial presentation. *Long-term memory or remote memory* is the reproduction, recognition, or recall of experiences or information from the distant past. That function is usually not disturbed early in cerebral disease.

7.13. **The answer is C** (*Synopsis VII*, pages 267–271).

The stress interview is a type of interview characterized by *confrontation of the patient by the psychiatrist* and by the avoidance of the usual ways of reducing anxiety during the session. Such interviews may be useful in diagnosis, but their repeated use is generally contraindicated in the course of psychotherapy. One situation in which the stress interview may be used is with patients who are monotonously repetitious or who show insufficient emotionality for motivation. Apathy, indifference, and emotional blunting are not conducive to a discussion of personality problems. In patients with such reactions, stimulation of their emotions can be constructive. The patients may require probing, challenging, or confrontation to arouse feelings that further their understanding.

The Social Readjustment Rating Scale, devised by Tomas H. Holmes, quantifies life events, assigning a point value to life changes that require adaptation. Research indicates a critical level at which too many of those events happening to a person during one year puts the person at great risk for illness.

The stress interview is not related to *intimidation* of any kind, nor should it be *destructive*. Anxiety may be present *in both the physician and the patient* during any initial interview.

7.14. **The answer is D** (*Synopsis VII*, pages 279 and 308).

Asking patients what they would do if they received someone else's mail among their own is a test of *judgment*. Judgment involves the process of evaluating choices within the framework of a given value system for the purpose of deciding on an appropriate course of action. The response that one would hand a misdirected letter back to the letter carrier or drop it into a mailbox reflects appropriate judgment. *Intelligence* is the ability to learn and the capacity to apply what one has learned. *Abstract thinking* is the ability to shift voluntarily from one aspect of a situation to another, to keep in mind simultaneously various aspects of a situation, and to think or to perform symbolically. *Insight* is the power or act of seeing into and recognizing the objective reality of a situation. *Cognition* involves the perceptual and intellectual level of mental functioning.

7.15. **The answer is C** (*Synopsis VII*, pages 287–293).

Amobarbital (Amytal) is the drug most commonly used in the drug-assisted psychiatric interview. It can be of use with patients who have difficulty in expressing themselves freely or who are suppressing anxiety-provoking material. In narcotherapy, regularly scheduled interviews use amobarbital as an adjunctive agent. The drug-assisted interview can also be of help in differentiating organic psychiatric disorder caused by brain damage from those caused by psychological factors.

Meprobamate, diazepam, and *chloral hydrate* are antianxiety agents used as sedatives or hypnotics. The *phenothiazines* are antipsychotics used in the treatment of schizophrenia.

7.16. **The answer is E (all)** (*Synopsis VII*, pages 267–271).

The reaction of patients toward the psychiatrist is influenced by *the psychiatrist's attitude*, style, and orientation. If patients believe that they will lose their psychiatrist's respect as they expose their problems, they may be unwilling to disclose such material. If, in their *previous experiences with physicians* (psychiatric or nonpsychiatric), patients felt ridiculed or their problems were minimized, those experiences influence what they do or do not tell the psychiatrist.

Transference is a process in which patients unconsciously and inappropriately displace onto persons in their current life those patterns of behavior and emotional reactions that originated in childhood. *The patient's view of authority figures in childhood* influences reactions to the psychiatrist. Differences in the social, educational, and intellectual backgrounds of each patient and the psychiatrist may also interfere with the development of rapport. It is an obvious advantage for the psychiatrist to acquire as much understanding and familiarity as possible with *the patient's cultural background*.

7.17. **The answer is A** (*Synopsis VII*, pages 267–271).

Conducting a stress interview may occasionally be helpful in evaluating a patient, but it is unusually confrontational and is not a method designed to facilitate the development of doctor-patient rapport. *Asking open-ended questions* or questions that cannot be answered merely with "yes" or "no" effectively allows the patient to reveal more about the patient's life and usually fosters rapport. *Using the patient's own words* as reassurance that the patient is being heard can also be helpful. *Uncovering feelings* by asking patients for specific examples of how and when they felt a certain way also helps establish a sense that the physician is interested in the nuances of their emotional lives. In general, a sense that the physician is *understanding the patient*, is listening to and hearing the patient, is often the most important element in establishing rapport and providing therapeutic relief.

7.18.   The answer is D (*Synopsis VII*, pages 267–271).

The physician should try to encourage the patient to express his angry feelings in order to get to the causes of those hostile thoughts. Asking *"Why do you have those feelings"* allows the physician to plan a treatment program that will deal with the patient's feelings during the course of therapy.

Saying *"You are expressing latent homosexual impulses"* is premature and may be inaccurate. It is an inappropriate interpretation and may have nothing to do with the patient's personal experiences with women. It may also cause the patient to reject the physician's attempt to interact with him. Saying *"Those feelings are oedipal in nature"* is also premature. And saying *"Your feelings of hostility toward women will make it impossible for us to work together"* provides the ultimate therapeutic rejection to the patient and only further reinforces the patient's problems. It is totally inappropriate during the first psychiatric interview for the treating physician to discuss her countertransference fears with the patient by saying *"You're bringing on feelings of fear in me."*

7.19.   The answer is B (*Synopsis VII*, pages 278–279).

Recent memory is the ability to remember what has been experienced within the past few hours, days, or weeks. It is assessed by asking patients to describe how they spent the last 24 hours, such as *what they had to eat for their last meal.*

Remote memory or long-term memory is the ability to remember events in the distant past. Memory for the remote past can be evaluated by inquiring about important dates in patients' lives, such as *their date of birth*. The answers must be verifiable.

To test patients' orientation to place, one can inquire whether patients know where they are—for instance, *the name of the hospital they are in*. Concentration may be tested by asking the patient *to subtract 7 from 100* serially. If patient cannot do that task, the clinician must determine whether anxiety or some disturbance of mood or consciousness seems to be responsible for the difficulty.

To test a patient's general knowledge or fund of information, one can ask *who is the President of the United States*. The interviewer must ask questions that have some relevance to the patient's educational and cultural background.

7.20.   The answer is E (all) (*Synopsis VII*, page 285).

A favorable therapeutic window—that is, the range within which a drug is most effective—is as-

sociated with all the drugs listed. Blood levels should be tested routinely when using *imipramine* (Tofranil), *nortriptyline* (Pamelor), or *desipramine* (Norpramin) in the treatment of depressive disorders. Taking blood levels may also be of use in patients with poor responses at normal dosage ranges and in high-risk patients when there is an urgent need to know whether a therapeutic or toxic plasma level of the drug has been reached. Blood level tests should also include the measurement of active metabolites (for example, imipramine is converted to desipramine, and *amitriptyline* (Elavil) is converted to nortriptyline).

7.21.   The answer is C (*Synopsis VII*, pages 287–293).

Amobarbital (Amytal) interviews *help recover repressed memories*. In addition, the interviews *are helpful in the differential diagnosis of muteness*, catatonia, and stupor. Organic conditions tend to worsen with infusions of amobarbital, but nonorganic or psychogenic conditions tend to get better.

Amobarbital interviews do not *cause a worsening of pseudodementia* but can be useful in the condition's differential diagnosis. Therapeutically, amobarbital interviews are useful in disorders of repression and dissociation—for example, in the recovery of memory in dissociative amnesia and fugue, in improving *the symptoms of conversion disorder*, in the recovery of function in conversion disorder, and in the facilitation of emotional expression *in posttraumatic stress disorder*.

7.22–7.26

7.22.   The answer is A (*Synopsis VII*, page 289).

7.23.   The answer is C (*Synopsis VII*, pages 289–290 and 373).

7.24.   The answer is E (*Synopsis VII*, page 292).

7.25.   The answer is D (*Synopsis VII*, pages 283–284, 290, and 293).

7.26.   The answer is B (*Synopsis VII*, page 290).

Hepatic encephalopathy is associated with *increased serum ammonia* caused by chronic liver disease. The psychiatric signs of hepatic encephalopathy include personality changes, impaired consciousness, agitation, a musty sweet breath odor, and fetor hepaticus.

Wilson's disease is associated with an *elevated* level of *copper* caused by a disturbance in copper metabolism. The rare disease is transmitted in an autosomal recessive fashion.

Carbamazepine (Tegretol) is used in psychiatry as a mood stabilizer in bipolar I disorder. The most serious potential adverse effect is agranulocytosis, including a *decrease in platelet count*.

Lithium (Eskalith) is used in the treatment of manic episodes of bipolar I disorder. A side effect is polyuria secondary to decreased resorption of fluid

Table 7.2
Medical Problems That May Present as Psychiatric Symptoms

Medical Problem	Sex and Age Prevalence	Common Medical Symptoms	Psychiatric Symptoms and Complaints	Impaired Performance and Behavior	Diagnostic Problems
Hyperthyroidism (thyrotoxicosis)	Females 3:1, 30 to 50	*Tremor,* sweating, loss of weight and strength	*Anxiety* if rapid onset; depression if slow onset	Occasional *hyperactivity* or grandiose behavior	Long lead time; a rapid onset resembles anxiety attack
Hypothyroidism (myxedema)	Females 5:1, 30 to 50	Puffy face, *dry skin,* cold intolerance	Anxiety with irritability, thought disorder, somatic delusions, hallucinations	*Myxedema madness;* delusional, paranoid, belligerent behavior	Madness may mimic schizophrenia; mental status is clear, even during most disturbed behavior
Porphyria—acute intermittent type	Females, 20 to 40	*Abdominal crises,* paresthesias, weakness	Anxiety—sudden onset, severe *mood swings*	Extremes of excitement or withdrawal; emotional or angry outbursts	Patients often have truly abnormal life styles; crises resemble conversion disorder or anxiety attacks
Hepatolenticular degeneration (Wilson's disease)	Males 2:1, adolescence	Liver and extrapyramidal symptoms, *Kayser-Fleischer rings*	Mood swings— sudden and changeable; anger— explosive	Eventual *brain damage* with memory and I.Q. loss; combativeness	In late teens, disorder may resemble adolescent storm, incorrigibility, or schizophrenia
Pancreatic carcinoma	Males 3:1, 50 to 70	Weight loss, abdominal pain, weakness, *jaundice*	Depression, *sense of imminent doom* but without severe guilt	Loss of drive and motivation	Long lead time; exact age and symptoms of involutional depression

from the distal tubule of the kidneys. *Creatinine clearance* is a good gauge of the patient's renal function and is part of the *pretreatment workup for lithium therapy.*

Stress is a physical or psychological event that produces strain or upsets physiological equilibrium (homeostasis). *Stress* is associated with *increased cortisone.*

7.27–7.31

7.27.   The answer is E (*Synopsis VII*, page 773).

7.28.   The answer is B (*Synopsis VII*, pages 281–282 and 772).

7.29.   The answer is D (*Synopsis VII*, pages 111 and 774).

7.30.   The answer is C (*Synopsis VII*, page 292).

7.31.   The answer is A (*Synopsis VII*, pages 281 and 772).

The clinician should be aware of the many medical problems that may present as psychiatric symptoms. For example, *tremor, anxiety, and hyperactivity* are often associated with *hyperthyroidism*; *dry skin* and *myxedema madness* (which may mimic schizophrenia) are associated with *hypothyroidism*; *abdominal crisis* and *mood swings* are associated with *porphyria*; *Kayser-Fleischer rings* and *brain*

damage are associated with *hepatolenticular degeneration*; and *jaundice* and a *sense of imminent doom* are associated with *pancreatic carcinoma.*

Table 7.2 gives some examples of medical problems that may present as psychiatric symptoms.

7.32–7.36

7.32.   The answer is A (*Synopsis VII*, pages 283 and 291).

7.33.   The answer is A (*Synopsis VII*, pages 283 and 291).

7.34.   The answer is B (*Synopsis VII*, pages 283, 291, and 717–718).

7.35.   The answer is A (*Synopsis VII*, pages 283 and 291).

7.36.   The answer is B (*Synopsis VII*, pages 283, 291, and 808).

The serotonin metabolite 5-hydroxyindoleacetic acid *(5-HIAA)* is *elevated* in the urine of patients with *carcinoid tumors* and at times in patients who take *phenothiazine medications* and in persons who eat foods high in L-tryptophan, the chemical precursor of serotonin (for example, walnuts, *bananas*, and avocados). The amount of 5-HIAA in cerebrospinal fluid is *decreased* in some persons who display *aggressive behavior* and in *suicidal patients* who have committed suicide in particularly violent ways.

Typical Signs and Symptoms of Psychiatric Illness Defined

What is the difference between a delusion and an illusion? Between a clang association and a neologism? Between an obsession and a compulsion? How does one describe subtle shadings of mood or affect, of motor behavior or thought, of speech or perception? What types of delusions and hallucinations are possible? What are the specific and typical disturbances in the process and the content of thought that are present in many mental disorders?

A skillful psychiatric practitioner must know the answers to those questions and many others to form a basis for diagnosis, treatment, and psychodynamic understanding of a variety of patients. Signs are objective data elicited or observed by the clinician; symptoms are subjective complaints as described and experienced by the patient. Examples of psychiatric signs are pressured speech and motor hyperactivity (psychomotor agitation); examples of the corresponding psychiatric symptoms are a feeling of not being able to stop talking and an inner experience of restlessness. A complex psychiatric symptom is the hearing of punishing and derogatory voices, but the only sign is a preoccupation with internal stimuli. A patient with a personality disorder may complain about others, instead of themselves: "I don't have any problems, but everyone else always has problems with me." In that case, the symptom is a chronic interpersonal dissatisfaction, and the sign is a rigid, inflexible defensive style.

A strict adherence to signs and symptoms when faced with the complexity of human behavior and emotion is inappropriate. Unlike physical medicine, psychiatry has no pathognomonic signs and symptoms, although highly suggestive clusters of signs and symptoms are associated with various pathological conditions.

The psychiatrist must be able to distinguish the signs and symptoms that are often associated with organic pathology. Apparent aphasias, cognitive deficits, and alterations in the level of consciousness should alert the clinician to the possibility of underlying organic pathology. Psychiatric signs and symptoms are a common pathway for initial insults, including purely organic insults. A thorough grounding in the recognition of signs and symptoms is the first step in helping the clinician make crucial diagnostic decisions.

Students should study Chapter 8 of *Kaplan and Sadock's Synopsis VII* and then assess their level of knowledge of the subject by studying the questions and answers below.

HELPFUL HINTS

The student should be able to define and categorize the signs and symptoms and other terms listed below.

disturbances of consciousness and attention	disturbances of perception, both those caused by brain diseases and those associated with psychological phenomena	disorientation
affect and mood		delirium
disturbances of conation		coma
disturbances in the form and the content of thought	hallucinations	distractibility
disturbances in speech	disturbances of memory	*folie à deux*
aphasic disturbances	disturbances of intelligence	hypnosis
	insight and judgment	anxiety
		panic

cerea flexibilitas	agnosias	*déjà pensé*
stereotypy	depersonalization	*déjà entendu*
aggression	synesthesia	*jamais vu*
delusion	illusions	dementia
phobias	*déjà vu*	pseudodementia
noesis		

QUESTIONS

DIRECTIONS: Each of the incomplete statements below is followed by five suggested completions. Select the *one* that is *best* in each case.

8.1. A medical student begins to fall asleep in class and is startled awake, thinking that the student's name was called; in reality, it was not. That is an example of
A. hypnagogic hallucination
B. hypnopompic hallucination
C. illusion
D. synesthesia
E. dissociation

8.2. A 27-year-old man comes to the emergency room complaining of having his thoughts controlled by the CIA. Such thinking is
A. dereistic
B. magical
C. depersonalized
D. obsessional
E. delirious

8.3. A psychiatric patient who, although coherent, never gets to the point has a disturbance in the form of thought called
A. word salad
B. circumstantiality
C. tangentiality
D. verbigeration
E. blocking

8.4. A 26-year-old man believes that the Mafia and his brother are putting horrible thoughts into his head. That is an example of
A. thought broadcasting
B. delusion of reference
C. nihilistic delusion
D. thought insertion
E. pseudologica phantastica

8.5. Loss of normal speech melody is known as
A. stuttering
B. stammering
C. aphonia
D. dysprosody
E. dyslexia

8.6. Perceptual disturbances include all the following *except*
A. hallucinations
B. hypnagogic experiences
C. echolalia
D. depersonalization
E. derealization

8.7. Asking a patient to interpret a proverb is used as a way of assessing
A. judgment
B. impulse control
C. abstract thinking
D. insight
E. intelligence

DIRECTIONS: Each group of questions below consists of lettered headings followed by a list of numbered phrases or statements. For each numbered phrase or statement, select the *one* lettered heading that is most associated with it. Each lettered heading may be selected once, more than once, or not at all.

Questions 8.8–8.12
A. Stupor
B. Delirium
C. Coma
D. Somnolence
E. Dreamlike state

8.8. Profound degree of unconsciousness

8.9. Lack of reaction to and an unawareness of one's surroundings

8.10. Restless, confused, and disoriented

8.11. Synonym for complex partial seizure or psychomotor epilepsy

8.12. Abnormal drowsiness

Questions 8.13–8.17
A. Anhedonia
B. Euphoria
C. Alexithymia
D. Euthymia
E. Expansive mood

8.13. "I don't know how I feel; I just can't say."

8.14. "I have no sex drive and no appetite; I just don't feel like doing anything."

8.15. "You can't keep me on this ward; I have to submit my plans for the country to the President."

8.16. "I feel fine—basically happy."

8.17. "I feel better today than I ever have in my life."

Questions 8.18–8.22
A. Echopraxia
B. Catalepsy
C. Cataplexy
D. Stereotypy
E. Tic

8.18. Weakness and temporary loss of muscle tone precipitated by emotional states

8.19. General term for an immobile position that is constantly maintained

8.20. Involuntary, spasmodic motor movement

8.21. Repetitive, fixed pattern of physical action or speech

8.22. Pathological imitation of another person's movements

Questions 8.23–8.27
A. Loosening of associations
B. Flight of ideas
C. Clang association
D. Blocking
E. Neologism

8.23. "I was gigglifying not just tempifying; you know what I mean."

8.24. "I was grocery training; but, when I ride the grocery, I drive the food everywhere on top of lollipops."

8.25. "Cain and Abel—they were cannibals. You see brothers kill brothers—that is laudable. If you ask me, though, never name your son Huxtibal. OK."

8.26. Patient: "I never wanted. . . ." Physician: "Go on. What were you saying?" Patient: "I don't know."

8.27. "Tired, mired, schmired, wired."

Questions 8.28–8.32
A. Delusion
B. Obsession
C. Compulsion
D. Phobia
E. Overvalued idea

8.28. Pathological need to act on a feeling

8.29. Pathological persistence of an irresistible thought or feeling

8.30. Fixed, false belief, based on incorrect inferences about external reality

8.31. Unreasonable, sustained false belief that is not fixed

8.32. Persistent, irrational, exaggerated dread of some specific type of stimulus or situation

Questions 8.33–8.36
A. Broca's (motor) aphasia
B. Sensory aphasia
C. Nominal aphasia
D. Global aphasia
E. Syntactical aphasia

8.33. Difficulty in finding the correct names for objects

8.34. Loss of the ability to comprehend the meaning of words

8.35. Loss of the ability to speak

8.36. Inability to arrange words in a proper sequence

Questions 8.37–8.40
A. Dysdiadochokinesia
B. Astereognosis
C. Visual agnosia
D. Autotopagnosia
E. Simultanagnosia

8.37. Inability to recognize a body part as one's own

8.38. Inability to distinguish by touch between a quarter and a dime

8.39. Inability to perform rapid alternating movements

8.40. Inability to recognize objects or people

Questions 8.41–8.44
    A. Déjà vu
    B. Déjà entendu
    C. Déjà pensé
    D. Jamais vu
    E. Confabulation

8.41. Illusion of auditory recognition

8.42. Regarding a new thought as a repetition of a previous thought

8.43. Feeling of unfamiliarity with a familiar situation

8.44. Regarding a new situation as a repetition of a previous experience

Questions 8.45–8.48
    A. Synesthesia
    B. Paramnesia
    C. Hypermnesia
    D. Eidetic images
    E. Lethologica

8.45. Exaggerated degree of retention and recall

8.46. Temporary inability to remember a name

8.47. Confusion of facts and fantasies

8.48. Sensations that accompany sensations of another modality

Questions 8.49–8.53
    A. Insight
    B. Abstract thinking
    C. Concrete thinking
    D. Pseudodementia
    E. Dementia

8.49. A 70-year-old woman can no longer remember her children's names

8.50. A severely depressed 36-year-old man can no longer balance his checkbook, something he had done for years

8.51. "People in glass houses shouldn't throw stones" means that the glass will break if a stone hits it

8.52. "A rolling stone gathers no moss" means that you cannot form solid friendships or foundations if you are never in one place

8.53. A 45-year-old man with alcohol dependence states that he will die if he continues to drink alcohol as he does

Questions 8.54–8.57
    A. Anxiety
    B. Ambivalence
    C. Guilt
    D. Abreaction

8.54. Coexistence of two opposing impulses

8.55. Emotional discharge after recalling a painful experience

8.56. Feeling of apprehension

8.57. Emotion resulting from doing something perceived as wrong

Questions 8.58–8.62

A. Tangentiality
B. Anosognosia
C. Dysprosody
D. Erotomania
E. Nominal aphasia

8.58. Associated with denial of physical disorder

8.59. Person never gets to the point

8.60. Disturbance in language output

8.61. Disordered rhythm of speech

8.62. Disturbance in content of thought

ANSWERS

Typical Signs and Symptoms
of Psychiatric Illness Defined

8.1. The answer is A (*Synopsis VII*, pages 306–307).

The phenomenon of the student who begins to fall asleep in class but is startled awake, thinking that the student's name was called, although it was not, is an example of a *hypnagogic hallucination*. A hypnagogic hallucination is a false sensory perception that occurs while the person is falling asleep; it is generally considered nonpathological.

In contrast, a *hypnopompic hallucination* is a false sensory perception that occurs while the person's awakening from sleep; it, too, is generally considered nonpathological.

An *illusion* is a misperception or a misinterpretation of real external sensory stimuli.

Synesthesia is a sensation or hallucination caused by another sensation (for example, a sound is experienced as being seen, or a visual experience is seemingly heard).

Dissociation is a defense mechanism. It is a temporary but drastic modification of a person's character or sense of personal identity to avoid emotional distress.

8.2. The answer is A (*Synopsis VII*, page 304).

The patient in the emergency room complaining of having his thoughts controlled by the CIA was using *dereistic* thinking—that is, thinking not concordant with logic or experience.

Magical thinking is a form of thought found in Jean Piaget's stage of preoperational thought in children, in which thoughts and words assume power (for example, they can cause or prevent events).

Depersonalized thinking is characterized by the sensation of unreality concerning oneself, parts of oneself, or one's environment that occurs under extreme stress or fatigue.

Obsessional thinking is a disturbance in the content of thought. It is a pathological persistence of an irresistible thought or feeling that cannot be eliminated from consciousness by logical effort.

A person who is *delirious* suffers from a disturbance of consciousness and is usually bewildered, restless, confused, and disoriented.

8.3. The answer is C (*Synopsis VII*, page 305).

Tangentiality is the inability to have a goal-directed association of thoughts. The patient never gets from the desired point to the desired goal.

Word salad is an incoherent mixture of words and phrases. *Circumstantiality* is indirect speech that is delayed in reaching the point but eventually gets there. Circumstantiality is characterized by an overinclusion of details and parenthetical remarks. *Verbigeration* is a meaningless repetition of specific words or phrases. *Blocking* is an abrupt interruption in the train of thinking before a thought or idea is finished. After a brief pause, the person indicates no recall of what was being said or what was going to be said. It is also known as thought deprivation.

8.4. The answer is D (*Synopsis VII*, pages 305–306).

All the lettered completions are examples of specific disturbances in the content of thought. *Thought insertion* is a type of delusion of control in which persons feel that thoughts are being implanted in their minds by other people or forces.

Thought broadcasting is a delusion of control in which persons feel that their thoughts can be heard by others, as though the thoughts were being broadcast into the air.

Delusions are false beliefs based on incorrect inferences about external reality that are not consistent with the patient's intelligence or cultural background and that cannot be corrected by reasoning. A *delusion of reference* is a false belief that the behavior of others refers to oneself and that events, objects, or other people have a particular and unusual significance, usually negative. The delusion is derived from an idea of reference in which one falsely feels that one is being talked about by others (for example, a belief that people on television or the radio are talking to or about the patient). A *nihilistic delusion* is a false feeling that oneself, others, or the world is nonexisting or ending.

Pseudologia phantastica is a type of lying in which persons appear to believe in the reality of their fantasies and, therefore, act on them. It is associated with Munchausen syndrome, which is a repeated feigning of illness.

8.5. The answer is D (*Synopsis VII*, page 306).

Loss of normal speech melody is known as *dysprosody*. A disturbance in speech inflection and rhythm results in a monotonous and halting speech pattern, which occasionally suggests a foreign accent. It can be the result of a brain disease, such as Parkinson's disease, or it can be a psychological defensive mechanism (seen in some people with schizophrenia). As a psychological device, it can serve the function of maintaining a safe distance in social encounters.

Stuttering is a speech disorder characterized by repetitions or prolongations of sound syllables and words and by hesitations or pauses that disrupt the flow of speech. It is also known as *stammering*. *Aphonia* is a loss of one's voice. *Dyslexia* is a specific learning disability involving a reading impairment that is unrelated to the person's intelligence.

8.6.   The answer is C (*Synopsis VII*, pages 305–307).

A disturbance in perception is a disturbance in the mental process by which data—intellectual, sensory, and emotional—are organized. Through perception, people are capable of making sense out of the many stimuli that bombard them. Perceptual disturbances do not include *echolalia*, which is the repetition of another's words or phrases. Echolalia is a disturbance of thought form and communication. Examples of perceptual disturbances are *hallucinations*, which are false sensory perceptions without concrete external stimuli. Common hallucinations involve sights or sounds, although any of the senses may be involved, and *hypnagogic experiences*, which are hallucinations that occur just before falling asleep. Other disturbances of perception include *depersonalization*, which is the sensation of unreality concerning oneself or one's environment, and *derealization*, which is the feeling of changed reality or the feeling that one's surroundings have changed.

8.7.   The answer is C (*Synopsis VII*, pages 279 and 308).

Asking a patient to interpret a proverb is generally used as a way of assessing whether the person has the capacity for *abstract thought*. Abstract thinking, as opposed to concrete thinking, is characterized primarily by the ability to shift voluntarily from one aspect of a situation to another, to keep in mind simultaneously various aspects of a situation, and to think symbolically. Concrete thinking is characterized by an inability to conceptualize beyond immediate experience or beyond actual things and events. Psychopathologically, it is most characteristic of persons with schizophrenia or organic brain disorders.

Judgment, the patient's ability to comprehend the meaning of events and to appreciate the consequences of actions, is often tested by asking how the patient would act in certain standard circumstances; for example, if the patient smelled smoke in a crowded movie theater. *Impulse control* is the ability to control acting on a wish to discharge energy in a manner that is, at the moment, felt to be dangerous, inappropriate, or otherwise ill-advised. *Insight* is a conscious understanding of forces that have led to a particular feeling, action, or situation. *Intelligence* is the capacity for learning, recalling, integrating, and applying knowledge and experience.

8.8–8.12

8.8.   The answer is C (*Synopsis VII*, page 300).

8.9.   The answer is A (*Synopsis VII*, page 300).

8.10.   The answer is B (*Synopsis VII*, page 300).

8.11.   The answer is E (*Synopsis VII*, page 300).

8.12.   The answer is D (*Synopsis VII*, page 300).

Consciousness is a person's state of awareness. The lettered responses represent varying degrees of disturbances in consciousness. The most *profound degree of unconsciousness* is *coma*.

Stupor is a *lack of reaction to and an unawareness of one's surroundings*. Stupor is caused by intoxication, infection, and a host of other sources.

Delirium is a bewildered, *restless, confused, and disoriented* state associated with fear and hallucinations. Delirium may be caused by many of the same sources resulting in stupor.

Someone who suffers a *complex partial seizure or psychomotor epilepsy* is said to suffer from a *dreamlike state*. The seizures usually arise from the temporal lobe—limbic cortex region; during the attack, memory and consciousness are either impaired or lost. Temporal lobe seizures may also produce a preseizure aura with feelings of *déjà vu, jamais vu*, micropsia, macropsia, or dreaminess.

Somnolence is *abnormal drowsiness*; it may be seen in such conditions as narcolepsy and sleep apnea.

8.13–8.17

8.13.   The answer is C (*Synopsis VII*, page 303).

8.14.   The answer is A (*Synopsis VII*, page 303).

8.15.   The answer is E (*Synopsis VII*, page 303).

8.16.   The answer is D (*Synopsis VII*, page 303).

8.17.   The answer is B (*Synopsis VII*, page 303).

Alexithymia is difficulty in describing or becoming aware of one's emotions or moods. *Anhedonia* is a loss of interest in and withdrawal from all regular and pleasurable activities; the condition is most often associated with depression. Persons in an *expansive mood* express their feelings without restraint and frequently with an overestimation of the person's significance or importance; this condition is often seen in patients who are manic. Someone who shows a normal range of mood, implying an absence of depressed or elevated mood, is said to be displaying *enthymia*. *Euphoria* is an intense elation with feelings of grandeur.

8.18–8.22

8.18.   The answer is C (*Synopsis VII*, page 304).

8.19.   The answer is B (*Synopsis VII*, page 304).

8.20.   The answer is E (*Synopsis VII*, page 304).

8.21.   The answer is D (*Synopsis VII*, page 304).

8.22. The answer is A (*Synopsis VII*, page 304).

Cataplexy is a *weakness and temporary loss of muscle tone precipitated by* a variety of *emotional states. Catalepsy* is a *general term for an immobile position that is constantly maintained* and is seen in certain types of schizophrenia. A *tic* is an *involuntary, spasmodic motor movement*; it is seen in such conditions as Tourette's disorder. A type of motor behavior with a *repetitive, fixed pattern of physical action or speech* is called *stereotypy. Echopraxia* is a *pathological imitation of another person's movements.*

8.23–8.27

8.23. The answer is E (*Synopsis VII*, page 305).

8.24. The answer is A (*Synopsis VII*, page 305).

8.25. The answer is B (*Synopsis VII*, page 305).

8.26. The answer is D (*Synopsis VII*, page 305).

8.27. The answer is C (*Synopsis VII*, page 305).

All the lettered responses are examples of specific disturbances in form of thought. Most are seen in schizophrenic patients. *Neologisms* are new words created by the patient, often by combining syllables of other words, for idiosyncratic psychological reasons. *Loosening of associations* is a flow of thoughts in which ideas shift from one subject to another in completely unrelated ways. When the condition is severe, the patient's speech may be incoherent. *Flight of ideas* is a rapid, continuous verbalization or play on words that produces a constant shifting from one idea to another; the ideas tend to be connected, and when the condition is not severe, a listener may be able to follow them; the thought disorder is most characteristic of someone in a manic state. *Blocking* is an abrupt interruption in a train of thinking before a thought or idea is finished; after a brief pause, the person indicates no recall of what was being said or what was going to be said. The condition is also known as thought deprivation. A person who is using *clang association* uses an association of words similar in sound but not in meaning; the words used have no logical connections and may include examples of rhyming and punning.

8.28–8.32

8.28. The answer is C (*Synopsis VII*, page 306).

8.29. The answer is B (*Synopsis VII*, page 306).

8.30. The answer is A (*Synopsis VII*, pages 305–306).

8.31. The answer is E (*Synopsis VII*, page 305).

8.32. The answer is D (*Synopsis VII*, page 306).

The lettered headings are examples of specific disturbances in content of thought. A *compulsion* is a pathological need to act on a feeling that, if resisted, produces anxiety. An *obsession* is a *pathological persistence of an irresistible thought or feeling* that cannot be eliminated from consciousness by logical effort and is associated with anxiety; it is also termed rumination. A *delusion* is a *fixed, false belief, based on incorrect inferences about external reality*, that cannot be corrected by reasoning. A person who maintains an *unreasonable, sustained false belief that is not fixed* is said to have an *overvalued idea*. A *phobia* is a *persistent, irrational, exaggerated*, and invariably pathological *dread of some specific type of stimulus or situation*; the dread results in a compelling desire to avoid the stimulus.

8.33–8.36

8.33. The answer is C (*Synopsis VII*, page 306).

8.34. The answer is B (*Synopsis VII*, page 306).

8.35. The answer is A (*Synopsis VII*, page 306).

8.36. The answer is E (*Synopsis VII*, page 306).

Nominal aphasia, also known as anomia, is *difficulty in finding the correct names for objects*. A person who experiences an organic *loss of the ability to comprehend the meaning of words* suffers from *sensory aphasia*; speech is fluid and spontaneous but incoherent and nonsensical. A person who retains language comprehension but who suffers the *loss of the ability to speak* has *Broca's (motor) aphasia*; speech is halting, laborious, and inaccurate. *Syntactical aphasia* is the *inability to arrange words in a proper sequence*. *Global aphasia* is a combination of a grossly nonfluent aphasia and a severe fluent aphasia; the person has difficulty in both the comprehension and the production of language.

8.37–8.40

8.37. The answer is D (*Synopsis VII*, page 307).

8.38. The answer is B (*Synopsis VII*, page 307).

8.39. The answer is A (*Synopsis VII*, page 307).

8.40. The answer is C (*Synopsis VII*, page 307).

The lettered responses are examples of cognitive disorders. *Autotopagnosia* is the *inability to recognize a body part as one's own*; it is also known as somatopagnosia. *Astereognosis* is the *inability to distinguish* objects *by touch*, such as a quarter and a dime. *Dysdiadochokinesia* is the *inability to perform rapid alternating movements*; it is usually a cerebellar dysfunction. *Visual agnosia* is the *inability to recognize objects or persons*. *Simultanagnosia* is the inability to comprehend more than one element of a visual scene at a time or to integrate the parts into a whole.

8.41–8.44

8.41. **The answer is B** (*Synopsis VII*, page 308).

8.42. **The answer is C** (*Synopsis VII*, page 308).

8.43. **The answer is D** (*Synopsis VII*, page 308).

8.44. **The answer is A** (*Synopsis VII*, page 308).

Déjà vu is *regarding a new situation as a repetition of a previous experience. Déjà entendu* is an *illusion of auditory recognition. Déjà pensé* is *regarding a new thought as a repetition of a previous thought. Jamais vu* is a *feeling of unfamiliarity with a familiar situation. Confabulation* is the unconscious filling in of memory by imagining experiences that have no basis in fact.

8.45–8.48

8.45. **The answer is C** (*Synopsis VII*, page 308).

8.46. **The answer is E** (*Synopsis VII*, page 308).

8.47. **The answer is B** (*Synopsis VII*, pages 307–308).

8.48. **The answer is A** (*Synopsis VII*, page 307).

In *synesthesia* the patient experiences *sensations that accompany sensations of another modality*; for example, an auditory sensation is accompanied by or triggers a visual sensation, or a sound is experienced as being seen or accompanied by a visual experience. *Paramnesia* is a *confusion of facts and fantasies*; it lends to a falsification of memory by the distortion of real events by fantasies. *Hypermnesia* is an *exaggerated degree of retention and recall* or an ability to remember material that ordinarily is not retrievable. *Eidetic images*, also known as primary memory images, are visual memories of almost hallucinatory vividness. *Lethologica* is the *temporary inability to remember a name* or a proper noun.

8.49–8.53

8.49. **The answer is E** (*Synopsis VII*, page 308).

8.50. **The answer is D** (*Synopsis VII*, page 308).

8.51. **The answer is C** (*Synopsis VII*, page 308).

8.52. **The answer is B** (*Synopsis VII*, page 308).

8.53. **The answer is A** (*Synopsis VII*, page 308).

Dementia is an organic and global deterioration of intellectual functioning without a clouding of consciousness. Dementia is caused by such illnesses as Alzheimer's disease, Huntington's disease, and acquired immune deficiency syndrome (AIDS).

A depressed person may have clinical features that resemble a dementia but have no underlying organic condition. That is known as *pseudodementia*.

Concrete thinking is one-dimensional thought. It results in the liberal use of metaphors without understanding the nuances of meaning.

Abstract thinking is the ability to appreciate the nuances of meaning. People who think abstractly are capable of multidimensional thought and use metaphors and hypotheses appropriately.

Insight is the ability to understand the true cause and meaning of a situation. For example, a person with alcohol dependence may be cognizant of the cause-and-effect relation of alcohol on his life expectancy.

8.54–8.57

8.54. **The answer is B** (*Synopsis VII*, page 303).

8.55. **The answer is D** (*Synopsis VII*, page 303).

8.56. **The answer is A** (*Synopsis VII*, page 303).

8.57. **The answer is C** (*Synopsis VII*, page 303).

Anxiety is a *feeling of apprehension* caused by anticipation of danger, which may be internal or external. *Ambivalence* is the *coexistence of two opposing impulses* toward the same thing in the same person at the same time. *Guilt* is an *emotion resulting from doing something perceived as wrong. Abreaction* is an *emotional discharge after recalling a painful experience*.

8.58–8.62

8.58. **The answer is B** (*Synopsis VII*, page 307).

8.59. **The answer is A** (*Synopsis VII*, pages 277 and 305).

8.60. **The answer is E** (*Synopsis VII*, page 306).

8.61. **The answer is C** (*Synopsis VII*, pages 277 and 306).

8.62. **The answer is D** (*Synopsis VII*, page 306).

The many typical signs and symptoms of psychiatric illness that the student needs to be able to define and recognize include disturbances of consciousness, emotion, motor behavior, thinking, perception, memory, intelligence, insight, and judgment.

Disturbances in the form of thought involve a disruption in the goal-directed flow of ideas and associations typical of the logical sequence of normal thinking. A formal thought disorder is a disturbance in the form, as opposed to the content, of thought. *Tangentiality* is a specific disorder in the form of thought that involves the patient's thinking in tangents that never return to the idea or question or origin; the *person never gets to the point.* Anosognosia is a disturbance associated with brain diseases of the nonlanguage sphere. *Anosognosia* is *associated with denial of a physical disorder.* The patient denies, suppresses, or is unable to recognize a physical disability. Aphasias are *disturbances in language output* and comprehension. They include motor (or Broca's) aphasia, which is characterized by difficulty in speaking, with comprehension intact; sensory (or Wernicke's) aphasia, which is characterized by impaired comprehension, with speech relatively fluent; and *nominal aphasia*, which is the defective use of words and the inability to name objects. *Dysprosody* is *disordered rhythm of speech* or the loss of normal speech melody; it may be caused by a frontal lesion that makes the patient's speech sound odd. *Erotomania*, also known as Clérembault's syndrome, is a delusional belief that another person is in love with the patient. It is an example of a *disturbance in content of thought*. Erotomania has been interpreted psychodynamically as a grandiose fantasy that defends against an underlying belief that the patient is unlovable.

Classification in Psychiatry and Psychiatric Rating Scales

Because so much of psychiatric diagnosis is descriptive in nature (no definitive laboratory or medical investigations confirm a specific diagnosis), diagnoses must be as reliable and valid as possible. For the practice of psychiatry to be coherent, psychiatrists must speak the same language, and what they speak about must be real entities. *Diagnostic and Statistical Manual of Mental Disorders* (DSM), first published in 1952, is an evolving attempt to standardize psychiatric language and diagnosis by making them increasingly reliable and valid. Four editions of DSM have been published since 1952: DSM-II was published in 1968, DSM-III in 1980, DSM-III-R in 1987, and DSM-IV in 1994.

The basic features of DSM-IV are an atheoretical descriptive approach, specified diagnostic criteria that must be present for each mental disorder diagnosed, a systematic description of essential and associated features in conjunction with known epidemiological data for each disorder, and provisions for diagnostic uncertainties. The criteria and data are based on extensive field trials and clinical research in an attempt to increase the degree of diagnostic validity.

DSM-IV uses a multiaxial approach that allows the diagnostician to describe the patient from a variety of perspectives, including medical, psychosocial, and global level of functioning. DSM-IV has made a number of both subtle and dramatic changes in the diagnosis and the description of essential and associated features of various disorders. The student of psychiatry must grasp those changes and understand their significance.

The DSM system has been controversial throughout its history, and it will continue to be so. Most psychiatrists do not argue that the most recent DSMs have increased the reliability and the validity of psychiatric diagnosis: psychiatrists now usually speak the same language about real entities. However, some psychiatrists use the manual in an unsophisticated and cookbook way; they rigidly adhere to the listed criteria, rather than pay attention to the complicated, often atypical patient sitting in front of them. Perhaps the best way to use DSM-IV is to be intimately familiar with it in order to use it intelligently and criticize it constructively.

Chapter 9 in *Kaplan and Sadock's Synopsis VII* addresses many of the issues in psychiatric classification. The questions below test the student's understanding of the issues.

HELPFUL HINTS

The student should be able to define the terms below, especially the diagnostic categories.

classification	impairment	age of onset
validity and reliability	predisposing factors	course
predictive validity	sex ratio	complications
bipolar I disorder	differential diagnosis	prevalence
diagnostic criteria	clinical syndromes	familial pattern
disability determination	personality disorders	multiaxial system
descriptive approach	competence	pervasive developmental disorders
associated and essential features	atheoretical	ICD-10

residual type	severity-of-stress rating	dissociative fugue
Global Assessment of Functioning Scale	highest level of functioning	depersonalization disorder
	partial and full remission	dysthymic disorder
reality testing	psychosis	psychological factors affecting medical condition
schizophrenia	alcohol delirium	
delusional disorder	obsessive-compulsive disorder	agoraphobia
mood disorders	cognitive disorders	somatization disorder
phobias	sexual dysfunctions	conversion disorder
gross social norms	ego-dystonic and ego-syntonic	hypochondriasis
panic disorder	Emil Kraepelin	amnestic disorders
generalized anxiety disorder	dementia precox	dissociative identity disorder
posttraumatic stress disorder	DSM-IV	paraphilias
general medical conditions	somatoform disorders	depressive disorders
psychosocial and environmental stressors	body dysmorphic disorder	premenstrual dysphoric disorder
	dissociative disorders	

QUESTIONS

DIRECTIONS: Each of the incomplete statements below is followed by five suggested completions. Select the *one* that is *best* in each case.

9.1. The fourth edition of *Diagnostic and Statistical Manual of Mental Disorders* (DSM-IV)
A. is used by Medicare in billing codes for reimbursement
B. provides the causes of the mental disorders
C. provides a list of treatment modalities for each disorder
D. is a multiaxial system
E. uses Axis I to list mental retardation

9.2. The term "psychotic"
A. applies to major and minor distortions of reality
B. is applied in the presence of either delusions or hallucinations
C. has a precise meaning in current clinical and research practice
D. is not used in DSM-IV
E. is used to describe a person with a phobia

9.3. All the following are classified as paraphilias *except*
A. fetishism
B. homosexuality
C. exhibitionism
D. sexual sadism
E. transvestic fetishism

9.4. The Social and Occupational Functioning Assessment Scale (SOFAS)
A. is scored independent of the person's psychological symptoms
B. does not include impairment in functioning that is due to a general medical condition
C. may not be used to rate functioning at the time of the evaluation
D. may not be used to rate functioning of a past period
E. is included on Axis III

9.5. DSM-IV conditions that have been termed neurotic disorders in other classification systems include
A. anxiety disorders
B. somatoform disorders
C. dissociative disorders
D. dysthymic disorder
E. all the above

DIRECTIONS: Each group of questions below consists of five lettered headings followed by a list of numbered phrases or statements. For each numbered phrase or statement, select the *one* lettered heading that is most closely associated with it. Each lettered heading may be selected once, more than once, or not at all.

Questions 9.6–9.7

A. Axis I
B. Axis II
C. Axis III
D. Axis IV
E. Axis V

9.6. Psychosocial and environmental problems

9.7. Global assessment of functioning

Questions 9.8–9.12

A. Paranoid personality disorder
B. Schizotypal personality disorder
C. Borderline personality disorder
D. Dependent personality disorder
E. Passive-aggressive personality disorder

9.8. Ideas of reference and magical thinking

9.9. Stubborn and procrastinates

9.10. Suspicious and hypervigilant

9.11. Impulsive and self-destructive

9.12. Clinging and subordinates own needs to those of others

Questions 9.13–9.17

A. Axis I
B. Axis II
C. Axis III
D. Axis IV
E. Axis V

9.13. Kidney failure

9.14. Borderline personality disorder

9.15. Mental retardation

9.16. Unemployment

9.17. Delusional disorder

ANSWERS

Classification in Psychiatry and Psychiatric Rating Scales

9.1. The answer is D (*Synopsis VII*, page 315).

The fourth edition of *Diagnostic and Statistical Manual of Mental Disorders* (DSM-IV) *is a multiaxial system* that contains five axes and evaluates the patient along several variables. Published in 1994, DSM-IV is the latest and most up-to-date classification of mental disorders.

DSM-IV correlates with the 10th revision of the World Health Organization's International Classification of Diseases and Related Health Problems (ICD-10), developed in 1992. Diagnostic systems used in the United States must be compatible with ICD to ensure uniform reporting of national and international health statistics. In addition, ICD, not DSM-IV, *is used by Medicare in billing codes for reimbursement*.

The approach in DSM-IV is atheoretical with regard to causes. Thus, DSM-IV describes what the manifestations of the mental disorders are; only rarely does DSM-IV attempt to *provide the causes of the mental disorders*. DSM-IV also describes each disorder in terms of its associated features: specific age, cultural, and gender-related features; prevalence, incidence, and risk; course; complications; predisposing factors; familial pattern; and differential diagnosis. In some instances, when many of the specific disorders share common features, that information is included in the introduction to the entire section. Laboratory findings and associated physical examination signs and symptoms are described when relevant.

DSM-IV does not *provide a list of treatment modalities for each disorder*. Nor does it mention management or controversial issues surrounding a particular diagnostic category.

Clinical syndromes and other conditions that may be a focus of clinical attention are included on Axis I. DSM-IV does not *use Axis I to list mental retardation*; they are included on Axis II.

9.2. The answer is B (*Synopsis VII*, page 325).

The term "psychotic" *is applied in the presence of either delusions or hallucinations* without patient insight into their pathological nature. With gross impairment in reality testing, persons incorrectly evaluate the accuracy of their perceptions and thoughts and make incorrect inferences about external reality, even in the face of contrary evidence.

The term "psychotic" *applies only to major distor-*

tions of reality; it does not apply to minor distortions of reality that involve matters of relative judgment. For example, depressed patients who underestimate their achievements are not described as psychotic, whereas patients who believe that they have caused natural catastrophes are described as psychotic.

Although the traditional meaning of the term "psychotic" emphasized the loss of reality testing and the impairment of mental functioning—manifested by delusions, hallucinations, confusion, and impaired memory—two other meanings have evolved during the past 50 years. In the most common psychiatric use of the term, "psychotic" became synonymous with the severe impairment of social and personal functioning characterized by social withdrawal and the inability to perform the usual household and occupational roles. The other use of the term specifies the degree of ego regression as the criterion for psychotic illness. As a consequence of those multiple meanings, the term "psychotic" *does not have a precise meaning in current clinical and research practice*. However, the term "psychotic" *is used in DSM-IV*.

The term "neurosis" is no longer used in DSM-IV, although that term is still found in the literature and in ICD-10. Neurosis has come to mean a chronic or recurrent nonpsychotic disorder characterized mainly by anxiety, which is experienced or expressed directly or is altered through defense mechanisms. Neurosis appears as a symptom, such as an obsession, a compulsion, a phobia, or a sexual dysfunction. Thus, "neurosis," not "psychotic" *is used to describe a person with a phobia*, a persistent, irrational dread of a stimulus or a situation.

9.3. The answer is B (*Synopsis VII*, pages 658–659).

Paraphilias are conditions associated with (1) preference for the use of a nonhuman object for sexual arousal, (2) repetitive sexual activity with humans involving real or simulated suffering or humiliation, or (3) repetitive sexual activity with nonconsenting or inappropriate partners.

Homosexuality is no longer classified as a paraphilia. Whether or not homosexuality should be classified as a mental disorder has been the focus of considerable controversy in the past. In December 1973 the Board of Trustees of the American Psychiatric Association voted to eliminate homosexuality as a mental disorder. DSM-IV lists persistent and marked distress about one's sexual orientation as an example of sexual disorder not otherwise specified. The removal of homosexuality as a paraphilia was supported by the following rationale: The crucial issue in determining whether or not homosexuality should be regarded as a mental disorder is not the cause of the condition but its consequences and the definition of mental disorder. A significant proportion of homosexuals are apparently satisfied with their sexual orientation, show no significant signs of manifest psychopathology, and are able to function socially and occupationally with no impairment. If one uses the criteria of distress or disability, homosexuality is not a mental disorder. If one uses the criterion of inherent disadvantage, it is not at all clear that homosexuality is a disadvantage in all cultures or subcultures.

Some common paraphilias are *fetishism*, pedophilia, *exhibitionism*, voyeurism, *sexual sadism*, sexual masochism, *transvestic fetishism*, and zoophilia.

9.4. The answer is A (*Synopsis VII*, page 330).

The Social and Occupational Functioning Assessment Scale (SOFAS) (Table 9.1) is a new scale included in a DSM-IV appendix. The scale differs from the Global Assessment of Functioning (GAF) Scale in that it focuses only on the person's level of social and occupational functioning. It *is scored independent of the severity of the person's psychological symptoms.* And unlike the GAF scale, the SOFAS *may include impairment in functioning that is due to a general medical condition. The SOFAS may be used to rate functioning at the time of the evaluation, or it may be used to rate functioning of a past period. The SOFAS is included on Axis V, not Axis III.*

9.5. The answer is E (all) (*Synopsis VII*, pages 325–326).

A neurosis is an ego-alien (ego-dystonic) nonorganic disorder in which reality testing is intact, anxiety is a major characteristic, and the use of various defense mechanisms plays a major role. As opposed to ICD-10, which contains a number of neurotic diagnostic classes, DSM-IV contains no diagnostic category of neuroses. However, a number of DSM-IV categories were termed neurotic disorders in the past, and many clinicians still use the term "neurosis" for those disorders. Those disorders include anx-

Table 9.1
Social and Occupational Functioning Assessment Scale (SOFAS)[1]

Consider social and occupational functioning on a continuum from excellent functioning to grossly impaired functioning. Include impairments in functioning due to physical limitations, as well as those due to mental impairments. To be counted, impairment must be a direct consequence of mental and physical health problems; the effects of lack of opportunity and other environmental limitations are not to be considered.

Code	(**Note:** Use intermediate codes when appropriate, e.g., 45, 68, 72.)	Code	
100 | 91	Superior functioning in a wide range of activities.	40 | 31	Major impairment in several areas, such as work or school, family relations (e.g., depressed man avoids friends, neglects family, and is unable to work; child frequently beats up younger children, is defiant at home, and is failing at school).
90 | 81	Good functioning in all areas, occupationally and socially effective.	30 | 21	Inability to function in almost all areas (e.g., stays in bed all day; no job, home, or friends).
80 | 71	No more than a slight impairment in social, occupational, or school functioning (e.g., infrequent interpersonal conflict, temporarily falling behind in schoolwork).	20 | 11	Occasionally fails to maintain minimal personal hygiene; unable to function independently.
70 | 61	Some difficulty in social, occupational, or school functioning, but generally functioning well, has some meaningful interpersonal relationships.	10 | 1	Persistent inability to maintain minimal personal hygiene. Unable to function without harming self or others or without considerable external support (e.g., nursing care and supervision).
60 | 51	Moderate difficulty in social, occupational, or school functioning (e.g., few friends, conflicts with peers or co-workers).	0	Inadequate information.
50 | 41	Serious impairment in social, occupational, or school functioning (e.g., no friends, unable to keep a job).		

[1]**Note:** The rating of overall psychological functioning on a scale of 0-100 was operationalized by Luborsky in the Health-Sickness Rating Scale (Luborsky L: Clinicians' judgments of mental health. Arch Gen Psychiatry *7:* 407, 1962). Spitzer and colleagues developed a revision of the Health-Sickness Rating Scale called the Global Assessment Scale (GAS) (Endicott J, Spitzer R L, Fleiss J L, et at: The Global Assessment Scale: A procedure for measuring overall severity of psychiatric disturbance. Arch Gen Psychiatry *33:* 766, 1976). The SOFAS is derived from the GAS and its development is described in Goldman H H, Skodol A E, Lave T R: Revising Axis V for DSM-IV: A review of measures of social functioning. Am J Psychiatry *149:* 1148, 1992.
Table from DSM-IV, *Diagnostic and Statistical Manual of Mental Disorders,* ed 4. Copyright American Psychiatric Association, Washington, 1994. Used with permission.

iety disorders, somatoform disorders, dissociative disorders, sexual and gender identity disorders, and *dysthymic disorder*.

9.6–9.7

9.6. The answer is D (*Synopsis VII*, pages 315–316).

9.7. The answer is E (*Synopsis VII*, pages 316–317 and 330).

Axis IV is used to code the *psychosocial and environmental problems* that significantly contribute to the development or the exacerbation of the patient's disorder. The evaluation of stressors is based on the clinician's assessment of the stress that an average person with similar sociocultural values and circumstances would experience from the psychosocial stressors. That judgment considers the amount of change in the person's life caused by the stressor, the degree to which the event is desired and under the person's control, and the number of stressors. Stressors may be positive (for example, a job promotion) or negative (for example, the loss of a loved one). Information about stressors may be important in formulating a treatment plan that includes attempts to remove the psychosocial stressors or to help the patient cope with them. Table 9.2 presents the psychosocial and environmental problems listed in DSM-IV.

Axis V is the *global assessment of functioning*, in which the clinician judges the patient's overall level of functioning during a particular time period (for example, the patient's level of functioning at the time of the evaluation or the patient's highest level of functioning for at least a few months during the past year). Functioning is conceptualized as a composite of three major areas: social functioning, occupational functioning, and psychological functioning. The Global Assessment of Functioning (GAF) Scale, based on a continuum of mental health and mental illness, is a 100-point scale; 100 represents the highest level of functioning in all areas. Table 9.3 presents the Global Assessment of Functioning (GAF) Scale as it is published in DSM-IV.

9.8–9.12

9.8. The answer is B (*Synopsis VII*, pages 315 and 736–737).

A person with *paranoid personality disorder is suspicious, hypervigilant*, secretive, and hypersensitive and has a generally restricted affect. A person with *schizotypal personality disorder uses ideas of reference and magical thinking* and may manifest an odd sense of speech, have recurrent depersonalization experiences or illusions, and be isolated and withdrawn. A person with *borderline personality disorder is impulsive and self-destructive*, shows patterns of unstable interpersonal relationships, and may make suicidal gestures. A person with dependent personality disorder is *clinging and subordinates*

Table 9.2
Axis IV: Psychosocial and Environmental Problems

Problems with primary support group—e.g., death of a family member; health problems in family; disruption of family by separation, divorce, or estrangement; removal from the home; remarriage of parent; sexual or physical abuse; parental overprotection; neglect of child; inadequate discipline; discord with siblings; birth of a sibling

Problems related to the social environment—e.g., death or loss of friend; social isolation; living alone; difficulty with acculturation; discrimination; adjustment to life-cycle transition (such as retirement)

Educational problems—e.g., illiteracy; academic problems; discord with teachers or classmates; inadequate school environment

Occupational problems—e.g., unemployment; threat of job loss; stressful work schedule; difficult work condition; job dissatisfaction; job change; discord with boss or coworkers

Housing problems—e.g., homelessness; inadequate housing; unsafe neighborhood; discord with neighbors or landlord

Economic problems—e.g., extreme poverty; inadequate finances; insufficient welfare support

Problems with access to health care services—e.g., inadequate health care services; transportation to health care facilities unavailable; inadequate health insurance

Problems related to interaction with the legal system/crime—e.g., arrest; incarceration; litigation; victim of crime

Other psychosocial problems—e.g., exposure to disasters, war, other hostilities; discord with nonfamily caregivers (such as counselor, social worker, physician), unavailability of social service agencies.

Table from DSM-IV, *Diagnostic and Statistical Manual of Mental Disorders*, ed 4. Copyright American Psychiatric Association, Washington, 1994. Used with permission.

---

own needs to the needs of others. Such a person is generally passive and finds it difficult to assume responsibility for major life duties. A person with *passive-aggressive personality disorder is stubborn and procrastinates* and shows long-standing social and occupational ineffectiveness.

9.9. The answer is E (*Synopsis VII*, pages 315 and 746–747).

9.10. The answer is A (*Synopsis VII*, pages 315 and 734–735).

9.11. The answer is C (*Synopsis VII*, pages 315 and 739–740).

9.12. The answer is D (*Synopsis VII*, pages 315 and 744–745).

9.13. The answer is C (*Synopsis VII*, pages 315–317).

Table 9.3
Global Assessment of Functioning (GAF) Scale[1]

Consider psychological, social, and occupational functioning on a hypothetical continuum of mental health-illness. Do not include impairment in functioning due to physical (or environmental) limitations.

Code	(**Note:** Use intermediate codes when appropriate, e.g., 45, 68, 72.)
100	**Superior functioning in a wide range of activities, life's problems never seem to get out of hand, is sought out by others because of his or her many positive qualities. No**
91	**symptoms.**
90	**Absent or minimal symptoms** (e.g., mild anxiety before an exam), **good functioning in all areas, interested and involved in a wide range of activities, socially effective, generally satisfied with life, no more than everyday problems or concerns** (e.g., an occasional argument with family
81	members).
80	**If symptoms are present, they are transient and expectable reactions to psychosocial stressors** (e.g., difficulty concentrating after family argument); **no more than slight impairment in social, occupational, or school functioning**
71	(e.g., temporarily falling behind in school work).
70	**Some mild symptoms** (e.g., depressed mood and mild insomnia) **OR some difficulty in social, occupational, or school functioning** (e.g., occasional truancy, or theft within the household), **but generally functioning pretty well, has some**
61	**meaningful interpersonal relationships.**
60	**Moderate symptoms** (e.g., flat affect and circumstantial speech, occasional panic attacks) **OR moderate difficulty in social, occupational, or school functioning** (e.g., few friends, conflicts
51	with peers or co-workers).
50	**Serious symptoms** (e.g., suicidal ideation, severe obsessional rituals, frequent shoplifting) **OR any serious impairment in social, occupational, or school functioning** (e.g., no friends, unable to
41	keep a job).

Code	
40	**Some impairment in reality testing or communication** (e.g., speech is at times illogical, obscure, or irrelevant) **OR major impairment in several areas, such as work or school, family relations, judgment, thinking, or mood** (e.g., depressed man avoids friends, neglects family, and is unable to work; child frequently beats up younger
31	children, is defiant at home, and is failing at school).
30	**Behavior is considerably influenced by delusions or hallucinations OR serious impairment in communication or judgment** (e.g., sometimes incoherent, acts grossly inappropriately, suicidal preoccupation) **OR inability to function in almost all areas** (e.g., stays in bed
21	all day; no job, home, or friends).
20	**Some danger of hurting self or others** (e.g., suicide attempts without clear expectation of death; frequently violent; manic excitement) **OR occasionally fails to maintain minimal personal hygiene** (e.g., smears feces) **OR gross impairment in communication** (e.g., largely
11	incoherent or mute).
10	**Persistent danger of severely hurting self or others** (e.g., recurrent violence) **OR persistent inability to maintain minimal personal hygiene OR serious suicidal acts with clear expectation**
1	**of death.**
0	Inadequate information.

[1]The rating of overall psychological functioning on a scale of 0-100 was operationalized by Luborsky in the Health-Sickness Rating Scale (Luborsky L: Clinicians' judgments of mental health. Arch Gen Psychiatry *7:* 407, 1962). Spitzer and colleagues developed a revision of the Health-Sickness Rating Scale called the Global Assessment Scale (GAS) (Endicott J, Spitzer R L, Fleiss J L, Cohen J: The Global assessment scale: A procedure for measuring overall severity of psychiatric disturbance. Arch Gen Psychiatry *33:* 766, 1976). A modified version of the GAS was included in DSM-III-R as the Global Assessment of Functioning (GAF) Scale.
Table from DSM-IV, *Diagnostic and Statistical Manual of Mental Disorders,* ed 4. Copyright American Psychiatric Association, Washington, 1994. Used with permission.

9.14. **The answer is B** (*Synopsis VII*, pages 315–317).

9.15. **The answer is B** (*Synopsis VII*, pages 315–317).

9.16. **The answer is D** (*Synopsis VII*, pages 315–317).

9.17. **The answer is A** (*Synopsis VII*, pages 315–317).

DSM-IV uses a multiaxial scheme of classification consisting of five axes, each of which covers a differ-

ent aspect of functioning. Each axis should be covered for each diagnosis. *Axis I* consists of all major clinical syndromes and other conditions that may be a focus of clinical attention. Examples include schizophrenia, mood disorders, and *delusional disorder*. *Axis II* consists of personality disorders, including *borderline personality disorder* and *mental retardation*. *Axis III* consists of general medical conditions. The condition may be causative (for example, *kidney failure* causing delirium), secondary (for example, acquired immune deficiency syndrome [AIDS] as a result of a substance-related disorder), or unrelated. *Axis IV* consists of psychosocial and environmental problems that are related to the current mental disorder. Examples include divorce, *unemployment*, and inadequate health insurance. *Axis V* is a global assessment of functioning in which the clinician evaluates the highest level of functioning by the patient in the past year. The Global Assessment of Functioning (GAF) Scale is a 100-point scale, with 100 representing the highest level of functioning in all areas.

Delirium, Dementia, Amnestic and Other Cognitive Disorders and Mental Disorders Due to a General Medical Condition

In its classification of the cognitive disorders, the fourth edition of *Diagnostic and Statistical Manual of Mental Disorders* (DSM-IV) follows in the tradition of the third edition (DSM-III) and the revised third edition (DSM-III-R) by choosing diagnostic nomenclature that is consistent with current clinical experience and reflective of advances in the understanding of those syndromes and disorders. Specifically, just as DSM-III removed references to unsupported theoretical models from its diagnostic criteria, DSM-IV has removed the classic but unsupported distinction between organic and functional psychiatric disorders.

Because of that assessment of the data, the concept of functional disorders has been determined to be misleading, and both the term "functional" and its historical opposite, "organic," are dropped from DSM-IV. Thus, the section called organic mental disorders in DSM-III-R is called delirium, dementia, and amnestic and other cognitive disorders in DSM-IV. Some diagnoses from the former DSM-III-R category of organic mental disorders are found in a new DSM-IV section, mental disorders due to a general medical condition not elsewhere classified.

All these disorders have clusters of signs and symptoms that indicate underlying abnormalities of neuroanatomy, neurochemistry, or neurophysiology. The disorders may be the results of primary dysfunctions originating in the brain or of secondary dysfunctions resulting from systemic disorders that have affected the brain. Mental disorders due to a general medical condition may include disorders of mood, anxiety, personality, reality testing, intoxication, and withdrawal. Psychiatrists must know the psychiatric manifestations of general medical disorders (such as systemic lupus erythematosus and Parkinson's disease) and neurological disorders (such as multiple sclerosis).

Psychiatrists need to be familiar with the many potential causes of delirium and to differentiate between delirium and dementia. They also need to be familiar with the most common types of dementia—in particular, dementia of the Alzheimer's type and how it is distinguished from vascular dementia.

An impairment of memory is the single or primary defect in the amnestic disorders. Psychiatrists must be able to differentiate between a loss of memory secondary to purely psychogenic causes (for example, dissociative disorders) and a loss of memory secondary to medical causes (for example, thiamine deficiency, head injury, and cerebral neoplasm).

Many mental disorders are due to a general medical condition. To make the diagnosis, the physician must find a medical cause that antedates the onset of the symptoms and that is known to be associated with the disorder. Thus, the physician needs to be aware of the possible psychiatric symptoms associated with a wide-ranging array of medical disorders. Symptoms of depression, mania, anxiety, psychosis, and changes in personality—all may be directly caused by such medical conditions as neurological, endocrine, systemic, inflammatory, and deficiency disorders.

The student should refer to Chapter 10 in *Kaplan and Sadock's Synopsis VII*. The questions and answers below test the student's knowledge of the subject.

HELPFUL HINTS

The student should be able to define the signs, symptoms, and syndromes listed below.

cognitive disorders	tactile or haptic hallucinations	parkinsonism
orientation	auditory, olfactory, and visual	Huntington's disease
memory	hallucinations	kuru
intellectual functions	Lilliputian hallucination	general paresis
delirium	hypnagogic and hypnopompic	normal pressure hydrocephalus
postoperative	hallucinations	multiple sclerosis
black-patch	delusional disorder	ALS
sundowner syndrome	mood disorder due to a general	SLE
dementia	medical condition	transient global amnesia
beclouded dementia	personality change due to a general	intracranial neoplasms
dementia of the Alzheimer's type	medical condition	hypoglycemic, hepatic, and uremic
short-term versus long-term	anxiety disorder due to a general	encephalopathy
memory loss	medical condition	diabetic ketoacidosis
abstract attitude	intoxication and withdrawal	AIP
catastrophic reaction	Pick's disease	myxedema
pseudodementia	Creutzfeldt-Jakob disease	cretinism
normal aging	Down's syndrome	Addison's disease
vascular dementia	senile plaques	Cushing's syndrome
amnestic disorders	neurofibrillary tangles	beriberi
dissociative amnesia	granulovacuolar degeneration	pellagra
retrograde versus anterograde	pseudobulbar palsy	pernicious anemia
amnesia	dysarthria	epilepsy
confabulation	TIA	partial versus generalized seizures
Korsakoff's syndrome	vertebrobasilar disease	interictal manifestations

---

QUESTIONS

DIRECTIONS: Each of the questions or incomplete statements below is followed by five suggested responses or completions. Select the *one* that is *best* in each case.

10.1. Patients with dementia
A. may show idiosyncratic responses to benzodiazepines
B. usually show equal impairment of short-term memory and long-term memory early in the course of the dementia
C. are believed to have a dopamine deficiency
D. often have an impairment of consciousness
E. usually have a marked disturbance of the sleep-wake cycle

10.2. A person with a complex partial seizure disorder
A. has no alteration in consciousness during the seizure
B. may exhibit a personality disturbance, such as religiosity
C. usually does not experience preictal events (auras)
D. usually displays a characteristic electroencephalogram (EEG) pattern
E. may have acute intermittent porphyria as the underlying cause

10.3. Delirium
A. has an insidious onset
B. rarely has associated neurological symptoms
C. generally causes a diffuse slowing of brain activity on an electroencephalogram (EEG)
D. generally has an underlying cause residing in the central nervous system
E. may be successfully treated with lithium

10.4. Korsakoff's syndrome
A. is due to folate deficiency
B. is equivalent to Wernicke's encephalopathy
C. is best treated with antipsychotic medications
D. often has confabulation as a prominent symptom
E. is a dissociative disorder

10.5. Which of the following drugs is best used to treat acute delirium?
A. Chlorpromazine (Thorazine)
B. Diazepam (Valium)
C. Haloperidol (Haldol)
D. Amobarbital (Amytal)
E. Physostigmine salicylate (Antilirium)

10.6 The incidence of delirium after open-heart and coronary-bypass surgery is
A. less than 10 percent
B. 20 percent
C. 30 percent
D. 40 percent
E. more than 50 percent

10.7. All the following statements about the clinical differentiation of delirium and dementia are true *except*
A. the onset of delirium is sudden
B. the duration of delirium is usually less than one month
C. in delirium, symptoms worsen at night
D. the sleep-wake cycle is disrupted in delirium
E. visual hallucinations and transient delusions are more common in dementia than in delirium

10.8. The electroencephalogram (EEG) shown in Figure 10.1 is an example of
A. partial seizure
B. grand mal epilepsy
C. petit mal epilepsy or absence seizure
D. psychomotor epilepsy
E. none of the above

10.9. Inpatient cognitive tests that are helpful in the diagnosis of dementia include assessing
A. Patients' ability to remember three objects after five minutes
B. Patients' ability to remember place of birth or what happened yesterday
C. Patients' fund of common information, such as past U.S. Presidents
D. Patients' ability to find similarities and differences between related words
E. all the above

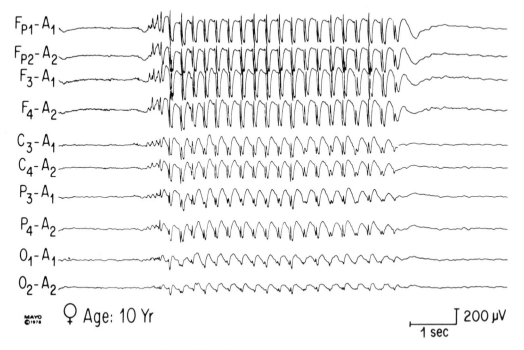

Figure 10.1. Electroencephalogram (EEG).

10.10. The organic causes of delirium include
A. hypoglycemia
B. hypokalemia
C. migraine
D. infectious mononucleosis
E. all the above

10.11. The diagnosis of vascular dementia is associated with
A. cerebrovascular disease
B. hypertension
C. a stepwise progression of focal motor symptoms
D. such personality changes as emotional lability and hypochondriasis
E. all the above

10.12. Features of amnestic disorders include
A. an impairment of memory as the single or predominant cognitive defect
B. retrograde amnesia and anterograde amnesia
C. preservation of the ability for immediate recall
D. evidence of a specific causative medical or substance-related factor
E. all the above

10.13. Amnestic disorders may be
A. transient
B. chronic
C. permanent
D. slowly progressive
E. all the above

10.14. Which of the following statements is true regarding personality change due to a general medical condition?
A. Many patients exhibit low drive and initiative
B. Emotions are typically labile and shallow
C. True sadness and depression are uncommon
D. The expression of impulses is characteristically disinhibited
E. All the above

DIRECTIONS: Each set of lettered headings below is followed by a list of numbered words or phrases. For each numbered word or phrase, select

A. if the item is associated with *A only*
B. if the item is associated with *B only*
C. if the item is associated with *both A and B*
D. if the item is associated with *neither A nor B*

Questions 10.15–10.24
A. Delirium
B. Dementia
C. Both
D. Neither

10.15. Sudden onset

10.16. Insidious onset

10.17. Clouding of consciousness

10.18. Reversible

10.19. Insight present

10.20. Hallucinations

10.21. Sundowning

10.22. Catastrophic reaction

10.23. High mortality rate

10.24. Decreased acetylcholine activity

Questions 10.25–10.28
A. Dementia of the Alzheimer's type
B. Pick's disease
C. Both
D. Neither

10.25. Unknown cause

10.26. Senile plaques and neurofibrillary changes

10.27. Lobar atrophy

10.28. Reversible

DIRECTIONS: Each group of questions below consists of lettered headings followed by a list of numbered phrases or statements. For each numbered phrase or statement, select the *one* lettered heading that is most closely associated with it. Each lettered heading may be used once, more than once, or not at all.

Questions 10.29–10.33
A. Creutzfeldt-Jakob disease
B. Normal pressure hydrocephalus
C. Neurosyphilis
D. Huntington's disease
E. Multiple sclerosis

10.29. Death occurs 15 to 20 years after the onset of the disease, and suicide is common

10.30. Slow virus, with death occurring within two years of the diagnosis

10.31. Manic syndrome with neurological signs in up to 20 percent of cases

10.32. Treatment of choice is a shunt

10.33. More prevalent in cold and temperate climates than in the tropics and subtropics

Questions 10.34–10.38
A. Mercury poisoning
B. Manganese madness
C. Thallium intoxication
D. Lead poisoning
E. Arsenic poisoning

10.34. Alopecia

10.35. Calcium disodium edetate

10.36. Mad Hatter syndrome

10.37. Masked facies

10.38. Increased pigmentation of the neck, eyelids, nipples, and axillae

ANSWERS

Delirium, Dementia, Amnestic and Other Cognitive Disorders and Mental Disorders Due to a General Medical Condition

10.1.   The answer is A (*Synopsis VII*, page 356).

The clinician may prescribe benzodiazepines for insomnia and anxiety but must be aware that patients with dementia *may show idiosyncratic responses to benzodiazepines.* In such patients, benzodiazepines may precipitate agitated, aggressive, or psychotic behavior.

Patients with dementia *do not usually show equal impairment of short-term memory and long-term memory early in the course of the dementia.* Memory impairment is typically an early and prominent feature in dementias, especially in dementias involving the cortex, such as dementia of the Alzheimer's type. Early in the course of dementia, memory impairment is mild and is usually most marked for recent events, such as forgetting telephone numbers, conversations, and events of the day. As the dementia progresses, memory impairment becomes severe, and only the most highly learned information (for example, place of birth) is retained.

Patients with dementia *are not believed to have a dopamine deficiency.* The neurotransmitters most implicated in the pathophysiology of dementia are acetylcholine and norepinephrine, both of which are hypothesized to be hypoactive in dementia of the Alzheimer's type. Several studies have reported data consistent with the hypothesis that a specific degeneration of cholinergic neurons is present in the nucleus basalis of Meynert in patients with dementia of the Alzheimer's type. Additional support for the cholinergic deficit hypothesis comes from the observation that cholinergic antagonists, such as scopolamine and atropine, impair cognitive abilities, whereas cholinergic agonists, such as physostigmine, have been reported to enhance cognitive abilities.

Patients with dementia *do not have an impairment of consciousness.* That symptom is characteristic of delirium, not dementia.

Patients with dementia *do not usually have a marked disturbance of the sleep-wake cycle.* Such disturbances are characteristic of delirium, not dementia.

10.2.   The answer is B (*Synopsis VII*, pages 365–366).

A person with a complex partial seizure disorder *may exhibit a personality disturbance, such as religiosity.* The most frequent psychiatric abnormalities reported in epileptic patients (especially patients with partial complex seizures of temporal lobe origin) are personality disturbances. In a person displaying religiosity, the religiosity may be striking and may be manifested not only by increased participation in overtly religious activities but also by unusual concern for moral and ethical issues, preoccupation with right and wrong, and heightened interest in global and philosophical concerns. The hyperreligious features can sometimes seem like the prodromal symptoms of schizophrenia and can result in a diagnostic problem in an adolescent or a young adult.

Partial seizures are classified as complex if they are associated with alterations in consciousness during the seizure episode. Thus, a person with a complex partial seizure disorder *always has an alteration in consciousness during the seizure.*

The person also *experiences preictal events (auras).* Preictal events in complex partial seizures include autonomic sensations (for example, fullness in the stomach, blushing, and changes in respiration), cognitive sensations (for example, *déjà vu, jamais vu,* forced thinking, and dreamy states), affective states (for example, fear, panic, depression, and elation), and, classically, automatisms (for example, lip smacking, rubbing, and chewing).

A person with a complex partial seizure disorder *does not display a characteristic electroencephalogram (EEG) pattern.* On the contrary, multiple normal EEGs are often obtained from a patient with complex partial seizures; therefore, normal EEGs cannot be used to exclude a diagnosis of complex partial seizures. The use of long-term EEG recordings (usually 24 to 72 hours) can help the clinician detect a seizure focus in some patients. Only in petit mal epilepsy does one see a characteristic EEG pattern of 3-per-second spike-and-wave activity.

Acute intermittent porphyria is not the underlying cause of complex partial seizures. The porphyrias are disorders of heme biosynthesis, resulting in the excessive accumulation of porphyrins. However, a disease that may lead to the development of complex partial seizures is herpes simplex encephalitis.

10.3.   The answer is C (*Synopsis VII*, pages 341, and 343–344).

Delirium *generally causes a diffuse slowing of brain activity on the electroencephalogram (EEG),* which may be useful in differentiating delirium from depression and psychosis. The EEG of a delirious patient sometimes shows focal areas of hyperactivity. In rare cases, differentiating delirium related to epilepsy from delirium related to other causes may be difficult.

In general, delirium *has a sudden onset, not an insidious onset.*

Patients with delirium *commonly have associated neurological symptoms*, including dysphasia, tremor, asterixis, incoordination, and urinary incontinence.

Delirium *does not have an underlying cause residing in the central nervous system.* Delirium has many causes, all of which result in a similar pattern of symptoms relating to the patient's level of consciousness and cognitive impairment. Most of the causes of delirium lie outside the central nervous system—for example, renal and hepatic failures.

Delirium *cannot be successfully treated with lithium (Eskalith).* Patients with lithium serum concentrations greater than 1.5 mEq per L are at risk for delirium.

Table 10.1 presents the diagnostic criteria for delirium due to a general medical condition.

10.4. The answer is D (*Synopsis VII*, page 359).

Korsakoff's syndrome *often has confabulation as a prominent symptom.*

Korsakoff's syndrome is the amnestic syndrome

Table 10.1
Diagnostic Criteria for Delirium Due to a General Medical Condition

---

A. Disturbance of consciousness (i.e., reduced clarity of awareness of the environment) with reduced ability to focus, sustain, or shift attention.

B. A change in cognition (such as memory deficit, disorientation, language disturbance) or the development of a perceptual disturbance that is not better accounted for by a preexisting, established, or evolving dementia.

C. The disturbance develops over a short period of time (usually hours to days) and tends to fluctuate during the course of the day.

D. There is evidence from the history, physical examination, or laboratory findings that the disturbance is caused by the direct physiological consequences of a general medical condition.

Coding note: If delirium is superimposed on a preexisting dementia of the Alzheimer's type or vascular dementia, indicate the delirium by coding the appropriate subtype of the dementia, e.g., dementia of the Alzheimer's type, with late onset, with delirium.

Coding note: Include the name of the general medical condition on Axis I, e.g., delirium due to hepatic encephalopathy; also code the general medical condition on Axis III.

Table from DSM-IV, *Diagnostic and Statistical Manual of Mental Disorders,* ed 4. Copyright American Psychiatric Association, Washington, 1994. Used with permission.

caused by thiamine deficiency; it is *not due to folate deficiency.* Folate deficiency may cause megaloblastic anemia. Thiamine deficiency is most commonly associated with the poor nutritional habits of persons with chronic alcohol abuse. Other causes of poor nutrition (for example, starvation), gastric carcinoma, hemodialysis, hyperemesis gravidarum, prolonged intravenous hyperalimentation, and gastric plication may also result in thiamine deficiency.

Korsakoff's syndrome is *not equivalent to Wernicke's encephalopathy*, but the two conditions are often associated. Wernicke's encephalopathy is characterized by confusion, ataxia, and ophthalmoplegia. In patients with those thiamine deficiency-related symptoms, the neuropathological findings include hyperplasia of the small blood vessels with occasional hemorrhages, hypertrophy of astrocytes, and subtle changes in neuronal axons. Although the delirium clears up within a month or so, the amnestic syndrome either accompanies or follows untreated Wernicke's encephalopathy in about 85 percent of all cases.

Korsakoff's syndrome *is not best treated with antipsychotics* but rather with thiamine, whose deficiency is the underlying cause of the syndrome. The administration of thiamine is the best treatment because it may prevent the development of additional amnestic symptoms, but rarely is the treatment able to reverse severe amnestic symptoms, once they are present. About a quarter to a third of all patients recover completely, and about a quarter of all patients have no improvement of their symptoms. Antipsychotics may be used to control the patient's agitated behavior.

Korsakoff's syndrome *is not a dissociative disorder*, although differentiating the conditions may sometimes be difficult. Patients with dissociative disorders are more likely to have lost their orientation to self and may have more selective memory deficits than do patients with amnestic disorders. Dissociative disorders are also often associated with emotionally stressful life events involving money, the legal system, or troubled relationships.

10.5 The answer is C (*Synopsis VII*, page 344).

The drug of choice for delirium is *haloperidol (Haldol)*, a butyrophenone. Depending on the patient's age, weight, and physical condition, the initial dose may range from 2 to 10 mg intramuscularly, repeated in an hour if the patient remains agitated. As soon as the patient is calm, oral medication in liquid concentrate or tablet form should begin. Two daily oral doses should suffice, with two thirds of the dose being given at bedtime. To achieve the same therapeutic effect, the clinician should give an oral dose about 1.5 times higher than a parenteral dose. The effective total daily dosage of haloperidol may range from 5 to 50 mg for the majority of delirious patients.

Phenothiazines, such as *chlorpromazine (Thorazine)*, should be avoided in delirious patients because those drugs are associated with significant anticholinergic activity. Benzodiazepines with long half-lives, such as *diazepam (Valium)*, and barbiturates, such as *amobarbital (Amytol)*, should be avoided unless they are being used as part of the treatment for the underlying disorder (for example, alcohol withdrawal). Sedatives can increase cognitive disorganization in delirious patients. When the delirium is due to anticholinergic toxicity, the use of *physostigmine salicylate (Antilirum)* 1 to 2 mg intravenously or intramuscularly, with repeated doses in 15 to 30 minutes, may be indicated; but it is not the first drug to be used in an acute delirium in which the cause has not been determined.

10.6.   The answer is C (*Synopsis VII*, page 338).

The incidence of delirium after open-heart and coronary-bypass surgery is about *30 percent*. Delirium is the psychiatric syndrome encountered most often by psychiatrists who are called to consult on patients in medical and surgical wards. 40 to 50 percent of patients who are recovering from surgery for hip fractures have an episode of delirium. An estimated 20 percent of patients with severe burns and 30 percent of patients with acquired immune deficiency syndrome (AIDS) have episodes of delirium while hospitalized.

10.7.   The answer is E (*Synopsis VII*, page 343).

The distinction between delirium and dementia may be difficult or, at times, impossible to make, particularly during the transition between delirium and dementia. *Visual hallucinations and transient delusions are more common in delirium than in dementia. The onset of delirium is generally sudden*, but prodromal symptoms (for example, daytime restlessness, anxiety, fearfulness, and hypersensitivity to light or sounds) may occur. *The duration of delirium is usually less than one month*. Also, *in delirium, symptoms worsen at night*, and *the sleep-wake cycle is disrupted*. Intellectual deterioration of more than one month is more likely in dementia than in delirium. Table 10.2 presents the frequency of clinical features of delirium contracted with dementia.

10.8.   The answer is C (*Synopsis VII*, pages 364–365).

Petit mal epilepsy or absence seizure is associated with a characteristic generalized, bilaterally synchronous, 3-hertz spike-and-wave pattern in the electroencephalogram (EEG) and is often easily induced by hyperventilation. Petit mal epilepsy occurs predominantly in children. It usually consists of simple absence attacks lasting 5 to 10 seconds, during which the patient has an abrupt alteration in awareness and responsiveness and an interruption in motor activity. The child often has a blank stare associated with an upward deviation of the eyes and some mild twitching movements of the eyes, eyelids, face, or extremities. Petit mal epilepsy is usually a

Table 10.2
Frequency of Clinical Features of Delirium Contrasted with Dementia

Feature	Delirium	Dementia
Impaired memory	+ + +	+ + +
Impaired thinking	+ + +	+ + +
Impaired judgment	+ + +	+ + +
Clouding of consciousness	+ + +	−
Major attention deficits	+ + +	+*
Fluctuation over course of a day	+ + +	+
Disorientation	+ + +	+ +*
Vivid perceptual disturbances	+ +	+
Incoherent speech	+ +	+*
Disrupted sleep-wake cycle	+ +	+*
Nocturnal exacerbation	+ +	+*
Insight	+ +†	+†
Sudden onset	+ +	−‡

+ + + Always present.
+ + Usually present.
+ Occasionally present.
− Usually absent.
*More frequent in advanced stages of dementia.
†Present during lucid intervals or on recovery from delirium; present during early stages of dementia.
‡Onset may be sudden in some dementias, e.g., vascular dementia, hypoxemia, certain reversible dementias.
Table adapted from E H Liston: Diagnosis and management of delirium in the elderly patient. Psychiatr Ann *14*: 117, 1984. Used with permission.

fairly benign seizure disorder, often resolving after adolescence.

A *partial seizure* (also known as jacksonian epilepsy) is a type of epilepsy characterized by recurrent episodes of focal motor seizures. It begins with localized tonic or clonic contraction, increases in severity, spreads progressively through the entire body, and terminates in a generalized convulsion with loss of consciousness. *Grand mal epilepsy* is the major form of epilepsy. Gross tonic-clonic convulsive seizures are accompanied by loss of consciousness and, often, incontinence of stool or urine. *Psychomotor epilepsy* is a type of epilepsy characterized by recurrent behavior disturbances. Complex hallucinations or illusions, frequently gustatory or olfactory, often herald the onset of the seizure, which typically involves a state of impaired consciousness resembling a dream, during which paramnestic phenomena, such as *déjà vu* and *jamais vu*, are experienced and the patient exhibits repetitive, automatic, or semipurposeful behaviors. In rare instances, violent behavior may be prominent. The EEG reveals a localized seizure focus in the temporal lobe.

10.9.   The answer is E (all) (*Synopsis VII*, pages 351–352).

Dementia is characterized by a loss of cognitive and intellectual abilities that is severe enough to impair social or occupational performance. The diagnostic criteria for dementia include impairment in short-term memory and long-term memory, which means an inability to learn new information and to remember information that was known in the past. *Patients' ability to remember three objects after five minutes* can assess their short-term memory; *patients' ability to remember their place of birth or what happened yesterday* or *patients' funds of common information*, such as past U.S. Presidents, can test their long-term memory. Other criteria for the diagnosis of dementia include impairment of abstract thinking, which can be indicated by *the patient's ability to find similarities and differences between related words.*

10.10. The answer is E (all) (*Synopsis VII*, page 339).

Delirium has many organic causes, including *hypoglycemia, hypokalemia, migraine* and *infectious mononucleosis*. The term "delirium" denotes a transient disturbance characterized by a global impairment of cognitive functions and a widespread disturbance of cerebral metabolism. Many cerebral and systemic diseases and toxic agents can lead to delirium. Table 10.3 lists common causes of delirium.

10.11. The answer is E (all) (*Synopsis VII*, pages 347 and 349–350).

The diagnosis of dementia is vascular associated with *cerebrovascular disease*. The disorder affects small and medium cerebral vessels, producing multiple, widely spread cerebral lesions that result in a combination of neurological and psychiatric symptoms. Vascular dementia is also associated with *hypertension* and manifests *a stepwise progression of focal*, sometimes fluctuating, *motor symptoms*. Those symptoms are accompanied by dementia. The clinical description of the disorder includes a variety of symptoms, ranging from headaches, dizziness, and transient focal neurological symptoms to *such personality changes as emotional lability and hypochondriasis*. Table 10.4 gives the diagnostic criteria for vascular dementia.

10.12. The answer is E (all) (*Synopsis VII*, pages 357–358).

Amnestic disorders have *an impairment of memory as the single or predominant cognitive defect*. The memory pathology is of two types: *retrograde amnesia and anterograde amnesia*. Retrograde amnesia is the loss of memory of events that took place before the onset of the illness. Anterograde amnesia is the reduced ability to recall current events. Although short-term memory is impaired, the patient has *preservation of the ability for immediate recall*, as tested by digit span. Since a number of organic pathological factors and conditions can give rise to amnestic disorders, *evidence of a specific causative medical or substance-related factor* is required for the diagnosis. Table 10.5 gives the diagnostic criteria for amnestic disorder due to a general medical condition.

10.13. The answer is E (all) (*Synopsis VII*, pages 357 and 361).

The mode of onset, the course, and the prognosis of amnestic disorders depend on their causes. The

Table 10.3
Causes of Delirium

Intracranial causes
  Epilepsy and postictal states
  Brain trauma (especially concussion)
  Infections
    Meningitis
    Encephalitis
  Neoplasms
  Vascular disorders
Extracranial causes
  Drugs (ingestion or withdrawal) and poisons
    Anticholinergic agents
    Anticonvulsants
    Antihypertensive agents
    Antiparkisonian agents
    Antipsychotic drugs
    Cardiac glycosides
    Cimetidine
    Clonidine
    Disulfiram
    Insulin
    Opiates
    Phencyclidine
    Phenytoin
    Ranitidine
    Salicylates
    Sedatives (including alcohol) and hypnotics
    Steroids
  Poisons
    Carbon monoxide
    Heavy metals and other industrial poisons
  Endocrine dysfunction (hypofunction or hyperfunction)
    Pituitary
    Pancreas
    Adrenal
    Parathyroid
    Thyroid
  Diseases of nonendocrine organs
    Liver
      Hepatic encephalopathy
    Kidney and urinary tract
      Uremic encephalopathy
    Lung
      Carbon dioxide narcosis
      Hypoxia
    Cardiovascular system
      Cardiac failure
      Arrhythmias
      Hypotension
    Deficiency diseases
      Thiamine, nicotinic acid, B_{12}, or folic acid deficiencies
    Systemic infections with fever and sepsis
    Electrolyte imbalance of any cause
    Postoperative states
    Trauma (head or general body)

Table adapted from Charles E. Wells, M.D.

syndrome may be *transient, chronic,* or *permanent*, and the outcome may be complete or partial recovery of memory function or an irreversible or even *slowly progressive* memory defect. The transient syndrome

Table 10.4
Diagnostic Criteria for Vascular Dementia

A. The development of multiple cognitive deficits manifested by both

   (1) memory impairment (impaired ability to learn new information or to recall previously learned information)
   (2) one (or more) of the following cognitive disturbances:

      (a) aphasia (language disturbance)
      (b) apraxia (impaired ability to carry out motor activities despite intact motor function)
      (c) agnosia (failure to recognize or identify objects despite intact sensory function)
      (d) disturbance in executive functioning (i.e., planning, organizing, sequencing, abstracting)

B. The cognitive deficits in criteria A1 and A2 each cause significant impairment in social or occupational functioning and represent a significant decline from a previous level of functioning.

C. Focal neurological signs and symptoms (e.g., exaggeration of deep tendon reflexes, extensor plantar response, pseudobulbar palsy, gait abnormalities, weakness of an extremity) or laboratory evidence indicative of cerebrovascular disease (e.g., multiple infarctions involving cortex and underlying white matter) that are judged to be etiologically related to the disturbance.

D. The deficits do not occur exclusively during the course of a delirium.

Code based on predominant features:
   With delirium: if delirium is superimposed on the dementia
   With delusions: if delusions are the predominant feature
   With depressed mood: if depressed mood (including presentations that meet full symptom criteria for a major depressive episode) is the predominant feature. A separate diagnosis of mood disorder due to a general medical condition is not given.
   Uncomplicated: if none of the above predominates in the current clinical presentation

Specify if:
   With behavioral disturbance

Coding note: Also code cerebrovascular condition on Axis III.

Table from DSM-IV, *Diagnostic and Statistical Manual of Mental Disorders,* ed 4. Copyright American Psychiatric Association, Washington, 1994. Used with permission.

Table 10.5
Diagnostic Criteria for Amnestic Disorder
Due to a General Medical Condition

A. The development of memory impairment as manifested by impairment in the ability to learn new information or the inability to recall previously learned information.

B. The memory disturbance causes significant impairment in social or occupational functioning and represents a significant decline from a previous level of functioning.

C. The memory disturbance does not occur exclusively during the course of a delirium or a dementia.

D. There is evidence from the history, physical examination, or laboratory findings that the disturbance is the direct physiological consequence of a general medical condition (including physical trauma).

Specify if:
   Transient: if memory impairment lasts for 1 month or less
   Chronic: if memory impairment lasts for more than 1 month

Coding note: Include the name of the general medical condition on Axis I, e.g., amnestic disorder due to head trauma; also code the general medical condition on Axis III (see Appendix G for codes).

Table from DSM-IV, *Diagnostic and Statistical Manual of Mental Disorders,* ed 4. Copyright American Psychiatric Association, Washington, 1994. Used with permission.

Table 10.6
Major Causes of Amnestic Disorders

Systemic medical conditions
   Thiamine deficiency (Korsakoff's syndrome)
   Hypoglycemia
Primary brain conditions
   Seizures
   Head trauma (closed and penetrating)
   Cerebral tumors (especially thalamic and temporal lobe)
   Cerebrovascular diseases (especially thalamic and temporal lobe)
   Surgical procedures on the brain
   Encephalitis due to herpes simplex
   Hypoxia (including nonfatal hanging attempts and carbon monoxide poisoning)
   Transient global amnesia
   Electroconvulsive therapy
   Multiple sclerosis
Substance-related causes
   Alcohol use disorders
   Neurotoxins
   Benzodiazepines (and other sedative-hypnotics)
   Many over-the-counter preparations

may result from a head injury, carbon monoxide poisoning, temporal lobe epilepsy, migraine, cardiac arrest, or electroconvulsive therapy. Chronic memory impairment may result from subarachnoid hemorrhage, cerebral infarction, or herpes simplex encephalitis. A slowly progressive disorder suggests a brain tumor or dementia of the Alzheimer's type. Table 10.6 lists the major causes of amnestic disorders.

10.14. The answer is E (all) (*Synopsis VII*, pages 362–363, 366, 369, and 749).

In personality change due to a general medical condition, *many patients exhibit low drive and initiative. Emotions are typically labile and shallow,* with euphoria or apathy predominating. Apathy may lead one to assume the presence of a depressed mood, but *true sadness and depression are uncommon.* Temper outbursts may occur with little or no provocation, resulting in violent behavior; *the expression of impulses is characteristically disinhibited,* resulting in inappropriate jokes, a crude manner, improper sexual advances, or outright antisocial behavior. Evidence of some causative organic factors must antedate the onset of the syndrome. Table 10.7 lists the diagnostic criteria for personality change due to a general medical condition.

10.15–10.24

10.15. The answer is A (*Synopsis VII*, pages 343–344).

10.16. The answer is B (*Synopsis VII*, page 343).

10.17. The answer is A (*Synopsis VII*, page 341).

10.18. The answer is C (*Synopsis VII*, pages 344 and 356).

10.19. The answer is D (*Synopsis VII*, pages 341–343 and 351–354).

10.20. The answer is C (*Synopsis VII*, pages 340 and 352).

10.21. The answer is C (*Synopsis VII*, pages 343 and 353).

10.22. The answer is B (*Synopsis VII*, page 352).

10.23. The answer is A (*Synopsis VII*, page 339).

10.24. The answer is C (*Synopsis VII*, pages 339 and 346).

The differentiation between delirium and dementia can be difficult. A number of clinical features help in the differentiation. In contrast to the *sudden onset* of delirium dementia usually has an *insidious onset*. Although both conditions include cognitive impairment, the changes in dementia are relatively stable over time and do not fluctuate over the course of a day, for example. A patient with dementia is usually alert; a patient with delirium has episodes of *clouding of consciousness*. Both delirium and dementia are *reversible*, although delirium has a better chance of reversing if treatment is timely. *Insight*, defined as the awareness that one is mentally ill, is absent in both conditions. *Hallucinations* can occur in both conditions and must be differentiated from those that occur in schizophrenia. In general, the hallucinations of schizophrenic patients are more constant and better formed than are the hallucinations of delirious patients. *Sundowning* is observed in both demented and delirious patients. Sundowning is characterized by drowsiness, confusion, ataxia, and accidental falls just about bedtime. Kurt Goldstein described a *catastrophic reaction* in demented patients; it is marked by agitation secondary to the subjective awareness of one's intellectual deficits under stressful circumstances. The presence of delirium is a bad prognostic sign. Patients with delirium have a *high mortality rate*. The three-month mortality rate of patients who have an episode of delirium is estimated to be 23 to 33 percent; the one-year mortality rate may be as high as 50 percent. The major neurotransmitter hypothesized to be involved in delirium and dementia is acetylcholine. Several types of

Table 10.7
Diagnostic Criteria for Personality Change Due to a General Medical Condition

A. A persistent personality disturbance that represents a change from the individual's previous characteristic personality pattern. (In children, the disturbance involves a marked deviation from normal development or a significant change in the child's usual behavior patterns lasting at least 1 year.)

B. There is evidence from the history, physical examination, or laboratory findings that the disturbance is the direct physiological consequence of a general medical condition.

C. The disturbance is not better accounted for by another mental disorder (including other mental disorders due to a general medical condition).

D. The disturbance does not occur exclusively during the course of a delirium and does not meet criteria for a dementia.

E. The disturbance causes clinically significant distress or impairment in social, occupational, or other important areas of functioning.

Specify type:
   Labile type: if the predominant feature is affective lability
   Disinhibited type: if the predominant feature is poor impulse control as evidenced by sexual indiscretions, etc.
   Aggressive type: if the predominant feature is aggressive behavior
   Apathetic type: if the predominant feature is marked apathy and indifference
   Paranoid type: if the predominant feature is suspiciousness or paranoid ideation
   Other type: if the predominant feature is not one of the above, e.g., personality change associated with a seizure disorder
   Combined type: if more than one feature predominates in the clinical picture
   Unspecified type

Coding note: Include the name of the general medical condition on Axis I, e.g., personality change due to temporal lobe epilepsy; also code the general medical condition on Axis III.

Table from DSM-IV, *Diagnostic and Statistical Manual of Mental Disorders,* ed 4. Copyright American Psychiatric Association, Washington, 1994. Used with permission.

studies of delirium and dementia have shown a correlation between *decreased acetylcholine activity* in the brain and both delirium and dementia.

10.25–10.28

10.25. The answer is C (*Synopsis VII*, pages 345–348).

10.26. The answer is A (*Synopsis VII*, pages 345–346).

10.27. The answer is B (*Synopsis VII*, page 347).

10.28. The answer is D (*Synopsis VII*, pages 345–348).

Dementia of the Alzheimer's type is characterized by a severe loss of intellectual function with an *unknown* cause. The specific lesions found in Alzheimer's disease include *senile plaques and neurofibrillary changes. Pick's disease* is a rare form of dementia that has an *unknown cause.*

The disorder is distinctive in that it is characterized by *lobar atrophy.* The frontal and temporal lobes are usually the most seriously affected, the occipital lobes are less affected, and the parietal lobes are still less affected. The neurofibrillary changes and senile plaques that characterize Alzheimer's disease are absent. Neither dementia of the Alzheimer's type nor Pick's disease is *reversible.* Treatment can be only supportive.

10.29–10.33

10.29. The answer is D (*Synopsis VII*, pages 348 and 363).

10.30. The answer is A (*Synopsis VII*, pages 348 and 370).

10.31. The answer is C (*Synopsis VII*, page 370).

10.32. The answer is B (*Synopsis VII*, pages 92 and 368).

10.33. The answer is E (*Synopsis VII*, pages 369–370).

Huntington's disease, inherited in an autosomal dominant pattern, leads to major atrophy of the brain with extensive degeneration of the caudate nucleus. The onset is usually insidious and most commonly begins in late middle life. The course is one of gradual progression; *death occurs 15 to 20 years after the onset of the disease, and suicide is common.*

Creutzfeldt-Jakob disease is a rare degenerative brain disease caused by a *slow virus, with death occurring within two years of the diagnosis.* A computed tomography (CT) scan shows cerebellar and cortical atrophy.

Neurosyphilis (also known as *general paresis*) is a chronic dementia and psychosis caused by the tertiary form of syphilis that affects the brain. The presenting symptoms include a *manic syndrome with neurological signs in up to 20 percent of cases.*

Normal pressure hydrocephalus is associated with enlarged ventricles and normal cerebrospinal fluid (CSF) pressure. The characteristic signs include dementia, a gait disturbance, and urinary incontinence. The *treatment of choice is a shunt* of the CSF from the ventricular space to either the atrium or the peritoneal space. Reversal of the dementia and associated signs is sometimes dramatic after treatment.

Multiple sclerosis is characterized by diffuse multifocal lesions in the white matter of the central nervous system (CNS). Its clinical course is characterized by exacerbations and remissions. It has no known specific cause, although research has focused on slow viral infections and autoimmune disturbances. Multiple sclerosis is much *more prevalent in cold and temperate climates than in the tropics and subtropics,* is more common in women than in men, and is predominantly a disease of young adults.

10.34–10.38

10.34. The answer is C (*Synopsis VII*, pages 362–373).

10.35. The answer is D (*Synopsis VII*, page 288).

10.36. The answer is A (*Synopsis VII*, page 372).

10.37. The answer is B (*Synopsis VII*, pages 345 and 362–373).

10.38. The answer is E (*Synopsis VII*, page 372).

In acute *mercury poisoning,* the central nervous system symptoms of lethargy and restlessness may occur, but the primary symptoms are secondary to severe gastrointestinal irritation, with bloody stools, diarrhea, and vomiting leading to circulatory collapse because of dehydration. *Mad Hatter syndrome,* named for the Mad Hatter in *Alice's Adventures in Wonderland,* is a parody of the madness resulting from the inhalation of mercury nitrate vapors, for mercury nitrate was used in the past in the processing of felt hats.

Early intoxication with manganese produces *manganese madness,* with symptoms of headache, irritability, joint pains, and somnolence. Lesions involving the basal ganglia and pyramidal system result in gait impairment, rigidity, monotonous or whispering speech, tremors of the extremities and tongue, *masked facies* (manganese mask), micrographia, dystonia, dysarthria, and loss of equilibrium.

Thallium intoxication initially causes severe pains in the legs, diarrhea, and vomiting. Within a week, delirium, convulsions, cranial nerve palsies, blindness, choreiform movements, and coma may occur. Behavioral changes include paranoid thinking and depression, with suicidal tendencies. *Alopecia is* a common and important diagnostic clue.

Chronic *lead poisoning* occurs when the amount of lead ingested exceeds the ability to eliminate it. Toxic symptoms appear after several months. Treatment should be instituted as rapidly as possible, even without laboratory confirmation, because of the high mortality. The treatment of choice to facilitate lead excretion is the intravenous administration of *calcium disodium edetate* (Calcium Disodium Versenate) daily for five days. One gram is given in each dose.

Chronic *arsenic poisoning* has an insidious onset, with weakness, lethargy, anorexia, diarrhea, nausea, inflammation of the nose and the upper respiratory tract, coughing, soreness of the mouth, and dermatitis, with *increased pigmentation of the neck, eyelids, nipples, and axillae.*

Neuropsychiatric Aspects of Human Immunodeficiency Virus (HIV) Infection and Acquired Immune Deficiency Syndrome (AIDS)

As knowledge about infection with the human immunodeficiency virus (HIV) has increased, so has the role of psychiatry in the treatment of HIV-positive people and people with acquired immune deficiency syndrome (AIDS). Psychiatrists are increasingly involved in the diagnosis, treatment, and management of the psychological and psychiatric sequelae of HIV infection. AIDS, in fact, is now considered part of most medical workups of psychotic patients, something to be ruled out as an underlying cause of psychiatric signs and symptoms. Virtually every psychiatric sign and symptom may be the direct result of central nervous system (CNS) HIV infection, from subtle cognitive deficits to frank psychosis.

The psychological ramifications of HIV infection and AIDS may also be immense. Dealing with a diagnosis that is almost invariably (at least initially) heard as a death sentence and that still carries with it social and cultural stigmatization can easily lead to complex feelings of depression, anger, guilt, anxiety, and fear. Although many physically and emotionally healthy persons are living with HIV infection, many others suffer psychological consequences. Psychiatrists must understand both the psychodynamic effects and the psychiatric syndromes that HIV infection may cause.

Physicians must also understand the epidemiology of HIV infection and AIDS: how the infection is transmitted, who is most at risk, how it is diagnosed, how it is treated, and how it can be prevented. Physicians must be comfortable when discussing the issues of HIV infection and AIDS with their patients and must feel secure in their ability to answer questions from their patients and their patients' families.

The reader is referred to Chapter 11 in *Kaplan and Sadock's Synopsis VII*. Students can assess their knowledge by studying the questions and answers below.

HELPFUL HINTS

The following terms should be known by the student.

HIV-1 and HIV-2	*Pneumocystis carinii* pneumonia	AZT
retrovirus	*Candida albicans*	ddI
astrocytes	tuberculosis	psychopharmacology
T4 lymphocytes	AIDS dementia complex	psychotherapy
Kaposi's sarcoma	HIV encephalopathy	worried well
transmission	CNS infections	institutional care
ELISA	neuropsychiatric syndromes	Western blot analysis
false-positives	AIDS in children	pretest and posttest counseling
seropositive	confidentiality	

QUESTIONS

DIRECTIONS: Each of the questions or incomplete statements below is followed by five suggested responses or completions. Select the *one* that is *best* in each case.

11.1. The human immunodeficiency virus (HIV)
A. is a deoxyribonucleic acid (DNA) retrovirus
B. is not present in the tears of infected persons
C. cannot be transmitted through breast feeding
D. has infected 10 million people worldwide
E. does not infect glial cells within the central nervous system (CNS)

11.2. In persons infected by HIV
A. seroconversion usually occurs two weeks after infection
B. the estimated length of time from infection to the development of AIDS is five years
C. 10 percent have neuropsychiatric complications
D. the T4 lymphocyte count usually falls to abnormal levels during the asymptomatic period
E. the vast majority are infected by HIV type 2 (HIV-2)

11.3. At the end of 1993, statistics regarding HIV and AIDS revealed that
A. the number of HIV-infected men is growing four times faster than the number of HIV-infected women
B. more women are infected by HIV through heterosexual intercourse than through intravenous (IV) substance use
C. New York, Los Angeles, San Francisco, and Miami account for 30 percent of all AIDS cases
D. not every state in the United States has reported cases of AIDS
E. more than 1 million deaths in the United States were caused by AIDS

11.4. In tests for HIV
A. assays usually detect the presence of viral proteins
B. the enzyme-linked immunosorbent assay (ELISA) is used to confirm positive test results of the Western blot analysis
C. the results cannot be shared with other members of a medical treatment team
D. pretest counseling should not inquire why a person desires HIV testing
E. a person may have a true negative result, even if the person is infected by HIV

11.5. In the treatment of HIV and HIV-related disorders
A. azidothymidine (AZT) acts by inhibiting the adherence of glycoprotein-120 (GP-120) to the CD4 receptor on T4 lymphocytes
B. AZT has caused increased neuropsychiatric symptoms
C. patients taking haloperidol (Haldol) have decreased sensitivity to the drug's extrapyramidal effects
D. the entire range of psychotherapeutic approaches may be appropriate
E. pentamidine is used prophylactically to guard against the development of Cryptosporidium

11.6. Diseases affecting the central nervous system (CNS) in patients with AIDS include
A. atypical aseptic meningitis
B. *Candida albicans* abscess
C. primary CNS lymphoma
D. cerebrovascular infarction
E. all the above

11.7. All of the following statements about the serum test for HIV are true *except*
A. false-positive results occur in about 1 percent of persons tested
B. the Western blot analysis is less likely to give a false-positive result than is the enzyme-linked immunosorbent assay (ELISA)
C. a person should be notified immediately if the result of the enzyme-linked immunosorbent assay (ELISA) is positive
D. blood banks must exclude sera that are ELISA-positive
E. about 1 million Americans are seropositive to HIV

11.8. Which drug should be chosen for a depressed AIDS patient with some signs of a cognitive disorder?
A. Nortriptyline (Aventyl)
B. Amitriptyline (Elavil)
C. Thioridazine (Mellaril)
D. Fluoxetine (Prozac)
E. Lorazepam (Ativan)

11.9. In the psychotherapy for a homosexual AIDS patient
A. therapy with the patient's lover is unwarranted
B. a discussion of safe-sex practices is not necessary
C. such issues as terminal care and life-support systems should be avoided
D. the psychiatrist can help the patient deal with feelings of guilt
E. the patient should be advised not to come out to the family

ANSWERS

Neuropsychiatric Aspects of Human Immunodeficiency Virus (HIV) Infection and Acquired Immune Deficiency Syndrome (AIDS)

11.1. The answer is D (*Synopsis VII*, page 376).

At the end of 1993, the World Health Organization (WHO) estimated that the human immunodeficiency virus (HIV) *has infected 10 million people worldwide.* HIV *is not a deoxyribonucleic acid (DNA) retrovirus*; rather, it is a ribonucleic acid (RNA) retrovirus that was isolated and identified in 1983. HIV is present in the blood, the semen, and cervical and vaginal secretions; to a small extent, HIV *is present in the tears*, breast milk, and cerebrospinal fluid *of infected persons.* HIV *can be transmitted through breast feeding*; children can also be infected in utero when their mothers are HIV-positive. Once a person is infected by HIV, the virus targets primarily CD4+ lymphocytes, which are also called T4 (helper) lymphocytes. HIV *does infect glial cells within the central nervous system (CNS).* It reflects primarily gland cells, particularly astrocytes. Astrocytes are glial cells, the nonneuronal cellular elements found on the CNS that are believed to carry out important metabolic functions.

11.2. The answer is D (*Synopsis VII*, page 378).

The T4 lymphocyte count usually falls to abnormal levels during the asymptomatic period of HIV infection. The normal values are 71,000/mm³, and grossly abnormal values can be <200/mm³.

Seroconversion is the change after infection with HIV from a negative HIV antibody test result to a positive HIV antibody test result. *Seroconversion usually occurs 6 to 12 weeks after infection.* In rare cases, seroconversion can take 6 to 12 months. *The estimated length of time from infection to the development of AIDS is 8 to 11 years*, although that time is gradually increasing because of the early implementation of treatment. At least *50 percent* of HIV-infected patients *have neuropsychiatric complications*, which may be the first signs of the disease in about 10 percent of patients. Two types of HIV have been identified, HIV type 1 (HIV-1) and HIV type 2 (HIV-2). *The vast majority* of HIV-positive patients *are infected by HIV-1.* However, HIV-2 infection seems to be increasing in Africa.

11.3. The answer is B (*Synopsis VII*, page 376).

Statistics at the end of 1993 revealed that *more women are infected by HIV through heterosexual in-tercourse than through intravenous (IV) substance use.* That finding is the opposite of what had been found in years past.

The ratio of men to women who are infected by HIV is estimated to be 8 to 1, but *the number of HIV-infected women is growing four times faster than the number of HIV-infected men*, not vice versa. Although the geographic distribution is heavily skewed toward large urban centers—for example, *the cities of New York, Los Angeles, San Francisco, and Miami account for more than 50 percent of all AIDS cases—every state in the United States has reported cases of AIDS.* At the end of 1993, *more than 185,000 deaths in the United States were caused by AIDS*; 340,000 cases of AIDS were reported.

11.4. The answer is E (*Synopsis VII*, pages 376–377).

A person may have a true negative result, even if the person is infected by HIV, if the test takes place after infection but before seroconversion. *Assays do not usually detect the presence of viral proteins. The enzyme-linked immunosorbent assay (ELISA) is not used to confirm positive test results of the Western blot analysis.* Rather, the ELISA is used as an initial screening test because it is less expensive than the Western blot analysis and more easily used to screen a large number of samples. The ELISA is sensitive and reasonably specific; although it is unlikely to report a false-negative result, it may indicate a false-positive result. For that reason, positive results from an ELISA are confirmed by using the more expensive and cumbersome Western blot analysis, which is sensitive and specific.

Confidentiality is a key issue in serum testing. No persons should be given HIV tests without their prior knowledge and consent, although various jurisdictions and organizations (for example, the military) now require HIV testing for all its inhabitants or members. *The results can be shared with other members of a medical treatment team* but should be provided to no one else.

Any person who wants to be tested should probably be tested, although *pretest counseling should inquire why a person desires HIV testing* to detect unspoken concerns and motivations that may merit psychotherapeutic intervention.

11.5. The answer is D (*Synopsis VII*, pages 381–382).

Classic psychiatric syndromes (for example, anxiety disorders, depressive disorders, and psychotic disorders) are commonly associated with HIV-related disorders. *The entire range of psychotherapeutic approaches may be appropriate* for patients with HIV-related disorders. Both individual therapy and group therapy can be effective. Individual therapy may be either short-term or long-term and may be supportive, cognitive, behavioral, or psychodynamic. Group therapy techniques can range from psychodynamic to completely supportive in nature.

In patients infected with HIV, secondary prevention involves modification of the disease course. Azidothymidine (AZT) is an inhibitor of reverse transcriptase; it slows the course of the disease in many patients and prolongs the survival of some patients. *AZT does not act by inhibiting the binding of glycoprotein-120 to the CD4 receptor on T4 lymphocytes.* Although that is how the virus gains entrance into T4 lymphocytes, no clinically available drug blocks the process.

A number of studies have reported that treatment with *AZT does not cause increased neuropsychiatric symptoms*; rather, it prevents or reverses the neuropsychiatric symptoms associated with HIV encephalopathy. Although dopamine receptor antagonists such as haloperidol (Haldol) may be required for control of agitation, they should be used in as low a dosage as possible because *patients taking haloperidol have increased sensitivity to the drug's extrapyramidal effects.* Also, the prophylactic use of aerosolized pentamidine (Nebeu-Pent) and of trimethoprim (Bactrim) and sulfamethoxazole (Gantanol) against the development of *Pneumocystis carinii* is now in common practice. Aerosolized *pentamidine is not used prophylactically to guard against the development of Cryptosporidium*, which causes intermittent or severe watery diarrhea, primarily in HIV-positive homosexual men. No treatment is available.

11.6. The answer is E (all) (*Synopsis VII*, pages 377–378).

Most of the infections secondary to HIV involvement of the central nervous system (CNS) are viral or fungal. *Atypical aseptic meningitis, Candida albicans abscess, primary CNS lymphoma,* and *cerebrovascular infarction* can all affect a patient with AIDS. Table 11.1 lists the most common diseases affecting the CNS in patients with AIDS.

11.7. The answer is C (*Synopsis VII*, pages 376–378).

A *person should not be notified immediately if the result of the ELISA is positive* until a confirmatory test, such as the Western blot analysis, is conducted. The serum test used to detect HIV is the enzyme-linked immunosorbent assay (ELISA). *False-positive results* (nondiseased persons with abnormal test re-

Table 11.1
Diseases Affecting the CNS in Patients with AIDS

Primary viral diseases
  HIV encephalopathy
  Atypical aseptic meningitis
  Vacuolar myelopathy
Secondary viruses (encephalitis, myelitis, retinitis, vasculitis)
  Cytomegalovirus
  Herpes simplex virus types 1 and 2
  Herpes varicella-zoster virus
  Papovavirus (PML)
Nonviral infections (encephalitis, meningitis, abscess)
  Toxoplasma gondii
  Cryptococcus neoformans
  Candida albicans
  Histoplasma capsulatum
  Aspergillus fumigatus
  Coccidiodes immitis
  Acremonium albamensis
  Rhizopus species
  Mycobacterium avium-intracellulare
  Mycobacterium tuberculosis hominis
  Mycobacterium kansasii
  Listeria monocytogenes
  Nocardia asteroides
Neoplasms
  Primary CNS lymphoma
  Metastatic systemic lymphoma
  Metastatic Kaposi's sarcoma
Cerebrovascular diseases
  Infarction
  Hemorrhage
  Vasculitis
Complications of systemic therapy

Table from A Beckett: The neurobiology of human immunodeficiency virus infection. In *American Psychiatric Press Review of Psychiatry*, vol 9, A Tasman, S M Goldfinger, C A Kaufman, editors, p 595. American Psychiatric Press, Washington, 1990. Used with permission.

sults) *occur in about 1 percent of persons tested* with ELISA. If an ELISA result is suspected of being incorrect, the serum can be subjected to a *Western blot analysis*, which *is less likely to give a false-positive* or false-negative *result* (diseased person with normal test result) *than is the ELISA*. However, *blood banks must exclude sera that are ELISA-positive. About 1 million Americans are seropositive to HIV.*

11.8. The answer is D (*Synopsis VII*, page 381).

Antidepressants, particularly those with few anticholinergic side effects, are of benefit in treating depression. If a cognitive disorder is present, drugs with anticholinergic effects must be used cautiously to prevent atropine psychosis. *Fluoxetine (Prozac)* is an antidepressant drug that is unrelated to tricyclic and tetracyclic drugs and other available antidepressant agents and that has few anticholinergic side effects. It is a serotonergic drug that works by blocking the uptake of serotonin. It is considered when one wants to avoid such anticholinergic actions. Similar serotonergic agents include sertraline (Zoloft) and peroxetine (Paxil). Among the other antidepressants, *nortriptyline (Aventyl)* has fewer anticholinergic effects than *amitriptyline (Elavil)*. *Thioridazine (Mellaril)* is an antipsychotic, and *lorazepam (Ativan)* is a benzodiazepine, neither of which has antidepressant effects.

11.9. The answer is D (*Synopsis VII*, pages 381–382).

Psychotherapy with a homosexual AIDS patient requires great flexibility. *The psychiatrist can help the patient deal with feelings of guilt* regarding behaviors that contributed to AIDS and that are disapproved of by segments of society. For example, the feeling that he is being punished for a deviant lifestyle. *Therapy with the patient's lover is warranted* in many cases. *A discussion of safe-sex practices*, such as using condoms in anal sex, *is necessary*. Difficult health care decisions and *such issues as terminal care and life-support systems should be explored*. The treatment of homosexuals and bisexuals with AIDS often involves both helping *the patient to come out to the family* (that is, telling the family that the patient is homosexual) and dealing with the possible issues of rejection, guilt, shame, and anger.

Substance-Related Disorders

Many of the terms uses when discussing substance-related disorders are confusing and used incorrectly. To become knowledgeable in the field of substance-related disorders, one must be clear about addiction, dependence, abuse, tolerance, cross-tolerance, intoxication, and withdrawal. For instance, the term "addiction" has essentially been replaced by the term "dependence." Dependence implies a psychological and physical reliance on a substance that leads to substance-seeking behavior, an inability to stop using the substance, an increasing tolerance to its effects, and a deterioration in physical and mental health as a result of continued use of the substance. A substance-related disorder implies both a pattern of pathological use of the substance and impairment of many functions because of the use of the substance. Examples of pathological use include an inability to reduce use of the substance and repeated intoxication. Examples of impairment of functions include absences from work because of substance use, legal problems, and the loss of friends and jobs.

Tolerance is an important indicator of substance dependence. Tolerance is defined in the fourth edition of *Diagnostic and Statistical Manual of Mental Disorders* (DSM-IV) as a "need for markedly increased amounts of the substance intoxication or to achieve desired effect" or a "markedly diminished effect with continued use of the same amount of the substance." Tolerance may develop to one substance as the result of exposure to another, a phenomenon termed cross-tolerance. For instance, to withdraw someone from alcohol, many clinicians use a protocol of gradually decreasing benzodiazepine doses—essentially substituting the benzodiazepines for the alcohol. Alcohol and benzodiazepines are cross-tolerant. Tolerance varies widely among persons and can differ because of ethnic background.

For instance, many Asian people have a very low tolerance for alcohol because of a genetically determined difference in their enzyme metabolism of alcohol.

Substance abuse is differentiated from substance dependence primarily on the basis of the severity of the pattern of use and the impairment in functioning. In other words, substance abuse is a pattern of substance use that does not meet all the criteria for substance dependence.

Many substances can lead to the characteristic patterns of substance abuse and dependence. Some substances are legal and readily available (for example, alcohol, tobacco, and caffeine), some are legal and generally prescribed by physicians (for example, benzodiazepines and sedative-hypnotics), and some are illegal (for example, phencyclidine, inhalants, heroin, and hallucinogens). Some substances, although usually considered illegal, may be legally prescribed for clearly specified medical disorders. Those drugs include amphetamines, cocaine, and opioids. An estimated 20 percent of the 1.4 billion prescriptions written each year in the United States are for mood-altering drugs, including anxiolytics, sedatives, stimulants, and analgesics.

The epidemiology of substance-related disorders reflects how common the disorders are in the general population. For instance, the lifetime prevalence of alcohol dependence is estimated to be 13 to 14 percent; the prevalence of alcohol abuse is most likely higher than that. The lifetime prevalence of nonalcohol substance abuse has been estimated to be 6 percent. Those figures represent millions of people, and the financial and emotional effects of the maladaptive patterns of substance use on their families and on society are immense.

Substance-related disorders are often associated with coexisting mental disorders. Anxi-

126

ety disorders and depressive disorders are particularly prevalent among substance abusers. The debate about which disorder comes first is an active one. Some specific relationships exist between mood and anxiety symptoms and certain substances of abuse (for example, cocaine, amphetamines, and benzodiazepines). However, it is often difficult to determine whether a patient who is anxious or depressed is self-medicating with substances or has caused the mood symptoms by using substances. In many patients, it is a vicious cycle, with the mood symptoms and the substance abuse interacting, so that each exacerbates the other.

In DSM-IV, substance-related disorders are divided into 11 "specific categories based on the substance involved. Those categories are associated with the use of alcohol, amphetamines (and amphetaminelike substances), caffeine, cannabis, cocaine, hallucinogens, inhalants, nicotine, opioids, phencyclidine (and phencyclidinelike substances), and sedatives, hypnotics, and anxiolytics. For each of the specific substance-related disorders, DSM-IV discusses its definition, epidemiology, clinical features, and course.

Students are referred to Chapter 12 in *Kaplan and Sadock's Synopsis VII* to prepare for the questions and answers below that assess their knowledge of the subject.

HELPFUL HINTS

The student should know each of the terms below and the DSM-IV diagnostic criteria.

intoxication	fetal alcohol syndrome	cocaine delirium
withdrawal	disulfiram	cocaine psychotic disorder
WHO definitions	Al-Anon	amphetamine
substance dependence	sedative-hypnotic-anxiolytic	psychedelics
patterns of pathological use	DEA	LSD
tolerance	AIDS	DPT
cross-tolerance	opioid intoxication	PCP
dispositional tolerance	MPTP-induced parkinsonism	MDMA
psychological dependence	DMT	DOM
physical dependence	hallucinogen	STP
abuse	flashback	alcohol intoxication; blood levels
misuse	arylcyclohexylamine	idiosyncratic alcohol intoxication
substance abuse	THC	alcohol withdrawal
pathological alcohol use	amotivational syndrome	DTs
AA	nitrous oxide	alcohol delirium
blackouts	volatile hydrocarbons	alcohol psychotic disorder
methadone withdrawal	belladonna alkaloids	Korsakoff's and Wernicke's
LAMM	anticholinergic side effects	syndromes
opioid antagonists	sympathomimetic signs	hallucinogen persisting perception
opioid withdrawal	miosis	disorder
NIDA	mydriasis	opioid
anabolic steroids	caffeine	opiate
dementia	cocaine intoxication and	inhalant
persisting amnestic disorder	withdrawal	

QUESTIONS

DIRECTIONS: Each of the questions or incomplete statements below is followed by five suggested responses or completions. Select the *one* that is *best* in each case.

12.1. In a person with an alcohol-related disorder
A. alcohol withdrawal delirium should be treated with antipsychotics
B. the most common hallucinations during alcohol withdrawal are visual
C. the person loses consciousness during a blackout
D. idiosyncratic alcohol intoxication usually occurs after excessive alcohol consumption
E. the classic sign of alcohol withdrawal is tremulousness

12.2. Amphetamines
A. have their primary effects mediated through the cholinergic system
B. do not cause substance dependence
C. are used in the treatment of obesity
D. cause an intoxication syndrome easily distinguished from cocaine intoxication
E. are not associated with adverse physical effects

12.3. Cannabis
A. has its euphoric effect a few hours after smoking it
B. can have a profound effect on the user's respiratory rate
C. may induce a short-lived anxiety state
D. depresses the user's sensitivity to external stimuli
E. intoxication does not impair motor skills

12.4. Cocaine
A. competitively blocks dopamine reuptake by the dopamine transporter
B. does not lead to physiological dependence
C. -induced psychotic disorders are most common in those who snort cocaine
D. had been used by 40 percent of the United States population as of 1991
E. is no longer used as a local anesthetic

12.5. Hallucinogens
A. cause physical dependence
B. cause withdrawal symptoms characterized by increased fatigue and somnolence
C. are associated with a phenomenon known as flashback
D. cause perceptions to become blunted
E. have a number of medical uses

12.6. The lifetime use of inhalants is highest in
A. young adults aged 18 to 25 years
B. adults aged 26 to 34 years
C. youths aged 12 to 17 years
D. middle-aged adults 40 to 65 years old
E. adults over the age of 65

12.7. Adverse effects on the brain that have been associated with long-term inhalant use include all the following *except*
A. rhabdomyolysis
B. brain atrophy
C. decreased intelligence quotient (I.Q.)
D. electroencephalographic (EEG) changes
E. decreased cerebral blood flow

12.8. Acute phencyclidine (PCP) intoxication is *not* treated with
A. diazepam (Valium)
B. cranberry juice
C. phentolamine (Regitine)
D. phenothiazines
E. all the above

12.9. All the following are associated with caffeine withdrawal symptoms *except*
A. headaches
B. nervousness
C. hallucinations
D. depression
E. insomnia

12.10. Which of the following statements about opioid abuse and opioid dependence is true?
A. About a fourth of all Americans with opioid dependence live in the New York City area
B. About 500,000 persons with opioid dependence are in the United States
C. An estimated 2 percent of the United States population have used heroin
D. The male-to-female ratio of persons with opioid dependence is 1 to 1
E. Most users of opiates and opioids started to use substances in their late 20s to mid-30s

12.11. Which of the following drugs is an opiate antagonist?
A. Naloxone
B. Naltrexone
C. Nalorphine
D. Apomorphine
E. All the above

12.12. The heroin behavior syndrome includes
A. depression
B. fear of failure
C. low self-esteem
D. need for immediate gratification
E. all the above

12.13. The symptoms of benzodiazepine withdrawal include
A. dysphoria
B. intolerance for bright lights
C. nausea
D. muscle twitching
E. all the above

Questions 12.14–12.15

An 18-year-old high school senior was brought to the emergency room by police after being picked up wandering in traffic on the Triborough Bridge. He was angry, agitated, and aggressive and talked of various people who were deliberately trying to confuse him by giving him misleading directions. His story was rambling and disjointed, but he admitted to the police that he had been using speed. In the emergency room he had difficulty focusing his attention and had to ask that questions be repeated. He was disoriented as to time and place and was unable to repeat the names of three objects after five minutes. His family gave a history of the patient's regular use of pep pills over the previous two years, during which time he was frequently high and did poorly in school.

12.14. Which of the following is *not* a clinical effect of amphetamine intoxication?
A. Increased libido
B. Formication
C. Delirium
D. Catatonia
E. All the above

12.15. Abrupt discontinuation of an amphetamine produces
A. fatigue
B. dysphoria
C. nightmares
D. agitation
E. all the above

Questions 12.16–12.18

12.16. The patient is a 20-year-old man who was brought to the hospital, trussed in ropes, by his four brothers. It was his seventh hospitalization in the past two years, each for similar behavior. One of his brothers reported that he "came home crazy" late one night, threw a chair through a window, tore a gas heater off the wall, and ran into the street. The family called the police, who apprehended him shortly thereafter as he stood, naked, directing traffic at a busy intersection. He assaulted the arresting officers, escaped, and ran home screaming threats at his family. There his brothers were able to subdue him.

On admission, the patient was observed to be agitated, his mood fluctuating between anger and fear. He had slurred speech, and he staggered when he walked. He remained extremely violent and disorganized for the first several days of his hospitalization, then he began having longer and longer lucid intervals, still interspersed with sudden, unpredictable periods during which his speech was slurred, he displayed great suspiciousness, and he assumed a fierce expression and clenched his fists.

After calming down, the patient denied ever having been violent or acting in an unusual way ("I'm a peaceable man") and said that he could not remember how he got to the hospital. He admitted to using alcohol and marijuana socially but denied phencyclidine (PCP) use except once, experimentally, three years previously. Nevertheless, blood and urine tests were positive for phencyclidine, and a brother said that "he gets dusted every day."

After three weeks of hospitalization, the patient was released, still sullen and watchful and quick to remark sarcastically on the smallest infringement of the respect due him. He was mostly quiet and isolated from others but was easily provoked to fury. His family reported that "this is as good as he gets now." He lived and ate most of his meals at home, and kept himself physically clean, but mostly he lay around the house, did no housework, and had not held a job for nearly two years. The family did not know how he got his spending money or how he spent his time outside the hospital.

Which of the following diagnoses does not apply in the above case?
A. Substance intoxication
B. Phencyclidine-induced psychotic disorders, with hallucinations
C. Substance dependence
D. Hallucinogen persisting perception disorder
E. All the above

12.17. A 55-year-old man with a long history of alcohol dependence was admitted to a medical ward. At the time of admission, he was noted to have alcohol on his breath. Two days after admission he became acutely agitated and reported hearing other patients calling him homosexual. He appeared to be alert and well-oriented. The patient was probably exhibiting symptoms of
A. schizophrenia
B. delirium tremens (alcohol withdrawal)
C. alcohol-induced psychotic disorder, with hallucinations
D. pathological intoxication (idiosyncratic alcohol intoxication)
E. methanol intoxication

12.18. A 20-year-old man was seen in the emergency room in a severely agitated state. He was labile emotionally, appeared to be frightened and markedly anxious, and showed slurred speech and dysarthria. According to a friend, the patient took angel dust about an hour before being seen in the emergency room. The reaction the patient was having was probably
A. caused by phencyclidine (PCP)
B. spontaneously cleared within 48 hours
C. diagnosed by urine testing for PCP
D. accompanied by violent acts
E. all the above

DIRECTIONS: Each set of lettered headings below is followed by a list of numbered words or phrases. For each numbered word or phrase, select

A. if the item is associated with *A only*
B. if the item is associated with *B only*
C. if the item is associated with *both A and B*
D. if the item is associated with *neither A nor B*

Questions 12.19–12.22
A. Alcohol withdrawal delirium
B. Alcohol-induced psychotic disorder, with hallucinations
C. Both
D. Neither

12.19. Withdrawal seizures

12.20. Auditory hallucinations

12.21. Clear sensorium

12.22. Benzodiazepine

Questions 12.23–12.27
A. Intoxication
B. Withdrawal
C. Both
D. Neither

12.23. Follows the recent ingestion and the presence in the body of a substance.

12.24. Follows the cessation or the reduction of the intake of a substance

12.25. Is a substance-specific syndrome

12.26. The clinical picture may correspond to one of the cognitive disorders

12.27. Requires maladaptive behavior as an essential diagnostic criterion

Questions 12.28–12.32
A. Benzodiazepines
B. Barbiturates
C. Both
D. Neither

12.28. Cause rapid eye movement (REM) sleep suppression

12.29. Symptoms of withdrawal usually appear within three days

12.30. High suicide potential

12.31. Clinically used as muscle relaxants

12.32. Antipsychotics

DIRECTIONS: The questions below consist of lettered headings followed by a list of numbered words or phrases. For each numbered word or phrase, select the *one* lettered heading that is most closely associated with it. Each lettered heading may be selected once, more than once, or not at all.

Questions 12.33–12.39
A. γ-Aminobutyric acid (GABA) receptor system
B. Opiate receptor system
C. Glutamate receptor system
D. Adenosine receptor system
E. Acetylcholine receptor system

12.33. Ethanol

12.34. Phenobarbital

12.35. Diazepam

12.36. Heroin

12.37. Phencyclidine (PCP)

12.38. Caffeine

12.39. Nicotine

ANSWERS

Substance-Related Disorders

12.1. The answer is E (*Synopsis VII*, pages 402 and 404–406).

In the diagnosed criteria for alcohol withdrawal in the fourth edition of *Diagnostic and Statistical Manual of Mental Disorders* (DSM-IV) (Table 12.1), *the classic sign of alcohol withdrawal is tremulousness.* Tremulousness (commonly called the shakes or jitters) develops six to eight hours after the cessation of drinking. The tremor of alcohol withdrawal can be similar to physiological tremor, with a continuous tremor of great amplitude and faster than 8 Hz, or to familial tremor, with bursts of tremor slower than 8 Hz.

Alcohol withdrawal delirium should not be treated with antipsychotics, which may reduce the seizure threshold in the patient. The best treatment for alcohol withdrawal delirium is its prevention. Patients who are withdrawing from alcohol who exhibit any withdrawal phenomena should receive a benzodiazepine, such as 25 to 50 mg of chlordiazepoxide (Librium) every two to four hours until they seem to be out of danger. Once the delirium appears, however, 50 to 100 mg of chlordiazepoxide should be given

Table 12.1
Diagnostic Criteria for Alcohol Withdrawal

A. Cessation of (or reduction in) alcohol use that has been heavy and prolonged.

B. Two (or more) of the following, developing within several hours to a few days after criterion A:

   (1) autonomic hyperactivity (e.g., sweating or pulse rate greater than 100)
   (2) increased hand tremor
   (3) insomia
   (4) nausea and vomiting
   (5) transient visual, tactile, or auditory hallucinations or illusions
   (6) psychomotor agitation
   (7) anxiety
   (8) grand mal seizures

C. The symptoms in criterion B cause clinically significant distress or impairment in social, occupational, or other important areas of functioning.

D. The symptoms are not due to a general medical condition and not better accounted for by another mental disorder.

Specify if:
   With perceptual disturbances

Table from DSM-IV, *Diagnostic and Statistical Manual of Mental Disorders*, ed 4. Copyright American Psychiatric Association, Washington, 1994. Used with permission.

every four hours orally, or intravenous lorazepam (Ativan) should be used if oral medication is not possible (Table 12.2).

The most common hallucinations during alcohol withdrawal are auditory, usually voices. The voices are characteristically maligning, reproachful, or threatening, although some patients report that the voices are pleasant and nondisruptive. Blackouts are not included in the DSM-IV diagnostic classification of alcohol use disorders (Table 12.3).

A *person does not lose consciousness during a blackout.* Instead, the person experiences anterograde amnesia, which can be distressing because the person may fear that he or she has unknowingly harmed someone or behaved imprudently while intoxicated.

Idiosyncratic alcohol intoxication (previously referred to as pathological intoxication) *does not usually occur after excessive alcohol consumption.* Instead, it is a severe behavioral syndrome that develops rapidly after the person consumes a small amount of alcohol that in most people has minimal behavioral effects. Idiosyncratic alcohol intoxication is an example of an alcohol use disorder not otherwise specified (Table 12.4).

12.2. The answer is C (*Synopsis VII*, page 411).

Amphetamines *are used in the treatment of obesity,* although their safety and efficacy for that indication are controversial. They are also used for attention-deficit/hyperactivity disorder, narcolepsy, and some depressive disorders.

Amphetamines do not have their primary effects mediated through the cholinergic system. Instead, they cause the release of catecholamines, particularly dopamine, from presynaptic terminals. The designer amphetamines (for example, MDMA, MDEA, MMDA, and DOM) also cause the release of serotonin.

Amphetamines *do cause substance dependence* (Table 12.5). Amphetamine dependence can result in a rapid down spiral of a person's abilities to cope with work-related and family-related obligations and stresses. An amphetamine-abusing person requires increasingly high doses of amphetamine to obtain the usual high, and physical signs of amphetamine abuse (for example, decreased weight and paranoid ideas) almost always develop with continued abuse. Table 12.6 lists the diagnostic criteria for substance abuse.

Amphetamines *cause an intoxication syndrome that is not easily distinguished from cocaine intoxi-*

Table 12.2
Drug Therapy for Alcohol Intoxication and Withdrawal

Clinical Problem	Drug	Route	Dosage	Comment
Tremulousness and mild to moderate agitation	Chlordiazepoxide	Oral	25–100 mg every 4–6 hrs	Initial dose can be repeated every 2 hours until patient is calm; subsequent doses must be individualized and titrated
	Diazepam	Oral	5–20 mg every 4–6 hrs	
Hallucinosis	Lorazepam	Oral	2–10 mg every 4–6 hrs	
Extreme agitation	Chlordiazepoxide	Intravenous	0.5 mg/kg at 12.5 mg/min	Give until patient is calm; subsequent doses must be individualized and titrated
Withdrawal seizures	Diazepam	Intravenous	0.15 mg/kg at 2.5 mg/min	
Delirium tremens	Lorazepam	Intravenous	0.1 mg/kg at 2.0 mg/min	

Table adapted from J K Weser, E M Sellers, H Kalant: Drug therapy: Alcohol Intoxication and withdrawal. N Engl J Med *294:* 757, 1976. Used with permission. Table from F A Rubino: Neurologic complications of alcoholism. Psychiatr Clin North Am *15:* 364, 1992. Used with permission.

Table 12.3
Alcohol-Related Disorders

Alcohol use disorders

Alcohol dependence
Alcohol abuse

Alcohol-induced disorders

Alcohol intoxication
Alcohol withdrawal
    Specify if: with perceptual disturbances
Alcohol intoxication delirium
Alcohol withdrawal delirium
Alcohol-induced persisting dementia
Alcohol-induced persisting amnestic disorder
Alcohol-induced psychotic disorder, with delusions
    Specify if: with onset during intoxication/with onset during withdrawal
Alcohol-induced psychotic disorder, with hallucinations
    Specify if: with onset during intoxication/with onset during withdrawal
Alcohol-induced mood disorder
    Specify if: with onset during intoxication/with onset during withdrawal
Alcohol-induced anxiety disorder
    Specify if: with onset during intoxication/with onset during withdrawal
Alcohol-induced sexual dysfunction
    Specify if: with onset during intoxication
Alcohol-induced sleep disorder
    Specify if: with onset during intoxication/with onset during withdrawal

Alcohol-related disorder not otherwise specified

Table based on DSM-IV, *Diagnostic and Statistical Manual of Mental Disorders,* ed 4. Copyright American Psychiatric Association, Washington, 1994. Used with permission.

Table 12.4
Diagnostic Criteria for Alcohol-Related Disorder Not Otherwise Specified

The alcohol-related disorder not otherwise specified category is for disorders associated with the use of alcohol that are not classifiable as alcohol dependence, alcohol abuse, alcohol intoxication, alcohol withdrawal, alcohol intoxication delirium, alcohol withdrawel delirium, alcohol-induced persisting dementia, alcohol-induced persisting amnestic disorder, alcohol-induced psychotic disorder, alcohol-induced mood disorder, alcohol-induced anxiety disorder, alcohol-induced sexual dysfunction, or alcohol-induced sleep disorder.

Table DSM-IV, *Diagnostic and Statistical Manual of Mental Disorders,* ed 4. Copyright American Psychiatric Association, Washington, 1994. Used with permission.

cation. Table 12.7 presents the diagnostic criteria for amphetamine intoxication.

Amphetamines *are associated with adverse physical effects.* Cerebrovascular, cardiac, and gastrointestinal effects are among the most serious adverse effects associated with amphetamine abuse. The specific life-threatening conditions include myocardial infarction, severe hypertension, cerebrovascular disease, and ischemic colitis. A continuum of neurological symptoms, from twitching to tetany to seizures to coma and death, is associated with increasingly high amphetamine doses. The less than life-threatening adverse effects include flushing, pallor, cyanosis, fever, headache, tachycardia, palpitations, nausea, vomiting, bruxism (teeth grinding), shortness of breath, tremor, and ataxia.

Table 12.5
Diagnostic Criteria for Substance Dependence

A maladaptive pattern of substance use, leading to clinically significant impairment or distress, as manifested by three (or more) of the following, occurring at any time in the same 12-month period:

(1) tolerance, as defined by either of the following:
    (a) need for markedly increased amounts of the substance to achieve intoxication or desired effect
    (b) markedly diminished effect with continued use of the same amount of the substance
(2) withdrawal, as manifested by either of the following:
    (a) the characteristic withdrawal syndrome for the substance (refer to criteria A and B of the criteria sets for withdrawal from the specific substances)
    (b) The same (or closely related) substance is taken to relieve or avoid withdrawal symptoms
(3) the substance is often taken in larger amounts or over a longer period than was intended
(4) there is a persistent desire or unsuccessful efforts to cut down or control substance use
(5) a great deal of time is spent in activities necessary to obtain the substance (e.g., visiting multiple doctors or driving long distances), use the substance (e.g., chain-smoking), or recover from its effects
(6) important social, occupational, or recreational activities given up or reduced because of substance use
(7) the substance use is continued despite knowledge of having a persistent or recurrent physical or psychological problem that is likely to have been caused or exacerbated by the substance (e.g., current cocaine use despite recognition of cocaine-induced depression, or continued drinking despite recognition that an ulcer was made worse by alcohol consumption)

Specify if:
    With physiological dependence: evidence of tolerance or withdrawal (i.e., either item 1 or 2 is present)
    Without physiological dependence: no evidence of tolerance or withdrawal (i.e., neither 1 nor 2 is present)

Course specifiers:
    Early full remission
    Early partial remission
    Sustained full remission
    Sustained partial remission
    On agonist therapy
    In a controlled environment

Table from DSM-IV, *Diagnostic and Statistical Manual of Mental Disorders*, ed 4. Copyright American Psychiatric Association, Washington, 1994. Used with permission.

12.3. The answer is C (*Synopsis VII*, page 422).

Cannabis *may induce a short-lived anxiety state*, diagnosed as cannabis-induced anxiety disorder (Table 12.8). Panic attacks may be induced, based on ill-defined and disorganized fears. The appearance of anxiety symptoms is correlated with the dose and is the most frequent adverse reaction to the moderate use of smoked cannabis. Inexperienced users are much more likely to experience anxiety symptoms than are experienced users.

Table 12.6
Diagnostic Criteria for Substance Abuse

A. A maladaptive pattern of substance use leading to clinically significant impairment or distress, as manifested by one (or more) of the following, occurring within a 12-month period:

    (1) recurrent substance use resulting in a failure to fulfill major role obligations at work, school, or home (e.g., repeated absences or poor work performance related to substance use; substance-related absences, suspensions, or expulsions from school; neglect of children or household)
    (2) recurrent substance use in situations in which it is physically hazardous (e.g., driving an automobile or operating a machine when impaired by substance use)
    (3) recurrent substance-related legal problems (e.g., arrests for substance-related disorderly conduct)
    (4) continued substance use despite having persistent or recurrent social or interpersonal problems caused or exacerbated by the effects of the substance (e.g., arguments with spouse about consequences of intoxication, physical fights)

B. The symptoms above never met the criteria for substance dependence for this class of substance.

Table from DSM-IV, *Diagnostic and Statistical Manual of Mental Disorders*, ed 4. Copyright American Psychiatric Association, Washington, 1994. Used with permission.

Table 12.7
Diagnostic Criteria for Amphetamine Intoxication

A. Recent use of amphetamine or a related substance (e.g., methylphenidate).

B. Clinically significant maladaptive behavioral or psychological changes (e.g., euphoria or affective blunting; changes in sociability; hypervigilance; interpersonal sensitivity; anxiety, tension, or anger; stereotyped behaviors; impaired judgment; or impaired social or occupational functioning) developing during, or shortly after, use of amphetamine or a related substance.

C. Two (or more) of the following, developing during, or shortly after, use of amphetamine or related substance:

    (1) tachycardia or bradycardia
    (2) pupillary dilation
    (3) elevated or lowered blood pressure
    (4) perspiration or chills
    (5) nausea or vomiting
    (6) evidence of weight loss
    (7) psychomotor agitation or retardation
    (8) muscular weakness, respiratory depression, chest pain, or cardiac arrhythmias
    (9) confusion, seizures, dyskinesias, dystonias, or coma

D. The symptoms are not due to a general medical condition and not better accounted for by another mental disorder.

Specify if:
    With perceptual disturbances

Table from DSM-IV, *Diagnostic and Statistical Manual of Mental Disorders*, ed 4. Copyright American Psychiatric Association, Washington, 1994. Used with permission.

Table 12.8
Diagnostic Criteria for Substance-Induced Anxiety Disorder

A. Prominent anxiety, panic attacks, obsessions or compulsions predominate in the clinical picture.

B. There is evidence from the history, physical examination, or laboratory findings of either (1) or (2):

(1) the symptoms in criterion A developed during, or within 1 month of, substance intoxication or withdrawal

(2) medical use is etiologically related to the disturbance

C. The disturbance is not better accounted for by an anxiety disorder that is not substance induced. Evidence that the symptoms are better accounted for by an anxiety disorder that is not substance induced might include the following: the symptoms precede the onset of the substance use (or medication use); the symptoms persist for a substantial period of time (e.g., about a month) after the cessation of acute withdrawal or severe intoxication or are substantially in excess of what would be expected given the type or amount of the substance used or the duration of use; or there is other evidence suggesting the existence of an independent non-substance-induced anxiety disorder (e.g., a history of recurrent non-substance-related panic episodes).

D. The disturbance does not occur exclusively during the course of a delirium.

E. The disturbance causes clinically significant distress or impairment in social, occupational, or other important areas of functioning.

Note: This diagnosis should be made instead of a diagnosis of Substance Intoxication or Substance Withdrawal only when the anxiety symptoms are in excess of those usually associated with the intoxication or withdrawal syndrome and when the anxiety symptoms are sufficiently severe to warrant independent clinical attention.

Code: [Specific substance]-induced anxiety disorder (Alcohol; amphetamine [or amphetamine-like substance]; caffeine; cannabis; cocaine; hallucinogen; inhalant; phencyclidine [or phencyclidine-like substance]; sedative, hypnotic, or anxiolytic; other [or unknown] substance)

Specify if:
With generalized anxiety: is excessive anxiety or worry about a number of events or activities predominates in the clinical presentation
With panic attacks: if panic attacks predominate in the clinical presentation
With obsessive-compulsive symptoms: if obsessions or compulsions predominate in the clinical presentation
With phobic symptoms: if phobic symptoms predominate in the clinical presentation

Specify if:
With onset during intoxication: if the criteria are met for intoxication with the substance and the symptoms develop during the intoxication syndrome
With onset during withdrawal: if criteria are met for withdrawal from the substance and the symptoms develop during, or shortly after, a withdrawal syndrome

When cannabis is smoked, *its euphoric effects appear within minutes,* peak in about 30 minutes, and last two to four hours. Some of the motor and cognitive effects last 5 to 12 hours.

Cannabis does *not have an effect on the user's respiratory rate.* Probably for that reason, no case of death caused by cannabis intoxication has been clearly documented.

Cannabis use commonly *heightens the user's sensitivity to external stimuli,* reveals new details, makes colors seem brighter and richer than in the past, and subjectively slows down the appreciation of time. In high doses, the user may also experience depersonalization and derealization.

Cannabis *intoxication* (Table 12.9) *does impair motor skills,* and the impairment remains after the subjective, euphoriant effects have resolved. For 8 to 12 hours after using cannabis, the impairment of motor skills interferes with the operation of motor vehicles and other heavy machinery. Moreover, those effects are additive to those of alcohol, which is commonly used in combination with cannabis.

12.4.   The answer is A (*Synopsis VII*, page 424).

Cocaine *competitively blocks dopamine reuptake by the dopamine transporter.* That primary pharmacodynamic effect is believed to be related to cocaine's behavioral effects, including elation, euphoria, heightened self-esteem, and perceived improvement on mental and physical tasks. Table 12.10 presents the diagnostic criteria for cocaine intoxication.

Cocaine *does lead to physiological dependence,* although cocaine withdrawal (Table 12.11) is mild compared with the effects of withdrawal from opiates and opioids. A psychological dependence on cocaine

Table 12.9
Diagnostic Criteria for Cannabis Intoxication

A. Recent use of cannabis.

B. Clinically significant maladaptive behavioral or psychological changes (e.g., impaired motor coordination, euphoria, anxiety, sensation of slowed time, impaired judgment, social withdrawal) that developed during, or shortly after, cannabis use.

C. Two (or more) of the following signs, developing within 2 hours of cannabis use:

(1) conjunctival injection
(2) increased appetite
(3) dry mouth
(4) tachycardia

D. The symptoms are not due to a general medical condition and are not better accounted for by another mental disorder.

Specify if:
With perceptual disturbances

Table 12.10
Diagnostic Criteria for Cocaine Intoxication

A. Recent use of cocaine.

B. Clinically significant maladaptive behavioral or psychological changes (e.g., euphoria or affective blunting; changes in sociability; hypervigilance; interpersonal sensitivity; anxiety, tension, or anger; stereotyped behaviors; impaired judgment; or impaired social or occupational functioning) that developed during, or shortly after, use of cocaine.

C. Two (or more) of the following, developing during, or shortly after, use:

(1) tachycardia or bradycardia
(2) pupillary dilation
(3) elevated or lowered blood pressure
(4) perspiration or chills
(5) nausea or vomiting
(6) evidence of weight loss
(7) psychomotor agitation or retardation
(8) muscular weakness, respiratory depression, chest pain, or cardiac arrhythmias
(9) confusion, seizures, dyskinesias, dystonias, or coma

D. The symptoms are not due to a general medical condition and are not better accounted for by another mental disorder.

Specify if:
With perceptual disturbances

Table from DSM-IV, *Diagnostic and Statistical Manual of Mental Disorders,* ed 4. Copyright American Psychiatric Association, Washington, 1994. Used with permission.

can develop after a single use because of its potency as a positive reinforcer of behavior.

Cocaine-*induced psychotic disorders are most common in intravenous (IV) users and crack users, not in those who snort cocaine.*

The National Institute of Drug Abuse (NIDA) reported that cocaine *had been used by 12 percent, not 40 percent, of the United States population as of 1991.* The highest use was in the 18-to-25-year-old age group; 18 percent of them had used cocaine at least once, and 2 percent were current users. In that age group, 3.8 percent had used crack at least once. Although cocaine use is highest among the unemployed, cocaine is also used by highly educated persons in high socioeconomic groups. Cocaine use among males is twice as frequent as cocaine use among females.

Despite its reputation as the most addictive commonly abused substance and one of the most dangerous, cocaine does have some important medical applications. Cocaine *is still used as a local anesthetic,* especially for eye, nose, and throat surgery, for which its vasoconstrictive effects are helpful.

12.5. The answer is C (*Synopsis VII*, pages 430–431).

Hallucinogens *are associated with a phenomenon known as flashback,* which involves hallucinogens symptoms that appear long after the ingestion of a hallucinogen. The syndrome is diagnosed as hallucinogen persisting perception disorder (Table 12.12).

Hallucinogens *do not cause physical dependence.* However, a user may experience a psychological dependence on the insight-inducing experiences seemingly associated with hallucinogen use. Hallucinogens *do not cause withdrawal symptoms.*

Hallucinogens *do not cause perceptions to become*

Table 12.11
Diagnostic Criteria for Cocaine Withdrawal

A. Cessation if (or reduction in) cocaine use that has been heavy and prolonged.

B. Dysphoric mood and two (or more) of the following physiological changes, developing within a few hours to several days after criterion A:

(1) fatigue
(2) vivid, unpleasant dreams
(3) insomnia or hypersomnia
(4) increased appetite
(5) psychomotor retardation or agitation

C. The symptoms in criterion B cause clinically significant distress or impairment in social, occupational, or other important areas of functioning.

D. The sypmtoms are not due to a general medical condition and are not better accounted for by another mental disorder.

Table from DSM-IV, *Diagnostic and Statistical Manual of Mental Disorders,* ed 4. Copyright American Psychiatric Association, Washington, 1994. Used with permission.

Table 12.12
Diagnostic Criteria for Hallucinogen Persisting Perception Disorder (Flashbacks)

A. The reexperiencing, following cessation of use of a hallucinogen, of one or more of the perceptual symptoms that were experienced while intoxicated with the hallucinogen (e.g., geometric hallucinations, false perceptions of movement in the peripheral visual fields, flashes of color, intensified colors, trails of images of moving objects, positive afterimages, halos around objects, macropsia, and micropsia).

B. The symptoms in criterion A cause clinically significant distress or impairment in social, occupational, or other important areas of functioning.

C. The symptoms are not due to a general medical condition (e.g., anatomical lesions and infections of the brain, visual epilepsies) and are not better accounted for by another mental disorder (e.g., delirium, dementia, schizophrenia) or hypnopompic hallucinations.

Table from DSM-IV, *Diagnostic and Statistical Manual of Mental Disorders,* ed 4. Copyright American Psychiatric Association, Washington, 1994. Used with permission.

blurred. Rather, perceptions become unusually brilliant and intense. Colors and textures seem to be richer than in the past, contours sharpened, music more emotionally profound, and smells and tastes heightened. Synesthesia is common; colors may be heard or sounds seen. Table 12.13 lists the diagnostic criteria for hallucinogen intoxication.

Hallucinogens *have no medical uses.*

12.6. The answer is A (*Synopsis VII*, page 433).

According to the National Institute of Drug Abuse (NIDA), *young adults aged 18 to 25 years* make up the largest group to have used inhalants in their lifetimes; 10.9 percent of that age group have used inhalants. Among the *adults aged 26 to 34 years,* 9.2 percent have used inhalants; 7 percent of *youths aged 12 to 17 years* have used inhalants, and only 2.5 percent of adults over 35, including *middle-aged adults 40 to 65 years old,* have used inhalants. Inhalant use is minimal in *adults over the age of 65.*

12.7. The answer is A (*Synopsis VII*, page 435).

Rhabdomyolysis does not affect the brain. It is a potentially fatal disease that entails destruction of skeletal muscles. It is a reported adverse effect of inhalant use that, if not fatal, results in permanent muscle damage.

The combination of organic solvents and high concentrations of copper, zinc, and heavy metals has been associated with the development of *brain atrophy,* temporal lobe epilepsy, *decreased intelligence quotient (I.Q.),* and a variety of *electroencephalographic (EEG) changes.* Several studies of house painters and factory workers who have been exposed to solvents for long periods have found evidence of brain atrophy on computed tomography (CT) scans and *decreased cerebral blood flow.*

12.8. The answer is D (*Synopsis VII*, pages 449–450).

Phenothiazines are not used in the treatment of acute phencyclidine (PCP) intoxication because they have anticholinergic effects that may potentiate the adverse effects of PCP, such as seizures. *Diazepam (Valium)* is of use in reducing agitation. If agitation is severe, however, the antipsychotic haloperidol (Haldol) may have to be used. *Cranberry juice* is used to acidify the urine and to promote the elimination of the drug. Ammonium chloride or ascorbic acid also serves the same purpose. *Phentolamine (Regitine)* is a hypotensive agent that may be needed to deal with severe hypertensive crises produced by PCP.

12.9. The answer is C (*Synopsis VII*, page 418).

Hallucinations are false sensory perceptions occurring in the absence of any relevant external stimulation of the sensory modality involved. Hallucinations do not occur during caffeine withdrawal.

According to laboratory experiments, the symptom of caffeine withdrawal most often reported is *headaches.* In nonlaboratory settings, as many as one third of the moderate and high caffeine consumers suffer that symptom if their daily caffeine intake is interrupted. The headaches, which seem to be remarkably consistent in different persons, are described as generalized and throbbing, proceeding from lethargy to a sense of cerebral fullness to a full-blown headache. They occur about 18 hours after the discontinuation of habitual caffeine intake and respond best to a renewed elevation of caffeine plasma levels, perhaps explaining why many tension headache-prone persons prefer over-the-counter analgesics that contain caffeine.

Other caffeine withdrawal symptoms include *nervousness,* a vague feeling of *depression,* drowsiness and lethargy, rhinorrhea, a disinclination to work, occasional yawning, nausea, and *insomnia* or sleep disturbances. Few recent reports have emphasized depression as a central feature of caffeinism. Surveys of psychiatric patients, however, revealed that the highest caffeine consumers (ingesting more than 750 mg daily) reported significantly high scores on the Beck Depression Inventory. Caffeine toxicity may induce psychosis in susceptible persons or exacerbate thinking disruptions in patients with diagnoses of schizophrenia.

In DSM-IV, caffeine withdrawal appears in an appendix of DSM-IV (Table 12.14) and is an example of caffeine use disorder not otherwise specified (Table 12.15).

Table 12.13
Diagnostic Criteria for Hallucinogen Intoxication

A. Recent use of a hallucinogen.

B. Clinically significant maladaptive behavioral or psychological changes (e.g., marked anxiety or depression, ideas of reference, fear of losing one's mind, paranoid ideation, impaired judgment, or impaired social or occupational functioning) that developed during, or shortly after, hallucinogen use.

C. Perceptual changes occurring in a state of full wakefulness and alertness (e.g., subjective intensification of perceptions, depersonalization, derealization, illusions, hallucinations, synesthesias) that developed during, or shortly after, hallucinogen use.

D. Two (or more) of the following signs, developing during, or shortly after, hallucinogen use:

(1) pupillary dilation
(2) tachycardia
(3) sweating
(4) palpitations
(5) blurring of vision
(6) tremors
(7) incoordination

E. The symptoms are not due to a general medical condition and are not better accounted for by another mental disorder.

Table from DSM-IV, *Diagnostic and Statistical Manual of Mental Disorders,* ed 4. Copyright American Psychiatric Association, Washington, 1994. Used with permission.

Table 12.14
Research Criteria for Caffeine Withdrawal

A. Prolonged daily use of caffeine.

B. Abrupt cessation of caffeine use, or reduction in the amount of caffeine used, closely followed by headache and one (or more) of the following symptoms:

   (1) marked fatigue or drowsiness
   (2) marked anxiety or depression
   (3) nausea or vomiting

C. The symptoms in criterion B cause clinically significant distress or impairment in social, occupational, or other important areas of functioning.

D. The sypmtoms are not due to the direct physiological effects of a general medical condition (e.g., migraine, viral illness) and are not better accounted for by another mental disorder.

Table from DSM-IV, *Diagnostic and Statistical Manual of Mental Disorders*, ed 4. Copyright American Psychiatric Association, Washington, 1994. Used with permission.

Table 12.15
Caffeine-Related Disorder Not Otherwise Specified

The caffeine-related disorder not otherwise specified category is for disorders associated with the use of caffeine that are not classifiable as caffeine intoxication, caffeine-induced anxiety disorder, or caffeine-induced sleep disorder. An example is caffeine withdrawal.

Table from DSM-IV, *Diagnostic and Statistical Manual of Mental Disorders*, ed 4. Copyright American Psychiatric Association, Washington, 1994. Used with permission.

12.10.   The answer is B (*Synopsis VII*, page 440).

About 500,000 persons with opioid dependence are in the United States. About half of them live in the New York City area. In 1991 an estimated 1.3 percent of the United States population had used heroin at least once. The male-to-female ratio of persons with opioid dependence is about 3 to 1. Typically, *users of opiates and opioids started to use substances in their teens and early 20s, not their late 20s to mid-30s.* Currently, most persons with opioid dependence are in their 30s and 40s. Opioid-related disorders are listed in Table 12.16.

12.11.   The answer is E (all) (*Synopsis VII*, page 446).

Opiate antagonists block or antagonize the effects of opiates and opioids. Unlike methadone, they do not in themselves exert narcotic effects and do not cause dependence. The antagonists include the following drugs: *naloxone*, which is used in the treatment of opiate and opioid overdose because it reverses the effects of narcotics; *naltrexone*, which is the longest-acting (72 hours) antagonist; *nalorphine*, levallorphan and *apomorpine*.

Table 12.16
Opioid-Related Disorders

Opioid use disorders

Opioid dependence
Opioid abuse

Opioid-induced disorders

Opioid intoxication
   Specify if: with perceptual disturbances
Opioid withdrawal
Opioid intoxication delirium
Opioid-induced psychotic disorder, with delusions
   Specify if: with onset during intoxication
Opioid-induced psychotic disorder, with hallucinations
   Specify if: with onset during intoxication
Opioid-induced mood disorder
   Specify if: with onset during intoxication
Opioid-induced sexual dysfunction
   Specify if: with onset during intoxication
Opioid-induced sleep disorder
   Specify if: with onset during intoxication/with onset during withdrawal

Opioid-related disorder not otherwise specified

Table based on DSM-IV, *Diagnostic and Statistical Manual of Mental Disorders,* ed 4. Copyright American Psychiatric Association, Washington, 1994. Used with permission.

12.12.   The answer is E (all) (*Synopsis VII*, page 441).

Some consistent behavior patterns seem to be especially pronounced in adolescents with opioid dependence. Those patterns have been called the heroin behavior syndrome: underlying *depression*, often of an agitated type and frequently accompanied by anxiety symptoms; impulsiveness expressed by a passive-aggressive orientation; *fear of failure*; use of heroin as an antianxiety agent to mask feelings of *low self-esteem*, hopelessness, and aggression; limited coping strategies and low frustration tolerance, accompanied by the *need for immediate gratification*; sensitivity to substance contingencies, with a keen awareness of the relation between good feelings and the act of substance taking; feelings of behavioral impotence counteracted by momentary control over the life situation by means of substances; and disturbances in social and interpersonal relationships with peers maintained by mutual substance experiences.

12.13.   The answer is E (all) (*Synopsis VII*, pages 452–453).

The severity of the withdrawal syndrome associated with the benzodiazepines varies significantly according to the average dose and the duration of use. However, a mild withdrawal syndrome can follow even short-term use of relatively low doses of benzodiazepines. A significant withdrawal syndrome is likely to occur at the cessation of dosages in the 40 mg a day range for diazepam, for example, although 10 to 20 mg a day, taken for a month, can also result in a withdrawal syndrome when the drug is stopped.

The onset of withdrawal symptoms usually occurs two to three days after the cessation of use, but with long-acting drugs, such as diazepam, the latency before onset may be five or six days.

The symptoms of benzodiazepine withdrawal include anxiety, *dysphoria, intolerance for bright lights* and loud noises, *nausea*, sweating, *muscle twitching*, and sometimes seizures (generally at dosages of 50 mg a day or more of diazepam).

Table 12.17 lists the diagnostic criteria for sedative, hypnotic, or anxiolytic withdrawal.

12.14–12.15

12.14.   The answer is D (*Synopsis VII*, pages 412–415).

Catatonia is not a clinical effect of amphetamine intoxication. When amphetamine is taken intravenously, the user experiences a characteristic rush of well-being and euphoria. Intoxication with high doses can lead to transient ideas of reference, paranoid ideation, *increased libido*, tinnitus, hearing one's name being called, and *formication* (tactile sensation of bugs crawling on the skin). Stereotyped movements may occur. *Delirium* (Table 12.18) with episodes of violence and substance: induced psychotic disorder (Table 12.19) may also be seen.

12.15.   The answer is E (all) (*Synopsis VII*, page 413).

Abrupt discontinuation of an amphetamine results in a letdown or crash characterized by the onset

of *fatigue, dysphoria, nightmares*, and *agitation*. According to DSM-IV, the syndrome may develop within a few hours to several days after the cessation of heavy amphetamine use. The withdrawal dysphoria may be treated with antidepressant medication. The agitation of the immediate letdown syndrome responds to diazepam (Valium). The diagnostic criteria for amphetamine (or related substance) withdrawal are listed in Table 12.20.

12.16.   The answer is D (*Synopsis VII*, pages 430–431 and 447–448).

Hallucinogen persisting perception disorder (Table 12.12) does not apply in this case. That disorder is characterized by the reexperiencing of the signs and symptoms of hallucinogen intoxication after having stopped the drug. The patient is mostly quiet and isolated and shows no loss of contact with reality or perceptual distortions unrelated to hallucinogen ingestion.

On the basis of the information given in the case of the 20-year-old man, the patient showed agitation, fluctuating mood, suspiciousness, and disorientation after the ingestion of a substance. Therefore, a general diagnosis of *substance intoxication* (Table 12.21) can apply. The substance, identified as phencyclidine (PCP), is an arylcyclohexylamine—a class of drugs (similar to hallucinogens) that produce hallucinations, loss of contact with reality, and other changes in thinking and feeling. PCP is a potent drug that may be taken orally, intravenously, or by sniffing. The disorder is diagnosed specifically as phencycli-

---

Table 12.17
Diagnostic Criteria for Sedative, Hypnotic, or Anxiolytic Withdrawal

A. Cessation of (or reduction in) sedative, hypnotic, or anxiolytic use that has been heavy and prolonged.

B. Two (or more) of the following, developing within several hours to a few days after criterion A:

   (1) autonomic hyperactivity (e.g., sweating or pulse rate greater than 100)
   (2) increased hand tremor
   (3) insomnia
   (4) nausea or vomiting
   (5) transient visual, tactile, or auditory hallucinations or illusions
   (6) psychomotor agitation
   (7) anxiety
   (8) grand mal seizures

C. The symptoms in criterion B cause clinically significant distress or impairment in social, occupational, or other important areas of functioning.

D. The symptoms are not due to a general medical condition and are not better accounted for by another mental disorder.

Specify if:
   With perceptual disturbances

Table from DSM-IV, *Diagnostic and Statistical Manual of Mental Disorders,* ed 4. Copyright American Psychiatric Association, Washington, 1994. Used with permission.

Table 12.18
Diagnostic Criteria for Substance Withdrawal Delirium

A. Disturbance of consciousness (i.e., reduced clarity of awareness of the environment) with reduced ability to focus, sustain, or shift attention.

B. A change in cognition (such as memory deficit, disorientation, language disturbance) or the development of a perceptual disturbance that is not better accounted for by a preexisting, established, or evolving dementia.

C. The disturbance develops over a short period of time (usually hours to days) and tends to fluctuate during the course of the day.

D. There is evidence from the history, physical examination, or laboratory findings that the symptoms in criteria A and B developed during, or shortly after, a withdrawal syndrome.

Note: This diagnosis should be made instead of a diagnosis of substance withdrawal only when the cognitive symptoms are in excess of those usually associated with the withdrawal syndrome and when the symptoms are sufficiently severe to warrant independent clinical attention.

Code: [Specific substance] withdrawal delirium
   (Alcohol; sedative, hypnotic, or anxiolytic; other [or unknown] substance)

Table from DSM-IV, *Diagnostic and Statistical Manual of Mental Disorders,* ed. 4. Copyright American Psychiatric Association, Washington, 1994. Used with permission.

Table 12.19
Diagnostic Criteria for Substance-Induced Psychotic Disorder

A. Prominent hallucinations or delusions. **Note:** Do not include hallucinations if the person has insight that they are substance-induced.

B. There is evidence from the history, physical examination, or laboratory findings of either (1) or (2):

   (1) the symptoms in criterion A developed during, or within a month of, substance intoxication or withdrawal

   (2) medication use is etiologically related to the disturbance

C. The disturbance is not better accounted for by a psychotic disorder that is not substance induced. Evidence that the symptoms are better accounted for by a psychotic disorder that is not substance induced might include the following: the symptoms precede the onset of the use (or medication use); the symptoms persist for a substantial period of time (e.g., about a month) after the cessation of acute withdrawal or severe intoxication, or are substantially in excess of what would be expected given the type or amount of the substance used or the duration of use; or there is other evidence that suggests the existence of an independent non-substance-induced psychotic disorder (e.g., a history of recurrent non-substance-related episodes).

D. The disturbance does not occur exclusively during the course of a delirium.

Note: This diagnosis should be made instead of a diagnosis of substance intoxication or substance withdrawal only when the symptoms are in excess of those usually associated with the intoxication or withdrawal syndrome and when the symptoms are sufficiently severe to warrant independent clinical attention.

Code: [Specific substance]-induced psychotic disorder (Alcohol, with delusions; alcohol, with hallucinations; amphetamine [or amphetamine-like substance], with delusions; amphetamine [or amphetamine-like substance], with hallucinations; cannabis, with delusions; cannabis, with hallucinations; cocaine, with delusions; cocaine, with hallucinations; hallucinogen, with delusions; hallucinogen, with hallucinations; inhalant, with delusions; inhalant, with hallucinations; opioid, with delusions; opioid, with hallucinations; phencyclidine [or phencyclidine-like substance], with delusions; phencyclidine [or phencyclidine-like substance], with hallucinations; sedative, hypnotic or anxiolytic, with delusions; sedative, hypnotic or anxiolytic, with hallucinations; other [or unknown] substance, with delusions; other [or unknown] substance, with hallucinations)

Specify if:

   With onset during intoxication: if criteria are met for intoxication with the substance and the symptoms develop during the intoxication syndrome

   With onset during withdrawal: if criteria are met for withdrawal from the substance and the symptoms develop during, or shortly after, a withdrawal syndrome

Table from DSM-IV, *Diagnostic and Statistical Manual of Mental Disorders,* ed 4. Copyright American Psychiatric Association, Washington, 1994. Used with permission.

Table 12.20
Diagnostic Criteria for Amphetamine Withdrawal

A. Cessation of (or reduction in) amphetamine (or related substance) use which has been heavy and prolonged.

B. Dysphoric mood and two (or more) of the following physiological changes, developing within a few hours to several days after criterion A:

   (1) fatigue
   (2) vivid, unpleasant dreams
   (3) insomnia or hypersomnia
   (4) increased appetite
   (5) psychomotor retardation or agitation

C. The symptoms in criterion B cause clinically significant distress or impairment in social, occupational, or other important areas of functioning.

D. The symptoms are not due to a general medical condition and not better accounted for by another mental disorder.

Table from DSM-IV, *Diagnostic and Statistical Manual of Mental Disorders,* ed 4. Copyright American Psychiatric Association, Washington, 1994. Used with permission.

Table 12.21
Diagnostic Criteria for Substance Intoxication

A. The development of a reversible substance-specific syndrome due to recent ingestion of (or exposure to) a substance. **Note:** Different substances may produce similar or identical syndromes.

B. Clinically significant maladaptive behavioral or psychological changes that are due to the effect of the substance on the central nervous system (e.g., belligerence, mood lability, cognitive impairment, impaired judgment, impaired social or occupational functioning) and develop during or shortly after use of the substance.

C. The symptoms are not due to a general medical condition and are not better accounted for by another mental disorder.

Table from DSM-IV, *Diagnostic and Statistical Manual of Mental Disorders,* ed 4. Copyright American Psychiatric Association, Washington, 1994. Used with permission.

dine intoxication. (Table 12.22). A patient who is found naked, directing traffic, screaming threats, and displaying great suspiciousness can be presumed to be suffering from either delusions, hallucinations, or both, and a diagnosis of *phencyclidine-induced psychotic disorder, with hallucinations,* can be made (Table 12.19). A history of the regular use of PCP with resultant impairment of functioning allows for a diagnosis of *substance dependence* (Table 12.5).

12.17.   The answer is C (*Synopsis VII*, page 408).

The usual case of *alcohol-induced psychotic disorder, with hallucinations,* differs from *schizophrenia* by the temporal relation to alcohol withdrawal, the short-lived course, and the absence of a past history of schizophrenia. Alcohol-induced psychotic dis-

Table 12.22
Diagnostic Criteria for Phencyclidine Intoxication

A. Recent use of phencyclidine (or a related substance).

B. Clinically significant maladaptive behavioral changes (e.g., belligerence, assaultiveness, impulsiveness, unpredictability, psychomotor agitation, impaired judgment, or impaired social or occupational functioning) that developed during, or shortly after, use of phencyclidine.

C. Within an hour (less when smoked, "snorted," or used intravenously), two (or more) of the following signs:

   (1) vertical or horizontal nystagmus
   (2) hypertension or tachycardia
   (3) numbness or diminished responsiveness to pain
   (4) ataxia
   (5) dysarthria
   (6) muscle rigidity
   (7) seizures or coma
   (8) hyperacusis

D. The symptoms are not due to a general medication condition and are not better accounted for by another mental disorder.

Specify if:
With perceptual disturbances

Table from DSM-IV, *Diagnostic and Statistical Manual of Mental Disorders*, ed 4. Copyright American Psychiatric Association, Washington, 1994. Used with permission.

order, with hallucinations, is usually manifested primarily by auditory hallucinations, sometimes accompanied by delusions, in the absence of symptoms of a mood disorder or a cognitive disorder.

Delirium tremens (DTs), another reaction to withdrawal from alcohol, usually occurs 72 to 96 hours after the cessation of heavy drinking. A distinctive characteristic is marked autonomic hyperactivity (tachycardia, fever, hyperhidrosis, and dilated pupils).

Pathological intoxication (called *idiosyncratic alcohol intoxication* in DSM-IV) is a syndrome of marked intoxication with subsequent amnesia for the period of intoxication. It is produced by the ingestion of an amount of alcohol insufficient to induce intoxication in most people. *Methanol intoxication* does not cause hallucinations but does cause blindness.

12.18. The answer is E (all) (*Synopsis VII*, pages 448–449).

The patient was having a reaction *caused by phencyclidine (PCP)*, which is known as angel dust. Reactions are related to the dose taken. Less than 5 mg of phencyclidine is considered a low dose, and doses above 10 mg are considered high. Experienced users report that the effects of 2 to 3 mg of smoked PCP begin within five minutes and plateau within half an hour. Reactions are sometimes *spontaneously cleared within 48 hours*. PCP can be *diagnosed by urine testing*. The patient's reaction may be *accompanied by violent acts*.

12.19–12.22

12.19. The answer is A (*Synopsis VII*, pages 404–406).

12.20. The answer is C (*Synopsis VII*, pages 404–406 and 408).

12.21. The answer is B (*Synopsis VII*, page 408).

12.22. The answer is C (*Synopsis VII*, pages 404–406 and 408).

Withdrawal seizures commonly precede the development of *alcohol-withdrawal delirium*, but the delirium can also appear unheralded. The essential feature of the syndrome is delirium that occurs within one week after the person stops drinking or reduces the intake of alcohol. In addition to the symptoms of delirium, the features include (1) autonomic hyperactivity, such as tachycardia, diaphoresis, fever, anxiety, insomnia, and hypertension; (2) perceptual distortions, which are most frequently visual or *auditory hallucinations*; and (3) fluctuating levels of psychomotor activity, ranging from hyperexcitability to lethargy. The best treatment for alcohol withdrawal delirium is its prevention. Patients who are withdrawing from alcohol who exhibit any withdrawal phenomena should receive a *benzodiazepine*, such as 25 to 50 mg of chlordiazepoxide (Librium) every two to four hours until they seem to be out of danger. Once the delirium appears, however, 50 to 100 mg of chlordiazepoxide should be given every four hours orally, or intravenous lorazepam (Ativan) should be used if oral medication is not possible.

In *alcohol-induced psychotic disorder, with hallucinations*, the patient may have *auditory hallucinations*, usually voices, but they are often unstructured. The voices are characteristically maligning, reproachful, or threatening, although some patients report that the voices are pleasant and nondisruptive. The hallucinations usually last less than a week, although during that week impaired reality testing is common. After the episode, most patients realize the hallucinatory nature of the symptoms. The hallucinations are differentiated from alcohol withdrawal delirium by the presence of a *clear sensorium* in patients with alcohol-induced psychotic disorder, with hallucinations.

12.23–12.27

12.23 The answer is A (*Synopsis VII*, pages 384 and 386).

12.24 The answer is B (*Synopsis VII*, pages 384 and 386).

12.25 The answer is C (*Synopsis VII*, pages 384 and 386).

12.26 The answer is D (*Synopsis VII*, pages 384 and 386).

12.27 The answer is A (*Synopsis VII*, pages 384 and 386).

Intoxication is a syndrome that *follows the recent ingestion and the presence in the body of a substance.* Withdrawal is the state that *follows the cessation or the reduction of the intake of a substance.* Both withdrawal and intoxication *are substance-specific syndromes.* The clinical picture in withdrawal and intoxication *does not correspond to any cognitive disorder. Maladaptive behavior is an essential diagnostic criterion* only for intoxication. The diagnostic criteria for substance withdrawal are listed in Table 12.23, and the diagnostic criteria for substance intoxication are based in Table 12.21.

12.28–12.32

12.28. The answer is B (*Synopsis VII*, pages 450–455).

12.29. The answer is C (*Synopsis VII*, pages 452–453).

12.30. The answer is B (*Synopsis VII*, pages 450–455).

12.31. The answer is A (*Synopsis VII*, pages 450–455).

12.32. The answer is D (*Synopsis VII*, page 450).

Barbiturates *cause rapid eye movement (REM) sleep suppression.* An abrupt withdrawal of a barbiturate will cause a marked increase or rebound in REM sleep. *Symptoms of withdrawal* from both benzodiazepines and barbiturates *usually appear within three days.* Barbiturates have a *high suicide potential.* Virtually no cases of successful suicide have occurred in patients taking benzodiazepines by themselves. In addition to treating anxiety, benzodiazepines are used in alcohol detoxification, for anesthetic induction, *as muscle relaxants,* and as anticonvulsants. Neither benzodiazepines nor barbiturates are *antipsychotics,* which are used to treat schizophrenia.

Table 12.23
Diagnostic Criteria for Substance Withdrawal

A. The development of a substance-specific syndrome due to the cessation of (or reduction in) substance use that has been heavy and prolonged.

B. The substance-specific syndrome causes clinically significant distress or impairment in social, occupational, or other important areas of functioning.

C. The symptoms are not due to a general medical condition and are not better accounted for by another mental disorder.

Table based on DSM-IV, *Diagnostic and Statistical Manual of Mental Disorders,* ed 4. Copyright American Psychiatric Association, Washington, 1994. Used with permission.

12.33–12.39

12.33. The answer is A (*Synopsis VII*, pages 392 and 400–401).

12.34. The answer is A (*Synopsis VII*, pages 392 and 451).

12.35. The answer is A (*Synopsis VII*, pages 392 and 451).

12.36. The answer is B (*Synopsis VII*, pages 392 and 440).

12.37. The answer is C (*Synopsis VII*, pages 392 and 447).

12.38. The answer is D (*Synopsis VII*, pages 392 and 416).

12.39. The answer is E (*Synopsis VII*, pages 392 and 437).

Ethanol acts on the γ-aminobutyric acid (GABA) receptor system and has effects on noradrenergic neurons in the locus ceruleus and on the dopaminergic neurons of the ventral tegmental area. Barbiturates, such as *phenobarbital,* also act primarily on the GABA system, specifically on the GABA receptor complex, which includes a binding site for the inhibitory amino acid GABA, a regulatory site that binds benzodiazepines, and a chloride ion channel. The binding of the barbiturate results in the facilitation of chloride ion influx into the neuron, making the neuron more negatively charged and less likely to be stimulated.

Diazepam (Valium), a benzodiazepine, affects the GABA receptor complex by binding to the site for benzodiazepines. When diazepam or another benzodiazepine binds to that site, the chloride ions flow through the channel, resulting in inhibition of the neuron. The benzodiazepine antagonist flumazenil (Mazicon) reverses the effects of benzodiazepines.

Opiates such as *heroin* bind to specific sites in the brain labeled opiate receptors. Changes in the number or the sensitivity of the opiate receptors may occur as the result of continuous exposure to an opiate, producing dependence on the substance. The activity of adrenergic neurons in the locus ceruleus also decreases with long-term use.

Phencyclidine (PCP) binds to specific receptor sites located in the ion channel associated with the receptor for glutamate, an excitatory amino acid. Tolerance to PCP does not occur.

The leading theory regarding a mechanism of action for *caffeine* involves antagonism of the adenosine receptors. Adenosine appears to function as a neuromodulator, possibly as a neurotransmitter in the brain. Caffeine may also affect dopaminergic systems and adrenergic systems.

Nicotine is believed to exert its effects on the central nervous system through the nicotinic receptors, one subclass of acetylcholine receptors. Nicotine affects the nicotinic receptors in the receptor-gated ion channels of the receptor system.

13 ||||||

Schizophrenia

Schizophrenia has sometimes been called "the cruelest disease" because it generally strikes young adults just at the beginning of their lives and because it is, in one form or another, a lifelong, chronic disorder that affects all that is most human in how a person interacts, experiences emotion, and processes information.

The contributions of Emil Kraepelin, Eugen Bleuler, and Kurt Schneider continue to provide valuable insights into schizophrenia. Much of the current thinking about the descriptive criteria necessary to making the diagnosis of schizophrenia stems directly from the early observations of those theorists.

Schizophrenia is often referred to as "the schizophrenias" to underscore the concept that the disorder now classified as schizophrenia most likely represents a spectrum of disorders. That spectrum encompasses some similar signs and symptoms but with varying presentations, responses to medication, levels of functioning, and prognoses.

The spectrum concept also underscores the idea that the cause of schizophrenia may, in fact, be many causes. Those causes probably encompass various insults in key areas of the brain—insults that lead ultimately to the common pathway of typical psychiatric and behavioral manifestations. For instance, the initial cause may be infectious, genetic, neurochemical, or traumatic and may affect the frontal lobes, the limbic system, or the basal ganglia; however, all the possible causes produce similar symptoms and signs of hallucinations, delusions, or loosening of associations, depending on what part of the brain was most affected. As the technology that allows researchers to view the brain's anatomy, chemistry, and physiology continues to expand, so will the definitions and diagnoses of the various schizophrenias become specific and sophisticated.

The major theories regarding the causes of schizophrenia are biological, and the current consensus is that schizophrenia is a disease of the brain. However, perhaps the most useful way to think about the cause of schizophrenia is to consider the stress-diathesis model. That model asserts that, for a disorder to be manifest, an underlying diathesis must be present. Thus, persons with no specific diathesis (be it viral, genetic, neurochemical, or traumatic) never become schizophrenic, no matter how much stress they may endure. They may become extremely anxious, severely depressed, floridly manic, or grossly personality-disordered, but they do not become schizophrenic. However, persons with specific diatheses (whatever they may be) do not require much stress to trigger the initial manifestation of the illness, and they may be sensitive to any type of biological or psychological stress, once the disorder has manifested itself. The stress-diathesis model is helpful because it emphasizes the intricate and complex interplay among biological, psychological, and environmental factors in schizophrenia.

Among the biological theories of the cause of schizophrenia, the dopamine hypothesis must be understood—both its strengths and its weaknesses. The student must be aware of how the system works, in which pathways and between which specific areas of the brain dopamine plays its role, and how that role is significant in terms of signs, symptoms, responses to medication, and medication side effects. The student must also be able to appreciate the significance of neurochemical studies of dopamine function and position emission tomography (PET) scan data related to the dopamine system.

The treatment of patients with schizophrenia requires a sophisticated knowledge of psychopharmacology and psychosocial interventions. Students need to become familiar with the medications that are used to treat the symptoms of schizophrenia and to be aware of the major side effects of those medications. The student must understand the mechanisms of those medications in the brain: in which pathways, on which neurotransmitters, in which areas of the brain those medications are working. The student must also be aware of alternative medication strategies if the traditional strategies fail.

Psychosocial interventions are crucial adjuncts to the biological treatment of schizophrenia. Many clinicians and researchers think that

the number of relapses, the frequency and the length of hospitalizations, and the amount of medication required to control a patient's symptoms may all be significantly reduced by optimal psychosocial treatment modalities. Those modalities range from supportive environments to family therapy to treatment of substance abuse to partial hospitalization and day treatment. The student needs to be educated about the available options and their applicability to individual patients.

Students are referred to Chapter 13 in *Kaplan and Sadock's Synopsis VII* and should then study the questions and answers below.

HELPFUL HINTS

The following names and terms, including the schizophrenic signs and symptoms listed, should be studied and the definitions memorized.

Emil Kraepelin	psychoimmunology and	*forme fruste*
Eugen Bleuler	psychoendocrinology	projective testing
Benedict Morel	RFLPs	disorganized type
Karl Kahlbaum	genetic hypothesis	catatonic type
Adolf Meyer	psychoanalytic and learning	paranoid type
Harry Stack Sullivan	theories	undifferentiated type
Gabriel Langfeldt	Gregory Bateson	residual type
Kurt Schneider	double bind	*bouffée délirante*
dementia precox	flat affect and blunted affect	autistic disorder
paranoia	hallucinations	schizoaffective disorder
fundamental and accessory	delusions	antipsychotics
symptoms	ego boundaries	tardive dyskinesia
dopamine hypothesis	thought disorders	ECT
mesocortical and mesolimbic tracts	impulse control, suicide, and	psychosocial treatments
neurotransmitters and	homicide	downward-drift hypothesis
neurodegeneration	orientation, memory, judgment,	social causation hypothesis
brain imaging—CT, PET, MRI	and insight	seasonality of birth
electrophysiology—EEG	soft signs	paraphrenia

QUESTIONS

DIRECTIONS: Each of the questions or incomplete statements below is followed by five suggested responses or completions. Select the *one* that is *best* in each case.

13.1. An 18-year-old female high school student was admitted for the first time to the psychiatry service because she had not spoken or eaten for three days. According to her parents, she had been a normal teenager, with good grades and friends, until about one year previously, when she began to stay at home, alone in her room, and seemed preoccupied and less animated than in the past. Six

months before her admission to the psychiatry service, she began to refuse to go to school, and her grades became barely passing. About a month later, she started to talk gibberish about spirits, magic, the devil—things that were totally foreign to her background. For the week preceding admission to the hospital, she had stared into space, immobile, allowing herself only to be moved from her bed to a chair or from one room to another.

The most likely diagnosis is

A. schizophreniform disorder
B. brief psychotic disorder
C. a mood disorder
D. schizophrenia
E. delusional disorder

13.2. A 44-year-old single unemployed man was brought into an emergency room by the police for striking an elderly woman in his apartment building. He complained that the woman he struck was a bitch and that she and "the others" deserved more than that for what they put him through.

The patient had been continuously ill since the age of 22. During his first year of law school, he gradually became more and more convinced that his classmates were making fun of him. He noticed that they would snort and sneeze whenever he entered the classroom. When a girl he was dating broke off the relationship with him, he believed that she had been replaced by a look-alike. He called the police and asked for their help in solving the "kidnapping." His academic performance in school declined dramatically, and he was asked to leave and seek psychiatric care.

The patient got a job as an investment counselor at a bank, which he held for seven months. However, he was getting an increasing number of distracting "signals" from coworkers, and he became more and more suspicious and withdrawn. At that time he first reported hearing voices. He was eventually fired and soon thereafter was hospitalized for the first time, at age 24. He had not worked since.

The patient had been hospitalized 12 times; the longest stay was for eight months. However, in the past five years he had been hospitalized only once, for three weeks. During the hospitalizations he had received various antipsychotic drugs. Although outpatient medication had been prescribed, he usually stopped taking it shortly after leaving the hospital. Aside from twice-yearly lunch meetings with his uncle and his contacts with mental health workers, he was totally isolated socially. He lived on his own and managed his own financial affairs, including a modest inheritance. He read *The Wall Street Journal* daily. He cooked and cleaned for himself.

The patient maintained that his apartment was the center of a large communication system that involved all three major television networks, his neighbors, and apparently hundreds of "actors" in his neighborhood. There were secret cameras in his apartment that carefully monitored all his activities. When he was watching television, many of his minor actions (for example, getting up to go to the bathroom) were soon directly commented on by the announcer. Whenever he went outside, the "actors" had all been warned to keep him under surveillance; everyone on the street watched him. His neighbors operated two "machines"; one was responsible for all his voices, except the "joker." He was not certain who controlled that voice, which visited him only occasionally and was very funny. The other voices, which he heard many times each day, were generated by that machine, which he sometimes thought was directly run by the neighbor whom he attacked. For example, when he was going over his investments, those "harassing" voices constantly told him which stocks to buy. The other machine he called "the dream machine." That machine put erotic dreams into his head, usually of black women.

The patient described other unusual experiences. For example, he recently went to a shoe store 30 miles from his home in the hope of getting some shoes that would not be "altered." However, he soon found out that, like the rest of the shoes he bought, special nails had been put into the bottoms of the shoes to annoy him. He was amazed that his decision about which shoe store to go to must have been known to his "harassers" before he himself knew it, so that they had time to get the altered shoes made up especially for him. He realized that great effort and "millions of dollars" were involved in keeping him under surveillance. He sometimes thought that was all part of a large experiment to discover the secret of his superior intelligence.

At the interview, the patient was well-groomed, and his speech was coherent and goal-directed. His affect was, at most, only mildly blunted. He was initially angry at being brought in by the police. After several weeks of treatment with an antipsychotic drug failed to control his psychotic symptoms, he was transferred to a long-stay facility with the plan to arrange a structured living situation for him.

As described, the patient's condition is best diagnosed as

A. schizophrenia, paranoid type
B. schizophrenia, disorganized type
C. schizophrenia, catatonic type
D. schizophrenia, undifferentiated type
E. schizophrenia, residual type

13.3. In the treatment of schizophrenia

A. the minimum length of an antipsychotic trial is usually two weeks
B. electroconvulsive therapy (ECT) is harmful to patients
C. clozapine is indicated in patients with tardive dyskinesia
D. short-term hospitalizations are less effective than long-term hospitalizations
E. patients are more likely to commit homicide than are the general population

13.4. Investigations into the cause of schizophrenia have revealed that
A. a particular genetic defect has been found in all schizophrenic patients
B. no abnormalities appear in the evoked potentials in schizophrenic patients
C. monozygotic twins have the highest concordance rate for schizophrenia
D. the efficacy and the potency of antipsychotics correlate with their ability to block acetylcholinesterase
E. a specific family pattern plays a causative role in the development of schizophrenia

13.5. Epidemiological studies of schizophrenia have found that
A. schizophrenia is more prevalent among men than among women
B. the lifetime prevalence is usually between 1 and 1.5 percent of the population
C. suicide is not a common cause of death among schizophrenic patients
D. schizophrenic patients are found equally among all socioeconomic groups
E. schizophrenic patients occupy less than 10 percent of all mental hospital beds

13.6. Hospital records suggest that for the past 100 years the incidence of schizophrenia in the United States has probably
A. increased greatly
B. increased slightly
C. decreased greatly
D. decreased slightly
E. remained unchanged

13.7. The mortality rate among schizophrenic patients
A. is higher than the rate for normal persons
B. is lower than the rate for normal persons
C. is the same as the rate for normal persons
D. has never been studied
E. is the same as the rate for patients with phobias

13.8. Having a schizophrenic family member, especially having one or two schizophrenic parents and a monozygotic twin who is schizophrenic
A. increases the risk for schizophrenia
B. decreases the risk for schizophrenia
C. has no effect on the risk for schizophrenia
D. may increase or decrease the risk for schizophrenia
E. has a variable effect on the risk for schizophrenia

13.9. Simple schizophrenia is characterized by
A. an insidious loss of drive and ambition
B. persistent hallucinations
C. persistent delusions
D. a desire for social and work-related situations
E. all the above

13.10. A schizophrenic patient who cuts off his penis is said to be suffering from
A. penis envy
B. castration complex
C. the Van Gogh syndrome
D. *bouffée délirante*
E. homosexual panic

13.11. A schizophrenic patient who feels a burning sensation in the brain is said to be experiencing a
A. delusional feeling
B. gustatory hallucination
C. cenesthetic hallucination
D. haptic hallucination
E. hypnopompic hallucination

13.12. A relapse in schizophrenia is most closely related to
A. the natural course of the illness
B. noncompliance in taking medicine
C. whether or not the patient is working
D. physical therapy
E. individual psychotherapy

13.13. Which of the following symptoms must be present before a psychiatrist can make a diagnosis of schizophrenia?
A. Thought broadcasting
B. Hallucinations
C. Flat affect
D. Disorganized behavior
E. All the above

13.14. The majority of computed tomographic (CT) studies of patients with schizophrenia have reported
A. enlarged lateral and third ventricles in 10 to 50 percent of patients
B. cortical atrophy in 10 to 35 percent of patients
C. atrophy of the cerebellar vermus
D. findings that are not artifacts of treatment
E. all the above

13.15. In general, pooled studies show expectancy rates for schizophrenia in monozygotic twins of
A. 0.1 percent
B. 5 percent
C. 25 percent
D. 40 percent
E. 50 percent

13.16. Paraphrenic schizophrenia is sometimes used as a synonym for
A. latent schizophrenia
B. simple deteriorative disorder (simple schizophrenia)
C. catatonic schizophrenia
D. hebephrenic schizophrenia
E. paranoid schizophrenia

13.17. The most common type of schizophrenic hallucination is
A. visual
B. auditory
C. tactile
D. olfactory
E. gustatory

13.18. A 33-year-old male psychiatric inpatient put on his dark sunglasses whenever he met with his doctor. He coherently stated that doing so made it impossible for the doctor to control his thoughts. The patient was exhibiting
A. social withdrawal
B. hypervigilance
C. fragmentation of thinking
D. delusional thinking
E. magical thinking

13.19. The schizophrenic patient shown in Figure 13.1 has the characteristic posture known as
A. catalepsy
B. mannerism
C. cataplexy
D. perseveration
E. none of the above

13.20. Features weighting toward a good prognosis in schizophrenia include all the following *except*
A. depression
B. a family history of mood disorders
C. paranoid features
D. undifferentiated or disorganized features
E. an undulating course

13.21. Thought disorders in schizophrenia are characterized by
A. delusions
B. loss of ego boundaries
C. sexual confusion
D. looseness of associations
E. all the above

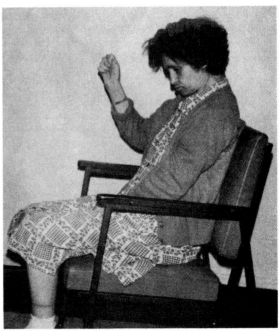

Figure 13.1. Schizophrenia patient. (Figure courtesy of Heinz E. Lehmann, M.D.)

13.22. Clozapine (Clorazil)
A. is an appropriate first-line drug for the treatment of schizophrenia
B. is associated with a 10-to-20 percent incidence of agranulocytosis
C. requires monthly monitoring of blood indexes
D. has not been associated with extrapyramidal side effects
E. is believed to exert its therapeutic effect by blocking dopamine receptors

13.23. Electrophysiological studies of persons with schizophrenia show
A. decreased alpha activity
B. spikes in the limbic area that correlate with psychotic behavior
C. increased frontal lobe slow-wave activity
D. increased parietal lobe fast-wave activity
E. all the above

DIRECTIONS: Each group of questions below consists of lettered headings followed by a list of numbered words or statements. For each numbered word or statement, select the *one* lettered heading that is most closely associated with it. Each lettered heading may be selected once, more than once, or not at all.

Questions 13.24–13.28
A. Eugen Bleuler
B. Benedict Morel
C. Karl Kahlbaum
D. Ewald Hecker
E. E. Gabriel Langfeldt

13.24. *Démence précoce*

13.25. Schizophrenia

13.26. Catatonia

13.27. Hebephrenia

13.28. Schizophreniform psychosis

Questions 13.29–13.32
A. Eugen Bleuler
B. Emil Kraeplin

13.29. Latinized the term *démence précoce*

13.30. Classified patients as being afflicted with manic-depressive psychoses, dementia precox, or paranoia

13.31. Coined the term schizophrenia

13.32. Described the four As of schizophrenia—associations, autism, affect, and ambivalence

Questions 13.33–13.37
A. Incoherence
B. Neologism
C. Mutism
D. Echolalia
E. Verbigeration

13.33. Functional inhibition of speech

13.34. New expression or word

13.35. Empty or obscure language

13.36. Repeating of the same words the questioner has asked

13.37. Senseless repetition of the same words or phrases

Questions 13.38–13.43
A. Schneiderian first-rank symptom
B. Schneiderian second-rank symptom

13.38. Sudden delusional ideas

13.39. Perplexity

13.40. Audible thoughts

13.41. Voices commenting

13.42. Thought withdrawal

13.43. The experience of having one's thoughts controlled

ANSWERS

Schizophrenia

13.1.   The answer is D (*Synopsis VII*, pages 470–474).

The most likely diagnosis in the 18-year-old female high school student is *schizophrenia*, based on the presence of delusions about supernatural phenomena, incoherence, and catatonic symptoms—for example, allowing herself to be passively moved. The diagnostic criteria for schizophrenia are listed in Table 13.1.

Her symptoms had been noted for about one year. That fact rules out *schizophreniform disorder*, which is diagnosed when the criteria for schizophrenia have been met but the symptoms have been present for at least one month but less than six months. *Brief psychotic disorder* is diagnosed when symptoms have been present for at least one day but less than one month.

The differential diagnosis of schizophrenia and *a mood disorder* can be difficult. In the case presented, the patient's mood was not reported to be disturbed. In *delusional disorder*, one expects nonbizarre delusions to be present but only in the absence of other symptoms of schizophrenia, such as incoherence and prominent hallucinations.

13.2.   The answer is A (*Synopsis VII*, pages 471–473).

The patient's condition is best diagnosed as *schizophrenia, paranoid type*. The patient's long illness apparently began with delusions of reference (his classmates making fun of him by snorting and sneezing when he entered the classroom). Over the years his delusions had become increasingly complex and bizarre (his neighbors were actually actors; his thoughts were monitored; a machine put erotic dreams into his head). In addition, he had prominent hallucinations of voices that harassed him.

All the patient's delusions and hallucinations seemed to involve the single theme of a conspiracy to harass him. That systematized persecutory delusion—in the absence of incoherence, marked loosening of associations, flat or grossly inappropriate affect, or catatonic or grossly disorganized behavior—indicates the paranoid type. Schizophrenia, paranoid type, is further specified as continuous if, as in this case, all past and present active phases of the illness have been the paranoid type.

Schizophrenia, disorganized type, is characterized by a marked regression to primitive, disinhibited, and unorganized behavior and by the absence of symptoms that meet the criteria for the catatonic type. The onset is usually early, before age 25. Disorganized patients are usually active but in an aimless, nonconstructive manner. Their thought disorder is pronounced, with symptoms such as marked loosening of associations, and their contact with reality is poor. Their personal appearance and their social behavior are dilapidated. Their emotional responses are inappropriate, and they often burst out laughing without any apparent reason. Incongruous grinning and grimacing are common in disorganized patients whose behavior is best described as silly or fatuous.

Schizophrenia, catatonic type, although common several decades ago, is now rare in Europe and North America. The classic feature of the catatonic type is a marked disturbance in motor function, which may involve stupor, negativism, rigidity, excitement, or posturing. Sometimes the patient shows a rapid alteration between extremes of excitement and stupor. Associated features include stereotypies, mannerisms, and waxy flexibility. Mutism is particularly common.

Frequently, patients who are clearly schizophrenic cannot be easily fitted into one of the other types. The fourth edition of *Diagnostic and Statistical Manual of Mental Disorders* (DSM-IV) diagnoses their condition as *schizophrenia, undifferentiated type*.

Schizophrenia, residual type is characterized by the presence of continuing evidence of the schizophrenic disturbance and the absence of a complete set of active symptoms. Emotional blunting, social withdrawal, eccentric behavior, illogical thinking, and mild loosening of associations are common in the residual type. If delusions or hallucinations are present, they are not prominent and are not accompanied by strong affect.

Table 13.2 lists the diagnostic criteria for the schizophrenia subtypes.

13.3.   The answer is C (*Synopsis VII*, page 482).

Clozapine is indicated in patients with tardive dyskinesia. The available data indicate that clozapine is an effective antipsychotic that is not associated with the development or the exacerbation of tardive dyskinesia, a movement disorder that develops after the prolonged use of antipsychotic medications.

The minimum length of an antipsychotic trial is usually four to six weeks, not two weeks. If the trial is unsuccessful, a different antipsychotic, usually from a different class, can be tried.

Electroconvulsive therapy (ECT) is not harmful to

Table 13.1
Diagnostic Criteria for Schizophrenia

A. *Characteristic symptoms:* Two (or more) of the following, each present for a significant portion of time during a 1-month period (or less if successfully treated):

    (1) delusions
    (2) hallucinations
    (3) disorganized speech (e.g., frequent derailment or incoherence)
    (4) grossly disorganized or catatonic behavior
    (5) negative symptoms, i.e., affective flattening, alogia, or avolition

    Note: Only one criterion A symptom is required if delusions are bizarre or hallucinations consist of a voice keeping up a running commentary on the person's behavior or thoughts, or two or more voices conversing with each other.

B. *Social/occupational dysfunction:* For a significant portion of the time since the onset of the disturbance, one or more major areas of functioning such as work, interpersonal relations, or self-care, ire markedly below the level achieved prior to the onset (or when the onset is in childhood or adolescence, failure to achieve expected level of interpersonal, academic, or occupational achievement).

C. *Duration:* Continuous signs of the disturbance persist for at least 6 months. This 6-month period must include at least 1 month of symptoms that meet criterion A (i.e., active- phase symptoms), and may include periods of prodromal or residual symptoms. During these prodromal or residual periods, the signs of the disturbance may be manifested by only negative symptoms or two or more symptoms listed in criterion A present in an attenuated form (e.g., odd beliefs, unusual perceptual experiences).

D. *Schizoaffective and mood disorder exclusion:* Schizoaffective disorder and mood disorder with psychotic features have been ruled out because either (1) no major depressive, manic, or mixed episodes have occurred concurrently with the active-phase symptoms; or (2) if mood episodes have occurred during active-phase symptoms, their total duration has been brief relative to the duration of the active and residual periods.

E. *Substance/general medical condition exclusion:* The disturbance is not due to the direct physiological effects of a substance (e.g., a drug of abuse, a medication) or a general medical condition.

F. *Relationship to a pervasive developmental disorder:* If there is a history of autistic disorder or another pervasive developmental disorder, the additional diagnosis of schizophrenia is made only if prominent delusions or hallucinations are also present for at least a month (or less if successfully treated).

Classification of longitudinal course (can be applied only after at least 1 year has elapsed since the initial onset of active-phase symptoms):
    Episodic with interepisode residual symptoms (episodes are defined by the reemergence of prominent psychotic symptoms); *also specify if:* **with prominent negative symptoms**
    Episodic with no interepisode residual symptoms
    Continuous (prominent psychotic symptoms are present throughout the period of observation); *also specify if:* **with prominent negative symptoms**
    Single episode in partial remission; *also specify if:* **with prominent negative symptoms**
    Single episode in full remission
    Other or unspecified pattern

Table from DSM-IV, *Diagnostic and Statistical Manual of Mental Disorders,* ed 4. Copyright American Psychiatric Association, Washington, 1994. Used with permission.

schizophrenic patients. Although ECT is much less effective than antipsychotics, it may be indicated for catatonic patients and for patients who for some reason cannot take antipsychotics.

Hospitalization decreases stress on patients and helps them structure their daily activities. The length of hospitalization depends on the severity of the patient's illness and the availability of outpatient treatment facilities. Research has shown that *short-term hospitalizations* (four to six weeks) *are just as effective as long-term hospitalizations* and that hospitals with active behavioral approaches are more effective than custodial institutions and insight-oriented therapeutic communities.

In spite of the sensational attention that the news media provide when a patient with schizophrenia murders someone, the available data indicate that

schizophrenic patients are no more likely to commit homicide than the general population. When a schizophrenic patient does commit homicide, it may be for unpredictable or bizarre reasons based on hallucinations or delusions.

13.4. The answer is C (*Synopsis VII*, page 463).

The cause of schizophrenia is not known. However, a wide range of genetic studies strongly suggest a genetic component to the inheritance of schizophrenia. *Monozygotic twins have the highest concordance rate for schizophrenia.* The studies of adopted monozygotic twins show that twins who are reared by adoptive parents have schizophrenia at the same rate as their twin siblings raised by their biological parents. That finding suggests that the genetic influence outweighs the environmental influence. In fur-

Table 13.2
Diagnostic Criteria for Schizophrenia Subtypes

Paranoid type

A type of schizophrenia in which the following criteria are met:

A. Preoccupation with one or more delusions or frequent auditory hallucinations.

B. None of the following is prominent: disorganized speech, disorganized or catatonic behavior, or flat or inappropriate affect or catatonic behavior.

Disorganized type

A type of schizophrenia in which the following criteria are met:

A. All of the following are prominent:

    (1) disorganized speech
    (2) disorganized behavior
    (3) flat or inappropriate affect

B. The criteria are not met for catatonic type.

Catatonic type

A type of schizophrenia in which the clinical picture is dominated by at least two of the following:

    (1) motoric immobility as evidenced by catalepsy (including waxy flexibility) or stupor
    (2) excessive motor activity (that is apparently purposeless and not influenced by external stimuli)
    (3) extreme negativism (an apparently motiveless resistance to all instructions or maintenance of a rigid posture against attempts to be moved) or mutism
    (4) peculiarities of voluntary movement as evidenced by posturing (voluntary assumption of inappropriate or bizarre postures), stereotyped movements, prominent mannerisms, or prominent grimacing
    (5) echolalia or echopraxia

Undifferentiated type

A type of schizophrenia in which symptoms that meet criterion A are present, but the criteria are not met for the paranoid, catatonic, or disorganized type.

Residual type

A type of schizophrenia in which the following criteria are met:

A. Absence of prominent delusions, hallucinations, disorganized speech, and grossly disorganized or catatonic behavior.

B. There is continuing evidence of the disturbance, as indicated by the presence of negative symptoms or two or more symptoms listed in criterion A for schizophrenia, present in an attenuated form (e.g., odd beliefs, unusual perceptual experiences).

Table from DSM-IV, *Diagnostic and Statistical Manual of Mental Disorders, ed. 4.* Copyright American Psychiatric Association, Washington 1994. Used with permission.

ther support of the genetic basis is the observation that the more severe the schizophrenia, the more likely the twins are to be concordant for the disorder.

Nevertheless, *a particular genetic defect has not been found in all schizophrenic patients.* Many associations between particular chromosomal sites and schizophrenia have been reported in the literature since the widespread application of the techniques of molecular biology. More than half of the chromosomes have been associated with schizophrenia in

those various reports, but the long arms of chromosomes 5, 11, and 18; the short arm of chromosome 19; and the X chromosome have been the most commonly reported. At this time, the literature is best summarized as indicating a potentially heterogeneous genetic basis for schizophrenia.

The research literature also report that *a large number of abnormalities appear in the evoked potentials in schizophrenic patients.* The P300 has been most studied and is defined as a large, positive evoked-potential wave that occurs about 300 milliseconds after a sensory stimulus is detected. The major source of the P300 wave may be located in the limbic system structures of the medial temporal lobes. In schizophrenic patients the P300 has been reported to be statistically smaller and later than in comparison groups.

Except for clozapine, *the efficacy and the potency of antipsychotics correlate with their ability to act as antagonists of the dopamine type 2 (D2) receptor, not with their ability to block acetylcholinesterase.*

No well-controlled evidence indicates that any *specific family pattern plays a causative role in the development of schizophrenia.* Some schizophrenic patients do come from dysfunctional families, just as many nonpsychiatrically ill persons come from dysfunctional families.

13.5. The answer is B (*Synopsis VII,* page 458).

The lifetime prevalence of schizophrenia is usually between 1 and 1.5 percent of the population. Consistent with that range, the National Institute of Mental Health (NIMH)—sponsored Epidemiologic Catchment Area (ECA) study reported a lifetime prevalence of 1.3 percent.

Schizophrenia is not more prevalent among men than among women; rather, it is equally prevalent in men and women. However, men have an earlier onset of schizophrenia than do women. The peak ages of onset for men are 15 to 25; for women the peak ages are 25 to 35.

Suicide is a common cause of death among schizophrenic patients. About 50 percent of all patients with schizophrenia attempt suicide at least once in their lifetimes, and 10 to 15 percent of schizophrenic patients die by suicide during a 20-year follow-up period.

Schizophrenia has been described in all cultures and socioeconomic status groups studied, but *schizophrenic patients are not found equally among all socioeconomic groups.* In industrialized nations a disproportionate number of schizophrenic patients are in the low socioeconomic groups.

Schizophrenic patients occupy more than 10 percent of all mental hospital beds. In fact they occupy about 50 percent of all hospital beds.

13.6. The answer is E (*Synopsis VII,* pages 458–463).

Hospital records suggest that the incidence of schizophrenia in the United States has probably *re-*

mained unchanged for the past 100 years and possibly throughout the entire history of the country, despite tremendous socioeconomic and population changes.

13.7. The answer is A (*Synopsis VII*, page 478).

The mortality rate among schizophrenic patients *is higher than the rate for normal persons*. The reasons for the high rate are not readily explainable.

13.8. The answer is A (*Synopsis VII*, page 468).

Having a schizophrenic family member, especially having one or two schizophrenic parents and a monozygotic twin who is schizophrenic, *increases the risk for schizophrenia*. Other risk factors include (1) having lived through a difficult obstetrical delivery, presumably with trauma to the brain; (2) having, for unknown reasons, a deviant course of personality maturation and development that has produced an excessively shy, daydreaming, withdrawn, friendless child; an excessively compliant, good, or dependent child; a child with idiosyncratic thought processes; a child who is particularly sensitive to separation; a child who is destructive, violent, incorrigible, and prone to truancy; or an anhedonic child; (3) having a parent who is overpossessive, hostile, or incapable of divining the child's needs or who has paranoid attitudes and formal disturbances of thinking; (4) having low levels of monoaminase oxidase, type B, in the blood platelets; (5) having abnormal pursuit eye movements; (6) having taken a variety of drugs— particularly lysergic acid diethylamide (LSD), amphetamines, cannabis, cocaine, and phencyclidine; and (7) having a history of temporal lobe epilepsy, Huntington's disease, homocystinuria, folic acid deficiency, and the adult form of metachromatic leukodystrophy.

None of those risk factors invariably occurs in schizophrenic patients; they may occur in various combinations. Not everyone who ingests psychotomimetic drugs later becomes schizophrenic. Not every schizophrenic patient has abnormal pursuit eye movements, and some well relatives of schizophrenic patients may also have abnormal pursuit eye movements.

13.9. The answer is A (*Synopsis VII*, pages 475 and 490).

The term "simple schizophrenia" was used during a period when schizophrenia had a broad diagnostic conceptualization. Simple schizophrenia was characterized by a gradual, *insidious loss of drive and ambition*. Patients with the disorder were usually not overtly psychotic and experienced *persistent hallucinations* or *delusions*. The primary symptom is the patient's loss of *desire for social and work-related situations*. The syndrome may reflect depression, a phobia, dementia, or an exacerbation of personality traits. The clinician should be sure that the patient truly meets the diagnostic criteria for schizophrenia before making that diagnosis. In spite of those res-

ervations, simple schizophrenia (now called simple deteriorative disorder) has reappeared as a diagnostic category in an appendix of DSM-IV.

13.10. The answer is C (*Synopsis VII*, pages 477–478).

Dramatic self mutilation in schizophrenic patients—for example, the gouging out of an eye or the cutting off of the penis—has been referred to as *The Van Gogh syndrome*. It may sometimes be the expression of dysmorphophobic delusions, the irrational conviction that a serious bodily defect exists, or some other complex, unconscious mechanisms.

Penis envy is Sigmund Freud's concept that the woman envies the man for his possession of a penis. In psychoanalytic theory, *castration complex* a group of unconscious thoughts and motives that are related to the fear of losing the genitalia, usually as punishment for forbidden sexual desires. *Bouffée délirante* is a term used in France and is considered a diagnostic category in its own right, not a type of schizophrenia. The criteria are similar to those for schizophrenia, but the symptoms must be present for less than three months, thereby approximating the diagnosis of schizophreniform disorder. French psychiatrists report that about 40 percent of patients with the diagnosis are later classified as having schizophrenia.

Homosexual panic is the sudden onset of severe anxiety precipitated by the unconscious fear or conflict that one may be a homosexual or act out homosexual impulses.

13.11. The answer is C (*Synopsis VII*, page 477).

A person with schizophrenia often experiences a *cenesthetic hallucination*, a sensation of an altered state in body organs without any special receptor apparatus to explain the sensation—for example, a burning sensation in the brain, a pushing sensation in the abdominal blood vessels, or a cutting sensation in the bone marrow.

A *delusional feeling* is a feeling of false belief, based on an incorrect inference about external reality. A *gustatory hallucination* involves primarily taste. A tactile or *haptic hallucination* involves the sense of touch (for example, formication—the feeling of bugs crawling under the skin). A *hypnopompic hallucination* is a hallucination that occurs as one awakes.

13.12. The answer is B (*Synopsis VII*, pages 480–483).

Noncompliance in taking medication after the first episode of schizophrenia is related to a subsequent relapse. Those patients who do not take their medications as prescribed have a higher than usual relapse rate.

The risk of personality deterioration increases with each schizophrenic relapse. Schizophrenic recoveries are often called remissions because many of the patients later relapse. With each schizophrenic episode, the patient has an increased probability of some permanent personality damage. *The natural course of the illness*, however, does not inevitably lead to intellectual deterioration or relapse. *Whether or not the patient is working, physical therapy*, and *individual psychotherapy* do not influence relapse as much as does medication.

13.13. The answer is E (all) (*Synopsis VII*, pages 470–471).

To make a diagnosis of schizophrenia, the psychiatrist must find at least one of the following symptoms: delusions (for example, *thought broadcasting*), *hallucinations*, disorganized speech, negative symptoms (for example, *flat affect*), and catatonic or grossly *disorganized behavior*. Table 13.1 lists the diagnostic criteria for schizophrenia.

13.14. The answer is E (all) (*Synopsis VII*, pages 465–466).

The majority of computed tomographic (CT) studies of patients with schizophrenia have reported *enlarged lateral and third ventricles in 10 to 50 percent of patients*, and *cortical atrophy in 10 to 35 percent of patients*. Controlled studies have also revealed *atrophy of the cerebellar vermis*, decreased radiodensity of brain parenchyma, and reversals of the normal brain asymmetries. Those *findings are not artifacts of treatment* and are not progressive or reversible. The enlargement of the ventricles seems to be present at the time of diagnosis, before the use of medication. Some studies have correlated the presence of CT scan findings with the presence of negative or deficit symptoms (for example, social isolation), neuropsychological impairment, frequent motor side effects from antipsychotics, and a poor premorbid adjustment.

13.15. The answer is E (*Synopsis VII*, pages 468 and 481).

In general, pooled studies show expectancy rates of about *50 percent* in monozygotic twins.

13.16. The answer is E (*Synopsis VII*, page 475).

Paraphrenic schizophrenia is not listed in DSM-IV as a diagnostic entity; however, it appears in the 10th revision of the International Classification of Diseases and Related Health Problems (ICD-10).

In paranoid schizophrenia there is a deterioration and splitting off of many of the psychic functions, whereas in paraphrenic schizophrenia the delusions are so logical, at least on the surface, as to appear to be little more than an extension of the premorbid personality. *Latent schizophrenia* is a form of schizophrenia in which, despite the existence of fundamental symptoms, no clear-cut psychotic episode or gross break with reality has occurred. It is not a term used in DSM-IV. In *simple deteriorative disorder (simple schizophrenia)* there is an insidious psychic impoverishment that affects the emotions, the intellect, and the will. Chronic dissatisfaction or complete

indifference to reality is characteristic, and the simple schizophrenic patient is isolated, estranged, and asocial. *Catatonic schizophrenia* is a state characterized by muscular rigidity and immobility. *Hebephrenic schizophrenia* is a complex of symptoms characterized by wild or silly behavior or mannerisms, an inappropriate affect, frequent hypochondriacal complaints, and delusions and hallucinations that are transient and unsystematized.

The term is sometimes used as a synonym for *paranoid schizophrenia*. In other usages the term is used for either a progressively deteriorating course of illness or the presence of a well-systemized delusional system.

13.17. The answer is B (*Synopsis VII*, page 477).

The most common schizophrenic hallucination is *auditory*, particularly the hearing of voices. Characteristically, two or more voices talk about the patient in the third person. Frequently, the voices address the patient, comment on the patient's activities and what is going on around that person, or are threatening or obscene and very disturbing to the patient. Many schizophrenic patients experience the hearing of their own thoughts. When they are reading silently, for example, they may be disturbed by hearing every word they are reading clearly spoken to them.

Visual hallucinations occur less frequently than auditory hallucinations in schizophrenic patients, but they are not rare. When visual hallucinations occur in schizophrenia, they are usually seen nearby, clearly defined, in color, life-size, in three dimensions, and moving. Visual hallucinations almost never occur by themselves but always in combination with hallucinations in one of the other sensory modalities. *Tactile, olfactory*, and *gustatory* hallucinations are less common than visual hallucinations.

13.18. The answer is D (*Synopsis VII*, pages 477–478).

The male psychiatric inpatient was exhibiting symptoms of *delusional thinking*. He believed that the doctor could control his thoughts.

Social withdrawal is a pathological retreat from interpersonal contact and social involvement. It is an extreme decrease of intellectual and emotional interest in the environment. It may be seen in schizophrenia and depression. *Hypervigilance* is the continual scanning of the environment for signs of threat. It is most often seen in paranoid disorders. *Fragmentation of thinking* is a disturbance in association, characterized by loosening, in which basic concepts become vague and incoherent and the thinking processes become so confused that they cannot result in a complete idea or action. It is a form of thinking often associated with schizophrenia. *Magical thinking* is a notion that thinking something is either the same thing as doing it or may cause it to happen. It is commonly experienced in dreams, in certain mental disorders, and by children.

13.19.   The answer is A (*Synopsis VII*, pages 304 and 476).

Catalepsy is a condition in which a person maintains the body position in which it has been placed. The position can be maintained for long periods of time, even though it may appear to be uncomfortable. The condition is also known as waxy flexibility and *cerea flexibilitas.*

A *mannerism* is a stereotyped gesture or expression that is peculiar to a given person. *Cataplexy* is the temporary sudden loss of muscle tone, causing weakness and immobilization. It can be precipitated by a variety of emotional states, and it is often followed by sleep. *Perseveration* speech, rather than motor, behavior and consists of the patient's giving the same verbal response to various questions.

13.20.   The answer is D (*Synopsis VII*, pages 480–481).

Poor prognostic features in schizophrenia include a family history of schizophrenia, poor premorbid social, sexual, and work histories, and *undifferentiated or disorganized features.* Features weighting toward a good prognosis in schizophrenia include mood symptoms (especially *depression*), *a family history of mood disorders, paranoid features*, and *an undulating course.* Table 13.3 presents a summary of the factors used to assess prognosis in schizophrenia.

13.21.   The answer is E (all) (*Synopsis VII*, pages 477–478).

Disordered thought is characteristic of schizophrenia. Thought disorders may be divided into disorders of content, form, and process. Disorders of content reflect ideas, beliefs, and interpretations of stimuli. *Delusions* are the most obvious examples of disorder of thought content. The delusions may be persecutory, grandiose, religious, or somatic. *Loss of ego boundaries* is the patient's lack of a clear sense of where the patient's own body, mind, and influence end and where those of other animate and inanimate

objects begin. For example, the content of thought may include ideas of reference that other people, persons on television, or newspaper items are making reference to the patient. Other symptoms include a sense of fusion with outside objects (for example, a tree or another person) or a sense of disintegration. Given that state of mind, patients with schizophrenia may have *sexual confusion* and doubts as to what sex they are or what their sexual orientation is. Disorders in thought form or process reflect how thoughts are conveyed. *Looseness of associations*, a disorder of thought form, was once thought to be pathognomonic for schizophrenia; however, that form of thought may be seen in other psychotic states as well. It is characterized by thoughts that are connected to each other by meanings known only to the patient and conveyed in a manner that is diffuse, unfocused, illogical, and even incoherent.

13.22.   The answer is D (*Synopsis VII*, pages 481–482).

Clozapine (Clozaril) *has not been associated with extrapyramidal side effects* or tardive dyskinesia. It is an antipsychotic medication that is appropriate in the treatment of schizophrenic patients who have not responded to first-line dopamine receptor antagonists or who have tardive dyskinesia. It *is not an appropriate first-line drug for the treatment of schizophrenia.* Clozapine *has been associated with a 1-to-2 percent (not 10-to-20 percent) incidence of agranulocytosis* and thus *requires weekly, not monthly, monitoring of blood indexes.* Clozapine *is believed to exert its therapeutic effect by blocking serotonin, not dopamine, receptors.*

13.23.   The answer is E (all) (*Synopsis VII*, pages 467–468).

Electrophysiological studies of schizophrenia patients include electroencephalogram (EEG) studies. Those studies indicate a higher than usual number of patients with abnormal recordings, increased sen-

Table 13.3
Features Weighting toward Good Prognosis and Poor Prognosis in Schizophrenia

Good Prognosis	Poor Prognosis
Late onset	Early onset
Obvious precipitating factors	No precipitating factors
Sudden onset	Insidious onset
Good premorbid social, sexual, and work histories	Poor premorbid social, sexual, and work histories
Mood disorder symptoms (especially depressive disorders)	Withdrawn, autistic behavior
Married	Single, divorced, or widowed
Family history of mood disorders	Family history of schizophrenia
Good support systems	Poor support systems
Positive symptoms	Negative symptoms
	Neurological signs and symptoms
	History of perinatal trauma
	No remissions in three years
	Many relapses
	History of assaultiveness

sitivity (for example, frequent spike activity) to activation procedures (for example, sleep deprivation), *decreased alpha activity*, increased theta and delta activity, possibly more epileptiform activity, and possibly more left-sided abnormalities. Evoked potential studies have generally shown increased amplitude of early components and decreased amplitude of late components. That difference may indicate that, although schizophrenia patients are more sensitive than other persons to sensory stimulation, they compensate for that increased sensitivity by blunting their processing of the information at higher cortical levels.

Other central nervous system (CNS) electrophysiological investigations have included depth electrodes and quantitative EEG (QEEG). One study reported that schizophrenic patients showed *spikes in the limbic area that correlate with psychotic behavior*, however, no control subjects were examined. QEEG studies of schizophrenia show *increased frontal lobe slow-wave activity* and *increased parietal lobe fast-wave activity*.

13.24–13.28.

13.24.   The answer is B (*Synopsis VII*, page 457).

13.25.   The answer is A (*Synopsis VII*, pages 452–458).

13.26.   The answer is C (*Synopsis VII*, page 457).

13.27.   The answer is D (*Synopsis VII*, page 457).

13.28.   The answer is E (*Synopsis VII*, page 458).

Key people in the history of schizophrenia include *Eugen Bleuler* (Swiss, 1857–1939), who coined the term *schizophrenia; Benedict Morel* (French, 1809–1873), who used the term *démence précoce* for deteriorated patients whose illnesses began in adolescence; *Karl Kalhbaum* (German, 1828–1899), who described symptoms of *catatonia; Ewald Hecker* (German, 1843–1909), who wrote about the extremely bizarre behavior of *hebephrenia*, and *E. Gabriel Langfeldt* (Norwegian, 1895–1900), who distinguished two groups of schizophrenias—process (nuclear) schizophrenia and the *schizophreniform psychosis*. Process schizophrenia has an insidious onset and a deteriorating course; schizophreniform psychosis has typical schizophrenic characteristics, but the patient has a relatively well-integrated premorbid personality with a sudden onset of illness and a good prognosis.

13.29–13.32

13.29.   The answer is A (*Synopsis VII*, page 457).

13.30.   The answer is A (*Synopsis VII*, page 457).

13.31.   The answer is B (*Synopsis VII*, pages 457–458).

13.32.   The answer is B (*Synopsis VII*, pages 457–458).

Emil Kraepelin (1856–1926) *latinized the term démence précoce* to dementia precox, a term that emphasized a distinct cognitive process (dementia) and the early onset (precox) that is characteristic of the disorder. Kraepelin *classified patients as being afflicted with manic-depressive psychoses, dementia precox, or paranoia*.

Eugen Bleuler (1857–1939) *coined the term "schizophrenia"* and *described the four As of schizophrenia—associations, autism, affect, and ambivalence*.

13.33–13.37

13.33.   The answer is C (*Synopsis VII*, pages 304 and 478).

13.34.   The answer is B (*Synopsis VII*, pages 305 and 478).

13.35.   The answer is A (*Synopsis VII*, pages 305 and 477–478).

13.36.   The answer is D (*Synopsis VII*, pages 305 and 478).

13.37.   The answer is E (*Synopsis VII*, pages 305 and 478).

Incoherence results from the use of *empty or obscure language*. A *neologism* is *new expression or word*.

Mutism is the *functional inhibition of speech*.

Echolalia is the *repeating of the same words the questioner has used*.

Verbigeration is the *senseless repetition of the same words or phrases*. It may, at times, go on for days.

13.38–13.43

13.38.   The answer is B (*Synopsis VII*, pages 458–459).

13.39.   The answer is B (*Synopsis VII*, pages 458–459).

13.40.   The answer is A (*Synopsis VII*, pages 458–459).

13.41.   The answer is A (*Synopsis VII*, pages 458–459).

13.42.   The answer is A (*Synopsis VII*, pages 458–459).

13.43.   The answer is A (*Synopsis VII*, pages 458–459).

Kurt Schneider (1887–1967) described a number of *first-rank symptoms* of schizophrenia that are considered of pragmatic value in making the diagnosis of schizophrenia, although they are not specific to the disease. The symptoms include *audible thoughts*, hearing one's thoughts aloud; *voices* or auditory hallucinations *commenting* on the patient's behavior; *thought withdrawal*, the removal of the patient's thoughts by others; and *the experience of having one's thoughts controlled.* Schneider pointed out that schizophrenia can be diagnosed by *second rank symptoms* when accompanied by a typical clinical presentation. Second-rank symptoms include *sudden delusional ideas, perplexity*, and feelings of emotional impoverishment. Schneider's diagnostic criteria for schizophrenia are listed in Table 13.4.

Table 13.4
Kurt Schneider's Diagnostic Criteria for Schizophrenia

1. First-rank symptoms

    a. Audible thoughts
    b. Voices arguing or discussing or both
    c. Voices commenting
    d. Somatic passivity experiences
    e. Thought withdrawal and other experiences of influenced thought
    f. Thought broadcasting
    g. Delusional perceptions
    h. All other experiences involving volition, made affects, and made impulses

2. Second-rank symptoms

    a. Other disorders of perception
    b. Sudden delusional ideas
    c. Perplexity
    d. Depressive and euphoric mood changes
    e. Feelings of emotional impoverishment
    f. "... and several others as well"

14

Other Psychotic Disorders

Psychotic disorders that do not meet the diagnostic criteria for schizophrenia or mood disorders with psychotic features are classified in the fourth edition of *Diagnostic and Statistical Manual of Mental Disorders* (DSM-IV) as other psychotic disorders. Those disorders include schizophreniform disorder, schizoaffective disorder, delusional disorder, brief psychotic disorder (called brief reactive psychosis in the revised third edition of DSM (DSM-III-R), and shared psychotic disorder (called induced psychotic disorder in DSM-III-R). DSM-IV also includes several new diagnoses under the classification of other psychotic disorders, including psychotic disorder due to a general medical condition and substance-induced psychotic disorder, postpsychotic depressive disorder of schizophrenia, and simple deteriorative disorder. In addition, DSM-IV includes several diagnoses under the classification of psychotic disorder not otherwise specified, including postpartum psychosis.

The DSM-IV classification of mental disorders includes a wide-ranging and diverse group of syndromes, with the major unifying element being the presence of psychotic symptoms. One ramification of the diverse classification is the underscoring of the concept of psychotic symptoms as a final common pathway from multiple initial causes.

The signs and symptoms of schizophreniform disorder are indistinguishable from schizophrenia except that they have been present for at least one month but less than six months. Schizoaffective disorder is characterized by symptoms of both schizophrenia and a mood disorder. Delusional disorder is characterized by the presence of nonbizarre delusions in the context of a generally intact personality without the presence of prominent hallucinations. Brief psychotic disorder is characterized by a schizophrenialike presentation that lasts at least one day but less than one month. Shared psychotic disorder (previously known as *folie à deux* and induced psychotic disorder) involves the development of a delusion in a person who has a close relationship with another person who already has an established delusion.

Psychotic disorder due to a general medical condition combines prominent hallucinations or delusions and a general medical condition causally related to the disorder. Substance-induced psychotic disorder is a combination of prominent hallucinations or delusions and substance intoxication or withdrawal. The full diagnosis should include the type of substance and whether the disorder began during intoxication or withdrawal.

Postpartum psychosis is characterized by depression, delusions, and thoughts by the new mother of harming either the infant or herself. All doctors should be familiar with the syndrome because of its serious potential. Atypical psychoses include Capgras's syndrome and Cotard's syndrome. Culture-bound psychotic syndromes include amok and koro.

Students should read Chapter 14 in *Kaplan and Sadock's Synopsis VII* and test their knowledge with the questions and answers below.

HELPFUL HINTS

Students should know the psychotic syndromes and other terms listed here.

paranoia	schizoaffective disorder	amok
paraphrenia	lifetime prevalence	koro
prevalence	suicidal incidence	*suk-yeong*
incidence	course	piblokto
age of onset	prognostic variables	Arctic hysteria
marital status	inclusion and exclusion criteria	windigo psychosis
SES	neuroendocrine function	autoscopic psychosis
family studies	TRH stimulation test	Ganser's syndrome
limbic system and basal ganglia	schizophreniform disorder	postpartum psychosis
neurological conditions	Gabriel Langfeldt	postpartum blues
reduplicative paramnesia	brief psychotic disorder	Cushing's syndrome
reaction formation	significant stressor	ICD-10
paranoid states	*bouffée délirante*	mental status examination
Clérambault's syndrome	good-prognosis schizophrenia	delusions
nihilistic delusion	psychodynamic formulation	erotomania
Cotard's syndrome	shared psychotic disorder	homicide
Capgras's syndrome	*folie à deux*	lycanthropy
Fregoli's syndrome	double insanity	neuropsychological testing
projection	psychosis of association	EEG and CT scan
denial	passive person and dominant	psychotherapy
Daniel Paul Schreber	person	antipsychotic drugs
homosexuality	atypical psychoses	dopamine receptor antagonists
paranoid pseudocommunity	culture-bound syndromes	clozapine
Norman Cameron	psychotic disorder NOS	lithium
delusional disorder	differential diagnosis	

QUESTIONS

DIRECTIONS: Each of the questions or incomplete statement below is followed by five suggested responses or completions. Select the *one* that is *best* in each case

14.1. A beautiful, successful 34-year-old interior designer was brought to a clinic by her 37-year-old husband, a prominent attorney. The husband lamented that for the past three years his wife had made increasingly shrill accusations that he was unfaithful to her. He declared that he had done everything in his power to convince her of his innocence, but there was no shaking her conviction. An examination of the facts revealed no evidence that the man had been unfaithful. When his wife was asked what her evidence was, she became vague and mysterious, declaring that she could tell such things by a faraway look in his eyes.

The patient was absolutely sure that she was right and felt highly insulted by the suggestion that she was imagining the disloyalty. Her husband reported that for the past year she had been increasingly bitter, creating a cold-war atmosphere in the household. Militantly entrenched against her husband, she refused to show him any affection except at social gatherings. She seemed intent on giving the impression socially that they had a good relationship; but, when they were alone, the coldness reentered the picture. She had physically assaulted her husband on occasion, but her account obscured the fact that she initiated the assaults; her description of the tussles began at the point at which the husband attempted to interrupt her assault by holding her arms. She declared that she would never forgive him for holding her down and squeezing her arms, and her account made it appear that she was unfairly restrained.

The patient experienced no hallucinations; her speech was well-organized; she interpreted proverbs with no difficulty; she seemed to have a good command of current events and generally displayed no difficulty in thinking, aside from her conviction of her husband's infidelity. She described herself as having a generally full life, with a few close friends and no problems except those centering on her experiences of unhappiness in the marriage. The husband reported that his wife was respected for her skills but that she had had difficulties for most of her life in close relationships with friends. She had lost a number of friends because of her apparent intolerance of differences in opinion. The patient reported that she did not want to leave the marriage, nor did she want her husband to leave her; instead, she was furious about his "injustice" and demanded that it be confessed and redeemed.

The patient's condition is best diagnosed as
A. schizophrenia, paranoid type
B. delusional disorder, jealous type
C. schizophreniform disorder
D. schizoaffective disorder, depressive type
E. delusional disorder, persecutory type

14.2. Delusional disorder
A. involves bizarre delusions that are impossible
B. has a prevalence in the United States of 5 percent
C. may lead to the development of a pseudocommunity
D. has a mean age of onset in the early 20s
E. of the somatic type is the most common

14.3. Schizoaffective disorder patients
A. tend to have a deteriorating course
B. do not usually respond to lithium
C. may exhibit symptoms of schizophrenia a mood disorder in an alternating fashion
D. tend to have a worse prognosis than do patients with schizophrenia
E. have a suicide rate of at least 50 percent

14.4. Ms. B was a 43-year-old married woman who entered the hospital in 1968 with a chief complaint of being concerned about her sex problem; she stated that she needed hypnotism to find out what was wrong with her sexual drive. Her husband supplied the history; he complained that she had had many extramarital affairs, with many different men, throughout their married life. He insisted that in one two-week period she had had as many as 100 sexual experiences with men outside the marriage. The patient agreed with that assessment of her behavior but would not speak of the experiences, saying that she blocked the memories out. She denied any particular interest in sexuality but said that apparently she felt a compulsive drive to go out and seek activity despite her lack of interest.

The patient had been married to her husband for more than 20 years. He was clearly the dominant partner in the marriage. The patient was fearful of his frequent jealous rages, and apparently it was he who suggested that she enter the hospital to receive hypotherapy. The patient maintained that she could not explain why she sought out other men, that she really did not want to do it. Her husband stated that on occasion he had tracked her down, when he found her, she acted as though she did not know him. She confirmed that statement and said she believed it was due to the fact that the episodes of her sexual promiscuity were blotted out by amnesia.

When the examining physician indicated that he questioned the reality of the woman's sexual adventures, her husband became furious and accused the physician and a ward attendant of having sexual relations with his wife.

Neither an amobarbital (Amybal) interview nor considerable psychotherapy with the wife was able to clear the blocked-out memory of periods of sexual activities. The patient did admit to a memory of having had two extramarital relationships in the past, one 20 years before her admission to the hospital and the other just a year before her admission. She stated that the last one had actually been planned by her husband and that he was in the same house at the time. She continued to believe that she had actually had countless extramarital sexual experiences, although she remembered only two of them.

On the basis of the woman's history, the most likely diagnosis is
A. amnestic disorder
B. dissociative amnesia
C. schizophrenia
D. shared psychotic disorder
E. brief psychotic disorder

14.5. A 45-year-old single woman was brought to the hospital by her parents. Over the preceding year, the patient had begun to believe that her parents and state government officials were involved in a plan to get her to give away a piece of land she owned in the country. She began accusing the officials of putting substances in her food that damaged her hair and caused her to have receding gums. She wrote numerous letters to federal officials complaining of those events, yet all the while she worked efficiently at her job of examining income tax forms. She had had no previous contact with mental health professionals. The mental status examination revealed no hallucinations, incoherence, or loosening of associations.

The most likely diagnosis is
A. schizophrenia, paranoid type
B. schizophreniform disorder
C. delusional disorder
D. a mood disorder with psychotic features
E. paranoid personality disorder

14.6. True statements concerning brief psychotic disorder include all the following *except*
A. the stressor must be of sufficient severity to cause significant stress to any person in the same socioeconomic and cultural class
B. many patients also have preexisting personality disorders
C. prodromal symptoms appear before the onset of the precipitating stressor
D. mood disorders may be common in the relatives of affected probands
E. good prognostic features include a severe precipitating stressor, acute onset, and confusion or perplexity during psychosis

14.7. Which of the following statements applies to schizoaffective disorders?
A. The patient presents with a mixture of psychotic and mood disorder features
B. Mood-incongruent delusions and hallucinations are part of the clinical picture
C. The diagnosis cannot be made if the patient is suffering from a cognitive disorder
D. Delusions of control and auditory hallucinations are common features
E. All the above

14.8. The major treatment methods used for schizoaffective disorder are all the following *except*
A. psychoanalysis
B. antipsychotic agents
C. tricyclic drugs
D. antimanic drugs
E. electroconvulsive therapy

14.9. Which of the following combinations best characterizes the occurrence of mental disorders among the relatives of patients with schizoaffective disorder?
A. A frequency of schizophrenia comparable to that seen among the relatives of schizophrenic patients and a frequency of mood disorders greater than that expected for the general population
B. A frequency of schizophrenia less than that seen in the general population and a frequency of mood disorders greater than that expected for the relatives of patients with mood disorders
C. A frequency of schizoaffective disorder greater than that seen in the general population and a frequency of mood disorders less than that seen among the relatives of patients with mood disorders
D. A frequency of schizophrenia less than that seen in the relatives of schizophrenic patients and a frequency of mood disorders comparable to that seen in the relatives of patients with mood disorders
E. A frequency of schizoaffective disorder comparable to that of the general population; frequency of schizophrenia greater than that of the general population

14.10. The main defense mechanism used in shared psychotic disorder is
A. projection
B. regression
C. reaction formation
D. displacement
E. identification with the aggressor

14.11. Most studies of normal pregnant women indicate that the percentage who report the blues in the early postpartum period is about
A. 10 percent
B. 25 percent
C. 50 percent
D. 75 percent
E. 100 percent

14.12. Postpartum psychosis is
A. found in 1 to 2 per 1,000 deliveries
B. usually experienced within days of delivery
C. a psychiatric emergency
D. not to be confused with postpartum blues
E. all the above

14.13. In schizoaffective disorder, all the following variables indicate a poor prognosis *except*
A. depressive type
B. no precipitating factor
C. a predominance of psychotic symptoms
D. bipolar type
E. early onset

14.14. Examples of atypical psychoses include
A. Capgras's syndrome
B. Cotard's syndrome
C. postpartum psychosis
D. koro
E. all the above

14.15. According to the fourth edition of *Diagnostic and Statistical Manual of Mental Disorders* (DSM-IV), postpartum psychosis is best classified as
A. an anxiety disorder
B. psychotic disorder not otherwise specified
C. a mood disorder
D. schizophrenia
E. a personality disorder

14.16. True statements concerning the treatment of shared psychotic disorder include
A. separation of the submissive person from the dominant person is the primary intervention
B. recovery rates have been reported to be as low as 10 percent
C. the submissive person often requires treatment with antipsychotic drugs
D. the submissive person and the dominant person usually move back together after treatment
E. all the above

14.17. Shared psychotic disorder occurs most frequently among
A. women
B. low socioeconomic groups
C. the deaf
D. members of the same family
E. all the above

14.18. Delusional disorder
A. is less common than schizophrenia
B. is caused by frontal lobe lesions
C. is an early stage of schizophrenia
D. usually begins by age 20
E. is more common in men than in women

14.19. The characteristic feature of conjugal paranoia is
A. somatic delusion
B. idea of reference
C. delusion of grandeur
D. delusion of infidelity
E. delusion of persecution

14.20. Which of the following statements is correct?
A. The delusions of schizophrenia, paranoid type, tend to be bizarre and fragmented, in contrast to the better-organized delusions of delusional disorder
B. In the few patients who have hallucinations in conjunction with delusional disorder, the hallucinations are associated with the delusions, whereas hallucinations in schizophrenia are not necessarily connected with the delusions
C. In paranoid patients with a depressed affect, the affect is secondary to the delusional system, whereas in depressed patients the delusions are secondary to the depression
D. Delusions seen in cognitive disorders are characterized by forgetfulness and disorientation, whereas delusional disorder is characterized by intact orientation and memory
E. All the above

14.21. A 17-year-old high school junior was brought to the emergency room by her distraught mother, who was at a loss to understand her daughter's behavior. Two days earlier, the patient's father had been buried; he had died of a sudden myocardial infarction earlier in the week. The patient had become wildly agitated at the cemetery, screaming uncontrollably and needing to be restrained by relatives. She was inconsolable at home, sat rocking in a corner, and talked about a devil that had come to claim her soul. Before her father's death, her mother reported, she was a "typical teenager, popular, a very good student, but sometimes prone to overreacting." The girl had no previous psychiatric history.
The most likely diagnosis is
A. grief
B. brief psychotic disorder
C. schizophrenia
D. substance intoxication
E. delusional disorder

14.22. Which of the following statements regarding paranoid psychosis (delusional disorder) in immigrants is true?
A. The development of delusional disorder is aggravated by the immigrant's appearance and mannerisms.
B. Uncertainty in the new environment tends to increase isolation.
C. The incidence of paranoid psychosis (delusional disorder) in immigrants is about three times as high as that among native-born American patients.
D. The increased incidence of delusional disorders in immigrants may be due to an increased immigration of persons with unstable personalities.
E. All the above

DIRECTIONS: Each group of questions below consist of lettered headings followed by a list of numbered words or statements. For each numbered word or statement, select the *one* lettered heading that is most closely associated with it. Each lettered heading may be selected once, more than once, or not at all.

Questions 14.23–14.25
A. Schizophreniform disorder
B. Brief psychotic disorder
C. Simple deteriorative disorder

14.23. Schizophrenic symptoms last at least one day but no more than one month

14.24. Characterized as the progressive development of symptoms of social withdrawal and other deficit symptoms of schizophrenia

14.25. Schizophrenic symptoms last least one month but less than six months

Questions 14.26–14.28
A. Amok
B. Koro
C. Wihtigo

14.26. Delusion that the person's penis is shrinking and may disappear

14.27. Affected persons believe that they may be transformed into a giant monster that eats human flesh

14.28. Sudden, unprovoked outburst of wild rage in which affected persons attack anything in their path

Questions 14.29–14.33
A. Delusions of guilt and somatic delusions
B. Delusions secondary to perceptual disturbances
C. Grandiose delusions
D. Bizarre delusions of being controlled
E. Delusions of jealousy and persecution

14.29. Delusional disorder

14.30. Schizophrenia

14.31. Mania

14.32. Depressive disorders

14.33. Cognitive disorders

Questions 14.34–14.38
A. Paranoid personality disorder
B. Delusional disorder
C. Schizophrenia
D. Manic episode
E. Major depressive episode

14.34. Psychomotor retardation

14.35. Thought broadcasting

14.36. Easily distracted with an elevated, expansive, or irritable mood

14.37. Persecutory or grandiose delusions

14.38. Suspiciousness and mistrust of people

ANSWERS

Other Psychotic Disorders

14.1. The answer is B (*Synopsis VII*, pages 506 and 508).

The patient's condition is best diagnosed as *delusional disorder, jealous type* (Table 14.1). Although not all complaints of infidelity are unfounded, in this case the evidence supported the idea that the wife's jealousy was delusional. Delusional jealousy may be seen in schizophrenia; but in the absence of the characteristic psychotic symptoms of schizophrenia—such as bizarre delusions, hallucinations, and dis-

organized speech—it is a symptom of delusional disorder. As is commonly the case in delusional disorder, the woman's impairment because of her delusion did not involve her daily functioning apart from her relationship with her husband.

The patient's condition cannot be diagnosed as *schizophrenia, paranoid type*, because of the absence of the characteristic psychotic symptoms of schizophrenia, such as bizarre delusions and hallucinations. Furthermore, the woman showed no evidence since the onset of the disturbance of a deterioration of functioning in the areas of work, self-care, and other interpersonal relationships not involved in the delusion. A person with *schizophreniform disorder* (Table 14.2) has symptoms identical to schizophrenia except that the symptoms last at least one month but less than six months; in schizophrenia, the symptoms must be present for at least six months. The patient's condition cannot be diagnosed as *schizoaffective disorder, depressive type* (Table 14.3) because she showed no evidence of schizophrenia or a major depressive episode. In *delusional disorder, persecutory type*, the delusion usually involves a single theme or a series of connected themes, such as being conspired against, cheated, spied on, followed, poisoned or drugged, maliciously maligned, harassed, or obstructed in the pursuit of long-term goals. The patient in this question did not have such a delusion.

Table 14.1
Diagnostic Criteria for Delusional Disorder

A. Nonbizarre delusions (i.e., involving situations that occur in real life, such as being followed, poisoned, infected, loved at a distance, or deceived by one's spouse or lover, or having a disease) of at least 1 month's duration.

B. Criterion A for schizophrenia has never been met. **Note:** Tactile and olfactory hallucinations may be present in delusional disorder if they are related to the delusional theme.

C. Apart from the impact of the delusion(s) or its ramifications, functioning is not markedly impaired and behavior is not obviously odd or bizarre.

D. If mood episodes have occurred concurrently with delusions, their total duration has been brief relative to the duration of the delusional periods.

E. The disturbance is not due to the direct physiological effects of a substance (e.g., a drug of abuse, a medication) or a general medical condition.

Specify type (the following types are assigned based on the predominant delusional theme):

    Erotomanic type: delusions that another person, usually of higher status, is in love with the individual
    Grandiose type: delusions of inflated worth, power, knowledge, identity, or special relationship to a deity or famous person
    Jealous type: delusions that the individual's sexual partner is unfaithful
    Persecutory type: delusions that the person (or someone to whom the person is close) is being malevolently treated in some way
    Somatic type: delusions that the person has some physical defect or general medical condition
    Mixed type: delusions characteristic of more than one of the above types but no one theme predominates.
    Unspecified type

14.2
Diagnostic Criteria for Schizophreniform Disorder

A. Criteria A, D, and E of schizophrenia are met.

B. An episode of the disorder (including prodromal, active, and residual phases) lasts at least 1 month but less than 6 months. (When the diagnosis must be made without waiting for recovery, it should be qualified as "provisional.")

Specify if:
    Without good prognostic features
    With good prognostic features as evidenced by two (or more) of the following:

    (1) onset of prominent psychotic symptoms within four weeks of the first noticeable change in usual behavior or functioning
    (2) confusion or perplexity at the height of the psychotic episode
    (3) good premorbid social and occupational functioning
    (4) absence of blunted or flat affect

14.2. The answer is C (*Synopsis VII*, pages 505–506).

Delusional disorder *may lead to the development of a pseudocommunity*. Elaboration of the delusion to include imagined persons and the attribution of malevolent motivations to both real and imagined people results in the organization of the pseudocommunity—that is, a perceived community of plotters. That delusional entity hypothetically binds together projected fears and wishes to justify the patient's aggression and to provide a tangible target for the patient's hostilities.

Delusional disorder, unlike schizophrenia, does not involve bizarre delusions that are impossible. For example, patients with delusional disorder may feel that they are being followed by the Federal Bureau of Investigation, which is possible; schizophrenia patients may feel that they are being controlled by Martians, which is impossible.

Delusional disorder has a prevalence *in the United States of 0.025 to 0.03 percent*. Thus, delusional disorder is much rarer than schizophrenia, which has a prevalence of about 1 percent, and the mood disorders, which have a prevalence of about 5 percent.

Delusional disorder *has a mean age of onset of about 40 years*, but the range for the age of onset runs from 18 to the 90s. Delusional disorder *of the somatic type is not the most common*. The persecutory type is the most common.

Table 14.3
Diagnostic Criteria for Schizoaffective Disorder

A. An uninterrupted period of illness during which, at some time, there is either a major depressive episode, a manic episode, or a mixed episode concurrent with symptoms that meet criterion A for schizophrenia.

   Note: The major depressive episode must include criterion A1: depressed mood.

B. During the same period of illness, there have been delusions or hallucinations for at least 2 weeks in the absence of prominent mood symptoms.

C. Symptoms that meet criteria for a mood episode are present for a substantial portion of the total duration of the active and residual periods of the illness.

D. The disturbance is not due to the direct physiological effects of a substance (e.g., a drug of abuse, a medication) or a general medical condition.

Specify type:
   Bipolar type: if the disturbance includes a manic or a mixed episode (or a manic or a mixed episode and major depressive episodes)
   Depressive type: if the disturbance only includes major depressive episodes

14.3. The answer is C (*Synopsis VII*, pages 500–501).

Schizoaffective disorder patients *may exhibit symptoms of schizophrenia and a mood disorder in an alternating fashion*. As a group, schizoaffective disorder patients *tend to have a nondeteriorating course* and *usually respond to lithium*. Also as a group, schizoaffective disorder patients tend to *have a better prognosis than do patients with schizophrenia* and a worse prognosis than do patients with mood disorders. Schizoaffective disorder patients *have a suicide rate of 10 percent, not 50 percent*.

14.4. The answer is D (*Synopsis VII*, pages 491–492).

The most likely diagnosis in the case of the 43-year-old woman is *shared psychotic disorder* (Table 14.4). The disorder occurs when the delusional system of the patient has developed out of a close relationship with another person who has a previously established delusion. The disorder has been popularly known as *folie à deux*. Shared psychotic disorder is characterized by a passive person who absorbs the more dominant person's delusion. The delusion is often something in the realm of possibility, not as bizarre as the delusions often seen in schizophrenia.

In the case described, one's first impression is that an *amnestic disorder* or *dissociative amnesia* should be considered. However, the woman was not suffering from a lack of memory of events as much as the husband was suffering from persecutory delusions that his wife was unfaithful, and his wife had accepted that delusion. She adopted his persecutory delusion and did not really have any kind of amnesia. She showed none of the essential features of *schizophrenia* (bizarre delusions, hallucinations, or incoherence), and the essential criteria for *brief* (the sudden onset of a florid psychosis immediately after a significant psychosocial stressor and lasting less than one month) were not present.

Table 14.4
Diagnostic Criteria for Shared Psychotic Disorder

A. A delusion develops in an individual in the context of a close relationship with another person(s), who has an already established-delusion.

B. The delusion is similar in content to that of the person who already has the established delusion.

C. The disturbance is not better accounted for by another psychotic disorder (e.g., schizophrenia) or a mood disorder with psychotic features and is not due to the direct physiological effects of a substance (e.g., a drug of abuse, a medication) or a general medical condition.

14.5. The answer is C (*Synopsis VII*, pages 506–510).

On the basis of the information given, the most likely diagnosis in the case described is *delusional disorder*. The central features are the nonbizarre delusions involving situations that occur in real life—such as being followed, poisoned, and deceived—of at least one month's duration. The age of onset for delusional disorder is usually between 40 and 55. Intellectual and occupational functioning is usually satisfactory, whereas social and marital functioning is often impaired. The diagnosis is made only when no organic factor can be found that has initiated or maintained the disorder.

By definition, delusional disorder patients do not have prominent or sustained hallucinations, and the nonbizarre quality of the delusions cited—for example, substances put in her food—rule out, *schizophrenia paranoid type*, and *schizophreniform disorder*. In addition, as compared with schizophrenia, delusional disorder usually produces less impairment in daily functioning. Another consideration in the diagnostic criteria of schizophreniform disorder is the specification that the episode lasts less than six months (the patient described had symptoms over one year). The differential diagnosis with *mood disorders with psychotic features* can be difficult, as the psychotic features associated with mood disorders often involve nonbizarre delusions, and prominent hallucinations are unusual. The differential diagnosis depends on the relation of the mood disturbance and the delusions. In a major depression with psychotic features, the onset of the depressed mood usually antedates the appearance of psychosis and is present after the psychosis remits. Also, the depressive symptoms are usually prominent and severe. If depressive symptoms occur in delusional disorder, they occur after the onset of the delusions, are usually mild, and often remit while the delusional symptoms persist. In *paranoid personality disorder* there are no delusions, although there is paranoid ideation.

14.6. The answer is C (*Synopsis VII*, pages 513–514).

No prodromal symptoms appear before the onset of the precipitating stressor in brief psychotic disorder. A significant stressor maybe a causative factor for brief psychotic disorder, and *the stressor must be of sufficient severity to cause significant stress to any person in the same socioeconomic and cultural class.* However, *many patients also have preexisting personality disorders.* Although schizophrenia has not been found to be common in the relatives of persons with brief psychotic disorder, *mood disorders may be common in the relatives of affected probands. Good prognostic features include a severe precipitating stressor, acute onset, and confusion or perplexity during the psychosis.* Table 14.5 lists the diagnostic criteria for brief psychotic disorder.

Table 14.5
Diagnostic Criteria for Brief Psychotic Disorder

A. Presence of one (or more) of the following symptoms:

   (1) delusions
   (2) hallucinations
   (3) disorganized speech (e.g., frequent derailment or incoherence)
   (4) grossly disorganized or catatonic behavior

   Note: Do not include a symptom if it is a culturally sanctioned response pattern.

B. Duration of an episode of the disturbance is at least 1 day but less than 1 month, with eventual full return to premorbid level of functioning.

C. The disturbance is not better accounted for by a mood disorder with psychotic features, schizoaffective disorder, or schizophrenia and is not due to the direct physiological effects of a substance (e.g., a drug of abuse, a medication) or a general medical condition.

Specify if:

   With marked stressor(s) (brief reactive psychosis): if symptoms occur shortly after and apparently in response to events that, singly or together, would be markedly stressful to almost anyone in similar circumstances in the person's culture

   Without marked stressor(s): if psychotic symptoms do not occur shortly after, or are not apparently in response to events that, singly or together, would be markedly stressful to almost anyone in similar circumstances in the person's culture

   With postpartum onset: if onset within 4 weeks postpartum

Table from DSM-IV, *Diagnostic and Statistical Manual of Mental Disorders,* ed 4. Copyright American Psychiatric Association, Washington, 1994. Used with permission.

14.7. The answer is E (all) (*Synopsis VII*, pages 501–502).

In schizoaffective disorder *the patient presents with a mixture of psychotic and mood disorder features. Mood-incongruent delusions and hallucinations are part of the clinical feature. The diagnosis* of schizoaffective disorder *cannot be made if the patient is suffering from a cognitive disorder.*

Two kinds of psychotic symptoms define schizoaffective disorders. In the first kind *delusions of control and* certain types of *auditory hallucinations are common,* suggesting schizophrenia if there were no accompanying mood disorder features. The second kind includes the symptoms that arise in the context of a mood disorder without an apparent relation to depression or elation.

14.8. The answer is A (*Synopsis VII*, page 503).

Since schizoaffective disorder includes psychotic symptoms that are part of the criterion list for schizophrenia, it follows that *psychoanalysis* is not be the treatment of choice. Rather, psychopharmacologic or biological treatments are indicated, perhaps ideally in conjunction with some form of supportive psychotherapy.

Most patients with schizoaffective disorder require hospitalization because of their psychotic and mood disorder features or their risk for suicide. *Antipsychotic agents* (such as the phenothiazines and butyrophenones), *tricyclic drugs, antimanic drugs* (such as lithium [Eskalith]), and *electroconvulsive therapy* (ECT) are the major treatment methods used.

14.9. The answer is D (*Synopsis VII*, pages 501–502).

The occurrence of mental disorders among the relatives of patients with schizoaffective disorder includes an increased risk of schizoaffective disorder, *a frequency of schizophrenia less than that seen in the relatives of schizophrenic patients and a frequency of mood disorders comparable to that seen in the relatives of patients with mood disorders* but greater than that expected for the general population. In fact, most of the ill relatives of patients with schizoaffective disorders suffer from uncomplicated mood disorders.

14.10. The answer is E (*Synopsis VII*, page 491.)

The main defense mechanism used in shared psychotic disorder is *identification with the aggressor*. The aggressor is the dominant member of the two persons who share the psychosis. The initiator of the psychosis is usually the sicker of the two, often a person with schizophrenia, paranoid type, on whom the other person is dependent. Identification with the aggressor is an unconscious process by which persons incorporate within themselves the mental image of a person who represents a source of frustration in the outside world. A primitive defense, it operates in the interest and the service of the developing ego.

Projection is an unconscious defense mechanism in which a person attributes to another those generally unconscious ideas, thoughts, feelings, and impulses that are personally undesirable or unacceptable. By externalizing whatever is unacceptable, such persons deal with it as a situation apart from themselves. *Regression* is an unconscious defense mechanism in which a person undergoes a partial or total return to early patterns of adaptation. Regression is observed in many psychiatric conditions, particularly schizophrenia. *Reaction formation* is an unconscious defense mechanism in which a person has an attitude or interest that is the direct antithesis of some unacceptable wish or impulse that the person harbors. *Displacement* is an unconscious defense mechanism by which the emotional component of an unacceptable idea or object is transferred to a more acceptable component.

14.11. The answer is C (*Synopsis VII*, pages 36 and 494–495).

Postpartum psychosis should not be confused with postpartum blues, a normal condition that occurs in about *50 percent* of women after childbirth. The blues are self-limited, last only a few days, and

are characterized by tearfulness, fatigue, anxiety, and irritability that begin shortly after childbirth and lessen in severity each day postpartum.

14.12. The answer is E (all) (*Synopsis VII*, pages 494–496).

Postpartum psychosis is *found in 1 to 2 per 1,000 deliveries*. The risk is increased if the patient or the patient's mother had a previous postpartum illness or mood disorder. The symptoms are *usually experienced within days of delivery*, and almost always within the first eight weeks after giving birth. The patient begins to complain of insomnia, restlessness, and fatigue, and she shows lability of mood with tearfulness. Later symptoms include suspiciousness, confusion, incoherence, irrational statements, and obsessive concerns about the baby's health. Delusional material may involve the idea that the baby is dead or defective. The birth may be denied, or ideas of persecution, influence, or perversity may be expressed. Hallucinations may involve voices telling the patient to kill her baby. Postpartum psychosis is *a psychiatric emergency*. In one study, 5 percent of patients killed themselves, and 4 percent killed the baby. Postpartum psychosis is *not to be confused with postpartum blues*.

14.13. The answer is D (*Synopsis VII*, pages 502–503).

The course and the prognosis of schizoaffective disorder are variable. As a group, patients with this disorder have a prognosis intermediate between patients with schizophrenia and patients with mood disorders. Schizoaffective disorder, *bipolar type*, is associated with a good prognosis. A poor prognosis is associated with the *depressive type* of schizoaffective disorder. A poor prognosis is also associated with the following variables: *no precipitating factor, a predominance of psychotic symptoms, early or insidious onset*, a poor premorbid history, and a positive family history of schizophrenia.

14.14. The answer is E (all) (*Synopsis VII*, pages 493–496).

Examples of atypical psychoses include *Capgras's syndrome, Cotard's syndrome, postpartum psychosis*, and *koro*. In general, they are rare, exotic, and unusual mental disorders; (1) syndromes that occur only at a particular time (for example, during the menses or postpartum); (2) syndromes that are restricted to a specific cultural setting—that is, culture-bound syndromes; (3) psychoses with unusual features, such as persistent auditory hallucinations; (4) syndromes that seem to belong to a well-known diagnostic entity but that show some features that cannot be reconciled with the generally accepted typical characteristics of that diagnostic category; and (5) psychoses about which information is inadequate to make a specific diagnosis.

Capgras's syndrome is characterized by the delusional conviction that other persons in the environment are not their real selves but are doubles who, like imposters, assume the roles of the persons they impersonate and behave like them.

In Cotard's syndrome, patients complain of having lost not only possessions, status, and strength but also the heart, blood, and intestines. The world outside is often reduced to nothingness.

Postpartum psychosis is a syndrome that occurs after childbirth and is characterized by delusions and severe depression. Thoughts of wanting to harm the newborn infant or oneself are common and represent a real danger. Most patients with this disorder have an underlying mental illness—most commonly a bipolar disorder and, less commonly, schizophrenia. A few cases result from a cognitive disorder associated with perinatal events. Those women with a prior history of schizophrenia or a mood disorder should be classified as having a recurrence of those disorders, rather than an atypical psychosis.

Koro is a culture-bound syndrome characterized by a patient's desperate fear that his penis is shrinking and may disappear into his abdomen. The syndrome is found in Southeast Asia and in some areas of China.

In the fourth edition of *Diagnostic and Statistical Manual of Mental Disorders* (DSM-IV), atypical psychoses are classified as psychotic disorders not otherwise specified (Table 14.6).

Table 14.6
Diagnostic Criteria for Psychotic Disorder Not Otherwise Specified

This category includes psychotic symptomatology (i.e., delusions, hallucinations, disorganized speech, grossly disorganized or catatonic behavior) about which there is inadequate information to make a specific diagnosis or about which there is contradictory information, or disorders with psychotic symptoms that do not meet the criteria for any specific psychotic disorder.

Examples include:

1. Postpartum psychosis that does not meet criteria for mood disorder with psychotic features, brief psychotic disorder, psychotic disorder due to a general medical condition, or substance-induced psychotic disorder
2. Psychotic symptoms that have lasted for less than 1 month but that have not yet remitted, so that the criteria for brief psychotic disorder are not met
3. Persistent auditory hallucinations in the absence of any other features
4. Persistent nonbizarre delusions with periods of overlapping mood episodes that have been present for a substantial portion of the delusional disturbance
5. Situations in which the clinician has concluded that a psychotic disorder is present, but is unable to determine whether it is primary, due to a general medical condition, or substance induced

Table from DSM-IV, *Diagnostic and Statistical Manual of Mental Disorders,* ed 4. Copyright American Psychiatric Association, Washington, 1994. Used with permission.

14.15.   The answer is B (*Synopsis VII*, page 494).

According to DSM-IV, postpartum psychosis is classified as a psychotic disorder not otherwise specified when no other psychotic disorder can be diagnosed. An *anxiety disorder* is a disorder in which anxiety is the most prominent disturbance or in which the patients experience anxiety if they resist giving in to their symptoms. A *mood disorder* is a mental disorder in which disturbance of mood is the primary characteristic; disturbances in thinking and behavior are secondary characteristics. *Schizophrenia* is a psychotic mental disorder characterized by disturbances in thinking, mood, and behavior. A *personality disorder* is a mental disorder characterized by inflexible, deeply ingrained, maladaptive patterns of adjustment to life that cause significant impairments of adaptive functioning.

14.16.   The answer is E (all) (*Synopsis VII*, page 492).

Separation of the submissive person from the dominant person is the primary intervention. Clinical reports vary, but *recovery rates have been reported to be as low as 10 percent. The submissive person often requires treatment with antipsychotic drugs,* just as the dominant person needs antipsychotic drugs. *The submissive person and the dominant person usually move back together after treatment.*

14.17.   The answer is E (all) (*Synopsis VII*, page 491).

Shared psychotic disorder is rare but is more common in *women* than in men. Persons in all socioeconomic classes may be affected, although it may be most common in *low socioeconomic groups.* Patients with physical disabilities, such as *the deaf,* are also at increased risk because of the dependent relationships that may develop among them. More than 95 percent of all cases involve two *members of the same family.* About a third of the cases involve two sisters; another third involve a husband and a wife or a mother and a child. Two brothers, a brother and a sister, and a father and a child have also been reported.

14.18.   The answer is A (*Synopsis VII*, page 504).

Delusional disorder *is less common than schizophrenia.* Its prevalence in the United States is estimated to be 0.03 percent—in contrast with schizophrenia, 1 percent, and mood disorders, 5 percent.

The neuropsychiatric approach to delusional disorder derives from the observation that delusions are a common symptom in many neurological conditions, particularly those involving the limbic systems and the basal ganglia. No evidence indicates that the disorder *is caused by frontal lobe lesions.* Long-term follow-up of patients with delusional disorder has found that their diagnoses are rarely revised as schizophrenia or mood disorders; hence, delusional disorder *is not an early stage of schizophrenia* or mood disorders. Moreover, delusional disorder has a later onset than does schizophrenia or mood disorders. The mean age of onset is 40 years; the disorder *does not usually begin by age 20*. The disorder *is slightly more common in women than in men*.

14.19.   The answer is D (*Synopsis VII*, page 508).

In *delusion of infidelity* the spouse is said to have conjugal paranoia or the Othello syndrome. Small bits of "evidence," such as disarrayed clothing and spots on the sheets, may be collected and used to justify the delusion. Delusional disorder, jealous type, is the diagnosis.

The characteristic feature of a *somatic delusion* is that the body is perceived to be disturbed or disordered in all or individual organs or parts. An *idea of reference* is a preoccupation with the idea that the actions of other persons relate to oneself. The characteristic feature of a *delusion of grandeur* is an exaggerated concept of one's importance, power, knowledge, or identity. A *delusion of persecution* involves the pathological belief that one is being attacked, harassed, cheated, or conjured against.

14.20.   The answer is E (all) (*Synopsis VII*, pages 503–512).

The delusions of schizophrenia, paranoid type, tend to be bizarre and fragmented, in contrast to the better-organized delusions of delusional disorder. In the few patients who have hallucinations in conjunction with delusional disorder, *the hallucinations are associated with the delusions,* whereas hallucinations in schizophrenia are not necessarily connected with the delusions. In paranoid patients with a depressed affect *the affect is secondary to the delusional system,* whereas in depressed patients the delusions are secondary to the depression. *Delusions seen in cognitive disorders are characterized by forgetfulness and disorientation,* whereas delusional disorder is characterized by intact orientation and memory.

14.21.   The answer is B (*Synopsis VII*, page 514).

The sudden onset of a florid psychotic episode immediately after a marked psychosocial stressor, such as the death of a loved one, in the absence of increasing psychopathology before the stressor indicates the diagnosis of *brief psychotic disorder. Grief* is an expected and normal reaction to the loss of a loved one. The girl's reaction, however, was not only more severe than would be expected (wildly agitated, screaming) but also involved psychotic symptoms (the devil). Typically, the psychotic symptoms in brief psychotic disorder last for more than a day but no more than a month. In *schizophrenia* the symptoms last for at least six months. *Substance intoxication* can mimic brief psychotic disorder, but the case presented shows no evidence of substance use. *Delusional disorder* presents with nonbizarre delusions of at least one month's duration, with otherwise apparently normal behavior.

14.22.   The answer is E (all) (*Synopsis VII*, pages 189 and 504).

The development of suspiciousness and paranoid ideas is commonly found in immigrants. Surrounded by strange people whose ways of emotional reaction are much different, *its development of delusional disorder is aggravated by the immigrant's appearance and mannerisms*, which often become objects of contempt or ridicule. Uncertainty in the new environment tends to increase isolation. The incidence of paranoid psychosis (delusional disorder) in immigrants is about three times as high as that among native-born American patients. *The increased incidence of delusional disorder in immigrants may be due to an increased immigration of persons with unstable personalities.*

14.23–14.25

14.23.   The answer is B (*Synopsis VII*, page 512).

14.24.   The answer is C (*Synopsis VII*, page 490).

14.25.   The answer is A (*Synopsis VII*, page 496).

Schizophreniform disorder is identical in every respect to schizophrenia except that its *symptoms last at least one month but less than six months*. Patients with schizophreniform disorder return to their baseline level of functioning once the disorder has resolved. In contrast, for a patient to meet the diagnostic criteria for schizophrenia, the symptoms must have been present for at least six months. *Brief psychotic disorder* is characterized primarily by the *fact that the schizophrenic symptoms last at least one day but less than one month*.

Simple deteriorative disorder,, a still controversial diagnostic category, is characterized as the progressive development of symptoms of social withdrawal and other symptoms similar to the deficit symptoms of schizophrenia (Table 14.7).

Table 14.7
Research Criteria for Simple Deteriorative Disorder

A. Progressive development over a period of at least a year of all of the following:

  (1) marked decline in occupational or academic functioning
  (2) gradual appearance and deepening of negative symptoms such as affective flattening, alogia, and avolition
  (3) poor interpersonal rapport, social isolation, or social withdrawal

B. Criterion A for schizophrenia has never been met.

C. The symptoms are not better accounted for by schizotypal or schizoid personality disorder, a psychotic disorder, a mood disorder, an anxiety disorder, a dementia, or mental retardation and are not due to the direct physiological effects of a substance or a general medical condition.

Table from DSM-IV, *Diagnostic and Statistical Manual of Mental Disorders,* ed 4. Copyright American Psychiatric Association, Washington, 1994. Used with permission.

14.26–14.28

14.26. The answer is B (*Synopsis VII*, pages 190 and 494).

14.27. The answer is C (*Synopsis VII*, page 494).

14.28. The answer is A (*Synopsis VII*, pages 190 and 493).

The Malayan word *"amok"* means to engage furiously in battle. The amok syndrome consists of a *sudden, unprovoked outburst of wild rage in which affected persons attack anything in their path.* Savage homicidal attack is generally preceded by a period of preoccupation, brooding, and mild depression. After the attack, the person feels exhausted, has no memory of the attack, and often commits suicide.

Koro is characterized by the *delusion that the person's penis is shrinking and may disappear* into his abdomen and that he may die. The koro syndrome occurs among the people of Southeast Asia and in some areas of China, where it is known as *suk-yeong.* A corresponding disorder in women involves complaints of the shrinkage of the vulva, the labia, and the breasts.

Wihtigo or windigo psychosis is a psychiatric disorder confined to the Cree, Ojibwa, and Salteaux Indians of North America. *Affected persons believe that they may be transformed into a giant monster that eats human flesh.* During times of starvation, affected persons may have the delusion that they have been transformed into a wihtigo, and they may feel and express a craving for human flesh. Because of the person's belief in witchcraft and in the possibility of such a transformation, symptoms concerning the alimentary tract, such as loss of appetite and nausea from trivial causes, may sometimes cause the person to become greatly excited for fear of being transformed into a wihtigo.

14.29–14.33

14.29. The answer is E (*Synopsis VII*, page 507).

14.30. The answer is D (*Synopsis VII*, pages 471–474 and 477).

14.31. The answer is C (*Synopsis VII*, pages 526 and 532).

14.32. The answer is A (*Synopsis VII*, pages 532–535).

14.33. The answer is B (*Synopsis VII*, page 352).

In *delusional disorder, delusions of jealousy and persecution* are mostly found. In *schizophrenia, bizarre delusions of being controlled* and delusions of persecution can occur. In *mania, grandiose delusions* are seen. In *depressive disorders, delusions of guilt and somatic delusions* may occur. In *cognitive disorders*, such as dementia, *delusions secondary to perceptual disturbances* are evident.

14.34–14.38

14.34. The answer is E (*Synopsis VII*, pages 523–524).

14.35. The answer is C (*Synopsis VII*, pages 306–and 477–478).

14.36. The answer is D (*Synopsis VII*, page 526).

14.37. The answer is B (*Synopsis VII*, page 507).

14.38. The answer is A (*Synopsis VII*, pages 734–735).

Psychomotor retardation is a general slowing of mental and physical activity. It is often a sign of a *major depressive episode*, which is characterized by feelings of sadness, loneliness, despair, low self-esteem, and self-reproach.

Thought broadcasting is the feeling that one's thoughts are being broadcast or projected into the environment. Such feelings are encountered in *schizophrenia*.

A patient in a *manic episode* is *easily distracted with an elevated, expansive, or irritable mood* with pressured speech and hyperactivity.

Delusional disorder is characterized by *persecutory or grandiose delusions* and related disturbances in mood, thought, and behavior.

The essential feature of *paranoid personality disorder* is a long-standing *suspiciousness and mistrust of people.* Patients with this disorder are hypersensitive and continually alert for environmental clues that will validate their original prejudicial ideas.

Mood Disorders

The two major mood disorders as defined by the fourth edition of *Diagnostic and Statistical Manual of Mental Disorders* (DSM-IV) are major depressive disorder and bipolar I disorder. Bipolar I disorder in the revised third edition of DSM (DSM-III-R) was referred to simply as bipolar disorder. Bipolar I disorder, termed manic-depressive disorder in the past, is used to classify persons who either present with only manic episodes or who have some history of both manic episodes and major depressive episodes. Persons who have a history of only depressive episodes received diagnoses of major depressive disorder.

Dysthymic disorder and cyclothymic disorder are two mood disorders that are less severe and more chronic than major depressive disorder and bipolar I disorder, respectively. DSM-IV includes a number of additional mood disorders, both in its main text and in the appendixes, related to both depression and bipolar I disorder. Disorders related to depression include minor depressive disorder, recurrent brief depressive disorder, and premenstrual dysphoric disorder. Related to bipolar I disorder is bipolar II disorder (recurrent major depressive episodes with hypomania). Two additional mood disorder diagnoses included under other categories in DSM-III-R are mood disorder due to a general medical condition and substance-induced mood disorder. DSM-IV also includes the diagnoses of mood disorder not otherwise specified, depressive disorder not otherwise specified, and bipolar disorder not otherwise specified to enable the clinician to make a mood disorder diagnosis when the patient exhibits depressive or manic symptoms that do not meet the diagnostic criteria for any specific mood disorder.

The description and the experience of mood is a subjective phenomenon. In particular, the term "depression" is used loosely to describe a wide range of dysphoric emotions, many of them considered normal. The normal expression and experience of emotion involves an equally wide range of feeling, from sadness to irritation to anger to joy. To classify a person with a mood disorder, the clinician must be able to recognize the differences between a normal range of mood and an abnormal range of mood. Persons with mood disorders are not in control of their moods; they have a constellation of signs and symptoms that indicate both psychological and biological dysregulation. Persons with mood disorders have varying degrees of disturbances in thought process and content, activity level, cognitive abilities, speech, and vegetative functions and in interpersonal, social, and occupational functioning. Persons with mood disorders often describe an ineffable but distinct change in the quality of their mood, which they can often point to as abnormal and out of their control.

Mood disorders are common disorders. The lifetime prevalence of major depressive disorder, for instance, is about 6 percent for men and 10 percent for women. The lifetime prevalence of bipolar I disorder is about 1 percent, similar to the lifetime prevalence of schizophrenia. Most people with florid and obvious bipolar I disorder come to the attention of a physician and receive treatment, but only about 50 percent of those with major depressive disorder come to the attention of medical and psychiatric caretakers. The symptoms of major depressive disorder are often either missed or misdiagnosed. In fact, the symptoms of major depressive disorder are often dismissed as expectable reactions to stress, self-indulgence, or attempts to achieve secondary gains.

Specific causes of mood disorders are not known, although the causative factors can be divided into biological factors, genetic factors, and psychosocial factors. That division is artificial, as health research and clinical observation indicate that those factors interact in a complex way. For example, biological and psychosocial factors can affect gene expression, and biological and genetic factors can influence the patient's responses to psychosocial factors.

Biologically, many studies have implicated heterogeneous dysregulations of the biogenic amines—in particular, norepinephrine and serotonin but also dopamine and the amino acid neurotransmitter γ-aminobutric acid (GABA). A variety of neuroendocrine dysregulations have been reported in patients with mood disorders, with particular focus on the adrenal, thyroid, and growth hormone axes. Other biological systems investigated with regard to their effects on mood include abnormalities in the sleep cycle, abnormal regulation of circadian rhythms, and kindling or seizurelike phenomena in the temporal lobes. Neuroanatomically, mood disorders appear to involve pathology of the limbic system, the basal ganglia, and the hypothalamus.

Genetic data support a pattern of definite but complex genetic inheritance; a stronger genetic component is posited for the transmission of bipolar I disorder than for the transmission of major depressive disorder. Although psychosocial factors are often clearly contributory to the onset of an episode, bipolar I disorder is considered one of the most genetically determined of all disorders in psychiatry. About 50 percent of all bipolar I patients have at least one parent with a mood disorder, most often major depressive disorder. If one parent has bipolar I disorder, there is a 25 percent chance that a child will have a mood disorder. If both parents have bipolar I disorder, there is a 50 to 75 percent chance that a child will have a mood disorder. Adoption and twin studies have supported those figures from family studies.

Psychosocial factors involved in the cause, the precipitation, and the maintenance of mood disorders are many and complex. Stressful life events more often precede the first episodes of mood disorders than subsequent episodes. The stress associated with the first episode may result in long-lasting changes in brain tissue. The net result of the changes is that the person becomes vulnerable and at high risk for subsequent episodes. In general, the effects of loss (both real and symbolic), family dynamics, and conflicts play pivotal roles in the onset, the course, and the recurrence of episodes of mood disorders.

Treatment of mood disorders is complex and must be based on a biopsychosocial approach. Accurate diagnosis is essential to answer the specific questions that arise with regard to medication choice and effective psychotherapy. Biological treatments are sophisticated and individualized. The choices that confront today's clinicians involve the use of a wide range of antidepressants, augmenting agents, and mood stabilizers—all with their own mechanisms of action, target symptoms, and side effects. Clinicians must be knowledgeable about when a specific drug should be used and when a combination of agents is indicated. Knowledge about the effective and safe use of electroconvulsive therapy (ECT) is essential.

Nonbiological psychotherapies are also diverse and complex, ranging from cognitive-behavioral approaches to psychodynamic-psychoanalytically oriented modalities. Clinicians must be knowledgeable about all aspects of each of the therapies and aware of when the techniques from each are most applicable and effective.

Students should become aware of the new diagnostic categories included in DSM-IV. Those new categories are bipolar II disorder (included in the body of the text) and minor depressive disorder, recurrent brief depressive disorder, and premenstrual dysphoric disorder (included in the appendixes).

Students are referred to Chapter 15 in *Kaplan and Sadock's Synopsis VII* to study in depth the material addressed in the questions and answers below.

HELPFUL HINTS

The student should know the following terms that relate to mood disorders.

mood	life events and stress	lithium
affect	premorbid factors	amphetamine
vegetative functions	Heinz Kohut	MAOIs
major depressive disorder	learned helplessness	ECT
folie circulaire	cognitive theories	antipsychotics
folie à double forme	melancholic feature	carbamazepine
Karl Kahlbaum	age-dependent symptoms	rapid cycling
Emil Kraepelin	mood-congruent and mood-	cognitive, behavioral, family, and
incidence and prevalence	incongruent psychotic feat	psychoanalytic therapies
sex ratios of disorders	depression rating scales	dysthymic (early and late onset)
biogenic amines	suicide	disorder
GABA	depressive equivalent	cyclothymic disorder
TSH, TRH	*forme fruste*	double depression
GH	seasonal pattern	hypomania
LH, FSH	melatonin	mania
5-HT	phototherapy	SSRIs
bipolar I disorder	differential diagnosis	norepinephrine
bipolar II disorder	pseudodementia	catatonic features
REM latency, density	clinical management	atypical features
hypothalamus	thymoleptics	postpartum onset
genetic studies	euthymic	mild depressive disorder
RFLPs	T3	premenstrual dysphoric disorder

QUESTIONS

DIRECTIONS: Each of the questions or incomplete statements below is followed by five suggested responses or completions. Select the *one* that is *best* in each case.

15.1. Major depressive disorder
A. may have catatonic symptoms
B. cannot have psychotic features as part of its symptoms
C. has its mean age of onset at 60 years
D. cannot have its onset in childhood
E. has a lifetime prevalence of 1 percent

15.2. In the treatment of a patient with a depressive disorder
A. tricyclic drugs are not lethal when taken at overdose levels
B. antidepressants do not have sexual adverse effects
C. monoamine oxidase inhibitors (MAOIs) are chosen as first-line drugs more often than are serotonin-specific reuptake inhibitors (SSRIs)
D. antidepressants alone are effective in the treatment of major depressive episode with psychotic features
E. a drug trial of adequate dosage can be considered unsuccessful if the patient does not respond favorably in four weeks

15.3. Patients with bipolar I disorder
A. have a better prognosis than do patients with major depressive disorder
B. are not emotionally labile when manic
C. are easily interrupted while they are speaking when manic
D. usually have had a depressive episode before exhibiting their first manic episode
E. do not have bizarre and mood-incongruent delusions and hallucinations when manic

15.4. Dysthymic disorder
A. cannot coexist with major depressive disorder
B. usually has an abrupt onset
C. is synonymous with minor depressive disorder
D. has not shown successful treatment with antidepressants
E. is common among unmarried and young persons

15.5. Which of the following is of help in the differential diagnosis and the formulation of a treatment plan for a patient with a mood disorder?
A. Family history of psychiatric illness
B. Knowledge of the type of psychiatric medication used in the past
C. Medical problems
D. Past or present substance abuse
E. All the above

15.6. The defense mechanism most commonly used in depression is
A. projection
B. introjection
C. sublimation
D. undoing
E. altruism

15.7. A 24-year-old single female copy editor was presented at a case conference two weeks after her first psychiatric hospitalization. Her hospital admission had followed an accident in which she wrecked her car while driving at high speed late at night when she was feeling energetic and thought that "sleep was a waste of time." The episode began while she was on vacation, when she felt high and on the verge of a great romance. She apparently took off all her clothes and ran naked through the woods. On the day of her hospital admission, she reported hearing voices telling her that her father and the emergency room staff were emissaries of the devil, out to get her for no reason that she could understand.

At the case conference, she was calm and cooperative and talked of the voices she had heard in the past, which she now acknowledged had not been real. She realized that she had an illness but was still irritated at being hospitalized. She was receiving lithium, 2,100 mg a day and had a blood level of 1.0 ml Eq per L.

The most likely diagnosis is
A. bipolar I disorder, most recent episode manic, with mood-incongruent psychotic features
B. bipolar I disorder, most recent episode manic, with mood-congruent psychotic features
C. bipolar I disorder, most recent episode mixed, with mood-congruent psychotic features
D. bipolar I disorder, most recent episode depressed, with mood-congruent psychotic features
E. cyclothymic disorder

15.8. Vegetative signs in depression include all the following *except*
A. weight loss
B. abnormal menses
C. obsessive rumination
D. decreased libido
E. fatigability

15.9. The percentage of depressed patients who eventually commit suicide is estimated to be
A. 0.5 percent
B. 5 percent
C. 15 percent
D. 25 percent
E. 35 percent

15.10. All the following statements about bipolar I disorder are true *except*
A. bipolar I disorder most often starts with depression
B. about 10 to 20 percent of patients experience only manic episodes
C. an untreated manic episode lasts about three months
D. as the illness progresses, the amount of time between episodes often increases
E. rapid cycling is much more common in women than in men

15.11. According to the fourth edition of *Diagnostic and Statistical Manual of Mental Disorders* (DSM-IV), the course specifier "with seasonal pattern" can be applied to
A. dysthymic disorder
B. cyclothymic disorder
C. major depressive disorder, single episode
D. bipolar II disorder
E. all the above

15.12. Life events are
A. a possible factor in the onset and the timing of a specific episode of depression
B. are most associated with the development of depression in later life when a parent is lost before age 11
C. are most associated with the onset of a depressive episode when a spouse is lost
D. are not significantly related to the onset and the timing of a specific episode of mania
E. all the above

15.13. Of the following neurological diseases, which is most often associated with depression?
A. Epilepsy
B. Brain tumors
C. Parkinson's disease
D. Dementia of the Alzheimer's type
E. Huntington's disease

15.14. A 59-year-old married attorney with a promising practice, two daughters, and a good marriage was noticed by his wife to be "not functioning properly" during the previous two months. He called his office frequently, telling his partners that he was ill, while actually he could not get out of bed in the mornings. His colleagues were concerned about his frequent cancellation of appointments and his change in behavior. He stopped taking pride in his appearance, lost his appetite for food and his interest in sex, and was sleeping many hours each day. He told his wife that he was unsure whether he wanted to go on living. He had no history of alcohol or other use. He had had a thorough physical examination three months earlier and was told that he was in good health.

Which of the following is the most likely diagnosis?
A. Bipolar I disorder
B. Major depressive disorder
C. Generalized anxiety disorder
D. Schizophrenia
E. None of the above

15.15. A 25-year-old junior executive was referred to a health service because he had been drinking excessively over the previous two weeks. The patient reported that he had been "down" for about a month, cried frequently, and had no interest in sex or work. His history revealed that he had suffered those down periods for several years; but he also described himself as having experienced periods of elation during which he was gregarious, productive, and optimistic. During those times, he said, he did not drink at all. The young man also stated that the behavior had been present on and off since he was about 15 years old.

The patient was suffering from
A. major depressive disorder
B. bipolar I disorder
C. cyclothymic disorder
D. dysthymic disorder
E. bipolar II disorder

15.16. A 40-year-old man was brought to the psychiatric emergency room after becoming involved in a fistfight at a bar. He was speaking rapidly, jumping from one thought to another in response to simple, specific questions (for example, "When did you come to New York?" "I came to New York, the Big Apple, it's rotten to the core, no matter how you slice it, I sliced a bagel this morning for breakfast . . ."). The patient described experiencing his thoughts as racing. He was unable to explain how he got into the fight other than to say that the other person was jealous of the patient's obvious sexual prowess, the patient having declared that he had slept with at least 100 women. He made allusions to his father as being God, and he stated that he had not slept in three days. "I don't need it," he said. The patient's speech was full of amusing puns, jokes, and plays on words.

Associated findings consistent with the patient's probable diagnosis are
A. emotional lability
B. delusions
C. hallucinations
D. nocturnal electroencephalographic (EEG) changes
E. all the above

15.17. A few days after a 27-year-old married woman's father had been killed in a car accident, she showed profound behavioral changes. Suddenly, she told her husband that she did not love him, she went on spending sprees, and she was arrested by the police for driving at excessive speeds. Her speech became disorganized, her mood became elated, and she showed psychomotor agitation. The woman was brought to a local psychiatric emergency room, where she revealed to the examining psychiatrist that she had no appetite, had not been able to sleep for days, and, in the past, had had periods of severe depression.

The most likely diagnosis is
A. schizoaffective disorder
B. major depressive disorder
C. bipolar I disorder, most recent episode mixed
D. schizophrenia, undifferentiated
E. none of the above

15.18. Cyclothymic disorder is considered an attenuated form of bipolar I disorder because of
A. a similarity of symptoms in the two disorders
B. the significant number of cyclothymic patients who eventually have bipolar I disorder
C. the two disorders' favorable response to lithium
D. be a hypomanic response to tricyclic drugs among cyclothymic disorder patients
E. all the above

15.19. The lifetime prevalence of dysthymic disorder is
A. 5 cases per 1,000 persons
B. 10 cases per 1,000 persons
C. 20 cases per 1,000 persons
D. 35 cases per 1,000 persons
E. 45 cases per 1,000 persons

15.20. Which of the following symptoms is incompatible with dysthymic disorder?
A. Weight change
B. Sleep difficulty
C. Delusions
D. Decreased sexual performance
E. Suicidal ideas

15.21. Age-associated features of major depressive disorder include
A. separation anxiety
B. antisocial behavior
C. running away
D. pseudodementia
E. all the above

15.22. The course of major depressive disorder usually includes
A. an untreated episode of depression lasting 6 to 13 months untreated
B. a treated episode of depression lasting about three months
C. the return of symptoms after the withdrawal of antidepressants before three months have elapsed
D. an average of five to six episodes over a 20-year period
E. all the above

15.23. A manic episode is differentiated from a schizophrenic episode by
A. quality of mood
B. psychomotor activity
C. speed of onset
D. family history
E. all the above

15.24. Which of the following medications may produce depressive symptoms?
A. Analgesics
B. Antibacterials
C. Antipsychotics
D. Antihypertensives
E. All the above

15.25. L-Tryptophan
A. is the amino acid precursor to serotonin
B. has been used as an adjuvant to both antidepressants and lithium
C. has been used as a hypnotic
D. has been associated with eosinophilia-myalgia syndrome
E. is characterized by all the above

15.26. Drugs that may precipitate mania include
A. amphetamine
B. levodopa
C. cimetidine
D. bromide
E. all the above

15.27. Major depressive disorder
A. is more common in men than in women
B. peaks in women after age 55
C. shows no conclusive evidence for any difference between blacks and whites
D. is highest in the poor
E. is characterized by all the above

DIRECTIONS: Each set of lettered headings below is followed by a list of phrases or statements. For each numbered phrase or statements; select

A. if the item is associated with *A only*
B. if the item is associated with *B only*
C. if the item is associated with *both A and B*
D. if the item is associated with *neither A nor B*

Questions 15.28–15.30
A. Minor depressive disorder
B. Recurrent brief depressive disorder
C. Both
D. Neither

15.28. Symptoms meet most of the diagnostic criteria for major depressive disorder

15.29. Symptoms are equal in duration but fewer in number than those in major depressive disorder

15.30. Treatment may include the use of antidepressants

Questions 15.31–15.35
A. Mood-incongruent delusion
B. Mood-congruent delusion
C. Both
D. Neither

15.31. A 52-year-old suicidal man believes that he is the new Messiah.

15.32. A 45-year-old elated man believes that he has been reincarnated as a millionaire.

15.33. A 12-year-old boy thinks that he hears voices telling him to jump out the window.

15.34. A 25-year-old depressed woman thinks that she has committed terrible crimes.

15.35. A 30-year-old depressed woman believes that she is the Virgin Mary.

Questions 15.36–15.39
A. Major depressive disorder, recurrent
B. Dysthymic disorder
C. Both
D. Neither

15.36. Episodic periods of depression

15.37. Some patients have a positive family history of mood disorders, decreased rapid eye movement latency, and a positive therapeutic response to antidepressants

15.38. DSM-IV defines subtypes based on onset before and after age 21

15.39. May have psychotic symptoms

Questions 15.40–15.45
A. Dysthymic disorder
B. Cyclothymic disorder
C. Both
D. Neither

15.40. Treatment with antidepressants may lead to hypomanic symptoms

15.41. Delusions and hallucinations

15.42. Favorable response to lithium

15.43. Alcohol abuse

15.44. Sexual promiscuity

15.45. Often confused with substance abuse

Questions 15.46–15.47
A. Cyclothymic disorder
B. Bipolar II disorder
C. Both
D. Neither

15.46. Characterized by episodes of hypomaniclike symptoms and periods of mild depression

15.47. Characterized by major depressive episodes and hypomanic episodes

ANSWERS

Mood Disorders

15.1.   The answer is A (*Synopsis VII*, page 529).

Major depressive disorder *may have catatonic features;* in fact, the fourth edition of *Diagnostic and Statistical Manual of Mental Disorders* (DSM-IV) includes catatonic features as an additional symptom feature that can be used to describe patients with various mood disorders. Table 15.1 lists the criteria for cross-sectional symptom features.

Major depressive disorder *can have psychotic features as part of its symptoms.* The presence of psychotic features in major depressive disorder reflects severe disease and is an indicator of a poor prognosis. The psychotic symptoms themselves are often categorized as either mood-congruent—that is, in harmony with mood disorder ("I deserve to be punished because I am so bad")—or mood-incongruent—that is, not in harmony with the mood disorder. The criteria for catatonic features appear in Table 15.2.

The *mean age of onset* for major depressive disorder is about *40 years, not 60 years*; 50 percent of all patients have an onset between the ages of 20 and 50. Major depressive disorder *can have its onset in childhood*, although that is unusual. A later onset is associated with the absence of a family history of mood disorders, antisocial personality disorder, and alcohol abuse.

Major depressive disorder *has a lifetime prevalence of about 6 percent, not 1 percent.*

15.2.   The answer is E (*Synopsis VII*, page 551).

The most common clinical mistake leading to an unsuccessful trial of an antidepressant drug is the use of too low a dosage for too short a time. Unless adverse events prevent it, *a drug trial of adequate*

Table 15.1
Criteria for Severity/Psychotic/Remission Specifiers for Current (or Most Recent) Major Depressive Episode

Note: Code in fifth digit. Can be applied to the most recent major depressive episode in major depressive disorder and to a major depressive episode in bipolar I or II disorder only if it is the most recent type of mood episode.

Mild: Few, if any, symptoms in excess of those required to make the diagnosis and symptoms result in only minor impairment in occupational functioning or in usual social activities or relationships with others.
Moderate: Symptoms or functional impairment between "mild" and "severe".
Severe without psychotic features: Several symptoms in excess of those required to make the diagnosis, **and** symptoms markedly interfere with occupational functioning or with usual social activities or relationships with others.
Severe with psychotic features: Delusions or hallucinations. If possible, specify whether the psychotic features are mood-congruent or mood-incongruent:

  Mood-congruent psychotic features: Delusions or hallucinations whose content is entirely consistent with the typical depressive themes of personal inadequacy, guilt, disease, death, nihilism, or deserved punishment.
  Mood-Incongruent psychotic features: Delusions or hallucinations whose content does not involve typical depressive themes of personal inadequacy, guilt, disease, death, nihilism, or deserved punishment. Included here are such symptoms as persecutory delusions (not directly related to depressive themes), thought insertion, thought broadcasting, and delusions of control.

In partial remission Intermediate between "in full remission" and "mild," **and** no previous dysthymic disorder. (If the major depressive episode was superimposed on dysthymic disorder, the diagnosis of dysthymic disorder alone is given once the full criteria for a major depressive episode are no longer met).
In full remission: During the past 2 months no significant signs or symptoms of the disturbance were present.
Unspecified.

Table from DSM-IV, *Diagnostic and Statistical Manual of Mental Disorders,* ed 4. Copyright American Psychiatric Association, Washington, 1994. Used with permission.

Table 15.2
Criteria for Catatonic Features Specifier

Specify if:
  With catatonic features (can be applied to the current or most recent major depressive episode, manic episode, or mixed episode in major depressive disorder, bipolar I disorder, or bipolar II disorder)

The clinical picture is dominated by at least two of the following:

(1) motoric immobility as evidenced by catalepsy (including waxy flexibility) or stupor
(2) excessive motor activity (that is apparently purposeless and not influenced by external stimuli)
(3) extreme negativism (an apparently motiveless resistance to all instructions or maintenance of a rigid posture against attempts to be moved) or mutism
(4) peculiarities of voluntary movement as evidenced by posturing (voluntary assumption of inappropriate or bizarre postures), stereotyped movements, prominent mannerisms, or prominent grimacing
(5) echolalia or echopraxia

Table adapted from DSM-IV, *Diagnostic and Statistical Manual of Mental Disorders,* ed 4. Copyright American Psychiatric Association, Washington, 1994. Used with permission.

dosage can be considered unsuccessful if the patient does not respond favorably in four weeks.

Tricyclic drugs may be lethal when taken in overdose levels. Tricyclic and tetracyclic drugs are, by far, the most lethal of the antidepressants; the serotonin-specific reuptake inhibitors (SSRIs), bupropion (Wellbutrin), trazodone (Desyrel) and the monoamine oxidase inhibitors (MAOIs) are much safer, although even those drugs can be lethal when taken in combination with alcohol or other substances.

Antidepressants do have sexual adverse effects. Almost all the antidepressants, except bupropion, have been associated with decreased libido, erectile dysfunction, or anorgasmia. The serotonergic drugs are probably more closely associated with sexual adverse effects than are the noradrenergic compounds.

The MAOIs are usually not chosen as first-line drugs more often than are SSR's because of the association with tyramine-induced hypertensive crises, which are caused when a patient taking conventional MAOIs ingests certain drugs or foods with a high tyramine content. Although that adverse interaction can be avoided by the patient's following simple dietary guidelines, the potentially life-threatening nature of a hypertensive crisis and the need for dietary restrictions limit the acceptability of MAOIs.

Antidepressants alone are not effective in the treatment of major depressive episodes with psychotic features. One exception may be amoxapine (Asendin) an antidepressant closely related to loxapine (Loxitane), an antipsychotic. The usual practice, however, is to use a combination of an antidepressant and an antipsychotic.

15.3.   The answer is D (*Synopsis VII*, page 539).

Patients with bipolar I disorder *usually have had a depressive episode* (Table 15.3) *before exhibiting their first manic episode* (Table 15.4). That has been found true 75 percent of the time in women and 67 percent of the time in men. Most patients experience both depressive and manic episodes, although 10 to 20 percent experience only manic episodes.

Patients with bipolar I disorder *have a poorer prognosis than do patients with major depressive disorder.* About 40 to 50 percent of bipolar I disorder patients may have a second manic episode within two years of the first episode. Although lithium (Eskalith) prophylaxis improves the course and the prognosis of bipolar I disorder, probably only 50 to 60 percent of patients achieve significant control of their symptoms with lithium.

Patients may be emotionally labile when manic, switching from laughter to irritability to depression in minutes or hours. Patients *are not easily interrupted while they are speaking when manic,* and they are often intrusive nuisances to those around them. Patients *do have bizarre and mood-incongruent delusions and hallucinations when manic.*

15.4.   The answer is E (*Synopsis VII*, page 556).

Dysthymic disorder *is common among unmarried and young persons* and in persons with low incomes.

Table 15.3
Criteria for Major Depressive Episode

A. Five (or more) of the following symptoms have been present during the same 2-week period and represent a change from previous functioning; at least one of the symptoms is either (1) depressed mood or (2) loss of interest or pleasure.

Note: Do not include symptoms that are clearly due to a general medical condition, or mood-incongruent delusions or hallucinations.

(1) depressed mood most of the day, nearly every day, as indicated by either subjective report (e.g., feels sad or empty) or observation made by others (e.g., appears tearful). **Note:** In children and adolescents, can be irritable mood.
(2) markedly diminished interest or pleasure in all, or almost all, activities most of the day, nearly every day (as indicated by either subjective account or observation made by others)
(3) significant weight loss when not dieting or weight gain (e.g., a change of more than 5% of body weight in a month), or decrease or increase in appetite nearly every day. **Note:** In children, consider failure to make expected weight gains.
(4) insomnia or hypersomnia nearly every day
(5) psychomotor agitation or retardation nearly every day (observable by others, not merely subjective feelings of restlessness or being slowed down)
(6) fatigue or loss of energy nearly every day
(7) feelings of worthlessness or excessive or inappropriate guilt (which may be delusional) nearly every day (not merely self-reproach or guilt about being sick)
(8) diminished ability to think or concentrate, or indecisiveness, nearly every day (either by subjective account or as observed by others)
(9) recurrent thoughts of death (not just fear of dying), recurrent suicidal ideation without a specific plan, or a suicide attempt or a specific plan for committing suicide

B. The symptoms do not meet criteria for a mixed episode.

C. The symptoms cause clinically significant distress or impairment in social, occupational, or other important areas of functioning.

D. The symptoms are not due to the direct physiological effects of a substance (e.g., a drug of abuse, a medication) or a general medical condition (e.g., hypothyroidism).

E. The symptoms are not better accounted for by bereavement, i.e., after the loss of a loved one, the symptoms persist for longer than 2 months or are characterized by marked functional impairment, morbid preoccupation with worthlessness, suicidal ideation, psychotic symptoms, or psychomotor retardation.

Table from DSM-IV, *Diagnostic and Statistical Manual of Mental Disorders,* ed 4. Copyright American Psychiatric Association, Washington, 1994. Used with permission.

Table 15.4
Criteria for Manic Episode

A. A distinct period of abnormally and persistently elevated, expansive, or irritable mood, lasting at least 1 week (or any duration if hospitalization is necessary).

B. During the period of mood disturbance, three (or more) of the following symptoms have persisted (four if the mood is only irritable) and have been present to a significant degree:

(1) inflated self-esteem or grandiosity
(2) decreased need for sleep (e.g., feels rested after only 3 hours of sleep)
(3) more talkative than usual or pressure to keep talking
(4) flight of ideas or subjective experience that thoughts are racing
(5) distractibility (i.e., attention too easily drawn to unimportant or irrelevant external stimuli)
(6) increase in goal-directed activity (either socially, at work or school, or sexually) or psychomotor agitation
(7) excessive involvement in pleasurable activities that have a high potential for painful consequences (e.g., engaging in unrestrained buying sprees, sexual indiscretions, or foolish business investments)

C. The symptoms do not meet criteria for a mixed episode.

D. The mood disturbance is sufficiently severe to cause marked impairment in occupational functioning or in usual social activities or relationships with others, or to necessitate hospitalization to prevent harm to self or others, or there are psychotic features.

E. The symptoms are not due to the direct physiological effects of a substance (e.g., a drug of abuse, a medication, or other treatment) or a general medical condition (e.g., hyperthyroidism).

Note: Manic-like episodes that are clearly caused by somatic antidepressant treatment (e.g., medication, electroconvulsive therapy, light therapy) should not count toward a diagnosis of bipolar I disorder.

Table from DSM-IV, *Diagnostic and Statistical Manual of Mental Disorders,* ed 4. Copyright American Psychiatric Association, Washington, 1994. Used with permission.

Moreover, dysthymic disorder *can coexists with major depressive disorders,* anxiety disorders (especially panic disorder), substance abuse, and, probably, borderline personality disorder. About 50 percent of dysthymic disorder patients *experience an insidious onset, not an abrupt onset,* of the symptoms before age 25.

Dysthymic disorder *is not synonymous with minor depressive disorder.* The difference between dysthymic disorder and minor depressive disorder is primarily the episodic nature of the symptoms in minor depressive disorder. Between episodes, patients with minor depressive disorder have a euthymic mood, whereas patients with dysthymic disorder have virtually no euthymic periods.

Dysthymic disorder *has shown successful treatment with antidepressants.* In general, however, monoamine oxidase inhibitors (MAOIs) may be more beneficial than tricyclic drugs. The relatively recent introduction of the well-tolerated serotonin-specific reuptake inhibitors (SSRIs) has led to their frequent use by patients with dysthymic disorder; preliminary reports indicate that the SSRIs may be the drugs of choice for the disorder. Similarly, initial reports indicate that bupropion may be an effective treatment for patients with dysthymic disorder.

15.5.   The answer is E (all) (*Synopsis VII,* pages 535–537).

A patient's history and *family history of psychiatric illness* can provide valuable information about the patient's clinical picture. Suicide in a parent, for example, increases the risk of suicide in the patient. If a patient has been depressed before, *knowledge of the type of medication used in the past* can provide the physician with a head start. Knowing if the patient has ever had a period of mania or if the patient has had a recent severe emotional trauma is essential in making the correct diagnosis and formulating an effective treatment plan. For example, a history of a manic episode is indicative of I bipolar disorder. *Medical problems*—such as cancer of the pancreas, multiple sclerosis, and a space-occupying lesion of the brain—can produce depression. *Past or present substances abuse* is also important, since certain substances, such as alcohol and amphetamines, can mimic the clinical picture of depression.

15.6.   The answer is B (*Synopsis VII,* page 523).

In Sigmund Freud's structural theory, the *introjection* of the lost object into the ego leads to the typical depressive symptoms of a lack of energy available to the ego. The superego, unable to retaliate against the lost object externally, flails out at the psychic representation of the lost object, now internalized in the ego as an introject. When the ego overcomes or merges with the superego, energy previously bound in the depressive symptoms is released, and a mania supervenes with the typical symptoms of excess.

Projection is the unconscious defense mechanism in which a person attributes to another person those generally unconscious ideas, thoughts, feelings, and impulses that are personally undesirable or unacceptable. *Sublimation* is an unconscious defense mechanism in which the energy associated with unacceptable impulses or drives is diverted into personally and socially acceptable channels. *Undoing* is an unconscious defense mechanism by which a person symbolically acts out in reverse something unacceptable that has already been done or against which the ego must defend itself. *Altruism* is regard for and dedication to the welfare of others.

15.7.   The answer is A (*Synopsis VII,* pages 524–525).

In the case of the 24-year-old single female copy editor, the most likely diagnosis is *bipolar I disorder, most recent episode manic, with mood-incongruent psychotic features.* The characteristic features of a manic episode were present in the patient: elevated mood (feeling high), increased energy, decreased need for sleep, and involvement in activities with a high potential for painful consequences (reckless driving). The reference to being on the verge of a great romance also suggested the presence of grandiosity. In DSM-IV the presence of a manic episode, even without a history of a depressive episode, is sufficient to make a diagnosis of bipolar I disorder, manic, as the familial history, course, and treatment response of unipolar mania are apparently the same as in disorders with both manic and major depressive episodes.

The presence of the persecutory delusions is noted by including "with psychotic features." Since the content of the delusions had no apparent connection with themes of either inflated worth, power, knowledge, identity, or a special relationship to a deity or famous person, the delusions were mood-incongruent. Since the psychotic features are mood-incongruent, *bipolar I disorder, most recent episode manic, with mood-congruent psychotic features*, is not warranted.

Bipolar I disorder, most recent episode mixed, with mood-congruent psychotic features, involves the full symptomatic picture of both mania and depression intermixed or rapidly alternating every few days, with psychotic features congruent with manic and depressed moods. *Bipolar I disorder, most recent episode depressed, with mood-congruent psychotic features*, involves a current presentation of a major depressive episode in a previously manic patient. The mood-congruent psychotic features would involve depressive themes, such as guilt, poverty, nihilism, or somatic concerns.

Cyclothymic disorder is a chronic disorder of at least two years' duration, characterized by both hypomanic episodes and numerous periods of depressed mood or loss of interest or pleasure. In cyclothymia the patient shows no psychotic features, and the disorder is a less severe mood disorder than bipolar I disorder.

15.8. The answer is C (*Synopsis VII*, pages 530–532).

Obsessive rumination is a state of tension in which a patient has a persistent thought that serves no adaptive purpose. It is seen in depression but is more common in obsessive-compulsive disorder and is usually classified not as a vegetative sign but as a disorder of thought content. Vegetative signs usually refer to functions that relate to the autonomic nervous system, which provides innervation to the blood vessels, heart, glands, viscera, and smooth muscle. Signs that point toward a slowing of the organism rather than to a quickening are also known as vegetative (for example, decreased libido). Vegetative signs in depression include *weight loss, abnormal menses, decreased libido*, and *fatigability*.

15.9. The answer is C (*Synopsis VII*, pages 531 and 533–535).

Approximately two thirds of depressed patients have suicidal ideation, and about *15 percent* do eventually commit suicide.

15.10. The answer is D (*Synopsis VII*, page 539).

As the illness progresses, the amount of time between episodes often decreases, not increases. After approximately five episodes, however, the interepisode interval often stabilizes at about six to nine months. *Bipolar I disorder most often starts with depression* (75 percent of the time in females, 67 percent in males). Most patients experience both depression and mania, although *about 10 to 20 percent of patients experience only manic episodes*. An untreated manic episode lasts about three months; therefore, it is unwise to discontinue drugs before that time. Some patients develop rapidly cycling bipolar I disorder episodes. *Rapid cycling is much more common in women than in men*, although it is not related temporally to the menstrual cycle. Rapid cycling may be associated with treatment with tricyclic drugs, and patients receiving those medications often respond to combination therapies of lithium and MAOIs.

15.11. The answer is D (*Synopsis VII*, page 530).

According to DSM-IV, the specifier "with seasonal pattern" can be applied to bipolar I disorder, *bipolar II disorder*, and major depressive disorder, recurrent. According to DSM-IV, the specifier "with seasonal pattern" cannot be applied to *dysthymic disorder, cyclothymic disorder*, or *major depressive disorder, single episode*. The criteria for the seasonal pattern specifier are listed in Table 15.5.

15.12. The answer is E (all) (*Synopsis VII*, pages 522–523 and 538–539).

Some clinicians believe that life events play the primary or principal role in depression; others are more conservative, believing that life events are *a possible factor in the onset and the timing of a specific episode of depression*. However, the research data to support that relation are inconclusive. The most robust data indicate that life event are *most associated with the development of depression in later life when parent is lost before age 11*. The environmental stressor *most associated with the onset of an episode of depression is the loss of a spouse*. Although reasonable data suggest some relation between life events and the onset of depression, life events *are not significantly related to the onset and the timing of a specific episode of mania*.

15.13. The answer is C (*Synopsis VII*, pages 110 and 535).

Parkinson's disease, is most often associated with depression. Up to 90 percent of Parkinson's disease patients may have marked depressive symptoms that are not correlated with their degree of physical disability or age or duration of their illness. The symptoms of depression may be masked by the almost identical motor symptoms of Parkinson's disease. The depressive symptoms of Parkinson's disease often respond to antidepressant drugs or electroconvulsive therapy.

Other neurological diseases less often associated with depression are *epilepsy, brain tumors, dementia of the Alzheimer's type*, and *Huntington's disease.*

15.14.   The answer is B (*Synopsis VII*, pages 523–525).

The most likely diagnosis is *major depressive disorder*. The patient had symptoms for two months and, according to DSM-IV, the minimal criterion for length of depression is two weeks. Other symptoms included loss of appetite, hypersomnia, loss of interest or pleasure in usual activities, decreased libido, loss of energy, and recurrent thoughts of death, suicidal ideation, and wishes to kill himself.

Bipolar I disorder, by definition, must involve an episode of mania—not seen in this case—either currently or in the past. *Generalized anxiety disorder* is ruled out by the absence of any prominent symptoms of anxiety. *Schizophrenia* is also ruled out because indications of psychotic symptoms—such as hallucinations, delusions, and disorganized thinking—were not present.

The diagnostic criteria for major depressive disorder, single episode, are listed in Table 15.6.

15.15.   The answer is C (*Synopsis VII*, pages 560–561).

The patient was suffering from *cyclothymic disorder* (Table 15.7); he had symptoms of both depression and hypomania. His down or depressed periods were marked by crying and loss of interest in sex and work, and his excessive use of alcohol during times a defense against depression and not the primary illness from which he suffered. When elated, the patient was gregarious, optimistic, and productive.

The essential feature of *major depressive disorder* is a severe dysphoric mood and persistent loss of interest or pleasure in all usual activities. Because of the patient's hypomanic episodes and mild depressive symptoms, major depressive disorder is ruled out.

Bipolar I disorder is characterized by severe alterations in mood that are usually episodic and recurrent. The patient in this case had mood changes similar to those seen in bipolar I disorder, but the mildness of his symptoms precluded the full diagnosis of bipolar I disorder.

A diagnosis of *dysthymic disorder* is excluded because the patient showed episodes of elated moods. In dysthymic disorder, the patient's mood is one of chronic depression; in adult patients, a two-year history of such depression is required before the diagnosis can be made.

Bipolar II disorder is characterized by one or more major depressive episodes, at least one hypomanic

Table 15.5
Criteria for Seasonal Pattern Specifier

Specify if:
With seasonal pattern (can be applied to the pattern of major depressive episodes in bipolar I disorder, bipolar II disorder, or major depressive disorder, recurrent)

A. There has been a regular temporal relationship between the onset of major depressive episodes in bipolar I or bipolar II disorder or major depressive disorder, recurrent, and a particular time of the year (e.g., regular appearance of the major depressive episode in the fall or winter).

   Note: Do not include cases in which there is an obvious effect of seasonal-related psychosocial stressors (e.g., regularly being unemployed every winter).

B. Full remissions (or a change from depression to mania or hypomania) also occurs at a characteristic time of the year (e.g., depression disappears in the spring).

C. In the last two years, two major depressive episodes have occurred that demonstrate the temporal seasonal relationships defined in criteria A and B, and no nonseasonal major depressive episodes have occurred during that same period.

D. Seasonal major depressive episodes (as described above) substantially outnumber the nonseasonal major depressive episodes that may have occurred over the individual's lifetime.

Table 15.6
Diagnostic Criteria for Major Depressive Disorder, Single Episode

A. Presence of a major depressive episode.

B. The major depressive episode is not better accounted for by schizoaffective disorder, and is not superimposed on schizophrenia, schizophreniform disorder, delusional disorder, or psychotic disorder not otherwise specified.

C. There has never been a manic episode, a mixed episode, or a hypomanic episode. **Note:** This exclusion does not apply if all of the manic-like, mixed-like, or hypomanic-like episodes are substance or treatment induced or are due to the direct physiological effects of a general medical condition.

Specify (for current or most recent episode):
   Severity/psychotic/remission specifiers
   Chronic
   With catatonic features
   With melancholic features
   With atypical features
   With postpartum onset

episode, and no manic episodes. This patient had no major depressive episodes.

15.16.   The answer is E (all) (*Synopsis VII*, pages 525–532).

The patient was experiencing a manic episode, characterized by a predominantly elevated, expansive, or irritable mood. The mood may be characterized by *emotional lability*, with rapid shifts to brief depression from mania. The essential feature of a manic episode is a distinct period of intense psychophysiological activation with a number of accompanying symptoms, such as lack of judgment of the consequences of actions, pressure of speech, flight of ideas, inflated self-esteem, and, at times, hypersexuality. *Delusions* of grandiosity, *hallucinations*, and ideas of reference may also be present. *Nocturnal electroencephalographic* (EEG) changes in mania include a decreased total sleep time, a decreased percentage of dream time, and an increased dream latency. Those findings have been interpreted as indicating that circadian rhythm activities are delayed in mania because the activity of the intrinsic pacemaker is increased. In DSM-IV the diagnosis of a manic episode requires not a specific duration, such

as three days, but, rather, only a distinct period of abnormally and persistently disordered mood. Table 15.4 lists the DSM-IV criteria for a manic episode.

15.17.   The answer is C (*Synopsis VII*, pages 524–526).

The most probable diagnosis for this patient is *bipolar I disorder, most recent episode mixed* (Table 15.8). The diagnostic criteria, according to DSM-IV, indicate that the patient is in a manic state, with the presence of mood swings and with a history of depressive episodes. The patient presented with the essential feature of a manic episode, which is a distinct period of intense psychophysiological activation. In that state, the predominant mood is elevated, expansive, or irritable, accompanied by at least three of the symptoms listed in Table 15.4.

In *schizoaffective disorder*, the patient has depressive or manic features that develop with symptoms of schizophrenia. Those psychotic symptoms were not present in the above case, which illustrated a classic clinical picture of a manic episode.

In *major depressive disorder* the patient must have experienced one or more major depressive episodes and must never have had a manic or hypomanic episode.

Patients with *schizophrenia, undifferentiated type* show the classic symptom of schizophrenia but do not meet the criteria for the paranoid, catatonic, or disorganized types of schizophrenia.

15.18.   The answer is E (all) (*Synopsis VII*, pages 560–562).

Although the manifestations of cyclothymic disorder are usually of insufficient severity to meet the

Table 15.7
Diagnostic Criteria for Cyclothymic Disorder

A. For at least 2 years, the presence of numerous periods with hypomanic symptoms and numerous periods with depressive symptoms that do not meet criteria for a major depressive episode. **Note:** In children and adolescents, the duration must be at least 1 year.

B. During the above 2-year period (1 year in children and adolescents), the person has not been without the symptoms in criterion A for more than 2 months at a time.

C. No major depressive episode, manic episode, or mixed episode has been present during the first 2 years of the disturbance.

   Note: After the initial 2 years (1 year in children or adolescents) of cyclothymic disorder, there may be superimposed manic or mixed episodes (in which case both bipolar I disorder and cyclothymic disorder may be diagnosed) or major depressive episodes (in which case both bipolar II disorder and cyclothymic disorder may be diagnosed).

D. The symptoms in criterion A are not better accounted for by schizoaffective disorder and are not superimposed on schizophrenia, schizophreniform disorder, delusional disorder, or psychotic disorder not otherwise specified.

E. The symptoms are not due to the direct physiological effects of a substance (e.g., a drug of abuse, a medication) or a general medical condition (e.g., hyperthyroidism).

F. The symptoms cause clinically significant distress or impairment in social, occupational, or other important areas of functioning.

Table from DSM-IV, *Diagnostic and Statistical Manual of Mental Disorders*, ed 4. Copyright American Psychiatric Association, Washington, 1994. Used with permission.

Table 15.8
Diagnostic Criteria for Bipolar Disorder, Most Recent Episode Mixed

A. Currently (or most recently) in a mixed episode.

B. There has previously been at least one major depressive episode, manic episode, or mixed episode.

C. The mood episodes in criteria A and B are not better accounted for by schizoaffective disorder and are not superimposed on schizophrenia, schizophreniform disorder, delusional disorder, or psychotic disorder not otherwise specified.

Specify (for current or most recent episode):
   Severity/psychotic/remission specifiers
   With catatonic features
   With postpartum onset

Specify:
   Longitudinal course specifiers (with and without interepisode recovery)
   With seasonal pattern (applies only to the pattern of major depressive episodes)
   With rapid cycling

Table from DSM-IV, *Diagnostic and Statistical Manual of Mental Disorders*, ed 4. Copyright American Psychiatric Association, Washington, 1994. Used with permission.

diagnostic criteria for bipolar I disorder, certain similarities have led to a consensus that cyclothymic disorder is an attenuated form of bipolar I disorder. Those similarities include a *similarity of symptoms in the two disorders*; a *significant number of cyclothymic patients who eventually have bipolar I disorder*, and pharmacological similarities (notably, *the two disorders favorably respond to lithium* and, frequently, *a hypomanic response to tricyclic drugs among cyclothymic disorder patients*).

15.19. The answer is E (*Synopsis VII*, page 556).

The lifetime prevalence of dysthymic disorder has been reported by a number of studies to be *45 cases per 1,000 persons*.

15.20. The answer is C (*Synopsis VII*, pages 557–558).

The presence of *delusions* and hallucinations is inconsistent with the diagnosis of dysthymic disorder. Among the associated symptoms are those commonly associated with depressive episodes, including poor appetite, *weight change, sleep difficulty* (particularly early morning wakening), loss of energy, fatigability, psychomotor retardation, loss of interest or pleasure in activities, decreased sexual drive, *decreased sexual performance*, feelings of guilt and self-reproach, obsessive preoccupation with health, complaints of difficulty in thinking, indecisiveness, *suicidal ideas*, feelings of helplessness and hopelessness, and pessimism.

The diagnostic criteria for dysthymic disorder are listed in Table 15.9.

15.21. The answer is E (all) (*Synopsis VII*, pages 530–532).

Excessive clinging to parents and school phobia, both of which reflect *separation anxiety*, may be symptoms of depression in children. In latency and in early adolescent boys especially, negative and *antisocial behavior* may occur (depressive equivalents). Sexual acting out, truancy, and *running away* are seen in older boys and girls. In the elderly, *pseudodementia*—that is, depression presenting primarily as a loss of intellectual functioning—must be carefully differentiated from true dementia caused by a medical condition.

15.22. The answer is E (all) (*Synopsis VII*, pages 532–553).

The course of major depressive disorder usually includes *an untreated episode of depression lasting 6 to 13 months; a treated episode of depression lasting about three months; the return of symptoms after the withdrawal of antidepressants before three months have elapsed*; and *an average of five to six episodes over a 20-year period*.

15.23. The answer is E (all) (*Synopsis VII*, pages 537–538).

Although differentiating between a manic episode and a schizophrenic episode can be difficult, the clin-

Table 15.9
Diagnostic Criteria for Dysthymic Disorder

A. Depressed mood for most of the day, for more days than not, as indicated either by subjective account or observation by others, for at least 2 years. **Note:** In children and adolescents, mood can be irritable and duration must be at least 1 year.

B. Presence, while depressed, of two (or more) of the following:

  (1) poor appetite or overeating
  (2) insomnia or hypersomnia
  (3) low energy or fatigue
  (4) low self-esteem
  (5) poor concentration or difficulty making decisions
  (6) feelings of hopelessness

C. During the 2-year period (1 year for children or adolescents) of the disturbance, the person has never been without the symptoms in criteria A and B for more than 2 months at a time.

D. No major depressive episode has been present during the first 2 years of the disturbance (1 year for children and adolescents); i.e., the disturbance is not better accounted for by chronic major depressive disorder, or major depressive disorder, in partial remission.

  Note: There may have been a previous major depressive episode, provided there was a full remission (no significant signs or symptoms for 2 months) before development of the dysthymic disorder. In addition, after the initial 2 years (1 year in children or adolescents) of dysthymic disorder, there may be superimposed episodes of major depressive disorder, in which case both diagnoses may be given when the criteria are met for a major depressive episode.

E. There has never been a manic episode, a mixed episode, or a hypomanic episode, and criteria have never been met for cyclothymic disorder.

F. The disturbance does not occur exclusively during the course of a chronic psychotic disorder, such as schizophrenia or delusional disorder.

G. The symptoms are not due to the direct physiological effects of a substance (e.g., a drug of abuse, a medication) or a general medical condition (e.g., hypothyroidism).

H. The symptoms cause clinically significant distress or impairment in social, occupational, or other important areas of functioning.

Specify if:
  Early onset: if onset is before age 21 years
  Late onset: if onset is age 21 years or older

Specify (for most recent 2 years of dysthymic disorder):
  With atypical features

Table from DSM-IV, *Diagnostic and Statistical Manual of Mental Disorders,* ed 4. Copyright American Psychiatric Association, Washington, 1994. Used with permission.

ical guidelines include the following: (1) *quality of mood*: merriment, elation, and infectiousness of mood are much more common in mania than in schizophrenia; (2) *psychomotor activity*: the combination of an elated mood, rapid or pressured speech, and hyperactivity heavily weights toward a diagnosis of mania, although hyperactivity can also occur in schizophrenia; (3) *speed of onset*: the onset in mania, as opposed to schizophrenia, is often more rapid, being a marked change from previous behavior; and (4) *family history*: half of bipolar I disorder patients have a family history of a mood disorder; schizophrenic patients do not have as high a correlation.

15.24. The answer is E (all) (*Synopsis VII*, pages 570–571).

Many substances used to treat somatic illnesses may trigger depressive symptoms. Commonly prescribed medications associated with depressive symptoms include *analgesics* (for example, ibuprofen [Advil]), *antibacterials* (for example, ampicillin), *antipsychotics* (for example, phenothiazines), and *antihypertensives* (for example, propranolol [Inderal]). Certain substances used to treat medical disorders may also trigger a manic response. The most commonly encountered manic response is to steroids. Cases exist in which spontaneous manic and depressive episodes originated some years later in patients whose first illness episode seemed to be triggered by the medical use of steroids. Other drugs are also known to have the potential for initiating a manic syndrome, including amphetamines and tricyclic drugs (for example, imipramine [Tofranil], amitriptyline [Elavil, Endep]). Table 15.10 lists drugs that can cause depression.

15.25. The answer is E (*Synopsis VII*, pages 551–553).

L-Tryptophan, *the amino acid precursor to serotonin, has been used as an adjuvant to both antidepressants and lithium* in the treatment of bipolar I disorder. L-Tryptophan *has also been used* alone *as a hypnotic* and an antidepressant. L-Tryptophan and L-tryptophan-containing products have been recalled in the United States because L-tryptophan *has been associated with eosinophilia-myalgia syndrome*. The symptoms include fatigue, myalgia, shortness of breath, rashes, and swelling of the extremities. Congestive heart failure and death can also occur. Although several studies have shown that L-tryptophan is an efficacious adjuvant in the treatment of mood disorders, the drug should not be used for any purpose until the problem with eosinophilia-myalgia syndrome is resolved. Current evidence points to a contaminant in the manufacturing process.

15.26. The answer is E (all) (*Synopsis VII*, pages 570–571).

Many pharmacological agents, such as *amphetamine, levodopa* (Larodopa), *cimetidine* (Tagamet), and *bromide*, may precipitate mania, as can antidepressant treatment or withdrawal. Table 15.11 lists drugs associated with manic symptoms.

15.27. The answer is C (*Synopsis VII*, page 517).

Major depressive disorder *shows no conclusive evidence for any difference between blacks and whites*, even though more blacks than whites are hospitalized for major depressive disorder. The disorder *is twice as common in women as in men*, and it *peaks in women between the ages of 35 and 45*. The disorder shows no pattern in social class, it *is not highest in the poor*.

15.28–15.30

15.28. The answer is B (*Synopsis VII*, pages 563–565).

15.29. The answer is A (*Synopsis VII*, pages 563–565).

15.30. The answer is C (*Synopsis VII*, pages 563–565).

Recurrent brief depressive disorder (Table 15.12) is characterized by multiple, relatively brief (less than two weeks) episodes of depressive *symptoms that meet most of the diagnostic criteria for major depressive disorder*. The clinical features of recurrent brief depressive disorder are almost identical to those of major depressive disorder. One subtle difference is that the lives of patients with recurrent brief depressive disorder may seem more disrupted or chaotic because of the frequent changes in their moods when compared with the lives of patients with major depressive disorder, whose depressive episodes occur at a measured pace.

The treatment of patients with recurrent brief depressive disorder should be similar to the treatment of patients with major depressive disorder. The main treatments should be psychotherapy (insight-oriented psychotherapy, cognitive therapy, interpersonal therapy, or behavior therapy), *treatment may include the use of antidepressants*.

In *minor depressive disorder the symptoms are equal in duration but fewer in number than those in major depressive disorder* (Table 15.13).

The treatment of minor depressive disorder can include psychotherapy or pharmacotherapy or both. *Treatment may include the use of antidepressants.*

15.31–15.35

15.31. The answer is A (*Synopsis VII*, pages 523–527).

15.32. The answer is B (*Synopsis VII*, pages 523–527).

15.33. The answer is D (*Synopsis VII*, pages 523–527).

15.34. The answer is B (*Synopsis VII*, pages 523–527).

Table 15.10
Pharmacological Causes of Depressive Symptoms

Analgesics and anti-inflammatory drugs	Antineoplastics
Ibuprofen	C-Asparaginase
Indomethacin	Azathioprine (AZT)
Opiates	6-Azauridine
Phenacetin	Bleomycin
Antibacterials and antifungals	Trimethoprim
Ampicillin	Vincristine
Cycloserine	Neurological and psychiatric drugs
Ethionamide	Amantadine
Griseofulvin	Antipsychotics (butyrophenones, phenothiazines,
Metronidazole	oxyindoles)
Nalidixic acid	Baclofen
Nitrofurantoin	Bromocriptine
Streptomycin	Carbamazepine
Sulfamethoxazole	Levodopa
Sulfonamides	Phenytoin
Tetracycline	Sedatives and hypnotics (barbiturates, benzodiazepines,
Antihypertensives and cardiac drugs	chloral hydrate)
Alphamethyldopa	Steroids and hormones
Bethanidine	Corticosteroids (including ACTH)
β-Blockers (propranolol)	Danazol
Clonidine	Oral contraceptives
Digitalis	Prednisone
Guanabenz acetate	Triamcinolone
Guanethidine	Miscellaneous
Hydralazine	Acetazolamide
Lidocaine	Choline
Prazosin	Cimetidine
Procainamide	Cyproheptadine
Rescinnamine	Diphenoxylate
Reserpine	Disulfiram
Veratrum	Methysergide
	Stimulants (amphetamines, fenfluramine)

15.35. **The answer is A** (*Synopsis VII*, pages 523–527).

A *mood-incongruent delusion* is characterized by content that is not consistent with the patient's mood. Thus, a depressed patient who has delusions of inflated worth, power, identity or a special relationship to a deity or a famous person has a mood-incongruent delusion, as in the cases of *a suicidal man who believes that he is the Messiah* and *a 30-year-old depressed woman who believes that she is the Virgin Mary. Mood-congruent delusions* are those that are consistent with the patient's mood. *An elated man who believes that he has been reincarnated as a millionaire* and *a depressed woman who thinks that she has committed terrible crimes* are suffering from mood-congruent delusions. The *boy who thinks that he hears voices* is experiencing a hallucination, and hallucinations can also be described as either mood-congruent or mood-incongruent.

15.36–15.39

15.36. **The answer is A** (*Synopsis VII*, page 525).

15.37. **The answer is C** (*Synopsis VII*, pages 522 and 556–557).

15.38. **The answer is B** (*Synopsis VII*, page 557).

Table 15.11
Drugs Associated with Manic Symptoms

Amphetamines
Baclofen
Bromide
Bromocriptine
Captopril
Cimetidine
Cocaine
Corticosteroids (including ACTH)
Cyclosporine
Disulfiram
Hallucinogens (intoxication and flashbacks)
Hydralazine
Isoniazid
Levodopa
Methylphenidate
Metrizamide (following myelography)
Opiates and opioids
Procarbazine
Procyclidine

Table 15.12
Research Criteria for Recurrent Brief Depressive Disorder

A. Criteria, except for duration, are met for a major depressive episode.

B. The depressive periods in criterion A last at least 2 days but less than 2 weeks.

C. The depressive periods occur at least once a month for 12 consecutive months and are not associated with the menstrual cycle.

D. The periods of depressed mood cause clinically significant distress or impairment in social, occupational, or other important areas of functioning.

E. The symptoms are not due to the direct physiological effects of a substance (i.e., a drug of abuse, a medication) or a general medical condition (e.g., hypothyroidism).

F. There has never been a major depressive episode, and criteria are not met for dysthymic disorder.

G. There has never been a manic episode, a mixed episode, or a hypomanic episode, and criteria are not met for cyclophymic disorder. **Note:** This exclusion does not apply if all of the manic-, mixed-, or hypomanic-like episodes are substance or treatment induced.

H. The mood disturbance does not occur exclusively during schizophrenia, schizophreniform disorder, schizoaffective disorder, delusional disorder, or psychotic disorder not otherwise specified.

Table from DSM-IV, *Diagnostic and Statistical Manual of Mental Disorders*, ed 4. Copyright American Psychiatric Association, Washington, 1994. Used with permission.

15.39. The answer is A (*Synopsis VII*, page 524).

Dysthymic disorder does not include patients who have *episodic periods of depression.* By definition, dysthymic disorder symptoms do not occur exclusively during the course of a chronic psychotic disorder; dysthymic disorder *does not have psychotic symptoms.* Dysthymic disorder has symptoms nonpsychotic signs and symptoms of depression that meet specific diagnostic criteria, but do not meet the diagnostic criteria for major depressive disorder. About 5 to 10 percent of patients with *major depressive disorder may have psychotic symptoms,* including both delusions and hallucinations. *Major depressive disorder, recurrent,* is characterized by *episodic periods of depression. Many patients* with major depressive disorder and some patients with dysthymic disorder *have a positive family history of mood disorders, decreased rapid eye movement latency, and a positive therapeutic response to antidepressants.*

DSM-IV defines subtypes of dysthymic disorder based on onset before and after age 21. Table 15.9 lists the diagnostic criteria for dysthymic disorder.

15.40–15.45

15.40. The answer is B (*Synopsis VII*, pages 556–562).

15.41. The answer is D (*Synopsis VII*, pages 556–562).

15.42. The answer is B (*Synopsis VII*, pages 556–562).

15.43. The answer is C (*Synopsis VII*, pages 556–562).

15.44. The answer is B (*Synopsis VII*, pages 556–562).

15.45. The answer is C (*Synopsis VII*, pages 556–562).

In cyclothymic disorder, *treatment with antidepressants may lead to hypomanic symptoms* and patients may have a *favorable response to lithium.* During the hypomanic phase of cyclothymia, *sexual promiscuity* may be seen. With regard to *alcohol abuse,* 25 to 50 percent of persons with alcohol abuse have dysthymic disorder, and mood swings, such as those seen in cyclothymic disorder, have also been described as part of the mood disorder related to alcohol abuse. Both dysthymic disorder and cyclothymic disorder may be *confused with substance abuse.* Steroids, amphetamines, barbiturates, and CNS depressants produce depression after periods of heavy use, and mood swings may be associated with the ingestion of steroids, cocaine, amphetamines, and hallucinogens.

Delusions and hallucinations are, by definition, *inconsistent with the diagnosis of both dysthymic disorder and cyclothymic disorder.*

15.46–15.47

15.46. The answer is A (*Synopsis VII*, page 559).

15.47. The answer is B (*Synopsis VII*, page 566).

Cyclothymic disorder is *characterized by episodes of hypomaniclike symptoms* (Table 15.14) *and periods of mild depression.* In DSM-IV, cyclothymic disorder is differentiated from *bipolar II disorder,* which is *characterized by major depressive episodes and hypomanic episodes* (Table 15.15).

Table 15.13
Research Criteria for Minor Depressive Disorder

A. A mood disturbance, defined as follows:

(1) at least two (but less than five) of the following symptoms have been present during the same 2-week period and represent a change from previous functioning; at least one of the symptoms is either (a) or (b):

(a) depressed mood most of the day, nearly every day, as indicated by either subjective report (e.g., feels sad or empty) or observation made by others (e.g., appears tearful). **Note:** In children and adolescents, can be irritable mood.

(b) markedly diminished interest of pleasure in all, or almost all, activities most of the day, nearly every day (as indicated by either subjective account or observation made by others)

(c) significant weight loss when not dieting or weight gain (e.g., a change of more than 5% of body weight in a month), or decrease or increase in appetite nearly every day. **Note:** In children, consider failure to make expected weight gains.

(d) insomnia or hypersomnia nearly every day

(e) psychomotor agitation or retardation nearly every day (observable by others, not merely subjective feelings of restlessness or being slowed down)

(f) fatigue or loss of energy nearly every day

(g) feelings of worthlessness or excessive or inappropriate guilt (which may be delusional) nearly every day (not merely self-reproach or guilt about being sick)

(h) diminished ability to think or concentrate, or indecisiveness, nearly every day (either by subjective account or as observed by others)

(i) recurrent thoughts of death (not just fear of dying), recurrent suicidal ideation without a specific plan, or a suicide attempt or a specific plan for committing suicide

(2) the symptoms cause clinically significant distress or impairment in social, occupational, or other important areas of functioning

(3) the symptoms are not due to the direct physiological effects of a substance (e.g., a drug of abuse, a medication) or a general medical condition (e.g., hypothyroidism)

(4) the symptoms are not better accounted for by bereavement (i.e., a normal reaction to the death of a loved one)

B. There has never been a major depressive episode, and criteria are not met for dysthymic disorder.

C. There has never been a manic episode, a mixed episode, or a hypomanic episode, and criteria are not met for cyclophymic disorder. **Note:** This exclusion does not apply if all of the manic-, mixed-, or hypomanic-like episodes are substance or treatment induced.

D. The mood disturbance does not occur exclusively during schizophrenia, schizophreniform disorder, schizoaffective disorder, delusional disorder, or psychotic disorder not otherwise specified.

Table from DSM-IV, *Diagnostic and Statistical Manual of Mental Disorders,* ed. 4. Copyright American Psychiatric Association, Washington, 1994. Used with permission.

Table 15.14
Criteria for Hypomanic Episode

A. A distinct period of persistently elevated, expansive, or irritable mood, lasting throughout at least 4 days, that is clearly different from the usual nondepressed mood.

B. During the period of mood disturbance, three (or more) of the following symptoms have persisted (four if the mood is only irritable) and have been present to a significant degree:

(1) inflated self-esteem or grandiosity

(2) decreased need for sleep (e.g., feels rested after only 3 hours of sleep)

(3) more talkative than usual or pressure to keep talking

(4) flight of ideas or subjective experience that thoughts are racing

(5) distractibility (i.e., attention too easily drawn to unimportant or irrelevant external stimuli)

(6) increase in goal-directed activity (either socially, at work or school, or sexually) or psychomotor agitation

(7) excessive involvement in pleasurable activities that have a high potential for painful consequences (e.g., the person engages in unrestrained buying sprees, sexual indiscretions, or foolish business investments)

C. The episode is associated with an unequivocal change in functioning that is uncharacteristic of the person when not symptomatic.

D. The disturbance in mood and the change in functioning are observable by others.

E. The episode is not severe enough to cause marked impairment in social or occupational functioning, or to necessitate hospitalization, and there are no psychotic features.

F. The symptoms are not due to the direct physiological effects of a substance (e.g., a drug of abuse, a medication, or other treatment) or a general medical condition (e.g., hyperthyroidism).

Note: Hypomanic-like episodes that are clearly caused by somatic antidepressant treatment (e.g., medication, electroconvulsive therapy, light therapy) should not count toward a diagnosis of bipolar II disorder.

Table from DSM-IV, *Diagnostic and Statistical Manual of Mental Disorders,* ed 4. Copyright American Psychiatric Association, Washington, 1994. Used with permission.

Table 15.15
Diagnostic Criteria for Bipolar II Disorder

A. Presence (or history) of one or more major depressive episodes.

B. Presence (or history) of at least one hypomanic episode.

C. There has never been a manic episode or a mixed episode.

D. The mood symptoms in criteria A and B are not better accounted for by schizoaffective disorder and are not superimposed on schizophrenia, schizophreniform disorder, delusional disorder, or psychotic disorder not otherwise specified.

E. The symptoms cause clinically significant distress or impairment in social, occupational, or other important areas of functioning.

Specify current or most recent episode:
   Hypomanic: if currently (or most recently) in a hypomanic episode
   Depressed: if currently (or most recently) in a major depressive episode

Specify (for current or most recent major depressive episode only if it is the most recent type of mood episode):
   Severity/psychotic/remission specifiers. Note: Fifth-digit codes cannot be used here because the code for bipolar II disorder already uses the fifth digit.
   Chronic
   With catatonic features
   With melancholic features
   With atypical features
   With postpartum onset

Specify:
   Longitudinal course specifiers (with and without interepisode recovery)
   With seasonal pattern (applies only to the pattern of major depressive episodes)
   With rapid cycling

Table from DSM-IV, *Diagnostic and Statistical Manual of Mental Disorders,* ed 4. Copyright American Psychiatric Association, Washington, 1994. Used with permission.

16 ||||||

Anxiety Disorders

Anxiety is an emotion familiar to everyone, and it can be viewed along a spectrum from normal and adaptive to pathological and maladaptive. Anxiety may be generated by one's perception and psychological interpretation of external stress, pressures, and realities and by one's biological reaction to internal biological changes. Anxiety in some cases is almost purely psychological in origin, with concomitant physiological manifestations; in other cases, it is almost purely biological in origin, with concomitant emotional and behavioral responses. In most cases, anxiety results from a complex interplay of psychology, temperament, environment, conditioning, and biology.

The causal theories of anxiety are both psychological and biological in origin. The psychological theories derive from three major schools—psychoanalytic, behavioral, and existential. The biological theories of anxiety generally focus on the autonomic nervous system (particularly the patient's degree of sympathetic tone, adaptation to repeated stimuli, and degree of response to moderate stimuli), the role of specific neurotransmitters (particularly norepinephrine, serotonin, and γ-aminobutyric acid [GABA]), and how anxiolytic drugs affect those neurotransmitters. Brain-imaging studies involve such instruments as computed tomography (CT), positron emission tomography (PET), magnetic resonance imaging (MRI), single photon emission computed tomography (SPECT), and electroencephalography (EEG). An early and conservative interpretation of much of the research data involves the belief that some patients with anxiety disorders have demonstrable cerebral pathology that may be causally related to their symptoms. Neuroanatomical considerations have also taken on increasing importance, with most attention directed at the locus ceruleus and the raphe nuclei and their projections to the limbic system and the cerebral cortex.

The fourth edition of *Diagnostic and Statistical Manual of Mental Disorders* (DSM-IV) lists the following anxiety disorders: panic disorder without agoraphobia, panic disorder with agoraphobia, agoraphobia without history of panic disorder, specific phobia, social phobia, obsessive-compulsive disorder, posttraumatic stress disorder, acute stress disorder, generalized anxiety disorder (including overanxious disorder of childhood), anxiety disorder due to a general medical condition, substance-induced anxiety disorder, and anxiety disorder not otherwise specified (NOS), including mixed anxiety-depressive disorder.

By studying Chapter 16 in *Kaplan and Sadock's Synopsis VII*, students will be able to test their knowledge of anxiety disorders with the questions and answers below.

HELPFUL HINTS

The student should know the following names, cases, terms, and acronyms related to anxiety disorders.

anxiety	repression	posttraumatic stress disorder
fear	panic disorder	generalized anxiety disorder
Charles Darwin	phobias: agoraphobia, social,	Sigmund Freud
stress	specific	GABA
conflict	obsessive-compulsive disorder	norepinephrine

MHPG	John B. Watson	clomipramine (Anafranil)
serotonin	ego-dystonic	aversive conditioning
aplysia	propranolol (Inderal)	thought stopping
limbic system	Joseph Wolpe	soldier's heart
cerebral cortex	systematic desensitization	Jacob M. DaCosta
acute stress disorder	flooding	shell shock
lactate infusion	hypnosis	trauma
PET	implosion	sleep EEG studies
panic attack	isolation	secondary gain
imipramine (Tofranil)	undoing	numbing
anticipatory anxiety	reaction formation	MMPI, Rorschach
Little Hans	aggression	time-limited psychotherapy
Little Albert	cleanliness	benzodiazepines
counterphobic attitude	ambivalence	dopamine
Otto Fenichel	magical thinking	adrenergic

QUESTIONS

DIRECTIONS: Each of the incomplete statements below is followed by five suggested completions. Select the *one* that is *best* in each case.

16.1. Anxiety
A. is associated with the awareness of being nervous or frightened.
B. may occur without physiological sensations
C. is a response to a known external threat
D. tends to sharpen concentration
E. tends to increase recall

16.2. The most common form of phobia is
A. photophobia
B. thanatophobia
C. acrophobia
D. agoraphobia
E. nyctophobia

16.3. The obsessive-compulsive disorder patient who tries to resist carrying out the compulsion generally experiences
A. anxiety
B. hypochondriasis
C. somatization disorder
D. dissociation
E. ambivalence

16.4. Sigmund Freud postulated that the defense mechanisms necessary in phobias are
A. repression, displacement, and avoidance
B. regression, condensation, and projection
C. regression, repression, and isolation
D. repression, projection, and displacement
E. regression, condensation, and dissociation

16.5. All the following may be used effectively in the treatment of phobias *except*
A. diazepam
B. chlordiazepoxide
C. imipramine
D. hypnosis
E. chlorpromazine

16.6. Counterphobic attitudes may be represented by
A. parachute jumping
B. rock climbing
C. burgee jumping
D. parasailing
E. all the above

16.7. Features associated with posttraumatic stress disorder include
A. reexperiencing of the trauma through dreams
B. emotional numbing
C. autonomic instability
D. cognitive difficulties
E. all the above

16.8. Therapy for phobias may include
A. systematic desensitization
B. flooding
C. propranolol (Inderal)
D. phenelzine (Nardil)
E. all the above

16.9. Posttraumatic stress disorder is associated with
A. an event outside the range of usual human experiences
B. a stress that would be distressing to anyone
C. biological vulnerability
D. decreased rapid eye movement (REM) latency
E. all the above

16.10. Medications used to treat posttraumatic stress disorder include
A. amitriptyline
B. imipramine
C. phenelzine
D. clonidine
E. all the above

16.11. In acute stress disorder the symptoms
A. must last for a minimum of two days
B. can last for a maximum of eight weeks
C. must occur within one year of the trauma
D. must occur within six months of the trauma
E. must occur within two months of the trauma

16.12. Unexpected panic attacks are required for
the diagnosis of
A. panic disorder
B. social phobia
C. specific phobia
D. generalized anxiety disorder
E. all the above

16.13. The symptoms of a panic attack can
include
A. sweating
B. chest pain
C. nausea
D. fear of dying
E. all the above

DIRECTIONS: Each set of lettered headings below is followed by a list of numbered words or
phrases. For each numbered word or phrase, select

    A. if the item is associated with *A only*
    B. if the item is associated with *B only*
    C. if the item is associated with *both A and B*
    D. if the item is associated with *neither A nor B*

Questions 16.14–16.19
    A. Obsessions
    B. Compulsions
    C. Both
    D. Neither

16.14. Idea or impulse intrudes insistently and
persistently into awareness

16.15. Are ego-alien

16.16. Patient feels a strong desire to resist them

16.17. Ideas or sensations

16.18. Acts or behaviors

16.19. Are ego-syntonic

Questions 16.20–16.23
    A. Little Hans
    B. Little Albert
    C. Both
    D. Neither

16.20. Fear of horses

16.21. Castration anxiety

16.22. Conditioned response

16.23. Fear of rabbits

Questions 16.24–16.28
    A. Panic disorder without agoraphobia
    B. Generalized anxiety disorder
    C. Both
    D. Neither

16.24. Discrete and episodic

16.25. Chronic and persistent

16.26. Dizziness and paresthesias

16.27. Other psychiatric symptoms are present

16.28. Obvious physical evidence of respiratory
alkalosis

DIRECTIONS: Each group of questions below consists of lettered headings followed by a list of numbered statements. For each numbered statement, select the *one* lettered heading that is most closely associated with it. Each lettered heading may be used once, more than once, or not at all.

Questions 16.29–16.32
A. Psychoanalytic theories of anxiety
B. Behavioral theories of anxiety
C. Existential theories of anxiety

16.29. Anxiety is a conditioned response to specific environmental stimuli

16.30. Persons become aware of a profound nothingness in their lives

16.31. Anxiety is a signal to the ego that an unacceptable drive is pressing for conscious representation

16.32. Treatment is usually with some form of desensitization to the anxiogenic stimulus

Questions 16.33–16.35
A. Norepinephrine
B. Serotonin
C. γ-Aminobutyric acid (GABA)

16.33. The cell bodies of the neurotransmitter's neurons are localized primarily to the locus ceruleus

16.34. Benzodiazepines enhance the neurotransmitter's effects at its receptors

16.35. The cell bodies of the neurotransmitter's neurons are localized primarily to the raphe nuclei

Questions 16.36–16.41
A. Generalized anxiety disorder
B. Obsessive-compulsive disorder
C. Specific phobia
D. Social phobia
E. Posttraumatic stress disorder

16.36. Fear of flying

16.37. Fear of public speaking

16.38. Isolation, undoing, and reaction formation

16.39. Shell shock

16.40. Buspirone is a drug of choice

16.41. May have associated Tourette's disorder

Questions 16.42–16.46
A. Walter Cannon
B. James Lange
C. Otto Rank
D. Harry Stack Sullivan
E. Melanie Klein

16.42. Trauma of birth

16.43. Transmission of maternal anxiety

16.44. Adrenal release of epinephrine

16.45. Anxiety in response to peripheral phenomena

16.46. Primitive superego anxiety

ANSWERS

Anxiety Disorders

16.1.

573–5

An
nervoɪ
tions,
not a
advers
It tenɑ
tends t

16.2.
and 59

Agoɪ
the moɪ
60 perc
agoraph
listed iɪ
panic di
16.2. Ph
termine
infectioɪ
in sever
is exposɪ
as a neu
bia is the
places. N

... fear of night or darkness.

16.3.   The answer is A (*Synopsis VII*, pages 598–599).

If the obsessive-compulsive disorder patient tries to resist carrying out the compulsion, the patient generally experiences *anxiety*.

Table 16.1
Diagnostic Criteria for Agoraphobia Without History of Panic Disorder

A. The presence of agoraphobia related to fear of developing panic-like symptoms (e.g., dizziness or diarrhea).

B. Criteria have never been met for panic disorder.

C. The disturbance is not due to the direct physiological effects of a substance (e.g., a drug of abuse, a medication) or a general medical condition.

D. If an associated general medical condition is present, the fear described in criterion A is clearly in excess of that usually associated with the condition.

Table from DSM-IV, *Diagnostic and Statistical Manual of Mental Disorders,* ed 4. Copyright American Psychiatric Association, Washington, 1994. Used with permission.

Hypochondriasis is a somatoform disorder characterized by excessive, morbid anxiety about one's health. *Somatization disorder* is a somatoform disorder characterized by recurrent and multiple physical complaints with no apparent physical cause. *Dissociation* is an unconscious defense mechanism involving the segregation of any group of mental or behavioral processes from the rest of the person's psychic activity. It may entail the separation of an idea from its accompanying emotional tone, as seen in dissociative disorders. When a patient experiences *ambivalence*, strong and often overwhelming simultaneous contrasting attitudes, ideas, feelings, and drives toward an object, person, or goal are present.

16.4.   The answer is A (*Synopsis VII*, page 593).

Sigmund Freud viewed phobias as resulting from conflicts centered on an unresolved childhood oedipal situation. In the adult, because the sexual drive continues to have a strong incestuous coloring, its arousal tends to arouse anxiety that is characteris-

Table 16.2
Diagnostic Criteria for Panic Disorder with Agoraphobia

A. Both (1) and (2):

   (1) recurrent unexpected panic attacks
   (2) at least one of the attacks has been followed by 1 month (or more) of one (or more) of the following:

      (a) persistent concern about having additional attacks
      (b) worry about the implications of the attack or its consequences (e.g., losing control, having a heart attack, "going crazy")
      (c) a significant change in behavior related to the attacks

B. The presence of agoraphobia

C. The panic attacks are not due to the direct physiological effects of a substance (e.g., a drug of abuse, a medication) or a general medical condition (e.g., hyperthyroidism).

D. The panic attacks are not better accounted for by another mental disorder, such as social phobia (e.g., occuring on exposure to feared social situations), specific phobia (e.g., on exposure to a specific phobia situation), obsessive-compulsive disorder (e.g., on exposure to dirt in someone with an obsession about contamination), posttraumatic stress disorder (e.g., in response to stimuli associated with a severe stressor), or separation anxiety disorder (e.g., in response to being away from home or close relatives).

Table from DSM-IV, *Diagnostic and Statistical Manual of Mental Disorders,* ed 4. Copyright American Psychiatric Association, Washington, 1994. Used with permission.

tically a fear of castration. The anxiety then alerts the ego to exert *repression* to keep the drive away from conscious representation and discharge. Because repression fails to be entirely successful in its function, the ego must call on auxiliary defenses. In phobic patients, the defenses, arising genetically from an earlier phobic response during the initial childhood period of the oedipal conflict, involves primarily the use of *displacement*—that is, the sexual conflict is transposed or displaced from the person who evoked the conflict to a seemingly unimportant, irrelevant object or situation, which then has the power to arouse the entire constellation of affects, including signal anxiety. The phobic object or situation thus selected has a direct associative connection with the primary source of the conflict and has thus come naturally to symbolize it. Furthermore, the situation or object is usually such that the patient is able to keep out of its way and, by the additional defense mechanism of *avoidance*, can escape suffering from serious anxiety.

Regression is an unconscious defense mechanism in which a person undergoes a partial or total return to early patterns of adaptation. *Condensation* is a mental process in which one symbol stands for a number of components. *Projection* is an unconscious defense mechanism in which persons attribute to another those generally unconscious ideas, thoughts, feelings, and impulses that are undesirable or unacceptable in themselves. Projection protects persons from anxiety arising from an inner conflict. By externalizing whatever is unacceptable, persons deal with it as a situation apart from themselves. In psychoanalysis, *isolation* is a defense mechanism involving the separation of an idea or memory from its attached feeling tone. Unacceptable ideational content is thereby rendered free of its disturbing or unpleasant emotional charge. *Dissociation* is an unconscious defense mechanism involving the segregation of any group of mental or behavioral processes from the rest of the person's psychic activity.

16.5. The answer is E (*Synopsis VII*, pages 597–598).

Chlorpromazine (Thorazine) is a phenothiazine derivative used primarily as an antipsychotic agent and in the treatment of nausea and vomiting. It is not used in phobias.

Diazepam (Valium) and *chlordiazepoxide* (Librium) may be useful in decreasing symptoms of anxiety. They should be prescribed with caution for those patients who have a history suggesting a tendency for psychological or physical dependence on substances. *Imipramine* (Tofranil) may be useful in decreasing phobic or depressive symptoms. All those drugs should be used with caution in patients suffering from posttraumatic stress disorder after accidents that have led to serious physical illness. Imipramine, in particular, may precipitate symptoms of delirium in patients suffering from serious medical illness.

Hypnosis is useful not only in enhancing the suggestion that is a part of the therapist's generally supportive approach but in directly combating the anxiety arising from the phobic situation. The psychiatrist can teach patients the techniques of autohypnosis, through which they can achieve a degree of relaxation when they are facing the phobic situation that will enable them to tolerate it. Those patients who cannot be hypnotized may be taught techniques of muscle relaxation.

16.6. The answer is E (all) (*Synopsis VII*, pages 593–594).

Many activities may mask phobic anxiety, which can be hidden behind attitudes and behavior patterns that represent a denial, either that the dreaded object or situation is dangerous or that one is afraid of it. Basic to this phenomenon is a reversal of the situation in which one is the passive victim of external circumstances to a position of attempting actively to confront and master what one fears. The counterphobic person seeks out situations of danger and rushes enthusiastically toward them. The devotee of dangerous sports, such as *parachute jumping, rock climbing, bungee jumping,* and *parasailing,* may be exhibiting counterphobic behavior. Such patterns may be secondary to phobic anxieties or may be used as a normal means of dealing with a realistically dangerous situation.

16.7. The answer is E (all) (*Synopsis VII*, pages 606–610).

Posttraumatic stress disorder (Table 16.3) develops in persons who have experienced emotional or physical stress that would be extremely traumatic for virtually anyone. The major features associated with the disorder are the *reexperiencing of the trauma through dreams* and waking thoughts; *emotional numbing* to other life experiences, including relationships; and associated symptoms of *autonomic instability*, depression, and *cognitive difficulties*, such as poor concentration.

16.8. The answer is E (all) (*Synopsis VII*, pages 597–598).

Both behavioral and pharmacological techniques have been used in treating phobias. The most common behavioral technique is *systematic desensitization*, in which the patient is exposed serially to a predetermined list of anxiety-provoking stimuli graded in a hierarchy from the least frightening to the most frightening. Patients are taught to self-induce a state of relaxation in the face of each anxiety-provoking stimulus. In *flooding*, patients are exposed to the phobic stimulus (actual [in vivo] or through imagery) for as long as they can tolerate the fear until they reach a point at which they can no longer feel it. The social phobia of stage fright in performers has been effectively treated with such β-adrenergic antagonists as *propranolol* (Inderal), which blocks the physiological signs of anxiety (for example, tachycardia).

Table 16.3
Diagnostic Criteria for Posttraumatic Stress Disorder

A. The person has been exposed to a traumatic event in which both of the following have been present:

    (1) the person experienced, witnessed, or was confronted with an event or events that involved actual or threatened death or serious injury, or a threat to the physical integrity of self or others

    (2) the person's response involved intense fear, helplessness, or horror. **Note:** In children, this may be expressed instead by disorganized or agitated behavior

B. The traumatic event is persistently reexperienced in one (or more) of the following ways:

    (1) recurrent and intrusive distressing recollections of the event, including images, thoughts, or perceptions. **Note:** In young children, repetitive play may occur in which themes or aspects of the trauma are expressed.

    (2) recurrent distressing dreams of the event. **Note:** In children, there may be frightening dreams without recognizable content.

    (3) acting or feeling as if the traumatic event were recurring (includes a sense of reliving the experience, illusions, hallucinations, and dissociative flashback episodes, including those that occur upon awakening or when intoxicated) **Note:** In young children, trauma-specific reenactment may occur.

    (4) intense psychological distress at exposure to internal or external cues that symbolize or resemble an aspect of the traumatic event

    (5) physiologic reactivity on exposure to internal or external cues that symbolize or resemble an aspect of the traumatic event

C. Persistent avoidance of stimuli associated with the trauma and numbing of general responsiveness (not present before the trauma), as indicated by three (or more) of the following:

    (1) efforts to avoid thoughts, feelings, or conversations associated with the trauma

    (2) efforts to avoid activities, places, or people that arouse recollections of the trauma

    (3) inability to recall an important aspect of the trauma

    (4) markedly diminished interest or participation in significant activities

    (5) feeling of detachment or estrangement from others

    (6) restricted range of affect (e.g., unable to have loving feelings)

    (7) sense of a foreshortened future (e.g., does not expect to have a career, marriage, children, or a normal life span)

D. Persistent symptoms of increased arousal (not present before the trauma), as indicated by two (or more) of the following:

    (1) difficulty falling or staying asleep

    (2) irritability or outbursts of anger

    (3) difficulty concentrating

    (4) hypervigilance

    (5) exaggerated startle response

E. Duration of the disturbance (symptoms in criteria B, C, and D) is more than 1 month.

F. The disturbance causes clinically significant distress or impairment in social, occupational, or other important areas of functioning.

Specify if:
    Acute: if duration of symptoms is less than 3 months
    Chronic: if duration of symptoms is 3 months or more

Specify if:
    With delayed onset: if onset of symptoms is at least 6 months after the stressor

Table from DSM-IV, *Diagnostic and Statistical Manual of Mental Disorders,* ed 4. Copyright American Psychiatric Association, Washington, 1994. Used with permission.

Phenelzine (Nardil), a monoamine oxidase inhibitor, is also of use in treating social phobia.

16.9. The answer is E (all) (*Synopsis VII*, pages 606–610).

The stress that precipitates posttraumatic stress disorder is usually *outside the range of usual human experiences*, such as from earthquakes, flood, or war. It is also *a stress that would be distressing to anyone.* The fact that a person finds the stressor disagreeable is not a sign of being psychologically abnormal. Each person has his or her threshold for developing symptoms of the disorder; that threshold is based on the character traits of the person, *biological vulnerability*, and the nature of the stressor. Research on the

biological theories of posttraumatic stress disorder have found labile autonomic nervous system reactions to stress, *decreased rapid eye movement (REM) latency* periods, and increased endogenous opioid secretion.

16.10. The answer is E (all) (*Synopsis VII*, pages 610–611).

Tricyclic drugs, especially *amitriptyline* (Elavil) and *imipramine* (Tofranil), and the monoamine oxidase inhibitor *phenelzine* (Nardil) are the drugs most often used to treat posttraumatic stress disorder. They are particularly indicated when depression or panic symptoms are present. Increasing numbers of clinicians report therapeutic success with *clonidine*

(Catapres), and a few reports suggest that propranolol (Inderal) may be an effective treatment. Antipsychotic medications may be necessary for brief periods during treatment if behavior is particularly agitated.

16.11.   The answer is A (*Synopsis VII*, pages 608–609).

In acute stress disorder (Table 16.4) the symptoms *must last for a minimum of two days, can last*

Table 16.4
Diagnostic Criteria for Acute Stress Disorder

A. The person has been exposed to a traumatic event in which both of the following were present:

   (1) the person been experienced, witnessed, or was confronted with an event or events that involved actual or threatened death or serious injury, or a threat to the physical integrity of self or others
   (2) the person's response involved intense fear, helplessness, or horror

B. Either while experiencing or after experiencing the distressing event, the individual has three (or more) of the following dissociative symptoms:

   (1) a subjective sense of numbing, detachment, or absence of emotional responsiveness
   (2) a reduction in awareness of his or her surroundings (e.g., "being in a daze")
   (3) derealization
   (4) depersonalization
   (5) dissociative amnesia (i.e., inability to recall an important aspect of the trauma)

C. The traumatic event is persistently reexperienced in at least one of the following ways: recurrent images, thoughts, dreams, illusions, flashback episodes, or a sense of reliving the experience; or distress on exposure to reminders of the traumatic event.

D. Marked avoidance of stimuli that arouse recollections of the trauma (e.g., thoughts, feelings, conversations, activities, places, people).

E. Marked symptoms of anxiety or increased arousal (e.g., difficulty sleeping, irritability, poor concentration, hypervigilance, exaggerated startle response, motor restlessness).

F. The disturbance causes clinically significant distress or impairment in social, occupational, or other important areas of functioning or impairs the individual's ability to pursue some necessary task, such as obtaining necessary assistance or mobilizing personal resources by telling family members about the traumatic experience.

G. The disturbance lasts for a minimum of 2 days and a maximum of 4 weeks and occur within 4 weeks of the traumatic event.

H. The disturbance is not due to the direct physiological effects of a substance (e.g., a drug of abuse, a medication) or a general medical condition, is not better accounted for by brief psychotic disorder, and is not merely an exacerbation of a preexisting Axis I or Axis II disorder.

Table from DSM-IV, *Diagnostic and Statistical Manual of Mental Disorders*, ed 4. Copyright American Psychiatric Association, Washington, 1994. Used with permission.

for a maximum of four weeks (not eight weeks), and must occur within four weeks (not one year, six months, or two months) of the trauma.

16.12.   The answer is A (*Synopsis VII*, page 585).

Unexpected panic attacks are required for the diagnosis of *panic disorder*, but panic attacks (Table 16.5) can occur in several anxiety disorders. The clinician must consider the context of the panic attack when making a diagnosis. Panic attacks can be divided into two types: (1) unexpected panic attacks, in which the panic attack is not associated with a situational trigger, and (2) situationally bound panic attacks, in which a panic attack occurs immediately after exposure in a situational trigger, or in anticipation of the situational trigger. Situationally bound panic attacks are most characteristic of *social phobia* and *specific phobia*. In *generalized anxiety disorder* the anxiety cannot be about having a panic attack.

16.13.   The answer is E (all) (*Synopsis VII*, pages 582–585).

The symptoms of a panic attack can include palpitations, *sweating*, trembling, *chest pain, nausea*, fear of going crazy, and *fear of dying*. Table 16.5 lists all the symptoms of panic attack in the diagnostic criteria of the fourth edition of *Diagnostic and Statistical Manual of Mental Disorders* (DSM-IV).

16.14–16.19

16.14.   The answer is C (*Synopsis VII*, pages 598–604).

16.15.   The answer is C (*Synopsis VII*, pages 598–604).

16.16.   The answer is C (*Synopsis VII*, pages 598–604).

16.17.   The answer is A (*Synopsis VII*, pages 598–604).

16.18.   The answer is B (*Synopsis VII*, pages 598–604).

16.19.   The answer is D (*Synopsis VII*, pages 598–604).

Obsessions and compulsions have certain features in common: (1) *an idea or an impulse intrudes insistently and persistently into awareness*; (2) a feeling of anxious dread accompanies the central manifestation and frequently leads the person to take countermeasures against the initial idea or impulse; (3) the obsession or compulsion is *ego-alien*; that is, it is experienced as being foreign to the person's experience of himself or herself as a psychological being; (4) the person recognizes the obsession or compulsion as absurd and irrational; and (5) *the person feels a strong desire to resist them. Obsessions* are thoughts, feelings, *ideas, or sensations. Compulsions* are *acts or behaviors. Neither* obsessions nor compulsions *are ego-syntonic.* A patient with obsessive-compulsive disorder recognizes the irrationality of the obsession, which means that both the obsession and the compulsion are ego-dystonic.

16.20–16.23

16.20. The answer is **A** (*Synopsis VII*, page 593).

16.21. The answer is **A** (*Synopsis VII*, page 593).

16.22. The answer is **B** (*Synopsis VII*, page 593).

16.23. The answer is **B** (*Synopsis VII*, page 593).

In Sigmund Freud's case history of *Little Hans*, a 5-year-old boy who had a *fear of horses*, Hans's fear of horses represented *castration anxiety*, a displaced fear that his penis would be cut off by his father.

In 1920 John B. Watson recounted his experiences with Little Albert, an infant with a phobia about rabbits. Unlike Freud's Little Hans, who showed his symptoms in the natural course of his maturation, Little Albert's difficulties were the direct result of the scientific experiments of two psychologists, who used techniques that had successfully induced *conditioned responses* in laboratory animals. They produced a loud noise paired with the rabbit, so that *fear of rabbits* resulted.

16.24–16.28

16.24. The answer is **A** (*Synopsis VII*, pages 582–590).

16.25. The answer is **B** (*Synopsis VII*, pages 611–614).

16.26. The answer is **C** (*Synopsis VII*, pages 582–590 and 611–614).

16.27. The answer is **D** (*Synopsis VII*, pages 582–590 and 611–614).

16.28. The answer is **A** (*Synopsis VII*, pages 582–590).

Panic disorder is characterized by *discrete and episodic* attacks of anxiety, whereas generalized anxiety disorder is characterized by anxiety that is *chronic and persistent.* Such symptoms as *dizziness, paresthesia*, restlessness, and palpitations are seen in both types of anxiety. The classifications of panic disorder without agoraphobia (Table 16.6) and generalized anxiety disorder (Table 16.7) are reserved for those patients in whom *other psychiatric symptoms*, such as obsessions and phobias *are absent.* Hyperventilation may be seen in both types of anxiety disorder but only in panic disorder without agoraphobia is sufficient carbon dioxide blown off to bring on *obvious evidence of respiratory alkalosis*, such as muscle twitching and tetany.

Table 16.5
Criteria for Panic Attack

Note: A panic attack is not a codable disorder. Code the specific diagnosis in which the panic attack occurs (e.g., panic disorder with agoraphobia).

A discrete period of intense fear or discomfort, in which four (or more) of the following symptoms developed abruptly and reached a peak within 10 minutes:

(1) palpitations, pounding heart, or accelerated heart rate
(2) sweating
(3) trembling or shaking
(4) sensations of shortness of breath or smothering
(5) feeling of choking
(6) chest pain or discomfort
(7) nausea or abdominal distress
(8) feeling dizzy, unsteady, lightheaded, or faint
(9) derealization (feelings of unreality) or depersonalization (being detached from oneself)
(10) fear of losing control or going crazy
(11) fear of dying
(12) paresthesias (numbness or tingling sensations)
(13) chills or hot flushes

Table from DSM-IV, *Diagnostic and Statistical Manual of Mental Disorders,* ed 4. Copyright American Psychiatric Association, Washington, 1994. Used with permission.

Table 16.6
Diagnostic Criteria for Panic Disorder Without Agoraphobia

A. Both (1) and (2):
  (1) recurrent unexpected panic attacks
  (2) at least one of the attacks has been followed by at least 1 month of one (or more) of the following:
    (a) persistent concern about having additional attacks
    (b) worry about the implications of the attack or its consequences (e.g., losing control, having a heart attack, "going crazy")
    (c) a significant change in behavior related to the attacks

B. Absense of agoraphobia

C. The panic attacks are not due to the direct physiological effects of a substance (e.g., a drug of abuse, a medication) or a general medical condition (e.g., hyperthyroidism).

D. The panic attacks are not better accounted for by another mental disorder, such as social phobia (e.g., occuring on exposure to feared social situations), specific phobia (e.g., on exposure to a specific phobic situation), obsessive-compulsive disorder (e.g., on exposure to dirt in someone with an obsession about contamination), posttraumatic stress disorder (e.g., in response to stimuli associated with a severe stressor), or separation anxiety disorder (e.g., in response to being away from home or close relatives).

Table from DSM-IV, *Diagnostic and Statistical Manual of Mental Disorders,* ed 4. Copyright American Psychiatric Association, Washington, 1994. Used with permission.

Table 16.7
Diagnostic Criteria for Generalized Anxiety Disorder

A. Excessive anxiety and worry (apprehensive expectation), occurring more days than not for at least 6 months, about a number of events or activities (such as work or school performance).

B. The person finds it difficult to control the worry.

C. The anxiety and worry are associated with three (or more) of the following six symptoms (with at least some symptoms present for more days than not for the past 6 months). **Note:** only one item is required for children.

   (1) restlessness or feeling keyed up or on edge
   (2) being easily fatigued
   (3) difficulty concentrating or mind going blank
   (4) irritability
   (5) muscle tension
   (6) sleep disturbance (difficulty falling or staying asleep, or restless unsatisfying sleep)

D. The focus of the anxiety and worry is not confined to features of an Axis I disorder, e.g., the anxiety or worry is not about having a panic attack (as in panic disorder), being embarrassed in public (as in social phobia), being contaminated (as in obsessive-compulsive disorder), being away from home or close relatives (as in separation anxiety disorder), gaining weight (as in anorexia nervosa), having multiple physical complaints (as in somatization disorder), or having a serious illness (as in hypochondriasis), and the anxiety and worry do not occur exclusively during posttraumatic stress disorder.

E. The anxiety, worry, or physical symptoms cause clinically significant distress or impairment in social, occupational, or other important areas of functioning.

F. The disturbance is not due to the direct physiological effects of a substance (e.g., a drug of abuse, a medication) or a general medical condition (e.g., hyperthyroidism) and does not occur exclusively during a mood disorder, a psychotic disorder, or a pervasive developmental disorder.

Table from DSM-IV, *Diagnostic and Statistical Manual of Mental Disorders,* ed 4. Copyright American Psychiatric Association, Washington, 1994. Used with permission.

16.29–16.32

16.29. The answer is B (*Synopsis VII*, page 576).

16.30. The answer is C (*Synopsis VII*, page 576).

16.31. The answer is A (*Synopsis VII*, page 575–576).

16.32. The answer is B (*Synopsis VII*, page 576).

Three major schools of psychological theory—psychoanalytic, behavioral, and existential—have contributed theories regarding the causes of anxiety. Within the *psychoanalytic* school of thought, Sigmund Freud proposed that *anxiety is a signal to the ego that an unacceptable drive is pressing for con-scious representation and discharge. Behavioral* theories state that *anxiety is a conditioned response to specific environmental stimuli.* In a model of classic conditioning, a person who does not have any food allergies may become sick after eating contaminated shellfish in a restaurant. Subsequent exposures to shellfish may cause that person to feel sick. Through generalization, such a person may come to distrust all food prepared by others.

Treatment is usually with some form of desensitization to the anxiogenic stimulus, coupled with cognitive psychotherapeutic approaches. In *existential* theories of anxiety, *persons become aware of a profound nothingness in their lives,* feelings that may be even more profoundly discomforting than an acceptance of their inevitable death. Anxiety is the person's response to that vast void.

16.33–16.35

16.33. The answer is A (*Synopsis VII*, pages 576–577).

16.34. The answer is C (*Synopsis VII*, pages 576–577).

16.35. The answer is B (*Synopsis VII*, pages 576–577).

The three major neurotransmitters associated with anxiety are norepinephrine, serotonin, and γ-aminobutyric acid (GABA). The general theory regarding the role of *norepinephrine* in anxiety disorders is that affected patients may have a poorly regulated noradrenergic system that has occasional bursts of activity. In that system *the cell bodies of the neurotransmitter's neurons are localized primarily to the locus ceruleus* in the rostral pons, and they project their axons to the cerebral cortex, the limbic system, the brainstem, and the spinal cord. Experiments in primates have shown that stimulations of the locus ceruleus produces a fear response.

The interest in *serotonin* was initially motivated by the observation that serotonergic antidepressants have therapeutic effects in some anxiety disorders—for example, clomipramine (Anafranil) in obsessive-compulsive disorder. The effectiveness of buspirone (BuSpar), a serotonergic type 1A (5-HT1A) receptor agonist in the treatment of anxiety disorders also suggests the possibility of an association between serotonin and anxiety. *The cell bodies of most of the serotonergic neurons are located in the raphe nuclei* in the rostral brainstem (especially the amygdala and the hippocampus) and the hypothalamus.

The role of *γ-aminobutyric acid (GABA)* in anxiety disorders is most strongly supported by the undisputed efficacy of *benzodiazepines, which enhance the activity of GABA at the GABA$_A$ receptor* in the treatment of some types of anxiety disorders.

16.36–16.41

16.36. **The answer is C** (*Synopsis VII*, pages 594–596).

16.37. **The answer is D** (*Synopsis VII*, pages 594–596).

16.38. **The answer is B** (*Synopsis VII*, page 600).

16.39. **The answer is E** (*Synopsis VII*, page 606).

16.40. **The answer is A** (*Synopsis VII*, page 615).

16.41. **The answer is B** (*Synopsis VII*, page 603).

Excessive *fear of flying* is an example of a *specific phobia* (Table 16.8). *Fear of public speaking* is an example of a *social phobia* (Table 16.9).

Sigmund Freud described three major psychological defense mechanisms that determine the form and the quality of *obsessive-compulsive disorder: isolation, undoing, and reaction formation*. Isolation is a defense mechanism in which the affect and the impulse of which it is a derivative are separated from the ideational component and are pushed out of consciousness. Undoing is a compulsive act that is performed in an attempt to prevent or undo the consequences that the patient irrationally anticipates from a frightening obsessional thought or impulse. Reaction formation involves manifest patterns of behavior and consciously experienced attitudes that are exactly the opposite of the underlying impulses.

In World War I *posttraumatic stress disorder* was called *shell shock* and was hypothesized to result from brain trauma caused by the explosion of shells. The psychiatric morbidity associated with Vietnam War veterans brought the concept of posttraumatic stress disorder into full fruition as it is known today (Table 16.3).

Buspirone is a drug of choice in *generalized anxiety disorder*. The drug is most likely effective in 60 to 80 percent of patients with the disorder. Data indicate that buspirone is more effective in reducing the cognitive symptoms of generalized anxiety disorder than in reducing the somatic symptoms.

Patients with *obsessive-compulsive disorder (Table 16.10), may have associated Tourette's disorder*. The characteristic symptoms of Tourette's disorder are motor and vocal tics that occur frequently and virtually every day. About 90 percent of Tourette's disorder patients have compulsive symptoms, and as many as two thirds meet the diagnostic criteria for obsessive-compulsive disorder.

16.42–16.46

16.42. **The answer is C** (*Synopsis VII*, pages 575–576).

16.43. **The answer is D** (*Synopsis VII*, page 576).

16.44. **The answer is A** (*Synopsis VII*, page 576).

16.45. **The answer is B** (*Synopsis VII*, page 576).

Table 16.8
Diagnostic Criteria for Specific Phobia

A. Marked and persistent fear that is excessive or unreasonable, cued by the presence or anticipation of a specific object or situation (e.g., flying, heights, animals, receiving an injection, seeing blood).

B. Exposure to the phobic stimulus almost invariably provokes an immediate anxiety response, which may take the form of a situationally bound or situationally predisposed panic attack. **Note:** In children, the anxiety may be expressed by crying, tantrums, freezing, or clinging.

C. The person recognizes that the fear is excessive or unreasonable. **Note:** In children, this feature may be absent.

D. The phobic situation(s) is avoided or else endured with intense anxiety or distress.

E. The avoidance, anxious anticipation, or distress in the feared situation(s) interferes significantly with the person's normal routine, occupational (or academic) functioning, or with social activities or relationships, or there is marked distress about having the phobia.

F. In individuals under age 18 years, the duration is at least 6 months.

G. The anxiety, panic attacks, or phobic avoidance associated with the specific object or situation are not better accounted for by another mental disorder, such as obsessive-compulsive disorder (e.g., fear of dirt in someone with an obsession about contamination), posttraumatic stress disorder (e.g., avoidance of stimuli associated with a severe stressor), separation anxiety disorder (e.g., avoidance of school), social phobia (e.g., avoidance of social situations because of fear of embarrassment), panic disorder with agoraphobia, or agoraphobia without history of panic disorder.

Specify type:
  Animal type
  Natural environment type (e.g., heights, storms, water)
  Blood-injection-injury type
  Situational type (e.g., planes, elevators, enclosed places)
  Other type (e.g., phobic avoidance of situations that may lead to choking, vomiting, or contracting an illness; in children, avoidance of loud sounds or costumed characters)

Table from DSM-IV, *Diagnostic and Statistical Manual of Mental Disorders,* ed 4. Copyright American Psychiatric Association, Washington, 1994. Used with permission.

16.46. **The answer is E** (*Synopsis VII*, pages 256–257 and 523).

Otto Rank traced the genesis of all anxiety back to the processes associated with the *trauma of birth*. *Harry Stack Sullivan* placed emphasis on the early relationship between the mother and the child and the importance of the *transmission of maternal anxiety* to the infant. *Melanie Klein* wrote that anxiety becomes fear of persecutory objects and later, through reintrojection of aggression in the form of internalized bad objects, the fear of outer and inner persecutors. Inner persecutors constitute the origin of *primitive superego anxiety*. *Walter Cannon* dem-

Table 16.9
Diagnostic Criteria for Social Phobia

A. A marked and persistent fear of one or more social or performance situations in which the person is exposed to unfamiliar people or to possible scrutiny by others. The individual fears that he or she will act in a way (or show anxiety symptoms) that will be humiliating or embarrassing. **Note:** In children, there must be evidence of the capacity for age-appropriate social relationships with familiar people and the anxiety must occur in peer settings, not just in interactions with adults.

B. Exposure to the feared social situation almost invariably provokes anxiety, which may take the form of a situationally bound or situationally predisposed panic attack. **Note:** In children, the anxiety may be expressed by crying, tantrums, freezing, or shrinking from social situations with unfamiliar people.

C. The person recognizes that the fear is excessive or unreasonable. **Note:** In children, this feature may be absent.

D. The feared social or performance situations are avoided or else are endured with intense anxiety or distress.

E. The avoidance, anxious anticipation, or distress in the feared social or performance situation(s) interferes significantly with the person's normal routine, occupational (academic) functioning, or social activities or relationships, or there is marked distress about having the phobia.

F. In individuals under age 18 years, the duration is at least 6 months.

G. The fear or avoidance is not due to the direct physiological effects of a substance (e.g., a drug of abuse, a medication) or a general medical condition and is not better accounted for by another mental disorder (e.g., panic disorder with or without agoraphobia, separation anxiety disorder, body dysmorphic disorder, a pervasive developmental disorder, or schizoid personality disorder).

H. If a general medical condition or another mental disorder is present, the fear in criterion A is unrelated to it, e.g., the fear is not of stuttering, trembling in Parkinson's disease, or exhibiting abnormal eating behavior in anorexia nervosa or bulimia nervosa.

Specify if:
Generalized: if the fears include most social situations (also consider the additional diagnosis of avoidant personality disorder)

Table from DSM-IV, *Diagnostic and Statistical Manual of Mental Disorders,* ed 4. Copyright American Psychiatric Association, Washington, 1994. Used with permission.

onstrated that cats exposed to barking dogs exhibited behavioral and physiological signs of fear associated with the *adrenal release of epinephrine*. The *James Lange* theory hypothesized that subjective *anxiety* is a *response to peripheral phenomena*.

Table 16.10
Diagnostic Criteria for Obsessive-Compulsive Disorder

A. Either obsessions or compulsions:

Obsessions as defined by (1), (2), (3), and (4):

(1) recurrent and persistent thoughts, impulses, or images that are experienced, at some time during the disturbance, as intrusive and inappropriate and that cause marked anxiety or distress

(2) the thoughts, impulses, or images are not simply excessive worries about real-life problems

(3) the person attempts to ignore or suppress such thoughts, impulses, or images, or to neutralize them with some other thought or action

(4) the person recognizes that the obsessional thoughts, impulses, or images are a product of his or her own mind (not imposed from without as in thought insertion)

Compulsions as defined by (1) and (2):

(1) repetitive behaviors (e.g., hand washing, ordering, checking) or mental acts (e.g., praying, counting, repeating words silently) that the person feels driven to perform in response to an obsession, or according to rules that must be applied rigidly

(2) the behaviors or mental acts are aimed at preventing or reducing distress or preventing some dreaded event or situation; however, these behaviors or mental acts either are not connected in a realistic way with what they are designed to neutralize or prevent or are clearly excessive

B. At some point during the course of the disorder, the person has recognized that the obsessions or compulsions are excessive or unreasonable. **Note:** This does not apply to children.

C. The obsessions or compulsions cause marked distress, are time consuming (take more than 1 hour a day), or significantly interfere with the person's normal routine, occupational (or academic) functioning, or usual social activities or relationships.

D. If another Axis I disorder is present, the content of the obsessions or compulsions is not restricted to it (e.g., preoccupation with food in the presence of an eating disorder; hair pulling in the presence of trichotillomania; concern with appearance in the presence of body dysmorphic disorder; preoccupation with drugs in the presence of a substance use disorder; preoccupation with having a serious illness in the presence of hypochondriasis; preoccupation with sexual urges or fantasies in the presence of a paraphilia; or guilty ruminations in the presence of major depressive disorder).

E. The disturbance is not due to the direct physiological effects of a substance (e.g., a drug of abuse, a medication) or a general medical condition.

Specify if:
With poor insight: if, for most of the time during the current episode, the person does not recognize that the obsessions and compulsions are excessive or unreasonable

Table from DSM-IV, *Diagnostic and Statistical Manual of Mental Disorders,* ed 4. Copyright American Psychiatric Association, Washington, 1994. Used with permission.

Somatoform Disorders

The somatoform disorders involve physical symptoms, preoccupations, or complaints for which no medical explanation can be found. The symptoms, preoccupations or complaints are severe enough to cause the patient significant distress or disability and are not the result of either malingering (conscious dissembling or lying about illness for overt secondary gain) or factitious disorders (feigning and creating of serious medical conditions for subtle, often unconscious motivations). To diagnose a somatoform disorder, the clinician must believe, on the basis of an in-depth medical evaluation, that the presenting symptoms are largely psychological in origin.

The specific somatoform disorders listed in the fourth edition of *Diagnostic and Statistical Manual of Mental Disorders* (DSM-IV) are somatization disorder, conversion disorder, hypochondriasis, body dysmorphic disorder, and pain disorder. The two residual diagnostic categories are undifferentiated somatoform disorder and somatoform disorder not otherwise specified (NOS).

One of the major problems in diagnosing many of the somatoform disorders is the difficulty in definitively ruling out a medical disorder. A thorough medical and neurological workup is essential before a clinician can feel relatively secure that no primary medical cause underlies the onset, the intensity, and the duration of the physical complaint. Many patients who ultimately receive a diagnosis of a somatoform disorder are initially seen and evaluated in the offices of nonpsychiatric physicians. A complicating and often confusing factor is the fact that often the patients do suffer from concomitant nonpsychiatric medical disorders that nonetheless do not account for the severity, the duration, or the presentation of the somatoform disorder. Those diagnosable medical conditions must be noted, evaluated, treated, and monitored.

The somatoform disorders share some characteristics, but they differ markedly in their presentations and epidemiological profiles. For example, somatization disorder is distinguished from other somatoform disorders by the multiplicity of complaints and the multiple organ systems affected, beginning before age 30. Conversion disorder is limited to neurological symptoms and may have its onset at any age.

Somatoform disorders appear to be most common among women, except that hypochondriasis appears to affect men and women equally. All the somatoform disorders are frequently associated with other mental disorders—in particular, anxiety disorders and depressive disorders but also personality disorders, substance-related disorders, and psychotic disorders. Some somatoform disorders are considered chronic (somatization disorder, body dysmorphic disorder, and pain disorder); others tend to run episodic courses (conversion disorder and hypochondriasis). In all the somatoform disorders, signs and symptoms are exacerbated by psychological stress.

Treatment of the somatoform disorders involves both psychological and biological strategies. Of paramount importance is diagnosing any other mental disorders that are present (for example, anxiety disorders, depressive disorders, psychotic disorders) and treating the underlying disorders first. Behavioral treatments, psychodynamic or insight-oriented treatments, and psychopharmacological treatments have all been useful in the management of somatoform disorders. Issues of secondary gain need to be evaluated and gently addressed. The signs and the symptoms of all somatoform disorders hold powerful, usually unconscious symbolic meanings for the patients afflicted with the disorders. A psychodynamic understanding of the possible meanings of the illness to the patient can help the physician care for the patient. Pharmacotherapy is generally most effective when the patient has an underlying drug-responsive condition. Tricyclic and tetracyclic drugs, monoamine oxidase inhibitors, serotonin-specific reuptake inhibitors, and dopamine receptor antagonists (antipsychotics) have all been used with varying success in somatoform disorders, and the student needs to be familiar with the medications that have proved to be most effective with specific disorders.

Students should study Chapter 17 in *Kaplan and Sadock's Synopsis VII* and the following questions and answers.

HELPFUL HINTS

The student should be able to define the somatoform disorder terms listed below.

somatization disorder	astasia-abasia	undoing
Briquet's syndrome	primary gain and secondary gain	generalized anxiety disorder
somatosensory input	*la belle indifférence*	body dysmorphic disorder
antisocial personality disorder	identification	dysmorphophobia
conversion disorder	amobarbital (Amytal) interview	symbolization and projection
instinctual impulse	pain disorder	anorexia nervosa
depression	endorphins	pimozide (Orap)
stocking-and-glove anesthesia	major depressive disorder	undifferentiated somatoform
hemianesthesia	antidepressants	disorder
conversion blindness	biofeedback	somatoform disorder NOS
pseudocyesis	hypochondriasis	secondary symptoms

QUESTIONS

DIRECTIONS: Each of the questions or incomplete statements below is followed by five suggested responses or completions. Select the *one* that is *best* in each case.

17.1. A 29-year-old mother of two children requested medical clearance for impending surgery for cysts in her breasts. She described the cysts as rapidly enlarging and unbearably painful. While drawing attention to her breasts, she said: "They're so large and so tender to the touch. And I just can't have relations. Forget that."

She also had disabling back pain that spread up and down her spine and made her legs give out on her suddenly, causing her to fall. When discussing that symptom, she winced visibly and said: "Oh, there it goes; my back keeps clicking. The pain is so severe it affects me with my kids. Pain like that will make anyone into a beast." (She had previously been suspected of child abuse.) She also complained of dyspnea and a dry cough that prevented her walking uphill.

Her medical history began at menarche with dysmenorrhea and menorrhagia. At 18 she had exploratory surgery for a possible ovarian cyst and later underwent another operation for suspected abdominal adhesions. She also had a history of recurrent urinary tract symptoms, although no organisms were ever clearly documented, and she had normal findings after a workup for "an enlarged thyroid." At various times she had received the diagnoses of spastic colon, migraine, and endometriosis.

Two marriages, both to alcoholic and abusive men who refused to pay child support, had ended in divorce. She had lost several clerical jobs because of excessive absences. During the periods when she felt worst, she spent most of the day at home in a bathrobe while her relatives cared for her children. She had a history of opiate dependence and claimed that she began using analgesics for her back pain and then, "I overdid it."

The physical examination at the time of her medical visit revealed inconsistencies in the breast tissue but no frank masses, and the mammography findings were normal.

The patient is probably suffering from
A. hypochondriasis
B. conversion disorder
C. pain disorder
D. somatization disorder
E. body dysmorphic disorder

17.2. A 38-year-old married woman had complained of nervousness since childhood. She also said she was sickly since her youth, with a succession of physical problems doctors often indicated were caused by her nerves or depression. She, however, believed that she had a physical problem that had not yet been discovered by the doctors. Besides nervousness, she had chest pain and had been told by a variety of medical consultants that she had a nervous heart. She also consulted doctors for abdominal pain and had been told she had a spastic colon. She had seen chiropractors and osteopaths for backaches, for pains in her extremities, and for anesthesia of her fingertips. Three months previously, she was vomiting and had chest pain and abdominal pain, and she was admitted to a hospital for a hysterectomy. Since the hysterectomy, she had had repeated anxiety attacks, fainting spells that she claimed were associated with unconsciousness that lasted more than 30 minutes, vomiting, food intolerance, weakness, and fatigue. She had been hospitalized several times for medical workups for vomiting, colitis, vomiting of blood, and chest pain. She had had a surgical procedure for an abscess of the throat. She said she felt depressed, but thought that it was all because her "hormones were not straightened out." She was still looking for a medical explanation for her physical and psychological problems.
The most likely diagnosis is
A. somatization disorder
B. conversion disorder
C. hypochondriasis
D. dysthymic disorder
E. none of the above

17.3. The treatment of hypochondriasis is characterized by
A. patients who are resistant to psychotherapy
B. patients who respond better to group psychotherapy than to individual therapy
C. frequent physical examinations
D. treatment of any underlying psychiatric disorder
E. all the above

17.4. Which of the following statements about conversion disorder is most accurate?
A. The inability to speak is intentionally produced in a conversion disorder
B. Conversion disorder is most common among patients in a high socioeconomic group
C. Psychoanalytic theory holds that the major defense mechanism in conversion disorder is suppression
D. Mutism is one of the most common symptoms of conversion disorder
E. *La belle indifférence* is a necessary component in making the diagnosis of conversion disorder

17.5. Characteristic behavioral features in patients with conversion disorder include
A. somatic compliance
B. *la belle indifférence*
C. autonomic dysfunction
D. sexual disturbances
E. all the above

17.6. The most accurate statement regarding hypochondriasis is
A. patients with hypochondriasis usually believe that they have multiple diseases
B. hypochondriasis may be the result of an unconscious desire to assume the sick role
C. the patient's belief that a particular disease is present can be of a delusional intensity
D. more men than women are affected by hypochondriasis
E. the incidence of hypochondriasis is affected by educational level and marital status

17.7. Characteristic signs of conversion disorder include
A. stocking-and-glove anesthesia
B. hemianesthesia of the body beginning precisely at the midline
C. astasia-abasia
D. normal reflexes
E. all the above

17.8. A third-year medical student returned to the student health services for the third time with a complaint of ulcerative colitis. After a thorough medical workup, he was told that no organic disease was present. Despite that reassurance, the student continued to test his stool for blood and continued to believe that his doctors had missed the correct diagnosis. The student is exhibiting
A. depersonalization
B. phobia
C. conversion disorder
D. bulimia nervosa
E. hypochondriasis

17.9. In body dysmorphic disorder
A. plastic surgery is usually beneficial
B. a comorbid diagnosis is unusual
C. anorexia nervosa may also be diagnosed
D. 50 percent of patients may attempt suicide
E. serotonin-specific drugs are effective in reducing the symptoms

17.10. A patient with somatization disorder
A. presents the initial physical complaints after age 30
B. has had physical symptoms for three months
C. has complained of pain, gastrointestinal, sexual, and pseudoneurological symptoms, which are not explained by a known medical condition
D. usually experiences minimal impairment in social or occupational functioning
E. may have a false belief of being pregnant and objective signs of pregnancy, such as decreased menstrual flow or amenorrhea

17.11. All the following are classified as somatoform disorders *except*
A. conversion disorder
B. hypochondriasis
C. somatization disorder
D. Munchausen syndrome
E. body dysmorphic disorder

17.12. Medical disorders to be considered in a differential diagnosis of somatization disorder include
A. multiple sclerosis
B. systemic lupus erythematosus
C. acute intermittent porphyria
D. hyperparathyroidism
E. all the above

17.13. Hypochondriasis enables patients to provide themselves with
A. denial of the pain of low self-esteem
B. gratification of their dependence needs
C. protection from their sense of guilt
D. various secondary gains
E. all the above

DIRECTIONS: The questions below consist of lettered headings followed by a list of numbered words or phrases. For each numbered word or phrase, select the *one* lettered heading that is most closely associated with it. Each heading may be used once, more than once, or not at all.

Questions 17.14–17.17
A. Conversion disorder
B. Pain disorder
C. Somatization disorder

17.14. *La belle indifférence*

17.15. Alexithymia

17.16. Briquet's syndrome

17.17. Astasia-abasia

DIRECTIONS: Each set of lettered headings below is followed by a list of numbered phrases. For each numbered phrase, select

A. if the item is associated with *A only*
B. if the item is associated with *B only*
C. if the item is associated with *both A and B*
D. if the item is associated with *neither A nor B*

Questions 17.18–17.22
A. Somatization disorder
B. Pain disorder
C. Both
D. Neither

17.18. Affects women more than men

17.19. Most often begins during a person's teens

17.20. Antidepressants are effective

17.21. Serotonin may be involved in the pathophysiology of the disorder

17.22. Anorexia nervosa is a commonly associated disturbance

Questions 17.23–17.26
A. Autonomic arousal disorder
B. Neurasthenia
C. Both
D. Neither

17.23. The symptom pattern seen in undifferentiated somatoform disorder

17.24. Complaints involving the cardiovascular, respiratory or gastrointestinal system

17.25. Complaints of mental and physical fatigue

17.26. Symptoms caused by a tic bite

Questions 17.27–17.32
A. Hypochondriasis
B. Somatization disorder
C. Both
D. Neither

17.27. Is found approximately equally in men and women

17.28. Peak incidence during the 40s or 50s

17.29. Likely to have a hysterical cognitive and interpersonal style

17.30. Includes disease conviction or disease fear

17.31. Associated with anhedonia

17.32. Hallucinations may be present

ANSWERS

Somatoform Disorders

17.1. The answer is D (*Synopsis VII*, pages 624–626).

The patient is probably suffering from *somatization disorder*, since she fits the diagnostic criteria listed in Table 17.1. The patient complained of at least four pain symptoms (breast pain, back pain, urinary, and migraine), two gastrointestinal symptoms (spastic colon and adhesions), one sexual symptom ("can't have relations"), and one pseudoneurological symptom (falling)—none of which is completely explained by physical or laboratory examinations. In addition, her symptoms had their onset before age 30.

Hypochondriasis is characterized by the false belief that one has a specific disease; in contrast, somatization disorder is characterized by concern with many symptoms. The symptoms of *conversion disorder* are limited to one or two neurological symptoms, rather than the wide-ranging symptoms of somatization disorder. *Pain disorder* is limited to one or two complaints of pain symptoms.

Body dysmorphic disorder is not distinguished by any type of symptoms. Instead, body dysmorphic disorder entails the preoccupation with an imagined defect in appearance. No such preoccupation was found in the patient described.

17.2. The answer is A (*Synopsis VII*, pages 617–621).

Nearly all the physical symptoms that the patient described were apparently without an organic basis. That suggested a somatoform disorder, and the large number of symptoms involving multiple organ systems suggested *somatization disorder*. She had symptoms relating to the gastrointestinal, cardiovascular, pulmonary, neurological, and gynecological systems, which meet the criteria for that diagnosis. *Conversion disorder* was ruled out because the patient's symptoms were not limited to the sensorimotor areas alone; they covered a far broader range. *Hypochondriasis* is distinguished from somatization disorder in that it includes the fear of disease and bodily preoccupation. In *dysthymic disorder*, patients show cognitive (slow thinking), behavioral (early morning awakening, lethargy), and mood (depression or suicidal ideation) symptoms.

17.3. The answer is E (all) (*Synopsis VII*, pages 625–626).

In the treatment of hypochondriasis, most *patients are resistant to psychotherapy*. Some hypochon-

Table 17.1
Diagnostic Criteria for Somatization Disorder

A. A history of many physical complaints beginning before age 30 years that occur over a period of several years and result in treatment being sought or significant impairment in social, occupational, or other important areas of functioning.

B. Each of the following criteria must have been met, with individual symptoms occurring at any time during the course of the disturbance:

   (1) *four pain symptoms:* a history of pain related to at least four different sites or functions (e.g., head, abdomen, back, joints, extremities, chest, rectum, during menstruation, during sexual intercourse, or during urination)

   (2) *two gastrointestinal symptoms:* a history of at least two gastrointestinal symptoms other than pain (e.g., nausea, bloating, vomiting other than during pregnancy, diarrhea, or intolerance of several different foods)

   (3) *one sexual symptom:* a history of at least one sexual or reproductive symptom other than pain (e.g., sexual indifference, erectile or ejaculatory dysfunction, irregular menses, excessive menstrual bleeding, vomiting throughout pregnancy)

   (4) *one pseudoneurologic symptom:* a history of at least one symptom or deficit suggesting a neurological condition not limited to pain (conversion symptoms such as impaired coordination or balance, paralysis or localized weakness, difficulty swallowing or lump in throat, aphonia, urinary retention, hallucinations, loss of touch or pain sensation, double vision, blindness, deafness, seizures; dissociative symptoms such as amnesia; or loss of consciousness other than fainting)

C. Either (1) or (2):

   (1) after appropriate investigation, each of the symptoms in criterion B cannot be fully explained by a known general medical condition or the direct effects of a substance (e.g., the effects of injury, medication, drugs, or alcohol)

   (2) when there is a related general medical condition, the physical complaints or resulting social or occupational impairment are in excess of what would be expected from the history, physical examination, or laboratory findings.

D. The symptoms are not intentionally feigned or produced (as in factitious disorder or malingering).

Table from DSM-IV, *Diagnostic and Statistical Manual of Mental Disorders,* ed 4. Copyright American Psychiatric Association, Washington, 1994. Used with permission.

driac patients accept psychiatric treatment if it takes place in a medical setting and focuses on stress reduction and education in coping with chronic illness. Such *patients respond better to group psychotherapy than to individual therapy*, perhaps because the group provides the social support and the social interaction that the patients need. Individual insight-oriented traditional psychotherapy for primary hypochondriasis is generally not successful. *Frequent physical examinations* should be performed; they reassure patients that they are not being abandoned by their physicians and that their complaints are being taken seriously. Invasive diagnostic and therapeutic procedures, however, should be undertaken only on the basis of objective evidence. When possible, the clinician should refrain from treating equivocal or incidental findings. Pharmacotherapy alleviates hypochondriacal symptoms only when the patient has an underlying drug-sensitive condition, such as an anxiety disorder or a major depressive disorder. When hypochondriasis is secondary to some other primary mental disorder, the *underlying psychiatric disorder* should be treated in its own right. When hypochondriasis is a transient situational reaction, patients must be helped to cope with the stress without reinforcing their illness behavior and their use of the sick role as solutions to their problems.

17.4. The answer is D (*Synopsis VII*, pages 621–624).

Mutism is one of the most common symptoms of conversion disorder. Other common symptoms are paralysis and blindness. Conversion disorder may be most commonly associated with passive-aggressive, dependent, antisocial, and histrionic personality disorders. Symptoms of depressive disorders and anxiety disorders often accompany the symptoms of conversion disorder, and affected patients are at risk for suicide.

The inability to speak is not intentionally produced in a conversion disorder. If the symptoms are under conscious voluntary control, malingering and factitious disorders must be considered. A factitious disorder is produced or feigned for the sole purpose of assuming the patient role. Malingering is motivated by some secondary gain (for example, money or shelter). In both of those disorders, the patient's history is usually more inconsistent and contradictory than is the conversion disorder patient's history.

Conversion disorder is most common among patients in a low socioeconomic group, rural populations, little-educated persons, those with low intelligence quotients (I.Q.s), and military personnel who have been exposed to combat situations.

Psychoanalytic theory holds that the major defense mechanism in conversion disorder is repression, not suppression. Suppression is the conscious or semiconscious act of inhibiting an impulse or idea. Repression is the active process of keeping out of consciousness those ideas and impulses that are

unacceptable to the patient. The conflict is between an instinctual impulse (for example, aggressive or sexual) and the prohibitions against its expression. The symptoms allow the partial expression of the forbidden wish or urge but disguise it, so that the patients need not consciously confront their unacceptable impulses. The conversion disorder symptoms also enable the patients to communicate that they need special consideration and special treatment. Such symptoms may function as a nonverbal means of controlling or manipulating others.

La belle indifférence, the patient's inappropriately cavalier attitude toward a serious symptom, is not always an accurate measure of whether a patient has conversion disorder, and so *la belle indifférence is not a necessary component in making the diagnosis of conversion disorder.*

Table 17.2 lists the diagnostic criteria for conversion disorder.

17.5. The answer is E (all) (*Synopsis VII*, pages 621–624).

A characteristic behavioral feature in patients with conversion disorder is what the French authors of the 19th century called *la belle indifférence*. Despite what appear to be the most extensive and crippling disturbances in function, the patient may be completely unconcerned and may not spontaneously

Table 17.2
Diagnostic Criteria for Conversion Disorder

A. One or more symptoms or deficits affecting voluntary motor or sensory function that suggest a neurological or other general medical condition.

B. Psychological factors are judged to be associated with the symptom or deficit because the initiation or exacerbation of the symptom or deficit is preceded by conflicts or other stressors.

C. The symptom or deficit is not intentionally produced or feigned (as in factitious disorder or malingering).

D. The symptom or deficit cannot, after appropriate investigation, be fully explained by a general medical condition, or by the direct effects of a substance, or as a culturally sanctioned behavior or experience.

E. The symptom or deficit causes clinically significant distress or impairment in social, occupational, or other important areas of functioning or warrants medical evaluation.

F. The symptom or deficit is not limited to pain or sexual dysfunction, does not occur exclusively during the course of somatization disorder, and is not better accounted for by another mental disorder.

Specify type of symptom or deficit:
With motor symptom or deficit
With sensory symptom or deficit
With seizures or convulsions
With mixed presentation

Table from DSM-IV, *Diagnostic and Statistical Manual of Mental Disorders*, ed 4. Copyright American Psychiatric Association, Washington, 1994. Used with permission.

mention such disturbances, which often results in their being overlooked. Unless specifically searched for, *la belle indifférence* is a calm mental attitude of acquiescence and complacency directed specifically at the physical symptom.

Somatic compliance is the degree to which a person's organic structures coincide with the psychological mechanisms in the symptomatic expression of the pathological defenses. In conversion symptoms, for instance, the entire cathexis of the objectionable impulses is condensed onto a definite physical function. The ability of the affected function to absorb the cathexis is its somatic compliance.

Autonomic dysfunctions may be reflected in various visceral symptoms, such as anorexia, vomiting, hiccoughs, and other abdominal complaints, which are considered a part of the classical syndrome of conversion disorders. Sensory disturbances—anesthesias, in particular—are also typical of the physical symptoms of hysterical neurosis.

A history of *sexual disturbances*—especially impotence, anorgasmia, and a lack of desire—is frequently seen along with conversion symptoms. According to psychoanalytic theory, conversion disorder has been linked to a psychosexual conflict arising from the failure to relinquish oedipal ties and to rid the normal adult libido of its incestuous ties.

17.6.   The answer is B (*Synopsis VII*, pages 624–626).

A number of theories attempt to explain the cause of hypochondriasis. One theory is that *hypochondriasis may be the result of an unconscious desire to assume the sick role* by a person facing seemingly insurmountable and insolvable problems. The sick role offers a way out, because the sick patient is allowed to avoid noxious obligations and to postpone unwelcome challenges and is excused from usually expected duties. The diagnostic criteria for hypochondriasis (Table 17.3) require that patients be preoccupied with the false belief that they have a serious disease and that the false belief be based on a misinterpretation of physical signs or sensations. *Patients with hypochondriasis usually believe that they have a specific disease, not multiple diseases. The patient's belief that a particular disease is present is not of delusional intensity.* If it were of such intensity, a delusional disorder, somatic type, would be diagnosed, since delusion is a fixed false idea. *Men are not affected by hypochondriasis more than women*; in fact, men and women are equally affected. *The incidence of hypochondriasis is not affected by educational level and marital status.*

17.7.   The answer is E (all) (*Synopsis VII*, pages 621–624).

In conversion disorder, anesthesia and paresthesia are common, especially of the extremities. All sensory modalities are involved, and the distribution of the disturbance is inconsistent with that of either central or peripheral neurological disease. Thus, one

Table 17.3
Diagnostic Criteria for Hypochondriasis

A. Preoccupation with fears of having, or the idea that one has, a serious disease based on the person's misinterpretation of bodily symptoms.

B. The preoccupation persists despite appropriate medical evaluation and reassurance.

C. The belief in criterion A is not of delusional intensity (as in delusional disorder, somatic type) and is not restricted to a circumscribed concern about appearance (as in body dysmorphic disorder).

D. The preoccupation causes clinically significant distress or impairment in social, occupational, or other important areas of functioning.

E. The duration of the disturbance is at least 6 months.

F. The preoccupation is not better accounted for by generalized anxiety disorder, obsessive-compulsive disorder, panic disorder, a major depressive episode, separation anxiety, or another somatoform disorder.

Specify if:
   With poor insight: if, for most of the time during the current episode, the person does not recognize that the concern about having a serious illness is excessive or unreasonable

Table from DSM-IV, *Diagnostic and Statistical Manual of Mental Disorders*, ed 4. Copyright American Psychiatric Association, Washington, 1994. Used with permission.

sees the characteristic *stocking-and-glove anesthesia* of the hands or feet or *hemianesthesia of the body beginning precisely at the midline*. Motor symptoms include abnormal movements and gait disturbance, which is often a wildly ataxic, staggering gait accompanied by gross, irregular, jerky truncal movements and thrashing and waving arms (also known as *astasia-abasia*). *Normal reflexes* are seen. The patient shows no fasciculations or muscle atrophy, and electromyography results are normal.

17.8.   The answer is E (*Synopsis VII*, pages 624–625).

In *hypochondriasis*, patients have an unrealistic interpretation of physical signs or sensations as abnormal, leading to a preoccupation with the fear or belief of having a disease.

Depersonalization is a nonspecific syndrome in which patients feel that they have lost their personal identity. As a result, they experience themselves as strange or unreal. It can be seen in schizophrenia, depersonalization disorder, and schizotypal personality disorder. A *phobia* is a persistent, pathological, unrealistic, intense fear of an object or situation. The phobic person may realize that the fear is irrational but is, nonetheless, unable to dispel it. In *conversion disorder* the anxiety that stems from an intrapsychic conflict is converted and expressed in a symbolic somatic symptom. In *bulimia nervosa* a large amount of food is ingested in a short period of time, usually less than two hours, and the patient then compensates by such maneuvers as self-induced vomiting.

17.9. The answer is E (*Synopsis VII*, pages 626–628).

Serotonin-specific drugs like clomipramine (Anafranil) and fluoxetine (Prozac) *are effective in reducing the symptoms* in at least 50 percent of patients with body dysmorphic disorder. In any patient with a coexisting mental disorder or an anxiety disorder, the coexisting disorder should be treated with the appropriate pharmacotherapy and psychotherapy. How long treatment should be continued when the symptoms of body dysmorphic disorder have remitted is unknown. *Plastic surgery is not usually beneficial* in the treatment of patients with body dysmorphic disorder. In fact, surgical, dermatological, dental, and other medical procedures to address the alleged defects rarely satisfy the patient.

A comorbid diagnosis is not unusual. Body dysmorphic disorder commonly coexists with other mental disorders. One study found that more than 90 percent of the body dysmorphic disorder patients had experienced a major depressive episode in their lifetimes, about 70 percent had had an anxiety disorder, and about 30 percent had a psychotic disorder. However, *anorexia nervosa should not be diagnosed* along with body dysmorphic disorder, since distortions of body image occur in anorexia nervosa, gender identity disorders, and some specific types of brain damage (for example, neglect syndromes).

The effects of body dysmorphic disorder on a person's life can be significant. Almost all affected patients avoid social and occupational exposure. As many as a third of the patients may be housebound by their concern about being ridiculed for their alleged deformities, and as many as *20 percent, not 50 percent, of patients attempt suicide.*

The diagnostic criteria for body dysmorphic disorder are listed in Table 17.4.

17.10. The answer is C (*Synopsis VII*, pages 617–621).

During the course of somatization disorder, the patient *has complained of pain, gastrointestinal, sex-*

ual, and pseudoneurological symptoms, which are not explained by a known medical condition. In addition, the patient *presents the initial physical complaints before, not after, age 30.* The patient *has had physical symptoms for years, not just three months.* The patient has had interpersonal problems and tremendous psychological distress and *usually experiences significant, not minimal, impairment in social or occupational functioning.* A patient who has *a false belief of being pregnant and objective signs of pregnancy, such as decreased menstrual flow or amenorrhea does not have somatization disorder.* Instead, the patient has pseudocyesis, a somatoform disorder not otherwise specified (Table 17.5).

17.11. The answer is D (*Synopsis VII*, page 634).

Munchausen syndrome is categorized as a factitious disorder with predominantly physical signs and symptoms; the essential feature is the ability of patients to present physical symptoms so well that they are able to gain admission to and stay in hospitals. The symptom production in somatoform disorders is not intentional. *Conversion disorder* is a condition in which psychological factors are judged to be causatively related to a loss or an alteration of physical functioning. *Hypochondriasis* involves preoccupation with the fear of having a serious disease. *Somatization disorder* is a chronic, polysymptomatic disorder that begins early in life. *Body dysmorphic disorder* is characterized by preoccupation with some imagined defect in one's appearance.

17.12. The answer is E (all) (*Synopsis VII*, page 620).

The clinician must always rule out organic causes for the patient's symptoms. Medical disorders that

Table 17.4
Diagnostic Criteria for Body Dysmorphic Disorder

A. Preoccupation with an imagined defect in appearance. If a slight physical anomaly is present, the person's concern is markedly excessive.

B. The preoccupation causes clinically significant distress or impairment in social, occupational, or other important areas of functioning.

C. The preoccupation is not better accounted for by another mental disorder (e.g., dissatisfaction with body shape and size in anorexia nervosa).

Table from DSM-IV, *Diagnostic and Statistical Manual of Mental Disorders,* ed 4. Copyright American Psychiatric Association, Washington, 1994. Used with permission.

Table 17.5
Diagnostic Criteria for Somatoform Disorder Not Otherwise Specified

---

This category includes disorders with somatoform symptoms that do not meet the criteria for any specific somatoform disorder. Examples include

1. Pseudocyesis: a false belief of being pregnant that is associated with objective signs of pregnancy, which may include abdominal enlargement (although the umbilicus does not become everted), reduced menstrual flow, amenorrhea, subjective sensation of fetal movement, nausea, breast engorgement and secretions, and labor pains at the expected date of delivery. Endocrine changes may be present, but the syndrome cannot be explained by a general medical condition that causes endocrine changes (e.g., a hormone-secreting tumor).
2. A disorder involving nonpsychotic hypochondriacal symptoms of less than 6 months' duration.
3. A disorder involving unexplained physical complaints (e.g., fatigue or body weakness) of less than 6 months' duration that are not due to another mental disorder.

Table from DSM-IV, *Diagnostic and Statistical Manual of Mental Disorders,* ed 4. Copyright American Psychiatric Association, Washington, 1994. Used with permission.

present with nonspecific, transient abnormalities pose the greatest diagnostic difficulty in the differential diagnosis of somatization disorder. The disorders to be considered include *multiple sclerosis, systemic lupus erythematosus, acute intermittent porphyria,* and *hyperparathyroidism*. In addition, the onset of many somatic symptoms late in life must be presumed to be caused by a medical illness until testing rules it out.

17.13. The answer is E (all) (*Synopsis VII*, pages 624–626).

Investigators see hypochondriacal symptoms as playing a primarily defensive role in the psychic economy. For Harry Stack Sullivan they represented a protective activity that enabled the patient to *deny the pain of low self-esteem*. In other words, persons can substitute an image of themselves as physically ill or deficient for the far more devastating view of themselves as worthless human beings. Hypochondriasis also enables patients to *gratify their dependence needs, protect themselves from their sense of guilt,* and provide themselves with *various secondary gains*. The obvious advantage that persons gain from their illness is secondary gain, such as gifts, attention, and release from responsibility.

17.14–17.17

17.14. The answer is A (*Synopsis VII*, page 622).

17.15. The answer is B (*Synopsis VII*, pages 628–630).

17.16. The answer is C (*Synopsis VII*, page 617).

17.17. The answer is A (*Synopsis VII*, page 622).

La belle indifférence is a psychological symptom often associated with *conversion disorder. La belle indifférence* is the patient's inappropriately cavalier attitude toward a serious symptom. The bland indifference may be lacking in some conversion disorder patients.

Alexithymia is the inability to articulate internal feelings that is often associated with *pain disorder*. Some patients who are unable to articulate their internal feelings do so by the body's expressing them in the form of a pain disorder. Patients who experience aches and pains in their bodies without identifiable physical causes may be symbolically expressing an intrapsychic conflict through the body. Table 17.6 lists the diagnostic criteria for pain disorder.

Briquet's syndrome is a synonym for *somatization disorder*. In 1859 Paul Briquet, a French physician, observed the multiplicity of the symptoms and affected organ symptoms and commented on the usually chronic course of the disorder. Somatization disorder became the standard name in 1980.

Astasia-abasia is gait disturbance seen in *conversion disorder*. A wildly ataxic, staggering gait is accompanied by gross, irregular, jerky truncal movements and thrashing and waving arm movements.

Table 17.6
Diagnostic Criteria for Pain Disorder

A. Pain in one or more anatomical sites is the predominant focus of the clinical presentation and is of sufficient severity to warrant clinical attention.

B. The pain causes clinically significant distress or impairment in social, occupational, or other important areas of functioning.

C. Psychological factors are judged to have an important role in the onset, severity, exacerbation, or maintenance of the pain.

D. The symptom or deficit is not intentionally produced or feigned (as in factitious disorder or malingering).

E. The pain is not better accounted for by a mood, anxiety, or psychotic disorder and does not meet criteria for dyspareunia.

Code as follows:
Pain disorder associated with psychological factors: psychological factors are judged to have a major role in the onset, severity, exacerbation, or maintenance of the pain. (If a general medical condition is present, it does not have a major role in the onset, severity, exacerbation, or maintenance of the pain.) This type of pain disorder is not diagnosed if criteria are also met for somatization disorder.

Specify if:
Acute duration of less than 6 months
Chronic duration of 6 months or longer

Pain disorder associated with both psychological factors and a general medical condition: both psychological factors and a general medical condition are judged to have important roles in the onset, severity, exacerbation, or maintenance of the pain. The associated general medical condition or anatomical site of the pain (see below) is coded on Axis III.

Specify if:
Acute duration of less than 6 months
Chronic duration of 6 months or longer

Note: The following is not considered to be a mental disorder and is included here to facilitate differential diagnosis.

Pain disorder associated with a general medical condition: a general medical condition has a major role in the onset, severity, exacerbation, or maintenance of the pain. (If psychological factors are present, they are not judged to have a major role in the onset, severity, exacerbation, or maintenance of the pain.) The diagnostic code for the pain is selected based on the associated general medical condition is one has been established or on the anatomical location of the pain if the underlying general medical condition is not yet clearly established—for example, low back, sciatic, pelvic, headache, facial, chest, joint, bone, abdominal, breast, renal, ear, eye, throat, tooth, and urinary.

Table from DSM-IV, *Diagnostic and Statistical Manual of Mental Disorders*, ed 4. Copyright American Psychiatric Association, Washington, 1994. Used with permission.

Patients with the symptoms rarely fall or if they do, are generally not injured.

17.18–17.22

17.18. **The answer is C** (*Synopsis VII*, pages 617 and 628).

17.19. **The answer is A** (*Synopsis VII*, pages 617–620).

17.20. **The answer is C** (*Synopsis VII*, pages 620–621 and 630).

17.21. **The answer is B** (*Synopsis VII*, page 628).

17.22. **The answer is D** (*Synopsis VII*, pages 617–621 and 628–630).

Both somatization disorder and pain disorder affect *women more than men*. Somatization disorder has a 5 to 1 female-to-male ratio. The lifetime prevalence of somatization disorder among women in the general population may be 1 to 2 percent. Pain disorder is diagnosed twice as frequently in women as in men.

Somatization disorder is defined as beginning before age 30, and it *most often begins during a person's teens*. As for pain disorder, the peak of onset is in the fourth and fifth decades, perhaps because the tolerance for pain decreases with age.

Antidepressants—such as amitriptyline (Elavil), imipramine (Tofranil), and doxepin (Sinequan)—*are effective* in the treatment of pain disorder and somatization disorder.

Serotonin may be involved in the pathophysiology of pain disorder. It is probably the main neurotransmitter in the descending inhibitory pathways. Endorphins also play a role in the central nervous system modulation of pain.

Anorexia nervosa is not commonly associated with either pain disorder or somatization disorder. Anorexia nervosa is an eating disorder that presents a dramatic picture of self-starvation, peculiar attitudes toward food, weight loss (leading to the maintenance of the patients's body weight at least 15 percent below that expected), and an intense fear of weight gain.

17.23–17.26

17.23. **The answer is C** (*Synopsis VII*, pages 630–631).

17.24. **The answer is A** (*Synopsis VII*, pages 91, 576, and 630–631).

17.25. **The answer is B** (*Synopsis VII*, pages 630–631

17.26. **The answer is D** (*Synopsis VII*, pages 630–631).

Both *autonomic arousal disorder and neurasthenia* are *symptom patterns seen in patients with un-*

Table 17.7
Diagnostic Criteria for Undifferentiated Somatoform Disorder

A. One or more physical complaints (e.g., fatigue, loss of appetite, gastrointestinal or urinary complaints)

B. Either (1) or (2):

  (1) after appropriate investigation, the symptoms cannot be fully explained by a known general medical condition or the direct effects of a substance (e.g., the effects of injury, medication, drugs, or alcohol)

  (2) when there is a related general medical condition, the physical complaints or resulting social or occupational impairment is in excess of what would be expected from the history, physical examination, or laboratory findings

C. The symptoms cause clinically significant distress or impairment in social, occupational, or other important areas of functioning.

D. The duration of the disturbance is at least 6 months.

E. The disturbance is not better accounted for by another mental disorder (e.g., another somatoform disorder, sexual dysfunction, mood disorder, anxiety disorder, sleep disorder, or psychotic disorder).

F. The symptom is not intentionally produced or feigned (as in factitious disorder or malingering).

Table from DSM-IV, *Diagnostic and Statistical Manual of Mental Disorders,* ed 4. Copyright American Psychiatric Association, Washington, 1994. Used with permission.

differentiated somatoform disorder (Table 17.7). In *autonomic arousal disorder*, patients are affected with somatoform disorder symptoms that are limited to bodily functions innervated by the autonomic nervous system. Such patients have *complaints involving the cardiovascular, respiratory, gastrointestinal*, urogenital, and dermatological *systems*. Other patients have *complaints of mental and physical fatigue*, physical weakness and exhaustion, and the inability to perform many everyday activities because of their symptoms. That syndrome is often referred to as *neurasthenia. Neither autonomic arousal disorder nor neurasthenia has symptoms caused by a tic bite.*

17.27–17.32

17.27. **The answer is A** (*Synopsis VII*, page 624).

17.28. **The answer is A** (*Synopsis VII*, pages 624–625).

17.29. **The answer is B** (*Synopsis VII*, pages 617–621).

17.30. **The answer is A** (*Synopsis VII*, pages 624–625).

17.31. **The answer is C** (*Synopsis VII*, pages 617–620 and 624–625).

17.32. **The answer is D** (*Synopsis VII*, pages 624–625).

Hypochondriasis, which is an excessive concern about disease and a preoccupation with one's health, *is found approximately equally in men and women*. Somatization disorder, which is a chronic syndrome of multiple somatic symptoms that cannot be explained medically, is much more common in women than in men. The *peak incidence* of hypochondriasis is thought to occur *during the 40s or 50s*, whereas somatization disorder begins before age 30.

Somatization disorder patients are *likely to have a hysterical cognitive and interpersonal style*, as opposed to obsessional hypochondriac patients. Somatization disorder does not *include disease conviction or disease fear*, as does hypochondriasis. *Anhedonia* (the inability to experience pleasure) is a sign of depression but may be present in both hypochondriasis and somatization disorders. *Hallucinations are not present* in either disorder.

18 ||||

Factitious Disorders

Factitious disorders occur in persons for whom being a patient and being hospitalized are the primary motivating factors. The disorders involve the compulsive, voluntary, and deliberate feigning of illness solely for the reason of becoming a patient. Obvious secondary gain—such as financial compensation, escape from legal authorities, avoidance of work, or getting a bed for the night—is not a feature of factitious disorders. The lack of obvious secondary gain is one of the major features distinguishing factitious disorders from malingering. Factitious disorders appear to occur most frequently among people who are health care workers and who have had extensive previous experience with illness, injury, or hospitalization during their early development. Theorists have speculated that some of those people may unconsciously be attempting to master the past trauma of early serious medical illness or hospitalization by reliving the painful and frightening experience over and over again. Many patients with factitious disorders fulfill the diagnostic criteria for borderline personality disorder, especially in terms of their rigid defensive structure and vulnerable identity formation. Other features associated with those patients include normal to above-average intelligence quotients (I.Q.s), absence of a formal thought disorder, confusion over sexual identity, and strong dependence needs.

In the fourth edition of *Diagnostic and Statistical Manual of Mental Disorders* (DSM-IV), factitious disorders are classified by type: with predominantly psychological signs and symptoms, with predominantly physical signs and symptoms, and with combined psychological and physical signs and symptoms. DSM-IV also includes the category of factitious disorder not otherwise specified (NOS); the most notable example, factitious disorder by proxy, is included in an appendix.

Factitious disorder with predominantly physical signs and symptoms is also known as Munchausen syndrome, hospital addiction, and professional patient syndrome. The term "gridiron abdomen" has been used to describe the appearance of some patients because of their multiple surgical scars. Their clinical presentations are diverse, including hematoma, hemoptysis, abdominal pain, fever, seizures, hypoglycemia, and hematuria. Patients characteristically travel from hospital to hospital, gaining readmission with a panoply of medical symptoms.

Factitious disorder with predominantly psychological signs and symptoms is a difficult diagnosis to make; it requires prolonged investigation. The presenting symptoms include depression, hallucinations, dissociated states, conversion symptoms, and bereavement. Pseudologia phantastica, which is also seen in the physical type of factitious disorder, is characterized by extensive and colorful fantasies associated with the presentation of the patient's story. In the case of factitious bereavement, for example, the patient may tell a dramatic story of violent or bloody deaths, often involving a child or a young adult.

In factitious disorder by proxy, someone intentionally produces physical signs or symptoms in another person who is under the first person's care. The most common scenario involves a mother who deceives medical personnel into believing that her child is ill. The deception can range from giving false medical information to inducing injury or illness in the child. The only apparent gain in the disorder is for the caretaker to assume the patient role indirectly.

Students should review Chapter 18 in *Kaplan and Sadock's Synopsis VII* and should then study the questions and answers below to test their knowledge of the area.

HELPFUL HINTS

The student should be able to define each of the terms below.

factitious disorder
  with predominantly physical
    signs and symptoms
  with predominantly
    psychological signs and
    symptoms
  NOS
  by proxy

as-if personality
regression
symbolization
Munchausen syndrome
gridiron abdomen
pseudomalingering
pseudologia phantastica
somatoform disorders

schizophrenia
malingering
substance abuse
Ganser's syndrome
approximate answers
unmasking ceremony
Briquet's syndrome

QUESTIONS

DIRECTIONS: Each of the incomplete statements below is followed by five suggested completions. Select the *one* that is *best* in each case.

18.1. Patients with factitious disorders
A. do not intentionally produce signs of medical or mental disorders
B. use the facsimile of genuine illness for secondary gains
C. do not seek out painful procedures
D. usually had a family of origin with either an absent father or a rejecting mother
E. are easily engaged in exploratory psychotherapy

18.2. In patients suspected of having a factitious disorder
A. emphasis should be placed on securing information from any available friend or relative
B. the examiner should ask pointed questions to reveal the false nature of the illness
C. their intelligence quotients (I.Q.s) are usually below average
D. there is evidence of a formal thought disorder
E. their tolerance to frustration is usually high

18.3. The differential diagnosis of a factitious disorder includes
A. somatization disorder
B. hypochondriasis
C. antisocial personality disorder
D. malingering
E. all the above

18.4. Factitious disorders
A. usually begin in childhood
B. are best treated with psychoactive drugs
C. usually have a good prognosis
D. are synonymous with Ganser's syndrome
E. may occur by proxy

18.5. Patients with factitious disorders
A. do not usually gain admission to a hospital
B. may take anticoagulants to simulate bleeding disorders
C. are usually easy to manage in the hospital
D. do not display symptoms of pseudologia phantastica
E. usually receive the codiagnosis of schizotypal personality disorder

Questions 18.6–18.7

A 29-year-old female laboratory technician was admitted to the medical service through the emergency room because of bloody urine. The patient said that she was being treated for lupus erythematosus by a physician in a different city. She also mentioned that she had had von Willebrand's disease (a rare hereditary blood disorder) as a child. On the third day of her hospitalization, a medical student told the resident that she had seen the patient several weeks before at a different hospital, where the patient had been admitted for the same problem. A search of the patient's belongings revealed a cache of anticoagulant medication. When confronted with the evidence, she refused to discuss the matter and hurriedly signed out of the hospital against medical advice.

18.6. The best diagnosis is
A. somatoform disorders
B. malingering
C. factitious disorder with predominantly physical signs and symptoms
D. factitious disorder with psychological symptoms
E. antisocial personality disorder

18.7. A leading predisposing factor in the development of factitious disorder with predominantly physical signs and symptoms is employment as a
A. teacher
B. health care worker
C. police officer
D. banker
E. waitress

Questions 18.8–18.10

18.8. Factitious disorder with predominantly physical signs and symptoms is synonymous with
A. Munchausen syndrome
B. hospital addiction
C. polysurgical addiction
D. professional patient syndrome
E. all the above

18.9. Factitious disorder with predominantly physical signs and symptoms is
A. under voluntary control, but the patient often denies the voluntary production of the illness
B. also known as Munchausen syndrome
C. frequently seen in patients with a family history of serious illness or disability
D. frequently seen in persons employed in health care jobs
E. characterized by all the above

18.10. Persons displaying a factitious disorder are often characterized by
A. a history of being exposed to genuine illness in a family member
B. employment in a health-related field
C. a history of early parental rejection
D. a tendency to view the physician as a loving parent
E. all the above

ANSWERS

Factitious Disorders

18.1. The answer is D (*Synopsis VII*, page 632).

Anecdotal case reports of patients with factitious disorders indicate that many of the patients suffered childhood abuse or deprivation, resulting in frequent hospitalizations during early development and that the patient *usually had a family of origin with either an absent father or a rejecting mother.* In such circumstances, an inpatient stay may have been regarded as an escape from a fragmented home situation, and the patient may have found the series of caretakers (such as doctors, nurses, and hospital workers) as loving and caring.

In factitious disorders, patients *do intentionally produce signs of medical or mental disorders* and misrepresent their histories and symptoms. The only apparent objective of the behavior is to assume the role of a patient. Patients also *use the facsimile of genuine illness to re-create the desired positive parent-child bond, not for secondary gains. Patients may seek out painful procedures,* such as surgical operations and invasive diagnostic tests. Those patients may have masochistic personalities in which pain serves as punishment for past sins, imagined or real.

Given the intentionally deceptive nature of factitious disorders, patients *are difficult to engage in exploratory psychotherapy.* They may insist that their symptoms are physical and, therefore, that psychologically oriented treatment is useless. The diagnostic criteria for factitious disorder in the fourth edition of *Diagnostic and Statistical Manual of Mental Disorders* (DSM-IV) are given in Table 18.1.

18.2. The answer is A (*Synopsis VII*, pages 632–633).

In patients suspected of having factitious disorder, *emphasis should be placed on recuring information from any available friend, relative,* or other informant, because interviews with reliable outside sources often reveal the false nature of the patient's illness. Although time-consuming and tedious, verifying all the facts presented by the patient concerning prior hospitalizations and medical care is essential.

The examiner should not ask accusatory or *pointed questions to reveal the false nature of the illness.* Such questions may provoke truculence, evasion, or flight from the hospital. There may be a danger of provoking frank psychosis if vigorous confrontation is used; in some instances the feigned illness serves an adaptive function and is a desperate attempt to ward off further disintegration.

Table 18.1
Diagnostic Criteria for Factitious Disorder

A. Intentional production or feigning of physical or psychological signs or symptoms.

B. The motivation for the behavior is to assume the sick role.

C. External incentives for the behavior (such as economic gain, avoiding legal responsibility, or improving physical well-being, as in malingering) are absent.

Code based on type:

With predominantly psychological signs and symptoms: if psychological signs and symptoms predominate in the clinical presentation

With predominantly physical signs and symptoms: if physical signs and symptoms predominate in the clinical presentation

With combined psychological and physical signs and symptoms: if both psychological and physical signs and symptoms are present but neither predominate in the clinical presentation

Table from DSM-IV, *Diagnostic and Statistical Manual of Mental Disorders,* ed 4. Copyright American Psychiatric Association, Washington, 1994. Used with permission.

Certain features are overrepresented in patients with factitious disorder. For example, *their intelligence quotients (I.Q.s) are usually normal or above average; there is an absence of a formal thought disorder*; the patients have a poor sense of identity, including confusion over sexual identity, and poor sexual adjustment; *their tolerance to frustration is usually low*; and they have strong dependence needs and narcissism.

18.3. The answer is E (all) (*Synopsis VII*, page 635).

A factitious disorder is differentiated from *somatization disorder* (Briquet's syndrome) by the voluntary production of factitious symptoms, the extreme course of multiple hospitalizations, and the patient's seeming willingness to undergo an extraordinary number of mutilating procedures.

Hypochondriasis differs from factitious disorder in that the hypochondriacal patient does not voluntarily initiate the production of symptoms, and hypochondriasis typically has a later age of onset. As is the case with somatization disorder, patients with hypochondriasis do not usually submit to potentially mutilating procedures.

Because of their pathological lying, lack of close

relationships with others, hostile and manipulative manner, and associated substance and criminal history, factitious disorder patients are often classified as having *antisocial personality disorder*; however, persons with antisocial personality disorder do not usually volunteer for invasive procedures or resort to a way of life marked by repeated or long-term hospitalizations.

Factitious disorders must be distinguished from *malingering*. Malingerers have an obvious, recognizable environmental goal in producing signs and symptoms. They may seek hospitalization to secure financial compensation, evade the police, avoid work, or merely obtain free bed and board for the night; but they always have some apparent end for their behavior.

18.4. **The answer is E** (*Synopsis VII*, pages 634–635).

Factitious disorders *may occur by proxy* (Table 18.2); such disorders are classified as factitious disorder not otherwise specified (Table 18.3).

Factitious disorders *usually begin in early adult life*, although they may appear during childhood or adolescence. The onset of the disorder or of discrete episodes of treatment seeking may follow a real illness, loss, rejection, or abandonment. Usually, the patient or a close relative had a hospitalization in childhood or early adolescence for a genuine physical

Table 18.2
Diagnostic Criteria for Factitious Disorder by Proxy

A. Intentional production or feigning of physical or psychological signs or symptoms in another person who is under the individual's care.

B. The motivation for the perpetrator's behavior is to assume the sick role by proxy.

C. External incentives for the behavior (such as economic gain) are absent.

D. The behavior is not better accounted for by another mental disorder.

Table from DSM-IV, *Diagnostic and Statistical Manual of Mental Disorders*, ed 4. Copyright American Psychiatric Association, Washington, 1994. Used with permission.

Table 18.3
Diagnostic Criteria for Factitious Disorder Not Otherwise Specified

This category includes disorders with factitious symptoms that do not meet the criteria for factitious disorder. An example is factitious disorder by proxy: the intentional production or feigning of physical or psychological signs or symptoms in another person who is under the individual's care for the purpose of indirectly assuming the sick role.

Table from DSM-IV, *Diagnostic and Statistical Manual of Mental Disorders*, ed 4. Copyright American Psychiatric Association, Washington, 1994. Used with permission.

illness. Thereafter, a long pattern of successive hospitalizations unfolds, beginning insidiously.

Factitious disorders *are not best treated with psychoactive drugs*. No specific psychiatric therapy has been effective in treating factitious disorders.

Although no adequate data are available about the ultimate outcome for the patients, a few of them probably die as a result of needless medication, instrumentation, or surgery. They *usually have a poor prognosis*.

Factitious disorders *are not synonymous with Ganser's syndrome*, a controversial condition most typically associated with prison inmates. It is characterized by the use of approximate answers. Ganser's syndrome may be a variant of malingering, in that the patients avoid punishment or responsibility for their actions. Ganser's syndrome is classified as a dissociative disorder not otherwise specified.

18.5. **The answer is B** (*Synopsis VII*, page 634).

Patients with factitious disorder *may take anticoagulants to simulate bleeding disorders*. The patients are able to present physical or psychological symptoms so well that they *are usually able to gain admission to a hospital*. They continue to be demanding and difficult and so *are not easy to manage in the hospital*. They may *display symptoms of pseudologia phantastica*, in which limited factual material is mixed with extensive and colorful fantasies. Patients with factitious disorders *do not usually receive the codiagnosis of schizotypal personality disorder*. However, many such patients have the poor identity formation and the disturbed self-image that are characteristic of someone with borderline personality disorder.

18.6–18.7

18.6. **The answer is C** (*Synopsis VII*, page 634).

The best diagnosis is *factitious disorder with predominantly physical signs and symptoms*. The unusual circumstances, such as the woman's possession of anticoagulants (taken to simulate bleeding disorders), her history of repeated hospitalizations, and her leaving the hospital when confronted, strongly suggest that her symptoms were under voluntary control and were not genuine symptoms of a physical disorder. The differential diagnoses to consider are malingering, somatoform disorder, and factitious disorders.

In *somatoform disorders* the production of symptoms is unconscious and involuntary; in the case presented the symptom production appeared to be under voluntary control. In *malingering* the patient have obvious environmental goals in producing their symptoms; from what is known in this case, it appears that the patient had no goal other than that of assuming the role of a patient. Since the feigned symptoms were physical (bloody urine), the diagnosis of *factitious disorder with predominantly psychological signs and symptoms* is ruled out. Because of pathological lying, a hostile and manipulative manner, and lack of close relationships with others, many factitious disorder patients also receive the diagnosis of *antisocial personality disorder*. However, persons with antisocial personality disorder rarely volunteer for invasive procedures or resort to hospitalization as a way of life, as the woman described did. Not enough information is available to determine whether the woman had a personality disorder.

18.7.   The answer is B (*Synopsis VII*, page 632).

Employment as a *health care worker* is considered a leading predisposing factor in the development of factitious disorder with predominantly physical signs and symptoms. Nurses make up one of the largest risk groups in the development of the disorder. In the case presented, the patient was a laboratory technician.

Employment as a *teacher, police officer, banker, waitress* is not a predisposing factor in the development of factitious disorders.

18.8.   The answer is D (*Synopsis VII*, page 634).

Factitious disorder with predominantly physical signs and symptoms has been designated by a variety of labels, the best known of which is *Munchausen syndrome*, named for Baron Münchausen. A German who lived in the 18th century, he wrote many fantastic travel and adventure stories and wandered from tavern to tavern, telling tall tales. Patients who suffer from Munchausen syndrome wander from hospital to hospital, where they manage to be admitted because of the dramatic stories they tell about being dangerously ill. Baron Münchausen never underwent any operations and was not known to be concerned about illness. Other names for the disorder are *hospital addiction, polysurgical addiction,* and *professional patient syndrome*; sometimes the patients are referred to as hospital hoboes.

18.9.   The answer is E (all) (*Synopsis VII*, page 634).

The essential feature of factitious disorder with predominantly physical signs and symptoms is the patient's plausible presentation of physical symptoms that are apparently *under voluntary control*, but *the patient often denies the voluntary production of the illness*. The disorder, *also known as Munchausen syndrome*, is *frequently seen in patients with a family history of serious illness or disability*, and is *frequently seen in persons employed in health care jobs*.

18.10.   The answer is E (all) (*Synopsis VII*, pages 632–634).

A frequent occurrence in the histories of factitious disorder patients is a personal history of serious illness or disability *or a history of being exposed to genuine illness in a family member* or significant extrafamilial figure. A history of prior or current *employment in a health-related field* as a nurse, laboratory technician, ambulance driver, or physician is so common that it suggests inclusion as a clinical feature and a causal factor. Consistent with the concept of poor identity formation is the observation that the patients oscillate between two separate roles—a health professional and a patient—with momentary confusion as to which role is being played at the time.

Psychological models of factitious disorders generally emphasize the causal significance of *a history of parental rejection*. The usual history reveals that one or both parents are experienced as rejecting figures who are unable to form close relationships.

The patients have *a tendency to view the physician as a loving parent*, a potential source of the sought-for love, and person who will fulfill their unmet dependence needs.

19 ||||

Dissociative Disorders

The fourth edition of *Diagnostic and Statistical Manual of Mental Disorders* (DSM-IV) lists specific diagnostic criteria for four dissociative disorders: dissociative amnesia (previously called psychogenic amnesia), dissociative fugue (previously called psychogenic fugue), dissociative identity disorder (previously called multiple personality disorder), and depersonalization disorder.

Dissociative amnesia is characterized by the apparent forgetting of information related to an event generally experienced as traumatic; dissociative fugue is characterized by sudden, unexpected travel away from one's home and family, associated with a loss of memory about one's past and usually the assumption of a new identity; dissociative identity disorder is characterized by the presence of two or more distinct personalities within a single person, usually with only one of the personalities being aware of the others; depersonalization disorder is characterized by a persistent or recurrent sense of estrangement, dislocation, or detachment from one's body or mind. DSM-IV also includes the category of dissociative disorder not otherwise specified (NOS), which includes those disorders that do not meet diagnostic criteria for other dissociative disorders, and dissociative trance disorder is an example of dissociative disorder NOS. Dissociative trance disorder is characterized by single or episodic alterations in consciousness in which the patient exhibits diminished responsivity to environmental stimuli. To make the diagnosis of dissociative trance disorder, the clinician must consider the trance not to be a normal part of a broadly accepted collective cultural or religious practice.

Dissociative experiences may range from normal to pathological. An example of dissociative state in a normal person is the phenomenon of hypnosis. Many studies have indicated an association between traumatic events and the development of dissociative symptoms and disorders. Physical and sexual abuse in childhood has been most frequently noted in association with the development of dissociative disorders, as have other traumatic events, such as war, natural disasters, and personal crises.

To make the diagnosis of a dissociative disorder, the clinician must rule out the presence of any potential underlying organic cause of the dissociative state. Examples of organic causes of dissociative amnesia, for example, include cerebral infections, cerebral neoplasms, substance-related disorders, seizure disorders, and metabolic disorders. Once an organic cause has been ruled out, the clinician can generally state that the essential motivating factor in the evolution of dissociative disorders is the desire to withdraw from emotionally painful experiences. When people are mentally healthy, they generally have a sense of integrated thoughts, feelings, and actions; some have termed that state a unitary consciousness with a unifying experience of self as a single human being with a single essential personality. In dissociative disorders, the patients lack that sense of integration, usually as a defense against trauma. A dissociative defensive reaction allows patients to remove themselves from the traumatic experience as it occurs (to be outside themselves) and to indefinitely delay the confrontation of the ongoing effects of the trauma on the person's life. In dissociative identity disorder, the most severe and chronic disorder, patients fragment into multiple manifestations of different personalities to protect the fragile core personality that has been fragmented.

Students should study Chapter 19 in *Kaplan*

and Sadock's Synopsis VII before testing their knowledge with the questions and answers below.

HELPFUL HINTS

The terms below relate to dissociative disorders and should be defined.

dissociative amnesia
epidemiology of dissociative
   disorders
localized amnesia
selective amnesia
continuous amnesia
transient global amnesia
anterograde amnesia
retrograde amnesia
dissociative fugue
wandering
temporal lobe functions

dissociative identity disorder
dominant personality
secondary gain
depersonalization
derealization
hemidepersonalization
paramnesia
double orientation
reduplicative paramnesia
Ganser's syndrome
dissociative trance disorder
possession state

automatic writing
crystal gazing
highway hypnosis
approximate answers
coercive persuasion
brainwashing
sleepwalking disorder
dissociation
denial
Korsakoff's syndrome
malingering
doubling

QUESTIONS

DIRECTIONS: Each of the incomplete statements below is followed by five suggested completions. Select the *one* that is *best* in each case.

19.1. Transient global amnesia is differentiated from dissociative amnesia by
A. the presence of anterograde amnesia in dissociative amnesia
B. the greater upset in patients with transient global amnesia
C. the loss of personal identity in patients with transient global amnesia
D. the older age of the dissociative amnesia patient
E. the absence of a psychological stressor in dissociative amnesia

9.2. The cause of dissociative identity disorder has been attributed to
A. a specific traumatic life event
B. an inborn biological tendency
C. generalized environmental factors
D. the absence of existing support
E. all the above

19.3. Each of the following statements about dissociative identity disorder is true *except*
A. the transition from one personality to another is often sudden and dramatic
B. the patient generally has amnesia for the existence of the other personalities
C. each personality has a characteristic behavioral pattern
D. the host personality rarely seeks treatment
E. the personalities may be of both sexes

19.4. Depersonalization disorder is characterized by
A. impaired reality testing
B. ego-dystonic symptoms
C. occurrence in the late decades of life
D. gradual onset
E. a brief course and a good prognosis

19.5. Clinical features of dissociative amnesia include
A. some precipitating emotional trauma
B. an abrupt onset
C. awareness of the memory loss
D. retaining the capacity to learn new information
E. all the above

19.6. Dissociative fugue is
A. rare
B. characterized by awareness of the loss of memory
C. characterized by behavior that appears extraordinary to others
D. usually long-lasting
E. all the above

19.7. Dissociative amnesia is
A. most common during periods of war and during natural disasters
B. the least common type of dissociative disorder
C. most common in elderly adults
D. more common in men than in women
E. ~~above~~

~~dissociative fugue~~

19.10. Signs of dissociative identity disorder include
A. reports by the patient of being recognized by people whom the patient does not know
B. the use of the word "we" by the patient
C. reports by the patient of time distortions and lapses
D. changes in behavior reported by a reliable observer
E. all the above

19.11. Dissociative identity disorder is
A. most common in early childhood
B. not nearly as rare as it thought to be
C. much more frequent in men than in women
D. not common in first-degree relatives of persons with the disorder

19.12. Dissociative disorders include all the following *except*
A. amnestic disorders
B. dissociative identity disorder
C. depersonalization disorder
D. Ganser's syndrome
E. dissociative trance disorder

...below are followed by a list of numbered phrases. For each

...is associated with *A only*
...is associated with *B only*
...is associated with *both A and B*
...is associated with *neither A nor B*

Questions 19.13–19.16
A. Dissociation
B. Splitting
C. Both
D. Neither

19.13. ....

19.14. Defense mechanism

19.15. Impulse control impaired

19.16. Memory affected

DIRECTIONS: The lettered headings below are followed by a list of numbered statements. For each numbered statement, select the one lettered heading that is most closely associated with it. Each lettered heading may be selected once, more than once, or not at all.

Questions 19.17–19.20
A. Dissociative amnesia
B. Dissociative fugue
C. Dissociative identity disorder
D. Depersonalization disorder

19.17. A 25-year-old man comes to the emergency room and cannot remember his name

19.18. A 35-year-old man states that his body feels unreal, not attached to him

19.19. A 16-year-old girl is found in another city far from her home and does not recall how she got there

19.20. A 30-year-old woman suddenly has a new childlike voice in the interview

ANSWERS

Dissociative Disorders

19.1.   The answer is B (*Synopsis VII*, page 641).

Transient global amnesia can be differentiated from dissociative amnesia in several ways, for example; *the greater upset in patients with transient global amnesia* than in those with dissociative amnesia; *the presence of anterograde amnesia in transient global amnesia but not in dissociative amnesia; the loss of personal identity in patients with dissociative amnesia but not in transient global amnesia; the older age of the transient global amnesia patient than the dissociative disorder patient*; and *the absence of a psychological stressor in transient global amnesia but not in dissociative amnesia.*

19.2.   The answer is E (all) (*Synopsis VII*, pages 644–645).

The cause of dissociative identity disorder is unknown, although the histories of the patients invariably involve a traumatic event, most often in childhood. In general, four types of causative factors have been identified: (1) *a specific traumatic life event*, (2) *an inborn biological or psychological tendency* for the disorder to develop, (3) *generalized environmental factors*, and (4) *the absence of external support.* The traumatic event is usually childhood physical or sexual abuse, commonly incestuous. Other traumatic events may include the death of a close relative or friend during childhood and witnessing a trauma or a death.

Table 19.1 lists the diagnostic criteria for dissociative identity disorder.

19.3.   The answer is D (*Synopsis VII*, pages 645–648).

In dissociative identity disorder, *the host personality is usually the one who seeks treatment. The transition from one personality to another is often sudden and dramatic. The patient generally has amnesia for the existence of the other personalities* and for the events that took place when another personality was dominant. *Each personality has a characteristic behavioral pattern. The personalities may be of both sexes*, of various races and ages, and from families different from the patient's family of origin. The most common subordinate personality is childlike. Often, the personalities are disparate and may even be opposites.

19.4.   The answer is B (*Synopsis VII*, page 648).

Depersonalization disorder is characterized by *ego-dystonic symptoms*—that is, symptoms at vari-

---

Table 19.1
Diagnostic Criteria for Dissociative Identity Disorder

A. The presence of two or more distinct identities or personality states (each with its own relatively enduring pattern of perceiving, relating to, and thinking about the environment and self).

B. At least two of these identities or personality states recurrently take control of the person's behavior.

C. Inability to recall important personal information that is too extensive to be explained by ordinary forgetfulness.

D. The disturbance is not due to the direct effects of a substance (e.g., blackouts or chaotic behavior during alcohol intoxication) or a general medical condition (e.g., complex partial seizures). **Note:** In children, the symptoms are not attributable to imaginary playmates or other fantasy play.

Table from DSM-IV, *Diagnostic and Statistical Manual of Mental Disorders,* ed 4. Copyright American Psychiatric Association, Washington, 1994. Used with permission.

---

ance with the ego. However, the person maintains *intact reality testing*; he or she is aware of the disturbances. Depersonalization has *rarely occurred in the late decades of life.* The disorder most often starts between the ages of 15 and 30 years. In the large majority of patients, the symptoms first appear suddenly; only a few patients report a *gradual onset.* A few follow-up studies indicate that, in more than half the cases, depersonalization disorder tends to have *a long-term course and a poor prognosis.* Table 19.2 lists the diagnostic criteria for depersonalization disorder.

19.5.   The answer is E (all) (*Synopsis VII*, pages 640–641).

Although some episodes of amnesia occur spontaneously, the history usually reveals *some precipitating emotional trauma* charged with painful emotions and psychological conflict. The disorder usually has *an abrupt onset*, and the patient usually has an *awareness of the memory loss. Retaining the capacity to learn new information* is another clinical feature. Table 19.3 lists the diagnostic criteria for dissociative amnesia.

19.6.   The answer is A (*Synopsis VII*, page 642).

Dissociative fugue is considered *rare* and, like dissociative amnesia, occurs most often during wartime, after natural disasters, and as a result of personal crises with intense conflict. Dissociative fugue

Table 19.2
Diagnostic Criteria for Depersonalization Disorder

A. Persistent or recurrent experiences of feeling detached from, and as if one is an outside observer of, one's mental processes or body (e.g., feeling like one is in a dream).

B. During the depersonalization experience, reality testing remains intact.

C. The depersonalization causes clinically significant distress or impairment in social, occupational, or other important areas of functioning.

D. The depersonalization experience does not occur exclusively during the course of another mental disorder, such as schizoprehnia, panic disorder, acute stress disorder, or another dissociative disorder, and is not due to the direct physiological effects of a substance (e.g., a drug of abuse, a medication) or a general medical condition (e.g., temporal lobe epilepsy).

Table from DSM-IV, *Diagnostic and Statistical Manual of Mental Disorders,* ed 4. Copyright American Psychiatric Association, Washington, 1994. Used with permission.

Table 19.3
Diagnostic Criteria for Dissociative Amnesia

A. The predominant disturbance is one or more episodes of inability to recall important personal information, usually of a traumatic or stressful nature, that is too extensive to be explained by ordinary forgetfulness.

B. The disturbance does not occur exclusively during the course of dissociative identity disorder, dissociative fugue, posttraumatic stress disorder, acute stress disorder, or somatization disorder and is not due to the direct physiological effects of a substance (e.g., a drug of abuse, a medication) or a neurological or other general medical condition (e.g., amnestic disorder due to head trauma).

C. The symptoms cause clinically significant distress or impairment in social, occupational, or other important areas of functioning.

Table from DSM-IV, *Diagnostic and Statistical Manual of Mental Disorders,* ed 4. Copyright American Psychiatric Association, Washington, 1994. Used with permission.

is *characterized by a lack of awareness of the loss of memory but not by behavior that appears extraordinary to others.* A dissociative fugue is *usually brief—hours to days.* Table 19.4 lists the diagnostic criteria for dissociative fugue.

19.7.   The answer is D (*Synopsis VII*, page 639).

Dissociative amnesia is *most common during periods of war and during natural disasters.* It is *the most common type of dissociative disorder, occurs most often in adolescents and young adults, and is more common in women than in men.*

19.8.   The answer is E (all) (*Synopsis VII*, page 642).

Heavy alcohol abuse may predispose a person to dissociative fugue, but the cause is thought to be ba-

Table 19.4
Diagnostic Criteria for Dissociative Fugue

A. The predominant disturbance is sudden, unexpected travel away from home or one's customary place of work, with inability to recall one's past.

B. Confusion about personal identity or assumption of new identity (partial or complete).

C. The disturbance does not occur exclusively during the course of dissociative identity disorder and is not due to the direct physiological effects of a substance (e.g., a drug of abuse, a medication) or a general medical condition (e.g., temporal lobe epilepsy).

D. The symptoms cause clinically significant distress or impairment in social, occupational, or other important areas of functioning.

Table from DSM-IV, *Diagnostic and Statistical Manual of Mental Disorders,* ed 4. Copyright American Psychiatric Association, Washington, 1994. Used with permission.

sically psychological. The essential motivating factor appears to be a desire to withdraw from emotionally painful experiences. Patients with *mood disorders* and certain personality disorders (for example, *borderline, schizoid,* and histrionic *personality disorders*) are predisposed to dissociative fugue.

19.9.   The answer is E (all) (*Synopsis VII*, pages 641–642).

The differential diagnosis of dissociative amnesia includes dissociative mental disorders in which the patient experiences a memory disturbance, especially *transient global amnesia.* In *alcohol persisting amnestic disorder,* short-term memory loss occurs. In *postconcussion amnesia,* the memory disturbance follows head trauma, is often retrograde, and usually does not extend beyond one week. *Epilepsy* leads to sudden memory impairment associated with motor and electroencephalogram abnormalities. A history of an aura, head trauma, or incontinence helps in the diagnosis.

19.10.   The answer is E (*Synopsis VI*, pages 645–646).

Dissociative identity disorder (formerly called multiple personality disorder) may be misdiagnosed as a schizophrenic disorder or a personality disorder. The clinician should listen for specific features suggestive of the disorder. Signs of the disorder include *reports by the patient of being recognized by people whom the patient does not know, the use of the word "we" by the patient, reports by the patient of time distortions and lapses,* and *changes in behavior reported by a reliable observer.* Table 19.5 lists the signs of multiplicity.

19.11.   The answer is B (*Synopsis VII*, pages 644–645).

Recent reports on dissociative identity disorder suggest that it is *not nearly as rare as it was once*

Table 19.5
Signs of Multiplicity

1. Reports of time distortions, lapses, and discontinuities
2. Being told of behavioral episodes by others that are not remembered by the patient
3. Being recognized by others or called by another name by people whom the patient does not recognize
4. Notable changes in the patient's behavior reported by a reliable observer; the patient may call himself or herself by a different name or refer to himself or herself in the third person
5. Other personalities are elicited under hypnosis or during amobarbital interviews
6. Use of the word "we" in the course of an interview
7. Discovery of writings, drawings, or other productions or objects (identification cards, clothing, etc.) among the patient's personal belongings that are not recognized or cannot be accounted for
8. Headaches
9. Hearing voices originating from within and not identified as separate
10. History of severe emotional or physical trauma as a child (usually before the age of 5 years)

Table from J L Cummings: Dissociative states, depersonalization, multiple personality, episodic memory lapses. In *Clinical Neuropsychiatry,* J L Cummings, editor, p 122. Grune & Stratton, Orlando, 1985. Used with permission.

thought to be. It is *most common in late adolescence and young adult life, not childhood,* and is *much more frequent in women than in men.* Several studies have indicated that the disorder is *more common in first-degree relatives of persons with the disorder* than in the general population. It is classified as *a dissociative disorder.*

19.12.   The answer is A (*Synopsis VII*, pages 336–337 and 638).

The *amnestic disorders* are classified with the cognitive disorders (for example, dementias), not the dissociative disorders.

The dissociative disorders comprise dissociative amnesia, dissociative fugue, *dissociative identity disorder, depersonalization disorder,* and dissociative disorder not otherwise specified (NOS). *Ganser's syndrome* is listed in the fourth edition of *Diagnostic and Statistical Manual of Mental Disorders* (DSM-IV) as an example of dissociative disorder NOS (Table 19.6). In Ganser's syndrome, patients (for example, give approximate answers to questions 2 + 2 = 5). Another example of dissociative disorder NOS is dissociative trance disorder (Table 19.7).

19.13–19.16

19.13.   The answer is C (*Synopsis VII*, pages 250–251 and 638).

19.14.   The answer is C (*Synopsis VII*, pages 250–251 and 638).

19.15.   The answer is B (*Synopsis VII*, pages 250 and 638).

19.16.   The answer is A (*Synopsis VII*, pages 251 and 638).

Dissociation and *splitting* have both similarities and differences. Both involve an active compartmentalization and *separation of mental contents.* Both are used as *defense mechanisms* to ward off unpleasant affects associated with the integration of contradictory parts of the self. They differ to some extent in the nature of the ego functions that are affected. With splitting, anxiety tolerance and *impulse control are impaired.* In dissociation, *memory* and consciousness are *affected.*

19.17–19.20

19.17.   The answer is A (*Synopsis VII*, pages 638–642).

19.18.   The answer is D (*Synopsis VII*, pages 648–650).

19.19.   The answer is B (*Synopsis VII*, pages 642–643).

19.20.   The answer is C (*Synopsis VII*, pages 644–646).

Dissociative amnesia, as in the case of the man who *cannot remember his name,* is characterized by an inability to remember information, usually related to a stressful or traumatic event, that cannot be explained by ordinary forgetfulness, the ingestion of substances, or a general medical condition. *Dissociative fugue,* as in the case of the girl who *is found in another city far from her home,* is characterized by sudden and unexpected travel away from home or work, associated with an inability to recall one's past and confusion about one's personal identity or the adoption of a new identity. *Dissociative identity disorder,* as in the case of the woman who *suddenly has a new childlike voice in the interview,* is characterized by the presence of two or more distinct personalities within a single person; dissociative identity disorder is generally considered the most severe and chronic of the dissociative disorders. *Depersonalization disorder,* as in the case of the man who *states that his body feels unreal,* is characterized by recurrent or persistent feelings of detachment from one's body or mind.

Table 19.6
Diagnostic Criteria for Dissociative Disorder Not Otherwise Specified

This category is included for disorders in which the predominant feature is a dissociative symptom (i.e., a disruption in the usually integrated functions of consciousness, memory, identity, or perception of the environment) that does not meet the criteria for any specific dissociative disorder. Examples include

1. Clinical presentations similar to dissociative identity disorder that fail to meet full criteria for this disorder. Examples include presentation in which a) there are not two or more distinct personality states, or b) amnesia for important personal information does not occur.
2. Derealization unaccompanied by depersonalization in adults.
3. States of dissociation that occur in individuals who have been subjected to periods of prolonged and intense coercive persuasion (e.g., brainwashing, thought reform, or indoctrination while a captive).
4. Dissociative trance disorder: single or episodic disturbances in the state of consciousness, identity, or memory that are indigenous to particular locations and cultures. Dissociative trance involves narrowing of awareness of immediate surroundings or stereotyped behaviors or movements that are experienced as being beyond one's control. Possession trance involves replacement of the customary sense of personal identity by a new identity, attributed to the influence of a spirit, power, deity, or other person, and associated with stereotyped "involuntary" movements or amnesia. Examples include *amok* (Indonesia), *bebainan* (Indonesia), *latah* (Malaysia), *pibloktoq* (Arctic), *ataque de nervios* (Latin America) and possession (India). The dissociative or trance disorder is not a normal part of a broadly accepted collective cultural or religious practice.
5. Loss of consciousness, stupor, or coma not attributable to a general medical condition.
6. Ganser's syndrome: the giving of approximate answers to questions (e.g., "2 plus 2 equals 5") when not associated with dissociative amnesia or dissociative fugue.

Table from DSM-IV, *Diagnostic and Statistical Manual of Mental Disorders*, ed 4. Copyright American Psychiatric Association, Washington, 1994. Used with permission.

Table 19.7
Research Criteria for Dissociative Trance Disorder

A. Either (1) or (2):

  (1) trance, i.e., temporary marked alteration in the state of consciousness or loss of customary sense of personal identity without replacement by an alternate identity, associated with at least one of the following:

   (a) narrowing of awareness of immediate surroundings, or unusually narrow and selective focusing on environmental stimuli
   (b) stereotyped behaviors or movements that are experienced as being beyond one's control

  (2) possession trance, a single of episodic alteration in the state of consciousness characterized by the replacement of customary sense of personal identity by a new identity. This is attributed to the influence of a spirit, power, deity, or other person, as evidenced by one (or more) of the following:

   (a) stereotyped and culturally determined behaviors or movements that are experienced as being controlled by the possessing agent
   (b) full or partial amnesia for the event

B. The trance or possession trance state is not accepted as a normal part of a collective cultural or religious practice.

C. The trance or possession trance state causes clinically significant distress or impairment in social, occupational, or other important areas of functioning.

D. The trance or possession trance state does not occur exclusively during the course of a psychotic disorder (including mood disorder with psychotic features and brief psychotic disorder) or dissociative identity disorder and is not due to the direct physiological effects of a substance or general medical condition.

Table from DSM-IV, *Diagnostic and Statistical Manual of Mental Disorders*, ed 4. Copyright American Psychiatric Association, Washington, 1994. Used with permission.

Human Sexuality

Sexual behaviors considered normal encompass a large and diverse spectrum. To a great extent, normal human sexuality is in the eye of the beholder, and abnormal sexuality is sexual behavior that is destructive, that cannot be directed toward a partner, that is overwhelmed by profound guilt and anxiety, or that is compulsive.

Several interrelated factors constitute a person's sexuality, and those factors are often misdefined and confused with one another. Those factors are sexual identity, gender identity, sexual orientation, sexual fantasy, and sexual behavior. Sexual identity consists of a person's biological sex characteristics that are genetically and hormonally determined. Gender identity is a person's sense of being clearly male or clearly female, which is most often determined by the person's sexual identity. Sexual orientation concerns the object of a person's sexual impulses; the orientation may be heterosexual, homosexual, or bisexual. Sexual fantasy and sexual behavior are a person's psychophysiological responses to psychological and physical stimuli; they are what a person thinks and does when sexually aroused.

The fourth edition of *Diagnostic and Statistical Manual of Mental Disorders* (DSM-IV) describes a four-phase sexual response cycle: phase 1 is desire, phase 2 is excitement, phase 3 is orgasm, and phase 4 is resolution. The desire phase is characterized by sexual fantasies and the desire to have sexual activity. The excitement phase is characterized by penile tumescence and erection in the male and by vaginal lubrication and clitoral engorgement in the female. The orgasm phase is characterized by a release of sexual tension and a series of involuntary muscle contractions. The resolution phase is characterized by detumescence of the genitalia, both male and female, and a variable refractory period to further orgasm in the male and no refractory period in the female.

DSM-IV divides the sexual disorders into sexual dysfunctions and paraphilias. Seven major sexual dysfunctions are described in DSM-IV: (1) sexual desire disorders, (2) sexual arousal disorders, (3) orgasm disorders, (4) sexual pain disorders, (5) sexual dysfunction due to a general medical condition, (6) substance-induced sexual dysfunction, and (7) sexual dysfunction not otherwise specified (NOS).

A useful way to conceptualize sexual dysfunctions is as disorders related to the phases of the sexual response cycle. For instance, sexual desire disorders are associated with the appetitive phase. Sexual dysfunctions may be biologically or psychologically determined, or they may be caused by a combination of other factors. For each sexual dysfunction, the clinician must rule out any potential underlying medical cause, including medications and other substances. If a sexual dysfunction is the result of a general medical condition or is substance-induced, it should be labeled as such.

Sexual desire disorders include the common hypoactive sexual desire disorder and the less common sexual aversion disorder. Sexual arousal disorders include female sexual arousal disorder, in which there is a persistent or recurrent failure to attain or maintain lubrication, and male erectile disorder, in which there is persistent or recurrent failure to attain or maintain an erection. Orgasm disorders include female orgasmic disorder, in which the woman is unable to achieve orgasm; inhibited male orgasmic disorder; in which there is persistent or recurrent delayed or absent orgasm after the man has a normal excitement phase; and premature ejaculation, which is characterized by the man's persistent or recurrent ejaculation before he wants it. Sexual pain disorders include dyspareunia—which is recurrent or persistent genital pain before, during, or after sexual intercourse in either the man or the woman—and vaginismus, which is characterized by an involuntary muscle constriction of the vagina that interferes with penile insertion. Examples of sexual dysfunction NOS include masturbatory pain and orgasmic anhedonia.

Treatment of sexual dysfunctions relies heavily on behavioral techniques, but other techniques are also used, including hypnotherapy, psychoanalytically oriented psychotherapy, dual-sex couple therapy, and pharmacotherapy.

Paraphilias are sexual disorders defined as specialized sexual fantasies and intense sexual impulses and behavior that are usually repetitive, compulsive, and disturbing to the person experiencing them. Often, the power of the fantasy and its compelling behavioral components come to pervade the person's life. The paraphilias described in DSM-IV are exhibitionism, fetishism, frotteurism, pedophilia, sexual masochism, sexual sadism, voyeurism, transvestite fetishism, and paraphilia NOS. The most com-

mon legally identified paraphilia is pedophilia. Exhibitionism and voyeurism are also common. Sexual masochism, sexual sadism, and fetishism are thought to be greatly underrepresented in any prevalence estimates. The paraphilias are most often described in men, and more than half of all paraphilias begin before the age of 18. Many persons have multiple paraphilias. Paraphilia NOS includes a variety of conditions, such as telephone scatologia (obscene telephone calling), necrophilia (sexual gratification from corpses), and zoophilia (sexual gratification from animals).

The clinician needs to differentiate a true paraphilia or sexual dysfunction from experimentation and an isolated incident. Pervasiveness, recurrence, persistence, or compulsivity is what characterizes a sexual dysfunction paraphilia.

Students are referred to Chapter 20 in *Kaplan and Sadock's Synopsis VII* to expand their knowledge about normal sexuality and sexual dysfunctions and paraphilias. The following questions and answers can then be addressed.

HELPFUL HINTS

The student should know the following terms and their definitions.

psychosexual stages	exhibitionism	hypoactive sexual desire disorder
sexual identity and gender identity	sexual masochism and sexual sadism	sexual aversion disorder
HIV, AIDS	moral masochism	vagina dentata
embryological studies	voyeurism	male erectile disorder
gender role	scoptophilia	female sexual arousal disorder
masturbation	fetishism	anorgasmia
Alfred Kinsey	transvestic fetishism	castration
William Masters and Virginia Johnson	frotteurism	nocturnal penile tumescence
tumescence and detumescence	zoophilia	Doppler effect
excitement	coprophilia	TFTs, FH, FSH
plateau	urophilia	cystometric examination
orgasm	partialism	penile arteriography
resolution	necrophilia	clitoral versus vaginal orgasm
sympathetic and parasympathetic nervous systems	hypoxyphilia	female organic disorder
erection and ejaculation	autoerotic asphyxiation	male orgasmic disorder
refractory period	telephone scatologia	retarded ejaculation
phases of sexual response	sexual desire disorders	retrograde ejaculation
intimacy	sexual arousal disorders	premature ejaculation
paraphilias	orgasm disorders	dyspareunia
steal phenomenon	sexual pain disorders	vaginismus
pedophilia	sexual dysfunction NOS	Peyronie's disease
	biogenic versus psychogenic	orgasmic anhedonia
		postcoital headache

postcoital dysphoria	sensate focus	prosthetic devices
unconsummated marriage	spectatoring	rape (male and female)
Don Juanism	squeeze technique	statutory rape
satyriasis	stop-start technique	spouse abuse
sexual orientation distress	desensitization therapy	incest
homosexuality	hymenectomy	infertility
coming out	vaginoplasty	sterilization
dual-sex therapy		

QUESTIONS

DIRECTIONS: Each of the questions or incomplete statements below is followed by five suggested responses or completions. Select the *one* that is *best* in each case.

20.1. Homosexuality
A. is listed in the fourth edition of *Diagnostic and Statistical Manual of Mental Disorders* (DSM-IV) as a mental disorder
B. among men has a prevalence of 15 percent
C. was perceived by Sigmund Freud as a mental illness
D. is socially stigmatized less for women than for men
E. does not have a genetic or biological component

20.2. Male erectile disorder is
A. sometimes situational
B. the chief complaint in less than 25 percent of all men presenting with sexual disorders
C. universal in aging men
D. organic in cause
E. all the above

20.3. Masturbation
A. is not common in infancy and childhood
B. leads to a decrease in sexual potency
C. is common among married couples
D. usually results in orgasmic anhedonia
E. is not associated with autoerotic asphyxiation

20.4. Paraphilias
A. are usually not distressing to the person with the disorder
B. are found equally among men and women
C. according to the classic psychoanalytic model, are due to a failure to complete the process of heterosexual adjustment
D. with an early age of onset are associated with a good prognosis
E. such as pedophilia usually involve vaginal or anal penetration of the victim

20.5. The prevalence of sexual dysfunctions among married couples has been estimated to be
A. 5 percent
B. 10 percent
C. 20 percent
D. 30 percent
E. more than 40 percent

20.6. Figure 20.1 shows a man with gynecomastia and small testes. He has positive Barr bodies and an XXY karyotype. The most likely diagnosis is
A. androgen insensitivity
B. Klinefelter's syndrome
C. Turner's syndrome
D. hermaphroditism
E. Cushing's syndrome

20.7. A fetish is
A. a nonliving inanimate object that is used as the preferred or necessary adjunct to sexual arousal
B. integrated into sexual activity with a human partner
C. a device that may function as a hedge against separation anxiety
D. a device with magical phallic qualities that is used to ward off castration anxiety
E. all the above

20.8. Which of the following has been associated with male erectile disorder due to a general medical condition?
A. Mumps
B. Atherosclerosis
C. Klinefelter's syndrome
D. Multiple sclerosis
E. All the above

20.9. Orgasm is characterized by all the following *except*
A. involuntary contractions of the anal sphincter
B. carpopedal spasm
C. absence of contractions of the uterus
D. blood pressure rise
E. slight clouding of consciousness

20.10. A married man with a chief complaint of premature ejaculation is best treated with
A. antianxiety agents
B. psychoanalysis
C. squeeze technique
D. cognitive therapy
E. none of the above

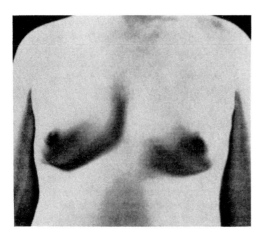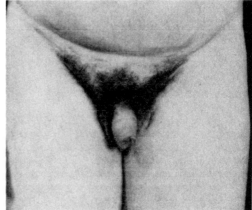

Figure 20.1. A man with gynecomastia and small testes. (Figure courtesy of Robert B. Greenblatt, M.D., and Virginia P. McNamara, M.D.)

20.11. Autoerotic asphyxiation is most commonly associated with
A. adolescent girls
B. middle-aged men
C. a heightened intensity of orgasm
D. adolescent boys
E. no other mental disorder

20.12. Measures used to help differentiate organically caused impotence from functional impotence include
A. monitoring of nocturnal penile tumescence
B. glucose tolerance tests
C. follicle-stimulating hormone (FSH) determinations
D. testosterone level tests
E. all the above

20.13. Each of the following statements about sexual masochism is true *except*
A. the most common finding is that the person with sexual masochism is unable to take the opposite role of the sexual sadist with arousal and pleasure
B. the essential feature is sexual excitement produced by the person's own suffering
C. masochistic sexual fantasies are likely to have been present in childhood
D. the disorder is usually chronic
E. self-mutilation, if it occurs, is likely to be recurrent

20.14. Premature ejaculation is associated with
A. stress
B. negative cultural conditioning
C. more frequency among college-educated men than among those with less education
D. general medical factors exclusively
E. all the above

20.15. Which of the following statements is true?
A. The effects of various drugs on sexual functioning in women have not been studied as extensively as they have been in men
B. Women are less vulnerable to pharmacologically induced sexual dysfunction than are men
C. Phenelzine decreases libido in some women
D. Sexual dysfunction associated with the use of a drug disappears when the drug is discontinued
E. All the above

20.16. Male orgasmic disorder is
A. also called retarded ejaculation
B. less common than premature ejaculation
C. sometimes a result of prostate surgery
D. sometimes caused by antihypertensive drugs
E. characterized by all the above

20.17. Which of the following surgical procedures may be used in treating sexual dysfunctions?
A. Insertion of a penile prosthesis
B. Penile revascularization
C. Hymenectomy
D. Vaginoplasty
E. All the above

DIRECTIONS: Each group of questions below consists of lettered headings followed by a list of numbered words or phrases. For each numbered word or phrase, select the *one* lettered heading that is most closely associated with it. Each lettered heading may be used once, more than once, or not at all.

Questions 20.18–20.28

A. Fetishism
B. Voyeurism
C. Frotteurism
D. Exhibitionism
E. Sexual masochism
F. Sexual sadism
G. Tranvestic fetishism
H. Hypoactive sexual desire disorder
I. Sexual aversion disorder
J. Dyspareunia
K. Vaginismus

20.18. Observing people who are naked or engaging in sexual activity

20.19. Rubbing up against a fully clothed woman to achieve orgasm

20.20. Sexual focus is on objects intimately associated with the human body

20.21. Urges by heterosexual men to dress in female clothes for purposes of arousal

20.22. Absence of sexual fantasies and of desire for sexual activity

20.23. Avoidance of genital sexual contact with a sexual partner

20.24. Involuntary muscle constriction

20.25. Persistent genital pain occurring before, during, or after intercourse

20.26. Fantasies involving harm to others

20.27. Fantasies involving the act of being humiliated

20.28. Recurrent urge to expose one's genitals to a stranger

Questions 20.29–20.33

A. Desire phase
B. Excitement phase
C. Orgasm phase
D. Resolution phase

20.29. Vaginal lubrication

20.30. Orgasmic platform

20.31. Testes increase in size by 50 percent

20.32. Slight clouding of consciousness

20.33. Detumescence

ANSWERS

Human Sexuality

20.1. The answer is D (*Synopsis VII*, page 659).

Homosexuality is socially stigmatized less for women than for men. Homosexual male couples are, therefore, more likely to be subjected to civil and social discrimination than are homosexual female couples. Although more stable male-male relationships exist than were previously thought, male-male relationships appear to be less stable and more fleeting than are female-female relationships.

Homosexuality *is not listed in the fourth edition* of Diagnostic and Statistical Manual of Mental Disorders *(DSM-IV) as a mental disorder*. In 1973 homosexuality was eliminated as a diagnostic category by the American Psychiatric Association and was removed from *Diagnostic and Statistical Manual of Mental Disorders*. Doing so was the result of the view that homosexuality is an alternative life-style, rather than a mental disorder, and that it occurs with some regularity as a variant of human sexuality. As David Hawkins wrote, "The presence of homosexuality does not appear to be a matter of choice; the expression of it is a matter of choice." However, if a person persistently finds his or her homosexuality markedly distressing, that person may be classified as having a sexual disorder not otherwise specified.

Although no sex surveys are wholly reliable, a 1988 survey by the U.S. Bureau of the Census concluded that homosexuality among men has a *prevalence of 2 to 3 percent, not 15 percent*. In 1993 the Alan Guttmacher Institute found that the percentage of men reporting exclusively homosexual activity in the previous year was 1 percent and that 2 percent reported a lifetime history of homosexual experiences. Other estimates of homosexual behavior are given in Table 20.1.

Homosexuality *was perceived by Sigmund Freud as an arrest of psychosexual development, not a mental illness*.

Recent studies indicate that homosexuality *may have a genetic or biological component*. Homosexual men reportedly exhibit lower levels of circulatory androgen than do heterosexual men. And women with hyperadrenocorticalism become bisexual or homosexual in greater proportion than does the general population. In addition, genetic studies have found a higher incidence of homosexual concordance among monozygotic twins than among dizygotic twins, which suggests a genetic predisposition; but chromosome studies have been unable to differentiate homosexuals from heterosexuals. Male homosexuals also show a familial distribution; homosexual men

have more brothers who are homosexual than do heterosexual men.

20.2. The answer is A (*Synopsis VII*, page 664).

Male erectile disorder (Table 20.2) is *sometimes situational*. In situational male erectile disorder the man is able to have coitus in certain circumstances but not in others; for example, a man may function effectively with a prostitute but be impotent with his wife.

Male erectile disorder is *the chief complaint in more than 50 percent of all men presenting with sexual disorders*. The incidence increases with age. However, male erectile disorder is *not universal in aging men*; having an available sex partner is closely related to continuing potency, as is a history of consistent sexual activity. Male erectile disorder may be *organic or psychological in cause* or a combination of both, but most patients have a psychological cause.

20.3. The answer is C (*Synopsis VII*, page 657).

Masturbation *is common among married couples*; Alfred Kinsey reported that it occurs, on average, once a month among married couples. Masturbation is a normal activity that is common in all stages of life, from infancy to old age. Longitudinal studies of development show that it *is common in infancy and childhood*.

No scientific evidence supports myths generated by moral taboos, such as the myth that masturbation *leads to a decrease in sexual potency*. Masturbation *does not result in orgasmic anhedonia*, a condition in which the person has no physical sensation of orgasm, even though the physiological component (for example, ejaculation) remains intact.

Masturbation *is associated with autoerotic asphyxiation*. Some masturbatory practices involve masturbating while hanging oneself by the neck to heighten erotic sensations and the intensity of the orgasm through the mechanism of mild hypoxia. Although the persons intend to release themselves from the noose after orgasm, an estimated 500 to 1,000 persons a year accidentally kill themselves by hanging.

20.4. The answer is C (*Synopsis VII*, page 675).

Paraphilias, *according to the classic psychoanalytic model, are due to a failure to complete the process of heterosexual adjustment*. However bizarre its manifestation, the paraphilia provides an outlet for the sexual and aggressive drives that would other-

Table 20.1
Estimates of Homosexual Behavior

Country	Sample	Findings
Canada	5,514 first-year college students under age 25	98% heterosexual 1% bisexual 1% homosexual
Norway	6,155 adults, ages 18–26	3.5% of males and 3% of females reported past homosexual experiences
France	20,055 adults	Lifetime homosexual experience: 4.1% for men and 2.6% for women
Denmark	3,178 adults, ages 18–59	Less than 1% of men exclusively homosexual
Britain	18,876 adults, ages 16–59	6.1% of men reported past homosexual experiences

Data reported by *The Wall Street Journal* (March 31, 1993) and *The New York Times* (April 15, 1993) from research studies on homosexual behavior.

Table 20.2
Diagnostic Criteria for Male Erectile Disorder

A. Persistent or recurrent inability to attain, or to maintain until completion of the sexual activity, an adequate erection.

B. The disturbance causes marked distress or interpersonal difficulty.

C. The erectile dysfunction is not better accounted for by another Axis I disorder (other than a sexual dysfunction) and is not due exclusively to the direct physiological effects of a substance (e.g., a drug of abuse, a medication) or a general medical condition.

Specify type:
Lifelong type
Acquired type

Specify type:
Generalized type
Situational type

Specify:
Due to psychological factors
Due to combined factors

Table from DSM-IV. *Diagnostic and Statistical Manual of Mental Disorders,* ed 4. Copyright American Psychiatric Association, Washington, 1994. Used with permission.

Table 20.3
Frequency of Paraphiliac Acts Committed by Paraphilia Patients Seeking Outpatient Treatment

Diagnostic Category	Paraphilia Patients Seeking Outpatient Treatment (%)	Paraphiliac Acts per Paraphilia Patient*
Pedophilia	45	5
Exhibitionism	25	50
Voyeurism	12	17
Frotteurism	6	30
Sexual masochism	3	36
Transvestic fetishism	3	25
Sexual sadism	3	3
Fetishism	2	3
Zoophilia	1	2

*Median number.
Table by Gene G. Abel, M.D.

wise have been channeled into proper sexual behavior.

Paraphilias *are usually distressing to the person with the disorder.* Paraphilias *are not found equally among men and women.* As usually defined, paraphilias seem to be largely male conditions.

Paraphilias *with an early age of onset are associated with a poor prognosis,* as are paraphilias with a high frequency of the acts (Table 20.3), no guilt or shame about the acts, and substance abuse.

Paraphilias *such as pedophilia* (Table 20.4) *usually do not involve vaginal or anal penetration of the victim.* The vast majority of child molestations involve genital fondling or oral sex.

20.5. The answer is E (*Synopsis VII,* pages 663–664).

The prevalence of sexual dysfunctions is not known, but most of the disorders are believed to be common, particularly in their mild forms. A survey of 100 relatively happily married well-to-do couples revealed that *40 percent of the men and 63 percent of the women* had arousal or orgasmic dysfunctions, a prevalence close to the patient population in William Masters and Virginia Johnson's series.

20.6. The answer is B (*Synopsis VII,* pages 654–685).

Klinefelter's syndrome is a chromosomal abnormality in which an extra sex chromosome exists; instead of the normal 46, the affected child is born with 47 chromosomes. For example, there is an XXY pattern, instead of the usual XX or XY pairs. The persons affected are male in development, with small firm testes, eunuchoid habitus, variable gynecomastia and other signs of androgen deficiency, and elevated gonadotropin levels.

Androgen insensitivity is a congenital disorder resulting from an inability of target tissues to respond to androgen. *Turner's syndrome* is a chromosome disorder affecting girls. Instead of an XX sex chromosome, an XO sex chromosome exists, and the girl has a total of 45 chromosomes, rather than the usual 46. *Hermaphroditism* is a state in which a person has

Table 20.4
Diagnostic Criteria for Pedophilia

A. Over a period of at least 6 months, recurrent, intense sexually arousing fantasies, sexual urges, or behaviors involving sexual activity with a prepubescent child or children (generally age 13 years or younger).

B. The fantasies, sexual urges, or behaviors cause clinically significant distress or impairment in social, occupational, or other important areas of functioning.

C. The person is at least age 16 years and at least 5 years older than the child or children in criterion A.

> **Note:** Do not include an individual in late adolescence involved in an ongoing sexual relationship with a 12- or 13-year-old.

Specify if:
Sexually attracted to males
Sexually attracted to females
Sexually attracted to both

Specify if:
Limited to incest

Specify type:
Exclusive type (attracted only to children)
Nonexclusive type

Table from DSM-IV. *Diagnostic and Statistical Manual of Mental Disorders,* ed 4. Copyright American Psychiatric Association, Washington, 1994. Used with permission.

both female and male gonads, usually with one sex dominating. *Cushing's syndrome* or hyperadrenocorticism is named for an American neurosurgeon, Harvey W. Cushing (1869–1939). The disorder is characterized by muscle wasting, obesity, osteoporosis, atrophy of the skin, and hypertension. Emotional lability is common, and frank psychoses are occasionally observed.

Table 20.5 lists and describes intersexual disorders.

20.7. The answer is E (all) (*Synopsis VII*, pages 675–676).

The essential feature of a fetish is *a nonliving object that is used as the preferred or necessary adjunct to sexual arousal*. Sexual activity may involve the fetish alone, or the fetish may be *integrated into sexual activities with a human partner*. In the absence of the fetish, there may be impotence in the male. According to psychoanalytic theory, the fetish *may function as a hedge against separation anxiety* from the love object and may be *used to ward off castration anxiety*. Table 20.6 lists the diagnostic criteria for fetishism.

Table 20.5
Classification of Intersexual Disorders*

Syndrome	Description
Virilizing adrenal hyperplasia (andrenogenital syndrome)	Results from excess androgens in a fetus with XX genotype; most common female intersex disorder; associated with enlarged clitoris, fused labia, hirsutism in adolescence
Turner's syndrome	Results from absence of second female sex chromosome (XO); associated with web neck, dwarfism, cubitus valgus; no sex hormones produced; infertile; usually assigned as females because of female-looking genitals
Klinefelter's syndrome	Genotype is XXY; male habitus presents with small penis and rudimentary testes because of low androgen production; weak libido; usually assigned as male
Androgen insensitivity (testicular-feminizing syndrome)	Congenital X-linked recessive disorder that results in inability of tissues to respond to androgens; external genitals look female and cryptorchid testes present; assigned as females, even though they have XY genotype; in extreme form patient has breasts, normal external genitals, short blind vagina, and absence of pubic and axillary hair
Enzymatic defects in XY genotype (e.g., 5-α-reductase deficiency, 17-hydroxysteroid deficiency)	Congenital interruption in production of testosterone that produces ambiguous genitals and female habitus; usually assigned as female because of female-looking genitalia
Hermaphroditism	True hermaphrodite is rare and characterized by both testes and ovaries in same person (may be 46 XX or 46 XY)
Pseudohermaphroditism	Usually the result of endocrine or enzymatic defect (e.g., adrenal hyperplasia) in persons with normal chromosomes; female pseudohermaphrodites have masculine-looking genitals but are XX; male pseudohermaphrodites have rudimentary testes and external genitals and are XY; assigned as males or females, depending on morphology of genitals

*Intersexual disorders include a variety of syndromes that produce persons with gross anatomical or physiological aspects of the opposite sex.

Table 20.6
Diagnostic Criteria for Fetishism

A. Over a period of at least 6 months, recurrent, intense sexually arousing fantasies, sexual urges, or behaviors involving the use of nonliving objects (e.g., female undergarments).

B. The fantasies, sexual urges, or behaviors cause clinically significant distress or impairment in social, occupational, or other important areas of functioning.

C. The fetish objects are not limited to articles of female clothing used in cross-dressing (as in transvestic fetishism) or devices designed for the purpose of tactile genital stimulation (e.g., vibrator).

Table from DSM-IV. *Diagnostic and Statistical Manual of Mental Disorders,* ed 4. Copyright American Psychiatric Association, Washington, 1994. Used with permission.

20.8.   The answer is E (all) (*Synopsis VII*, pages 667–668).

The incidence of psychological as opposed to organic male erectile disorder has been the focus of many studies. Statistics indicate that 20 to 50 percent of men with erectile disorder have an organic basis for the disorder. Organic causes of male erectile disorder include mumps, atherosclerosis, Klinefelter's syndrome, multiple sclerosis, surgery, and many other medical conditions.

Mumps is an acute infectious and contagious disease caused by Paramyxovirus; it is characterized by inflammation and swelling of the parotid gland and sometimes of other glands, and occasionally there is inflammation of the testes, ovaries, pancreas, and meninges.

Atherosclerosis is characterized by irregularly distributed lipid deposits in the intima of large and medium-sized arteries. The deposits are associated with fibrosis and calcification and are almost always present to some degree in middle-aged and elderly adults. In its severe form, atherosclerosis may lead to arterial narrowing, and the following disorders can occur: angina pectoris, myocardial infarction, cerebrovascular disease, intermittent claudication, and gangrene of the lower extremities.

Klinefelter's syndrome is a chromosomal anomaly in which the person has an extra X chromosome. The affected person is male in development with small firm testes, eunuchoid habitus, variable gynecomastia and other signs of androgen deficiency, and elevated gonadotropin levels.

Multiple sclerosis is one of the demyelinating diseases of the central nervous system and, at least in temperate zones, one of the most common neurological disorders. It is characterized pathologically by swelling and then demyelination of the medullary sheath, which is followed by glial proliferation. The result is an irregular scattering of well-demarcated sclerotic plaques throughout the white and gray matter of the brain and spinal cord.

20.9.   The answer is C (*Synopsis VII*, pages 655 and 666).

In the woman, orgasm is characterized by 3 to 15 involuntary contractions of the lower third of the vagina and by *strong sustained contractions of the uterus,* flowing from the fundus downward to the cervix. Both men and women have *involuntary contractions of the anal sphincter.* Those and the other contractions during orgasm occur at intervals of 0.8 second. Other manifestations include voluntary and involuntary movements of the large muscle groups, including facial grimacing and *carpopedal spasm.* Systolic *blood pressure rises* 20 mm, diastolic blood pressure rises 40 mm, and the heart rate increases up to 160 beats a minute. Orgasm lasts from 3 to 15 seconds and is associated with a *slight clouding of consciousness.*

20.10.   The answer is C (*Synopsis VII*, page 672).

A married man with a chief complaint of premature ejaculation is best treated with the *squeeze technique.* In that method the woman squeezes the coronal ridge of the erect penis just before ejaculation or the time of ejaculatory inevitability. That moment is signaled to the woman by the man in a manner previously agreed to, at which time the woman forcefully applies the squeeze technique. The erection subsides slightly, and ejaculation is postponed. Eventually, the threshold of ejaculatory inevitability is raised, and the condition thereby improves.

Even though premature ejaculation is accompanied by anxiety, drug therapy with *antianxiety agents* is not indicated. *Psychoanalysis* may reveal unconscious fears of women that contribute to premature ejaculation, but it is not considered the most effective therapy. Psychoanalysis can be used if the patient does not respond to the squeeze technique because of deep-seated psychological conflicts. *Cognitive therapy* is used as a treatment of depression and is of limited use as a primary treatment approach to any of the sexual disorders. If the patient has a depression secondary to the sexual disorder, however, cognitive therapy may be of use.

Table 20.7 lists the diagnostic criteria for premature ejaculation.

20.11.   The answer is D (*Synopsis VII*, pages 671 and 679).

Autoerotic asphyxiation is a masturbatory phenomenon most common among *adolescent boys,* not *adolescent girls or middle-aged men.* The practice involves hanging oneself by the neck while masturbating to induce hypoxia. Hypoxia does produce a slightly altered state of consciousness, but it does *not heighten the intensity of orgasm.* The practice is associated with *severe mental disorders.* Although death is accidental, an estimated 500 to 1,000 deaths by hanging occur each year as a result of the masturbatory practice. Some apparent, hanging suicides by adolescent boys are actually caused by autoerotic asphyxiation.

20.12. The answer is E (all) (*Synopsis VII*, pages 664 and 667).

A variety of measures are used to help differentiate organically caused impotence from psychologically caused impotence. The *moniterling of nocturnal penile tumescence* is a noninvasive procedure; normally, erections occur during sleep and are associated with rapid eye movement (REM) sleep periods. Tumescence may be determined with a simple strain gauge. In most cases in which organic factors account for the impotence, the man has no nocturnal erections. Conversely, in most cases of psychologically caused or psychogenic impotence, erections do occur during REM sleep.

Other diagnostic tests that delineate organic bases of impotence include *glucose tolerance tests, follicle-stimulating hormone (FSH) determinations,* and *testosterone level tests.* The glucose tolerance curve measures the metabolism of glucose over a specific period of time and is useful in diagnosing diabetes, of which impotence may be a symptom. FSH is a hormone produced by the anterior pituitary that stimulates the secretion of estrogen from the ovarian follicle in the female; it is also responsible for the production of sperm from the testes in men. An abnormal finding suggests an organic cause for impotence. Testosterone is the male hormone produced by the interstitial cells of the testes. In the male, a low testosterone level produces a lack of desire as the chief complaint, which may be associated with impotence. If the measure of nocturnal penile tumescence is abnormal, indicating the possibility of organic impotence, a measure of plasma testosterone is indicated.

Table 20.7
Diagnostic Criteria for Premature Ejaculation

A. Persistent or recurrent ejaculation with minimal sexual stimulation before, on, or shortly after penetration and before the person wishes it. The clinician must take into account factors that affect duration of the excitement phase, such as age, novelty of the sexual partner or situation, and recent frequency of sexual activity.

B. The disturbance causes marked distress or interpersonal difficulty.

C. The premature ejaculation is not due exclusively to the direct effects of a substance (e.g., withdrawal form opioids).

Specify type:
  Lifelong type
  Acquired type

Specify type:
  Generalized type
  Situational type

Specify:
  Due to psychological factors
  Due to combined factors

Table from DSM-IV, *Diagnostic and Statistical Manual of Mental Disorders,* ed 4. Copyright American Psychiatric Association, Washington, 1994. Used with permission.

20.13. The answer is A (*Synopsis VII*, page 677).

Sexual masochism is *sexual excitement produced by the person's own suffering. Masochistic sexual fantasies are likely to have been present in childhood,* although the age of onset of overt masochistic activities with partners is variable. *The disorder is usually chronic,* and *self-mutilation, if it occurs, is likely to be recurrent.*

The most common finding is that the person with sexual masochism is able to take the opposite role of the sexual sadist with arousal and pleasure.

The diagnostic criteria for sexual masochism are listed in Table 20.8.

20.14. The answer is E (all) (*Synopsis VII*, pages 665–666).

In premature ejaculation, the man recurrently achieves orgasm and ejaculation before he wishes to. *Stress* clearly plays a role in exacerbating the condition; for example, in ongoing relationships, the partner has been found to have great influence on the premature ejaculator, and a stressful marriage exacerbates the disorder. Difficulty in ejaculatory control may also result from *negative cultural conditioning.* For example, men who experience most of their early sexual contacts with prostitutes who demand that the sexual act proceed quickly or in situations in which discovery would be embarrassing (the back seat of a car or the parental home) may become conditioned to achieve orgasm rapidly. Premature ejaculation is associated with *more frequency among college-educated men than among men with less education.* The condition is thought to be related to their concern for partner satisfaction, which may induce performance anxiety, or to their greater awareness of the availability of therapy. As with other sexual dysfunctions, premature ejaculation is not caused by *general medical factors exclusively.*

20.15. The answer is E (all) (*Synopsis VII*, pages 669–670).

The effects of various drugs on sexual functioning in women have not been studied as extensively as they have been in men. In general, however, *women are less vulnerable to pharmacologically induced sexual dysfunction than are men.* Oral contraceptives are

Table 20.8
Diagnostic Criteria for Sexual Masochism

A. Over a period of at least 6 months, recurrent, intense sexually arousing fantasies, sexual urges, or behaviors involving the act (real, not simulated) of being humiliated, beaten, bound, or otherwise made to suffer.

B. The fantasies, sexual urges, or behaviors cause clinically significant distress or impairment in social, occupational, or other important areas of functioning.

Table from DSM-IV, *Diagnostic and Statistical Manual of Mental Disorders,* ed 4. Copyright American Psychiatric Association, Washington, 1994. Used with permission.

reported to decrease libido in some women, and the monoamine oxidase inhibitor *phenelzine* (Nardil) *decreases libido in some women. Sexual dysfunction associated with the use of a drug disappears when the drug is discontinued.*

Psychiatric drugs implicated in female orgasmic disorder are listed in Table 20.9, and the diagnostic criteria for female orgasmic disorder are listed in Table 20.10.

20.16. The answer is E (all) (*Synopsis VII*, pages 665 and 668).

In male orgasmic disorder, which is *also called retarded ejaculation,* the man achieves climax during coitus with great difficulty, if at all. Male orgasmic disorder is *less common than premature ejaculation* and impotence. The problem is more common among men with obsessive-compulsive disorders than among other men. Male orgasmic disorder may have physiological causes and *is sometimes a result of prostate surgery.* It may also be associated with Parkinson's disease and other neurological disorders involving the lumbar or sacral sections of the spinal cord. It is *sometimes caused by antihypertensive drugs,* such as guanethidine (Ismelin) and methyldopa (Aldomet), and the phenothiazines. The diagnostic criteria for male orgasmic disorder are listed in Table 20.11.

Table 20.9
Psychiatric Drugs Implicated in Female Orgasmic Disorder*

Amoxapine (Asendin)[†]
Clomipramine (Anafranil)[‡]
Fluoxetine (Prozac)[§]
Imipramine (Tofranil)
Isocarboxazid (Marplan)[**]
Nortriptyline (Aventyl)[§]
Phenelzine (Nardil)[**]
Thioridazine (Mellaril)
Tranylcypromine (Parnate)[**]
Trifluoperazine (Stelazine)

*The interrelation between female sexual dysfunctions and pharmacological agents has been less extensively evaluated than have male reactions. Oral contraceptives are reported to decrease libido in some women, and some drugs with anticholinergic side effects may impair arousal and orgasm, Benzodiazepines have been reported to decrease libido, but in some patients the diminution of anxiety caused by those drugs enhances sexual function. Both increases and decreases in libido have been reported with psychoactive agents. It is difficult to separate those effects from the underlying condition or from improvement of the condition. Sexual dysfunction associated with the use of a drug disappears when the drug is discontinued.
[†]Bethanachol (Urecholine) can reverse the effects of amoxepine-induced anorgasmia.
[‡]Clomipramine is also reported to increase arousal and orgasmic potential.
[§]Cyproheptadine (Perlactin) reverses fluoxetine- and nortriptyline-induced anorgasmia.
[**]Monoamine oxidase inhibitor (MAOI)-induced anorgasmia may be a temporary reaction to the medication that disappears even though administration of the drug is continued.
Table by Virginia A. Sadock, M.D.

Table 20.10
Diagnostic Criteria for Female Orgasmic Disorder

A. Persistent or recurrent delay in, or absence of, orgasm following a normal sexual excitement phase. Women exhibit wide variability in the type or intensity of stimulation that triggers orgasm. The diagnosis of female orgasmic disorder should be based on the clinician's judgment that the woman's orgasmic capacity is less than would be reasonable for her age, sexual experience, and the adequacy of sexual stimulation she receives.

B. The disturbance causes marked distress or interpersonal difficulty.

C. The orgasmic dysfunction is not better accounted for by another Axis I disorder (except another sexual dysfunction) and is not due exclusively to the direct physiological effects of a substance (e.g., a drug of abuse, a medication) or a general medical condition.

Specify type:
   Lifelong type
   Acquired type

Specify type:
   Generalized type
   Situational type

Specify:
   Due to psychological factors
   Due to combined factors

Table from DSM-IV, *Diagnostic and Statistical Manual of Mental Disorders,* ed 4. Copyright American Psychiatric Association, Washington, 1994. Used with permission.

Table 20.11
Diagnostic Criteria for Male Orgasmic Disorder

A. Persistent or recurrent delay in, or absence of, orgasm following a normal sexual excitement phase during sexual activity that the clinician, taking into account the person's age, judges to be adequate in focus, intensity, and duration.

B. The disturbance causes marked distress or interpersonal difficulty.

C. The orgasmic dysfunction is not better accounted for by another Axis I disorder (except another sexual dysfunction) and is not due exclusively to the direct physiological effects of a substance (e.g., a drug of abuse, a medication) or a general medical condition.

Specify type:
   Lifelong type
   Acquired type

Specify type:
   Generalized type
   Situational type

Specify:
   Due to psychological factors
   Due to combined factors

Table from DSM-IV, *Diagnostic and Statistical Manual of Mental Disorders,* ed 4. Copyright American Psychiatric Association, Washington, 1994. Used with permission.

20.17. The answer is E (all) (*Synopsis VII*, pages 671–674).

The *insertion of a penile prosthesis* in a man with inadequate erectile responses who is resistant to other treatment methods or who has organically caused deficiencies is sometimes effective. Some physicians use *penile revascularization* as a direct approach to treating erectile dysfunction attributable to vascular disorders. Such surgical procedures may be indicated in patients with corporal shunts, in which normally entrapped blood leaks from the corporal space, leading to inadequate erections.

Among the surgical approaches to female dysfunctions are *hymenectomy* (excision of the hymen) in dyspareunia or in the treatment of an unconsummated marriage because of hymenal obstruction. *Vaginoplasty* (plastic surgery involving the vagina) in multiparous women complaining of lessened vaginal sensations is sometimes used.

20.18–20.28

20.18. The answer is **B** (*Synopsis VII*, page 677).

20.19. The answer is **C** (*Synopsis VII*, page 676).

20.20. The answer is **A** (*Synopsis VII*, page 676).

20.21. The answer is **G** (*Synopsis VII*, pages 677–678).

20.22. The answer is **H** (*Synopsis VII*, pages 662–663).

20.23. The answer is **I** (*Synopsis VII*, pages 662–663).

20.24. The answer is **K** (*Synopsis VII*, pages 666–667).

20.25. The answer is **J** (*Synopsis VII*, page 666).

20.26. The answer is **F** (*Synopsis VII*, page 677).

20.27. The answer is **E** (*Synopsis VII*, page 677).

20.28. The answer is **D** (*Synopsis VII*, page 676).

In *fetishism* the *sexual focus is on objects* (such as shoes, gloves, pantyhose, and stockings) *that are intimately associated with the human body* (Table 20.6). The particular fetish is linked to someone closely involved with the patient during childhood and has some quality associated with that loved, needed, or even traumatizing person. *Voyeurism* is the recurrent preoccupation with fantasies and acts that involve *observing people who are naked or engaging in sexual activity* (Table 20.12). It is also known as scopophilia. Masturbation to orgasm usually occurs during or after the event.

Frotteurism is usually characterized by the male's *rubbing up against a fully clothed woman to achieve orgasm* (Table 20.13). The acts usually occur in crowded places, particularly subways and buses.

Exhibitionism is the *recurrent urge to expose one's genitals to a stranger* or an unsuspecting person (Table 20.14). Sexual excitement occurs in anticipation of the exposure, and orgasm is brought about by masturbation during or after the event.

Persons with *sexual masochism* have a recurrent preoccupation with sexual urges and *fantasies involving the act of being humiliated*, beaten, bound, or otherwise made to suffer (Table 20.8).

Persons with *sexual sadism* (Table 20.15). have *fantasies involving harm to others*. According to psychoanalytic theory, sexual sadism is a defense against fears of castration—the persons with sexual sadism do to others what they fear will happen to them. Pleasure is derived from expressing the aggressive instinct.

Table 20.12
Diagnostic Criteria for Voyeurism

A. Over a period of at least 6 months, recurrent, intense sexually arousing fantasies, sexual urges, or behaviors involving the act of observing an unsuspecting person who is naked, in the process of disrobing, or engaging in sexual activity.

B. The fantasies, sexual urges, or behaviors cause clinically significant distress or impairment in social, occupational, or other important areas of functioning.

Table from DSM-IV, *Diagnostic and Statistical Manual of Mental Disorders,* ed 4. Copyright American Psychiatric Association, Washington, 1994. Used with permission.

Table 20.13
Diagnostic Criteria for Frotteurism

A. Over a period of at least 6 months, recurrent, intense sexually arousing fantasies, sexual urges, or behaviors involving touching and rubbing against a nonconsenting person.

B. The fantasies, sexual urges, or behaviors cause clinically significant distress or impairment in social, occupational, or other important areas of functioning.

Table from DSM-IV, *Diagnostic and Statistical Manual of Mental Disorders,* ed 4. Copyright American Psychiatric Association, Washington, 1994. Used with permission.

Table 20.14
Diagnostic Criteria for Exhibitionism

A. Over a period of at least 6 months, recurrent, intense sexually arousing fantasies, sexual urges, or behaviors involving the exposure of one's genitals to an unsuspecting stranger.

B. The fantasies, sexual urges, or behaviors cause clinically significant distress or impairment in social, occupational, or other important areas of functioning.

Table from DSM-IV, *Diagnostic and Statistical Manual of Mental Disorders,* ed 4. Copyright American Psychiatric Association, Washington, 1994. Used with permission.

Transvestic fetishism is marked by fantasies and sexual *urges by heterosexual men to dress in female clothes for purposes of arousal* and as an adjunct to masturbation or coitus (Table 20.16). Transvestic fetishism typically begins in childhood or early adolescence. As years pass, some men with transvestic fetishism want to dress and live permanently as women. Such persons are classified as persons with transvestic fetishism with gender dysphoria.

Sexual desire disorders are divided into two classes: *hypoactive sexual desire disorder*, characterized by a deficiency or the *absence of sexual fantasies and of desire for sexual activity* (Table 20.17), and *sexual aversion disorder*, characterized by an aversion to and *avoidance of genital sexual contact with a sexual partner* (Table 20.18). Hypoactive sexual desire disorder is more common than sexual aversion disorder. An estimated 20 percent of the total population have hypoactive sexual desire disorder.

Dyspareunia is recurrent or *persistent genital pain occurring before, during, or after intercourse* in either the man or the woman. Dyspareunia should not be diagnosed when an organic basis for the pain is found or when, in a woman, it is caused exclusively by vaginismus or by a lack of lubrication (Table 20.19).

Vaginismus is an *involuntary muscle constriction* of the outer third of the vagina that interferes with penile insertion and intercourse. The diagnosis is not made if the dysfunction is caused exclusively by organic factors or if it is symptomatic of another Axis I mental disorder (Table 20.20).

Table 20.15
Diagnostic Criteria for Transvestic Fetishism

A. Over a period of at least 6 months, in a heterosexual male, recurrent, intense sexually arousing fantasies, sexual urges, or behaviors involving cross-dressing.

B. The fantasies, sexual urges, or behaviors cause clinically significant distress or impairment in social, occupational, or other important areas of functioning.

Specify if:
With gender dysphoria: if the person has persistent discomfort with gender role or identity.

Table from DSM-IV, *Diagnostic and Statistical Manual of Mental Disorders,* ed 4. Copyright American Psychiatric Association, Washington, 1994. Used with permission.

Table 20.16
Diagnostic Criteria for Sexual Sadism

A. Over a period of at least 6 months, recurrent, intense sexually arousing fantasies, sexual urges, or behaviors involving acts (real, not simulated) in which the psychological or physical suffering (including humiliation) of the victim is sexually exciting to the person.

B. The fantasies, sexual urges, or behaviors cause clinically significant distress or impairment in social, occupational, or other important areas of functioning.

Table from DSM-IV, *Diagnostic and Statistical Manual of Mental Disorders,* ed 4. Copyright American Psychiatric Association, Washington, 1994. Used with permission.

Table 20.17
Diagnostic Criteria for Hypoactive Sexual Desire Disorder

A. Persistently or recurrently deficient (or absent) sexual fantasies and desire for sexual activity. The judgment of deficiency or absence is made by the clinician, taking into account factors that affect sexual functioning, such as age and the context of the person's life.

B. The disturbance causes marked distress or interpersonal difficulty.

C. The sexual dysfunction is not better accounted for by another Axis I disorder (except another sexual dysfunction) and is not due exclusively to the direct physiological effects of a substance (e.g., a drug of abuse, a medication) or a general medical condition.

Specify type:
Lifelong type
Acquired type

Specify type:
Generalized type
Situational type

Specify:
Due to psychological factors
Due to combined factors

Table from DSM-IV, *Diagnostic and Statistical Manual of Mental Disorders,* ed 4. Copyright American Psychiatric Association, Washington, 1994. Used with permission.

Table 20.18
Diagnostic Criteria for Sexual Aversion Disorder

A. Persistent or recurrent extreme aversion to, and avoidance of, all (or almost all) genital sexual contact with a sexual partner.

B. The disturbance causes marked distress or interpersonal difficulty.

C. The sexual dysfunction is not better accounted for by another Axis I disorder (except another sexual dysfunction).

Specify type:
Lifelong type
Acquired type

Specify type:
Generalized type
Situational type

Specify:
Due to psychological factors
Due to combined factors

Table from DSM-IV, *Diagnostic and Statistical Manual of Mental Disorders,* ed 4. Copyright American Psychiatric Association, Washington, 1994. Used with permission.

Table 20.19
Diagnostic Criteria for Dyspareunia

A. Recurrent or persistent genital pain associated with sexual intercourse in either a male or a female.

B. The disturbance causes marked distress or interpersonal difficulty.

C. The disturbance is not caused exclusively by vaginismus or lack of lubrication, is not better accounted for by another Axis I disorder (except another sexual dysfunction) and is not due exclusively to the direct physiological effects of a substance (e.g., a drug of abuse, a medication) or a general medical condition.

Specify type:
Lifelong type
Acquired type

Specify type:
Generalized type
Situational type

Specify:
Due to psychological factors
Due to combined factors

Table from DSM-IV, *Diagnostic and Statistical Manual of Mental Disorders,* ed 4. Copyright American Psychiatric Association, Washington, 1994. Used with permission.

Table 20.20
Diagnostic Criteria for Vaginismus

A. Recurrent or persistent involuntary spasm of the musculature of the outer third of the vagina that interferes with sexual intercourse.

B. The disturbance causes marked distress or interpersonal difficulty.

C. The disturbance is not better accounted for by another Axis I disorder (e.g., somatization disorder) and is not due exclusively to the direct physiological effects of a general medical condition.

Specify type:
Lifelong type
Acquired type

Specify type:
Generalized type
Situational type

Specify:
Due to psychological factors
Due to combined factors

Table from DSM-IV, *Diagnostic and Statistical Manual of Mental Disorders,* ed 4. Copyright American Psychiatric Association, Washington, 1994. Used with permission.

20.29–20.33

20.29. **The answer is B** (*Synopsis VII*, pages 655–657).

20.30. **The answer is B** (*Synopsis VII*, pages 655–657).

20.31. **The answer is B** (*Synopsis VII*, pages 655–657).

20.32. **The answer is C** (*Synopsis VII*, pages 655–657).

20.33. **The answer is D** (*Synopsis VII*, pages 655–657).

The fourth edition of *Diagnostic and Statistical Manual of Mental Disorders* (DSM-IV) defines a four-phase sexual response cycle: phase 1, desire; phase 2, excitement; phase 3, orgasm; phase 4, resolution.

The *desire phase* is distinct from any phase identified solely through physiology, and it reflects the psychiatrist's fundamental concern with motivations, drives, and personality. The phase is characterized by sexual fantasies and the desire to have sexual activity.

The *excitement phase* is brought on by psychological stimulation (fantasy or the presence of a love object) or physiological stimulation (stroking or kissing) or a combination of the two. It consists of a subjective sense of pleasure. The excitement phase is characterized by penile tumescence leading to erection in the man and by *vaginal lubrication* in the woman. Initial excitement may last several minutes to several hours. With continued stimulation, the woman's vaginal barrel shows a characteristic constriction along the outer third, known as the orgasmic platform, and the man's testes increase in size 50 percent and elevate.

The *orgasm phase* consists of a peaking of sexual pleasure, with the release of sexual tension and the rhythmic contraction of the perineal muscles and the pelvic reproductive organs. A subjective sense of ejaculatory inevitability triggers the man's orgasm. The forceful emission of semen follows. The male orgasm is also associated with four to five rhythmic spasms of the prostate, seminal vesicles, vas, and urethra. In the woman, orgasm is characterized by 3 to 15 involuntary contractions of the lower third of the vagina and by strong sustained contractions of the uterus, flowing from the fundus downward to the cervix. Blood pressure rises 20 to 40 mm (both systolic and diastolic), and the heart rate increases up to 160 beats a minute. Orgasm lasts from 3 to 25 seconds and is associated with a *slight clouding of consciousness.*

The *resolution phase* consists of the disgorgement of blood from the genitalia *(detumescence),* and that detumescence brings the body back to its resting state. If orgasm occurs, resolution is rapid; if it does not occur, resolution may take two to six hours and may be associated with irritability and discomfort.

Tables 20.21 and 20.22 describe the male and female sexual response cycles.

Table 20.21
Male Sexual Response Cycle

Organ	Excitement Phase	Orgasmic Phase	Resolution Phase
	Lasts several minutes to several hours; heightened excitement before orgasm, 30 seconds to 3 minutes	3 to 15 seconds	10 to 15 minutes; if no orgasm, ½ to 1 day
Skin	Just before orgasm; sexual flush inconsistently appears; maculopapular rash originates on abdomen and spreads to anterior chest wall, face, and neck and can include shoulders and forearms	Well-developed flush	Flush disappears in reverse order of appearance; inconsistently appearing film of perspiration on soles of feet and palms of hands
Penis	Erection in 10 to 30 seconds caused by vasocongestion of erectile bodies of corpus cavernosa of shaft; loss of erection may occur with introduction of asexual stimulus, loud noise; with heightened excitement, size of glans and diameter of penile shaft increase further	Ejaculation: emission phase marked by three to four contractions of 0.8 second of vas, seminal vesicles, prostate; ejaculation proper marked by contractions of 0.8 second of urethra and ejaculatory spurt of 12 to 20 inches at age 18, decreasing with age to seepage at 70	Erection: partial involution in 5 to 10 seconds with variable refractory period; full detumescence in 5 to 30 minutes
Scrotum and testes	Tightening and lifting of scrotal sac and elevation of testes; with heightened excitement, 50% increase in size of testes over unstimulated state and flattening against perineum, signaling impending ejaculation	No change	Decrease to baseline size because of loss of vasocongestion; testicular and scrotal descent within 5 to 30 minutes after orgasm; involution may take several hours if no orgasmic release takes place
Cowper's glands	2 to 3 drops of mucoid fluid that contain viable sperm are secreted during heightened excitement	No change	No change
Other	Breasts: inconsistent nipple erection with heightened excitement before orgasm Myotonia: semispastic contractions of facial, abdominal, and intercostal muscles Tachycardia: up to 175 a minute Blood pressure: rise in systolic 20 to 80 mm; in diastolic 10 to 40 mm Respiration: increased	Loss of voluntary muscular control Rectum: rhythmical contractions of sphincter Heart rate: up to 180 beats a minute Blood pressure: up to 40 to 100 mm systolic; 20 to 50 mm diastolic Respiration: up to 40 respirations a minute	Return to baseline state in 5 to 10 minutes

Table by Virginia A. Sadock, M.D.

Table 20.22
Female Sexual Response Cycle

Organ	Excitement Phase	Orgasmic Phase	Resolution Phase
	Lasts several minutes to several hours; heightened excitement before orgasm, 30 seconds to 3 minutes	3 to 15 seconds	10 to 15 minutes; if no orgasm, ½ to 1 day
Skin	Just before orgasm: sexual flush inconsistently appears; maculopapular rash originates on abdomen and spreads to anterior chest well, face, and neck; can include shoulders and forearms	Well-developed flush	Flush disappears in reverse order of appearance; inconsistently appearing film of perspiration on soles of feet and palms of hands
Breasts	Nipple erection in two thirds of women, venous congestion and areolar enlargement; size increases to one fourth over normal	Breasts may become tremulous	Return to normal in about ½ hour
Clitoris	Enlargement in diameter of glans and shaft; just before orgasm, shaft retracts into pupuce	No change	Shaft returns to normal position in 5 to 10 seconds; detumescence in 5 to 30 minutes; if no orgasm, detumescence takes several hours
Labia majora	Nullipara: elevate and flatten against perineum Multipara: congestion and edema	No change	Nullipara: increase to normal size in 1 to 2 minutes Multipara: decrease to normal size in 10 to 15 minutes
Labia minora	Size increase two to three times over normal; change to pink, red, deep red before orgasm	Contractions of proximal labia minora	Return to normal within 5 minutes
Vagina	Color change to dark purple; vaginal transudate appears 10 to 30 seconds after arousal; elongation and ballooning of vagina; lower third of vagina constricts before orgasm	3 to 15 contractions of lower third of vagina at intervals of 0.8 second	Ejaculate forms seminal pool in upper two thirds of vagina; congestion disappears in seconds or, if no orgasm, in 20 to 30 minutes
Uterus	Ascends into false pelvis; laborlike contractions begin in heightened excitement just before orgasm	Contractions throughout orgasm	Contractions cease, and uterus descends to normal position
Other	Myotonia A few drops of mucoid secretion from Bartholin's glands during heightened excitement Cervix swells slightly and is passively elevated with uterus	Loss of voluntary muscular control Rectum: rhythmical contractions of sphincter Hyperventilation and tachycardia	Return to baseline status in seconds to minutes Cervix color and size return to normal, and cervix descends into seminal pool

Table by Virginia A. Sadock, M.D.

Gender Identity Disorders

The terms "sex," "sexual orientation," "gender role," and "gender identity" refer to specific concepts that must be clearly differentiated to understand the gender identity disorders. "Sex," in this context, refers strictly to the anatomical and physiological characteristics that distinguish males from females (for example, a penis or a vagina). "Sexual orientation" refers to whether one is aroused by men or by women. Sexual orientation may be defined by one's object choice (for example, a man or a woman) and by one's erotic fantasy life. One's sexual orientation may be heterosexual, homosexual, or bisexual. "Gender role" refers to the way in which a person behaves that reflects and communicates an inner sense of maleness or femaleness. Gender role, when defined in that way, is irrevocably tied to cultural and social definitions of maleness and femaleness and, thus, may be different from culture to culture. "Gender identity" is a person's internal psychological sense and conviction of being either male or female, as reflected in the certainty to declare unequivocally, "I am a woman" or "I am a man." Gender identity disorders occur in persons who experience a persistent and intense sense of distress that their assigned gender is wrong. An anatomically and culturally defined male with a gender identity disorder may express the feeling that he is a woman trapped inside a man's body.

The fourth edition of *Diagnostic and Statistical Manual of Mental Disorders* (DSM-IV) simplifies the classification of gender identity disorders used in previous editions. In DSM-IV, only three diagnoses are described: gender identity disorder in children, gender identity disorder in adolescents and adults, and gender identity disorder not otherwise specified (NOS). In the revised third edition of *Diagnostic and Statistical Manual of Mental Disorders* (DSM-III-R), those disorders were classified under the

heading of disorders usually first evident in infancy, childhood, or adolescence. DSM-IV lists gender identity disorders under the heading of sexual and gender identity disorders. Onset in childhood or adolescence is no longer considered a defining criterion.

Traditionally, gender identity disorders have been described as occurring far more frequently in males than in females, with figures from gender identity clinics and sex-reassignment surgery centers reporting clear male preponderance. Whether those figures reflect true disparities between the sexes or a greater sensitivity to and concern about cross-gender-identified boys versus girls is unclear.

The causes of gender identity disorders are unclear. Some researchers have focused on biological factors—in particular, the role of prenatal sex hormones on the masculinization or the feminization of brain organization. Those studies are controversial. Most researchers in gender identity disorders have focused on psychosocial and postnatal factors that influence the development of gender identity, including such issues as the temperamental interplay between the child and the parents, the quality of the mother-child relationship in the first years of life, the role of the father, the effects of child abuse, and the child's reactions to a mother's death, extended absence, or depression.

The student should become familiar with the DSM-IV criteria required to make the diagnosis of gender identity disorder. Before a clinician can make the diagnosis, patients must have intense and persistent discomfort about their assigned sex and the desire to be the other sex or insistence that they are the other sex. The disorders do not cover persons who do not rigidly adhere to societal expectations or notions with regard to stereotypical male or female behavior. The disorders do cover patients with a strong conviction that they are not the sex they have been assigned and an all-consuming need or wish to be the opposite sex. Those patients often experience their genitals and secondary sex characteristics as repulsive, disgusting, and a continual source of distress.

According to DSM-IV, once the diagnosis of gender identity disorder is made, the patient's object of sexual attraction should be specified (male, female, both, or neither). In almost all cases, the patients do not consider themselves homosexual.

DSM-IV lists three examples of gender identity disorders not otherwise specified (NOS): (1) persons with intersex conditions and gender dysphoria; (2) adults with transient, stress-related cross-dressing behavior; and (3) persons who have a persistent preoccupation with castration or penectomy without a desire to acquire the sex characteristics of the opposite sex. Examples of intersex conditions include Turner's syndrome, Klinefelter's syndrome, adrenogenital syndrome, pseudohermaphroditism, and androgen insensitivity syndrome. The student should also be aware of the differences among transvestism, transsexualism, homosexuality, and heterosexuality.

Treatment of gender identity disorders involves a variety of behavioral, psychological, familial, pharmacological, and, at times, surgical approaches.

By studying Chapter 21 in *Kaplan and Sadock's Synopsis VII*, students will be prepared to test their knowledge with the questions and answers below.

HELPFUL HINTS

The student should know the gender identity syndromes and terms listed below.

gender identity	Turner's syndrome	gender confusion
gender role	dysgenesis	sex of rearing
gender identity disorder not	Klinefelter's syndrome	homosexual orientation
otherwise specified	adrenogenital syndrome	agenesis
transsexualism	pseudohermaphroditism	dysgenesis
cross-gender	hermaphroditism	male habitus
cross-dressing	androgen insensitivity syndrome	ambiguous genitals
assigned sex	testicular feminization syndrome	virilized genitals
transvestic fetishism	sex steroids	cryptorchid testis
homosexuality	genotype	buccal smear
asexual	phenotype	Barr chromatin body
intersex conditions	X-linked	

QUESTIONS

DIRECTIONS: Each of the incomplete statements below is followed by five suggested completions. Select the *one* that is *best* in each case.

21.1. Persons with gender identity disorder
A. usually try to maintain the gender role assigned by biological sex
B. are usually adults
C. usually assert that they will grow up to be members of the opposite sex
D. usually desire sex-change operations
E. usually achieve sexual excitement when cross-dressing

21.2. A boy with gender identity disorder
A. usually begin to display signs of the disorder after age 9
B. experiences sexual excitement when he cross-dresses
C. has boys as his preferred playmates
D. is treated with testosterone
E. may say that his penis or testes are disgusting

21.3. Girls with gender identity disorder in childhood
A. regularly have male companions
B. may refuse to urinate in a sitting position
C. may assert that they have or will grow a penis
D. give up masculine behavior by adolescence
E. are characterized by all the above

DIRECTIONS: Each group of questions below consists of lettered headings followed by a list of numbered statements. For each numbered statement, select the *one* lettered heading that is most closely associated with it. Each heading can be used once, more than once, or not at all.

Questions 21.4–21.7
A. Sexual identity
B. Sexual orientation
C. Gender identity
D. Gender role

21.4. Anatomical and physiological characteristics that indicate whether one is male or female

21.5. Reflects the inner sense of oneself as being male or female

21.6. The image of maleness versus femaleness that is communicated to others

21.7. A person's erotic-response tendency toward men or women or both

Questions 21.8–21.11

A 25-year-old patient called Charles requested a sex-change operation. Charles had for three years lived socially and been employed as a man. For the past two years, Charles had been the housemate, economic provider, and husband-equivalent of a bisexual woman who had fled from a bad marriage. Her two young children regarded Charles as their stepfather, and they had a strong affectionate bond.

In social appearance the patient passed as a not very virile man whose sexual development in puberty could be conjectured to have been delayed or hormonally deficient. Charles's voice was pitched low but was not baritone. Bulky clothing was worn to camouflage tightly bound, flattened breasts. A strap-on penis produced a masculine-looking bulge in the pants; it was so constructed that, in case of social necessity, it could be used as a urinary conduit in the standing position. Without success

the patient had tried to obtain a mastectomy so that in summer only a T-shirt could be worn while working outdoors as a heavy construction machine operator. Charles had also been unsuccessful in trying to get a prescription for testosterone to produce male secondary sex characteristics and to suppress menses. The patient wanted a hysterectomy and an oophorectomy and looked forward to obtaining a successful phalloplasty.

The patient's history was straightforward in its account of progressive recognition in adolescence of being able to fall in love only with a woman, following a tomboyish childhood that had finally consolidated into the transsexual role and identity.

A physical examination revealed normal female anatomy, which the patient found personally repulsive, incongruous, and a source of continual distress. The endocrine laboratory results were within normal limits for a woman.

A. Gender identity
B. Gender role
C. Sexual identity
D. Sexual orientation

21.8. Charles recognized in adolescence that she could fall in love only with a woman

21.9. Charles was regarded by the two young children of her housemate as their stepfather

21.10. The physical examination revealed normal female anatomy, and the endocrine laboratory results were within normal limits for a woman

21.11. In a subsequent interview, Charles stated that she viewed herself as a man

Questions 21.12–21.16

A. Klinefelter's syndrome
B. Turner's syndrome
C. Congenital virilizing adrenal hyperplasia
D. True hermaphroditism
E. Androgen insensitivity syndrome

21.12. A 17-year-old girl presented to a clinic with primary amenorrhea and no development of secondary sex characteristics. She was short in stature and had a webbed neck

21.13. A baby was born with ambiguous external genitalia. Further evaluation revealed that both ovaries and testes were present

21.14. A baby was born with ambiguous external genitalia. Further evaluation revealed that ovaries, a vagina, and a uterus were normal and intact. No testes were found

21.15. A buccal smear from a phenotypically female patient revealed that the patient was XY. A further workup revealed undescended testes

21.16. A tall, thin man who presented for infertility problems was found to be XXY

ANSWERS

Gender Identity Disorders

21.1. The answer is C (*Synopsis VII*, pages 682–683).

Persons with gender identity disorder *usually assert that they will grow up to be members of the opposite sex*. The essential feature of gender identity disorder is a persistent and intense distress about their assigned sex and the desire to be the other sex or an insistence that they are the other sex. Therefore, they *do not usually try to maintain the gender role assigned by biological sex*. The patients may be *adults* or children. Table 21.1 lists the diagnostic criteria for gender identity disorder.

The desire for sex-reassignment surgery occurs in less than 10 percent of gender identity disorder patients. Therefore, they *do not usually desire sex-change operations*. Persons who *achieve sexual excitement when cross-dressing* are given the diagnosis of transvestic fetishism, not gender identity disorder. The cross-dressing in gender identity disorder does not usually cause sexual excitement.

21.2. The answer is E (*Synopsis VII*, page 683).

A boy with gender identity disorder *may say that his penis or testes are disgusting* and that he would be better off without them. Persons with the disorder *usually begin to display signs of the disorder before age 4*, although it may present at any age. Cross-dressing may be part of the disorder, but boys *do not experience sexual excitement when they cross-dress*. A boy with a gender identity disorder is usually preoccupied with female stereotypical activities and usually *has girls as his preferred playmates, not boys*. Gender identity disorder *is not treated with testosterone*.

21.3. The answer is E (all) (*Synopsis VII*, page 683).

Girls with gender identity disorder in childhood *regularly have male companions* and an avid interest in sports and rough-and-tumble play; they show no interest in dolls and playing house. In a few cases a girl with the disorder *may refuse to urinate in a sitting position, may assert that she has or will grow a penis*, does not want to grow breasts or menstruate, and asserts that she will grow up to become a man. Most girls *give up masculine behavior by adolescence*.

21.4–21.7

21.4. The answer is A (*Synopsis VII*, pages 654–655 and 682).

21.5. The answer is C (*Synopsis VII*, pages 654–655 and 682).

21.6. The answer is D (*Synopsis VII*, pages 654–655 and 682).

21.7. The answer is B (*Synopsis VII*, pages 654–655 and 682).

Sexual identity (also known as biological sex), is strictly limited to the *anatomical and physiological characteristics that indicate whether one is male or female*.

Sexual orientation is a *person's erotic-response tendency toward men or women or both*. Sexual orientation takes into account one's object choice (man or woman) and one's fantasy life—for example, erotic fantasies about men or women or both.

Gender identity is a psychological state that *reflects the inner sense of oneself as being male or female*. Gender identity is based on culturally determined sets of attitudes, behavior patterns, and other attributes usually associated with masculinity or femininity. The person with a healthy gender identity is able to say with certainty, "I am male" or "I am female."

Gender role is the external behavioral pattern that reflects the person's inner sense of gender identity. It is a public declaration of gender; it is *the image of maleness versus femaleness that is communicated to others*.

21.8–21.11

21.8. The answer is D (*Synopsis VII*, pages 682–685).

21.9. The answer is B (*Synopsis VII*, pages 682–685).

21.10. The answer is C (*Synopsis VII*, pages 682–685).

21.11. The answer is A (*Synopsis VII*, pages 682–685).

When *Charles stated that she viewed herself as a man*, that was a statement of her *gender identity*. *Since Charles was regarded by the two young children of her housemate as their stepfather*, that revealed her masculine *gender role*. Charles's *sexual identity* was confirmed when *the physical examination revealed normal female anatomy, and the endocrine laboratory results were within normal limits for a woman*. Charles's expressed *sexual orientation* was

Table 21.1
Diagnostic Criteria for Gender Identity Disorder

A. A strong and persistent cross-gender identification (not merely a desire for any perceived cultural advantages of being the other sex).

In children, the disturbance is manifested by four (or more) of the following:

(1) repeatedly stated desire to be, or insistence that he or she is, the other sex
(2) in boys, preference for cross-dressing or simulating female attire; in girls, insistence on wearing only stereotypical masculine clothing
(3) strong and persistent preferences for cross-sex roles in make-believe play or persistent fantasies of being the other sex
(4) intense desire to participate in the stereotypical games and pastimes of the other sex
(5) strong preference for playmates of the other sex

In adolescents and adults, the disturbance is manifested by symptoms such as a stated desire to be the other sex, frequent passing as the other sex, desire to live or be treated as the other sex, or the conviction that one has the typical feelings and reactions of the other sex.

B. Persistent discomfort with his or her sex or sense of inappropriateness in the gender role of that sex.

In children, the disturbance is manifested by any of the following: in boys, assertion that his penis or testes are disgusting or will disappear or assertion that it would be better not to have a penis, or aversion toward rough-and-tumble play and rejection of male stereotypical toys, games, and activities; in girls, rejection of urinating in a sitting position, assertion that she has or will grow a penis, or assertion that she does not want to grow breasts or menstruate, or marked aversion towards normative feminine clothing.

In adolescents and adults, the disturbance is manifested by symptoms such as preoccupation with getting rid of one's primary and secondary sex characteristics (e.g., request for hormones, surgery, or other procedures to physically alter sexual characteristics to simulate the other sex) or belief that one was born the wrong sex.

C. The disturbance is not concurrent with a physical intersex condition.

D. The disturbance causes clinically significant distress or impairment in social, occupational, or other important areas of functioning.

Code based on current age:
    Gender identity disorder in childhood
    Gender identity disorder in adolescents or adults

Specify if (for sexually mature individuals):
    Sexually attracted to males
    Sexually attracted to females
    Sexually attracted to both
    Sexually attracted to neither

Table from DSM-IV, *Diagnostic and Statistical Manual of Mental Disorders*, ed 4. Copyright American Psychiatric Association, Washington, 1994. Used with permission.

---

toward the same sex, as was shown when she stated that she *recognized in adolescence that she could fall in love only with a woman.*

21.12–21.16

21.12. The answer is B (*Synopsis VII*, page 685).

21.13. The answer is D (*Synopsis VII*, page 686).

21.14. The answer is C (*Synopsis VII*, pages 685–686).

21.15. The answer is E (*Synopsis VII*, page 686).

21.16. The answer is A (*Synopsis VII*, page 685).

In *Turner's syndrome*, one sex chromosome is missing (XO). The result is an absence (agenesis) or minimal development (dysgenesis) of the gonads; no significant sex hormones, male or female, are produced in fetal life or postnatally. The sexual tissues remain in a female resting state. Because the second X chromosome, which seems to be responsible for full femaleness, is missing, the girls have an incomplete sexual anatomy and, lacking adequate estrogens, have *amenorrhea* and *develop no secondary sex characteristics* without treatment. They often suffer other stigmata, such as *webbed neck*, low posterior hairline margin, *short stature*, and cubitus valgus. The infant is born with normal-appearing female external genitals and so is unequivocally assigned to the female sex and is so reared. All the children develop as unremarkably feminine, heterosexually oriented girls.

True hermaphroditism is characterized by the presence of *both ovaries and testes* in the same person. The genitals' appearance at birth determines the sex assignment, and the core gender identity is male, female, or hermaphroditic, depending on the family's conviction about the child's sex. Usually, a panel of experts determine the sex of rearing; they base their decision on buccal smears, chromosome studies, and parental wishes.

Congenital virilizing adrenal hyperplasia results from an excess of androgen acting on the fetus. When the condition occurs in girls, excessive fetal androgens from the adrenal gland cause *ambiguous external genitals*, ranging from mild clitoral enlargement to external genitals that look like a normal scrotal sac, testes, and a penis; but they also have *ovaries, a vagina, and a uterus.*

Androgen insensitivity syndrome, a congenital X-linked recessive trait disorder, results from an inability of the target tissues to respond to androgens. Unable to respond, the fetal tissues remain in their female resting state, and the central nervous system is not organized as masculine. The infant at birth appears to be female, although she is later found to have *undescended testes*, which produce the testosterone to which the tissues do not respond, and minimal or absent internal sexual organs. Secondary sex characteristics at puberty are female because of the small but sufficient amounts of estrogens typically produced by the testes. The patients invariably sense themselves to be females and are feminine. Androgen insensitivity syndrome is diagnosed as a gender identity disorder not otherwise specified (Table 21.2).

In *Klinefelter's syndrome* the person (usually *XXY*) has a male habitus, under the influence of the Y chromosome, but the effect is weakened by the presence of the second X chromosome. Although the patient is born with a penis and testes, the testes are small and infertile, and the penis may also be small. Beginning in adolescence, some patients develop gynecomastia and other feminine-appearing contours. Their sexual desire is usually weak. Sex assignment and rearing should lead to a clear sense of maleness, but the patients often have gender disturbances, ranging from transsexualism to an intermittent desire to put on women's clothes. As a result of lessened androgen production, the fetal hypogonadal state in some patients seems to have interfered with the completion of the central nervous system organization that should underlie masculine behavior. In fact, many patients have a wide variability of psychopathology, ranging from emotional instability to mental retardation.

Table 21.2
Diagnostic Criteria for Gender Identity Disorder Not Otherwise Specified

This category is included for coding disorders in gender identity that are not classifiable as a specific gender identity disorder. Examples include

1. Intersex conditions (e.g., androgen insensitivity syndrome or congenital adrenal hyperplasia) and gender dysphoria
2. Transient, stress-related cross-dressing behavior
3. Persistent preoccupation with castration or penectomy without a desire to acquire the sex characteristics of the other sex

Table from DSM-IV, *Diagnostic and Statistical Manual of Mental Disorders,* ed 4. Copyright American Psychiatric Association, Washington, 1994. Used with permission.

Eating Disorders

Anorexia nervosa and bulimia nervosa are characterized by the wish to be thin and varying degrees of body-image distortion.

In the fourth edition of *Diagnostic and Statistical Manual of Mental Disorders* (DSM-IV), anorexia nervosa is characterized by a pervasive fear of becoming fat and such signs as the absence of at least three consecutive menstrual cycles. DSM-IV has two subtypes: restricting type and binge eating/purging type. In the restricting type the person restricts food intake but does not engage regularly in binge eating, purging, or vomiting; in the binge eating/purging type the person does regularly engage in those activities. Anorexia nervosa runs a course ranging from spontaneous remission to death.

Both anorexia nervosa and bulimia nervosa are most common in young women, usually beginning in the midteenage years, and are most common in highly developed countries. Bulimia nervosa is more common than anorexia nervosa and is characterized by recurrent episodes of eating large amounts of food and by recurrent behaviors aimed at ridding the body of food (self-induced vomiting, misuse of diuretics and laxatives, fasting, and excessive exercise). One difference between anorexia and bulimia nervosa is that persons with bulimia nervosa tend to maintain their normal weight, whereas persons with anorexia nervosa refuse to maintain their weight at or above a minimum expected level. DSM-IV has two types of bulimia nervosa: purging type and nonpurging type. In the purging type the person regularly engages in

self-induced vomiting or the misuse of laxatives or diuretics; in the nonpurging type the person uses other behaviors to control weight, such as fasting and excessive exercise.

Biological, social and psychological factors have all been investigated as causes of eating disorders. The serotonin and norepinephrine transmitters have been implicated, as have endogenous opiates and endorphins. A family history of depression has been recognized in both anorexia nervosa and bulimia nervosa. The persons with the disorders tend to be high achievers who respond to many internal and external expectations and who struggle with issues of autonomy, control, and psychological separation from their families.

The treatment of eating disorders involves a complex interaction of individual therapy, group therapy, family therapy, and pharmacotherapy. Although patients with anorexia nervosa and patients with bulimia nervosa are similar in a number of respects, they differ in many other respects. For example, they differ in their responses to antidepressant medications. Bulimia nervosa patients tend to have a much more favorable response to pharmacotherapy than do anorexia nervosa patients, who usually do not respond well to any specific medication.

Students should study Chapter 22 of *Kaplan and Sadock's Synopsis VII*. They can then test their knowledge by studying the questions and answers below.

HELPFUL HINTS

The student should know and be able to define the terms below.

anorexia nervosa
bulimia nervosa
geophagia
Kleine-Levin syndrome
pyloric stenosis
aversive conditioning
amenorrhea
obsessive-compulsive disorder
lanugo
edema
hypothermia

LH
ACTH
MHPG
T waves
denial
hypokalemic alkalosis
ST segment depression
ECT
binge eating
postbinge anguish

Klüver-Bucy-like syndrome
hypersexuality
hyperphagia
borderline personality disorder
hypersomnia
imipramine (Tofranil)
eating disorder not otherwise
   specified
cyproheptadine (Periactin)
self-stimulation

QUESTIONS

DIRECTIONS: Each of the incomplete statements below is followed by five suggested completions. Select the *one* that is *best* in each case.

22.1. Studies of anorexia nervosa have found that
A. the most common age of onset is the late 20s
B. good sexual adjustment is frequently described
C. most patients are interested in psychiatric treatment
D. sisters of anorexia nervosa patients are not likely to be afflicted
E. compulsive stealing, usually of candy and laxatives, is common

22.2. A person with anorexia nervosa
A. disproportionately consumes foods high in carbohydrates
B. usually retains her menstrual period
C. may not also have somatization disorder
D. may have either the restricting type or the binge eating/purging type
E. rarely has a family history of other mental disorders

22.3. Patients with bulimia nervosa
A. experience a postbinge euphoria
B. are usually underweight
C. usually do not induce vomiting
D. feel a lack of control of their eating during binge episodes
E. usually describe their parents as loving and accepting

22.4. Anorexia nervosa occurs
A. 10 to 20 times more often in females than in males
B. five times more often in males than in females
C. in 4 percent of adolescent girls
D. predominantly in the upper economic classes
E. with greatest frequency among young women in professions associated with food preparation

22.5. The patient in Figure 22.1 has rejected all food and has lost more than 30 percent of her original body weight. No physical illness has been found to account for the weight loss. One may also expect to find
A. an intense fear of becoming fat
B. denial of emaciation by the patient
C. feelings of hunger
D. a warm, seductive, and passive father
E. all the above

22.6. Anorexia nervosa has a mortality rate of up to
A. 1 percent
B. 18 percent
C. 30 percent
D. 42 percent
E. 50 percent

22.7. Anorexia nervosa is characterized by all the following *except*
A. self-imposed dietary limitations
B. weight loss
C. normal menses
D. intense fear of gaining weight
E. disturbed body image

22.8. Characteristics of binge eating disorder include
A. recurrent episodes of binge eating
B. inappropriate compensatory behaviors characteristic of bulimia nervosa
C. binge eating that occurs at least twice a week for less than six months
D. fixation on body weight
E. all the above

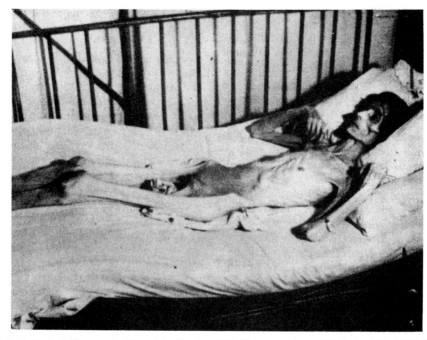

Figure 22.1. Patient who lost 30 percent of her original body weight. (Figure courtesy of Katherine Halmi, M.D.)

Questions 22.9–22.10

Mary was a gaunt 15-year-old high school student evaluated at the insistence of her parents, who were concerned about her weight loss. She was 5 feet 3 inches tall and had obtained her greatest weight of 100 pounds a year earlier. Shortly thereafter she decided to lose weight to be more attractive. She felt chubby and thought she would be more appealing if she were thinner. She first eliminated all carbohydrate-rich foods and gradually increased her dieting until she was eating only a few vegetables a day. She also started a vigorous exercise program. Within six months, she was down to 80 pounds. She then became preoccupied with food and started to collect recipes from magazines to prepare gourmet meals for her family. She had difficulty in sleeping and was irritable and depressed, having several crying spells every day. Her menses had started last year, but she had had only a few normal periods.

Mary had always obtained high grades in school and had spent a great deal of time studying. She had never been active socially and had never dated. She was conscientious and perfectionistic in everything she undertook. She had never been away from home as long as a week. Her father was a business manager. Her mother was a housewife who for the past two years had had a problem with hypoglycemia and had been on a low-carbohydrate diet.

During the interview, Mary said she felt fat, even though she weighed only 80 pounds, and she described a fear of losing control and eating so much food that she would become obese. She did not feel she was ill and thought that hospitalization was unnecessary.

22.4. The diagnosis of anorexia nervosa can be made on the basis of Mary's
A. 20-pound weight loss
B. her feeling fat at a weight of 80 pounds and a height of 5 feet 3 inches
C. her having had only a few normal periods
D. her fear of becoming obese
E. all the above

22.10. Features associated with anorexia nervosa include
A. onset between the ages of 10 and 30
B. lanugo
C. mortality rates from 5 to 18 percent
D. the fact that 4 to 6 percent of those affected are male

DIRECTIONS: The questions below consist of lettered headings followed by a list of numbered phrases. For each numbered phrase, select

    A.   if the item is associated with *A only*
    B.   if the item is associated with *B only*
    C.   if the item is associated with *both A and B*
    D.   if the item is associated with *neither A nor B*

Questions 22.11–22.18

    A.   Anorexia nervosa
    B.   Bulimia nervosa
    C.   Both
    D.   Neither

22.11. Must have the absence of at least three consecutive menstrual cycles

22.12. May engage in binge eating and purging behaviors

22.13. Preoccupied with weight, food, and body shape

22.14. Most remain sexually active

22.15. Denies symptoms and resists treatment

22.16. Body weight of less than 85 percent of the patient's normal weight

22.17. Tricyclic drugs have been successfully used

22.18. Usually experiences loss of appetite

ANSWERS

Eating Disorders

22.1. The answer is E (*Synopsis VII*, page 691).

Compulsive stealing, usually of candy and laxatives, is common. The *most common age of onset is between the ages of 13 and 20 years.* In few patients does the disorder develop in the late 20s. *Poor sexual adjustment is frequently described* in patients with the disorder. Many adolescent anorexia nervosa patients have delayed psychosocial sexual development, and adults often have a markedly decreased interest in sex. *Most patients are uninterested in psychiatric treatment* and even resistant to it; they are brought to a doctor's office unwillingly by agonizing relatives or friends. The patients rarely accept the recommendation of hospitalization without arguing and criticizing the program being offered. The intense fear of gaining weight undoubtedly contributes to the patients' lack of interest and even resistance to therapy. *Sisters of anorexia nervosa patients are likely to be afflicted,* but that association may reflect social influences more than genetic factors.

22.2. The answer is D (*Synopsis VII*, pages 691–692).

A person with anorexia nervosa *may have either the restricting type or the binge eating/purging type.* Persons with the restricting type limit their food selection, take in as few calories as possible, and often have obsessive-compulsive traits with respect to food and other matters. However, they do not regularly engage in binge eating or purging behavior (for example, self-induced vomiting or the misuse of laxatives or diuretics) during the episode of anorexia nervosa. Persons with the binge eating/purging type do regularly engage in binge eating or purging behavior during the episode of anorexia nervosa.

Regardless of type, persons with anorexia nervosa *disproportionately decrease their consumption of foods high in carbohydrates* and fats.

For anorexia nervosa to be diagnosed (Table 22.1), a woman who is postmenarche must have experienced the absence of at least three consecutive menstrual cycles. Thus, a woman with anorexia nervosa *does not retain her menstrual period.*

Weight fluctuations, vomiting, and peculiar food handling may occur in somatization disorder. On rare occasions a patient fulfills the diagnostic criteria for both somatization disorder and anorexia nervosa; in such a case both diagnoses should be made. Therefore, patients with anorexia nervosa *may also have somatization disorder.*

A patient with anorexia nervosa *is likely to have*

Table 22.1
Diagnostic Criteria for Anorexia Nervosa

A. Refusal to maintain body weight at or above a minimally normal weight for age and height (e.g., weight loss leading to maintenance of body weight less than 85% of that expected; or failure to make expected weight gain during period of growth, leading to body weight less than 85% of that expected).

B. Intense fear of gaining weight or becoming fat, even though underweight.

C. Disturbance in the way in which one's body weight or shape is experienced, undue influence of body weight or shape on self-evaluation, or denial of the seriousness of the current low body weight.

D. In post-menarchal females, amenorrhea, i.e., the absence of at least three consecutive menstrual cycles. (A woman is considered to have amenorrhea if her periods occur only following hormone, e.g., estrogen, administration.)

Specify type:
   Restricting type: during the current episode of anorexia nervosa, the person has not regularly engaged in binge-eating or purging behavior (i.e., self-induced vomiting or the misuse of laxatives, diuretics, or enemas)
   Binge eating/purging type: during the current episode of anorexia nervosa, the person has regularly engaged in binge-eating or purging behavior (i.e., self-induced vomiting or the misuse of laxatives, diuretics, or enemas)

Table from DSM-IV, *Diagnostic and Statistical Manual of Mental Disorders,* ed 4. Copyright American Psychiatric Association, Washington, 1994. Used with permission.

a family history of other mental disorders, such as depressive disorders, alcohol use disorder, and eating disorders.

22.3. The answer is D (*Synopsis VII*, pages 695–696).

Patients with bulimia nervosa (Table 22.2) *feel a lack of control of their eating during binge episodes.* The binge eating is often followed by feelings of guilt, depression, or self-disgust. Bulimia nervosa patients *do not experience a postbinge euphoria.* Unlike anorexia nervosa patients, those with bulimia nervosa *are not usually underweight.* Patients with bulimia nervosa *usually induce vomiting* by sticking a finger down the throat, although some patients are able to vomit at will. Bulimia nervosa patients usually *describe their parents as neglectful and rejecting, not loving and accepting.*

Table 22.2
Diagnostic Criteria for Bulimia Nervosa

A. Recurrent episodes of binge eating. An episode of binge eating is characterized by both of the following:

(1) eating, in a discrete period of time (e.g., within any 2-hour period), an amount of food that is definitely larger than most people would eat during a similar period of time and under similar circumstances

(2) a sense of lack of control over eating during the episode (e.g., a feeling that one cannot stop eating or control what or how much one is eating)

B. Recurrent inappropriate compensatory behavior in order to prevent weight gain, such as self-induced vomiting; misuse of laxatives, diuretics, enemas, or other medications; fasting; or excessive exercise.

C. The binge eating and inappropriate compensatory behaviors both occur, on average, at least twice a week for 3 months.

D. Self-evaluation is unduly influenced by body shape and weight.

E. The disturbance does not occur exclusively during episodes of anorexia nervosa.

Specify type:

Purging type: during the current episode of bulimia nervosa, the person has regularly engaged in self-induced vomiting or the misuse of laxatives, diuretics, or enemas

Nonpurging type: during the current episode of bulimia nervosa, the person has used other inappropriate compensatory behaviors, such as fasting or excessive exercise, but has not regularly engaged in self-induced vomiting or the misuse of laxatives, diuretics, or enemas

Table from DSM-IV, *Diagnostic and Statistical Manual of Mental Disorders,* ed 4. Copyright American Psychiatric Association, Washington, 1994. Used with permission.

22.4.   The answer is A (*Synopsis VII*, page 689).

Anorexia nervosa occurs *10 to 20 times more often in females than in males.* Anorexia nervosa is estimated to occur *in about 0.5 percent of adolescent girls.* Although the disorder was initially reported *predominantly in the upper economic classes,* recent epidemiological surveys do not show that distribution. The disorder may be seen *with greatest frequency among young women in professions that require thinness,* such as modeling and ballet, *not professions associated with food preparation.*

22.5.   The answer is E (all) (*Synopsis VII*, pages 689–692).

The patient is suffering from anorexia nervosa, which is characterized by a weight loss leading to the maintenance of body weight less than 85 percent of that expected. Anorexia nervosa patients have *an intense fear of becoming fat,* a disturbance of body image, and amenorrhea patients *deny that they are emaciated,* and they *do not lose their feelings of hunger* but steadfastly refuse to eat.

Psychodynamic theories in anorexia nervosa postulate that the patients reject, through starvation, a wish to be pregnant and have fantasies of oral impregnation. Other dynamic formulations have included a dependent relationship with *a warm, seductive, and passive father* and guilt over aggression toward an ambivalently regarded mother.

22.6.   The answer is B (*Synopsis VII*, page 693).

Studies have shown that anorexia nervosa has a range of mortality rates from 5 percent to *18 percent.*

22.7.   The answer is C (*Synopsis VII*, pages 689–693).

Anorexia nervosa is characterized in women by *amenorrhea, not normal menses.* It is also characterized by *self-imposed dietary limitations,* behavior directed toward losing weight, peculiar patterns of handling food, *weight loss, intense fear of gaining weight and disturbance of body image.*

22.8.   The answer is A (*Synopsis VII*, page 698).

Binge eating disorder (Table 22.3) is characterized by *recurrent episodes of binge eating* in *the absence of the inappropriate compensatory behaviors characteristic of bulimia nervosa.* The binge eating *occurs,* on average, *at least twice a week for at least six months.* Patients with eating disorder are *not fixated on body weight.* Binge eating disorder is an example of eating disorder not otherwise specified (Table 22.4).

22.9.   The answer is E (all) (*Synopsis VII*, pages 690–692).

The diagnosis of anorexia nervosa can be made on the basis of *Mary's 20-pound weight loss, her feeling fat at a weight of 80 pounds and a height of 5 feet 3 inches, her having had only a few normal periods,* and *her fear of becoming obese.*

22.10.   The answer is E (all) (*Synopsis VII*, pages 689–693).

Features associated with anorexia nervosa include *onset between the ages of 10 and 30, lanugo* (neonatallike body hair), *mortality rates from 5 to 18 percent,* and *the fact that 4 to 6 percent of those affected are male.*

22.11–22.18

22.11.   The answer is A (*Synopsis VII*, pages 689–693).

22.12.   The answer is C (*Synopsis VII*, pages 689–693 and 695–607).

22.13.   The answer is C (*Synopsis VII*, pages 689–693 and 695–697).

22.14.   The answer is B (*Synopsis VII*, pages 695–697).

Table 22.3
Research Criteria for Binge Eating Disorder

A. Recurrent episodes of binge eating. An episode of binge eating is characterized by both of the following:

(1) eating, in a discrete period of time (e.g., within any 2-hour period) an amount of food that is definitely larger than most people would eat in a similar period of time under similar circumstances

(2) a sense of lack of control over eating during the episode (e.g., a felling that one cannot stop eating or control what or how much one is eating)

B. The binge-eating episodes are associated with three (or more) of the following:

(1) eating much more rapidly than normal
(2) eating until feeling uncomfortably full
(3) eating large amounts of food when not feeling physically hungry
(4) eating alone because of being embarrassed by how much one is eating
(5) feeling disgusted with oneself, depressed, or feeling very guilty after overeating

C. Marked distress regarding binge eating is present.

D. The binge eating occurs, on average, at least 2 days a week for 6 months.

Note: The method of determining frequency differs from that used for bulimia nervosa; future research should address whether the preferred method of setting a frequency threshold is counting the number of days on which binges occur or counting the number of episodes of binge eating.

E. The binge eating is not associated with the regular use of inappropriate compensatory behaviors (e.g., purging, fasting, excessive exercise) and does not occur exclusively during the course of anorexia nervosa or bulimia nervosa.

Table from DSM-IV, *Diagnostic and Statistical Manual of Mental Disorders,* ed 4. Copyright American Psychiatric Association, Washington, 1994. Used with permission.

22.15. **The answer is A** (*Synopsis VII*, pages 689–693).

22.16. **The answer is A** (*Synopsis VII*, pages 689–693).

22.17. **The answer is C** (*Synopsis VII*, pages 694 and 697–698).

22.18. **The answer is D** (*Synopsis VII*, pages 689–693 and 695–697).

To meet the diagnostic criteria for *anorexia nervosa*, postmenarchal females *must have an absence of at least three consecutive menstrual cycles*. Patients

Table 22.4
Diagnostic Criteria for Eating Disorder Not Otherwise Specified

The eating disorder not otherwise specified category is for disorders of eating that do not meet the criteria for any specific eating disorder. Examples include

1. For females, all of the criteria for anorexia nervosa are met except the individual has regular menses.
2. All of the criteria for anorexia nervosa are met except that, despite significant weight loss, the individual's current weight is in the normal range.
3. All of the criteria for bulimia nervosa are met except that the binge eating and inappropriate compensatory mechanisms occur at a frequency of less than twice a week or for a duration of less than 3 months.
4. The regular use of inappropriate compensatory behavior by an individual of normal body weight after eating small amounts of food (e.g., self-induced vomiting after the consumption of two cookies).
5. Repeatedly chewing and spitting out, but not swallowing, large amounts of food.
6. Binge-eating disorder: recurrent episodes of binge eating in the absence of the regular use of inappropriate compensatory behaviors characteristic of bulimia nervosa.

Table from DSM-IV, *Diagnostic and Statistical Manual of Mental Disorders,* ed 4. Copyright American Psychiatric Association, Washington, 1994. Used with permission.

with anorexia nervosa are often secretive, *deny their symptoms, and resist treatment.* The diagnostic criteria include a persistent refusal to maintain body weight at or above a minimum expected weight (for example, loss of weight leading to a *body weight of less than 85 percent of the patient's expected weight*) or a failure to gain the expected weight during a period of growth, leading to a body weight less than 85 percent of the expected weight.

Most bulimia nervosa patients remain sexually active, in contrast to anorexia nervosa patients, who are not interested in sex. Antidepressant medications can reduce binge eating and purging independent of the presence of a mood disorder. Thus, for particularly difficult binge-purge cycles that are not responsive to psychotherapy alone, *tricyclic drugs have been successfully used.*

Both bulimia nervosa patients and patients with the binge eating/purging type of anorexia nervosa *may engage in binge eating and purging behaviors. Both* persons with anorexia nervosa and persons with bulimia nervosa are excessively *preoccupied with weight, food, and body shape.*

Neither anorexia nervosa patients nor bulimia nervosa patients *experience loss of appetite.*

Normal Sleep
and Sleep Disorders

Research into sleep tends to focus on two areas: (1) basic sleep architecture and physiology and (2) sleep problems. Sleep architecture is divided into two physiological states: nonrapid eye movement (NREM) sleep and rapid eye movement (REM) sleep.

NREM sleep comprises four stages and accounts for about 75 percent of all sleep. Stage 1, the lightest stage of sleep, is characterized by low-voltage, regular activity on an electroencephalogram (EEG). Stage 2 is characterized by frequent spindle-shaped tracings and slow triphasic waves. Stage 3 is characterized by the initial appearance of high-voltage delta waves. Stage 4 is characterized by the predominance of delta waves. Stages 3 and 4 are often described as delta sleep or slow-wave sleep because of how they appear on an EEG. Most physiological functioning is greatly reduced during NREM sleep.

REM sleep is characterized by a highly active brain and accounts for about 25 percent of all sleep. REM latency is the amount of time between sleep onset and the appearance of the first REM episode of the night. The typical REM latency in normal adults is 90 minutes. A decreased REM latency may characteristically appear in such disorders as major depressive disorder and narcolepsy.

In general, NREM sleep is normally a quiescent state. The person's pulse rate, respiration, blood pressure, and resting muscle potential are lower in NREM sleep than when awake. Cerebral blood flow is reduced, rapid eye movements are few, and penile erections are rare. The deepest stages of NREM sleep, stages 3 and 4, may be associated with unusual arousal patterns. Typically, if a person is awakened in stage 3 or 4, the person experiences disorganization, confusion, and amnesia for events that

occur during the arousal. Several specific sleep disorders, such as sleepwalking disorder and sleep terror disorder are associated with slow-wave or stages 3 and 4 sleep.

REM sleep has been termed paradoxical sleep because, from polysomnographic recordings and various physiological monitorings during REM periods, the person shows patterns close to waking patterns. The person's pulse, respiration, blood pressure, and brain oxygen use are all increased during REM sleep. Partial or full penile erections occur during almost every REM period, a fact that helps in the workup of the cause of impotence. The person experiences near-total paralysis of the skeletal or postural muscles and alterations in the body's thermoregulation during REM sleep. The most distinctive feature of REM sleep is dreaming. Sixty to 90 percent of all persons awakened during REM sleep report that they were dreaming.

Normal sleep is regularly cyclical. A REM period occurs about every 90 minutes during the night. The first REM period is the shortest, and most REM periods normally occur in the last third of the night. Most stage 4 sleep occurs in the first third of the night. In some disorders the regularity of the cycle is disrupted. For instance, in a significant number of people with major depressive disorder, the sleep cycle is backward: The REM latency is often 20 to 40 minutes; the highest percentage of REM sleep occurs early in the sleep cycle, usually in the first third of sleep; and the REM periods are longest in the early parts of the night. Concomitantly, stage 4 sleep is decreased overall and is pushed into the late parts of the night.

Sleep regulation involves a complex interaction of neurotransmitters, including serotonin, norepinephrine, acetylcholine, and dopamine. Many antidepressants suppress REM sleep, perhaps rebalancing the relationship between REM and NREM sleep.

Disorders of sleep are common. About one third of all American adults experience some type of sleep disorder in their lifetimes. Insomnia is the most common sleep disorder.

The fourth edition of *Diagnostic and Statistical Manual of Mental Disorders* (DSM-IV) lists three major categories of sleep disorders: primary sleep disorders, sleep disorders related to another mental disorder, and other sleep disorders—in particular, sleep disorder due to a general medical condition and substance-induced sleep disorder.

The primary sleep disorders are dyssomnias and parasomnias. The dyssomnias, a heterogeneous group of disorders involving disrupted sleep, include primary insomnia, primary hypersomnia, narcolepsy, breathing-related sleep disorder, circadian rhythm sleep disorder, and dyssomnia not otherwise specified (NOS). The parasomnias are unusual or undesirable phenomena that occur suddenly during sleep or on the boundary between waking and sleeping. Parasomnias usually occur during stages 3 and 4 of NREM sleep; thus, recall of the phenomenon is usually impaired. The parasomnias include nightmare disorder (dream anxiety disorder), sleep terror disorder, sleepwalking disorder, and parasomnia not otherwise specified (NOS).

Primary insomnia occurs independently of any known physical or mental condition. It is characterized by persistent difficulty in initiating or maintaining sleep. Primary hypersomnia is characterized by persistent excessive sleepiness associated with manifestations of disordered REM sleep. In narcolepsy, REM latency is reduced to only 10 minutes of sleep onset. Other manifestations of narcolepsy include hypnopompic and hypnagogic hallucinations, vivid and often frightening perceptual experiences, cataplexy, and persistent sleep paralysis while awake and conscious.

Breathing-related sleep disorder is characterized by apnea, hypoapnea, and oxygen depletion, which usually produce hypersomnia but can also lead to insomnia. Circadian rhythm sleep disorder is associated with a misalignment between desired and actual sleep pe-

riods. Examples of conditions leading to circadian rhythm sleep disorder include jet lag, shift work, and delayed sleep phase (difficulty in falling asleep at a desired conventional time, often associated with daytime sleepiness).

Dyssomnia NOS includes nocturnal myoclonus (abrupt leg jerking during sleep), restless legs syndrome (relentless deep sensations of creeping inside the calves, associated with irresistible urges to move the legs, leading to sleep disruption), menstrual-associated syndrome (intermittent marked hypersomnia at or shortly before the onset of menses), and sleep drunkenness (an abnormal type of awakening in which the transition from sleep to being fully awake is prolonged and exaggerated).

Parasomnias include nightmare disorder, sleep terror disorder, sleepwalking disorder, and parasomnia NOS. Nightmare disorder, unlike most other parasomnias, occurs during REM sleep, usually after a long REM period late in the night. Most persons with recurrent nightmares awake frightened and are able to recall and describe the details of the dream. Sleep terror disorder occurs during deep NREM sleep, stages 3 and 4 sleep. Persons with sleep terror disorder often sit up in bed, appear to be terrified, and may either remain awake but disoriented and confused or, more commonly, fall asleep and have no memory of the episode. Drugs that suppress REM sleep, such as tricyclic drugs, may help reduce the frequency of nightmares; drugs that suppress stages 3 and 4 sleep, such as benzodiazepines, may help eliminate sleep terror disorder. Sleepwalking disorder is also a disorder of deep NREM sleep and is most often associated with lack of memory of the episode. It is most often treated with drugs that suppress stages 3 and 4 sleep. Sleepwalking is common in both children and adults. It occurs in all stages of sleep and, if not accompanied by sleep terror disorder, requires no treatment. Parasomnia NOS includes medical conditions exacerbated during sleep—for example, nocturnal angina.

Sleep disorders related to another mental disorder include insomnia related to Axis I or Axis II disorder (for example, insomnia due to major depressive disorder) and hypersomnia related to Axis I or Axis II disorder (for example, hypersomnia due to bipolar I disorder).

In sleep disorder due to a general medical condition, an accurate diagnosis can lead to effective treatment of the underlying general medical condition. Examples include sleep-related epileptic seizures (seizures that occur almost exclusively during sleep), sleep-related cluster headaches and chronic paroxysmal hemicrania (sleep-exacerbated vascular headaches associated with REM sleep), sleep-related asthma (asthma exacerbated by sleep), and sleep-related gastroesophageal reflex (awakening from sleep with burning, substernal pain or a sour taste in the mouth).

Substances such as central nervous system (CNS) stimulants, antidepressants, and sedative-hypnotics can cause many types of sleep disorders, including hypersomnia, insomnia, and parasomnias. The sleep disorders can be caused by substance intoxication or withdrawal. Sleep disorders can also be caused by a wide variety of other drugs, including antimetabolites and other anticancer drugs, anticonvulsants, antidepressants, and oral contraceptives.

Students should review Chapter 23 in *Kaplan and Sadock's Synopsis VII* before challenging their level of knowledge with the questions and answers below.

HELPFUL HINTS

The student should know and be able to define each of the terms listed below.

normal sleep	narcolepsy	sleep-related bruxism
EEG	variable sleepers	sleep-related (nocturnal)
REM, NREM	sleep apnea	myoclonus syndrome
K complexes	alveolar hypoventilation syndrome	dysesthesia
poikilothermic	sleep paralysis, sleep attacks	jactatio capitis nocturna
L-Tryptophan	idiopathic CNS hypersomnolence	familial sleep paralysis
melatonin	microsleeps	sleep-related cluster headaches
sleep deprivation, REM-deprived	Kleine-Levin syndrome	and chronic paroxysmal
dyssomnias	sleep drunkenness	hemicrania
parasomnias	circadian rhythm sleep disorder	sleep-related abnormal swallowing
insomnia	delayed sleep phase syndrome	syndrome
transient	advanced sleep phase syndrome	sleep-related asthma
persistent	sleepwalking disorder	sleep-related cardiovascular
nonorganic	somniloquy	symptoms
organic	pavor nocturnus, incubus	sleep-related gastroesophageal
primary	nightmares	reflux
secondary	nightmare disorder	paroxysmal nocturnal
hypersomnia	sleep terror disorder	hemoglobinuria
somnolence	sleep-related epileptic seizures	

QUESTIONS

DIRECTIONS: Each of the questions or incomplete statements below is followed by five suggested responses or completions. Select the *one* that is *best* in each case.

23.1. The characteristic electroencephalographic (EEG) patterns from a wakeful state to sleep are
A. alpha waves, delta waves, 3 to 7 cycles a second, sleep spindles and K complexes
B. alpha waves, 3 to 7 cycles a second, delta waves, sleep spindles and K complexes
C. alpha waves, sleep spindles and K complexes, delta waves, 3 to 7 cycles a second
D. alpha waves, delta waves, sleep spindles and K complexes, 3 to 7 cycles a second
E. alpha waves, 3 to 7 cycles a second, sleep spindles and K complexes, delta waves

23.2. During rapid eye movement (REM) sleep
A. the pulse rate is typically 5 to 10 beats below the level of restful waking
B. a poikilothermic condition is present
C. frequent, involuntary body movements are seen
D. dreams are typically lucid and purposeful
E. sleepwalking may occur

23.3. In the fourth edition of *Diagnostic and Statistical Manual of Mental Disorders* (DSM-IV) category of dyssomnias
A. psychotherapy has been useful in the treatment of primary insomnia
B. narcolepsy is a psychogenic disturbance
C. nasal continuous positive airway pressure is the treatment of choice for obstructive sleep apnea
D. Kleine-Levin syndrome has insomnia as a major symptom
E. sleep drunkenness results from sleep deprivation

23.4. Sleep apnea is
A. pure obstructive sleep apnea when air flow and respiratory effort cease
B. believed to be a benign condition
C. usually found in men in their early 30s
D. called Pickwickian syndrome in obese patients
E. all the above

23.5. A 40-year-old man who snores loudly while sleeping and at times seems to stop breathing is likely to be suffering from
A. narcolepsy
B. catalepsy
C. sleep apnea
D. Kleine-Levin syndrome
E. hypersomnia primary

23.6. An 11-year old girl asked her mother to take her to a psychiatrist because she feared she was going crazy. Several times during the past two months she had awakened confused about where she was until she realized that she was on the living room couch or in her little sister's bed, even though she went to bed in her own room. When she woke up in her older brother's bedroom, she became concerned and felt guilty about it. Her younger sister said that she had seen the patient walking during the night, looking like "a zombie," that she did not answer when called, and that she had walked at night several times but usually went back to her bed. The patient feared she had amnesia because she had no memory of anything happening during the night.

The patient had no history of seizures or of similar episodes during the day. Electroencephalogram and physical examination results were normal. The patient's mental status was unremarkable except for some anxiety about her symptoms and the usual early adolescent concerns. Her school and family functioning were excellent.

The most likely diagnosis is
A. nightmare disorder
B. familial sleep paralysis
C. somniloquy
D. sleepwalking disorder
E. sleep terror disorder

23.7. Which of the following is involved in sleep and waking mechanisms?
A. Serotonin
B. Dopamine
C. Norepinephrine
D. Acetylcholine
E. All the above

23.8. Hypersomnia related to an Axis I or Axis II disorder may be the result of
A. major depressive disorder
B. amphetamine withdrawal
C. alcohol intoxication
D. jet lag
E. all the above

23.9. The symptoms of narcolepsy include
A. daytime sleepiness
B. cataplexy
C. sleep paralysis
D. hallucinations
E. all the above

23.10. Hypersomnia is associated with
A. Kleine-Levin syndrome
B. trypanosomiasis
C. depression
D. amphetamine withdrawal
E. all the above

DIRECTIONS: Each group of questions below consists of lettered headings followed by a list of numbered words or phrases. For each numbered word or phrase, select the *one* lettered heading that is most closely associated with it. Each lettered heading may be selected once, more than once, or not at all.

Questions 23.11–23.13
  A. Rapid eye movement (REM) sleep
  B. Nonrapid eye movement (NREM) sleep

23.11. Sleep terror disorder

23.12. Nightmare disorder

23.13. Sleepwalking disorder

Questions 23.14–23.18
  A. Sleep terror disorder
  B. Nocturnal myoclonus
  C. Jactatio capitis nocturnus
  D. Sleep-related hemolysis
  E. Sleep-related bruxism

23.14. Urge to move the legs

23.15. Brownish-red morning urine

23.16. Patient wakes up screaming

23.17. Head banging

23.18. Damage to the teeth

Questions 23.19–23.22
  A. REM sleep
  B. NREM sleep

23.19. Sleepwalking

23.20. Bed-wetting (enuresis)

23.21. Paroxysmal hemicrania

23.22. Erections

Questions 23.23–23.27
  A. Nightmares
  B. Night terrors

23.23. REM sleep

23.24. NREM sleep

23.25. Perseverative movements

23.26. Usually recalled in some detail

23.27. Usually followed by amnesia

Normal Sleep and Sleep Disorders

23.1. The answer is E (*Synopsis VII,* page 699).

The characteristic electroencephalographic (EEG) changes from a wakeful state to sleep are *alpha waves, 3 to 7 cycles a second, sleep spindles and K complexes, and delta waves.* The waking EEG is characterized by alpha waves of 8 to 12 cycles a second and low-voltage activity of mixed frequency. As the person falls asleep, alpha activity begins to disappear. Stage 1, considered the lightest stage of sleep, is characterized by low-voltage, regular activity at 3 to 7 cycles a second. After a few seconds or minutes, that stage gives way to stage 2, a pattern showing frequent spindle-shaped tracings at 12 to 14 cycles a second (sleep spindles) and slow triphasic waves known as K complexes. Soon thereafter, delta waves—high-voltage activity at 0.5 to 2.5 cycles a second—make their appearance and occupy less than 50 percent of the tracing (stage 3). Eventually, in stage 4, delta waves occupy more than 50 percent of the record. It is common practice to describe stages 3 and 4 as delta sleep or slow-wave sleep because of their characteristic appearance on the EEG record.

23.2. The answer is B (*Synopsis VII,* pages 700–701).

During rapid eye movement (REM) sleep *a poikilothermic condition is present.* Poikilothermia is a state in which body temperature varies with the temperature of the surrounding medium. In contrast, a homeothermic condition is present during wakefulness and nonrapid eye movement (NREM) sleep; in that condition the body temperature remains constant regardless of the temperature of the surrounding medium.

In REM sleep *the pulse rate is not typically 5 to 10 beats below the level of restful waking;* that is characteristic of NREM sleep. In fact, pulse, respiration, and blood pressure in humans are all high during REM sleep—much higher than during NREM sleep and often higher than during waking. Because of motor inhibition, *body movement is absent* during REM sleep. *Dreams* during REM sleep *are typically abstract and unreal.* Dreaming does occur during NREM sleep, but it is typically lucid and purposeful. *Sleepwalking does not occur* in REM sleep but does occur during stages 3 and 4 of NREM sleep. The diagnostic criteria for sleepwalking disorder are listed in Table 23.1.

23.3. The answer is C (*Synopsis VII,* page 709).

Nasal continuous positive airway pressure is the treatment of choice for obstructive sleep apnea. Other

Table 23.1
Diagnostic Criteria for Sleepwalking Disorder

A. Repeated episodes of rising from bed during sleep and walking about, usually occurring during the first third of the major sleep episode.

B. While sleepwalking, the person has a blank, staring face, is relatively unresponsive to the efforts of others to communicate with him or her, and can be awakened only with great difficulty.

C. On awakening (either from the sleepwalking episode or the next morning), the person has amnesia for the episode.

D. Within several minutes after awakening from the sleepwalking episode, there is no impairment of mental activity or behavior (although there may initially be a short period of confusion or disorientation).

E. The sleepwalking causes clinically significant distress or impairment in social, occupational, or other important areas of functioning.

F. The disturbance is not due to the direct physiological effects of a substance (e.g., a drug of abuse, a medication) or a general medical condition.

Table from DSM-IV, *Diagnostic and Statistical Manual of Mental Disorders,* ed 4. Copyright American Psychiatric Association, Washington, 1994. Used with permission.

procedures include weight loss, nasal surgery; tracheotomy, and uvulopalatoplasty. No medications are consistently effective in normalizing sleep in specific patients.

Psychotherapy has not been useful in the treatment of primary insomnia. The condition is commonly treated with benzodiazepine hypnotics, chloral hydrate (Noctec), and other sedatives. Hypnotic drugs should be used with care. Various nonspecific measures—so called sleep hygiene—can be helpful in improving sleep. Light therapy is also used.

It is an abnormality of the sleep mechanisms—specifically, REM-inhibiting mechanisms.

Kleine-Levin syndrome does not have insomnia as a major symptom: in fact, just the opposite is true. Kleine-Levin syndrome is a relatively rare condition consisting of recurrent periods of prolonged sleep (from which the patient may be aroused) with intervening periods of normal sleep and alert waking.

Sleep drunkenness is an abnormal form of awakening in which the lack of a clear sensorium in the transition from sleep to full wakefulness is prolonged and exaggerated. *Sleep drunkenness does not result from sleep deprivation.*

The diagnostic criteria for breathing-related sleep

disorder are listed in Table 23.2. The diagnostic criteria for primary insomnia are listed in Table 23.3.

23.4. The answer is D (*Synopsis VII,* pages 709–710).

Sleep apnea, the cessation of air flow at the nose or the mouth, is *called Pickwickian syndrome in obese patients.* It is *pure obstructive sleep apnea when air flow ceases but respiratory effort increases* during apneic periods because that combination indicates an obstruction in the airway and increasing efforts by the abdominal and thoracic muscles to force air past the obstruction. Sleep apnea is *not believed to be a benign condition;* in fact it can be dangerous and is thought to account for a number of unexplained deaths. Sleep apnea is *not usually found in men in their 30s.* The most characteristic picture is of middle-aged or elderly men who report tiredness and in-

ability to stay awake in the daytime, sometimes associated with depression, mood changes, and daytime sleep attacks.

23.5. The answer is C (*Synopsis VII,* pages 708–709).

Sleep apnea is characterized by multiple apneas during sleep, loud snoring, and daytime sleepiness. *Narcolepsy* (Table 23.4) is a dyssomnia characterized by recurrent, brief, uncontrollable episodes of sleep. *Catalepsy* is a condition in which a person maintains the body position in which the body is placed. It is a symptom observed in severe cases of catatonic schizophrenia. It is also known as waxy flexibility and *cerea flexibilitas. Kleine-Levin syndrome* is a condition characterized by periodic episodes of hypersomnia and bulimia; it is most often seen in adolescent boys; it eventually disappears spontaneously. *Primary hypersomnia* (Table 23.5) is characterized by excessive time spent sleeping. It is not related to narcolepsy.

23.6. The answer is D (*Synopsis VIII,* page 712).

The most likely diagnosis of the 11-year-old girl's condition is *sleepwalking disorder.* Sleepwalking disorder consists of a sequence of complex behaviors initiated in the first third of the night during deep non-rapid eye movement (NREM) sleep (stages 3 and 4). The disorder consists of arising from bed during sleep and walking about, appearing unresponsive during the episode, amnestic for the sleepwalking on awakening, and no impairment in consciousness several minutes after awakening. Sleepwalking usually begins between ages 6 and 12 and tends to run in families.

Nightmare disorder consists of repeated awakenings from long, frightening dreams. The awakening usually occurs during the second half of the sleep period, during REM sleep. *Familial sleep paralysis* is

Table 23.2
Diagnostic Criteria for Breathing-Related Sleep Disorder

A. Sleep disruption, leading to excessive sleepiness or insomnia, that is judged to be due to a sleep-related breathing condition (e.g., obstructive or central sleep apnea syndrome or central alveolar hypoventilation syndrome).

B. The disturbance is not better accounted for by another mental disorder and is not due to the direct physiological effects of a substance (e.g., a drug of abuse, a medication) or another general medical condition (other than a breathing-related disorder).

Coding notes: Also code sleep-related breathing disorder on Axis III.

Table from DSM-IV, *Diagnostic and Statistical Manual of Mental Disorders,* ed 4. Copyright American Psychiatric Association, Washington, 1994. Used with permission.

Table 23.3
Diagnostic Criteria for Primary Insomnia

A. The predominant complaint is difficulty initiating or maintaining sleep, or nonrestorative sleep, for at least 1 month.

B. The sleep disturbance (or associated daytime fatigue) causes clinically significant distress or impairment in social, occupational, or other important areas of functioning.

C. The sleep disturbance does not occur exclusively during the course of narcolepsy, breathing-related sleep disorder, circadian rhythm sleep disorder, or a parasomnia.

D. The disturbance does not occur exclusively during the course of another mental disorder (e.g., major depressive disorder, generalized anxiety disorder, a delirium).

E. The disturbance is not due to the direct physiological effects of a substance (e.g., a drug of abuse, a medication) or a general medical condition.

Table from DSM-IV, *Diagnostic and Statistical Manual of Mental Disorders,* ed 4. Copyright American Psychiatric Association, Washington, 1994. Used with permission.

Table 23.4
Diagnostic Criteria for Narcolepsy

A. Irresistible attacks of refreshing sleep that occur daily over at least 3 months.

B. The presence of one or both of the following:

   (1) cataplexy (i.e., brief episodes of sudden bilateral loss of muscle tone, most often in association with intense emotion)
   (2) recurrent intrusions of elements of rapid eye movement (REM) sleep into the transition between sleep and wakefulness, as manifested by either hypnopompic or hypnagogic hallucinations or sleep paralysis at the beginning or end of sleep episodes

C. The disturbance is not due to the direct physiological effects of a substance (e.g., a drug of abuse, a medication) or another general medical condition.

Table from DSM-IV, *Diagnostic and Statistical Manual of Mental Disorders,* ed 4. Copyright American Psychiatric Association, Washington, 1994. Used with permission.

Table 23.5
Diagnostic Criteria for Primary Hypersomnia

A. The predominant complaint is excessive sleepiness for at least 1 month (or less if recurrent) as evidenced by either prolonged sleep episodes or daytime sleep episodes that occur almost daily.

B. The excessive sleepiness causes clinically significant distress or impairment in social, occupational, or other important areas of functioning.

C. The excessive sleepiness is not better accounted for by insomnia and does not occur exclusively during the course of another sleep disorder (e.g., narcolepsy, breathing-related sleep disorder, circadian rhythm sleep disorder, or a parasomnia) and cannot be accounted for by an inadequate amount of sleep.

D. The disturbance does not occur exclusively during the course of another mental disorder.

E. The disturbance is not due to the direct physiological effects of a substance (e.g., a drug of abuse, a medication) or a general medical condition.

Specify if:
   Recurrent: if there are periods of excessive sleepiness that last at least 3 days occurring several times a year for at least 2 years

Table from DSM-IV, *Diagnostic and Statistical Manual of Mental Disorders,* ed 4. Copyright American Psychiatric Association, Washington, 1994. Used with permission.

Table 23.6
Diagnostic Criteria for Nightmare Disorder

A. Repeated awakenings from the major sleep period or naps with detailed recall of extended and extremely frightening dreams, usually involving threats to survival, security, or self-esteem. The awakenings generally occur during the second half of the sleep period.

B. On awakening from the frightening dream, the person rapidly becomes oriented and alert (in contrast to the confusion and disorientation seen in sleep terror disorder and some forms of epilepsy).

C. The dream experience, or the sleep disturbance resulting from the awakening, causes clinically significant distress or impairment in social, occupational, or other important areas of functioning.

D. The nightmares do not occur exclusively during the course of another mental disorder (e.g., a delirium, posttraumatic stress disorder) and are not due to the direct physiological effects of a substance (e.g., a drug of abuse, a medication) or a general medical condition.

Table from DSM-IV, *Diagnostic and Statistical Manual or Mental Disorders,* ed 4. Copyright American Psychiatric Association, Washington, 1994. Used with permission.

characterized by a sudden inability to execute voluntary movements either just at the onset of sleep or on awakening during the night or in the morning. *Somniloquy,* sleeptalking, occurs in all stages of sleep. The talking usually involves a few words that are difficult to distinguish, and sleep talking by itself requires no treatment. *Sleep terror disorder* is characterized by terrified arousal in the first third of the night during deep NREM sleep. The patient generally has no dream recall. The arousal is inaugurated by a piercing scream and is accompanied by behavioral manifestations of intense anxiety. Most often, patients fall back to sleep and, as with sleepwalking, forget the episode.

Table 23.1 lists the diagnostic criteria for sleepwalking disorder. Table 23.6 lists the diagnostic criteria for nightmare disorder.

23.7   The answer is E (all) (*Synopsis VII,* pages 701–702).

The neurohumor most clearly involved in sleep and waking mechanisms is brain *serotonin.* The administration of the serotonin precursor L-tryptophan induces sleep (reduces sleep latency) and tends to increase total sleep and to increase rapid eye movement (REM) sleep time without altering the states and stages of sleep.

Dopamine seems to be involved in sleep-waking mechanisms. Pharmacological methods of increasing brain dopamine tend to produce arousal and wakefulness, whereas dopamine blockers, such as pimo-

zide (Orap) and the phenothiazines, tend to increase sleep time somewhat.

Norepinephrine may also be involved in the control of sleep. There seems to be an inverse relation between functional brain norepinephrine and REM sleep. Drugs and manipulations that increase the available brain norepinephrine produce a marked decrease in REM sleep whereas reducing brain norepinephrine levels increases REM sleep. That action of norepinephrine almost certainly involves α-adrenergic receptors, because an α-blocker, such as phenoxybenzamine, increases REM sleep, but a β-blocker, such as propranolol (Inderal), has no effect.

Acetylcholine is also involved in sleep. Physostigmine and similar cholinergic agents can trigger REM sleep in humans.

23.8.   The answer is A (*Synopsis VII,* pages 713–714).

Hypersomnia related to an Axis I or Axis II disorder (Table 23.7) may be the result of *major depressive disorder.* Hypersomnia due to *amphetamine withdrawal* is diagnosed as substance-induced sleep disorder with onset during withdrawal, hypersomnia type (Table 23.8). Hypersomnia due to *alcohol intoxication* is diagnosed as substance-induced sleep disorder with onset during intoxication, hypersomnia type. *Jet lag* is diagnosed as circadian rhythm sleep disorder, jet lag type (Table 23.9).

23.9.   The answer is E (all) (*Synopsis VII,* pages 707–708).

Excessive *daytime sleepiness* and naps and the accessory symptoms of *cataplexy, sleep paralysis,* and hypnagogic *hallucinations* are the classically recog-

Table 23.7
Diagnostic Criteria for Hypersomnia Related to [Axis I or Axis II Disorder]

A. The predominant complaint is excessive sleepiness for at least 1 month as evidenced by either prolonged sleep episodes or daytime sleep episodes that occur almost daily.

B. The excessive sleepiness causes clinically significant distress or impairment in social, occupational, or other important areas of functioning.

C. The hypersomnia is judged to be related to another Axis I or Axis II disorder (e.g., major depressive disorder, dysthymic disorder), but is sufficiently severe to warrant independent clinical attention.

D. The disturbance is not better accounted for by another sleep disorder (e.g., narcolepsy, breathing-related sleep disorder, a parasomnia) or by an inadequate amount of sleep.

E. The disturbance is not due to the direct physiological effects of a substance (e.g., a drug of abuse, a medication) or a general medical condition.

Table from DSM-IV, *Diagnostic and Statistical Manual of Mental Disorders,* ed 4. Copyright American Psychiatric Association, Washington, 1994. Used with permission.

Table 23.8
Diagnostic Criteria for Substance-induced Sleep Disorder

A. A prominent disturbance in sleep that is sufficiently severe to warrant independent clinical attention.

B. There is evidence from the history, physical examination, or laboratory findings of either (1) or (2):

(1) the symptoms in criterion A developed during, or within a month of, substance intoxication or withdrawal
(2) medication use is etiologically related to the sleep disturbance

C. The disturbance is not better accounted for by a sleep disorder that is not substance induced. Evidence that the symptoms are better accounted for by a sleep disorder that is not substance induced might include the following: the symptoms precede the onset of the substance use (or medication use); the symptoms persist for a substantial period of time (e.g., about a month) after the cessation of acute withdrawal or severe intoxication, or are substantially in excess of what would be expected given the type or amount of the substance used or the duration of use; or there is other evidence that suggests the existence of an independent non-substance-induced sleep disorder (e.g., a history of recurrent non-substance-related episodes).

D. The disturbance does not occur exclusively during the course of a delirium.

E. The sleep disturbance causes clinically significant distress or impairment in social, occupational, or other important areas of functioning.

Note: This diagnosis should be made instead of a diagnosis of substance intoxication or substance withdrawal only when the sleep symptoms are in excess of those usually associated with the intoxication or withdrawal syndrome and when the symptoms are sufficiently severe to warrant independent clinical attention.

Code [specific substance]-induced sleep disorder:
(alcohol; amphetamine; caffeine; cocaine; opioid; sedative, hypnotic, or anxiolytic; other [or unknown] substance)

Specify type:
Insomnia type: if the predominant sleep disturbance is insomnia
Hypersomnia type: if the predominant sleep disturbance is hypersomnia
Parasomnia type: if the predominant sleep disturbance is a parasomnia
Mixed type: if more than one sleep disturbance is present and none predominates

Specify if:
With onset during intoxication: if the criteria are met for intoxication with the substance and the symptoms develop during the intoxication syndrome
With onset during withdrawal: if criteria are met for withdrawal from the substance and the symptoms develop during, or shortly after, a withdrawal syndrome

Table from DSM-IV, *Diagnostic and Statistical Manual of Mental Disorders,* ed 4. Copyright American Psychiatric Association, Washington, 1994. Used with permission.

nized symptoms of narcolepsy. Patients generally first report the onset of daytime sleepiness before the accessory symptoms are noted.

The sleepiness may persist throughout the day, but more often it is periodic and may be relieved by a sleep attack or by a nap from which the patient characteristically awakens refreshed. Thus, there are often refractory periods of two or three hours of almost normal alertness. The sleep attacks are usually associated with characteristic times of the day, such as after meals, when some degree of sleepiness is quite normal. The attacks are typically irresistible and may even occur while eating, riding a bicycle, or actively conversing and also during sexual relations.

Cataplexy, which occurs in two thirds to 95 percent of the cases, represents the paralysis or the paresis of the antigravity muscles in the awake state. A cataplectic attack often begins during expressions of emotion, such as laughter, anger, and exhilaration. The attacks vary in intensity and frequency; they can consist of a weakening of the knees, a jaw drop, a head drop, or a sudden paralysis of all the muscles of the body—except for the eyes and the diaphragm—leading to a complete collapse.

Sleep paralysis is a neurological phenomenon that is most likely due to a temporary dysfunction of the reticular activating system. It consists of brief episodes of an inability to move or speak when awake or asleep.

Hypnagogic hallucinations are vivid perceptual dreamlike experiences occurring at sleep onset or on awakening. They occur in about 50 percent of the patients. The accompanying affect is usually fear or dread. The hallucinatory imagery is remembered

Table 23.9
Diagnostic Criteria for Circadian Rhythm Sleep Disorder

A. A persistent or recurrent pattern of sleep disruption leading to excessive sleepiness or insomnia that is due to a mismatch between the sleep-wake schedule required by a person's environment and his or her circadian sleep-wake pattern.

B. The sleep disturbance causes clinically significant distress or impairment in social, occupational, or other important areas of functioning.

C. The disturbance does not occur exclusively during the course of another sleep disorder or other mental disorder.

D. The disturbance is not due to the direct physiological effects of a substance (e.g., a drug of abuse, a medication) or a general medical condition.

Specify type:
   Delayed sleep phase type: a persistent pattern of late sleep onset and late awakening times, with an inability to fall asleep and awaken at a desired earlier time
   Jet lag type: sleepiness and alertness that occur at an inappropriate time of day relative to local time, occurring after repeated travel across more than one time zone
   Shift work type: insomnia during the major sleep period or excessive sleepiness during the major awake period associated with night shift work or frequently changing shift work
   Unspecified type

Table from DSM-IV, *Diagnostic and Statistical Manual of Mental Disorders*, ed 4. Copyright American Psychiatric Association, Washington, 1994. Used with permission.

best after a brief narcoleptic sleep attack, when it is often described as a dream.

23.10.   The answer is E (all) (*Synopsis VII,* pages 704–705).

Hypersomnia manifests as excessive amounts of sleep and excessive daytime sleepiness (somnolence). In some situations both symptoms are present.

Kleine-Levin syndrome is characterized by recurrent periods of hypersomnia, usually associated with hyperphagia, and also by periodic episodes of bulimia. The hypersomnia is characterized by prolonged sleep from which the patient is incapable of being aroused.

Infectious causes of hypersomnolence as an isolated symptom are extremely rare or nonexistent at present in the United States, but they are common in Africa and have been seen at times in many parts of the world. The best-known such condition is *trypanosomiasis,* which produces sleeping sickness.

Excessive sleep and *depression* are typical symptoms of *amphetamine withdrawal.* Withdrawal from other stimulant drugs, including caffeine, can produce similar effects.

Table 23.10 lists some common causes of hypersomnia. As with insomnia, hypersomnia is associated with borderline conditions, situations that are hard to classify, and idiopathic cases.

23.11–23.13

23.11.   The answer is B (*Synopsis VII,* page 711.)

23.12.   The answer is A (*Synopsis VII,* page 711).

23.13.   The answer is B (*Synopsis VII,* page 712).

Nightmare disorder is associated with *rapid eye movement (REM) sleep. Sleep terror disorder* and *sleepwalking disorder* are associated with *nonrapid eye movement (NREM) sleep.*

The diagnostic criteria for nightmare disorder are listed in Table 23.6. The diagnostic criteria for sleep terror disorder are listed in Table 23.11.

23.14–23.18

23.14.   The answer is B (*Synopsis VII,* page 710).

23.15.   The answer is D (*Synopsis VII,* pages 714–715).

23.16.   The answer is A (*Synopsis VII,* page 711).

23.17.   The answer is C (*Synopsis VII,* page 713).

23.18.   The answer is E (*Synopsis VII,* page 713).

Nocturnal myoclonus consists of highly stereotyped contractions of certain leg muscles during sleep. Though rarely painful, the syndrome causes an almost irresistible *urge to move the legs,* thus interfering with sleep.

Sleep-related hemolysis (paroxysmal nocturnal hemoglobinuria) is a rare, acquired, chronic hemolytic anemia in which intravascular hemolysis results in hemoglobinemia and hemoglobinuria. Accelerated during sleep, the hemolysis and consequent hemoglobinuria color the *morning urine a brownish red.* Sleep-related hemolysis is diagnosed as sleep disorder due to a general medical condition (Table 23.12).

In *sleep terror disorder* (Table 23.11) the *patient* typically sits up in bed with a frightened expression, and *wakes up screaming,* often with a feeling of intense terror; patients are often amnestic for the episode.

Sleep-related *head banging (jactatio capatis nocturnus)* consists chiefly of rhythmic to-and-fro head rocking, less commonly of total body rocking, occurring just before or during sleep, rarely persisting into or occurring in deep nonrapid eye movement (NREM) sleep.

According to dentists, 5 to 10 percent of the population suffer from *sleep-related bruxism* (tooth grinding) severe enough to produce noticeable *damage to the teeth.* Although the condition often goes unnoticed by the sleeper, except for an occasional feeling of jaw ache in the morning, the bed partner and roommates are acutely cognizant of the situation, as they are repeatedly awakened by the sound.

Sleep-related head banging and sleep-related bruxism are diagnosed as parasomnia not otherwise specified (Table 23.13).

Table 23.10
Common Causes of Hypersomnia

Symptom	Chiefly Medical	Chiefly Psychiatric or Environment
Excessive sleep (hypersomnia)	Kleine-Levin syndrome Menstrual-associated somnolence Metabolic or toxic conditions Encephalitic conditions Alcohol and depressant medications Withdrawal from stimulants	Depression (some) Avoidance reactions
Excessive daytime sleepiness	Narcolepsy and narcolepsylike syndromes Sleep apneas Hypoventilation syndrome Hyperthyroidism and other metabolic and toxic conditions Alcohol and depressant medications Withdrawal from stimulants Sleep deprivation or insufficient sleep Any condition producing serious insomnia	Depression (some) Avoidance reactions Circadian rhythm sleep disorder

Table by Ernest Hartmann, M.D.

Table 23.11
Diagnostic Criteria for Sleep Terror Disorder

A. Recurrent episodes of abrupt awakening from sleep, usually occurring during the first third of the major sleep episode and beginning with a panicky scream.

B. Intense fear and signs of autonomic arousal, such as tachycardia, rapid breathing, and sweating, during each episode.

C. Relative unresponsiveness to efforts of others to comfort the person during the episode.

D. No detailed dream is recalled and there is amnesia for the episode.

E. The episodes cause clinically significant distress or impairment in social, occupational, or other important areas of functioning.

F. The disturbance is not due to the direct physiological effects of a substance (e.g., a drug of abuse, a medication) or a general medical condition.

Table from DSM-IV, *Diagnostic and Statistical Manual of Mental Disorders,* ed 4. Copyright American Psychiatric Association, Washington, 1994. Used with permission.

23.19–23.22

23.19.   The answer is B (*Synopsis VII,* page 712).

23.20.   The answer is B (*Synopsis VII,* page 699).

23.21.   The answer is A (*Synopsis VII,* pages 700–701).

23.22.   The answer is A (*Synopsis VII,* page 701).

Sleepwalking occurs during the first third of the night during *NREM sleep,* stages 3 and 4. *Bed-wetting (enuresis),* a repetitive and inappropriate passage of urine during sleep, is associated with *NREM sleep,* stages 3 and 4. *Paroxysmal hemicrania* is a

Table 23.12
Diagnostic Criteria for Sleep Disorder Due to a General Medical Condition

A. A prominent disturbance in sleep that is sufficiently severe to warrant independent clinical attention.

B. There is evidence from the history, physical examination, or laboratory findings that the sleep disturbance is the direct physiological consequence of a general medical condition.

C. The disturbance is not better accounted for by another mental disorder (e.g., an adjustment disorder in which the stressor is a serious medical illness).

D. The disturbance does not occur exclusively during the course of a delirium.

E. The disturbance does not meet the criteria for breathing-related sleep disorder or narcolepsy.

F. The sleep disturbance causes clinically significant distress or impairment in social, occupational, or other important areas of functioning.

Specify type:
    Insomnia type: if the predominant sleep disturbance is insomnia
    Hypersomnia type: if the predominant sleep disturbance is hypersomnia
    Parasomnia type: if the predominant sleep disturbance is a parasomnia
    Mixed type: if more than one sleep disturbance is present and none predominates

Coding note: Include the name of the general medical condition on Axis I, e.g., sleep disorder due to chronic obstructive pulmonary disease insomnia type; also code the general medical condition on Axis III.

Table from DSM-IV, *Diagnostic and Statistical Manual of Mental Disorders,* ed 4. Copyright American Psychiatric Associaton, Washington, 1994. Used with permission.

Table 23.13
Diagnostic Criteria for Parasomnia Not Otherwise Specified

The parasomnia not otherwise specified category is for disturbances that are characterized by abnormal behavioral or physiological events during sleep or sleep-wake transitions, but that do not meet criteria for a more specific parasomnia. Examples include

1. REM sleep behavior disorder: motor activity, often of a violent nature, that arises during rapid eye movement (REM) sleep. Unlike sleepwalking, these episodes tend to occur later in the night and are associated with vivid dream recall.

2. Sleep paralysis: an inability to perform voluntary movement during the transition between wakefulness and sleep. The episodes may occur at sleep onset (hypnagogic) or with awakening (hypnopompic). The episodes are usually associated with extreme anxiety and, in some cases, fear of impending death. Sleep paralysis occurs commonly as an ancillary symptom of narcolepsy and, in such cases, should not be coded separately.

3. Situations in which the clinician has concluded that a parasomnia is present but is unable to determine whether it is primary, due to a general medical condition, or substance induced.

Table from DSM-IV, *Diagnostic and Statistical Manual of Mental Disorders*, ed 4. Copyright American Psychiatric Association, Washington, 1994. Used with permission.

type of unilateral vascular headache that is sleep-exacerbated and occurs only in association with *REM sleep. Erections* are associated with *REM sleep.* Almost every REM period is accompanied by a partial or full penile erection (or clitoral erection in women).

23.23–23.27

23.23. The answer is A (*Synopsis VII,* page 711).

23.24. The answer is B (*Synopsis VII,* pages 711–712).

23.25. The answer is B (*Synopsis VII,* pages 711–712).

23.26. The answer is A (*Synopsis VII,* page 711).

23.27. The answer is B (*Synopsis VII,* pages 711–712).

Night terrors need to be clearly distinguished from nightmares. *Nightmares* occur during *REM sleep* and manifest with less intense anxiety than do night terrors. Nightmares are usually not forgotten and, in fact, are *usually recalled in some detail. Night terrors* occur during *NREM sleep* and manifest with severe anxiety, being heralded by a panicky scream. They are accompanied by disorientation and *perservative movements* and are *usually followed* by *amnesia* for the event.

Impulse Control Disorders Not Elsewhere Classified

Persons who experience difficulty in controlling their impulses share a number of features. For example, they are unable, consciously or unconsciously, to resist harmful impulses or temptations that may or may not be planned. Before acting on impulses or temptations, they feel an increasing sense of tension; during the act, they feel a sense of release; after the act, they may or may not feel regret or guilt. The fourth edition of *Diagnostic and Statistical Manual of Mental Disorders* (DSM-IV) lists six categories of impulse control disorders: intermittent explosive disorder, kleptomania, pyromania, pathological gambling, trichotillomania, and impulse control disorder not otherwise specified (NOS).

Both biological and psychosocial factors have been investigated with regard to the causes of impulse control disorders. Psychosocially, some recurrent themes include exposure to violence in the home, alcohol abuse, erratic and unstable sexual relationships, antisocial behavior, and parental figures who have impulse control problems.

Biological factors have been extensively investigated in impulse control disorder patients, especially those exhibiting violent behavior. Some reported associations include areas of the brain, such as the limbic system; hormones, such as testosterone; histories of head trauma; and the adult residue of childhood attention-deficit/hyperactivity disorder. Much study has been directed at the serotonin 5-hydroxytryptamine (5-HT) neurotransmitter system. A relation has been suggested between cerebrospinal fluid (CSF) levels of 5-hydroxyindoleacetic

acid (5-HIAA) and impulsive aggression. In some suicide victims, brainstem and CSF levels of 5-HIAA are decreased, and 5-HT binding sites are increased.

Intermittent explosive disorder occurs in persons who experience several discrete episodes of losing control, resulting in serious harm to other persons or property. The degree of aggressiveness in the disorder is grossly out of proportion to the identified triggers. Kleptomania is associated with an inability to resist impulses to steal. The stolen objects are not needed for their monetary value or for personal use. In kleptomania the object stolen is not the goal; the goal is the act of stealing. Pathological gambling is characterized by a pervasive pattern of maladaptive gambling behavior. The behavior may include a preoccupation with gambling, a need to gamble with increasing amounts of money, lying to conceal the extent of the gambling, and the jeopardizing of personal relationships or a career because of gambling. Trichotillomania is the recurrent pulling out of one's hair, leading to noticeable hair loss. Impulse control disorder not otherwise specified includes compulsive shopping, compulsive sexual behavior, and addiction to video games.

Each impulse control disorder has its own epidemiology, causes, psychodynamic formulation, course, prognosis, and treatment. Each must be viewed individually, even though common threads are found in them. Students should study Chapter 24 in *Kaplan and Sadock's Synopsis VII* and the questions and answers below.

HELPFUL HINTS

The terms below relate to impulse control disorders and should be defined by the student.

impulse control disorder	limbic system	progressive-loss stage
intermittent explosive disorder	testosterone	desperate stage
kleptomania	epileptoid personality	enuresis
pyromania	anticonvulsants	multidetermined
pathological gambling	benzodiazepines	trichophagy
trichotillomania	lithium	alopecia
impulse control disorder NOS	lust angst	hydroxyzine hydrochloride
pleasure principle, reality principle	behavior therapy	biofeedback
psychodynamics	winning phase	hypnotherapy

QUESTIONS

DIRECTIONS: Each of the questions or incomplete statements below is followed by five suggested responses or completions. Select the *one* that is *best* in each case.

24.1. Which of the following statements is *not* true regarding impulse control disorders?
A. The patients cannot resist the temptation to perform an act
B. The patients feel an increasing surge of tension before they commit the act
C. The patients feel a burst of pleasure while committing the act
D. The act is ego-syntonic
E. After the act the patients rarely feel guilt or self-reproach

24.2. Biological factors involved in the causes of impulse control disorders include all the following *except*
A. limbic system
B. testosterone
C. tyrosine levels
D. temporal lobe epilepsy
E. mixed cerebral dominance

24.3. Which of the following drugs has been found effective in impulse control disorders?
A. Phenothiazines
B. Lithium (Eskalith)
C. Phenytoin (Dilantin)
D. Trazodone (Desyrel)
E. All the above

24.4. All the following statements about trichotillomania are true *except*
A. the diagnosis should not be made if the hair pulling is the result of another mental disorder
B. pulling out hair causes gratification
C. the disorder is more common in males than in females
D. the most common site is the scalp
E. trichobezoars may result

24.5. The estimated number of pathological gamblers in the United States is
A. less than 100,000
B. 250,000
C. 500,000
D. 750,000
E. 1 million or more

DIRECTIONS: Each set of lettered headings below is followed by a list of numbered words or phrases. For each numbered word or phrase, select

    A. if the item is associated with *A only*
    B. if the item is associated with *B only*
    C. if the item is associated with *both A and B*
    D. if the item is associated with *neither A nor B*

Questions 24.6–24.12
    A. Trichotillomania
    B. Pyromania
    C. Both
    D. Neither

24.6. More common in females than in males

24.7. Onset generally in childhood

24.8. Sense of gratification or relief during the behavior

24.9. Treated with lithium

24.10. Associated with truancy

24.11. May be a response to an auditory hallucination

24.12. Associated with mental retardation

Questions 24.13–24.16
    A. Intermittent explosive disorder
    B. Kleptomania
    C. Both
    D. Neither

24.13. Greater prevalence among males than among females

24.14. Associated with organic brain disease

24.15. Treatment with carbamazepine (Tegretol)

24.16. May be due to antisocial personality disorder

ANSWERS

Impulse Control Disorders Not Elsewhere Classified

24.1.   The answer is E (*Synopsis VII*, page 717).

After the act the patients may feel guilt or self-reproach. Patients with impulse control disorders share the following features: (1) *The patients cannot resist the temptation to perform an act* that is harmful to themselves or others. They may or may not consciously resist the impulse and may or may not plan the act. (2) *The patients feel an increasing sense of tension before they commit the act.* (3) *They feel a burst of of pleasure while committing the act.* The act is ego-syntonic in that it is consonant with the patient's immediate conscious wishes.

24.2.   The answer is C (*Synopsis VII*, pages 717–718).

Tyrosine levels have not been implicated in impulse control disorders. Specific brain regions, such as the *limbic system,* are associated with impulsive and violent activity; other brain regions are associated with the inhibition of such behaviors. Certain hormones, especially *testosterone,* have been associated with violent and aggressive behavior. Some reports have described a relation between *temporal lobe epilepsy* and certain impulsive violent behaviors, an association of aggressive behavior in patients with histories of head trauma, increased numbers of emergency room visits, and other potential organic antecedents. A high incidence of *mixed cerebral dominance* may be found in some violent populations.

24.3.   The answer is E (*Synopsis VII*, page 719).

Anticonvulsants have long been used in treating explosive patients, with mixed results. *Phenothiazines* and antidepressants have been effective in some cases. Benzodiazapines have been reported to produce a paradoxical reaction of dyscontrol in some cases. *Lithium (Eskalith)* has been reported to be useful in generally lessening aggressive behavior, and carbamazepine (Tegretol) and *phenytoin (Dilantin)* have also been reported to be helpful. Propanolol (Inderal), buspirone (BuSpar), and *trazodone (Desyrel)* have also been effective in some cases. Increasing reports indicate that fluoxetine (Prozac) and other strotonin-specific reuptake inhibitors are useful in reducing impulsivity and aggression.

24.4.   The answer is C (*Synopsis VII*, pages 724–725).

Trichotillomania *is apparently more common in females than in males. The diagnosis should not be made if the hair pulling is the result of another men-* *tal disorder* (for example, those disorders manifesting delusions or hallucinations) or a general medical disorder (for example, a preexisting lesion of the skin). The diagnosis criteria are listed in Table 24.1. Before engaging in the behavior, trichotillomaniac patients experience an increasing sense of tension. *Pulling out hair causes* a sense of release or *gratification.* All areas of the body may be affected. *The most common site is the scalp.* Other areas involved are the eyebrows, eyelashes, and the beard; less commonly, the trunk, armpits, and the pubic area are involved. Trichophagy, mouthing of the hair, may follow the hair plucking. *Trichobezoars,* malnutrition, and intestinal obstruction result.

24.5.   The answer is E (*Synopsis VII*, page 722).

Estimates place the number of pathological gamblers in the United States at *1 million or more.* The disorder is thought to be more common in men than in women. Males with fathers with the disorder and females with mothers with the disorder are more likely to have the disorder than the population at large. The diagnostic criteria for pathological gambling are listed in Table 24.2.

24.6–24.12

24.6.   The answer is A (*Synopsis VII*, page 724).

24.7.   The answer is C (*Synopsis VII*, pages 722 and 725).

24.8.   The answer is C (*Synopsis VII*, pages 721 and 724).

Table 24.1
Diagnostic Criteria for Trichotillomania

A. Recurrent putting out of one's hair resulting in noticeable hair loss.

B. An increasing sense of tension immediately before pulling out the hair or when attempting to resist the behavior.

C. Pleasure, gratification, or relief when pulling out the hair.

D. The disturbance is not better accounted for by another mental disorder and is not due to a general medical condition (e.g., a dermatological condition).

E. The disturbance causes clinically significant distress or impairment in social, occupational, or other important areas of functioning.

Table from DSM-IV, *Diagnostic and Statistical Manual of Mental Disorders,* ed 4. Copyright American Psychiatric Association, Washington, 1994. Used with permission.

Table 24.2
Diagnostic Criteria for Pathological Gambling

A. Persistent and recurrent maladaptive gambling behavior as indicated by five (or more) of the following:

(1) is preoccupied with gambling (e.g., preoccupied with reliving past gambling experiences, handicapping or planning the next venture, or thinking of ways to get money with which to gamble)

(2) needs to gamble with increasing amounts of money in order to achieve the desired excitement

(3) has repeated unsuccessful efforts to control, cut back, or stop gambling

(4) is restless or irritable when attempting to cut down or stop gambling

(5) gambles as a way of escaping from problems or of relieving a dysphoric mood (e.g., feelings of helplessness, guilt, anxiety, depression)

(6) after losing money gambling, often returns another day to get even ("chasing" one's losses)

(7) lies to family members, therapist, or others to conceal the extent of involvement with gambling

(8) has committed illegal acts such as forgery, fraud, theft, or embezzlement to finance gambling

(9) has jeopardized or lost a significant relationship, job, or educational or career opportunity because of gambling

(10) relies on others to provide money to relieve a desperate financial situation caused by gambling

B. The gambling behavior is not better accounted for by a manic episode.

Table from DSM-IV, *Diagnostic and Statistical Manual of Mental Disorders*, ed 4. Copyright American Psychiatric Association, Washington, 1994. Used with permission.

Table 24.3
Diagnostic Criteria for Pyromania

A. Deliberate and purposeful fire setting on more than one occasion.

B. Tension or affective arousal before the act.

C. Fascination with, interest in, curiosity about, or attraction to fire and its situational contexts or associated characteristics (e.g., paraphernalia, uses, consequences).

D. Pleasure, gratification, or relief when setting fires, or when witnessing or participating in their aftermath.

E. The fire setting is not done for monetary gain, as an expression of sociopolitical ideology, to conceal criminal activity, to express anger or vengeance, to improve one's living circumstances, in response to a delusion or hallucination, or as a result of impaired judgment (e.g., in dementia, mental retardation, substance intoxication).

F. The fire setting is not better accounted for by conduct disorder, a manic episode, or antisocial personality disorder.

Table from DSM-IV, *Diagnostic and Statistical Manual of Mental Disorders*, ed 4. Copyright American Psychiatric Association, Washington, 1994. Used with permission.

24.13–24.16

24.13.   The answer is A (*Synopsis VII*, page 718).

24.14.   The answer is C (*Synopsis VII*, pages 718 and 720).

24.15.   The answer is A (*Synopsis VII*, page 719).

24.16.   The answer is D (*Synopsis VII*, pages 718–720).

Intermittent explosive disorder is apparently very rare and appears to have a *greater prevalence among males than females*, Kleptomania is also rare, and the sex ratio is unknown. Most patients with intermittent explosive disorder are treated with a combined pharmacological and psychotherapeutic approach. Psychotherapy with violent patients is exceedingly difficult because of potential problems with countertransference and limit setting. Anticonvulsants, phenothiazines, and antidepressants have all been effective in some cases of intermittent explosive disorder, and studies have shown that both lithium and *carbamazepine* are useful in certain cases. The latter has not been used in the treatment of kleptomania.

Both disorders may be *associated with organic brain disease*. Lesions in the limbic system, for example, have been associated with violent behavior and loss of control of aggressive impulses. Kleptomania has also been associated with brain disease and mental retardation.

Neither intermittent explosive disorder nor kleptomania can be diagnosed when impulsiveness, ag-

24.9.   The answer is D (*Synopsis VII*, pages 722 725).

24.10.   The answer is B (*Synopsis VII*, page 721).

24.11.   The answer is D (*Synopsis VII*, pages 721 and 724).

24.12.   The answer is C (*Synopsis VII*, pages 721 and 724–725).

Both pyromania and trichotillomania have their *onset in childhood* and are characterized by a *sense of gratification or release during the act. Trichotillomania* is apparently *more common in females than in males.* People who set fires are more likely to be moderately retarded than people who do not set fires, and the inability to resist the impulse to pull out one's own hair is also associated with *mental retardation. Pyromania* is associated with antisocial traits, such as *truancy,* running away from home, and delinquency. *Neither disorder* is *treated with lithium* (Eskalith), and *neither is a response to an auditory hallucination.*

Table 24.3 lists the diagnostic criteria for pyromania. Table 24.1 lists the diagnostic criteria for trichotillomania.

gressiveness, or stealing is *due to antisocial personality disorder.*

Table 24.4 lists the diagnostic criteria for kleptomania. Table 24.5 lists the diagnostic criteria for intermittent explosive disorder.

Table 24.4
Diagnostic Criteria for Kleptomania

A. Recurrent failure to resist impulses to steal objects not needed for personal use or for their monetary value.

B. Increasing sense of tension immediately before committing the theft.

C. Pleasure, gratification, or relief at the time of committing the theft.

D. The stealing is not committed to express anger or vengeance and is not in response to a delusion or hallucination.

E. The stealing is not better accounted for by conduct disorder, a manic episode, or antisocial personality disorder.

Table from DSM-IV, *Diagnostic and Statistical Manual of Mental Disorders,* ed 4. Copyright American Psychiatric Association, Washington, 1994. Used with permission.

Table 24.5
Diagnostic Criteria for Intermittent Explosive Disorder

A. Several discrete episodes of failure to resist aggressive impulses that result in serious assaultive acts or destruction of property.

B. The degree of aggressiveness expressed during the episodes is grossly out of proportion to any precipitating psychosocial stressors.

C. The aggressive episodes are not better accounted for by another mental disorder (e.g., antisocial personality disorder, borderline personality disorder, a psychotic disorder, a manic episode, conduct disorder, or attention-deficit/hyperactivity disorder) and are not due to the direct physiological effects of a substance (e.g., a drug of abuse, a medication) or a general medical condition (e.g., head trauma, Alzheimer's disease).

Table from DSM-IV, *Diagnostic and Statistical Manual of Mental Disorders,* ed 4. Copyright American Psychiatric Association, Washington, 1994. Used with permission.

Adjustment Disorders

A person experiences a personal setback, misfortune, or adverse event. The person responds with marked distress that exceeds what is normally expected in response to the event and, as a result, experiences significant impairment in social, occupational, or academic functioning. The person's response occurs within three months of the event and either lessens in intensity as the event recedes or, if the event continues, achieves a new level of adaptation. According to the fourth edition of *Diagnostic and Statistical Manual of Mental Disorders* (DSM-IV), the person experiencing the described sequence of emotions and behaviors is suffering from adjustment disorder.

Common precipitating events that trigger adjustment disorder include marital problems, divorce, relocation, and financial crises. However, the severity of the precipitating event does not always predict a person's response. One person may react to relatively minor stress with adjustment disorder, but a second person may react to a much more obviously stressful event with equanimity. The degree to which a precipitating stress is experienced as severe depends on many factors, including duration, reversibility, context, and personality structure. The clinician must explore both the conscious and the unconscious meanings of the precipitating stressful event to the patient. For instance, a current event may trigger memories of an early traumatic event or may stimulate unconscious conflict stemming from an early

stress. The person's phase of development (for example, having one's first child or facing retirement) may play a pivotal role in producing a maladaptive response to an event that, if experienced at a different developmental phase, would elicit a different response.

As defined in DSM-IV, adjustment disorder does not have to begin immediately after a stressor occurs. If the stressor continues, the disorder may become chronic. The disorder may have its onset at any age and may have a variety of clinical presentations. DSM-IV describes six types of adjustment disorder: (1) with depressed mood, (2) with anxiety, (3) with mixed anxiety and depressed mood, (4) with disturbance of conduct, (5) with mixed disturbance of emotions and conduct, and (6) unspecified. The student should be able to define each of those six types and be able to differentiate them from each other and from such conditions as bereavement, major depressive disorder, posttraumatic stress disorder, and brief psychotic disorder.

The treatment of adjustment disorder includes combinations of crisis intervention strategies, insight-oriented psychotherapy, environmental and behavioral manipulations, and, if indicated, brief focused pharmacotherapy.

Students should study Chapter 25 in *Kaplan and Sadock's Synopsis VII* and then test themselves with the following questions and answers.

HELPFUL HINTS

The student should know the terms and types of adjustment disorder below.

maladaptive reaction	with anxiety	bereavement
psychosocial stressor	with mixed disturbance of	posttraumatic stress disorder
Donald Winnicott	emotions and conduct	mass catastrophes
good-enough mother	with disturbance of conduct	severity of stress scale
adjustment disorder	with mixed anxiety and	secondary gain
with depressed mood	depressed mood	recovery rate

QUESTIONS

DIRECTIONS: Each of the statements or questions below is followed by five suggested responses or completions. Select the *one* that is *best* in each case.

25.1. A 39-year-old divorced woman was referred for psychiatric evaluation after a brief hospitalization for complaints of intermittent numbness in her arms and the right side of her face. Extensive neurological evaluation revealed stenosis of the outlets of several cervical vertebrae; intermittently compromised nerve roots were thought to account for the physical symptoms. The patient, an artist who composed large structures from various work materials, was advised by her physicians to stop for the next several months all lifting, reaching, raising her arms, and other strenuous activities requisite to her work. She had felt despondent for more than two months, with episodes of tearfulness, anxiety, and increased irritability. She continued to supervise her assistants but was increasingly disinterested in work. She had no sleep or appetite change, but her libido was diminished. She was still able to enjoy music. The patient had no prior personal or familial history of a mood disorder.

The best diagnosis is
A. major depressive disorder
B. dysthymic disorder
C. adjustment disorder with depressed mood
D. adjustment disorder with anxiety
E. adjustment disorder, unspecified

25.2. For a diagnosis of adjustment disorder, the reaction to a psychosocial stressor must occur within
A. one week
B. two weeks
C. one month
D. two months
E. three months

25.3. Adjustment disorder
A. correlates with the severity of the stressor
B. occurs more often in males than in females
C. is a type of bereavement
D. usually requires years of treatment
E. occurs in all age groups

25.4. Adjustment disorder is
A. an exacerbation of a preexisting verbal disorder
B. a normal response to a nonspecific stressor
C. a normal response to a clearly identifiable event
D. a maladaptive reaction to an identifiable stressor
E. a type of brief psychotic disorder

25.5. Adjustment disorder may be associated with
A. beginning school
B. leaving home
C. getting married
D. becoming a parent
E. all the above

25.6. Vulnerability to adjustment disorder is affected by
A. a previous history of a personality disorder
B. severity of the stress
C. adolescence
D. poor mothering experiences
E. all the above

25.7. In adjustment disorder
A. the severity of the stress is not always predictive of the severity of the disorder
B. a premorbid personality disorder may increase vulnerability
C. constitutional factors play a role
D. early mothering experiences affect the person's capacity to respond to stress
E. all the above are true

25.8. Adjustment disorder is characterized by
A. impairment in social functioning
B. symptoms in excess of a normal reaction to a stressor
C. symptoms occurring within three months of the stressor
D. spontaneous remission after the stressor ceases
E. all the above

25.9. From a psychodynamic viewpoint, persons are vulnerable to adjustment disorder if
A. they have lost a parent during adolescence
B. they have concurrent personality disorder
C. they use mature defense mechanisms
D. their parents were supportive and nurturing in early childhood
E. they are in their childhood years

DIRECTIONS: The lettered headings below are followed by a list of numbered phrases. For each numbered phrase, select

    A.   if the item is associated with *A only*
    B.   if the item is associated with *B only*
    C.   if the item is associated with *both A and B*
    D.   if the item is associated with *neither A nor B*

Questions 25.10–25.12
    A.   Posttraumatic stress disorder
    B.   Adjustment disorder
    C.   Both
    D.   Neither

25.10. Induced by stressors

25.11. Stressors producing the disorder are expected to do so in the average human being

25.12. Psychotherapy is usually not recommended

ANSWERS

Adjustment Disorder

25.1. The answer is C (*Synopsis VII*, pages 728–729)

The best diagnosis for the case study of the 39-year-old woman is *adjustment disorder with depressed mood* (Table 25.1). The patient had stressors—a physical illness and the directive to minimize for several months the use of her arms. As a result, the patient was unable to continue her artistic endeavors, which were crucial to her sense of self. In response, she experienced the emergence of a depressive constellation with less than a full vegetative set of symptoms; therefore, *major depressive disorder* could not be diagnosed. *Dysthymic disorder* was ruled out because her depressive symptoms were episodic. *Adjustment disorder with anxiety* would be diagnosed if the patient had such complaints as palpitations, agitation, jitters, and other symptoms of anxiety. Although the patient's response was maladaptive, it was not atypical, which is required for a diagnosis of *adjustment disorder, unspecified.*

25.2. The answer is E (*Synopsis VII*, page 728).

According to the fourth edition of *Diagnosis and Statistical Manual of Mental Disorders* (DSM-IV), symptoms of adjustment disorder must occur within *three months* of the onset of the stressor. If a longer time intervenes between the onset of the psychiatric symptoms and an identifiable psychosocial stressor, the clinician should not make a diagnosis of adjustment disorder. Symptoms can occur as early as *one week, two weeks, one month,* or *two months*, but DSM-IV allows more time between the stressor and the onset of the symptoms.

25.3. The answer is E (*Synopsis VII*, pages 727–729).

Adjustment disorder *occurs in all age groups*. The disorder *does not always correlate with the severity of the stressor* and appears to *occur more often in females than in males*. Adjustment disorder *is not a type of bereavement*. The overall prognosis for a person with adjustment disorder is generally favorable with appropriate treatment. Most patients return to their previous level of functioning within three months and *do not require years of therapy*.

25.4. The answer is D (*Sypnosis VII*, page 727).

According to DSM-IV, adjustment disorder is *a maladaptive reaction to an identifiable stressor*. The disorder is *not an exacerbation of a preexisting mental disorder*. The patient's response is to an identifiable stressor rather than to a nonspecific stressor. The response must be identified by significant impairment in social or occupational functioning or by symptoms that are in marked excess of a normal and expectable reaction to the stressor. Thus, the disorder is *not a normal response to either a nonspecific stressor or to a clearly identifiable event*. Adjustment disorder is not *a type of brief psychotic disorder*. Even if a precipitant stressor can be identified, the diagnosis of brief psychotic disorder is assigned only if the patient shows evidence of psychotic thinking, speech, or behavior.

25.5. The answer is E (*Sypnosis VII*, page 727).

Specific developmental stages—such as *beginning school, leaving home, getting married, becoming a*

Table 25.1
Diagnostic Criteria for Adjustment Disorder

A. The development of emotional or behavioral symptoms in response to a identifiable stressor(s) occurring within 3 months of the onset of the stressor(s).

B. These symptoms or behaviors are clinically significant as evidenced by either of the following:
   (1) marked distress that is in excess of what would be expected from exposure to the stressor
   (2) significant impairment in social or occupational (academic) functioning

C. The stress-related disturbance does not meet the criteria for any specific Axis I disorder and is not merely an exacerbation of a preexisting Axis I or Axis II disorder.

D. Does not represent bereavement.

E. Once the stressor (or its consequences) has terminated, the symptoms do not persist for more than an additional 6 months.

Specify if:
   Acute: if the disturbance lasts less than 6 months
   Chronic: if the disturbance lasts for 6 months or longer

Adjustment Disorders are coded based on the subtype, which is selected according to the predominant symptoms. The specific stressor(s) can be specified on Axis IV.
   With depressed mood
   With anxiety
   With mixed anxiety and depressed mood
   With disturbance of conduct
   With mixed disturbance of emotions and conduct
   Unspecified

Table from DSM-IV, *Diagnostic and Statistical Manual of Mental Disorders,* ed 4. Copyright American Psychiatric Association, Washington, 1994. Used with permission.

parent, failing to achieve occupational goals, the last child's leaving home, and retiring—are often associated with adjustment disorder.

25.6.   The answer is E (all) (*Synopsis VII,* pages 727–728).

Vulnerability to adjustment disorder is affected by many factors. Persons with *a previous history of a personality disorder* or a cognitive disorder are susceptible. *The severity of the stressor* also increases vulnerability (for example, the loss of a young child is a greater stress than the loss of an aged parent.) Adjustment disorder may occur at any age, but it is most common during *adolescence* and young adulthood. Vulnerability is increased by *poor mothering experiences.* Providing the infant with an environment in which anxiety is attended to appropriately enables the growing child to tolerate the frustrations in life. Vulnerability is also associated with the lack of a parent during infancy and childhood.

25.7.   The answer is E (all) (*Synopsis VII,* pages 727–729).

The severity of the stressor is not always predictive of the severity of the disorder. Cultural or group norms and values play roles in the responses to stressors, and *a premorbid personality disorder may increase vulnerability. Constitutional factors play a role* in adjustment disorder. *Early mothering experiences affect the person's capacity to respond to stress.* Particularly important was Donald Winnicott's concept of the good-enough mother, and a person who adapts to the infant's needs.

25.8.   The answer is E (all) (*Synopsis VII,* page 728).

Adjustment disorder produces *impairment in social* or occupational *functioning.* The stressor produces *symptoms in excess of a normal portion to a*

stressor. The *symptoms occur within these months of the stressor,* and there is *a spontaneous remission after the stressor ceases.*

25.9.   The answer is B (*Synopsis VII,* pages 727–728).

Persons who *have a concurrent personality disorder* or organic impairment are vulnerable to adjustment disorder. Vulnerability is also increased if *they lost a parent during infancy, not during adolescence.* Actual or perceived support from key relationships may mediate behavioral and emotional responses to stressors. Persons who use *mature defense mechanisms* are not vulnerable; they bounce back quickly from the stressor. Studies of trauma repeatedly indicate that if *parents were supportive and nurturing in early childhood,* traumatic incidents do not cause permanent psychological damage. No increased vulnerability to adjustment disorder is found *in childhood years;* adjustment disorder may occur at any age.

25.10–25.12

25.10.   The answer is C (*Synopsis VII,* pages 607–608 and 727–728).

25.11.   The answer is A (*Synopsis VII,* pages 607–608).

25.12.   The answer is D (*Synopsis VII,* pages 610–611 and 730).

Both adjustment disorder and posttraumatic stress disorder are *induced by stressors. Stressors producing posttraumatic stress disorder are expected to do so in the average human being.* The response to a stressor in adjustment disorder is beyond the normal, usual, or expected response to such a stressor. *Psychotherapy is the treatment of choice for both adjustment disorder and posttraumatic stress disorder.*

Personality Disorders

Personality is a constellation of behavioral, temperamental, and psychological characteristics that are molded by a complex interaction of development, environment, and biology that translates into how a person interacts with and adapts to other people and the world. Healthy personalities present a wide spectrum of characteristics but all are flexible and adaptive. A person's personality is largely stable and predictable; it is shaped early in life but is continually refined throughout life.

A personality disorder indicates a breakdown somewhere in the growth of a healthy personality. The breakdown occurs as the result of an intricate interplay among all the factors that shape personality—developmental issues, temperament, biology, genetics, and environment.

When confronted with stress, everyone exhibits inflexible or maladaptive traits. A personality disorder occurs when those inflexible or maladaptive traits are sustained and pervasive. Persons with personality disorders are generally significantly impaired with regard to their ability to get along with other people and in their capacity for happiness and satisfaction in their lives. They often do not perceive themselves to be the source of their own dissatisfactions or unhappiness; rather, they externalize their sense of grievance or malaise to the outside world. A person with a personality disorder experiences problems in relating to the world as *"their* fault, not my fault." Such persons may experience distress, discomfort, anxiety, rage, or unhappiness but generally attribute those subjective states to something outside themselves, to something others are doing to them. Thus, their experiences are ego-syntonic: they are generally not consciously in inner conflict or turmoil over their own roles in creating problems with others. Persons with personality disorders may or may not be aware that they are lonely, unhappy, or unable to achieve an expected level of satisfaction in their lives. Whether or not they are aware, they often find it difficult or impossible to change their deeply ingrained patterns of relating to others. The reasons for the difficulty in changing the patterns are complex; in general, the reasons concern the unconscious defensive and self-protective, albeit maladaptive, functions of the persons' personality styles; they act the way they do in order, on some level, to decrease conscious anxiety and depression. The personality style is a maladaptive attempt to control some underlying anxiety.

In the fourth edition of *Diagnostic and Statistical Manual of Mental Disorders* (DSM-IV), personality disorders are grouped into three clusters. In cluster A—paranoid, schizoid, and schizotypal personality disorders—are those persons who most often appear odd, reclusive, or eccentric. In cluster B—antisocial, borderline, histrionic, and narcissistic personality disorders—are those persons who appear dramatic, overly emotional, erratic, volatile, or unstable in their relationships. In cluster C—avoidant, dependent, and obsessive-compulsive personality disorders—are those persons who appear overly anxious, fearful, or needy. Personality disorder not otherwise specified (NOS) is included in DSM-IV for disorders that do not fit into any of the previously described personality disorders. The two examples given in DSM-IV are passive-aggressive personality disorder and depressive personality disorder.

Although psychodynamic formulations remain basic and critically useful to any causal understanding of personality disorders, other causal factors are also recognized. For instance, significantly more persons with schizotypal personality disorder are found in the families of schizophrenic patients than in controls, leading many researchers to suspect a genetic link between the disorders. Similarly, borderline personality disorder patients have more relatives with mood disorders than do control groups, and borderline personality disorder and mood disorders often coexist.

The treatment of personality disorders is difficult and long-term. The disorders reflect chronic, inflexible, and tenacious patterns of functioning. The disorders are in the basic makeup of the person. Any treatment must often combine psychotherapy, cognitive behavioral techniques, pharmacotherapy, and family, substance abuse, and group interventions.

Students are referred to Chapter 26 in *Kaplan and Sadock's Synopsis VII* to prepare for the questions and answers below.

HELPFUL HINTS

The student should be able to define the terms below.

alloplastic	oral character	Wilhelm Reich
autoplastic	Heinz Kohut	character armor
ego-dystonic	mask of sanity	Erik Erikson
ego-syntonic	ambulatory schizophrenia	fantasy
paranoid	as-if personality	dissociation
schizoid	psychotic character	denied affect
schizotypal	emotionally unstable personality	isolation
histrionic	micropsychotic episodes	projection
narcissistic	identity diffusion	counterprojection
antisocial	panphobia	repression
borderline	pananxiety	hypochondriasis
avoidant	panambivalence	secondary gain
dependent	chaotic sexuality	splitting
obsessive-compulsive	timid temperament	turning anger against the self
depressive	inferiority complex	acting out
passive-aggressive	Sigmund Freud	*la belle indifferénce*
extroversion	free association	dependence
introversion	sadomasochistic personality	Stella Chess, Alexander Thomas
Carl Gustav Jung	Marquis de Sade	goodness of fit
clusters A, B, and C	castration anxiety	ideas of reference
Briquet's syndrome	Leopold von Sacher-Masoch	magical thinking
platelet MAO	self-defeating personality	macropsia
saccadic movements	sadistic personality	organic personality disorder
endorphins	anal triad	ICD-10
object choices	three Ps	

QUESTIONS

DIRECTIONS: Each of the questions or incomplete statements below is followed by five suggested responses or completions. Select the *one* that is *best* in each case.

26.1. A 21-year-old man was interviewed by a psychiatrist while he was being detained in jail awaiting trial for attempted robbery. The patient had a history of arrests for substance abuse, robbery, and assault and battery.

The patient's past history revealed that he had been expelled from junior high school for truancy, fighting, and generally poor academic performance. After his theft of a car when he was 14 years old, he was placed in a juvenile detention center.

Subsequently, he spent brief periods in a variety of institutions, from which he usually ran away. At times, his parents attempted to let him live at home, but he was disruptive and threatened them with physical harm. After one incident in which he threatened them with a knife, he was admitted to a psychiatric hospital; but he signed himself out against medical advice one day later.

The patient had never formed close personal relationships with his parents, his two older brothers, or friends of either sex. He was a loner and a drifter, and he had not worked for more than two months at any one job in his life. He was recently terminated, because of fighting and poor attendance, from a vocational training program in which he had been enrolled for about three weeks.

The most likely diagnosis is
A. narcissistic personality disorder
B. borderline personality disorder
C. antisocial personality disorder
D. schizoid personality disorder
E. paranoid personality disorder

26.2. True statements concerning antisocial personality disorder include all the following *except*
A. the prevalence of antisocial personality disorder is 3 percent in men and 1 percent in women
B. a familial pattern is present
C. the patients often show abnormalities in their electroencephalograms and soft neurological signs
D. antisocial personality disorder is synonymous with criminality
E. the patients appear to lack a conscience

26.3. Leon was a 45-year-old postal service employee who was evaluated at a clinic specializing in the treatment of depression. He claimed to have felt constantly depressed since the first grade, without a period of normal mood for more than a few days at a time. His depression had been accompanied by lethargy, little or no interest or pleasure in anything, trouble in concentrating, and feelings of inadequacy, pessimism, and resentfulness. His only periods of normal mood occurred when he was home alone, listening to music or watching TV.

On further questioning, Leon revealed that he could never remember feeling comfortable socially. Even before kindergarten, if he was asked to speak in front of a group of family friends, his mind would go blank. He felt overwhelming anxiety at children's social functions, such as birthday parties, which he either avoided or, if he went, attended in total silence. He could answer questions in class only if he wrote down the answers in advance; even then, he frequently mumbled and could not get the answer out. He met new children with his eyes lowered, fearing their scrutiny, expecting to feel humiliated and embarrassed. He was convinced that everyone around him thought he was dumb or a jerk.

As he grew up, Leon had a couple of neighborhood playmates, but he never had a best friend. His school grades were good but suffered when oral classroom participation was expected. As a teenager, he was terrified of girls and to this day had never gone on a date or even asked a girl for a date. That bothered him, although he was so often depressed that he felt he had little energy or interest in dating.

Leon attended college and did well for a while;

then he dropped out as his grades slipped. He remained self-conscious and terrified of meeting strangers. He had trouble finding a job because he was unable to answer questions in interviews. He worked at a few jobs for which only a written test was required. He passed a civil service examination at age 24 and was offered a job in the post office on the evening shift. He enjoyed the job, since it involved little contact with others. He was offered but refused several promotions because he feared the social pressure. Although by now he supervised a number of employees, he still found it difficult to give instructions, even to people he had known for years. He had no friends and avoided all invitations to socialize with coworkers. During the past several years, he had tried several therapies to help him get over his shyness and depression. Leon had never experienced sudden anxiety or a panic attack in social situations or at other times. Rather, his anxiety gradually built to a constant level in anticipation of social situations. He had never experienced any psychotic symptoms.

The best diagnosis is
A. avoidant personality disorder
B. schizoid personality disorder
C. schizotypal personality disorder
D. social phobia
E. adjustment disorder with anxiety

26.4. True statements regarding borderline personality disorder include all the following *except*
A. patients with borderline personality disorder have more relatives with mood disorders than do control groups
B. borderline personality disorder and mood disorders often coexist
C. first-degree relatives of persons with borderline personality disorder show an increased prevalence of alcohol dependence
D. smooth pursuit eye movements are abnormal in borderline personality disorder
E. monoamine oxidase inhibitors are used in the treatment of borderline personality disorder patients

26.5. Adult patients with borderline personality disorders who pigeonhole people into all-good and all-bad categories are demonstrating which of the following mechanisms?
A. Undoing
B. Intellectualization
C. Projection
D. Splitting
E. Displacement

26.6. The defense mechanism most often associated with paranoid personality disorder is
A. hypochondriasis
B. splitting
C. isolation
D. projection
E. dissociation

26.7. A pervasive pattern of grandiosity, lack of empathy, and need for admiration suggests the diagnosis of which of the following personality disorders?
A. Schizotypal
B. Passive-aggressive
C. Borderline
D. Narcissistic
E. Paranoid

26.8. All the following characteristics of the dependent personality disorder apply *except*
A. more often diagnosed in men than in women
B. more common in youngest children of a sibship than in the older children
C. pessimism
D. marked lack of self-confidence
E. getting others to assume responsibility for major areas of the patient's life

26.9. People who are prone to dependent personality disorder include all the following *except*
A. men
B. younger children
C. persons with chronic physical illness in childhood
D. persons with a history of separation anxiety disorder
E. children of mothers with panic disorder

26.10. Sadomasochistic personality disorder is
A. not included in the fourth edition of *Diagnostic and Statistical Manual of Mental Disorders* (DSM-IV)
B. characterized by unconscious castration anxiety
C. characterized by severe guilt about sex
D. best treated with insight-oriented psychotherapy
E. all the above

DIRECTIONS: Each group of questions below consists of lettered headings followed by a list of numbered statements. For each numbered phrase or statement, select the *one* lettered heading that is most closely associated with it. Each lettered heading may be selected once, more than once, or not at all.

Questions 26.11–26.15
A. Schizoid personality disorder
B. Schizotypal personality disorder

26.11. Strikingly odd or eccentric behavior

26.12. Magical thinking

26.13. Ideas of reference

26.14. Formerly called simple or latent schizophrenia

26.15. Suspiciousness or paranoid ideation

Questions 26.16–26.22
A. Dependent personality disorder
B. Organic personality disorder
C. Obsessive-compulsive personality disorder
D. Paranoid personality disorder
E. Histrionic personality disorder
F. Borderline personality disorder
G. Avoidant personality disorder

26.16. Cognitive disturbances, suspiciousness, and paranoid ideation

26.17. Preoccupied with orderliness, perfectionism, rigid and stubborn

26.18. Patients feel helpless when alone, have difficulty in doing things on their own

26.19. Want to be the center of attention, preoccupied with physical appearance

26.20. Unwilling to get involved with people unless certain of being liked

26.21. Identity disturbance, impulsivity, and recurrent suicidal behavior

26.22. Read hidden demeaning or threatening meanings into benign events and comments

ANSWERS

Personality Disorders

26.1.   The answer is C (*Synopsis VII,* pages 737–738)

The most likely diagnosis is *antisocial personality disorder.* Antisocial personality disorder is characterized by continual antisocial or criminal acts and an inability to conform to social norms that involves many aspects of the patient's adolescent and adult development. In the case of the 21-year-old man described, the many arrests for criminal acts, the aggressiveness, and the inability to maintain an enduring attachment to a sexual partner all suggest antisocial personality disorder. The fourth edition of *Diagnostics and Statistical Manual of Mental Disorders* (DSMMD-IV) requires evidence of conduct disorder before age 15 to make the diagnosis of antisocial personality disorder; in the case described, the history of truancy, expulsion from school, fighting, and thefts, all before age 15, confirms the diagnosis.

Narcissistic personality disorder is characterized by a heightened sense of self-importance, grandiose feelings of uniqueness, lack of empathy, and need for admiration. *Borderline personality disorder* is characterized by severely unstable mood, affect, behavior, object relations, and self-image. Antisocial personality disorder is frequently associated with narcissistic and borderline personality disorders. *Schizoid personality disorder* is diagnosed in patients with a lifelong pattern of social withdrawal. Such persons are often seen by others as eccentric, isolated, or lonely. *Paranoid personality disorder* is characterized by longstanding suspiciousness and mistrust of people in general. The essential feature of disorder is a pervasive and unwarranted tendency to interpret other people's actions as deliberately demeaning or threatening. The history provided in the case described does not justify the diagnosis of either schizoid personality disorder or paranoid personality disorder.

Table 26.1 lists the diagnostic criteria for antisocial personality disorder.

26.2.   The answer is D (*Synopsis VII,* pages 737–738).

Antisocial personality disorder is characterized by continual antisocial or criminal acts, but it *is not synonymous with criminality.* Rather, it is a pattern of irresponsible and antisocial behavior that pervades the patient's adolescence and adulthood. *The prevalence of antisocial personality disorder is 3 percent in men and 1 percent in women. A familial pattern is*

Table 26.1
Diagnostic Criteria for Antisocial Personality Disorder

A. There is a pervasive pattern of disregard for and violation of the rights of others occurring since age 15 years, as indicated by three (or more) of the following:

   (1) failure to conform to social norms with respect to lawful behaviors as indicated by repeatedly performing acts that are grounds for arrest
   (2) deceitfulness, as indicated by repeated lying, use of aliases, or conning others for personal profit or pleasure
   (3) impulsivity or failure to plan ahead
   (4) irritability and aggressiveness, as indicated by repeated physical fights or assaults
   (5) reckless disregard for safety of self or others
   (6) consistent irresponsibility, as indicated by repeated failure to sustain consistent work behavior or honor financial obligations
   (7) lack of remorse, as indicated by being indifferent to or rationalizing having hurt, mistreated, or stolen from another

B. The individual is at least age 18 years.

C. There is evidence of conduct disorder with onset before age 15 years.

D. The occurrence of antisocial behavior is not exclusively during the course of schizophrenia or a manic episode.

Table from DSM-IV, *Diagnostic and Statistical Manual of Mental Disorders,* ed 4. Copyright American Psychiatric Association, Washington, 1994. Used with permission.

present in that it is five times more common among first degree relatives of males with the disorder than among controls. A notable finding is a lack of remorse; that is, *the patients appear to lack a conscience.*

The patients often show abnormalities in their electroencephalograms and soft neurological signs suggestive of minimal brain damage in childhood.

26.3.   The answer is A (*Synopsis VII,* page 743).

The best diagnosis is *avoidant personality disorder.* Although feeling constantly depressed caused him to seek treatment, the pervasive pattern of social avoidance, fear of criticism, and lack of close peer relationships was of equal importance. Persons with avoidant personality show an extreme sensitivity to rejection, which may lead to social withdrawal. They are not asocial but are shy and show a great desire for companionship; they need unusually strong guarantees of uncritical acceptance. In the case presented, the patient exhibited a long-standing pattern of difficulty in relating to others. Persons with *schiz-oid personality disorder* do not evince the same strong desire for affection and acceptance; they want to be alone. *Schizotypal personality disorder* is characterized by strikingly odd or strange behavior, magical thinking, peculiar ideas, ideas of reference, illusions, and derealization. The patient described did not exhibit those characteristics. *Social phobia* is an irrational fear of social or performance situations such as public speaking and eating in public. A social phobia is anxiety concerning social identified situations, not relationships in general.

A person with a personality disorder can have a superimposed adjustment disorder but only if the current episode includes new clinical features not characteristic of the person's personality. No evidence in the case described indicated that the anxiety was qualitatively different from what the patient always experienced in social situations. Thus, an additional diagnosis of *adjustment disorder with anxiety* is not made.

The diagnostic criteria for avoidant personality disorder are listed in Table 26.2.

26.4. The answer is D (*Synopsis VII*, pages 739–741).

Smooth pursuit eye movements are normal in borderline personality disorder. They are abnormal in schizophrenic patients and patients with schizotypal personality disorder.

Patients with borderline personality disorders have more *relatives with mood disorders* than do control groups, and *borderline personality disorder and mood disorder often coexist. First-degree relatives of persons with borderline personality disorder show an increased prevalence of alcohol dependence* and substance abuse.

Monoamine oxidase inhibitors are used in the treatment of borderline personality disorder patients and have been effective in modulating affective instability and impulsivity in a number of patients.

Table 26.3 lists the diagnostic criteria for borderline personality disorder.

26.5. The answer is D (*Synopsis VII*, page 733 and 740).

Adult patients with borderline personality disorder distort their present relationships by pigeonholing people into all-good and all-bad categories, a defense mechanism known as *splitting*. People are seen as either nurturant and attachment figures or hateful and sadistic persons who deprive the patients of security needs and threaten them with abandonment whenever they feel dependent.

Undoing is an unconscious defense mechanism by which a person symbolically acts out in reverse something unacceptable that has already been done or against which the ego must defend itself. A primitive defense mechanism, undoing is a form of magical expiatory action. Repetitive in nature, it is commonly observed in obsessive-compulsive disorder. *Intellec-*

Table 26.2
Diagnostic Criteria for Avoidant Personality Disorder

A pervasive pattern of social inhibition, feelings of inadequacy, and hypersensitivity to negative evaluation, beginning by early adulthood and present in a variety of contexts, as indicated by four (or more) of the following:

   (1) avoids occupational activities that involve significant interpersonal contact, because of fears of criticism, disapproval, or rejection
   (2) is unwilling to get involved with people unless certain of being liked
   (3) shows restraint within intimate relationships because of the fear of being shamed or ridiculed
   (4) is preoccupied with being criticized or rejected in social situations
   (5) is inhibited in new interpersonal situations because of feelings of inadequacy
   (6) views self as socially inept, personally unappealing, or inferior to others
   (7) is unusually reluctant to take personal risks or to engage in any new activities because they may prove embarrassing

Table from DSM-IV, *Diagnostic and Statistical Manual of Mental Disorders,* ed 4. Copyright American Psychiatric Association, Washington, 1994. Used with permission.

Table 26.3
Diagnostic Criteria for Borderline Personality Disorder

A pervasive pattern of instability of interpersonal relationships, self-image, and affects, and marked impulsivity beginning by early adulthood and present in a variety of contexts, as indicated by five (or more) of the following:

   (1) frantic efforts to avoid real or imagined abandonment. **Note:** Do not include suicidal or self-mutilating behavior covered in criterion 5.
   (2) a pattern of unstable and intense interpersonal relationships characterized by alternating between extremes of idealization and devaluation
   (3) identity disturbance: markedly and persistently unstable self-image or sense of self
   (4) impulsivity in at least two areas that are potentially self-damaging (e.g., spending, sex, substance abuse, reckless driving, binge eating). **Note:** Do not include suicidal or self-mutilating behavior covered in criterion 5.
   (5) recurrent suicidal behavior, gestures, or threats, or self-mutilating behavior
   (6) affective instability due to a marked reactivity of mood (e.g., intense episodic dysphoria, irritability, or anxiety usually lasting a few hours and only rarely more than a few days)
   (7) chronic feelings of emptiness
   (8) inappropriate, intense anger or difficulty controlling anger (e.g., frequent displays of temper, constant anger, recurrent physical fights)
   (9) transient, stress-related paranoid ideation or severe dissociative symptoms

Table from DSM-IV, *Diagnostic and Statistical Manual of Mental Disorders,* ed 4. Copyright American Psychiatric Association, Washngton, 1994. Used with permission.

tualization is an unconscious defense mechanism in which reasoning or logic is used in an attempt to avoid confrontation with an objectionable impulse and thus defend against anxiety. It is also known as brooding compulsion and thinking compulsion. *Projection* is an unconscious defense mechanism in which persons attribute to another those generally unconscious ideas, thoughts, feelings, and impulses that are personally undesirable or unacceptable. Projection protects persons from anxiety arising from an inner conflict. By externalizing whatever is unacceptable, persons deal with it as a situation apart from themselves. *Displacement* is an unconscious defense mechanism by which the emotional component of an unacceptable idea or object is transferred to a more acceptable one.

26.6. The answer is D (*Synopsis VII*, pages 733–734).

The defense mechanism most often associated with paranoid personality disorder is *projection*. The patients externalize their own emotions and attribute to others impulses and thoughts that they are unable to accept in themselves. Excessive fault finding, sensitivity to criticism, prejudice, and hypervigilance to injustice can all be understood as examples of projecting unacceptable impulses and thoughts onto others.

Hypochondriasis is as a defense mechanism in some personality disorders, particularly in borderline, dependent, and passive-aggressive personality disorders. Hypochondriasis disguises reproach; that is, the hypochondriac complaint that others do not provide help often conceals bereavement, loneliness, or unacceptable aggressive impulses. The mechanism of hypochondriasis permits covert punishment of others with the patient's own pain and discomfort.

Splitting is used by patients with borderline personality disorder in particular. With splitting, the patient divides ambivalently regarded people, both past and present, into all-good or all-bad, rather than synthesizing and assimilating less-than-perfect caretakers.

Isolation is the defense mechanism characteristic of the orderly, controlled person, often labeled an obsessive-compulsive personality. Isolation allows the person to face painful situations without painful affect or emotion and, thus, to remain always in control.

Dissociation consists of a replacement of unpleasant affects with pleasant ones. It is most often seen in patients with histrionic personality disorder.

The diagnostic criteria for paranoid personality disorder are listed in Table 26.4.

26.7. The answer is D (*Synopsis VII*, page 742).

A pervasive pattern of grandiosity (in fantasy or behavior), lack of empathy, and need for admiration suggests the diagnosis of *narcissistic* personality disorder. The fantasies of narcissistic patients are of unlimited success, power, brilliance, beauty, and ideal

Table 26.4
Diagnostic Criteria for Paranoid Personality Disorder

A. A pervasive distrust and suspiciousness of others such that their motives are interpreted as malevolent, beginning by early adulthood and present in a variety of contexts, as indicated by four (or more) of the following:

  (1) suspects, without sufficient basis, that others are exploiting, harming, or deceiving him or her
  (2) is preoccupied with unjustified doubts about the loyalty or trustworthiness of friends or associates
  (3) is reluctant to confide in others because of unwarranted fear that the information will be used maliciously against him or her
  (4) reads hidden demeaning or threatening meanings into benign remarks or events
  (5) persistently bears grudges, i.e., is unforgiving of insults, injuries, or slights
  (6) perceives attacks on his or her character or reputation that are not apparent to others and is quick to react angrily or to counterattack
  (7) has recurrent suspicions, without justification, regarding fidelity of spouse or sexual partner

B. Does not occur exclusively during the course of schizophrenia, a mood disorder with psychotic features, or another psychotic disorder and is not due to the direct physiological effects of a general medical condition.

Note: If criteria are met prior to the onset of schizophrenia, add "premorbid," e.g., "paranoid personality disorder (premorbid)."

Table from DSM-IV, *Diagnostic and Statistical Manual of Mental Disorders,* ed 4. Copyright American Psychiatric Association, Washington, 1994. Used with permission.

love; their demands are for constant attention and admiration. Narcissistic personality disorder patients are indifferent to criticism or respond to it with feelings of rage or humiliation. Other common characteristics are a sense of entitlement, surprise and anger that people do not do what the patient wants, and interpersonal exploitiveness.

Schizotypal personality disorder is characterized by various eccentricities in communication or behavior, coupled with defects in the capacity to form social relationships. The term emphasizes a possible relation with schizophrenia. The manifestation of aggressive behavior in passive ways—such as obstructionism, pouting, stubbornness, and intentional inefficiency—typify *passive-aggressive* personality disorder. *Borderline* personality disorder is marked by instability of mood, interpersonal relationships, and self-image. *Paranoid* personality disorder is characterized by rigidity, hypersensitivity, unwarranted suspicion, jealousy, envy, an exaggerated sense of self-importance, and a tendency to blame and ascribe evil motives to others.

Table 26.5 lists the diagnostic criteria for narcissistic personality disorder.

26.8. The answer is A (*Synopsis VII*, page 744).

Dependent personality disorder is *more often diagnosed in women than in men*. It is *more common*

Table 26.5
Diagnostic Criteria for Narcissistic Personality Disorder

A pervasive pattern of grandiosity (in fantasy or behavior), need for admiration, and lack of empathy, beginning by early adulthood and present in a variety of contexts, as indicated by five (or more) of the following:

(1) has a grandiose sense of self-importance (e.g., exaggerates achievements and talents, expects to be recognized as superior without commensurate achievements)
(2) is preoccupied with fantasies of unlimited success, power, brilliance, beauty, or ideal love
(3) believes that he or she is "special" and unique and can only be understood by, or should associate with, other special or high-status people (or institutions)
(4) requires excessive admiration
(5) has a sense of entitlement, i.e., unreasonable expectations of especially favorable treatment or automatic compliance with his or her expectations
(6) is interpersonally exploitative, i.e., takes advantage of others to achieve his or her own ends
(7) lacks empathy: is unwilling to recognize or identify with the feelings and needs of others
(8) is often envious of others or believes that others are envious of him or her
(9) shows arrogant, haughty behaviors or attitudes

Table from DSM-IV, *Diagnostic and Statistical Manual of Mental Disorders,* ed 4. Copyright American Psychiatric Association, Washington, 1994. Used with permission.

Table 26.6
Diagnostic Criteria for Dependent Personality Disorder

A pervasive and excessive need to be taken care of that leads to submissive and clinging behavior and fears of separation, beginning by early adulthood and present in a variety of contexts, as indicated by five (or more) of the following:

(1) has difficulty making everyday decisions without an excessive amount of advice and reassurance from others
(2) needs others to assume responsibility for most major areas of his or her life
(3) has difficulty expressing disagreement with others because of fear of loss of support or approval. **Note:** Do not include realistic fears of retribution
(4) has difficulty initiating projects or doing things on his or her own (because of a lack of self-confidence in judgment or abilities rather than a lack of motivation or energy)
(5) goes to excessive lengths to obtain nurturance and support from others, to the point of volunteering to do things that are unpleasant
(6) feels uncomfortable or helpless when alone because of exaggerated fears of being unable to care for himself or herself
(7) urgently seeks another relationship as a source of care and support when a close relationship ends
(8) is unrealistically preoccupied with fears of being left to take care of himself or herself

Table from DSM-IV, *Diagnostic and Statistical Manual of Mental Disorders,* ed 4. Copyright American Psychiatric Association, Washington, 1994. Used with permission.

in the youngest children of a sibship than in the older children.

Pessimism, marked lack of self-confidence, passivity, and fears about expressing sexual and aggressive feelings characterize the behavior of the person with dependent personality disorder. *Getting others to assume responsibility for major areas of the patient's life* is characteristic.

The diagnostic criteria for dependent personality disorder are listed in Table 26.6.

26.9.   The answer is A (*Synopsis VII,* page 744).

People who are prone to dependent personality disorder include *women (not men), younger children,* and *persons with chronic physical illness in childhood.* Some workers believe that *a history of separation anxiety disorder* predisposes to the development of dependent personality disorder. Separation anxiety disorder has its onset before the age of 18 and is characterized by excessive anxiety concerning separation from people to whom the child is attached. Separation anxiety disorder itself may be frequent in *children of mothers with panic disorder,* and that factor may predispose to the development of dependent personality disorder.

26.10.   The answer is E (all) (*Synopsis VII,* page 748).

Sadomasochistic personality disorder is characterized by elements of sadism, masochism or a com-

bination of the two. Although *not included in DSM-IV,* the personality disorder is of clinical interest.

Sigmund Freud believed that sadists warded off *unconscious castration anxiety* and were able to achieve sexual pleasure only when they were able to do to others what they feared would be done to them.

Freud believed that masochists' ability to achieve orgasm is disturbed by anxiety and *severe guilt about sex* that are alleviated by their own suffering and punishment. Clinical observations indicate that elements of both sadistic and masochistic behavior are usually present in the same person. *Treatment with insight-oriented psychotherapy,* including psychoanalysis, has been effective in some cases. As a result of therapy, the patient becomes aware of the need for self-punishment secondary to excessive unconscious guilt and also comes to recognize repressed aggressive impulses that have their origins in early childhood.

26.11–26.25

26.11.   The answer is B (*Synopsis VII,* pages 735–737).

26.12.   The answer is B (*Synopsis VII,* pages 735–737).

26.13.   The answer is B (*Synopsis VII,* pages 735–737).

26.14. **The answer is B** (*Synopsis VII*, pages 735–737).

26.15. **The answer is B** (*Synopsis VII*, pages 735–737).

Unlike schizoid personality disorder (Table 26.7), *schizotypal personality disorder* (Table 26.8) manifests with *strikingly odd or eccentric behavior. Magical thinking, ideas of reference,* illusions, and derealization are common; their presence formerly led to defining disorder as borderline, *simple, or latent schizophrenia. Suspiciousness or paranoid ideation* occurs in schizotypal personality disorder, not schizoid personality disorder.

26.16–26.22

26.16. **The answer is B** (*Synopsis VII*, page 749).

26.17. **The answer is C** (*Synopsis VII*, page 745).

26.18. **The answer is A** (*Synopsis VII*, page 744).

26.19. **The answer is E** (*Synopsis VII*, page 741).

26.20. **The answer is G** (*Synopsis VII*, page 743).

26.21. **The answer is F** (*Synopsis VII*, pages 739–740).

26.22. **The answer is D** (*Synopsis VII*, page 734).

Organic personality disorder (Table 26.9) is characterized by *cognitive disturbances, suspiciousness, and paranoid ideation.* In the 10th revision of the International Classification of Disease (ICD-10), the disorder is classified with personality and behavioral disorders due to brain disease, damage and dysfunction.

Patients with *obsessive-compulsive personality disorder* (Table 26.10) are *preoccupied with orderliness and perfectionism and are rigid and stubborn.* In ICD-10 the disorder is called anankastic personality disorder. In *dependent personality disorder patients feel helpless when alone, and have difficulty in doing things on their own.* Patients with *histrionic personality disorder* (Table 26.11) *want to be the center of attention,* and are *preoccupied with physical appearance.* Patients with *avoidant personality disorder* are *unwilling to get involved with people unless certain of being liked.* In ICD-10 the disorder is called anxious personality disorder. *Borderline personality disorder* is characterized by *identity disturbance, im-*

Table 26.7
Diagnostic Criteria for Schizoid Personality Disorder

A. A pervasive pattern of detachment from social relationships and a restricted range of expression of emotions in interpersonal settings, beginning by early adulthood and present in a variety of contexts, as indicated by four (or more) of the following:

  (1) neither desires nor enjoys close relationships, including being part of a family
  (2) almost always chooses solitary activities
  (3) has little, if any, interest in having sexual experiences with another person
  (4) takes pleasure in few, if any, activities
  (5) lacks close friends or confidants other than first-degree relatives
  (6) appears indifferent to the praise or criticism of others
  (7) shows emotional coldness, detachment, or flattened affectivity

B. Does not occur exclusively during the course of schizophrenia, a mood disorder with psychotic features, another psychotic disorder, or a Pervasive Developmental Disorder and is not due to the direct physiological effects of a general medical condition.

Note: If criteria are met prior to the onset of schizophrenia, add "premorbid," e.g., "schizoid personality disorder (premorbid)."

Table from DSM-IV, *Diagnostic and Statistical Manual of Mental Disorders,* ed 4. Copyright American Psychiatric Association, Washington, 1994. Used with permission.

Table 26.8
Diagnostic Criteria for Schizotypal Personality Disorder

A. A pervasive pattern of social and interpersonal deficits marked by acute discomfort with, and reduced capacity for, close relationships as well as by cognitive or perceptual distortions and eccentricities of behavior, beginning by early adulthood and present in a variety of contexts, as indicated by five (or more) of the following:

  (1) ideas of reference (excluding delusions of reference)
  (2) odd beliefs or magical thinking that influence behavior and are inconsistent with subcultural norms (e.g., superstitiousness, belief in clairvoyance, telepathy, or "sixth sense"; in children and adolescents, bizarre fantasies or preoccupations)
  (3) unusual perceptual experiences, including bodily illusions
  (4) odd thinking and speech (e.g., vague, circumstantial, metaphorical, overelaborate, or stereotyped)
  (5) suspiciousness or paranoid ideation
  (6) inappropriate or constricted affect
  (7) behavior or appearance that is odd, eccentric, or peculiar
  (8) lack of close friends or confidants other than first-degree relatives
  (9) excessive social anxiety that does not diminish with familiarity and tends to be associated with paranoid fears rather than negative judgments about self

B. Does not occur exclusively during the course of schizophrenia, a mood disorder with psychotic features, another psychotic disorder, or a pervasive development disorder.

Note: If criteria are met prior to the onset of schizophrenia, add "premorbid," e.g., "schizotypal personality disorder (premorbid)."

Table from DSM-IV, *Diagnostic and Statistical Manual of Mental Disorders,* ed. 4, Copyright American Psychiatric Association, Washington, 1994. Used with permission.

Table 26.9
ICD-10 Diagnostic Criteria for Organic Personality Disorder

This disorder is characterized by a significant alteration of the habitual patterns of premorbid behaviour. The expression of emotions, needs, and impulses is particularly affected. Cognitive functions may be defective mainly or even exclusively in the areas of planning and anticipating the likely personal and social consequences, as in the so-called frontal lobe syndrome. However, it is now known that this syndrome occurs not only with frontal lobe lesions but also with lesions to other circumscribed areas of the brain.

Diagnostic guidelines
In addition to an established history or other evidence of brain disease, damage, or dysfunction, a definitive diagnosis requires the presence of two or more of the following features:

(a) consistently reduced ability to persevere with goal-directed activities, especially those involving longer periods of time and postponed gratification;

(b) altered emotional behaviour, characterized by emotional lability, shallow and unwarranted cheerfulness (euphoria, inappropriate jocularity), and easy change to irritability or short-lived outbursts of anger and aggression; In some instances apathy may be a more prominent feature;

(c) expression of needs and impulses without consideration of consequences or social convention (the patient may engage in dissocial acts, such as stealing, inappropriate sexual advances, or voracious eating, or may exhibit disregard for personal hygiene);

(d) cognitive disturbances, in the form of suspiciousness or paranoid ideation, and/or excessive preoccupation with a single, usually abstract, theme (e.g. religion, ''right'' and ''wrong'');

(e) marked alteration of the rate and flow of language production, with features such as circumstantiality, over-inclusiveness, viscosity, and hypergraphia;

(f) altered sexual (hyposexuality or change of sexual preference).

Table from World Health Organization: *The ICD-10 Classification of Mental and Behavioural Disorders: Clinical Disorders and Diagnostic Guidelines* World Health Organization, Geneva, 1992. Used with permission.

pulsivity, and recurrent suicidal behavior. In ICD-10 the disorder is called emotionally unstable personality disorder. Patients with *paranoid personality disorder read hidden demeaning or threatening meanings into benign events and comments.*

Table 26.10
Diagnostic Criteria for Obsessive-Compulsive Personality Disorder

A pervasive pattern of preoccupation with orderliness, perfectionism, and mental and interpersonal control, at the expense of flexibility, openness, and efficiency, beginning by early adulthood and present in a variety of contexts, as indicated by four (or more) of the following:

(1) is preoccupied with details, rules, lists, order, organization, or schedules to the extent that the major point of the activity is lost

(2) shows perfectionism that interferes with task completion (e.g., is unable to complete a project because his or her own overly strict standards are not met)

(3) is excessively devoted to work and productivity to the exclusion of leisure activities and friendships (not accounted for by obvious economic necessity)

(4) is overconscientious, scrupulous, and inflexible about matters of morality, ethics, or values (not accounted for by cultural or religious identification)

(5) is unable to discard worn-out or worthless objects even when they have no sentimental value

(6) is reluctant to delegate tasks or to work with others unless they submit to exactly his or her way of doing things

(7) adopts a miserly spending style toward both self and others; money is viewed as something to be hoarded for future catastrophes

(8) shows rigidity and stubbornness

Table from DSM-IV, *Diagnostic and Statistical Manual of Mental Disorders*, ed. 4, Copyright American Psychiatric Association, Washington, 1994. Used with permission.

Table 26.11
Diagnostic Criteria for Histrionic Personality Disorder

A pervasive pattern of excessive emotionality and attention seeking, beginning by early adulthood and present in a variety of contexts, as indicated by five (or more) of the following:

(1) in uncomfortable in situations in which he or she is not the center of attention

(2) interaction with others is often characterized by inappropriate sexually seductive or provocative behavior

(3) displays rapidly shifting and shallow expression of emotions

(4) consistently uses physical appearance to draw attention to self

(5) has a style of speech that is excessively impressionistic and lacking in detail

(6) shows self-dramatization, theatricality, and exaggerated expression of emotion

(7) is suggestible, i.e., easily influenced by others or circumstances

(8) considers relationships to be more intimate than they actually are

Table from DSM-IV, *Diagnostic and Statistical Manual of Mental Disorders*, ed 4. Copyright American Psychiatric Association, Washington, 1994. Used with permission.

Psychological Factors Affecting Medical Condition (Psychosomatic Disorders)

Body and mind are connected and each affects the other in a variety of complex ways, both subtle and overt. In other words, psychology and biology are inextricably intertwined and, to one degree or another, always affect each other's functioning. The fourth edition of *Diagnostic and Statistical Manual of Mental Disorders* (DSM-IV) includes a diagnostic category that specifies that psychological factors do affect a patient's medical condition in a variety of ways. DSM-IV's diagnostic criteria include the proviso that there be a close temporal association between the psychological factors and the course of the medical condition. The diagnostic criteria also require that the nature of the psychological factor be specified and give five choices: mental disorder, psychological symptoms, personality traits or coping styles, maladaptive health behaviors, and unspecified psychological factors. The medical condition that is being affected is coded on Axis III. Excluded from DSM-IV's diagnostic criteria for psychological factors affecting medical condition are the somatoform disorders (such as somatization disorder, hypochondriasis, and conversion disorder) and physical complaints associated with either substance-related disorders or specific mental disorders.

How psychological factors affect medical conditions is still largely unknown. The most likely explanation is a combination of interacting factors, including the character of the stress, the genetic and biological vulnerability of the patient, the physiological stage, the patient's personality and psychological resilience, the health of the patient's immune system. How all those factors interact to produce disease is still a controversial and ongoing area of inquiry.

A number of specific disorders have been investigated with regard to the effects of psychological factors on their course and management. Included among the disorders are those involving the cardiovascular system (for example, coronary artery disease, essential hypertension, congestive heart failure, and Raynaud's phenomenon), the respiratory system (for example, bronchial asthma, hay fever, and hyperventilation syndrome), the gastrointestinal system (for example, peptic ulcer and ulcerative colitis), the musculoskeletal system (for example, rheumatoid arthritis and low back pain), the endocrine system (for example, diabetes mellitus, menopausal distress, and premenstrual syndrome), and the immune system (for example, infectious diseases, allergic disorders, organ transplantation and autoimmune diseases). Disorders such as headaches, chronic pain, cocaine abuse, and dermatological disorders have also been extensively studied with regard to the effects of psychological factors.

The field of consultation-liaison psychiatry most directly addresses the interaction of medicine and psychiatry. The consultation-liaison psychiatrist generally serves as a consultant to general medical colleagues, providing expertise with regard to mental disorders that may present with or complicate general medical symptoms and the many medical illnesses that can present with psychiatric symptoms. The major task of the consultation-liaison psychiatrist is to help identify any existing mental disorders and psychological responses to the medical illness. Part of that task is to recognize and describe the patient's personality style and coping techniques are to recommend effective therapeutic interventions. Some of the most common problems for which a consultation-liaison psychiatrist may be consulted include suicidal ideation, depression, agitation, hallucinations, sleep disorders, disorientation, noncompliance, and disorders with no apparent organic basis. Some of the settings in which a consultation-liaison psychiatrist provides advice and support include intensive care units, hemodialysis units, and surgical units.

The treatment of the psychological factors affecting medical condition almost invariably involves both psychotherapeutic and medical management. A combined treatment approach requires close collaboration between the psychiatrist (who addresses the psychiatric aspects of the case) and the medical specialist (who handles the nonpsychiatric aspects). Psychiatric therapies that have been effectively used include psychodynamic psychotherapy, cognitive therapy, behavior therapy (such as biofeedback and relaxation therapy) and pharmacotherapy (such as antidepressants and anxiolytics).

Students are referred to Chapter 27 in *Kaplan and Sadock's Synopsis VII* for detailed information on the topic. After studying Chapter 27, students will be prepared to address the questions and answers below.

HELPFUL HINTS

The terms relating to psychophysiological medicine listed below should be defined.

psychosomatic	propranolol (Inderal)	pain clinics
psychophysiological	bronchial asthma	immune disorders
psyche and soma	hay fever	immune response
conversion disorder	hyperventilation syndrome	immediate and delayed
somatization disorder	peptic ulcer	hypersensitivity
hypochondriasis	ulcerative colitis	cell-mediated immunity
dysthymic disorder	compulsive personality traits	humoral immunity
Thomas Holmes and Richard Rahe	obesity	AIDS
social readjustment rating scale	bulimia nervosa and anorexia	allergic disorders
life-change units	nervosa	organ transplantation
specific versus nonspecific stress	rheumatoid arthritis	autoimmune diseases
Flanders Dunbar	low back pain	systemic lupus erythematosus
Meyer Friedman and Roy	migraine	skin disorders
Rosenman	tension headaches	pruritus
Franz Alexander	obsessional personalities	hyperhidrosis
general adaptation syndrome	hyperthyroidism	C-L psychiatry
alexithymia	thyrotoxicosis	myxedema madness
coronary artery disease	diabetes mellitus	Wilson's disease
postcardiotomy delirium	PMS	pancreatic carcinoma
type A and type B personalities	premenstrual dysphoric disorder	command hallucination
essential hypertension	dysmenorrhea	gun-barrel vision
biofeedback	menopausal distress	pheochromocytoma
relaxation therapy	climacteric	ICUs
congestive heart failure	IgM and IgA	hemodialysis units
vasomotor syncope	atopic	dialysis dementia
personality types	idiopathic amenorrhea	surgical patients
specificity hypothesis	chronic pain	crisis intervention
vasovagal attack	pain threshold and perception	Hans Selye
cardiac arrhythmias	undermedication	vasomotor syncope
psychogenic cardiac nondisease	behavior modification,	giving up-given up concept
neurocirculatory asthenia	deconditioning program	hormonal personality factors
Jacob DaCosta	analgesia	

QUESTIONS

DIRECTIONS: Each of the questions or incomplete statements below is followed by five responses or completions. Select the *one* that is *best* in each case.

27.1. The key difference between the revised third edition of *Diagnostic and Statistical Manual of Mental Disorders* (DSM-III) and the fourth edition (DSM-IV) in regard to the diagnostic criteria for psychological factors affecting medical condition is that DSM-IV allows for emphasis on
A. environmental stimuli
B. psychological stimuli
C. somatoform disorders
D. conversion disorder
E. all the above

27.2. A decrease in T lymphocytes has been reported in all the following *except* in
A. bereavement
B. caretakers of patients with dementia of the Alzheimer's type
C. women who are having extramarital affairs
D. nonpsychotic inpatients
E. medical students during final examinations

27.3. Each of the following statements about the relative importance of various stresses is true *except*
A. divorce is a greater stress than marriage
B. marital separation is a greater stress than pregnancy
C. retirement from work is a greater stress than major illness
D. in-law troubles are a greater stress than trouble with the boss
E. changing to a new school is a greater stress than going on vacation

27.4. The major worker in the application of psychoanalytic concepts to the study of psychosomatic disorders was
A. George Mahl
B. Harold Wolff
C. Franz Alexander
D. Robert Ader
E. Meyer Friedman

27.5. Dialysis dementia is characterized by
A. loss of memory
B. disorientation
C. dystonias
D. seizures
E. all the above

27.6. Each of the following statements about psychoneuroimmunology is false *except*
A. immunological reactivity is not affected by hypnosis
B. lymphocytes cannot produce neurotransmitters
C. the immune system is affected by conditioning
D. growth hormone does not affect immunity
E. marijuana does not affect the immune system

27.7. Therapies that are considered alternatives to standard psychotherapy include all the following *except*
A. acupuncture
B. cognitive therapy
C. homeopathy
D. ozone therapy
E. chiropractic

27.8. The percentage of cancer patients who later have mental disorders is
A. 13 percent
B. 50 percent
C. 68 percent
D. 90 percent
E. 8 percent

27.9. A highly emetogenic anticancer agent is
A. cisplatin
B. doxorubicin
C. vincristine
D. vinblastine
E. bleomycin

27.10. Mood disorder and psychotic disorder symptoms are found most often with the use of
A. hexamethylmelamine
B. steroids
C. interferon
D. hydroxyurea
E. L-asparaginase

27.11. A patient presenting with mood disturbances, psychoses, fever, photosensitivity, butterfly rash, and joint pains is least given a diagnosis of
A. acute intermittent porphyria
B. hypoparathyroidism
C. systematic lupus erythematosus
D. hepatic encephalopathy
E. pheochromocytoma

27.12. Each of the following statements about common consultation-liaison problems is true *except*
A. agitation is often associated with cognitive disorders and withdrawal from drugs
B. in a disoriented patient, delirium must be differentiated from dementia
C. negative transference to a doctor is the most common cause of noncompliance
D. in a hospital the most common cause of hallucinations is schizophrenia
E. a major high-risk factor for men over 45 in a hospital is suicide

27.13. In the psychotherapeutic treatment of the psychological factors relevant to an exacerbation of peptic ulcer, the most difficult problem is
A. the patients' resistance to entering psychotherapy
B. the patients' erotic transference to the psychotherapist
C. the patients' positive response to the interpretation of the physiological meaning of their symptoms
D. the patients' recognition of the psychological correlation with their physiological symptoms
E. none of the above

27.14. Acute cerebellar syndrome with ataxia is a common complication of chemotherapy with
A. methotrexate
B. 5-fluorouracil
C. cisplatin
D. misonidazole
E. intrathecal thiotepa

27.15. Disorders in which autoimmune diseases have been implicated include all the following *except*
A. Graves' disease
B. rheumatoid arthritis
C. peptic ulcer
D. regional ileitis
E. pernicious anemia

27.16. The giving up-given up concept in psychology is associated with
A. Arthur Schmale
B. Walter Cannon
C. Jurgen Ruesch
D. Hans Selye
E. Flanders Dunbar

27.17. Phantom limb occurs after leg amputation in what percentage of patients?
A. 98 percent
B. 90 percent
C. 80 percent
D. 50 percent
E. 10 percent

27.18. The most common symptom associated with chronic headaches is
A. depression
B. hallucinations
C. perseveration
D. memory disturbance
E. altered body image

27.19. The most common cause of time lost from work in this country is
A. hypochondriasis
B. low back pain
C. angina pectoris
D. gout
E. dental pain

27.20. The number of patients who go to a physician with headaches as their main complaint has been estimated to be
A. less than 10 percent
B. 10 to 20 percent
C. 20 to 30 percent
D. 30 to 40 percent
E. more than 50 percent

27.21. In hypothyroidism a psychosis that occurs is called
A. hypothyroid crisis
B. schizophrenia, paranoid type
C. bipolar I disorder
D. myxedema madness
E. delirium

27.22. The scratching of the skin in generalized pruritus is often said to represent
A. aggression turned against the self
B. poor body image
C. anal sadism
D. orality
E. orgasm

27.23. Correct statements about persons with asthma include which of the following?
A. They are overly dependent on their mothers
B. Attacks follow episodes of frustration
C. Poor impulse control may be seen
D. Attacks follow separation from parents or parental figures
E. All the above

27.24. Which of the following may be associated with a complaint of chronic pain?
A. Depression
B. Mourning
C. Psychosis
D. Delusions
E. All the above

27.25. In evaluating patients with complaints of chronic pain of whatever cause, the physician must be alert to
A. the patient's use of an over-the-counter medication
B. alcohol dependence
C. withdrawal symptoms during the evaluation
D. an underlying medical illness
E. all the above

27.26. Factors associated with a risk for obesity include
A. socioeconomic status
B. social mobility
C. age
D. sex
E. all the above

DIRECTIONS: The questions below consist of five lettered headings followed by a list of numbered phrases. For each numbered select the *one* lettered heading that is most closely associated with it. Each lettered heading may be selected once, more than once, or not at all.

Questions 27.27–27.30

A. Wilson's disease
B. Pheochromocytoma
C. Systemic lupus erythematosus
D. Acquired immune deficiency syndrome (AIDS)
E. Pancreatic cancer

27.27. Dementia syndrome with global impairment and seropositivity

27.28. Resembles steroid psychosis

27.29. Explosive anger and labile mood

27.30. Symptoms of a classic panic attack

ANSWERS

Psychological Factors Affecting Medical Condition
(Psychosomatic Disorders)

27.1. The answer is B (*Synopsis VII,* page 752).

The important change in the fourth edition of *Diagnostic and Statistical Manual of Mental Disorders* (DSM-IV) from the revised third edition (DSM-III-R) is that DSM-IV allows clinicians to specify the *psychological stimuli* that affect the patient's medical condition. In DSM-III-R, psychologically meaningful *environmental stimuli* were temporally related to the physical disorder. Excluded in DSM-III-R were *somatoform disorders,* such as *conversion disorder,* in which the physical symptoms are not based on organic pathology. The DSM-IV emphasis on psychological factors permits a wide range of psychological stimuli to be noted (for example, personality traits, maladaptive health behaviors).

Table 27.1 lists the DSM-IV diagnostic criteria for psychological factors affecting medical condition.

27.2. The answer is C (*Synopsis VII,* page 765).

There are no studies on the T cells of *women who are having extramarital affairs.* Investigators have found a decrease in lymphocytic response in *bereavement* (conjugal and anticipatory), the *caretakers of patients with dementia of the Alzheimer's type,* in *nonpsychotic inpatients,* in resident physicians, in *medical students during final examinations,* in women who were separated or divorced, in the elderly with no social support, and in the unemployed.

27.3. The answer is C (*Synopsis VII,* page 753–755).

Stressful situations are weighted in the social readjustment rasing scale of Thomas Holmes and Richard Rahe. (Table 27.2). According to the scale, retirement from work is not a major illness. *Divorce is a greater stress than marriage. Marital separation is a greater stress than pregnancy. In-law troubles are a greater stress than trouble with the boss. And changing to a new school is a greater stress than going on vacation.*

27.4. The answer is C (*Synopsis VII,* pages 753 and 758–760).

Franz Alexander applied psychoanalytic concepts to the study of peptic ulcers, bronchial asthma, and essential hypertension. He studied specific repressed unconscious conflicts associated with those diseases.

George Mahl was an experimental animal psychologist who studied ulcer development in animals.

Table 27.1
Diagnostic Criteria for Psychological Factors Affecting Medical Condition

A. A general medical condition (coded on Axis III) is patient.

B. Psychological factors adversely affect the general medical condition in one of the following ways:

(1) the factors have influenced the course of the general medical condition as shown by a close temporal association between the psychological factors and the development or exacerbation of, or delayed recovery from, the general medical condition

(2) the factors interfere with the treatment of the general medical condition

(3) the factors constitute additional health risks for the individual

(4) stress-related physiologic responses precipitate or exacerbate symptoms of the general

Choose name based on the nature of the psychological factors (if more than one factor is present, indicate the most prominent):

Mental disorder affecting medical condition (e.g., an Axis I disorder such as major depressive disorder delaying recovery from a myocardial infarction)
Psychological symptoms affecting medical condition (e.g., depressive symptoms delaying recovery from surgery; anxiety exacerbating asthma)
Personality traits or coping style affecting medical condition (e.g., pathological denial of the need for surgery in a patient with cancer; hostile, pressured behavior contributing to cardiovascular disease)
Maladaptive health behaviors affecting medical condition (e.g., overeating; lack of exercise; unsafe sex)
Stress-related physiological response affecting medical condition (e.g., stress-related exacerbations of ulcer, hypertension, arrhythmia, or tension headache)
Other or unspecified psychological factors affecting medical condition (e.g., interpersonal, cultural, or religious factors)

Table from DSM-IV, *Diagnostic and Statistical Manual of Mental Disorders,* ed 4. Copyright American Psychiatric Association, Washington, 1994. Used with permission.

He concluded that chronic anxiety caused by any conflict is causally important.

Harold Wolff and Stewart Wolf attempted to correlate life stress with physiological protective human responses.

Robert Ader studied the immune response and psychoneuroimmunology in psychosomatic disorders.

Table 27.2
Social Readjustment Rating Scale

Life Event	Mean Value
1. Death of spouse	100
2. Divorce	73
3. Marital separation from mate	65
4. Detention in jail or other institution	63
5. Death of a close family member	63
6. Major personal injury or illness	53
7. Marriage	50
8. Being fired at work	47
9. Marital reconciliation with mate	45
10. Retirement from work	45
11. Major change in the health or behavior of a family member	44
12. Pregnancy	40
13. Sexual difficulties	39
14. Gaining a new family member (through birth, adoption, oldster moving in, etc.)	39
15. Major business readjustment (merger, reorganization, bankruptcy, etc.)	39
16. Major change in financial state (a lot worse off or a lot better off than usual)	38
17. Death of a close friend	37
18. Changing to a different line of work	36
19. Major change in the number of arguments with spouse (either a lot more or a lot less than usual regarding child rearing, personal habits, etc.)	35
20. Taking on a mortgage greater than $10,000 (purchasing a home, business, etc.)*	31
21. Foreclosure on a mortgage or loan	30
22. Major change in responsibilities at work (promotion, demotion, lateral transfer)	29
23. Son or daughter leaving home (marriage, attending college, etc.)	29
24. In-law troubles	29
25. Outstanding personal achievement	28
26. Wife beginning or ceasing work outside the home	26
27. Beginning or ceasing formal schooling	26
28. Major change in living conditions (building a new home, remodeling, deterioration of home or neighborhood)	25
29. Revision of personal habits (dress, manners, associations, etc.)	24
30. Troubles with the boss	23
31. Major change in working hours or conditions	20
32. Change in residence	20
33. Changing to a new school	20
34. Major change in usual type or amount of recreation	19
35. Major change in church activities (a lot more or a lot less than usual)	19
36. Major change in social activities (clubs, dancing, movies, visiting, etc.)	18
37. Taking on a mortgage or loan less than $10,000 (purchasing a car, TV, freezer, etc.)	17
38. Major change in sleeping habits (a lot more or a lot less sleep or change in part of day when asleep)	16
39. Major change in number of family get-togethers (a lot more or a lot less than usual)	15
40. Major change in eating habits (a lot more or a lot less food intake or very different meal hours or surroundings)	15
41. Vacation	15
42. Christmas	12
43. Minor violations of the law (traffic tickets, jaywalking, disturbing the peace, etc.)	11

*This figure no longer has any relevance in the light of inflation; what is significant is the total amount of debt from all sources.
Table from T Holmes: Life situations, emotions, and disease. Psychosom Med *19:* 747, 1978. Used with permission.

Meyer Friedman correlated personality types (type A and type B) with certain psychosomatic disorders, such as coronary heart disease.

27.5. The answer is E (all) (*Synopsis VII,* page 777).

Dialysis dementia is a rare condition characterized by *loss of memory, disorientation, dystonias, and seizures.* The dementia occurs in patients who have been receiving dialysis treatment for many years. The cause is unknown.

27.6. The answer is C (*Synopsis VII,* pages 765–766).

The immune system is affected by conditioning. According to Ader, *immunological reactivity is affected by hypnosis, lymphocytes can produce neurotransmitters, growth hormone does affect immunity,* and *marijuana does affect the immune system.* Robert Ader has summarized the psychoneuroimmunology factors (Table 27.3).

Table 27.3
Summary of Psychoneuroimmunology Factors
by Robert Ader

Nerve endings have been found in the tissues of the immune system. The central nervous system is linked both to the bone marrow and the thymus, where immune system cells are produced and developed, and to the spleen and the lymph nodes, where those cells are stored.

Changes in the central nervous system (the brain and the spinal cord) alter immune responses, and triggering all immune response alters central nervous system activity. Animal experiments dating back to the 1960s show that damage to different parts of the brain's hypothalamus can either suppress or enhance the allergics-type response. Recently, researchers have found that inducing an immune response causes nerve cells in the hypothalamus to become more active and that the brain cell anxiety peaks at precisely the same time that levels of antibodies are at their highest. Apparently, the brain monitors immunological changes closely.

Changes in hormone and neurotransmitter levels alter immune responses, and vice versa. The stress hormones generally suppress immune responses. But other hormones, such as growth hormone, also seem to affect immunity. Conversely, when experimental animals are immunized, they show changes in various hormone levels.

Lymphocytes are chemically responsive to hormones and neurotransmitters. Immune system cells have receptors—molecular structures on the surface of their cells—that are responsive to endorphins, stress hormones, and a wide range of other hormones.

Lymphocytes can produce hormones and neurotransmitters. When an animal is infected with a virus, lymphocytes produce minuscule amounts of many of the same substances produced by the pituitary gland.

Activated lymphocytes—cells actively involved in an immune response—produce substances that can be perceived by the central nervous system. The interleukins and interferons—chemicals that immune system cells use to talk to each other—can also trigger receptors on cells in the brain, more evidence that the immune system and the nervous system speak the same chemical language.

Psychosocial factors may alter the susceptibility to or the progression of autoimmune disease, infectious disease, and cancer. Evidence for those connections comes from many researchers.

Immunological reactivity may be influenced by stress. Chronic or intense stress, in particular, generally makes immune system cells less responsive to a challenge.

Immunological reactivity can be influenced by hypnosis. In a typical study, both of a subject's arms are exposed to a chemical that normally causes an allergic reaction. But the subject is told, under hypnosis, that only one arm will show the response—and that, in fact, is often what happens.

Immunological reactivity can be modified by classical conditioning. As Ader's own key experiments showed, the immune system can learn to react in certain ways as a conditioned response.

Psychoactive drugs and drugs of abuse influence immune function. A range of drugs that affect the nervous system—including alcohol, marijuana, cocaine, heroin, and nicotine have all been shown to affect the immune response, generally suppressing it. Some psychiatric drugs, such as lithium (prescribed for bipolar I disorder) also modulate the immune system.

Table adapted from D Goleman, J Guerin: *Mind Body Medicine*. Consumer Reports, Yonkers, N. Y. 1993. Used with permission.

27.7.   The answer is B (*Synopsis VII*, page 778 and 859).

Cognitive therapy is considered standard psychotherapy. It is based on the theory that behavior is secondary to the way in which persons think about themselves and their roles in the world. Maladaptive behavior is secondary to ingrained stereotyped thoughts that can lead to cognitive distortions or errors in thinking. The therapy is aimed at correcting those cognitive distortions and the self-defeating behaviors that result from them. It is especially useful in treating depressive disorders.

Acupuncture is the use of needles to stimulate areas that are supposed to have neural connections with specific organs and body functions. In *homeopathy*, medication is based on the premise that disease can be cured with diluted doses of various substances. *Ozone therapy* is the introduction of ozone gas into the bloodstream as a way to fight disease. *Chiropractic* is the manipulation or subluxation of the spinal vertebrae to relieve back problems and other ailments.

27.8.   The answer is B (*Synopsis VII*, pages 767–768).

About *50 percent* of cancer patients later have mental disorders; 68 percent of these disorders are adjustment disorder; 15 percent of those with psychiatric symptoms have major depressive disorder, and 8 percent have deliria. Although cancer patients may express suicidal wishes, the actual suicide incidence is only 1.4 to 1.9 times that of the general population. Vulnerability to suicide is increased by the factors listed in Table 25.4.

27.9.   The answer is A (*Synopsis VII*, page 768).

Cisplatin (Platinol) is highly emetogenic. *Doxorubicin* is moderately emetogenic, and *vincristine* (Oncovin), *vinblastine* (Velban), and *bleomycin* (Blenoxane) are minimally emetogenic. Table 27.5 summarizes the emetogenic problems with various chemotherapeutic agents.

27.10.   The answer is B (*Synopsis VII*, pages 768–769).

Steroids produce marked alterations of the patient's mental status, particularly from mania to depression—even to a suicidal degree. Dacarbazine produces depression and suicide, especially when used with hexamethylmelamine. *Interferon* produces anxiety and depression with suicidal ideation. Hallucinations have been reported with *hydroxyurea*. *L-Asparaginase* produces reversible depression.

Table 27.6 lists chemotherapy agents with mood and psychotic symptoms.

27.11.   The answer is C (*Synopsis VII*, pages 771–775).

Although the psychological symptoms are similar in all the conditions listed, a medical workup would

Table 27.4
Suicide Vulnerability Factors in Cancer Patients

Depression and hopelessness
Poorly controlled pain
Mild delirium (disinhibition)
Feeling of loss of control
Exhaustion
Anxiety
Preexisting psychopathology (substance abuse, character
  pathology, major psychiatric disorder)
Acute family problems
Threats or history of prior attempts at suicide
Positive family history of suicide
Other usually described risk factors in psychiatric patients

Table adapted from W. Breitbart: Suicide in cancer patients. Oncology 1: 49, 1987. Used with permission.

Table 27.5
Emetogenic Potential of Some Commonly Used Anticancer Agents

Highly emtogenic	Cisplatin
	Dacarbazine
	Streptozocin
	Actinomycin
	Nitrogen mustard
Moderately emetogenic	Doxorubicin
	Daunorubicin
	Cyclophosphamide
	Nitrosoureas
	Mitomycin-C
	Procarbazine
Minimally emetogenic	Vincristine
	Vinblastine
	5-Fluorouracil
	Bleomycin

Table by Marguerite S. Lederberg, M.D., and Jimmie C. Holland, M.D.

Table 27.6
Chemotherapy Agents with Mood and Psychotic Symptoms

Dacarbazine: depression and suicide reported, especially
  when used with hexamethylamine
Vinblastine: frequent reversible depression
Vincristine: 5 percent incidence of hallucinations; depression
  noted
L-Asparaginase: reversible depression noted
Procarbazine: MAOI; concurrent tricyclic drugs are
  contraindicated; associated with mania and depression;
  potentiales alcohol, barbiturates, phenothiazines
Hydroxyurea: hallucinations reported
Interferon: anxiety, depression with suicidal ideation common
  at doses above 40 million units
Steroids: frequent alterations of mental state ranging from
  emotional lability through mania or severe, suicidal
  depression to frank psychosis

Table by Marguette B. Loderberg, M.D., and Jimmie C. Holland, M.D.

reveal that fever, photosensitivity, butterfly rash, and joint pains are diagnostic of *systemic lupus erythematosus.*

In *acute intermittent porphyria,* abdominal pain, fever, peripheral neuropathy, and elevated porphobilinogen are significant. In *hypoparathyroidism* the patient has constipation, polydipsia, and nausea with increased calcium and variable parathyroid hormone (PTH) levels. In *hepatic encephalopathy* the patient has asterixis, spider angioma, and abnormal liver function test results. In *pheochromocytoma* the patient has paroxysmal hypertension, headache, elevated vanillylmandelic acid (VMA), and tachycardia.

27.12.   The answer is D (*Synopsis VII,* pages 775–776).

In a hospital the most common cause of hallucinations is not schizophrenia, but rather delirium tremens. *Agitation is often associated with cognitive disorders and withdrawal from drugs. In a disoriented patient, delirium must be differentiated from dementia. Negative transference to a doctor is the most common cause of noncompliance.* And *a major high-risk factor for men over 45 in a hospital is suicide.* Table 27.7 presents common consultation-liaison problems encountered in hospital practice.

27.13.   The answer is A (*Synopsis VII,* pages 780–781).

The most difficult problem in the treatment of psychosomatically ill patients is *the patients' resistance to entering psychotherapy* and to recognizing the psychological factors in their illness. Generally, clinicians have difficulty in forming a positive transference with the patients. *The patients' erotic transference to the psychotherapist does not develop. The patients usually react negatively to the interpretation of the physiological meaning of their symptoms* and do not recognize the psychological correlation with their physiological symptoms.

27.14.   The answer is B (*Synopsis VII,* page 768).

Acute cerebellar syndrome with ataxia is a common complication of chemotherapy with *5-fluorouracil* (Efudex). *Methotrexate* often produces encephalopathy. *Cisplatin* (Platinol) and *misonidazole* may manifest ototoxicity, and *intrathecal thiotepa* produces myelopathy. Table 27.8 lists neurological complications of chemotherapy.

27.15.   The answer is C (*Synopsis VII,* page 767).

Peptic ulcer is not considered an autoimmune disease. Disorders in which an autoimmune component has been implicated include *Graves' disease,* Hashimoto's disease, *rheumatoid arthritis,* ulcerative colitis, *regional ileitis,* systemic lupus erythematosus, psoriasis, myasthenia gravis, and *pernicious anemia.*

27.16.   The answer is A (*Synopsis VII,* page 757).

Arthur Schmale developed the giving up-given up concept for psychosomatic disorders. It is associated

Table 27.7
Common Consultation-Liaison Problems

Reason for Consultation	Comments
Suicide attempt or threat	High-risk factors are men over 45, no social support, alcohol dependence, previous attempt, incapacitating medical illness with pain, and suicidal ideation. If risk is present, transfer to psychiatric unit or start 24-hour nursing care.
Depression	Suicidal risks must be assessed in every depressed patient (see above); presence of cognitive defects in depression may cause diagnostic dilemma with dementia; check for history of substance abuse or depressant drugs (e.g., reserpine, propranolol); use anti-depressants cautiously in cardiac patients because of conduction side effects, orthostatic hypotension.
Agitation	Often related to cognitive disorder, withdrawal from drugs (e.g., opioids, alcohol, sedative-hypnotics); haloperidol most useful drug for excessive agitation; use physical restraints with great caution; examine for command hallucinations or paranoid ideation to which patient is responding in agitated manner; rule out toxic reaction to medication.
Hallucinations	Most common cause in hospital is delirium tremens; onset three to four days after hospitalization. In intensive care units, check for sensory isolation; rule out brief psychotic disorder, schizophrenia, cognitive disorder. Treat with antipsychotic medication.
Sleep disorder	Common cause is pain; early morning awakening associated with depression; difficulty in falling asleep associated with anxiety. Use antianxiety or antidepressant agent, depending on cause. Those drugs have no analgesic effect, so prescribe adequate painkillers. Rule out early substance withdrawal.
No organic basis for symptoms	Rule out conversion disorder, somatization disorder, factitious disorder, and malingering; glove and stocking anesthesia with autonomic nervous system symptoms seen in conversion disorder; multiple body complaints seen in somatization disorder; wish to be hospitalized seen in factitious disorder; obvious secondary gain in malingering (e.g., compensation case).
Disorientation	Delirium versus dementia; review metabolic status, neurological findings, substance history. Prescribe small dose of antipsychotics for major agitation; benzodiazepines may worsen condition and cause sundowner syndrome (ataxia, confusion); modify environment so patient does not experience sensory deprivation.
Noncompliance or refusal to consent to procedure	Explore relationship of patient and treating doctor; negative transference is most common cause of noncompliance; fears of medication or of procedure require education and reassurance. Refusal to give consent is issue of judgment; if impaired, patient can be declared incompetent but only by a judge; cognitive disorder is main cause of impaired judgment in hospitalized patients.

with a feeling of learned helplessness. *Walter Cannon* showed that the physiological concomitants of certain conditions are mediated by the autonomic nervous system. *Jurgen Ruesch* emphasized the importance of the communication between people in the development of psychosomatic disorders. *Hans Selye* showed that, under stress, a general adaption syndrome may produce physiological reactions that may eventuate in psychosomatic disorders. *Flanders Dunbar* correlated specific conscious personality types with specific psychosomatic disorders.

27.17. The answer is A (*Synopsis VII,* pages 776–779).

Phantom limb occurs in *98 percent* of patients who have undergone leg amputation. The experience may last for years. Sometimes the sensation is painful, and a neuroma at the stump should be ruled out. The condition has no known cause or treatment and usually stops spontaneously.

27.18. The answer is A (*Synopsis VII,* pages 761–762).

The most common symptom associated with chronic headaches is *depression*. The depression apparently has no organic basis but, rather, is secondary to the stress of having to deal with a chronic illness. The converse is also true; that is, headaches may also be seen as the presenting symptom of depression.

Hallucinations (false sensory perceptions) and *perseveration* (verbal repetition of words or phrases) are typically seen in psychotic illnesses and cognitive disorders and are not associated with headaches. *Memory disturbance* is most often evidence of an organic dysfunction, toxic or otherwise, and is not typical of headaches. *Altered body image,* the idea that one's body is shaped differently than it really is, is seen in the eating disorders anorexia nervosa and bulimia nervosa.

Table 27.8
Neurological Complications of Chemotherapy

Encephalopathy	Myelopathy
Methotrexate with	Intrathecal methotrexate
radiotherapy	Intrathecal cytarabine
Hexamethylmelamine	Intrathecal thiotepa
5-Fluorouracil	
Procarbazine	Neuropathy
Carmustine (BCNU)	Vinca alkaloids*
(intracarotid)	Cisplatin
Cisplatin (intracarotid)	Procarbazine
Cyclophosphamide	5-Azacytidine
5-Azacytidine	Vasopressin 16
Spirogermanium	VM 26
Misonidazole	Misonidazole
Cystarabine (high dose)	Methyl-G
L-Asparaginase	Cytarabine
Acute cerebellar syndrome,	Ototoxicity
ataxia	Cisplatin
5-Fluorouracil	Misonidazole
Cytarabine	
Procarbazine	
Hexamethylmelamine	

*Also involve cranial nerves.
Table by Marguerite S. Lederberg, M.D., and Jimmie C. Holland, M.D.
Table adapted from R A Patchell, J B Posner: Neurologic complications of systemic cancer. In *Symposium on Neuro-oncology Neurologic Clinics,* N A Vick, D D Bigner, editors, vol 3, p 729. Saunders, Philadelphia, 1985. Used with permission.

27.19. **The answer is B** (*Synopsis VII,* pages 764–765).

Chronic *low back pain* is the most common cause of time lost from work in this country. *Hypochondriasis* is a somatoform disorder characterized by excessive, morbid anxiety about one's health. Hypochondriacal patients exhibit a predominant disturbance in which the physical symptoms or complaints are not explainable on the basis of demonstrable organic findings and are apparently linked to psychological factors. *Angina pectoris* is severe constricting pain in the chest that is usually caused by coronary artery disease. *Gout* is an inherited metabolic disorder most commonly occurring in men. It is characterized by an elevated blood uric acid level and recurrent acute arthritis of sudden onset, which then leads to progressive and chronic arthritis. *Dental pain* is a general term referring to any pain in the mouth, teeth, or gums caused by various oral disorders.

27.20. **The answer is B** (*Synopsis VII,* pages 761–762).

Every year about 80 percent of the population are estimated to suffer from at least one headache, and *10 to 20 percent* of the population go to a physician with headaches as their primary complaint.

27.21. **The answer is D** (*Synopsis VII,* pages 772).

A high proportion of patients with adult onset of hypothyroidism show evidence of mental distur-

bance as part of the syndrome. *Myxedema madness* is a psychosis in which a wide range of organicity, from minimal to marked, may be manifest. It is often characterized by paranoid suspicions and auditory hallucinations.

Hypothyroid crisis is marked by a sudden reduction in thyroid function. *Schizophrenia* is paranoid type, characterized by the presence of persecutory or grandiose delusions, often accompanied by hallucinations. *Bipolar disorder* is a mood disorder in which the patient exhibits both manic and depressive episodes. *Delirium* is an acute, reversible cognitive disorder characterized by confusion and some impairment of consciousness. It is generally associated with emotional lability, hallucinations or illusions, and inappropriate, impulsive, irrational, or violent behavior.

27.22. **The answer is A** (*Synopsis VII,* page 770).

In generalized pruritus the rubbing of the skin represents *aggression turned against the self.* The emotions that most frequently lead to generalized psychogenic pruritus are repressed anger and repressed anxiety. An inordinate need for affection is a common characteristic of the patients. Frustrations of that need elicit aggressiveness that is then inhibited.

Body image is the conscious and unconscious perception of one's body at any particular time. One can perceive one's body image to be *poor,* good, or altered in some way. *Anal sadism* is the aggression, destructiveness, negativism, and externally directed rage that are typical components of the anal stage of development between the ages of 1 and 3. *Orality,* the earliest stage in psychosexual development, lasts through the first 18 months of life. During that period the oral zone is the center of the infant's needs, expression, and pleasurable erotic experiences. An *orgasm* is a sexual climax or peak psychophysiological reaction to sexual stimulation.

27.23. **The answer is E (all)** (*Synopsis VII,* pages 759–760)

Clinical research on asthmatic patients, especially children, has been guided by these main principles: (1) No single or uniform personality type has bronchial asthma. (2) Many asthmatic patients (about half) have strong unconscious wishes for protection and for being encompassed by another person; *they are overly dependent on their mothers.* Their wishes for protection sensitize some patients to separation from the mother. In other patients, the wish produces such an intense conflict that separation from the mother or her surrogate produces remission from asthmatic attacks. (3) The specific wishes for protection or envelopment are said to be caused by the mother's attitudes toward her asthmatic child. Studies of asthmatic children and their families, however, have shown that no single pattern of mother-child relationship obtains. The mother may be overprotective and oversolicitous of the child; perfectionistic and overambitious for the child; overtly domineering, punitive, or cruel to the child; or helpful and generative. Presumably, those attitudes both antecede the illness and are responsible for the child's conflicts and failure to develop psychologically. There is, however, no proof of those assumptions. In fact, the attitude of the mother is probably related to the child's social adjustment—his or her truancy or invalidism—than to the asthmatic attacks. (4) Asthmatic *attacks follow episode of frustration* by the mother or some other person, or they are activated and produce conflict. In both instances, strong emotions are aroused. (5) Some adult asthmatic patients have various psychological conflicts other than the ones already described.

Many asthmatic children have age-inappropriate behaviors and traits, and *poor impulse control may be seen.* Some children may be seen as timid, babyish, and overly polite; others are tense, restless, rebellious, irritable, and explosive in their emotional outbursts. Asthmatic boys, in particular, tend to be passively dependent, timid, and immature, and at times they become irritable when frustrated. Asthmatic girls tend to depend on their fathers more than their mothers and try to be self-sufficient but are frequently chronically depressed. Asthmatic children are also dominated by a fear of losing parental support. They attempt to defend against that fear by a show of independence, maturity, and masculinity. The mothers of some of the children are seductive; others overemphasize achievement and self-control. Regardless of the quality of the parental attitudes, *attacks follow separation from parents or parental figures.*

27.24.   The answer is E (all) (*Synopsis VII,* pages 764–765).

A large number of emotional states and mental disorders may lead to chronic pain. *Patients* with *depression* are especially prone to chronic pain, and if depression is severe, the patients may have delusions of cancer, rotting, or other metaphors of decay and death to explain the chronic pain.

A *mourning* person may have pain similar to that experienced by the lost person as a means of identifying with and introjecting part of the person in an attempt to deny the loss. Patients with *psychosis* may have bizarre forms of pain that are often attributed to some persecuting external force. Psychotic patients are also at risk for incorporating the pain of an organic illness—for example, myocardial infarction or perforated ulcer—into *delusions* and not seeking medical help.

27.25.   The answer is E (all) (*Synopsis VII,* pages 764–765).

Most chronic pain patients attempt to treat themselves before seeking medical help. Billions of dollars are spent annually by people seeking relief through *over-the-counter preparations* or other nonmedical means. Those persons often have *alcohol dependence* and other substance-related disorders. Therefore, the physician should be alert for substance toxicity (especially overmedication) and *withdrawal symptoms during the evaluation* and treatment of chronic pain patients. Explaining to the patient and family that sensitivity to pain may greatly increase during substance withdrawal may partially decrease anxiety and increase pain sensitivity caused by weaning. A physician should always remember that a psychiatric diagnosis does not preclude the existence of *an underlying medical illness.*

27.26.   The answer is E (all) (*Synopsis VII,* page 761).

The most striking influence on obesity is *socioeconomic status.* Obesity is six times more common among women of low status than among those of high status. A similar, although weaker, relationship is found among men. Obesity is also far more prevalent among lower-class children than it is among upper-class children; significant differences are already apparent by age 6. *Social mobility,* ethnic factors, and generation in the United States also influence the prevalence of obesity.

Age is the second major influence on obesity. There is a monotonic increase in the prevalence of obesity between childhood and age 50; a threefold increase occurs between ages 20 and 50. At age 50, prevalence falls sharply, presumably because of the high mortality of obese persons from cardiovascular disease in the elderly.

Sex also plays a role. *Women* show a higher prevalence of obesity than do men; the difference is particularly pronounced past age 50 because of the higher mortality rate among obese men after that age.

27.27–27.30

27.27.   The answer is D (*Synopsis VII,* page 772).

27.28.   The answer is C (*Synopsis VII,* page 773).

27.29.   The answer is A (*Synopsis VII,* page 774).

27.30.   The answer is B (*Synopsis VII,* page 774).

Wilson's disease, hepatolenticular degeneration, is a familial disease of adolescence that tends to have a long-term course. The pathology is caused by defective copper metabolism, leading to excessive copper deposits in tissues. The earliest psychiatric symptoms are *explosive anger and labile mood*—sudden and rapid changes from one mood to another. As the illness progresses, eventual brain damage occurs with memory and intelligence quotient (I.Q.) loss. The lability and combativeness tend to persist even after the brain damage develops.

Pheochromocytoma is a tumor of the adrenal medulla that causes headaches, paroxysms of severe hypertension, and the physiological and psychological *symptoms of a classic pain attack*—intense anxiety, tremulousness, apprehension, dizziness, palpitations, and diaphoresis. The tumor tissue secretes catecholamines that are responsible for the symptoms.

Systemic lupus erythematosus is an autoimmune disorder in which the body makes antibodies against its own cells. Those cells are then attacked by the antibodies as if they were infectious agents and, depending on which cells are being attacked, give rise to various symptoms. Frequently, the arteries in the cerebrum are affected, causing a cerebral arteritis, which alters the blood flow to various parts of the brain. The decreased blood flow can give rise to psychotic symptoms, such as a thought disorder with paranoid delusions and hallucinations. The symptoms can *resemble steroid psychosis* or schizophrenia.

The diagnosis of *acquired immune deficiency syndrome (AIDS)* includes a *dementia syndrome with global impairment and seropositivity*. The dementia can be caused by the direct attack on the central nervous system by the human immunodeficiency virus (HIV) or by secondary infections, such as toxoplasmosis.

Although any chronic illness can give rise to depression, some diseases, such as *pancreatic cancer,* are more likely causes than are others. The depression of pancreatic cancer patients is often associated with a sense of imminent doom.

Relational Problems

The fourth edition of *Diagnostic and Statistical Manual of Mental Disorders* (DSM-IV) describes problems in relationships that result in clinically significant impairment in one or more persons involved in the relationship. The category includes (1) relational problem related to a mental disorder or general medical condition, (2) parent-child relational problem, (3) partner relational problem, (4) sibling relational problem, and (4) relational problem not otherwise specified (NOS).

Relational problem related to a mental disorder or medical condition is diagnosed when a pattern of impaired interaction is associated with a mental disorder or a general medical condition in a family member. Examples include caring for elderly parents with a chronic illness, such as dementia of the Alzheimer's type, and caring for an adult child with schizophrenia.

Parent-child relational problem is reflected in a pattern of interaction that leads to clinically significant impairment in individual or family functioning or clinically significant symptoms. Examples include divorced parents and trouble with either the custodial parent or the noncustodial parent, remarriage and step-parent conflicts, the birth of a second child, the development of a fatal or chronic illness in a parent or a child.

Partner relational problem is diagnosed when a pattern of interaction between partners is characterized by dysfunctional communication and clinically significant impairment in individual or family functioning or symptoms in one or both partners. Examples of dysfunctional communication include patterns of criticism, unrealistic expectations, and withdrawal.

Sibling relational problem involves a pattern of interaction between siblings that leads to clinically significant impairment in individual or family functioning or symptoms in one or more of the siblings. Examples include excessive sibling rivalry and labeling specific children as good or bad, with resultant self-fulfilling behaviors.

Relational problem not otherwise specified includes such examples as patterns of difficulties with coworkers, neighbors, friends, and social groups.

Students should study Chapter 28 in *Kaplan and Sadock's Synopsis VII* and test their knowledge with the questions and answers below.

HELPFUL HINTS

The student should know the terms below.

stress relationships	sibling rivalry	sibling relational problem
dual-career families	relational problem related to a	relational problem not otherwise
birth of a child	mental disorder or general	specified (NOS)
chronic illness	medical condition	prejudice
role reversal	parent-child relational problem	racism
elderly abuse	partner relational problem	religious bigotry

QUESTIONS

DIRECTIONS: Each of the questions or incomplete statements below is followed by five suggested responses or completions. Select the *one* that is *best* in each case.

28.1. When a child has a congenital defect such as deafness
A. parents generally adapt quickly to the extra demands of the handicapped child
B. parent-child problems may arise with the unaffected siblings
C. money for hearing aids is provided by the government
D. divorce occurs in 80 percent of the families
E. the siblings are at an increased risk for childhood schizophrenia

28.2. Partner relational problem
A. may occur with a first episode of bipolar I disorder
B. rarely presents after the birth of a child
C. have associated sibling relational problems
D. usually occurs among the low socioeconomic group
E. is best handled through psychoanalysis

28.3. Which of the following statements about marital stress is *not* correct?
A. If the partners are from similar backgrounds, conflicts are not likely to arise
B. The birth of a child often precipitates a problem period
C. Abortion is not generally included as a potential conflict in a seemingly healthy marriage
D. Sexual dissatisfaction is involved in most cases of marital maladjustment
E. Complaints of female orgasmic disorder or male orgasmic disorder are usually indicative of deeper problems

DIRECTIONS: The questions below consist of lettered headings followed by a list of numbered statements. For each numbered statement, select the *one* lettered heading that is most closely associated with it. Each lettered heading may be used once, more than once, or not at all.

Questions 28.4–28.8
A. Relational problem related to a mental disorder or general medical condition
B. Parent-child relational problem
C. Partner relational problem
D. Sibling relational problem
E. Relational problem not otherwise specified

28.4. A woman with cancer resented being taken care of by her husband

28.5. A 54-year-old married man had problems with his neighbor; because of differences between the two, the police were called numerous times; otherwise, the man had many good friends

28.6. The oldest daughter in a family of four siblings refused to come home for any family gatherings if her oldest brother also came home

28.7. An adopted child continually felt that the family who adopted him paid more attention to their biological daughter than to him; he became increasingly withdrawn and irritable

28.8. A child accidently drowned in a neighborhood swimming pool; the mother blamed the father for lax parental supervision and was asking for a divorce

Relational Problems

28.1. **The answer is B** (*Synopsis VII*, pages 783–784).

When a child has a congenital defect such as deafness, the situation can stress the healthiest family, and *parent-child problems may arise with the unaffected siblings,* as well as the handicapped child. The unaffected siblings may be resented, preferred, or neglected because the ill child requires so much time and attention. *Parents generally do not adapt quickly to the extra demands of the handicapped child.*

If the handicap is severe, it often places an economic burden on the family. Currently, *money for hearing aids is not provided by the government* and is not included in the health care bill proposed by President Bill Clinton.

No statistics report that *divorce occurs in 80 percent of the families* with handicapped children. *The siblings are not at an increased risk for childhood schizophrenia.*

28.2. **The answer is A** (*Synopsis VII*, page 784).

A partner relational problem *may occur with a first episode of bipolar I disorder.* Bipolar I disorder is a mood disorder with alternating periods of mania and depression.

A partner relational problem *may be precipitated by the birth of a child,* abortion or miscarriage, economic stresses, moves to new areas, episodes of illness, major career changes, and any situations that involve a significant change in marital roles. Illness in a child exerts the greatest strain on a marriage, and marriages in which a child has died through illness or an accident end in divorce more often than not.

People with partner relational problems rarely *have associated sibling relational problems.* And partner relational problem does not *usually occur among the low socioeconomic group.*

Socioeconomic status in itself does not predispose a person to partner relational problem. It can, however, be a problem if the partners are of different backgrounds and have been raised with different value systems.

Partner relational problem *is best handled through marital therapy, not psychoanalysis.*

28.3. **The answer is C** (*Synopsis VII*, page 784).

Abortion is generally included as a potential conflict in a seemingly healthy marriage, as are economic stresses, moves to new areas, and unplanned pregnancies.

If the partners are from different backgrounds conflicts are more likely to arise than if they came from similar backgrounds. The areas of potential conflict that should be explored include sexual relations; attitudes toward contraception, childbearing, and child rearing; handling of money; relationships with in-laws; and attitudes toward social life.

28.4–28.8

28.4. **The answer is A** (*Synopsis VII*, page 783).

28.5. **The answer is E** (*Synopsis VII*, page 785).

28.6. **The answer is D** (*Synopsis VII*, page 784).

28.7. **The answer is B** (*Synopsis VII*, pages 783–784).

28.8. **The answer is C** (*Synopsis VII*, page 784).

The woman who resented being taken care of by her husband is classified as having *relational problem related to a mental disorder or general medical condition.*

The 54-year-old man who had problems with his neighbor is classified as having *relational problem not otherwise specified.*

The classification of *sibling relational problem* is best for the daughter who refused to attend family gatherings if her oldest brother was also present.

Parent-child *relational problem* is the appropriate diagnosis for the adopted child in a family with a biological daughter.

Partner relational problem is in the case of the marital discord related to the accidental drowning of the child.

Problems Related to Abuse or Neglect

The fourth edition of *Diagnostic and Statistical Manual of Mental Disorders* (DSM-IV) lists five problems related to abuse or neglect: (1) physical abuse of child, (2) sexual abuse of child, (3) neglect of child, (4) physical abuse of adult, and (5) sexual abuse of adult.

Child abuse and neglect occur frequently; 3 million cases were reported in 1992, and 1 million were substantiated. Child abuse and neglect are associated with many emotional, psychiatric, and medical problems. The psychiatric sequelae of child abuse and neglect include manifestations in childhood and when the children become adults. In children, common presentations include anxiety, aggressive behavior, paranoia, depression, suicidal ideation, dissociative symptoms, and posttraumatic stress disorder. In adults who were abused or neglected as children, possible presentations include borderline personality disorder, antisocial personality disorder, paranoid personality disorder, dissociative disorders, posttraumatic stress disorder, depressive disorders, substance-related disorders, reenactment of the abuse, and neglect of their own children.

The causes of child abuse and neglect are multifactorial. Many abusing and neglectful parents were abused and neglected as children. Other causative factors include stressful living conditions, social isolation, parental substance abuse, and mental disorders.

The diagnosis of abuse or neglect requires that official caretakers become educated about the characteristic signs and symptoms that should alert suspicion. For instance, symmetrical patterns of bruises and marks are not likely to have been caused accidentally. Physical indicators of sexual abuse include bruising, pain or itching in the genital region, and recurrent urinary tract infections or vaginal discharges. Behaviorally, physically and sexually abused children present myriad signs and symptoms, including withdrawal, depression, anxiety, increased aggression, and detailed knowledge or precocious displays of sexual acts. Poor impulse control and self-destructive and suicidal behaviors are common. Incest is a particularly common form of sexual abuse of children; 75 percent of reported cases involve father-daughter incest. Sibling incest is also common and is generally thought to be underreported.

Child neglect often presents as a general failure to thrive, malnutrition, poor skin hygiene, chronic infections, and inappropriate social interaction. The prognosis for children who have been physically or sexually abused or neglected depends on the severity of the abuse or neglect, the nature of the abuse, and the child's vulnerabilities. Treatment involves interventions with both the child and the parents and often begins with accurate diagnosis and timely reporting by educated clinicians.

Physical and sexual abuse of adults is a major problem that has only recently been discussed and emphasized. Spouse abuse—in particular, wife abuse—is estimated to occur in 2 million to 12 million families in the United States. Abusive husbands tend to experience strong feelings of inadequacy and high degrees of immaturity, dependence, and need to humiliate and bully to bolster their low self-esteem. Abuse occurs most often in families with problems of substance abuse.

The sexual abuse of adults is epitomized by the act of rape. The crime of rape requires only slight penile penetration of the outer vulva; full erection and ejaculation are not required by law to define an act as rape. Most rapes occur in the victim's own neighborhood and are premeditated; about 50 percent are committed by men known to their victims. Students should be familiar with the findings of recent research that categorize male rapists into separate groups, with the psychological sequelae of rape, and with the effective treatment of those sequelae.

Date rape and the rape of men are also topics with which every student needs to be familiar.

Students are referred to Chapter 29 and Chapter 50 in *Kaplan and Sadock's Synopsis VII* and then to the questions and answers below to test their knowledge on the subject.

HELPFUL HINTS

Each of the terms below should be defined by the student.

mood disorders	REM latency	annual deaths
major depressive disorder	secondary complications	low-birth-weight children
dysthymic disorder	functional impairment	premature children
irritable versus depressed mood	learning disabilities	family characteristics
mania	psychotic symptoms	diagnosis of child abuse
hypomania	suicide	incest
cyclothymic disorder	differential diagnosis	child pornography
schizoaffective disorder	hospitalization	father-daughter and mother-son
genetic factors	psychotherapy	incest
environmental factors	psychopharmacology	physician's responsibility
psychobiology	imipramine (Tofranil)	treatment
cortisol	child abuse	prevention
polysomnographic findings		

QUESTIONS

DIRECTIONS: Each of the questions or incomplete statements below is followed by five suggested responses or completions. Select the *one* that is *best* in each case.

29.1. Spouse abuse is
A. carried out by men who tend to be independent and assertive
B. a recent phenomenon
C. least likely to occur when the woman is pregnant
D. directed at specific actions of the spouse
E. an act that is self-reinforcing

29.2. Incestuous behavior
A. occurs most often in families of low socioeconomic status
B. is easily hidden by economically stable families
C. is perpetrated by men and women equally
D. occurs with a daughter who was emotionally distant from her father throughout childhood
E. usually begins before the child is 5 years old

29.3. Which of the following statements is true?
A. More than 50 percent of abused or neglected children were born prematurely or had low birth weight
B. Many abused children are perceived by their parents as slow in development or mentally retarded
C. More than 80 percent of abused children are living with married parents at the time of the abuse
D. Ninety percent of abusing parents were abused by their own mothers or fathers
E. All the above

29.4. The best way to establish a cause-and-effect relation between the type of mothering received and the symptoms of infant abuse is to show that
A. the child appears to be unduly afraid
B. the child shows evidence of repeated skin injuries
C. the child is undernourished
D. significant recovery occurs in the infant when the mothering is altered
E. the child is dressed inappropriately for the weather conditions

29.5. The estimated number of deaths from child maltreatment throughout the country each year is
A. 1,000 to 1,500
B. 2,000 to 4,000
C. 5,000 to 6,000
D. 7,000 to 8,000
E. 10,000

29.6. Which of the following statements about incest is true?
A. About 15 million women in the United States have been the object of incestuous attention
B. One-third of incest cases occur before the age of 9
C. It is most frequently reported in families of low socioeconomic status
D. Father-daughter incest is the most common type
E. All the above

29.7. Rape is predominately used to express power and anger in all the following cases *except*
A. rape of elderly women
B. homosexual rape
C. rape of young children
D. statutory rape
E. all the above

DIRECTIONS: The questions below consist of lettered headings followed by a list of numbered phrases or statements. For each numbered phrase or statement, select

A. if the item is associated with *A only*
B. if the item is associated with *B only*
C. if the item is associated with *both A and B*
D. if the item is associated with *neither A nor B*

Questions 29.8–29.10
A. Battered child syndrome
B. Sexual abuse

29.8. Usually perpetrated by men

29.9. Premature children are most vulnerable

29.10. Hyperactivity is a risk factor for the victim

ANSWERS

Problems Related to Abuse or Neglect

29.1.   The answer is E (*Synopsis VII,* page 793).

Spouse abuse is an *act that is self-reinforcing;* once a man has beaten his wife, he is likely to do so again. Abusive husbands *tend to be* immature, *dependent, and nonassertive* and to suffer from strong feelings of inadequacy. Spouse abuse is *not a recent phenomenon;* it is a problem of long standing that is *most likely to occur when the woman is pregnant;* 15 to 25 percent of pregnant women are physically abused while pregnant, and the abuse often results in birth defects. The *abuse is not directed at specific actions of the spouse.* Rather, impatient and impulsive, abusive husbands physically displace aggression provoked by others onto their wives.

29.2.   The answer is B (*Synopsis VII,* pages 789–790).

Incest is easily hidden by economically stable families. Incestuous behavior *does occur most often in families of low socioeconomic status.*

Incestuous behavior *is usually perpetrated by men:* fathers, stepfathers, uncles, and older siblings. In father-daughter incest the *daughter frequently had a close relationship with her father throughout childhood* and may be pleased at first when he approaches her sexually. The incestuous behavior *usually begins when the daughter is 10 years old.*

29.3.   The answer is E (all) (*Synopsis VII,* pages 786–792).

More than 50 percent of abused or neglected children were born prematurely or had low birth weight. Many abused children are perceived by their parents as difficult, *slow in development or mentally retarded,* bad, selfish, or hard to discipline. *More than 80 percent of abused children are living with married parents at the time of the abuse. Ninety percent of abusing parents were abused by their own mothers or fathers.*

29.4.   The answer is D (*Synopsis VII,* pages 789–791).

The only way to establish an unchallengeable cause-and-effect relation between the mothering received and the symptoms of infant abuse is to show that *significant recovery occurs in the infant when the mothering is altered.* That single criterion can make the diagnosis of maternal deprivation syndrome possible and, once made, calls for the development of a treatment plan based on immediate intervention and continued persistent surveillance. All markedly deprived infants should have an investigation of the social-environmental condition of the family and the psychological status of the mother to determine the factors responsible for inefficient mothering.

Child abuse and neglect may be suspected when several of the following factors are in evidence: the *child appears to be unduly afraid,* especially of the parents; the child is kept confined—as in a crib, playpen, or cage—for overlong periods of time; *the child shows evidence of repeated skin injuries;* the child's injuries are inappropriately treated in terms of bandages and medication; *the child is undernourished;* the child is given inappropriate food, drink, or medicine; *the child is dressed inappropriately for the weather conditions;* the child shows evidence of overall poor care; the child cries often; and the child takes over the role of a parent and tries to be protective or to take care of the parent's needs.

29.5.   The answer is B (*Synopsis VII,* page 786).

The National Center on Child Abuse and Neglect in Washington, D.C., has estimated that there are more than 300,000 instances of child maltreatment reported to central registries throughout the country every year and *2,000 to 4,000* deaths from abuse annually.

29.6.   The answer is E (all) (*Synopsis VII,* pages 787–790).

About 15 million women in the United States have been the object of incestuous attention, and *one-third of incest cases occur before the age of 9.* Incestuous behavior *is most frequently reported in families of low socioeconomic status.* That finding may be the result of their families' greater than usual contact with welfare workers, public health personnel, law enforcement agents, and other reporting officials; it is not a true reflection of higher incidence in that demographic group. *Father-daughter incest is the most common type.*

29.7.   The answer is D (*Synopsis VII,* page 790).

Statutory rape varies dramatically from the other kinds of rape in being nonassaultive and in being a sexual act, not a violent act. Statutory rape is intercourse that is unlawful because of the age of the participants. Intercourse is unlawful between a male over 16 years of age and a female under the age of consent, which ranges from 14 to 21 years, depending on the jurisdiction.

Other types of rape—including *the rape of elderly women, homosexual rape,* and *the rape of young chil-*

dren—are predominantly used to express power and anger. Studies of convicted rapists suggest that the crime is committed to relieve pent-up aggressive energy against persons of whom the rapist is in some awe. Although the awesome persons are usually men, the retaliatory violence is displaced toward women.

29.8–29.10

29.8.   The answer is B (*Synopsis VII*, pages 786–787).

29.9.   The answer is C (*Synopsis VII*, pages 786–787).

29.10.   The answer is A (*Synopsis VII*, pages 786–787).

Sexual abuse is usually perpetrated by men, although women acting in concert with men or alone have also been involved, especially in child pornography. *Premature children are vulnerable to both* battered child syndrome and sexual abuse. *Hyperactivity is also a risk factor for the victim.*

Additional Conditions That May Be a Focus of Clinical Attention

The fourth edition of *Diagnostic and Statistical Manual of Mental Disorders* (DSM-IV) lists 13 conditions that may bring a person into contact with the mental health system but are not mental disorders. However, the conditions may be associated with mental disorders or may be early manifestations of an undiagnosed mental disorder. Whenever someone presents with any of the conditions, the clinician must rule out any concomitant diagnosis of mental disorder. The 13 conditions are bereavement, borderline intellectual functioning, academic problem, occupational problem, childhood or adolescent antisocial behavior, adult antisocial behavior, malingering, phase of life problem, noncompliance with treatment for a mental disorder, identity problem, religious or spiritual problem, acculturation problem, and age-associated memory decline. Borderline intellectual functioning, academic problem, childhood or adolescent antisocial behavior, and identity problem are discussed in Chapter 48, "Child Psychiatry: Additional Conditions That May Be a Focus of Clinical Attention." All 13 conditions are coded on Axis IV.

Bereavement is distinguished from major depressive disorder on the basis of a variety of issues, including degree of guilt, suicidal ideas, psychomotor retardation, impaired functioning, hallucinations, and prolonged symptoms.

Occupational problem is exemplified by job dissatisfaction and uncertainty about career choices. Persons are particularly vulnerable during times of transition: entry into the working world, promotion or transfer, unemployment, and retirement. Stress is also produced by specific job situations: working for a demanding boss and having responsibility with-

out authority. Women in the workplace face many conflicts and stressors.

Adult antisocial behavior occurs outside the context of such mental disorders as antisocial personality disorder and impulse control disorder. Examples include the behavior of some professional thieves and dealers in illegal substances. Antisocial behavior can be observed in people with psychotic disorders and cognitive disorders. Patients may engage in antisocial behavior when influenced by the impaired judgment inherent in manic episodes.

Malingering is differentiated from such disorders as factitious disorders and somatoform disorders by the presence of an external goal that depends on the intentional production of false symptoms. The symptoms are consciously produced for a clear secondary gain. Malingering may be used in the service of adaptation, such as feigning illness when a captive in wartime.

Phase of life problem is exemplified in DSM-IV by problems associated with entering school, leaving parental control, starting a new career, and changes involved in marriage, divorce, and retirement.

Noncompliance with treatment for a mental disorder is exemplified in DSM-IV by irrationally motivated noncompliance due to denial of illness and decisions based on personal judgments about the advantages and disadvantages of the proposed treatment.

Religious or spiritual problem encompasses such issues as a loss or questioning of faith, problems associated with conversion to a new faith, and joining a religious cult.

Acculturation problem results from adjustment to a new culture because of migration or social transplantation. "Culture shock" is the colloquial term for the condition.

Age-associated memory decline is a decline in memory function within the normal limits given the person's age. The condition should be considered only after the clinician has clearly determined that the memory decline is not the result of a medical or neurological condition, such as dementia.

Students should study Chapter 30 in *Kaplan and Sadock's Synopsis VII* before turning to the questions and answers below.

HELPFUL HINTS

The student should know the following words and terms.

antisocial behavior	marital problems	coping mechanisms
kleptomania	noncompliance	phase of life problem
adoption studies	compliance	mature defense mechanisms
superego lacunae	adherence	cultural transition
emotional deprivation	doctor-patient match	culture shock
sociopathic	patient contract	bereavement
conditioning	occupational problem	normal grief
malingering	job-related stress	religious or spiritual problem
medicolegal context of presentation	noncustodial parent	cults
age-associated memory decline	dual-career families	acculturation problem
galvanic skin response	stress	brainwashing

QUESTIONS

DIRECTIONS: Each of the questions or incomplete statements below is followed by five suggested responses or completions. Select the *one* that is *best* in each case.

30.1. Which of the following is not considered a mental disorder?
A. Factitious disorder
B. Antisocial personality disorder
C. Malingering
D. Hypochondriasis
E. Somatization disorder

30.2. Adult antisocial behavior
A. has been effectively treated by psychotherapy
B. can be diagnosed in the presence of a mental disorder
C. is not influenced by genetic factors
D. is not associated with the use and abuse of alcohol and other substances
E. must be distinguished from temporal lobe epilepsy in the differential diagnosis

30.3. Exit therapy is designed to help people
A. with adult antisocial behavior
B. with acculturation problems
C. who are involved in cults
D. with occupational problems
E. in bereavement

30.4. Bereavement
A. usually leads to a full depressive disorder
B. is the same cross-culturally in terms of duration
C. includes guilt about things other than actions taken or not taken at the time of the death
D. includes preoccupation with thoughts about the deceased, tearfulness, irritability, and insomnia
E. can involve hallucinatory experiences other than hearing or seeing the deceased

30.5. The field of occupational or industrial psychiatry has found that
A. overwhelming ambition can usually overcome poor education and training and lead to success
B. few corporations are willing to employ a husband and a wife in the same firm
C. some people may fear success because of their inability to tolerate envy from others
D. fathers and mothers use unpaid parental leaves equally
E. the transition from outside employment to homemaking is stress-free

30.6. A person who malingers
A. often expresses subjective, ill-defined symptoms
B. should be confronted by the treating clinician
C. is usually found in settings with a preponderance of women
D. rarely seeks secondary gains
E. can achieve symptom relief by suggestion or hypnosis

30.7. Antisocial behavior is generally characterized by
A. lack of social charm and poor intelligence
B. heightened nervousness with neurotic manifestations
C. often successful suicide attempts
D. lack of remorse or shame
E. all the above

30.8. Factors most often associated with job-related stress include
A. unclear work objectives
B. conflicting demands
C. too much or too little work
D. responsibility for the professional development of others
E. all the above

30.9. Which one of the following conditions is motivated by financial gain?
A. Factitious disorder
B. Conversion disorder
C. Somatization disorder
D. Malingering
E. Body dysmorphic disorder

30.10. Occupational problem may arise from psychodynamic conflicts that include
A. problems with authority figures
B. competitive rivalries
C. pathological envy
D. fear of hostility from others
E. all the above

30.11. In dual-career families
A. mothers are vulnerable to guilt and anxiety regarding their maternal role
B. mothers emphasize the importance of discipline
C. the parents assume equal responsibility for child rearing and homemaking
D. the children are likely to have academic difficulties and psychological problems
E. the divorce rate is higher than in single-career families

DIRECTIONS: The questions below consist of lettered headings followed by a list of numbered phrases. For each numbered phrase, select

    A. if the item is associated with *A only*
    B. if the item is associated with *B only*
    C. if the item is associated with *both A and B*
    D. if the item is associated with *neither A nor B*

Questions 30.12–30.14
    A. Adult antisocial behavior
    B. Antisocial personality disorder
    C. Both
    D. Neither

30.12. Previous diagnosis of conduct disorder with onset before age 15

30.13. Mental disorder

30.14. Occurs more often in males than in females

ANSWERS

Additional Conditions That May Be a Focus of Clinical Attention

30.1. The answer is C (*Synopsis VII,* page 796).

Malingering is not considered a mental disorder. Malingering is characterized by the voluntary production and presentation of false or grossly exaggerated physical or psychological symptoms. The patient always has an external motivation, which falls into one of three categories: (1) to avoid difficult or dangerous situations, responsibilities, or punishment; (2) to receive compensation, free hospital room and board, a source of drugs, or haven from the police; and (3) to retaliate when the patient feels guilt or suffers a financial loss, legal penalty, or job loss.

Factitious disorder, antisocial personality disorder, hypochondriasis, and somatization disorder are all considered mental disorders. The presence of a clearly definable goal is the main factor that differentiates malingering from *factitious disorder. Antisocial personality disorder* requires evidence of conduct disorder that began before the age of 15. Hypochondriasis and somatization disorder are both somatoform disorders, which are characterized by physical symptoms that suggest physical disease, although no demonstrable organ pathology or pathophysiological mechanism can be identified. In *hypochondriasis* the patient is excessively concerned about disease and health. In *somatization disorder,* multiple somatic symptoms cannot be explained medically and are associated with psychosocial distress and medical help seeking.

Table 30.1 lists malingering features usually not found in genuine illness.

30.2. The answer is E (*Synopsis VII,* page 798).

Adult antisocial behavior *must be distinguished from temporal lobe epilepsy in the differential diagnosis.* When a clear-cut diagnosis of temporal lobe epilepsy or encephalitis can be made, that may contribute to the adult antisocial behavior. Abnormal electroencephalogram (EEG) findings are prevalent among violent offenders. An estimated 50 percent of aggressive criminals have abnormal EEG findings.

Adult antisocial behavior has not been effectively treated by psychotherapy, and there have been no major breakthroughs with biological treatments, including the use of medications. More enthusiasm is found for the use of therapeutic communities and other forms of group treatment. Many adult criminals who are incarcerated and in institutional settings have shown some response to group therapy approaches.

Table 30.1
Malingering Features Usually Not Found in Genuine Illness

Symptoms are vague, ill-defined, overdramatized, and not in conformity with known clinical conditions.

The patient seeks addicting drugs, financial gain, the avoidance of onerous (e.g., jail) or other unwanted conditions.

History, examination, and evaluative data do not elucidate complaints.

The patient is uncooperative and refuses to accept a clean bill of health or an encouraging prognosis.

The findings appear compatible with self-inflicted injuries.

History or records reveal multiple past episodes of injury or undiagnosed illness.

Records or test data appear to have been tampered with (e.g., erasures, unprescribed substances in urine).

Table by Arthur T. Meyerson, M.D.

Adult antisocial behavior *cannot be diagnosed in the presence of a mental disorder,* but it *is influenced by genetic factors.* A 60 percent concordance rate has been found in monozygotic twins and about a 30 percent concordance rate in dizygotic twins. Adoption studies show a high rate of antisocial behavior in the biological relatives of adoptees identified with antisocial behavior and a high incidence of antisocial behavior in the adopted-away offspring of those with antisocial behavior.

Adult antisocial behavior *is associated with the use and abuse of alcohol and other substances.*

Table 30.2 lists the major symptoms of adult antisocial behavior.

30.3. The answer is C (*Synopsis VII,* page 801).

Exit therapy is designed to help people *who are involved in cults;* it works only if their lingering emotional ties to persons outside the cult can be mobilized. Most potential cult members are in their adolescence or otherwise struggling with establishing their own identities. The cult holds out the false promise of emotional well-being and purports to offer the sense of direction for which the persons are searching. Cult members are encouraged to proselytize and to draw new members into the group. They are often encouraged to break with family members and friends and to socialize only with other group members. Cults are invariably led by charismatic personalities, who are often ruthless in their quest

Table 30.2
Symptoms of Adult Antisocial Behavior

Life Area	Antisocial Patients with Significant Problems in Area (%)
Work problems	85
Marital problems	81
Financial dependence	79
Arrests	75
Alcohol abuse	72
School problems	71
Impulsiveness	67
Sexual behavior	64
Wild adolescence	62
Vagrancy	60
Belligerence	58
Social isolation	56
Military record (of those serving)	53
Lack of guilt	40
Somatic complaints	31
Use of aliases	29
Pathological lying	16
Substance abuse	15
Suicide attempts	11

Data from L Robins: *Deviant Children Grown Up: A Sociological and Psychiatric Study of Sociopathic Personality.* Williams & Wilkins, Baltimore, 1966. Used with permission.

for financial, sexual, and power gains and in their insistence on conformity to the cult's ideological belief system, which may have strong religious or quasireligious overtones.

Exit therapy is not designed to help people with adult antisocial behavior with acculturation or occupational *problems,* or in bereavement. *Adult antisocial behavior* has no clearly successful mode of treatment. *Occupational problems* may bring a person into contact with the mental health field, and psychotherapy may aid in working through some occupational problems.

30.4. The answer is D (*Synopsis VII,* page 796).

Bereavement, a normal process, *includes* feelings of sadness, *preoccupation with thoughts about the deceased,* tearfulness, irritability, insomnia, and difficulties in concentrating and carrying out one's daily activities. Many of the symptoms are similar to those in major depressive disorder, but that diagnosis is generally not given unless the depressive symptoms persist two months after the loss. Bereavement *does not usually lead to a full depressive disorder.* In different cultures the length of bereavement varies, and so bereavement *is not the same cross-culturally in terms of duration.*

Bereavement *does not include guilt about things other than actions taken or not taken at the time of the death,* nor does it involve hallucinatory experiences other than hearing or seeing the deceased. Those symptoms are indicative of a major depressive episode.

30.5. The answer is C (*Synopsis VII,* page 797).

Some people may fear success because of their inability to tolerate envy from others. Other people may suffer from a pathological envy of the success of others. And *overwhelming ambition cannot usually overcome poor education and training and lead to success.*

In the past 25 years, major changes have occurred in the business world in the United States. Formerly, many businesses considered the employment of a husband and a wife taboo. That situation has changed. *Many corporations are now willing to employ a husband and a wife in the same firm.*

The Family Leave Law allows three months of unpaid maternal and paternal leave to employees, both men and women. However, *fathers and mothers do not use unpaid parental leaves equally.*

The transition from outside employment to homemaking is not stress-free. Researchers have found that women are specifically at risk for stress when they leave outside employment for homemaking.

30.6. The answer is A (*Synopsis VII,* page 800).

A person who malingers *often expresses subjective, ill-defined symptoms*—for example, headache; pains in the patient's neck, lower back, chest, or abdomen; dizziness; vertigo; amnesia; anxiety; and depression—and the symptoms often have a family history, in all likelihood not organically based but incredibly difficult to refute.

A patient suspected of malingering should be thoroughly and objectively evaluated, and the physician should refrain from showing any suspicion.

The patient *should not be confronted by the treating clinician.* If the clinician becomes angry (a common response to malingerers), a confrontation may occur, with two consequences: (1) The doctor-patient relationship is disrupted, and no further positive intervention is possible. (2) The patient is even more on guard, and proof of deception may become virtually impossible. Preserving the doctor-patient relationship is often essential to the diagnosis and long-term treatment of the patient. Careful evaluation usually reveals the relevant issue without the need for a confrontation.

Malingering *is usually found in settings with a preponderance of men,* such as the military, prisons, factories, and other industrial settings. The malingerer *always seeks secondary gains,* such as money, food, and shelter. The malingerer *cannot usually achieve symptom relief by suggestion or hypnosis.*

30.7. The answer is D (*Synopsis VII,* page 798).

Antisocial behavior is generally characterized by *lack of remorse or shame.* Other characteristics are a *superficial charm and good intelligence, an absence of nervousness and neurotic manifestations, and rarely successful suicide attempts.*

30.8. The answer is E (all) (*Synopsis VII,* pages 796–797).

Job-related stress is most likely to develop in the presence of *unclear work objectives, conflicting de-*

mands, *too much or too little work,* and *responsibility for the professional development of others* and little control over decisions that affect them.

30.9. The answer is D (*Synopsis VII,* pages 799–800).

Malingering, characterized by the voluntary production and presentation of false or grossly exaggerated physical or psychological symptoms, always has an external motivation, such as financial gain or the avoidance of responsibility. The presence of a clearly definable goal is the main factor that differentiates malingering from *factitious disorder.* Evidence of an intrapsychic need to maintain the sick role suggests factitious disorder.

Conversion disorder and *somatization disorder* do not show intentionality; the patient has no obvious, external incentives. Patients with *body dysmorphic disorder* believe that they are physically misshapen or defective in some way, despite an objectively normal appearance. The clinical features of the disorder are not motivated by the prospect of financial gain.

30.10. The answer is E (all) (*Synopsis VII,* page 797).

Occupational problem may arise from psychodynamic conflicts that include *problems with authority figures.* People with unresolved conflicts over *competitive rivalries* may experience great difficulty at work. They may suffer from a *pathological envy* of the success of others or *fear hostility from others.* Those conflicts are also present in other areas of the patient's life.

30.11. The answer is A (*Synopsis VII,* page 797).

In dual-career families, defined as families in which both spouses have careers, *mothers are vulnerable to guilt and anxiety regarding their maternal role* and their relative lack of availability to their children. The *mothers* usually accept middle-class or upper-middle-class values that *emphasize the importance of psychological health and the individual de-* velopment *of the child, not discipline.* They espouse sophisticated child-rearing practices that use sensitivity and communication to impart values to the child, rather than punishment. Despite the high educational levels and the intellectual sophistication of the couples, *the women generally still assume the major responsibility for child rearing and homemaking.* The husbands do contribute more than in previous generations, but their help is frequently couched in the form of "helping out their wives," rather than as a fully shared, equal burden. No evidence suggests that *the children are likely to have academic difficulties and psychological problems* as a result of the familial arrangements. No evidence indicates that *the divorce rate is higher in dual career families than in single-career families.*

30.12–30.14

30.12. The answer is B (*Synopsis VII,* pages 737–739 and 798–799).

30.13. The answer is B (*Synopsis VII,* pages 737–739 and 798–799).

30.14. The answer is C (*Synopsis VII,* pages 737–739).

The diagnosis of *antisocial personality disorder,* in contrast to *adult antisocial behavior,* requires evidence of preexisting psychopathology, such as *previous diagnosis of conduct disorder with onset before age 15,* and a long-standing pattern of irresponsible and antisocial behavior since the age of 15. Illegal behavior is not considered the equivalent of psychopathology and, without evidence of preexisting psychological disturbance, is not deemed secondary to antisocial personality disorder.

Adult antisocial behavior is not considered a *mental disorder,* but antisocial personality disorder is. *Both adult* antisocial behavior and antisocial personality disorder *occur more often in males than in females.* Familial patterns for both diagnostic classes have also been reported.

Psychiatric Emergencies

Psychiatric emergencies are either (1) situations in which persons are gravely disabled and unable to care for themselves or are in imminent risk of harming themselves or someone else or (2) the results of mental disorders that impair the persons' judgment, impulse control, or reality testing.

The prototypical psychiatric emergency is suicide. Suicide is the eighth leading cause of death in the United States, with a reported incidence of about 30,000 deaths a year or about 13 per 100,000 population each year. The number of attempted suicides is much higher than the number of completed suicides. Specific indicators of increased risk for suicide include such factors as age, sex, race, religion, marital status, occupation, physical and mental health, family history, current mental state, and previous history of suicidal behavior. For instance, an elderly white spiritually alienated unmarried unemployed and physically ill man with a substance-abuse problem and major depressive disorder who has a family history of depression and suicide, a current cognitive state of hopelessness, and a history of a failed suicide attempt is statistically at high risk for a completed suicide. However, not all suicidal persons fall into such neat categories, and the clinician must always treat the individual patient, not the presumed statistical risk. Nevertheless, a knowledge of the known risk factors can help guide both prediction and intervention.

Suicidal behavior most likely has biological, genetic, psychological, and social antecedents. Suicide does tend to run in families, which suggests both psychodynamic and biological hypotheses about causes. Twin and adoption studies of persons who have committed suicide support a genetic influence in suicide. The evidence most likely reflects genetic influences on such mental disorders as major depressive disorder, alcohol abuse, and schizophrenia—all of which are associated with higher than usual risks for suicide. However, the evidence also suggests the genetic transmittal of such factors as a tendency toward impulsivity, which has been associated with a deficiency in cerebral serotonin. Complex psychodynamic theories of suicide have been formulated by such diverse theorists as Sigmund Freud, Karl Menninger, and Aaron Beck.

Although suicide provides the prototype of a psychiatric emergency, many other clinical situations may present as emergencies. The most common psychiatric diagnoses associated with emergencies include major mood disorders (both manic and depressive episodes), schizophrenia, alcohol and other substance dependence, borderline personality disorder, and toxic conditions.

The clinician must have a clearly established strategy when interviewing patients in psychiatric emergencies. For instance, the clinician must be knowledgeable about self-protection, the prevention of harm to the patient and others, the ruling out of organic conditions, and impending psychotic decompensation. Knowledge about the guidelines for the use of restraints, including the use of pharmacological and chemical restraints, is also essential.

To become knowledgeable about suicide and other psychiatric emergencies, students are referred to Chapter 31 in *Kaplan and Sadock's Synopsis VII*. The following questions and answers can then be addressed.

HELPFUL HINTS

The terms below relate to psychiatric emergencies and should be defined.

suicide rate	adolescent suicide	delirium
anniversary suicides	ECT	dementia
age of suicides	amnesia	Wernicke's encephalopathy
methods	hypnosis	alcohol dependence
the suicide belt	panic	acute intoxication
Emile Durkheim	homosexual panic	blackouts
drugs and suicide	posttraumatic stress disorder	alcohol withdrawal
egoistic, altruistic, anomic suicides	mania	DTs
"Mourning and Melancholia"	catatonic stupor	opioids
Karl Menninger	psychotic withdrawal	sedative, hypnotic, or anxiolitic
Thanatos	catatonic excitement	withdrawal
Aaron Beck	akinetic mutism	nystagmus
5-HIAA in CSF	insomnia	lethal catatonia
platelet MAO activity	anorexia nervosa	delirious state
suicidal thoughts	bulimia nervosa	hypertoxic schizophrenia
suicidal threats	headache	exhaustion syndrome
copycat suicide	dysmenorrhea	hyperthermia
Werther syndrome	premenstrual dysphoric disorder	hypothermia
prevention centers	hyperventilation	mydriasis
crisis listening posts	alkalosis	miosis
suicidal depression	grief and bereavement	

QUESTIONS

DIRECTIONS: Each of the questions or incomplete statements below is followed by five suggested responses or completions. Select the *one* that is *best* in each case.

31.1. The patient was a 25-year-old female graduate student in physical chemistry who was brought to the emergency room by her roommates, who found her sitting in her car with the motor running and the garage door closed. The patient had entered psychotherapy two years before, complaining of long-standing unhappiness, feelings of inadequacy, low self-esteem, chronic tiredness, and a generally pessimistic outlook on life. While she was in treatment, as before, periods of well-being were limited to a few weeks at a time. During the two months before her emergency room visit, she had become increasingly depressed, had had difficulty in falling asleep and trouble in concentrating, and had lost 10 pounds. The onset of those symptoms coincided with a rebuff she had received from a chemistry instructor to whom she had become attracted.
The treatment of the patient could include
A. hospitalization
B. outpatient treatment
C. antidepressants
D. electroconvulsive therapy
E. all the above

31.2. Suicide rates
A. are equal among men and women
B. decrease with age
C. are higher among blacks than among whites
D. increase during December and other holiday periods
E. among Catholics are lower than the rates among Protestants and Jews

31.3. An increased risk for suicide is found in
A. patients with mood disorders
B. patients with schizophrenia
C. patients with alcohol dependence
D. patients with panic disorder
E. all the above

31.4. For patients seen in psychiatric emergency rooms
A. haloperidol can be given only every six hours
B. electroconvulsive therapy (ECT) may be used to control psychotic violence
C. restraints are illegal in most states
D. cognitive psychotherapy is the treatment modality of choice
E. extrapyramidal emergencies are treated with antipsychotic medications

31.5. Suicide
A. is usually a random or pointless act
B. rates in the United States are at the high point of the national rates reported to the United Nations by the industrialized countries
C. accounts for about 30,000 deaths in the United States each year
D. does not run in families
E. is characterized by all the above

31.6. Which of the following neurobiological findings is associated with suicide?
A. Increased 5-hydroxyindoleacetic acid (5-HIAA) levels in the cerebrospinal fluid (CSF)
B. Changes in the dopaminergic system
C. Serotonin deficiency
D. Increased levels of platelet monoamine oxidase (MAO)
E. Normal findings on electroencephalograms (EEGs)

31.7. Which of the following statements about the predictability of suicide is true?
A. Of persons who eventually kill themselves, 50 percent give warnings of their intent
B. Of persons who eventually kill themselves, 50 percent say openly that they want to die
C. A patient who openly admits to a plan of suicidal action is at less risk for suicide than is a patient who has only vague ideas about suicide
D. A patient who has been threatening suicide who becomes quiet and less agitated is at less risk for suicide than is a patient who remains agitated
E. A previously suicidal patient who begins to show a positive response to the pharmacological treatment of depression is not at risk for suicide

31.8. The psychodynamics of persons who commit suicide includes which of the following?
A. It is a means to a better life
B. Someone is telling them to kill themselves
C. It is a way to get revenge against a loved person
D. It is a release from illness
E. All the above

31.9. Suicide attempts may
A. provide a sense of mastery over a situation
B. represent a turning in of murderous rage
C. be part of an attempt at reunion
D. represent self-punishment
E. be characterized by all the above

31.10. Among men, suicide peaks after age 45; among women, it peaks after age
A. 35
B. 40
C. 45
D. 50
E. 55

DIRECTIONS: Each group of questions below consists of lettered headings followed by a list of numbered phrases or statements. For each numbered phrase or statement, select the *one* lettered heading that is most closely associated with it. Each lettered heading may be selected once, more than once, or not at all.

Questions 31.11–31.13
    A. Emile Durkheim
    B. Sigmund Freud
    C. Karl Menninger

31.11. Divided suicide into three social categories: egoistic, altruistic, and anomic

31.12. Described three components of hostility in suicide: the wish to kill, the wish to be killed, and the wish to die

31.13. Wrote that suicide represents aggression turned inward

Questions 31.14–31.19

A. Opiates
B. Barbiturates
C. Phencyclidine (PCP)
D. Monoamine oxidase inhibitors (MAOIs)
E. Acetaminophen (Tylenol)

31.14. Hypertensive crisis can occur

31.15. Pinpoint pupils after overdose

31.16. Cross-tolerant with diazepam (Valium)

31.17. Treated with propranolol (Inderal)

31.18. Toxic interaction with meperidine hydrochloride (Demerol)

31.19. Phenothiazines are contraindicated

ANSWERS

Psychiatric Emergencies

31.1. **The answer is E (all)** (*Synopsis VII,* pages 809–811).

The treatment of the depressed, suicidal 25-year-old female graduate student could include *hospitalization* or *outpatient treatment, antidepressants,* or *electroconvulsive therapy* (ECT). Whether to hospitalize the patient with suicidal ideation is a crucial clinical decision. Not all such patients require hospitalization; some may be treated as outpatients. Indications for hospitalization include the lack of a strong social support system, a history of impulsive behavior, and a suicidal plan of action. Most psychiatrists believe that the young woman described should be hospitalized because she had made a suicide attempt and so was clearly at increased risk. Other psychiatrists believe that they could treat the patient on an outpatient basis, provided certain conditions were met, such as (1) reducing the patient's psychological pain by modifying her stressful environment through the aid of a friend, a relative, or her employer; (2) building realistic support by recognizing that the patient may have legitimate complaints and offering alternatives to suicide; (3) securing commitment on the part of the patient to agree to call when she reached a point beyond which she was uncertain of controlling further suicidal impulses; and (4) assuring commitment on the part of the psychiatrist to be available to the patient 24 hours a day. Also, if the patient is not to be hospitalized, the family must take the responsibility of being with the patient 24 hours a day until the risk is passed. Because it is difficult to meet many of those conditions, hospitalization is often the safest route to take.

Many depressed suicidal patients require treatment with antidepressants or ECT. The young woman described had a recent is sustained and severely depressed mood that was associated with insomnia, trouble in concentrating, weight loss, and a suicide attempt. Those factors indicate the presence of a major depressive episode. There was also evidence of long-standing mild depressive symptoms (pessimism, feelings of inadequacy, and low energy level) that, although insufficient to meet the diagnostic criteria for a major depressive episode, do meet the criteria for dysthymic disorder. With those clinical features, the indication for the use of antidepressants is clear; ECT may be necessary if the patient was unresponsive to antidepressants or so severely depressed and suicidal that she required faster-acting treatment than is possible with antidepressants.

31.2. **The answer is E** (*Synopsis VII,* pages 804 and 807).

Suicide rates *among Catholics are lower than the rates among Protestants and Jews.* A religion's degree of orthodoxy and integration may be a more accurate measure of risk for suicide than is religious affiliation.

Suicide rates *are not equal among men and women.* Men commit suicide more than three times as often as do women. Women, however, are four times as likely to attempt suicide as are men. The higher rate of completed suicide for men is related to the methods they use. Men use firearms, hanging, or jumping from high places. Women are likely to take an overdose of psychoactive substances or a poison, but they are beginning to use firearms more often than previously. The use of guns has decreased as a method of suicide in those states with gun control laws.

Suicide rates *increase with age.* The significance of the mid-life crisis is underscored by suicide rates. Rates of 40 suicides per 100,000 population are found in men aged 65 and older. The elderly attempt suicide less often than do younger people but are successful more often. The elderly account for 25 percent of the suicides, although they make up only 10 percent of the total population. The rate for those 75 or older is more than three times the rate among the young.

Suicide rates *are higher among whites than among blacks.* In 1989 the suicide rate for white males (19.6 per 100,000 persons) was 1.6 times that for black males (12.5), 4 times that for white females (4.8), and 8.2 times that for black females (2.4). Among ghetto youth and certain Native American and Alaskan Indian groups, suicide rates have greatly exceeded the national rate. Suicide among immigrants is higher than in the native-born population. Two out of every three suicides are white males.

Contrary to popular belief, suicide rates *do not increase during December and other holiday periods.*

31.3. **The answer is E (all)** (*Synopsis VII,* pages 805–806).

Patients with mood disorders are at greatest risk for suicide in both sexes. The age-adjusted suidice rates for patients suffering from mood disorders have been estimated to be 400 per 100,000 for male patients and 180 per 100,000 for female patients. The suicide risk is also high among *patients with schizo-*

phrenia; up to 10 percent die by committing suicide. In the United States an estimated 4,000 schizophrenic patients commit suicide each year. *Patients with alcohol dependence* also are at high risk for committing suicide. Up to 15 percent of all alcohol-dependent persons commit suicide. Their suicide rate is estimated to be 270 per 100,000 a year; in the United States, between 7,000 and 13,000 alcohol-dependent persons are suicide victims each year. *Patients with panic disorder* also have an increased suicide risk. One study reported that such patients have a suicide rate more than seven times the age-adjusted and sex-adjusted rate for the general population, but the rate is similar to that of other clinical psychiatric populations.

31.4. The answer is B *(Synopsis VII, page 815).*

Electroconvulsive therapy (ECT) may be used to control psychotic violence. One or several ECT sessions within several hours usually end an episode of psychotic violence. However, haloperidol (Haldol) is one of the most useful emergency treatments of violent psychotic patients and is generally used instead of ECT. *Haloperidol may be given more than every six hours.* In some instances, haloperidol 5 to 10 mg every half hour to an hour is needed until a patient is stabilized. A contraindication is the use of haloperidol if the patient has suffered a head injury, because the medication can confuse the clinical picture.

Restraints are not illegal in most states, and restraints should be applied when patients are so dangerous to themselves or to others that they pose a severe threat that cannot be controlled in any other way. Most often, patients in restraints quiet down after some time has elapsed. On a psychodynamic level, such patients may even welcome the control of their impulses that restraints provide. Table 31.1 lists the guidelines for the use of restraints.

In emergency room psychiatry, *no one form of psychotherapy is the treatment modality of choice.* In an emergency psychiatric intervention, all attempts are made to help patients maintain self-esteem. More than one form of psychotherapy is frequently used in emergency therapy. The emphasis is on how various psychiatric modalities act synergistically to enhance recovery.

Extrapryamidal emergencies are not treated with antipsychotic medications. Extrapyramidal emergencies are usually the result of the adverse effects of antipsychotic medications. Patients in such emergencies usually respond to benztropine (Cogentin) 2 mg orally or intramuscularly (IM) or diphenhydramine (Benadryl) 50 mg IM or intravenously (IV). Some patients respond to diazepam (Valium) 5 to 10 mg orally or IV.

31.5. The answer is C *(Synopsis VII, page 803).*

Suicide *accounts for about 30,000 deaths in the United States each year.* That figure is for completed suicides; the number of attempted suicides is estimated to be 8 to 10 times that number. Lost in the

Table 31.1
Use of Restraints

Preferably five or a minimum of four persons should be used to restrain the patient. Leather restraints are the safest and surest type of restraints.

Explain to the patient why he or she is going into restraints.

A staff member should always be visible and reassuring the patient who is being restrained. Reassurance helps alleviate the patient's fear of helplessness, impotence, and loss of control.

The patient should be restrained with legs spread-eagled and one arm restrained to one side and the other arm restrained over the patient's head.

Restraints should be placed so that intravenous fluids can be given if necessary.

The patient's head should be raised slightly to decrease the patient's feelings of vulnerability and to reduce the possibility of aspiration.

The restraints should be checked periodically for safety and comfort.

After the patient is in restraints, the clinician should begin treatment, using verbal intervention.

Even in restraints, a majority of patients still take antipsychotic medication in concentrated form.

After the patient is under control, one restraint at a time should be removed at five-minute intervals until the patient has only two restraints on. Both of the remaining restraints should be removed at the same time, because it is inadvisable to keep a patient in only one restraint.

Always thoroughly document the reason for the restraints, the course of treatment, and the patient's response to treatment while in restraints.

Table data from W R Dubin, K J Weiss: Emergency psychiatry. In *Psychiatry,* vol 2, R Michaels, A Cooper, S B Guze, L L Judd, G L Klerman, A J Solnit, A J Sunkard, P J Wilner, editors. Lippincott, Philadelphia, 1991. Used with permission.

reporting are intentional misclassifications of the cause of death, accidents of undetermined cause, deaths through alcohol and other substance abuse, and consciously poor adherence to medical regimens for diabetes, obesity, and hypertension.

Suicide *rates in the United States are at the midpoint, not the high point, of the national rates reported to the United Nations by the industrialized countries.* Internationally, suicide rates range from highs of more than 25 per 100,000 people in Scandinavia, Switzerland, Germany, Austria, the eastern European countries (the suicide belt), and Japan to fewer than 10 per 100,000 in Spain, Italy, Ireland, Egypt, and the Netherlands.

Suicide is intentional self-inflicted death. Suicide *is not a random or pointless act.* On the contrary, it is a way out of a problem or a crisis that is invariably causing intense suffering. Suicide is associated with thwarted or unfulfilled needs, feelings of hopelessness and helplessness, ambivalent conflicts between survival and unbearable stress, a narrowing of perceived options, and a need for escape; the suicidal person sends out signals of distress.

Suicide *does run in families.* At all stages of the life cycle, a family history of suicide is present more often among persons who have attempted suicide than among those who have not. One major study found that the suicide risk for first-degree relatives of psychiatric patients was almost eight times greater than that for the relatives of controls. Furthermore, the suicide risk among the first-degree relatives of the psychiatric patients who had committed suicide was four times greater than that found among the relatives of patients who had not committed suicide.

31.6.   The answer is C (*Synopsis VII,* page 808).

A *serotonin deficiency,* as measured by *decreased (not increased) 5-hydroxyindoleacetic acid (5-HIAA) in the cerebrospinal levels fluid (CSF),* has been found in some patients who attempted suicide. In addition, some postmortem studies have reported *changes in the noradrenergic system (not dopaminergic system). Decreased (not increased) levels of platelet monoamine oxidase (MAO)* have been discovered in some suicidal patients. When blood samples from normal volunteers were analyzed, it was found that those persons with the lowest level of MAO in their platelets had eight times the prevalence of suicide in their families. *Abnormal findings on electroencephalograms (EEGs), not normal findings,* and ventricular enlargement have been found in a few studies of suicidal patients.

31.7.   The answer is B (*Synopsis VII,* page 809).

Of persons who eventually kill themselves, 50 percent say openly that they want to die, but *80 percent (not 50 percent) give warnings of their intent. A patient who openly admits to a plan of action is at greater (not less) risk for suicide than is a patient who has only vague suicidal ideas about suicide. A patient who has been threatening suicide who becomes quiet and less agitated may be at increased (not less) risk,* as may be *a previously suicidal patient who begins to show a positive response to the pharmacological treatment of depression.* Such patients may still harbor suicidal thoughts, and, because they are energized, they can carry out their plans. Depressed patients are most likely to commit suicide at the onset or at the end of a depressive episode. The risk of suicide also increases in the immediate period after discharge from inpatient psychiatric treatment.

31.8.   The answer is E (all) (*Synopsis VII,* pages 803–809).

Schneidman and Farberow classified suicides into four groups: (1) patients who conceive of suicide as *a means to a better life;* (2) patients who commit suicide as a result of psychosis with associated delusions or hallucinations—for example, *someone is telling them to kill themselves;* (3) patients who commit suicide *to get revenge against a loved person;* and (4) patients who are old or infirm for whom suicide is *a release from illness.*

31.9.   The answer is E (all) (*Synopsis VII,* pages 805–808).

Suicide attempts and the possibility of suicide seem to *provide a sense of mastery over a situation* through the control of life and death. In many young, severely disturbed, and seriously suicidal patients, suicide *represents a turning in of murderous rage* that is far from repressed. The act of dying can be conceived of as *sort of an attempt a reunion* with deceased parental figures or with wives, husbands, or siblings substituting as parents. Suicide attempts may also *represent self-punishment.*

31.10.   The answer is E (*Synopsis VII,* pages 803–804).

Among women suicide peaks after age 55. Rates of 40 per 100,000 population are found in men age 65 and older; the elderly attempt suicide less often than do younger people but are successful more frequently, accounting for 25 per cent of all completed suicides, although the elderly make up only 10 per cent of the total population. A decline in suicide in men begins between the ages 75 to 85. A peak risk among males is also found in late adolescence, when death by suicide is exceeded only by death attributed to accidents and cancer.

31.11–31.13

31.11.   The answer is A (*Synopsis VII,* page 807).

31.12.   The answer is C (*Synopsis VII,* page 807).

31.13.   The answer is B (*Synopsis VII,* page 807).

The first major contribution to the study of the social and cultural influences on suicide was made at the end of the 19th century by the French sociologist *Émile Durkheim.* In an attempt to explain statistical patterns, Durkheim *divided suicides into three social categories: egoistic, altruistic, and anomic.* Egoistic suicide applies to those who are not strongly integrated into any social group. The lack of family integration can be used to explain why the unmarried are more vulnerable to suicide than are the married and why couples with children are the best-protected group of all. Rural communities have more social integration than do urban areas and, thus, less suicide. Protestantism is a less cohesive religion than Catholicism is, and so Protestants have a higher suicide rate than do Catholics. Altruistic suicide applies to those whose proneness to suicide stems from their excessive integration into a group, with suicide being the outgrowth of that integration—for example, the Japanese soldier who sacrifices his life in battle. Anomic suicide applies to those persons whose integration into society is disturbed, thereby depriving them of the customary norms of behavior. Anomie can explain why those whose economic situation has changed drastically are more vulnerable than they were before their change in fortune. Anomie also refers to social instability, with a breakdown of society's standards and values.

The first important psychological insight into suicide came from *Sigmund Freud.* In his paper "Mourning and Melancholia, Freud *wrote that suicide represents aggression turned inward* against an introjected, ambivalently cathected love object. Freud doubted that there would be a suicide without the repressed desire to kill someone else.

Building on Freud's concepts, *Karl Menninger* in *Man Against Himself* conceived of suicide as a retroflexed murder, inverted homicide as a result of the patient's anger toward another person, which is either turned inward or used as an excuse for punishment. He also described a self-directed death instinct (Freud's concept of Thanatos). He *described three components of hostility in suicide: the wish to kill, the wish to be killed, and the wish to die.*

31.14–31.19

31.14. **The answer is D** (*Synopsis VII,* pages 819– and 974–975).

31.15. **The answer is A** (*Synopsis VII,* pages 442– 443 and 820).

31.16. **The answer is B** (*Synopsis VII,* pages 451– 454 and 818).

31.17. **The answer is C** (*Synopsis VII,* pages 449– 450 and 820).

31.18. **The answer is D** (*Synopsis VII,* pages 819 and 975).

31.19. **The answer is C** (*Synopsis VII,* pages 449– 450 and 820).

Substance abuse is one of the many reasons for visits to psychiatric emergency rooms. Patients who take overdoses of *opiates* (for example, heroin) tend to be pale and cyanotic (a dark bluish or purplish coloration of the skin and mucous membranes), with *pinpoint pupils* and absent reflexes. After blood is drawn for a study of drug levels, those patients should be given intravenous naloxone hydrochloride (Narcan), a narcotic antagonist that reverses the opiate effects, including respiratory depression, within two minutes of the injection.

The use of barbiturates and anxiolytics is widespread, and withdrawal from sedative-hypnotic drugs is a common reason for psychiatric emergencies. The first symptom of withdrawal can start as soon as eight hours after the last pill has been taken and may consist of anxiety, confusion, and ataxia. As withdrawal progresses, the patient may have seizures; occasionally, a psychotic state erupts, with hallucinations, panic, and disorientation. *Barbiturates* are *cross-tolerant with* all antianxiety agents, such as *diazepam (Valium).* In the treatment of sedative, hypnotic, or anxiolytic withdrawal, one must take into account the usual daily substance intake.

Phencyclidine (PCP or angel dust) is a common cause of psychotic drug-related hospital admissions. The presence of dissociative phenomena, nystagmus (ocular ataxia), muscular rigidity, and elevated blood pressure in a patient who is agitated, psychotic, or comatose strongly suggests PCP intoxication. In the treatment of PCP overdose, the patient should have gastric lavage to recover the drug, diazepam to reduce anxiety, an acidifying diuretic program consisting of ammonium chloride and furosemide (Lasix), which will enhance PCP excretion, and the treatment of hypertension with *propranolol (Inderal).* Acidification is not recommended with hepatic or renal failure or when barbiturate use is suspected. *Phenothiazines are contraindicated,* because muscle rigidity and seizures are side effects of PCP and can be exacerbated by phenothiazines, as can the anticholinergic effects of PCP.

Monoamine oxidase inhibitors (MAOIs) are useful in treating depression, but a *hypertensive crisis can occur* if the patients have eaten food with a high tyramine content while on their medication. Hypertensive crisis is characterized by severe occipital headaches, nausea, vomiting, sweating, photophobia, and dilated pupils. When a hypertensive crisis occurs, the MAOI should be discontinued, and therapy should be instituted to reduce blood pressure. Chlorpromazine (Thorazine) and phentolamine (Regitine) have both been found useful in those hypertensive crises. MAOIs have a *toxic interaction with meperidine hydrochloride (Demerol),* which can be fatal. When patients combine the two drugs, they become agitated, disoriented, cyanotic, hyperthermic, hypertensive, and tachycardic.

Acetaminophen (Tylenol) is an analgesic and antipyretic. Overdose with acetaminophen is characterized by fever, pancytopenia, hypoglycemic coma, renal failure, and liver damage. Treatment should begin with the induction of emesis or gastric lavage, followed by the administration of activated charcoal. Early treatment is critical to protect against hepatotoxicity.

Psychotherapies

Unlike many other fields of medicine, psychiatry is fundamentally a multiparadigmatic field—that is, it has not one but many theories about what makes human beings behave the way they do. Those theories have led to the development of a variety of treatments aimed at addressing what each theorist believes is the primary underlying constellation of forces producing the disturbance. Many times the varying theories and treatments are complementary, even synergistic; at other times they appear to be in conflict—even diametrically opposed. In reality, most skilled clinicians are knowledgeable about many types of treatment and adept at more than one type. They use their knowledge to choose techniques and insights derived from various schools of thought on the basis of what the patient most needs at any given time. Knowledgeable clinicians know when a specific type of therapy is indicated and which therapies work most effectively together.

Psychoanalysis, psychoanalytically oriented psychotherapy, and the brief dynamic psychotherapies are all based on the Freudian theory of a dynamic unconscious, psychic determination, and unconscious conflict. The underlying premise of those therapies is that only through psychological insight into the nature of one's unconscious conflicts can one hope to resolve the issues of the past that continue to influence one's behavior in the present. The techniques of each of those therapies derive from the basic goal of making the unconscious conscious. Each is different in terms of its length, intensity, development of transference, and specific contracts made with the patient before and during therapy. Patients in those types of uncovering therapies need to have adequate ego strength to tolerate frustration without decompensating or resorting to self-destructive acting out.

Family therapy and marital therapy are based on general systems theory, which states that a system, such as a family or a couple, attempts to maintain homeostasis even if doing so requires maladaptive relational patterns. One premise of those therapies is that the identified patient reflects the person in the family or the couple onto whom a central conflict has been displaced or projected. The goal of those therapies is to help the system understand how identifying that person as the disturbed member is, in reality, maintaining a particular pattern of relating for some particular reason.

Behavior therapy is based on learning theory; its techniques derive directly from the principles of operant and classical conditioning. The premises of behavior therapy are that insight is not required for behavioral change and that behavior is not a symptom of some underlying unconscious conflict. Behaviorists take behavior at face value, focusing concretely on the extinction of undesired responses and the substitution of favorable responses. Behavioral techniques are most effectively used in the treatment of specific, concrete maladaptive behavioral patterns, such as in smoking cessation, weight reduction, stuttering, and phobias.

Biofeedback is a particular type of behavior therapy; it is based on the premise that the autonomic nervous system can be regulated by using appropriate feedback signals. Autonomic functions that a person can learn to regulate include skin temperature, muscle tension, blood pressure, and heart rate.

Cognitive therapy is based on the theory that distortions in how persons think are based on inflexible, unspoken assumptions about themselves and their place in the world that lead to symptoms and maladaptive behavior. Cognitive therapy has been applied primarily to the treatment of depression. Aaron Beck's cognitive theory of depression provides the principal paradigm for the therapy. Beck's cognitive triad of depression consists of a negative view of the self (bad things happen because the person is bad), a negative view of the future (the anticipation of failure), and a negative view of the past and the present (the person has always been a failure). The goals of cognitive therapy include allowing the patient to recognize and to test negative thoughts and the assumptions on which those thoughts are based and to develop alternative flexible responses. Treatment involves exercises and homework (for example, putting oneself in a potentially stressful situation and recording what one automatically thinks at the time).

Group psychotherapy may be based on any of the theoretical paradigms, from purely supportive to cognitive-behavioral to psychoanalytic. In purely supportive group therapy, just as in supportive individual therapy, the techniques involve structuring, limit setting, and reality testing. Supportive therapy (group or individual) is used for the persons whose ego strengths are too fragile to tolerate intensive insight-oriented or interpretive therapies. Two advantages of group therapy over individual therapy are the opportunity to get immediate peer feedback and the elicitation of multiple transference responses.

Hypnosis shares some of the theoretical premises of the insight-oriented therapies by its appreciation and understanding of unconscious processes. During a hypnotic trance, a patient's attention is focused inward, and there is increased receptivity to inner experiences. Theoretically, through hypnosis, a patient is able to retrieve repressed memories and other memory processes, thus allowing the mechanisms of alertness and defense to relax. Hypnosis has been used in the treatment of amnestic disorders and dissociative disorders, in the treatment of such conditions as nicotine dependence and obesity, in the management of such conditions as chronic pain and asthma, and in the induction of anesthesia.

Students should study Chapter 32 in *Kaplan and Sadock's Synopsis VII* before turning to the questions and answers below.

HELPFUL HINTS

The names of the workers, their theories, and the therapy techniques should be known to the student.

psychoanalysis	countertransference	evidence of change, termination
psychoanalytic psychotherapy	self-analysis	interpersonal psychotherapy
transference, transference	therapeutic alliance	crisis theory
neurosis, negative transference	resistance	crisis intervention
Anna O.	expressive therapy	group psychotherapy
hysteria	insight-oriented psychotherapy	combined individual and group
ego psychology	supportive therapy	psychotherapy
object relations	relationship or superficial	psychodrama
Studies on Hysteria	psychotherapy	Eric Berne
The Interpretation of Dreams	Franz Alexander	here and now
The Ego and the Id	confidentiality	Frederick Perls
parapraxes	regression	Gestalt group therapy
structural theory	brief dynamic psychotherapy	Carl Rogers
Otto Fenichel	Thomas French	transactional group therapy
tabula rasa	Eric Lindemann	behavioral group therapy
analyst incognito	Michael Balint	authority anxiety
free association	Daniel Malan	dyad
Jacques Lacan	James Mann	peer anxiety
fundamental rule of psychoanalysis	Habib Davanloo	time-extended therapy
free-floating attention	time-limited psychotherapy	homogeneous versus heterogeneous
rule of abstinence	psychotherapeutic focus	groups
narcissistic transference	Peter Sifneos	reality testing
splitting	patient-therapist encounter	universalization
manifest and latent dream content	early therapy	cohesion
day's residue	height of the treatment	intellectualization, interpretation

ventilation and catharsis	Jacobson's exercise	four-way session
abreaction	mental imagery	group psychotherapy
inpatient versus outpatient groups	H. J. Eysenck	combined therapy
self-help groups	B. F. Skinner	behavioral medicine
AA, GA, OA	operant conditioning	disorders of self-control
Jacob Moreno	Joseph Wolpe	graded exposure
protagonist, auxiliary ego	systematic desensitization	participant modeling
role reversal	reciprocal inhibition	aversive therapy
double and multiple double	behavior therapy	positive reinforcement
mirror technique	relaxation training	token economy
Nathan Ackerman	hierarchy construction	disulfiram (Antabuse) therapy
family therapy	hypnosis	Jean-Martin Charcot
family sculpting	flooding	Hippolyte Bernheim
self-observation	assertiveness	autogenic therapy
Murray Bowen	social skills training	hypnotic capacity and induction
family systems	behavior rehearsal	eye-roll sign
triangulation	implosion	posthypnotic suggestion
genogram	reward of desired behavior	Aaron Beck
structural model	noxious stimulus	schemata
indicated patient	social network therapy	cognitive triad of depression
family group therapy	long-term reciprocity	testing automatic thoughts
Neal Miller	psychodynamic model	identifying maladaptive
thermistor	experimental model	assumptions
the bell and the pad	relational equitability	cognitive rehearsal
thermal biofeedback	marriage counseling	Paul Schilder
galvanic skin response	marital therapy	guided imagery
yoga, Zen	individual	flexible schemata
relaxation response	conjoint	

QUESTIONS

DIRECTIONS: Each of the questions or incomplete statements below is followed by five suggested responses or completions. Select the *one* that is *best* in each case.

32.1. Patients with poor frustration tolerance and poor reality testing are best treated with
A. supportive psychotherapy
B. insight-oriented psychotherapy
C. expressive therapy
D. intensive psychoanalytic psychotherapy
E. all the above

32.2. The most effective psychotherapeutic method for patients with pathological gambling is
A. activity groups
B. self-help groups
C. family therapy
D. psychodrama
E. individual therapy

32.3. The use of disulfiram (Antabuse) therapy in the treatment of alcohol abuse is an example of
A. relaxation training
B. graded exposure
C. aversion therapy
D. positive reinforcement
E. token economy

32.4. A patient with a fear of heights is brought to the top of a tall building and is required to remain there until the anxiety dissipates. That is an example of
A. graded exposure
B. participant modeling
C. aversion therapy
D. flooding
E. systematic desensitization

32.5. Which one of the following conditions is *not* amenable to hypnosis?
A. Paranoia
B. Pruritus
C. Alcohol dependence
D. Obesity
E. Asthma

32.6. Systematic desensitization is applicable in the treatment of
A. obsessive-compulsive disorder
B. sexual disorders
C. stuttering
D. bronchial asthma
E. all the above

32.7. The therapeutic factors in group therapy include
A. multiple transferences
B. collective transference
C. universalization
D. cohesion
E. all the above

32.8. Patients who experience anxiety in group therapy include
A. patients who are fearful in the presence of authority
B. patients who have had destructive relationships with peers
C. patients who were isolated from peers
D. children without siblings
E. all the above

32.9. Cotherapy in groups may be characterized by
A. each therapist's being as active as the other
B. neither therapist's being in a position of greater authority than the other
C. having a male therapist and a female therapist
D. replication of parental surrogates
E. all the above

32.10. Which of the following methods is *not* used in biofeedback?
A. Electromyography
B. Electroencephalography
C. Galvanic skin response
D. Strain gauge
E. All the above

32.11. The cognitive therapy approach includes
A. eliciting automatic thoughts
B. testing automatic thoughts
C. identifying maladaptive underlying assumptions
D. testing the validity of maladaptive assumptions
E. all the above

DIRECTIONS: The questions below consist of five lettered headings followed by a list of numbered statements. For each numbered statement, select the *one* lettered heading that is most closely associated with it. Each lettered heading may be selected once, more than once, or not at all.

Questions 32.12–32.16
A. Biofeedback
B. Behavior therapy
C. Crisis intervention
D. Cognitive therapy
E. Hypnosis

32.12. Based on the principles of learning theory

32.13. Based on the concept that autonomic responses can be controlled through the process of operant or instrumental conditioning

32.14. Based on an underlying theoretical rationale that affect and behavior are largely determined by the way a person structures the world

32.15. Emphasizes not only immediate responses to an immediate situation but also long-term development of psychological adaptation aimed at preventing future problems

32.16. The essential feature is subjective experiential change

DIRECTIONS: The lettered headings below are followed by a list of numbered statements. For each numbered statement, select

    A. if the item is associated with *A only*
    B. if the item is associated with *B only*
    C. if the item is associated with *both A and B*
    D. if the item is associated with *neither A nor B*

Questions 32.17–32.20
    A. Psychoanalytic psychotherapy
    B. Psychoanalysis
    C. Both
    D. Neither

32.17. The patient lies on a couch

32.18. Uncovers and works through infantile conflicts

32.19. Takes as its focus the patient's current conflicts and current dynamic patterns

32.20. Uses free association and the analysis of the transference neurosis

ANSWERS

Psychotherapies

32.1.   The answer is A (*Synopsis VII,* pages 830–831).

Patients with poor frustration tolerance and poor reality testing are best treated with *supportive psychotherapy.* Supportive psychotherapy (also called relationship-oriented psychotherapy) offers the patient support by an authority figure during a period of illness, turmoil, or temporary decompensation. It has the goal of restoring and strengthening the patient's defenses and integrating capacities that have been impaired. It provides a period of acceptance and dependence for a patient who is in need of help in dealing with guilt, shame, and anxiety and in meeting the frustrations or the external pressures that may be too great to handle. Supportive therapy uses a number of methods, either singly or in combination, including (1) warm, friendly, strong leadership; (2) gratification of dependence needs; (3) support in the ultimate development of legitimate independence; (4) help in the development of pleasurable sublimations (for example, hobbies); (5) adequate rest and diversion; (6) the removal of excessive external strain if possible; (7) hospitalization when indicated; (8) medication to alleviate symptoms; and (9) guidance and advice in dealing with current issues. It uses the techniques that help the patient feel secure, accepted, protected, encouraged, and safe and not anxious.

Insight-oriented psychotherapy (also called *expressive therapy* and *intensive psychoanalytic psychotherapy*) is not the best treatment for patients with poor frustration tolerance and poor reality testing. The psychiatrist's emphasis in insight-oriented therapy is on the value to patients of gaining a number of new insights into the current dynamics of their feelings, responses, behavior, and, especially, current relationships with other persons. Insight-oriented therapy is the treatment of choice for a patient who has adequate ego strength but who, for one reason or another, should not or cannot undergo psychoanalysis.

Table 32.1 summarizes the indication for insight-oriented (expressive) therapy versus supportive therapy.

32.2.   The answer is B (*Synopsis VII,* page 843).

Self-help groups are the most effective psychotherapeutic method for patients with pathological gambling. Gamblers seldom come forward voluntarily for treatment. Legal difficulties, family pressures, or other psychiatric complaints are what bring the

Table 32.1
Indications for Expressive or Supportive Emphasis in Psychotherapy

Insight-Oriented (Expressive)	Supportive
Strong motivation to understand	Significant ego defects of a long-term nature
Significant suffering	Severe life crisis
Ability to regress in the service of the ego	
Tolerance for frustration	Poor frustration tolerance
Capacity for insight (psychological mindedness)	Lack of psychological-mindedness
Intact reality testing	Poor reality testing
Meaningful object relations	Severely impaired object relations
Good impulse control	Poor impulse control
Ability to sustain work	Low intelligence
Capacity to think in terms of analogy and metaphor	Little capacity for self-observation
Reflective responses to trial interpretations	Organically based cognitive dysfunction
	Tenuous ability to form a therapeutic alliance

Table from G O Gabbard: *Psychodynamic Psychotherapy in Clinical Practice,* p. 86. American Psychiatric Press, Washington, 1990. Used with permission.

gamblers into treatment. Gamblers Anonymous (GA) was founded in 1957 and was modeled after Alcoholics Anonymous (AA); both GA and AA are self-help groups led and organized by nonprofessional group members. A distinguishing characteristic of the self-help group is its homogeneity. Members suffer from the same disorder, and they share their experiences—good and bad, successful and unsuccessful—with one another. By so doing, they educate one another, provide mutual support, and alleviate the sense of alienation that is usually felt by the person drawn to the group. Self-help groups emphasize cohesion.

Activity groups are a type of group therapy introduced and developed by S. R. Slavson and designed for children and young adolescents. Activity group therapy assumes that poor experiences have led to deficits in personality development of children; thus, corrective experiences in a therapeutic environment will modify them. Activity group therapy uses interview techniques, verbal explanations of fantasies, group play, work, and other communications. *Family therapy* is the treatment of more than one member of a family in the same session. Family relationships and processes are viewed as part of a family system, which has a stake in maintaining the status quo. The family believes that one or several family members are the source of all family problems. Family therapy may be helpful to pathological gamblers, in conjunction with GA. *Psychodrama* is a psychotherapy method originated by Jacob L. Moreno in which personality makeup, interpersonal relationships, conflicts, and emotional problems are expressed and explored through dramatization. The therapeutic dramatization of emotional problems includes the protagonist (patient), auxiliary egos (other group members), and the director (leader or therapist). The protagonist presents and acts out his or her emotional problems with the help of the auxiliary egos, who represent persons or things in the protagonist's experience. The auxiliary egos help account for the great range of therapeutic effects available in psychodrama. The director encourages the members of the group (members of the psychodrama and the audience) to be spontaneous and so has a catalytic function. The director must be available to meet the group's needs and not superimpose his or her values on it. Traditionally, psychodrama has not been the treatment of choice for pathological gamblers. *Individual therapy* is the traditional dyadic therapeutic technique, in which a psychotherapist treats one patient during a given therapeutic session. Individual therapy techniques are useful with some impulse disorders, but, in such disorders as pathological gambling, results are better when groups are composed of other gamblers who have mastered the problem.

32.3. The answer is C (*Synopsis VII,* page 855).

The use of disulfiram (Antabuse) therapy in the treatment of alcohol abuse is an example of *aversion therapy.* The alcohol-free patient is given a daily dose of disulfiram, which produces severe physiological consequences if alcohol is ingested while it is in the system (for example, nausea, vomiting, hypertension, and epilepsy). Another type of aversion therapy is to make the alcohol-abusing patient vomit by adding an emetic to an alcoholic drink, which is then imbibed.

Relaxation training is a method in which the patient is taught to relax major muscle groups to relieve anxiety. *Graded exposure* teaches phobic patients to approach a feared object in small increments until the phobia is extinguished. In *positive reinforcement* a desirable behavioral response is followed by a reward, such as food, the avoidance of pain, or praise. The person repeats the behavior to receive the reward. In *token economy* a patient is rewarded with a token that is used to purchase luxury items or certain privileges. It is used on inpatient hospital wards to modify behavior.

32.4. The answer is D (*Synopsis VII,* page 854).

Flooding is a technique in which, for example, a patient with a fear of heights is brought to the top of a tall building and is required to remain there until the anxiety dissipates. Flooding is based on the premise that escaping from an anxiety-provoking experience reinforces the anxiety through conditioning. Thus, if the person is not allowed to escape, anxiety can be extinguished, and the conditioned avoidance behavior can be prevented. In clinical situations, flooding consists of having the patient confront the anxiety-inducing object or situation at full intensity for prolonged periods of time, resulting in the patient's being flooded with anxiety. The confrontation may be done in imagination, but results are better when real-life situations are used.

In *graded exposure* the patient is exposed over a period of time to objects that cause increasing levels of anxiety. It is similar to flooding except that the phobic object or situation is approached through a series of small steps, rather than all at once. *Participant modeling* is based on imitation, whereby patients learn to confront a fearful situation or object by modeling themselves after the therapist. *Aversion therapy* involves the presentation of a noxious stimulus immediately after a specific behavioral response, leading to the response's being inhibited and extinguished. The negative stimulus (punishment) is paired with the undesired behavior, which is thereby suppressed. *Systematic desensitization,* like graded exposure, is based on the concept that a person can overcome maladaptive anxiety elicited by a situation or object by approaching the feared situation gradually and in a psychophysiological state that inhibits anxiety. The patient attains a state of complete relaxation and then is exposed to the anxiety-producing stimulus. The negative reaction of anxiety is inhibited by the relaxed state. Systematic desensitization differs from graded exposure in two respects: (1) systematic desensitization uses relaxation training, whereas graded exposure does not, and (2) systematic desensitization uses a graded list or hierarchy of anxiety-provoking scenes that the patient imagines, as opposed to graded exposure, in which the treatment is carried out in a real-life context.

32.5. The answer is A (*Synopsis VII,* page 859).

Paranoia is not amenable to hypnosis, simply because paranoid patients are suspicious and usually avoid or resist efforts to be hypnotized. Any patient who has difficulty with basic trust or who has problems with giving up control is not a good candidate for hypnosis. However, a variety of conditions have been treated with varying degrees of success with hypnosis, including *pruritus, alcohol dependence, obesity, asthma,* substance-released disorders, smoking, warts, and chronic pain.

32.6. The answer is E (all) (*Synopsis VII,* pages 852–854).

Systematic desensitization is applicable in the treatment of *obsessive-compulsive disorder, sexual disorders, stuttering, bronchial asthma,* and other conditions. Joseph Wolpe first described systematic desensitization, a behavioral technique in which the patient is trained in muscle relaxation; a hierarchy of anxiety-provoking thoughts or objects are paired with the relaxed state until the anxiety is systematically decreased and eliminated.

Obsessive-compulsive disorder (recurrent, intrusive mental events and behavior) is mediated by the anxiety elicited by specific objects or situations. Through systematic desensitization, the patient can be conditioned not to feel anxiety when around those objects or situations and thus to diminish the intensity of the obsessive-compulsive behavior. Desensitization has been used effectively with some stutterers by deconditioning the anxiety associated with a range of speaking situations. Some sexual disorders—such as male orgasmic disorder, female orgasmic disorder and premature ejaculation—are amenable to desensitization therapy.

32.7. The answer is E (all) (*Synopsis VII,* pages 837–841).

Many factors account for therapeutic change in group therapy. *Multiple transferences* are possible because a variety of group members stand for people significant in a patient's past or current life situation. Group members may take the roles of wife, mother, father, siblings, and employer. The patient can then work through actual or fantasized conflicts with the surrogate figures to a successful resolution.

Collective transference is a member's pathological personification of the group as a single transferential figure, generally the mother or the father. It is a phenomenon unique to group therapy. The therapist attempts to encourage the patient to respond to members of the group as individuals and to differentiate them.

Universalization is the process by which patients recognize that they are not alone in having an emotional problem. It is one of the most important processes in group therapy.

Cohesion is a sense of "we-ness," a sense of belonging. The members value the group, which engenders loyalty and friendliness among them. The members are willing to work together and take responsibility for one another in achieving their common goals. And they are willing to endure a certain degree of frustration to maintain the group's integrity. The more cohesion a group has, the more likely it is that it will have a successful outcome. Cohesion is considered the most important therapeutic factor in group therapy.

32.8. The answer is E (all) (*Synopsis VII,* page 838).

Many patients experience anxiety when placed in a group or when group therapy is suggested. They include *patients who are fearful in the presence of authority figures*—real or projected persons in a position of power who are, transferentially, projected parents. *Patients who have destructive relationships with peers or who were isolated from peers* generally react negatively or with increased anxiety when placed in a group setting, as do *patient without siblings.*

32.9. The answer is E (all) (*Synopsis VII,* pages 837–841).

Ideally, cotherapy in groups is characterized by *each therapist's being as active as the other, so that neither is in a position of greater authority than the other.* Having a male therapist and a female therapist can stimulate the *replication of parental surrogates* in the group; if the two interact harmoniously, they can serve as a corrective emotional experience for the members. Even if the cotherapists are of the same sex, one often tends to be confrontative and interpretative and is seen as masculine, and the other tends to be evocative of feelings and is seen as feminine. Styles of leadership and the personality characteristics of the cotherapists, regardless of their genders, also elicit transferential reactions.

32.10. The answer is D (*Synopsis VII,* pages 850–851).

In *electromyography* (EMG) muscle fibers generate electrical potentials that can be measured on an electromyograph. Electrodes placed in or on a specific muscle group—for example, masseter, deltoid, or temporalis—can be monitored for relaxation training. In *electroencephalography* (EEG) the evoked potential of the EEG is monitored to determine relaxation. Alpha waves are generally indicative of meditative states, but wave frequency and amplitude are also measured. In *galvanic skin response* (GSR), skin conductance of electricity is measured as an indicator of autonomic nervous system activity. Stress increases electrical conduction and the GSR; conversely, relaxation is associated with lowered autonomic activity and changes in skin response. Similarly, skin temperature as a measure of peripheral vasoconstriction is decreased under stress and can be measured with thermistors (thermal feedback).

A *strain gauge* is a device for measuring nocturnal penile tumescence that is used to determine if erections occur during sleep. It has no biofeedback applications.

32.11. The answer is E (all) (*Synopsis VII,* page 861).

The cognitive therapy approach includes four processes: (1) *eliciting automatic thoughts,* (2) *testing automatic thoughts,* (3) *identifying maladaptive underlying assumptions,* and (4) *testing the validity of maladaptive assumptions.* Automatic thoughts are cognitions that intervene between external events and the patient's emotional reaction to the event. An example of an automatic thought is the belief that "everyone is going to laugh at me when they see how badly I bowl"—a thought that occurs to someone who has been asked to go bowling and responds negatively. The therapist, acting as a teacher, helps the patient test the validity of automatic thoughts. The goal is to encourage patients to reject inaccurate or exaggerated automatic thoughts after careful examination. Patients often blame themselves for things that go wrong that may well have been outside their control. The therapist reviews with the patient the entire situation and helps to reattribute the blame or cause of the unpleasant events. Generating alternative explanations for events is another way of undermining inaccurate and distorted automatic thoughts.

32.12–32.16

32.12. **The answer is B** (*Synopsis VII,* page 852).

32.13. **The answer is A** (*Synopsis VII,* pages 850–851).

32.14. **The answer is D** (*Synopsis VII,* pages 859–860).

32.15. **The answer is C** (*Synopsis VII,* page 833).

32.16. **The answer is E** (*Synopsis VII,* pages 856–857).

Behavior therapy is *based on the principles of learning theory*—in particular, operant and classical conditioning. Behavior therapy is most often directed at specific habits of reacting with anxiety to objectively nondangerous stimuli (for example, phobias, compulsions, psychophysiological reactions, and sexual dysfunctions).

Biofeedback provides information to a person regarding one or more physiological processes in an effort to enable the person to gain some element of voluntary control over bodily functions that normally operate outside consciousness. Biofeedback is *based on the concept that autonomic responses can be controlled through the process of operant or instrumental conditioning.* Physiological manifestations of anxiety or tension (for example, headaches, tachycardia, and pain) can be reduced by teaching the patient to be aware of the physiological differences between tension and relaxation. The teaching involves immediate feedback to the patient through visible or audible recordings of the patient's biological functioning during anxiety versus relaxation states; the procedure reinforces the patient's awareness of which state is present and helps the patient control it.

Cognitive therapy—according to its originator, Aaron Beck—is *based on an underlying theoretical rationale that affect and behavior* are *largely determined by the way a person structures the world.* A person's structuring of the world is based on cognitions (verbal or pictorial ideas available to consciousness), which are based on assumptions (schemata developed from previous experiences).

Crisis intervention, by definition, is a therapy limited by the parameters of whatever crisis has led the patient to the clinician. Crisis intervention is based on crisis theory, which *emphasizes not only immediate responses to an immediate situation but also long-term development of psychological adaptation aimed at preventing future problems.*

Hypnosis is a state or condition in which a person is able to respond to appropriate suggestions by experiencing alterations of perceptions, memory, or mood. *The essential feature is subjective experiential change.*

32.17–32.20

32.17. **The answer is B** (*Synopsis VII,* page 826).

32.18. **The answer is B** (*Synopsis VII,* page 826).

32.19. **The answer is A** (*Synopsis VII,* page 828).

32.20. **The answer is B** (*Synopsis VII,* page 826).

In *psychoanalysis the patient lies on a couch,* and the analyst sits behind, partially or totally outside the patient's field of vision. The couch helps the analyst produce the controlled regression that favors the emergence of repressed material. The patient's reclining position in the presence of an attentive analyst almost re-creates symbolically the early parent-child situation, which varies from patient to patient. The position also helps the patient focus on inner thoughts, feelings, and fantasies, which can then become the focus of free associations. Psychoanalysis *uncovers and works through infantile conflicts* and *uses free association and the analysis of transference neurosis. Psychoanalytic psychotherapy takes as its focus the patient's current conflicts and current dynamic patterns*—that is, the analysis of the patient's problems with other persons and with themselves. Psychoanalytic psychotherapy is characterized by interviewing and discussion techniques that infrequently use free association. And unlike psychoanalysis, psychoanalytic psychotherapy usually limits its work on transference to a discussion of the patient's reactions to the psychiatrist and others. The reaction to the psychiatrist is not interpreted to as great a degree as it is in psychoanalysis.

Biological Therapies

Until recently, medications used to treat psychiatric disorders were largely classified as belonging to one of five categories: antidepressants, antipsychotics, antimanics, anxiolytics, and sedative-hypnotics. As knowledge about psychiatric medications has become increasingly sophisticated, that classification has generally been felt to be too simplistic and even misleading. For instance, many of the medications used to treat psychotic disorders are not specific to one disorder and, in fact, are currently used to treat disorders not included in the old categories. Many psychiatric medications from one category are also used adjunctively or synergistically in combination with psychiatric medications from another category. Some medications used to treat psychiatric disorders are not traditionally thought of as psychiatric medications and might not have been included in the old classifications, and some medications are used almost solely to treat the side effects of other medications.

For example, (1) some traditionally labeled antidepressant medications are used in the treatment of impulse control disorders, eating disorders, and anxiety disorders; (2) some traditionally labeled anticonvulsant medications are used as antimanic agents; (3) thyroid hormones and lithium (Eskalith) are used as augmenters in the treatment of depression; (4) some drugs traditionally used in the management of blood pressure—such as calcium channel blockers, β-blockers, and α-adrenergic agonists—are used in the management of a variety of psychiatric conditions; (5) anticholinergic drugs and dopamine agonists are used in the treatment of the side effects of dopamine receptor antagonists; and (6) anxiolytics are used as adjuncts in the treatment of psychotic disorders.

In addition, atypical agents have been introduced that were not easily classified under the old system. Examples include the serotonin-specific reuptake inhibitors, bupropion (Wellbutrin), buspirone (BuSpar), and clozapine (Clozaril). Even newer agents, either recently introduced or on the verge of introduction, such as zolpidem (Ambien) and risperidone (Risperdal), are being added to the psychiatrist's armamentarium.

In the first half of the 20th century, such organic therapies as electroconvulsive therapy (ECT), sedative and hypnotics, and psychosurgery were a part of psychiatric treatment. The evolution in the techniques, degree of sophistication, specificity of diagnostic indications, and effectiveness of ECT has been dramatic and profound. Students need to be highly educated with regard to those advances, especially in regard to ECT, to educate patients about that helpful and safe procedure. The development of biological therapies in psychiatry, in association with revolutionary advances in neuroscience, has enhanced the world's knowledge of neurochemistry, neurophysiology, and neuroanatomy.

Along with the progress and the advances has come the awareness of the downside of many of the biological therapies. Understanding the adverse side effects of major biological therapies has both elucidated the underlying mechanisms of action of the therapies and increased the knowledge of how the therapies should be used. The development of new biological regimens is often fueled by the desire to create more precise, cleaner drugs with fewer disturbing negative effects than the traditional approaches.

The side effects of psychiatric biological therapies are often tied to the specific neurotransmitter receptor systems they affect. Thus, one can understand the common side effects of dry mouth, blurred vision, urinary hesitancy, impaired sexual functioning, and constipation as the results of anticholinergic action. Anticholinergic side effects are seen with a variety of psychotropic drugs. Orthostatic hypotension, a common side effect of many psychotropic agents, is the result of an adrenergic receptor blockade. The fourth edition of *Diagnostic and Statistical Manual of Mental Disorders* (DSM-IV) introduced a new diagnostic category, medication-induced movement disorders. When one of the diagnoses is made and included as a focus of treatment, the movement disorder or adverse effect diagnosis should be listed on Axis I of the DSM-IV multiaxial diagnostic formulation. The DSM-IV medication-induced movement disorders includes neuroleptic-induced parkinsonism, neuroleptic malignant syndrome, neuroleptic-induced acute dystonia, neuroleptic-induced acute akathisia, neuroleptic-induced tardive dyskinesia, medication-induced postural tremor, and medication-induced movement disorder not otherwise specified (NOS). DSM-IV also includes adverse effects of medication not otherwise specified (NOS) under the category of other medication-induced disorders.

The clinician must know how to recognize, treat, and prevent the side effects of psychotropic medications and how to educate patients with regard to the medications' risks and benefits. Such information as indications, contraindications, drug-drug interactions, and adverse side effects is essential to any clinician prescribing psychotherapeutic medications.

Students need to be aware of the pharmacokinetics of the major psychotherapeutic drugs, including the general principles of absorption, distribution, metabolism, and excretion. Students also need to be familiar with such pharmacodynamic concepts as receptor mechanisms, dose-response curves, therapeutic indexes, and the development of tolerance, dependence, and withdrawal phenomena. Students need to know why one psychotherapeutic drug is used instead of another and which drugs may not work well together. Pharmacokinetics, pharmacodynamics, and drug profiles need to be assessed and weighed; and such patient characteristics as age, physical condition, and suicide potential must be considered. For instance, a clinician should know why and when to choose a high-potency dopamine receptor antagonist and when to choose a low-potency drug and when to choose a drug with more dopamine type 1 (D_1) antagonist activity than dopamine type 2 (D_2) antagonist activity. A clinician must understand when to use lithium instead of carbamazepine (Tegretol) or valproate in the management of bipolar I disorder and when to use a tricyclic drug instead of a serotonin-specific reuptake inhibitor or a monoamine oxidase inhibitor (MAOI) in the treatment of a depressive disorder. A clinician must know and understand the rationale for the pretreatment medical workup for such procedures as ECT and such medications as lithium, tricyclic and tetracylic drugs, carbamazepine, valproate, clozapine, and the MAOIs and must know how to monitor the effects of the procedures and medications during treatment.

Other biological therapies—such as light therapy for the treatment of mood disorders with seasonal pattern and sleep disorders, drug-assisted interviewing, and acupuncture—are treatments with varying degrees of general acceptance and success. In particular, light therapy has been shown to be an effective treatment for major depressive disorder characterized by symptoms that appear and disappear on a seasonal basis.

Students are directed to Chapter 33 in *Kaplan and Sadock's Synopsis VII* for an extensive and detailed description and examination of psychopharmacology, pharmacotherapy, and other biological therapies. Students can then tackle the questions and answers below.

HELPFUL HINTS

The student should know the terms and specific drugs listed below.

ECT
Ugo Cerletti
Lucio Bini
insulin coma therapy
psychosurgery
Egas Moniz
Julius Wagner-Jauregg
John Cade
artificial hibernation
Rauwolfia serpentina
buspirone (BuSpar)
pharmacokinetics
pharmacodynamics
biotransformation
half-life
therapeutic index
TD_{50}
dose-response curve
haloperidol (Haldol)
combination drugs
tricyclic and tetracyclic drugs
CYPD26
medication-induced movement
  disorders
SSRIs
dopamine receptor antagonists
MAOIs
benzodiazepine receptor agonists
  and antagonists
sympathomimetic
parkinsonian symptoms
akathisia
amantadine (Symmetrel)
adrenergic blockade
pilocarpine
physostigmine
atropine sulfate
prolactin
retrograde ejaculation
allergic dermatitis
photosensitivity
retinitis pigmentosa
cardiac effects
weight gain
sudden death
hematological effects
jaundice
overdoses
epileptogenic effects

oculogyric crisis
tardive dyskinesia
pill-rolling tremor
rabbit syndrome
demethylation
hydroxylation and glucuronidation
reuptake blockade
FDA
DEA
therapeutic trial
BPRS
informed consent
teratogenic
Ebstein's anomaly
antipsychotics
deinstitutionalization
positive and negative symptoms
protein binding
distribution volume
lipid solubility
metabolic enzymes
metabolites
potency—high and low
D_2 receptors
mesolimbic
mesocortical
monoamine hypothesis
down-regulation of receptors
secondary depression
panic disorder with agoraphobia
generalized anxiety disorder
obsessive-compulsive disorder
clomipramine (Anafranil)
eating disorders
side-effect profiles
L-triiodothyronine
tapering
prophylactic treatment
neuroendocrine tests
drug-induced mania
BPH
triplicate prescriptions
clonazepam (Klonopin)
clonidine (Catapres)
renal clearance
phosphatidylinositol
bipolar I disorder, bipolar II
  disorder

schizoaffective disorder
schizophrenia
impulse control disorders
TFTs
electrolyte screen
receptor blockade
noradrenergic, histaminic,
  cholinergic receptors
cholinergic rebound
idiopathic psychosis
secondary psychosis
drug intoxications
movement disorders
anticholinergic side effects
CNS depression
narrow-angle glaucoma
noncompliance
plasma levels
megadose therapy
rapid neuroleptization
orthostatic (postural) hypotension
drug holidays
depot preparations
dystonias
use in pregnancy
tonic, clonic phases
EEG, EMG
status epilepticus
apnea
ECT contraindications
stereotactic
psychosurgery
light therapy
zeitgebers
melatonin
sleep deprivation
drug-assisted interviewing
narcotherapy
mute patients
catatonia
acupuncture and acupressure
orthomolecular therapy
megavitamin therapy
hemodialysis
carbon dioxide therapy
electrosleep therapy
continuous sleep treatment
fluoxetine (Prozac)

QUESTIONS

DIRECTIONS: Each of the questions or incomplete statements below is followed by five suggested responses or completions. Select the *one* that is *best* in each case.

33.1. The primary synoptic effect of fluoxetine (Prozac) is on serotonin synaptic
A. synthesis
B. release
C. storage
D. reuptake
E. metabolism

33.2. An antihistamine that has been used for the treatment of male and female orgasmic disorders caused by serotonergic agents, such as fluoxetine (Prozac), is
A. cyproheptadine (Periactin)
B. diphenhydramine (Benadryl)
C. hydroxyzine hydrochloride (Atarax)
D. hydroxyzine pamoate (Vistaril)
E. cimetidine (Tagamet)

33.3. A drug that is usually effective in the treatment of lithium-induced tremor is
A. propranolol (Inderal)
B. amiloride (Midamor)
C. levothyroxine (Synthroid)
D. benztropine (Cogentin)
E. amantadine (Symmetrel)

33.4. An increase in lithium concentrations is *not* likely to result from the use of
A. indomethacin (Indocin)
B. caffeine
C. phenylbutazon (Azolid)
D. ibuprofen (Motrin)
E. naproxan (Naprosyn)

33.5. Yohimbine (Yocon) is used
A. by female patients only
B. by patients with renal disease
C. as a treatment for both idiopathic and drug-induced male sexual dysfunctions
D. by patients with cardiac disease
E. with clonidine (Catapres)

33.6. A hypertensive reaction to a monoamine oxidase inhibitor (MAO) can occur with
A. nifedipine (Procardia)
B. phentolamine (Regitine)
C. chlorpromazine (Thorazine)
D. liothyronine (Cytomel)
E. dextromethorphan

33.7. At risk during electroconvulsive therapy (ECT) are patients
A. with aneurysms
B. who are pregnant
C. with neuroleptic malignant syndrome
D. with intractable seizure disorders
E. with hypopituitarism

33.8. An epidemic of eosinophilia-myalgia syndrome related to a contaminant during manufacturing led to the withdrawal from the market of
A. lactate
B. tyrosine
C. L-tryptophan
D. niacin
E. lecithin

33.9. An antidepressant drug that is *not* associated with a significant effect on the reuptake of serotonin, norepinephrine, or dopamine is
A. maprotiline (Ludiomil)
B. amitriptyline (Elavil)
C. amoxapine (Asendin)
D. desipramine (Norpramin)
E. bupropion (Wellbutrin)

33.10. Calcium channel inhibitor drugs, such as verapamil (Calan) and nimodipine (Nimotop), are effective in the treatment of all the following *except*
A. schizophrenia
B. bipolar I disorder
C. tardive dyskinesia
D. Tourette's disorder
E. Huntington's disease

33.11. When sodium valproate (Depakene) is used
A. the ingestion of food with the drug decreases the ultimate amount of valproate absorbed
B. the total daily dose can be given as a single nighttime dose
C. the most serious adverse effects of treatment involve the pancreas and the liver
D. coadministration with lithium (Eskalith) and antipsychotics should be avoided
E. the dosage on the first day should be three doses of 250 mg each

33.12. Which of the following statements concerning monoamine oxidase inhibitors (MAOIs) is true?
A. Phenelzine (Nardil) acts by inhibiting monoamine oxidase, type A
B. The use of MAOIs and tricyclic drugs in combination does not pose a severe risk
C. MAOIs generally work in two to five days
D. Toxic reactions from MAOI overdoses do not usually appear until after several weeks of use
E. Clinical improvement with MAOI treatment usually occurs within one week

33.13. The lethal dose of tricyclic drugs is estimated to be
A. 5 to 10 times the daily dose level
B. 10 to 30 times the daily dose level
C. 30 to 50 times the daily dose level
D. 50 to 80 times the daily dose level
E. 70 to 100 times the daily dose level

33.14. The generally accepted therapeutic range of blood levels for lithium carbonate (Eskalith) is
A. 0.05 to 0.09 mEq per L
B. 0.5 to 0.9 mEq per L
C. 0.8 to 1.5 mEq per L
D. 2.5 to 8.2 mEq per L
E. 8 to 15 mEq per L

33.15. Pigmentary retinopathy is associated with daily doses of thioridazine (Mellaril) that exceed
A. 400 mg
B. 600 mg
C. 800 mg
D. 1,200 mg
E. 1,600 mg

33.16. The first behavioral sign of a convulsion during electroconvulsive therapy (ECT) consists of
A. movement of the big toe
B. movement of the fingers
C. gooseflesh
D. apnea
E. a slight plantar extension of the feet

33.17. The indications for lithium (Eskalith) include
A. schizophrenia
B. major depressive disorder
C. impulse control disorders
D. bipolar I disorder
E. all the above

33.18. Persons most responsive to electroconvulsive therapy (ECT) include those with
A. major depressive disorder with psychotic features
B. major depressive disorder with melancholic features
C. nonsuppression on the dexamethasone-suppression test
D. a blunted response of thyroid-stimulating (TSH) or thyrotropin-releasing hormone (TRH) infusion
E. all the above

33.19. Succinylcholine (Anectine)
A. is a fast-acting depolarizing blocking agent
B. stops most major ictal body movements
C. may have to be augmented with curare
D. may result in prolonged apnea
E. is characterized by all the above

33.20. Dystonias are
A. observed in about 10 percent of all patients taking an antipsychotic medication
B. usually observed in the first few hours or days of treatment
C. most common in young males
D. rare with thioridazine (Mellaril)
E. all the above

33.21. Figure 33.1 illustrates
A. a plasma level-clinical response curve
B. a plasma level-toxicity curve
C. a dose-response curve
D. a therapeutic window curve
E. none of the above

DIRECTIONS: Each set of lettered headings below is followed by a list of numbered phrases or statements. For each numbered phrase or statement, select

A. if the item is associated with *A only*
B. if the item is associated with *B only*
C. if the item is associated with *both A and B*
D. if the item is associated with *neither A nor B*

Questions 33.22–33.23
A. Antipsychotic drugs
B. Tricyclic drugs
C. Both
D. Neither

33.22. Abrupt withdrawal can reveal latent tardive dyskinesia

33.23. May produce parkinsonian symptoms

Questions 33.24–33.27

A. Clozapine (Clozaril)
B. Clonazepam (Klonopin)
C. Both
D. Neither

33.24. Treatment of psychotic disorders

33.25. Increased incidence of agranulocytosis

33.26. Increased incidence of seizures

33.27. Treatment of bipolar I disorder

DIRECTIONS: Each group of questions below consists of five lettered headings followed by a list of numbered words or phrases. For each numbered word or phrase, select the *one* lettered heading that is most closely associated with it. Each lettered heading may be selected once, more than once, or not at all.

Questions 33.28–33.33

A. Schedule I
B. Schedule II
C. Schedule III
D. Schedule IV
E. Schedule V

33.28. Low abuse potential and limited psychological and physical dependence liability

33.29. Moderate physical dependence and high psychological dependence liability

33.30. No accepted medical use in the United States

33.31. Amphetamine, morphine

33.32. Heroin, marijuana

33.33. Lowest abuse potential of all controlled substances

Questions 33.34–33.37

A. Light therapy
B. Psychosurgery
C. Amobarbital (Amytal) interview
D. Acupuncture

33.34. Catatonia

33.35. Major depressive disorder with seasonal pattern

33.36. Chronic, severe, intractable major depressive disorder

33.37. Substance dependence

ANSWERS

Biological Therapies

33.1. The answer is D (*Synopsis VII,* page 976).

Fluoxetine (Prozac) inhibits serotonin *reuptake* by presynaptic neurons. Fluoxetine, sertraline (Zoloft), paroxetine (Paxil), and two agents in widespread clinical use in Europe—fluvoxamine and citalopram—are referred to as serotonin-specific reuptake inhibitors or as selective serotonin reuptake inhibitors (SSRIs). In contrast, the tricyclic drugs inhibit the reuptake of all monoamine neurotransmitters, such as norepinephrine, dopamine, and serotonin. SSRIs typically increase extracellular serotonin levels to about three times their baseline levels. Compensatory decreases in the synthesis and the release of serotonin keep the levels from increasing further.

Serotonin can also be manipulated in other ways. For example, *synthesis* can be enhanced to some degree by administering large doses of L-tryptophan, the amino acid precursor of serotonin. L-Hydroxytryptophan, the immediate precursor of serotonin, can also increase the rate of serotonin synthesis. Experiments involving the use of tryptophan-free protein diets indicate that extracellular serotonin is reduced.

Fenfluramine (Pondimin) and cocaine trigger the *release* of serotonin and other monoamine neurotransmitters. Reserpine (Serpasil) interferes with the *storage* of those neurotransmitters. Monoamine oxidase inhibitor drugs, such as phenelzine (Nardil), decrease the rate of serotonin *metabolism*.

33.2. The answer is A (*Synopsis VII,* page 900).

Cyproheptadine (Periactin) has been used for the treatment of male and female orgasmic disorders caused by serotonergic agents, such as fluoxetine (Prozac). *Diphenhydramine (Benadryl)* is used for the treatment of neuroleptic-induced parkinsonism and neuroleptic-induced acute dystonia and sometimes as a hypnotic. *Hydroxyzine hydrochloride (Atarax)* and *hydroxyzine pamoate (Vistaril)* are used as anxiolytics. Although these drugs are generally referred to as antihistamines, another class of antihistamines that block the histamine type 2 (H_2) receptor—for example, *cimetidine (Tagamet)*—are used for the treatment of gastric ulcer. Unlike the other antihistamines, cyproheptadine is an antagonist of the serotonin type 2 ($5\text{-}HT_2$) receptor, which most likely accounts for its effectiveness in reversing drug-induced female orgasmic disorder.

33.3. The answer is A (*Synopsis VII,* page 893).

The significance of drug-induced tremors is recognized in the fourth edition of *Diagnostic and Sta-* *tistical Manual of Mental Disorders* (DSM-IV) by the inclusion of the diagnosis medication-induced postural tremor (Table 33.1). The tremor is usually a 8–10 Hz tremor and is most notable in outstretched hands, especially in the fingers. The tremor is sometimes worse during times of peak drug levels. The tremor can be reduced by dividing the daily dosage and reducing caffeine intake. *Propranolol (Inderal)* (30 to 160 mg a day in divided doses) is usually effective in reducing the tremor in most patients. When a lithium (Eskalith)-treated patient has a severe tremor, the possibility of lithium toxicity should be suspected and evaluated.

The most common adverse renal effect of lithium is polyuria with secondary polydipsia. Treatment consists of fluid replacement, the use of the lowest effective dosage of lithium, and single daily dosing of lithium. Treatment can also involve the use of a thiazide or potassium-sparing diuretic—for example, *amiloride (Midamor)* or amiloride-hydrochlorothiazide (Moduretic). If treatment with a diuretic is initiated, the lithium dosage should be halved, and the diuretic should not be started for five days, because the diuretic is likely to increase the retention of lithium.

Table 33.1
Diagnostic and Research Criteria for Medication-Induced Postural Tremor

---

Fine tremor occurring during attempts to maintain a posture that develops in association with the use of medication (e.g., lithium, antidepressants, valproate).

A. A fine postural tremor which has developed in association with the use of a medication (e.g., lithium, antidepressants, valproic acid).

B. The tremor (i.e., a regular, rhythmic, oscillation of the limbs, head, mouth, or tongue) has a frequency between 8 and 12 cycles per second.

C. The symptoms are not due to a preexisting nonpharmacologically induced tremor. Evidence that the symptoms are due to a preexisting tremor might include the following: the tremor was present prior to the introduction of the medication, the tremor does not correlate with serum levels of the medication, and the tremor persists after discontinuation of the medication.

D. The symptoms are not better accounted for by neuroleptic-induced parkinsonism.

Table from DSM-IV, *Diagnostic and Statistical Manual of Mental Disorders*, ed 4. Copyright American Psychiatric Association, Washington, 1994. Used with permission.

Lithium also affects thyroid function, causing a generally benign and often transient diminution in the concentrations of circulating thyroid hormones. If symptoms of hypothyroidism are present, treatment with *levothyroxine (Synthroid)* is indicated.

Benztropine (Cogentin) and *amantadine (Symmetral)* are used in psychiatry to treat extrapyramidal symptoms caused by dopamine receptor antagonists. They are not used in the treatment of lithium-associated side effects.

33.4. The answer is B (*Synopsis VII,* page 966.)

Most diuretics (for example, thiazides, potassium-sparing, and loop) can increase lithium levels; when treatment with such a diuretic is stopped, the clinician may need to increase the patient's daily lithium dosage. Osmotic diuretics, carbonic anhydrase inhibitors, and xanthines (including *caffeine*) may reduce lithium levels to below therapeutic levels. A wide range of nonsteroidal anti-inflammatory drugs can decrease lithium clearance, thereby increasing lithium concentrations; those drugs include *indomethacin (Indocin), phenylbutazone (Azolid),* diclofenac (Voltaren), ketoprofen (Orudis), oxyphenbutazone (Oxalid), *ibuprofen (Motrin),* piroxicam (Feldene), and *naproxan (Naprosyn).* Aspirin and sulindac do not affect lithium concentrations.

33.5. The answer is C (*Synopsis VII,* page 1004).

Yohimbine (Yocon) is an α_2-adrenergic receptor antagonist that has been used *as a treatment for both idiopathic and drug-induced male sexual dysfunctions.* Yohimbine *should not be used by female patients* or *by patients with renal disease, cardiac disease,* glaucoma, or a history of gastric or duodenal ulcers. Yohimbine should not be used *with clonidine (Catapres),* an α_2-adrenergic receptor agonist, because the two drugs have mutually canceling pharmacodynamic effects.

33.6. The answer is E (*Synopsis VII,* page 975).

A hypertensive reaction to a monoamine oxidase inhibitor (MAO) can occur with *dextromethorphan.* The inhibition of MAO can cause severe and even fatal interactions with various other drugs (Table 33.2). Patients should be instructed to tell any other physicians who are treating them that they are taking an MAOI. An MAOI-induced hypertensive crisis can be treated with *nifedipine (Procardia);* however, some controversy exists regarding that practice because nifedipine produces a rapid drop in arterial pressure. That drop is a concern if a patient mistakes a headache resulting from the rebound of MAOI-induced orthostatic hypotension for a hypertensive-related headache. When nifedipine is used, the patient should bite into a 10 mg nifedipine capsule and swallow its contents with water. Additional treatment can include the use of α-adrenergic antagonists—for example, *phentolamine (Regitine)* or *chlorpromazine (Thorazine).*

If an MAOI trial is not successful after six weeks,

Table 33.2
Drugs to Be Avoided during MAOI Treatment

Never use:
Anesthetics—never spinal anesthetic or local anesthetic containing epinephrine (lidocaine and procaine are safe)
Antiasthmatic medications
Antihypertensives (α-methyldopa, guanethidine, reserpine, pargyline)
L-Dopa, L-tryptophan
Narcotics (especially meperidine [Demerol]; morphine or codeine may be less dangerous)
Over-the-counter cold, hay fever, and sinus medications, especially those containing dextromethorphan (aspirin, acetaminophen, and menthol lozenges are safe)
Sympathomimetics (amphetamine, cocaine, methylphenidate, dopamine, metaraminol, epinephrine, norepinephrine, isoproterenol)
Serotonin-specific reuptake inhibitors, clomipramine

Use carefully:
Antihistamines
Hydralazine (Apresoline)
Propranolol (Inderal)
Terpin hydrate with codeine
Tricyclic and tetracyclic drugs

---

lithium (Eskalith) or L-triiodothyronine. (T_3 or *liothyronine [Cytomel]*) augmentation is warranted. Those combinations are not associated with a hypertensive reaction.

33.7. The answer is A (*Synopsis VII,* page 1010).

Patients who have increased intracerebral pressure or are at risk for cerebral bleeding (for example, patients with cerebrovascular diseases and *aneurysms*) are at risk during electroconvulsive therapy (ECT) because of the increased cerebral blood flow during the seizure. That risk can be lessened, although not eliminated, by control of the patient's blood pressure during the treatment.

ECT is not contraindicated in patients *who are pregnant,* and fetal monitoring is generally thought to be unnecessary unless the pregnancy is high-risk or complicated. ECT has been reported to be useful in patients with such medical conditions as *neuroleptic malignant syndrome, intractable seizure disorders, hypopituitarism,* and the on-off phenomenon of Parkinson's disease.

33.8. The answer is C (*Synopsis VII,* page 999).

L-Tryptophan was withdrawn from the market in the United States by the Food and Drug Administration (FDA) in 1990 because a contaminant from the production process at one particular manufacturing site caused an eosinophilia-myalgia syndrome in some patients taking the drug.

Lactate is used both as a nutrient and as a provocative agent in testing for panic disorder. *Tyrosine* is an amino acid precursor of the catecholamines. *Niacin* is a vitamin. *Lecithin* is used as a nutritional supplement.

33.9.   The answer is E (*Synopsis VII,* page 919).

Bupropion is an antidepressant drug that is not associated with a significant effect on the reuptake of serotonin, norepinephrine, or dopamine. *Maprotiline (Ludiomil), amitriptyline (Elavil), amoxapine (Asendin),* and *desipramine (Norpramin)* have significant inhibitory effects on the monoamine neurotransmitters. Those effects are thought to account for the drugs' therapeutic activities.

33.10.   The answer is A (*Synopsis VII,* page 923).

Well-controlled studies have found a lack of efficacy for calcium channel inhibitors in *schizophrenia* and depressive disorders. Data do support the use of verapamil (Calan) for the treatment of *bipolar I disorder,* although verapamil should be considered a fourth-line drug, following trials of lithium (Eskalith), carbamazepine (Tegretol), and valproate (Depakene). Preliminary data indicate that nimodipine (Nimotop) may be particularly effective in the treatment of rapid-cycling bipolar I disorder. Using a calcium channel inhibitor for *tardive dyskinesia* may be worth a therapeutic trial in severely affected patients. Case reports and small studies provide preliminary evidence of the efficacy of calcium channel inhibitors in *Tourette's disorder, Huntington's disease,* panic disorder, premenstrual dysphoric disorder, and intermittent explosive disorder.

33.11.   The answer is C (*Synopsis VII,* page 1000).

Peak plasma levels of valproate vary, depending on the preparation and whether food is ingested with the drug. *The ingestion of food with the drug* delays the absorption of the drug but *does not affect the ultimate amount of drug absorbed.* The half-life of valproate is 8 to 17 hours, commonly making three-times-daily dosing necessary to maintain stable plasma concentrations.

The most serious adverse effects of treatment with sodium valproate (Depakene) involve the pancreas and the liver. Rare cases of pancreatitis have been reported; they occur most often in the first six months of treatment, and the condition occasionally results in death. The most attention has been paid to an association between valproate and fatal hepatotoxicity. A result of that focus has been the identification of risk factors, including young age (less than 2 years), the use of multiple anticonvulsants, and the presence of neurological disorders. Therefore, *the total daily dose cannot given as a single nighttime dose.*

Valproate *is commonly coadministered with lithium (Eskalith) and antipsychotics.* The only consistent drug interaction with lithium is the exacerbation of drug-induced tremors, which can usually be treated with β-adrenergic receptor antagonists.

The dosage of valproate *on the first day should be one dose, not three doses, of 250 mg* administered with a meal. The dosage can be raised up to 250 mg orally three times daily over the course of three to six days.

33.12.   The answer is B (*Synopsis VII,* pages 974–975).

A number of large-scale studies in the European literature indicate that *the use of monoamine oxidase inhibitors (MAOIs) and tricyclic drugs does not pose a severe risk.* However, the combination is not in standard use in the United States because of fear of producing a hypertensive crisis.

A serotonergic syndrome has been described when MAOIs are coadministered with serotonergic drugs, such as serotonin-specific reuptake inhibitors and clomipramine (Anafranil), thus resulting in the recommendation that those combinations be avoided. The initial symptoms of a serotonin syndrome can include tremor, hypertonicity, myoclonus, and autonomic signs, which can then progress to hallucinosis, hyperthermia, and even death.

Phenelzine (Nardil) does not act by inhibiting either monoamine oxidase, type A or monoamine oxidase, type B.

MAOIs may take two weeks or longer before any clinical improvement is seen. *Toxic reactions from MAOI overdoses generally appear within hours of ingestion.*

33.13.   The answer is B (*Synopsis VII,* pages 880 and 995–997).

The lethal dose of tricyclic drugs is estimated to be *10 to 30 times the daily dose level.*

33.14.   The answer is C (*Synopsis VII,* pages 968–969).

The precise amount of lithium (Eskalith) required by an individual patient is determined by continuous periodic observations of the clinical state, achievement of a blood lithium level of *0.8 to 1.5 mEq per L,* and the avoidance of side effects. The amount of lithium in the blood is measured by atomic absorption photometry or flame emission photometry, using a few milliliters of venous blood drawn from the patient's arm.

33.15.   The answer is C (*Synopsis VII,* page 949).

Daily doses of thioridazine (Mellaril) of more than *800 mg* are to be avoided because of the drug's association with pigmentary retinopathy, also known as retinitis pigmentosa, a progressive atrophy of the retinal neuroepithelium. The disease is also seen with other phenothiazine drugs when they are used in high dosages over long periods of time.

33.16.   The answer is E (*Synopsis VII,* page1009).

A slight plantar extension of the feet can be noticed as evidence of the tonic phase of a convulsion in electroconvulsive therapy (ECT). After about 10 seconds, some *toe, finger,* or other movements should indicate the clonic phase. If none of the manifestations is noted, it is wise to give a second stimulus. A nonmotor manifestation of a convulsion is the appearance of *gooseflesh.*

The manifestations of electrically induced convulsions resemble those of a spontaneous convulsion with certain differences. If the amount of current given is not sufficient, the nonanesthetized patient only loses consciousness (petit mal response). If somewhat more current is given, the patient may have a delayed convulsion—that is, the patient loses consciousness and, after only a few seconds of *apnea*, goes slowly into the tonic phase, followed by the clonic phase. If still more current is used, there is an immediate convulsion in which the tonic phase starts at the moment of the stimulation.

BIOLOGICAL THERAPIES ☐ 343

The manifestations of electrically induced convulsions resemble those of a spontaneous convulsion with certain differences. If the amount of current given is not sufficient, the nonanesthetized patient only loses consciousness (petit mal response). If somewhat more current is given, the patient may have a delayed convulsion—that is, the patient loses consciousness and, after only a few seconds of *apnea*, goes slowly into the tonic phase, followed by the clonic phase. If still more current is used, there is an immediate convulsion in which the tonic phase starts at the moment of the stimulation.

33.17.   The answer is E (all) (*Synopsis VII,* pages 962–963).

The indications for lithium (Eskalith) include *schizophrenia, major depressive disorder, impulse control disorders,* and *bipolar I disorder.* Lithium is the major pharmacological treatment for bipolar I disorder and is effective in its treatment and prophylaxis in about 70 to 80 percent of patients. The symptoms of about one fifth to one half of all schizophrenic patients are further reduced when lithium is added to their antipsychotic drug. Some schizophrenic patients who cannot take antipsychotics may benefit from lithium treatment. Lithium is used in major depressive disorder as an adjuvant to tricyclic and tetracyclic drugs or monoamine oxidase inhibitors to convert an antidepressant nonresponder into a responder. Lithium alone may be effective for depressed patients who actually have bipolar I disorder but have not yet had their first manic episode. It is also used to treat the impulse control disorders of episodic violence and rage. Such episodic outbursts in mentally retarded patients may be reduced with lithium.

33.18.   The answer is E (all) (*Synopsis VII,* page 1006).

The most common indication for electroconvulsive therapy (ECT) is major depressive disorder. *Major depressive disorder with psychotic feature* is particularly responsive to ECT, whereas the response of that disorder to antidepressants alone is poor. *Major depressive disorder with melancholic features* (for example, markedly severe symptoms, psychomotor retardation, early morning awakening, diurnal variation, decreased appetite and weight, and agitation) is the type of depressive disorder most likely to respond to ECT. Patients with *nonsuppression on the dexamethasone-suppression test,* which is called a positive test result, and *a blunted response of thyroid-stimulating hormone (TSH) or thyrotropin-releasing hormone (TRH) infusion* are also likely to respond.

33.19.   The answer is E (all) (*Synopsis VII,* pages 1007–1008).

Succinylcholine (Anectine), a *fast-acting depolarizing blocking agent,* has gained virtually universal acceptance for the purpose of producing muscle relaxation during a course of electroconvulsive therapy (ECT). The optimal succinylcholine dose provides enough relaxation to *stop most major ictal body movements.* A typical starting dose is 60 mg for a medium-sized adult. If musculoskeletal or cardiac disease necessitates the use of total relaxation, increased succinylcholine *may have to be augmented with curare* (3 to 6 mg intravenously) several minutes before an esthetic induction. The presence of seizure activity under circumstances of complete relaxation can be monitored either by electroencephalogram or by the prevention of succinylcholine flow to one of the forearms, using an inflated blood pressure cuff. In cases of inborn or acquired pseudocholinesterase deficiency or when the metabolism of succinylcholine is disrupted by drug interaction, the drug *may result in prolonged apnea.*

33.20.   The answer is E (all) (*Synopsis VII,* page 950).

Dystonias are *observed in about 10 percent of all patients taking an observed antipsychotic medication.* The dystonias are *usually in the first few hours or days of treatment.* Dystonic movements result from a slow, sustained muscular contraction or spasm that can result in an involuntary movement. Dystonias can involve the eyes, neck, jaw, tongue, or entire body. They are *most common in young males* but can occur at any age in either sex. They are most common with intramuscular doses of high-potency antipsychotics (for example, haloperidol [Haldol]), but dystonias can occur with any antipsychotic. They are *rare with thioridazine (Mellaril).*

33.21.   The answer is C (*Synopsis VII,* pages 867–868).

The conceptually correct way to think about high and low dosage in psychiatry is in terms of *dose-response curves.* One is illustrated in Figure 33.1. When a very low dosage is given, patients have no clinical response. Above a certain dosage range, an increase in dosage produces a proportionately increased therapeutic response (the linear portion of the curve). When all the responses that can occur do occur, a point of diminishing return is reached, and increasing the dosage does not increase the response;

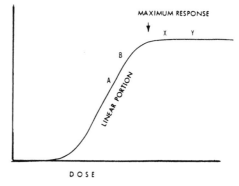

Figure 33.1.

that is, there is a ceiling effect. The inflection point at which the linear portion changes to diminished returns is often referred to as the optimal part of the dose-response curve, the point that indicates the lowest dosage necessary to achieve maximal clinical effects. A given dose-response curve applies to only one patient at a particular time, and a given patient may have different dose-response curves at different times.

The curve shown in Figure 33.2 illustrates *a plasma level-clinical response curve.* The first portion of the curve shows the relative lack of clinical response at low drug plasma levels. The linear portion of the curve shows a progressively better clinical response as more of the drug reaches the receptor site. Beyond the linear part of the curve, as large amounts of the drug are introduced, an area of diminishing returns appears.

Figure 33.3 illustrates *a plasma level-toxicity curve.* A plasma level-toxicity relation exists with regard to various side effects. If one thinks in terms of the total clinical benefit for the patient and plots that benefit against plasma levels, it is expected that, as plasma levels rise, the patient exhibits an improved clinical response. As the curve begins to level off, the patient enters the area of optimal benefit. When plasma levels are markedly elevated, the resulting detrimental side effects may outweigh the beneficial therapeutic effects.

Figure 33.4 illustrates *a therapeutic window curve.* Combining the therapeutic curve and the side-effects curve results in an inverted U-shaped curve.

When the plasma level of some drugs rises to a high level, the therapeutic effect may be lowered. A possible explanation is that, at a given range of concentration, some drugs may stimulate a receptor and, at a higher range, inhibit the receptor. Most drugs show increasing side effects as the plasma level increases. A drug that has neither of those high-dose effects—loss of clinical efficacy and serious toxicity—may not display a descending limb of the inverted U-shaped curve.

33.22–33.23

33.22.   The answer is A (*Synopsis VII,* pages 951–952).

33.23.   The answer is D (*Synopsis VII,* pages 883, 951–952 and 994).

Abrupt withdrawal of antipsychotic drugs can reveal latent tardive dyskinesia. Although tardive dyskinesia often emerges while the patient is taking a steady dosage of an antipsychotic medication, it is even more likely to emerge when the dosage is reduced. Once tardive dyskinesia is recognized, the clinician should consider reducing the dosage of the antipsychotic or even stopping the medication altogether. Alternatively, the clinician may switch the patient to clozapine (Clozaril) or to one of the new dopamine receptor antagonists, such as risperidone. Withdrawal of tricyclic drugs is not associated with tardive dyskinesia.

Both antipsychotic drugs and tricyclic drugs *may produce parkinsonian symptoms.* Among the tricyclic drugs, amoxapine (Asendin) is unique in causing parkinsonian symptoms, akathisia, and even dyskinesia because of the dopaminergic blocking activity of one of its metabolities. Amoxapine may also cause neuroleptic malignant syndrome in rare cases. According to DSM-IV, parkisonism caused by a medication other than a neuroleptic (for example, tricyclic drug) is diagnosed as medication-induced movement disorder not otherwise specified (Table 33.3). Parkinsonian adverse effects occur in about 15 percent of patients who are treated with antipsychotics, usually in 5 to 90 days of the initiation of treatment. Symptoms include muscle stiffness (lead-pipe rigidity), cogwheel rigidity, shuffling gait, stooped pos-

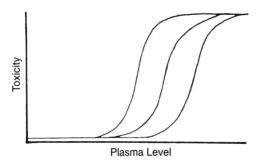

Figure 33.2.   A plasma level-clinical response curve.

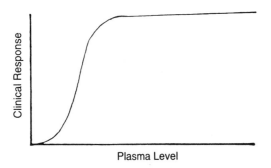

Figure 33.3.   A plasma level-toxicity curve.

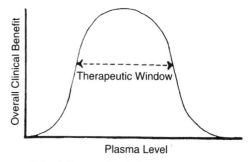

Figure 33.4.   A therapeutic window curve.

Table 33.3
Diagnostic Criteria for Medication-Induced Movement Disorder Not Otherwise Specified

This category is for medication-induced movement disorders not classified by any of the specific disorders listed above. Examples include 1) parkinsonism, acute akathisia, acute dystonia, or dyskinetic movement that is associated with a medication other than a neuroleptic; 2) a presentation that resembles neuroleptic malignant syndrome that is associated with a medication other than a neuroleptic; or 3) tardive dystonia.

Table from DSM-IV, *Diagnostic and Statistical Manual of Mental Disorders,* ed 4. Copyright American Psychiatric Association, Washington, 1994. Used with permission.

ture, and drooling. All antipsychotics can cause the symptoms, especially high-potency drugs with low anticholinergic activity. Chlorpromazine and thioridazine are not likely to be involved. The blockade of dopaminergic transmission in the nigrostriatal tract is the cause of neuroleptic-induced parkinsonism.

The diagnostic and research criteria for neuroleptic-induced tardive dyskinesia appear in Table 33.4. The diagnostic and research criteria for neuroleptic-induced parkinsonism are listed in Table 33.5.

33.24–33.27

33.24. **The answer is A** (*Synopsis VII,* page 932).

33.25. **The answer is A** (*Synopsis VII,* page 934).

33.26. **The answer is A** (*Synopsis VII,* page 934).

33.27. **The answer is B** (*Synopsis VII,* page 910).

Clozapine (Clozaril) is alternative drug for the *treatment of psychotic disorders,* particularly schizophrenia. Clozapine is a dibenzodiazepine but should not be confused with the drug clonazepam (Klonopin), which is a benzodiazepine. Clozapine is unique among the antipsychotics in that it is not associated with extrapyramidal adverse effects and probably does not cause either tardive dyskinesia or neuroleptic malignant syndrome. The major disadvantage of clozapine is an *increased incidence (1 to 2 percent) of agranulocytosis* in patients who take the drug. Agranulocytosis can appear precipitously or gradually; it most often develops in the first six months of treatment, although it can appear much later. Clozapine is also associated with an *increased incidence of seizures.* About 14 percent of patients taking more than 600 mg a day of clozapine, 1.8 percent of patients taking 300 to 600 mg a day, and 0.6 percent of patients taking less than 300 mg a day have seizures. *Clonazepam (Klonopin)* has been useful in the treatment of *bipolar I disorder.* Clonazepam is effective in the treatment of acute mania. It is also used as an adjuvant to lithium (Eskalith) in lieu of antipsychotics. As an adjuvant to lithium, clonazepam may result in a longer time between cycles and in fewer depressive episodes.

Table 33.4
Diagnostic and Research Criteria for Neuroleptic-Induced Tardive Dyskinesia

Involuntary choreiform, athetoid, or rhythmic movements (lasting at least a few weeks) of the tongue, jaw, or extremities developing in association with the use of neuroleptic medication for at least a few months (may be for a shorter period of time in elderly persons).

A. Involuntary movements of the tongue, jaw, trunk, or extremities have developed in association with the use of nueroleptic medication.

B. The involuntary movements are present over a period of at least 4 weeks and occur in any of the following patterns:

   (1) choreiform movements (i.e., rapic, jerky, nonrepetitive)
   (2) athetoid movements (i.e., slow, sinuous, continual)
   (3) rhythmic movements (i.e., stereotypes)

C. The signs or symptoms in criteria A and B develop during exposure to a neuroleptic medication or within 4 weeks of withdrawal from an oral (or within 8 weeks of withdrawal from a depot) neuroleptic medication.

D. There has been exposure to neuroleptic medication for at least 3 months (1 month if age 60 years or older).

E. The symptoms are not due to a neurological or general medical condition (e.g., Huntington's disease, Sydenham's chorea, spontaneous dyskinesia, hyperthyroidism, Wilson's disease), ill-fitting dentures, or exposure to other medications that cause acute reversible dyskinesia (e.g., L-dopa, bromocriptine). Evidence that the symptoms are due to one of these etiologies might include the following: the symptoms precede the exposure to the neuroleptic medication or unexplained focal neurological signs are present.

F. The symptoms are not better accounted for by a neuroleptic-induced acute movement disorder (e.g., neuroleptic-induced acute dystonia, neuroleptic-induced acute akathisia).

Table from DSM-IV, *Diagnostic and Statistical Manual of Mental Disorders,* ed 4. Copyright American Psychiatric Association, Washington, 1994. Used with permission.

33.28–33.33

33.28. **The answer is D** (*Synopsis VII,* pages 868–869).

33.29. **The answer is C** (*Synopsis VII,* pages 868–869).

33.30. **The answer is A** (*Synopsis VII,* pages 868–869).

33.31. **The answer is B** (*Synopsis VII,* pages 868–869).

33.32. **The answer is A** (*Synopsis VII,* pages 868–869).

33.33. **The answer is E** (*Synopsis VII,* pages 868–869).

The Drug Enforcement Administration (DEA) control levels were established to limit the abuse of

Table 33.5
Diagnostic and Research Criteria for Neuroleptic-Induced Parkinsonism

Parkinsonian tremor, muscular rigidity, or akinesia developing within a few weeks of starting or raising the dose of a neuroleptic medication (or after reducing a medication used to treat extrapyramidal symptoms).

A. One (or more) of the following signs of symptoms has developed in association with the use of neuroleptic medication:

    (1) parkinsonian tremor (i.e., a coarse, rhythmic, resting tremor with a frequency between 3 and 6 cycles per second, affecting the limbs, head, mouth, or tongue)

    (2) parkinsonian muscular rigidity (i.e., cogwheel rigidity or continuous "lead-pipe" rigidity)

    (3) akinesia (i.e., a decrease in spontaneous facial expressions, gestures, speech, or body movements)

B. The symptoms in criterion A developed within a few weeks of starting or raising the dose of a neuroleptic medication, or of reducing a medication used to treat (or prevent) acute extrapyramidal symptoms (e.g., anticholinergic agents).

C. The symptoms in criterion A are not better accounted for by a mental disorder (e.g., catatonic or negative symptoms in schizophrenia, psychomotor retardation in a major depressive episode). Evidence that the symptoms are better accounted for by a mental disorder might include the following: the symptoms precede the exposure to neuroleptic medication or are not compatible with the pattern of pharmacological intervention (e.g., no improvement after lowering the neuroleptic dose or administering anticholinergic medication).

D. The symptoms in criterion A are not due to a nonneuroleptic substance or to a neurological or other general medical condition (e.g., Parkinson's disease, Wilson's disease). Evidence that the symptoms are due to a general medical condition might include the following: the symptoms precede exposure to neuroleptic medication, unexplained focal neurological signs are present, or the symptoms progress despite a stable medication regimen.

Table from DSM-IV, *Diagnostic and Statistical Manual of Mental Disorders,* ed 4. Copyright American Psychiatric Association, Washington, 1994. Used with permission.

various substances prescribed by physicians or obtained illicitly. For example, such drugs as *heroin and marijuana* are listed on *Schedule I* and have *no accepted medical use in the United States* and are associated with a high abuse potential. Drugs such as *amphetamine and morphine* are listed on *Schedule II* and are also associated with a high abuse potential. Drugs such as morphine and methyprylon are listed on *Schedule III* and are associated with a

moderate physical dependence and high psychological dependence liability. Drugs such as chloral hydrate and benzodiazepines are listed on *Schedule IV* and are associated with a *low abuse potential and limited psychological and physical dependence liability.* However, in New York State, benzodiazepines are treated as Schedule II substances, which require a triplicate prescription for a maximum of one month's supply. Drugs listed on *Schedule V* include drugs with the *lowest abuse potential of all controlled substances.* Table 33.6 lists the DEA schedules and gives examples of drugs and their characteristics at each control level.

33.34–33.37

33.34. The answer is C (*Synopsis VII,* pages 1012–1013).

33.35. The answer is A (*Synopsis VII,* page 1011).

33.36. The answer is B (*Synopsis VII,* page 1013).

33.37. The answer is D (*Synopsis VII,* page 1014).

Light therapy, also called phototherapy, involves exposing patients to artificial light sources. The major indication for the treatment is *major depressive disorder with seasonal pattern,* a constellation of depressive symptoms that occurs during the fall and the winter and disappears during the spring and the summer.

In *psychosurgery* the brain is modified to reduce the symptoms of severely ill psychiatric patients who have not responded to traditional treatments. A reasonable guideline is that the disorder should have been present for at least three years, during which a variety of alternative treatments were attempted. *Chronic, severe, intractable major depressive disorder* is one of the disorders sometimes responsive to psychosurgery, although it is a treatment of last resort and is rarely used or recommended.

To gather information during a psychiatric interview, some psychiatrists advocate an *amobarbital (Amytal) interview.* The most common reasons for an amobarbital interview are uninformative or mute patients, catatonia, and conversion disorder.

Acupuncture is the stimulation of specific points on the body with electricity or transcutaneous needle insertion. Several American investigators have reported that acupuncture is an effective treatment of some patients with *substance dependence*—for example, dependence on nicotine, caffeine, cocaine, and heroin.

Table 33.6
Characteristics of Drugs at Each Drug Enforcement Administration (DEA) Control Level

DEA Control Level (Schedule)	Characteristics of Drug at Each Control Level	Examples of Drugs at Each Control Level
I	High abuse potential No accepted use in medical treatment in the United States at the present time and, therefore, not for prescription use	LSD, heroin, marijuana, peyote, mescaline, psilocybin, tetrahydrocannabinols, nicodeine, nicomorphine, and others
II	High abuse potential Severe physical dependence liability Severe psychological dependence liability	Amphetamine, opium, morphine, codeine, hydromorphine, phenmetrazine, cocaine, amobarbital, secobarbital, pentobarbital, methylphenidate
III	Abuse potential less than levels I and II Moderate or low physical dependence liability High psychological liability	Glutethimide, methyprylon, nalorphine, sulfonmethane, benzphetamine, phendimetrazine, clortermine, mazindol, chlorphentermine, compounds containing codeine, morphine, opium, hydrocodone, dihydrocodeine, and others.
IV	Low abuse potential Limited physical dependence liability Limited psychological dependence liability	Phenobarbital, benzodiazepines, chloral hydrate, ethchlorvynol, ethinamate, meprobamate, paraldehyde.
V	Lowest abuse potential of all controlled substances	Narcotic preparations containing limited amounts of nonnarcotic active medicinal ingredients

Child Psychiatry: Assessment, Examination, and Psychological Testing

Psychiatric assessment of a child integrates information from clinical interviews with the child and the child's parents. A great deal of important information—especially information pertaining to such inner experiences as mood, fears, anxiety, and psychotic phenomena—can be elicited from the child. Very young children, particularly children under the age of 5 years, are better at showing their feelings in a play situation than in words. Parents are generally the best informants about developmental milestones and chronological information.

The goals of the assessment are, first, to engage the child and, second, to identify developmental functions and psychiatric symptoms. To understand the significance of a child's or a parent's disclosure, the clinician must be able to compare it with age-appropriate experiences and behaviors. For example, normative separation anxiety and temper tantrums in a 3-year-old occur at a different rate and intensity than in a teenager.

A mental status examination is part of the assessment of a child of any age. Physical appearance, parent-child interactions, and separation and reunion behavior with parents are included in the mental status examination. The examiner should also observe mannerisms, sociability, and motor activity. During the mental status examination the clinician should note the child's speech and language development and the child's mood.

An assessment of suicidal ideation should be included in the mental status examination of all children who comprehend that concept. A child of average intelligence who is more than 4 years old usually understands the notion of real versus make-believe. Children are able to express whether they have thought about suicide even when they do not have a firm understanding of the permanence of death. An estimate of the child's cognitive abilities is also part of the mental status examination.

A comprehensive psychiatric evaluation often includes a standardized assessment of intellectual function and a report of the child's academic achievement and overall school functioning. The most widely used test of intelligence in school-age children is the Wechsler Intelligence Scale for Children-III (WISC-III). It gives a verbal intelligence quotient (I.Q.), a performance I.Q., and a combined or full-scale I.Q. The average full-scale I.Q. is 100; an I.Q. between 80 and 120 falls within the range of normal intelligence. The Stanford-Binet Intelligence Scale can be administered to children as young as 2 years of age, since it relies on nonverbal stimuli; it can also be used to assess intelligence in adults with verbal deficits. A standardized measure of adaptive behavior, such as the Vineland Adaptive Behavior Scales, is used to complete an assessment of mental retardation in a child who scores below the average range in an intelligence test. Achievement tests, such as the Wide-Range Achievement Test-Revised (WRAT-R) and the Peabody Individual Achievement Test (PIAT), are performance measures of knowledge and skills in various subjects—including reading, spelling, and arithmetic—that are mastered in school.

Standardized developmental scales—such as the Bayley Infant Scale of Development, the Gesell Infant Scale, and the Denver Developmental Screening Test—are used to assess motor, social, and some language development in infants 2 months to several years old.

Projective psychological tests, including the Rorschach test and the Children's Apperception Test (CAT), are tools that help elicit themes and fantasies from the child. Although the tests cannot be used diagnostically, the assumption is that a child's interpretation of the ambiguous stimuli presented by the tests reflects the child's themes and feelings.

After gathering the available information,

the clinician can then assess the child's functioning, taking into account the psychodynamic, developmental, family, and environmental influences.

Students should read the material in Chapter 34 in *Kaplan and Sadock's Synopsis VII*. By studying the questions and answers below, they can then assess their knowledge of the area.

HELPFUL HINTS

The student should memorize the following terms and their definitions.

developmental milestones	rapport	intelligence quotient (I.Q.)
clinical interview	limit setting	psychological tests
structured interview	motor activity level	adaptive function
best-estimate diagnosis	attention span	developmental delay
symbolic play	social relatedness	suicidal ideation
unstructured play	judgment	family psychiatric history
confidentiality	speech and language	family functioning
temperament	neurological soft signs	squiggle game
mental status examination	minor physical anomaly	three wishes
separation and reunion	cognitive function	Draw-a-Person

QUESTIONS

DIRECTIONS: Each of the questions or incomplete statements below is followed by five suggested responses or completions. Select the *one* that is *best* in each case.

34.1. The psychiatric assessment of a 3-year-old child includes all the following *except*
A. using an unstructured playroom to observe symbolic play
B. directing questions to a doll or a puppet
C. playing peekaboo games
D. observing separation and reunion behavior with the child's parents
E. noting motor activity and activity level

34.2. Techniques that are helpful in eliciting information and feelings from a school-age child include all the following *except*
A. asking the child to disclose three wishes
B. asking the child to draw a family
C. using Donald Winnicott's squiggle game
D. using only open-ended questions
E. using indirect commentary

34.3. All the following are components of the mental status examination of a child *except*
A. parent-child interaction
B. the child's activity level
C. the child's social relatedness
D. the child's intelligence quotient (I.Q.)
E. mood and affect

34.4. The mental status examination of children includes
A. fantasies and inferred conflicts
B. judgment and insight
C. positive attributes
D. self-esteem
E. all the above

34.5. The psychiatric assessment of adolescents include
A. giving adolescents the choice of being seen first alone or being present during the initial interview with their parents
B. seeing each parent in a separate interview to discern differences in their views of the child's problem
C. asking adolescents about sexual experiences and the use of drugs
D. sharing information with the parents
E. all the above

34.6. Hostility by an adolescent in the initial psychiatric interview may reflect all the following *except*
A. a test of how much the clinician can be trusted
B. a defense against anxiety
C. borderline intellectual functioning
D. a transference phenomenon
E. depression

34.7. Countertransference phenomena include all the following *except*
A. expectations that exceed the child's developmental level
B. identification with the child or the adolescent
C. ambivalent feelings toward the child's siblings
D. reactions by the child to the therapist as if the therapist were a parent
E. repeated arguing with the child or the adolescent

34.8. Which of the following statements about personality tests for children is true?
A. Personality tests and tests of ability are of equal reliability and validity
B. Both the Children's Apperception Test (CAT) and the Thematic Apperception Test (TAT) use pictures of people in situations
C. The Rorschach test has not been developed for children or adolescents
D. The Mooney Problem Check List is basically a checklist of personal problems
E. All the above

34.9. During a psychiatric examination of a child, the psychiatrist should
A. encourage the child to sit quietly in a chair
B. avoid looking at the child
C. always have the parent in the same room with the child
D. use a conversational approach and encourage the child to take the initiative
E. all the above

34.10. Figure 34.1 is part of a series of drawings used to test children for
A. depression
B. elation
C. frustration
D. anger
E. all the above

Figure 34.1. (Figure reproduced by permission of Saul Rosenzweig.)

DIRECTIONS: Each group of questions below consists of lettered headings followed by a list of numbered phrases or statements. For each numbered phrase or statement, select the *one* lettered heading that is most closely associated with it. Each lettered heading may be selected once, more than once, or not at all.

Questions 34.11–34.13
A. Rorschach test
B. Blacky Pictures
C. Toy tests and dolls

34.11. Bilaterally symmetrical inkblots

34.12. Reveals through play the child's attitudes toward the family, sibling rivalries, fears, aggressions, and conflicts

34.13. Cartoons of a small dog, its parents, and a sibling are designed to elicit sexual conflicts

Questions 34.14–34.18

A. Vineland Adaptive Behavior Scales
B. Children's Apperception Test (CAT)
C. Wide-Range Achievement Test-Revised (WRAT-R)
D. Peabody Picture Vocabulary Test-Revised (PPVT-R)
E. Wechsler Intelligence Scale for Children-III (WISC-III)

34.14. Measures receptive word understanding, with resulting standard scores, percentiles, and age equivalents

34.15. Measures communication, daily living skills, socialization, and motor development, yielding a composite expressed in a standard score, percentiles, and age equivalents

34.16. Generates stories from picture cards of animals that reflect interpersonal functioning

34.17. Measures functioning in reading, spelling, and arithmetic, with resulting grade levels, percentiles, and standard scores

34.18. Measures verbal, performance, and full-scale ability, with scaled subtest scores permitting specific skill assessment

ANSWERS

Child Psychiatry: Assessment, Examination, and Psychological Testing

34.1. The answer is C (*Synopsis VII,* page 1017).

Playing peekaboo games is appropriate with infants of 18 months or younger, but children over 2 years of age should be able to engage in symbolic play with the examiner and with toys. Assessments of young children generally include *using an unstructured playroom to observe symbolic play.* Many young children reveal more in play than in response to conversation. Children under the age of 6 years often reveal information most easily if the examiner *directs questions to a doll or a puppet. Observing separation and reunion behavior with the child's parents* is part of the mental status examination, and assessments of very young children usually begin with their parents present, since young children may be frightened by the interview situation. *Noting motor behavior and activity-level* is important in the assessment of young children.

34.2. The answer is D (*Synopsis VII,* page 1017).

Open-ended questions can overwhelm a school-age child and result in withdrawal or a shrugging of the shoulders; multiple-choice questions and partially open-ended questions may elicit more information from a school-age child. Techniques that can structure and facilitate the disclosure of feelings include *asking the child to disclose three wishes.* If a child is not adept with verbal skills, *asking the child to draw a family* is often a way to break the ice. Games such as *Donald Winnicott's squiggle,* in which the examiner draws a curved line and then takes turns with the child in continuing the drawing, may also help open up communication with the child. *Using indirect commentary*—such as, "I once knew a child about your age who felt very sad when he moved away from all his friends . . ."—helps elicit feelings from the child, although the clinician must be careful not to lead children into confirming what they think the clinician wants to hear.

34.3. The answer is D (*Synopsis VII,* pages 1019–1020).

Although intelligence affects the mental status examination, the *child's intelligence quotient (I.Q.),* a numerical figure derived from a standardized assessment of the child's intellectual abilities, is not a component of the mental status examination. The

mental status examination in a child includes *parent-child interaction, the child's activity level* and *social relatedness, mood,* and *affect.*

34.4. The answer is E (all) (*Synopsis VII,* pages 1019–1020).

Included in the mental status examination of children (Table 34.1) is the evaluation of fantasies and inferred conflicts, judgment and insight, positive attributes, and self-esteem. *Fantasies and inferred conflicts* can be assessed by direct questioning about the child's dreams, drawings, doodles, or spontaneous play. *Judgment and insight* can be assessed by exploring what the child thinks caused the presenting problem, how upset the child appears to be about the problem, what the child thinks may help solve the problem, and how the child thinks the clinician can help. *Positive attributes* include physical health, attractive appearance, normal height and weight, normal vision and hearing, even temperament, normal intelligence, appropriate emotional responses, recognition of feelings and fantasies, a good command of language, and good academic and social performance at school. Low *self-esteem* is often heralded by the child who makes such remarks as, "I can't do that" or "I'm no good at anything."

34.5. The answer is E (all) (*Synopsis VII,* pages 1017 and 1152–1153).

The psychiatric assessment of adolescents should include *giving adolescents the choice of being seen*

Table 34.1
Mental Status Examination of Children

1. Physical appearance
2. Parent-child interaction
3. Separation and reunion
4. Orientation to time, place, and person
5. Speech and language
6. Mood
7. Affect
8. Thought process and content
9. Social relatedness
10. Motor behavior
11. Cognition
12. Memory
13. Judgment and insight

first alone or being present during the initial interview with their parents. In addition to seeing the parents together, the clinician should *see each parent in a separate interview to discern differences in their views of the problem.* Eventually, the clinician should *ask adolescents about sexual experiences and the use of drugs. Sharing information with the parents* is part of the assessment. The younger a child or adolescent is, the more information has to be shared with the parents.

34.6. The answer is C (*Synopsis VII,* page 1017).

In the initial psychiatric interview, hostility by an adolescent *does not reflect borderline intellectual functioning.* The hostility is often *a test of how much the clinician can be trusted, a defense against anxiety, a transference phenomenon,* or evidence of a *depression.* In adolescents, poor academic performance, substance abuse, antisocial behavior, sexual promiscuity, truancy, and running away from home may all be symptoms of a depressive disorder. Transference phenomena involve reactions toward the clinician that derive from unconscious feelings toward childhood authority figures, rather than from the real relationship with the clinician. That real relationship must also be examined, and the experienced clinician always asks whether the patient's reaction is justified.

34.7. The answer is D (*Synopsis VII,* pages 6–7 and 826–827).

Reactions by the child to the therapist as if the therapist were a parent is an example of transference, not countertransference. In countertransference the therapist responds to the patient as if the patient were an important figure from the therapist's past. Examples of countertransference include (1) the clinician's setting *expectations that exceed the child's developmental level;* (2) the regressive pull experienced by the clinician, causing the clinician's *identification with the child or the adolescent;* (3) *ambivalent feelings toward the child's siblings,* which may be due to residual feelings from the clinician's own childhood relationships; (4) *repeated arguing with the child or the adolescent,* which may suggest that the clinician has become enmeshed with the patient.

34.8. The answer is D (*Synopsis VII,* pages 1020–1023).

The Mooney Problem Check List is basically a checklist of personal problems. It is a self-report inventory, a series of questions concerning emotional problems, worries, interests, motives, values, and interpersonal traits. The major usefulness of personality inventories is in the screening and identifying of children in need of further evaluation. *Personality tests and tests of ability are not of equal reliability and validity.* Personality tests are much less satisfactory with regard to norms, reliability, and validity. *The Children's Apperception Test (CAT) is different from the adult Thematic Apperception Test (TAT)*

in that *the TAT uses pictures of people, whereas the CAT uses pictures of animals* on the assumption that children respond more readily to animal characters than to people. *The Rorschach test,* one of the most widely used projective techniques, *has been developed for children* between the ages of 2 and 10 years *and for adolescents* between the ages of 10 and 17.

34.9. The answer is D (*Synopsis VII,* pages 1016–1017).

During a psychiatric examination of a child, the psychiatrist should *use a conversational approach and encourage the child to take the initiative.* The psychiatrist should *not encourage the child to sit quietly in a chair* and should *not avoid looking the child.* Nor should the psychiatrist *always have the parent in the same room with the child.*

34.10. The answer is C (*Synopsis VII,* pages 1016–1024).

Figure 34.1 is part of the Rosenzweig Picture-*Frustration* Study. The test presents a series of cartoons in which one person frustrates another. In the blank space provided, the child writes what the frustrated person replies. From that reply, the examiner determines the effect of frustration on the child; the effect can range from extreme passivity to extreme violence. The test is not used to measure *depression, elation,* or *anger.*

34.11–34.13

34.11. The answer is A (*Synopsis VII,* pages 1022–1023).

34.12. The answer is C (*Synopsis VII,* page 1017).

34.13. The answer is B (*Synopsis VII,* pages 1017–1023).

One of the most widely used projective techniques is the *Rorschach test,* in which the subjects are shown a set of *bilaterally symmetrical inkblots* and asked to tell what they see or what the blot represents. Another projective test is the *Blacky Pictures* in which *cartoons showing a small dog, its parents, and a sibling are designed to elicit sexual conflicts.* Drawings, *toy tests, and dolls* are used in other applications of projective methods. The objects are usually selected because of their associative value, often including dolls representing adults and children, bathroom and kitchen fixtures, and other household furnishings. Play with such articles is expected to *reveal the child's attitudes toward the family, sibling rivalries, fears, aggressions, and conflicts.* They are of particular use in eliciting sexual abuse problems in children.

34.14–34.18

34.14. The answer is D (*Synopsis VII,* page 1021).

34.15. The answer is A (*Synopsis VII,* page 1021).

34.16. **The answer is B** (*Synopsis VII,* page 1023).

34.17. **The answer is C** (*Synopsis VII,* pages 1021 and 1023).

34.18. **The answer is E** (*Synopsis VII,* pages 1021 and 1023).

The *Vineland Adaptive Behavior Scales are used to measure communication, daily living skills, socialization, and motor development, yielding a composite expressed in a standard score, percentiles, and age equivalents.* The scales are standardized for normal and mentally retarded people. A measure of adaptive function, as well as a standardized measure of intelligence, is a prerequisite when a diagnosis of mental retardation is being considered.

The *Children's Apperception Test (CAT)* is an adaptation for children of the Thematic Apperception Test (TAT). The CAT *generates stories from picture cards of animals that reflect interpersonal functioning.* The cards show ambiguous scenes related to family issues and relationships. The child is asked to describe what is happening and to tell a story about the outcome of the scene in the card. Animals are used because it was hypothesized that children respond more readily to animal images than to human figures.

The *Wide-Range Achievement Test-Revised (WRAT-R) measures functioning in reading, spelling, and arithmetic, with resulting grade levels, percentiles, and standard scores.* It can be used in children 5 years of age and older. It yields a score that is compared with the average expected score for the child's chronological age and grade level.

The *Peabody Picture Vocabulary Test-Revised (PPVT-R) measures receptive word of understanding, with resulting standard scores—percentile and age equivalents* can be used for children 4 years of age and older. The *Wechsler Intelligence Scale for Children-III (WISC-III),* the most widely used test of intelligence for school-age children, *measures verbal, performance, and full-scale ability, with scaled subtest scores permitting specific skill assessment.* In a full-scale intelligence quotient (I.Q.), 70 to 80 indicates borderline intelligence, 80 to 90 indicates low-average intelligence, 90 to 109 indicates average intelligence, and 110 to 119 indicates high average intelligence.

Table 34.2 lists some commonly used child and adolescent assessment instruments.

Table 34.2
Commonly Used Child and Adolescent Assessment Instruments

Test	Ages or Grades	Comments and Data Generated
Intellectual Ability		
Wechsler Intelligence Scale for Children (WISC-III) (Psychological Corporation)	6–16	Standard scores: verbal, performance, and full-scale I.Q.; scaled subtest scores permitting specific skill assessment
Wechsler Adult Intelligence Scale-Revised (WAIS-R) (Psychological Corporation)	16–adult	Same as WISC-R
Wechsler Preschool and Primary Scale of Intelligence (WPPSI) (Psychological Corporation)	4–6	Same as WISC-R
McCarthy Scales of Children's Abilities (MSCA) (Psychological Corporation)	2.6–8	Scores: general cognitive index (I.Q. equivalent), language, perceptual performance, quantitative memory and motor domain scores; percentiles
Kaufman Assessment Battery for Children (K-ABC) (American Guidance Service)	2.6–12.6	Well-grounded in theories of cognitive psychology and neuropsychology. Allows immediate comparison of intellectual capacity with acquired knowledge. Scores: mental processing composite (I.Q. equivalent); sequential and simultaneous processing and achievement standard scores; scaled mental processing and achievement subtest scores; age equivalents, percentiles
Stanford Binet, 4th edition (SB:FE) (Riverside Publishing Company)	2–23	Scores: I.Q., verbal, abstract-visual, and quantitative reasoning; short-term memory; standard age
Peabody Picture Vocabulary Test-Revised (PPVT-R) (American Guidance Service)	4–adult	Measures receptive vocabulary acquisition. Standard scores, percentiles, age equivalents
Development		
Gesell Infant Scale	8 wk–3 1/2 yr	Mostly motor development in the first year, with some social and language assessment
Bayley Infant Scale of Development	8 wk–2 1/2 yr	Motor and social
Denver Developmental Screening Test	2 mo–6 yr	Screening
Yale Revised Developmental Schedule	4 wk–6 yr	Gross motor, fine motor, adaptive, personal-social, language
Achievement		
Woodcock-Johnson Psycho-Educational Battery (DLM/Teaching Resources)	K–12	Scores: reading and mathematics (mechanics and comprehension), written language, other academic achievement; grade and age scores, standard scores, percentiles
Wide-Range Achievement Test-Revised, Levels 1 and 2 (WRAT-R) (Jastak Associates)	Level 1: 5–11 Level 2: 12–75	Permits screening for deficits in reading, spelling, and arithmetic; grade levels, percentiles, stanines, standard scores
Kaufman Test of Educational Achievement, Brief and Comprehensive Forms (K-TEA) (American Guidance Service)	1–12	Standard scores: reading, mathematics, and spelling; grade and age equivalents, percentiles, stanines. Brief form sufficient for most clinical applications; comprehensive form allows error analysis and more detailed curriculum planning
Adaptive Behavior		
Vineland Adaptive Behavior Scales (American Guidance Service)	Normal: 0–19 Retarded: all ages	Standard scores: adaptive behavior composite and communication, daily living skills, socialization and motor domains; percentiles, age equivalents, developmental age scores. Separate standardization groups for normal, visually handicapped, hearing-impaired, emotionally disturbed, and retarded
Scales of Independent Behavior (DLM Teaching Resources)	Newborn–adult	Standard scores: four adaptive (motor, social interaction and communication, personal living, community living) and three maladaptive (internalized, asocial, and externalized) areas; general maladaptive index and broad independence cluster

Continued

Table 34.2
Continued

Test	Ages or Grades	Comments and Data Generated
Projective		
Rorschach test (Huber, Haus; U.S. Distrib.: Grune & Stratton)	3–adult	Special scoring systems. Most recently developed and increasingly universally accepted is Exner's (1974) Comprehensive System. Assesses perceptual accuracy, integration of affective and intellectual functioning, reality testing, and other psychological processes
Thematic Apperception Test (TAT) (Harvard University Press)	6–adult	Generates stories that are analyzed qualitatively. Assumed to provide especially rich data regarding interpersonal functioning
Machover Draw-A-Person Test (DAP) (Charles C Thomas)	3–adult	Qualitative analysis and hypothesis generation, especially regarding subject's feelings about self and significant others
Kinetic Family Drawing (KFD) (Brunner/Mazel)	3–adult	Qualitative analysis and hypothesis generation regarding a person's perception of family structure and sentient environment. Some objective scoring systems in existence
Rotter Incomplete Sentences Blank (Psychological Corporation)	Child, adolescent, and adult forms	Primarily qualitative analysis, although some objective scoring systems have been developed
Personality		
Minnesota Multiphasic Personality Inventory (MMPI) (University of Minnesota Press)	16–adult	Most widely used personality inventory. Standard scores: 3 validity scales and 14 clinical scales
Millon Adolescent Personality Inventory (MAPI) (National Computer Systems)	13–18	Standard scores for 20 scales grouped into three categories: personality styles, expressed concerns, behavioral correlates. Normed on adolescent population. Focuses on broad functional spectrum, not just problem areas
Children's Personality Questionnaire (Institute for Personality and Ability Testing)	8–12	Measures 14 primary personality traits, including emotional stability, self-concept level, excitability, and self-assurance. Generates combined broad trait patterns, including extroversion and anxiety
Neuropsychological		
Beery-Buktenika Developmental Test of Visual-Motor Integration (VMI) (Modern Curriculum Press)	2–16	Screening instrument for visual-motor deficits. Standard scores, age equivalents, percentiles
Benton Visual Retention Test (Psychological Corporation)	6–adult	Assesses presence of deficits in visual-figural memory. Mean scores by age
Bender Visual-Motor Gestalt Test (American Orthopsychiatric Association)	5–adult	Assesses visual-motor deficits and visual-figural retention. Age equivalents
Reitan-Indiana Neuropsychological Test Battery for Children (Neuropsychology Press)	5–8	Cognitive and perceptual-motor tests for children with suspected brain damage
Halstead-Reitan Neuropsychological Test Battery for Older Children (Neuropsychology Press)	9–14	Same as Reitan-Indiana
Luria-Nebraska Neuropsychological Battery: Children's Revision (LNNB-C) (Western Psychological Services)	8–12	Sensory-motor, perceptual, and cognitive tests measuring 11 clinical and 2 additional domains of neuropsychological functioning. Provides standard scores

Table from G R Racusin, N E Moss: Psychological assessment of children and adolescents. In *Child and Adolescent Psychiatry: A Comprehensive Textbook,* M Lewis, editor, p 475. Williams & Wilkins, Baltimore, 1991. Used with permission. Adapted by Melvin Lewis, M.B.

Mental Retardation

Mental retardation consists of significantly subaverage intellectual functioning and impairments in adaptive functioning before the age of 18 years. The disorder is influenced by genetic, environmental, and psychosocial factors. Recently, such biological determinants as chromosomal abnormalities, hereditary syndromes, and prenatal noxious exposures have been recognized as contributing to mental retardation. Along with the stresses of coping with intellectual limitations, persons with mental retardation have higher than average rates of a variety of mental disorders, including mood disorders, schizophrenia, and attention-deficit and disruptive behavior disorders.

Intellectual functioning is determined by the use of standardized tests of intelligence; significantly subaverage intelligence is defined as a full-scale intelligence quotient (I.Q.) of less than 70—that is, at least two standard deviations below the mean for the test. Adaptive functioning can be measured by using a standardized scale, such as the Vineland Adaptive Behavior Scales, that generates a composite measure, taking into account the domains of communication, daily living skills, socialization, and motor skills.

The fourth edition of *Diagnostic and Statistical Manual of Mental Disorders* (DSM-IV) divides mental retardation into four categories that depends on severity:

Mild: I.Q. 50–55 to approximately 70
Moderate: I.Q. 35–40 to 50–55
Severe: I.Q. 20–25 to 35–40
Profound: I.Q. below 20 or 25

Mental retardation, severity unspecified, is diagnosed when there is a strong presumption of mental retardation but the person is untestable by standard intelligence tests.

About 85 percent of all persons with mental retardation fall into the mild mental retardation category. Persons with borderline intellectual functioning—that is, persons with intelligence quotients that fall at least one but less than two standard deviations below the mean (I.Q. between 71 and 84)—are not considered mentally retarded, but resulting limitations may become a focus of psychiatric treatment.

A specific biological cause of mental retardation can be identified in about 25 percent of all mentally retarded persons. The more severe the mental retardation, the more likely it is that a cause can be identified. The cause of the mental retardation is known in up to 75 percent of all persons with severe mental retardation. There are 1.5 times more males than females with mental retardation.

The causes of mental retardation include genetic and inherited conditions, prenatal exposure to infections and toxins, perinatal trauma, and possibly sociocultural factors. Among the chromosomal and metabolic causes, Down's syndrome, fragile X syndrome, and phenylketonuria (PKU) are the most common disorders associated with mild and moderate mental retardation.

Down's syndrome can be the result of any of three chromosomal aberrations: (1) trisomy 21, the most common underlying abnormality, in which three of chromosome 21 are present; (2) nondisjunction, in which both normal and trisomic cells are found in various tissues (mosaicism); and (3) translocation, in which two chromosomes, usually 21 and 15, fuse; that aberration is usually inherited. Down's syndrome is diagnosed in a baby by noting its oblique palpebral fissures, small flattened skull, single palmar crease, high cheek-bones, and protruding tongue. Children and adolescents with Down's syndrome are often characterized as sociable and good-natured; they tend to show a marked deterioration in language, memory, self-care skills, and problem-solving abilities after the age of 30 years.

Fragile X syndrome is the second most common single cause of mental retardation. It results from a mutation on the X chromosome at the fragile site. The fragile site is expressed in only some cells. The typical phenotype includes a large long head, short stature, hyperextensible joints, and macro-orchidism after puberty. Persons with fragile X syndrome have relatively strong skills in socialization, but their language is often characterized by perseverative speech, with abnormal modes of combining words into phrases. Persons with fragile X syndrome have higher than average rates of attention-deficit/hyperactivity disorder, learning disorders, and pervasive developmental disorders.

Prader-Willi syndrome is a mental retardation syndrome postulated to be due to a small deletion involving chromosome 15 manifested by compulsive eating, obesity, small stature, and hypogonadism. Children with Prader-Willi syndrome are often reported to be oppositional and defiant.

Prenatal noxious exposures, such as that resulting in fetal alcohol syndrome, can also result in a child with mental retardation. In fetal alcohol syndrome, hypertelorism, microcephaly, short palpebral fissures, and inner epicanthal folds are present. Behaviorally, children whose mothers consumed alcohol regularly during pregnancy often present with attention-deficit disorders and learning disorders whether or not they exhibit the facial dysmorphism of fetal alcohol syndrome.

The types of mental disorders that occur in mentally retarded persons run the gamut of those seen in persons who are not retarded. The risk factors for mental disorders in mentally retarded persons include neurological impairments, such as seizure disorders; genetic syndromes, including those associated with particular behavioral presentations (fragile X syndrome, Prader-Willi syndrome, Lesch-Nyhan syndrome); and psychosocial factors. Frustrations related to intellectual limitations and social ineptness may lead to a negative self-image and poor self-esteem among mentally retarded persons. Their social isolation and feelings of inadequacy can lead to anxiety and depression.

Treatment of the various mental disorders in mentally retarded persons are generally the same as for persons who are not mentally retarded. However, the clinician should individualize the psychotherapy to make it appropriate for the patient's intellectual level.

Students should study Chapter 35 in *Kaplan and Sadock's Synopsis VII* and then address the questions and answers below.

HELPFUL HINTS

The student should define the terms listed below.

mental retardation	Bayley Infant Scale of	Turner's syndrome
intelligence quotient (I.Q.)	Development	neurofibrillary tangles
AAMD	Cattell Infant Scale	Prader-Willi syndrome
adaptive functioning	chromosomal abnormality	cri-du-chat syndrome
Vineland Adaptive Behavior Scales	Down's syndrome	PKU
mental deficiency	fragile X syndrome	neurofibromatosis
WHO	nondysjunction	Lesch-Nyhan syndrome
borderline intellectual functioning	rubella	prenatal expposure

QUESTIONS

DIRECTIONS: Each of the questions or incomplete statements below is followed by five suggested responses or completions. Select the *one* that is *best* in each case.

35.1. Which of the following mental disorders is seen with a greater frequency in mentally retarded persons than in the general population?
A. Autistic disorder
B. Schizophrenia
C. Depressive disorders
D. Stereotypic movement disorder
E. All the above

35.2. Risk factors for psychopathology among mentally retarded persons include all the following *except*
A. neurological impairments
B. genetic syndromes
C. family dysfunctions
D. borderline intellectual functioning
E. communication limitations

35.3. Children born to mothers affected with rubella may present with
A. congenital heart disease
B. deafness
C. cataracts
D. microcephaly
E. all the above

35.4. Profoundly retarded preschool-age children respond to
A. social and communicative skills training
B. training in self-help
C. motor development training
D. constant aid and supervision only
E. all the above

35.5. The genetic finding most likely to be associated with advancing maternal age is
A. translocation between chromosome 14 and chromosome 21
B. mitotic nondisjunction of chromosome 21
C. partially trisomic karyotype
D. meiotic nondisjunction of chromosome 21
E. all the above

35.6. Which of the following chromosomal abnormalities is most likely to cause mental retardation?
A. Fusion of chromosomes 21 and 15
B. XO (Turner's syndrome)
C. XXY (Klinefelter's syndrome)
D. Extra chromosome 21 (trisomy 21)
E. XXYY (Klinefelter's syndrome variation)

35.7. Mental retardation should be diagnosed when the intelligence quotient (I.Q.) falls below
A. 20
B. 40
C. 70
D. 90
E. 100

35.8. Which of the following statements about mental retardation is true?
A. Idiopathic intellectual impairment is usually severe and associated with intelligence quotients (I.Q.s) below 40
B. Psychosocial deprivation is not believed to contribute to mental retardation
C. Rubella is second only to syphilis as the major cause of congenital malformations and mental retardation attributable to maternal infection
D. The prevalence of mental retardation at any one time is estimated to be about 1 percent of the general population
E. All the above

35.9. Fragile X syndrome
A. has a phenotype that includes postpubertal micro-orchidism
B. affects only males
C. usually causes severe to profound mental retardation
D. is associated with schizoid personality disorder in adulthood
E. has a phenotype that includes a large head and large ears

DIRECTIONS: Each group of questions below consists of lettered headings followed by a list of numbered words or phrases. For each numbered word or phrase, select the *one* lettered heading that is most closely associated with it. Each lettered heading may be selected once, more than once, or not at all.

Questions 35.10–35.14

A. Fragile X syndrome
B. Prader-Willi syndrome
C. Down's syndrome
D. Fetal alcohol syndrome
E. Lesch-Nyhan syndrome

35.10. Compulsive eating behavior, obesity, hypogonadism, and small stature

35.11. Compulsive self-mutilation by biting of the mouth and the fingers

35.12. Microcephaly, hypertelorism, short palpebral fissures, attention-deficit/hyperactivity disorder, and learning disorders

35.13. Long head and ears, short stature, hyperextensible joints, postpubertal macro-orchidism, and a risk for pervasive developmental disorders

35.14. A marked deterioration in language, memory, self-care, and problem-solving abilities in the patient's 30s

Questions 35.15–35.19

A. Phenylketonuria (PKU)
B. Rett's disorder
C. Acquired immune deficiency syndrome (AIDS)
D. Rubella
E. Cytomegalic inclusion disease

35.15. Mental retardation with cerebral calcifications, jaundice, microcephaly, and hepatosplenomegaly

35.16. Progressive encephalopathy, mental retardation, and seizures within the first year of life

35.17. An X-linked mental retardation syndrome that is degenerative and affects only females

35.18. Mental retardation, eczema, vomiting, and seizures

35.19. Mental retardation, microcephaly, microphthalmia, congenital heart disease, deafness, and cataracts

Questions 35.20–35.24

A. Hyperglycinemia
B. Histidinemia
C. Homocystinuria
D. Oculocerebrorenal dystrophy
E. Cystathioninuria

35.20. Cataracts

35.21. Severe ketosis

35.22. Positive ferric chloride test result

35.23. Treatment with pyridoxine

35.24. Patients resemble those with Marfan's syndrome

ANSWERS

Mental Retardation

35.1. The answer is E (all) (*Synopsis VII,* pages 1038–1039).

Persons with severe mental retardation have especially high rates of *autistic disorder* and other pervasive developmental disorders. About 2 to 3 percent of mentally retarded persons meet the *diagnostic* criteria for *schizophrenia;* that figure is several times greater than the figure for the general population. Up to half of all mentally retarded persons have *depressive disorders,* according to structured interviews and rating scales given to samples. The prevalence of depressive disorders in mentally retarded persons is not known, but it appears to be higher than in the general population. *Stereotypic movement disorder is* known to occur at a high rate in certain mental retardation syndromes (for example, Lesch-Nyhan syndrome) and is more prevalent in mentally retarded persons than in the general population.

35.2. The answer is D (*Synopsis VII,* page 1025).

Borderline intellectual functioning is defined as an intelligence quotient between 71 and 84. It is not a category of mental retardation, but results in some limitations that can become a focus of psychiatric intervention.

The risk for psychopathology increases with *neurological impairments,* such as seizure disorders. Increased neurological impairment is frequently present with severe mental retardation, which also presents a risk factor for psychopathology.

Various known *genetic syndromes* (for example, fragile X syndrome, Prader-Willi syndrome, and Down's syndrome) have predictable aberrant behavioral components. People with fragile X syndrome have high rates (up to 75 percent) of attention-deficit hyperactivity disorder and language dysfunction. Prader-Willi syndrome is almost always associated with hyperphagia and obesity, often along with oppositional defiant disorder; temper tantrums, irritability, and poor socialization skills seem to characterize persons with the syndrome in adolescence. In Down's syndrome, language function is relatively weak compared with social skills and interpersonal engagement. A variety of mental disorders occur in persons with Down's syndrome, but pervasive developmental disorders are lower in that population than in other groups of mentally retarded persons.

Family dysfunctions, leading to an inability to provide a supportive home environment for mentally retarded persons, may exacerbate their already frustrating interactions with society. A lack of appropriate expectations and support may further increase vulnerability in a mentally retarded person, leading to an increase in anxiety, anger, dysphoria, and depression.

Communication limitations result in chronic frustration and may increase the negative self-image and poor self-esteem that many mentally retarded persons exhibit. Persons who have trouble communicating often withdraw and become isolated and depressed.

35.3. The answer is E (all) (*Synopsis VII,* page 1034).

The children of mothers affected with rubella may present with a number of abnormalities, including *congenital heart disease,* mental retardation, *deafness, cataracts, microcephaly,* and microphthalmia. Timing is crucial, as the extent and the frequency of the complications are inversely related to the duration of pregnancy at the time of the maternal infection. When mothers are infected in the first trimester of pregnancy, 10 to 15 percent of the children are affected, but the incidence rises to almost 50 percent when the infection occurs in the first month of pregnancy. The situation is often complicated by subclinical forms of maternal infection, which often go undetected. Maternal rubella can be prevented by immunization.

35.4. The answer is D (*Synopsis VII,* pages 1040–1041).

Profoundly retarded preschool-age children require nursing care that they are able to get with *constant aid and supervision only.* Those children who have the capacity to respond to *social and communicative skills training* are considered mildly retarded. Children who are able to profit from *training in self-help* and *motor development training* are categorized as moderately or mildly retarded.

35.5. The answer is D (*Synopsis VII,* page 1027).

Meiotic nondisjunction of chromosome 21 not only produces the majority of cases of Down's syndrome—almost 85 percent—but also has been most closely linked to advancing maternal age. Paternal age has also been implicated as a factor in some studies.

Translocation events, by contrast, constitute only 5 percent of Down's syndrome cases. Furthermore, in many cases in which an asymptomatic parent carries the aberrant chromosome in the genotype, the incidence of Down's syndrome is obviously unrelated to parental age. If the *translocation* occurs *between chromosome 14 and chromosome 21* (14/21), the proband carries 46 chromosomes, including two normal 21 chromosomes, one normal 14 chromosome, and the 14/21 translocation, which carries parts of both chromosomes. Any asymptomatic parent or sibling who is a carrier of the translocation has only 45 chromosomes—missing one chromosome 21 and thus being spared the excessive genetic complement.

Mitotic nondisjunction of chromosome 21, which occurs in 1 percent of all Down's syndrome cases, occurs after fertilization of a presumably healthy ovum and may thus be considered independent of maternal age.

Partially trisomic karyotype may refer to the mosaicism—some cells normal, others with trisomy 21—seen in mitotic nondisjunction or to the excessive complement of chromosome 21 produced by translocation. Neither case is as closely tied to maternal age as is meiotic nondisjunction.

35.6.   The answer is D (*Synopsis VII,* page 1027).

An *extra chromosome 21* is *trisomy 21,* the most common genetic abnormality found in Down's syndrome and the abnormality most likely to cause mental retardation. Abnormalities in autosomal chromosomes are, in general, associated with mental retardation. The chromosomal aberration represented by 46 chromosomes with *fusion of chromosomes 21 and 15* produces a type of Down's syndrome that, unlike trisomy 21, is usually inherited.

Aberrations in sex chromosomes are not always associated with mental retardation—for example, *XO (Turner's syndrome),* XXY (Klinefelter's syndrome) and *XXYY* and *XXXY (Klinefelter's syndrome variations).* Some children with Turner's syndrome have normal to superior intelligence.

In Turner's syndrome one sex chromosome is missing (XO). The result is an absence (agenesis) or minimal development (dysgenesis) of the gonads; no significant sex hormone, male or female, is produced in fetal life or postnatally. The sexual tissues thus retain a female resting state. Because the second X chromosome, which seems responsible for full femaleness, is missing, the affected girls are incomplete in their sexual anatomy and, lacking adequate estrogens, develop no secondary sex characteristics without treatment. They often suffer other stigmata, such as web neck.

In Klinefelter's syndrome the person (usually XXY) has a male habitus, under the influence of the Y chromosome, but that effect is weakened by the presence of the second X chromosome. Although born with a penis and testes, the child has small and infertile testes, and the penis may also be small. In adolescence, some patients begin to show gynecomastia and other feminine-appearing contours.

35.7.   The answer is C (*Synopsis VII,* pages 1025–1026).

Mental retardation should be diagnosed when the intelligence quotient (I.Q.) falls below *70.* According

to the fourth edition of *Diagnostic and Statistical Manual of Mental Disorders* (DSM-IV), the following classification of mental retardation is used: mild (I.Q. 50–55 to approximately 70), moderate (I.Q. 35–40 to 50–55), severe (I.Q. 20–25 to 35–40), and profound (I.Q. below 20 or 25). Table 35.1 lists the diagnostic criteria for mental retardation.

35.8.   The answer is D (*Synopsis VII,* page 1026).

The prevalence of mental retardation at any one time is estimated to be about 1 percent of the population. Persons with profound mental retardation—intelligence quotient (I.Q.) below 20 or 25—constitute 1 to 2 percent of the mentally retarded population; mild cases (I.Q. 50–55 to approximately 70) make up 85 percent; moderate retardation (I.Q. 35–40 to 50–55), 10 percent; and severe retardation (I.Q. 20–25 to 35–40), 3 to 4 percent. The level of intellectual impairment of persons with no known cause (for example, *idiopathic intellectual impairment) is usually mild and associated with I.Q.s between 50 and 70.* No specific biological cause of mental retardation can be found in 75 percent of cases. *Psychosocial* (social, linguistic, intellectual) *deprivation has been believed to contribute to idiopathic mental retardation. Rubella has surpassed syphilis as the major cause of congenital malformations and mental retardation attributable to maternal infection.*

35.9.   The answer is E (*Synopsis VII,* pages 1027–1028).

Fragile X syndrome *has a phenotype that includes a large head and large ears,* long and narrow face,

Table 35.1
Diagnostic Criteria for Mental Retardation

A. Significantly subaverage intellectual functioning: an IQ of approximately 70 or below on an individually administered IQ test (for infants, a clinical judgment of significantly subaverage intellectual functioning).

B. Concurrent deficits or impairments in present adaptive functioning (i.e., the person's effectiveness in meeting the standards expected for his or her age by his or her cultural group) in at least two of the following areas: communication, self-care, home living, social/interpersonal skills, use of community resources, self-direction, functional academic skills, work, leisure, health, and safety.

C. The onset is before age 18 years.

Code based on degree of severity reflecting level of intellectual impairment:

   Mild mental retardation: IQ level 50–55 to approximately 70
   Moderate mental retardation: IQ level 35–40 to 50–55
   Severe mental retardation: IQ level 20–25 to 35–40
   Profound mental retardation: IQ level below 20 or 25
   Mental retardation, severity unspecified: when there is strong presumption of mental retardation but the person's intelligence is untestable by standard tests

---

Table from DSM-IV, *Diagnostic and Statistical Manual of Mental Disorders,* ed 4. Copyright American Psychiatric Association, Washington, 1994. Used with permission.

short stature, and *postpubertal macro-orchidism, not micro-orchidism*. The syndrome affects both males and females. Female carriers are usually less impaired than males but can manifest the typical physical characteristics and mild mental retardation. In males the syndrome usually causes *low average intelligence to severe mental retardation (not severe to profound mental retardation)*. The syndrome is associated *with antisocial, not schizoid, personality disorder in adulthood*. Those affected by the syndrome may also have attention-deficit/hyperactivity disorder and learning disorders.

35.10–35.14

35.10. The answer is B (*Synopsis VII*, page 1028).

35.11. The answer is E (*Synopsis VII*, page 1032).

35.12. The answer is D (*Synopsis VII*, page 1034).

35.13. The answer is A (*Synopsis VII*, pages 1027–1028).

35.14. The answer is C (*Synopsis VII*, page 1027).

In *Prader-Willi syndrome, compulsive eating behavior, obesity,* and *hypogonadism* are common. *Small stature,* along with small hands and feet, usually accompanies the syndrome.

Lesch-Nyhan syndrome is characterized by severe *compulsive self-mutilation by biting of the mouth and the fingers,* microcephaly, mental retardation, seizures, and choreoathetosis.

Children with *fetal alcohol syndrome* exhibit a characteristic phenotype consisting of *microcephaly, hypertelorism, short palpebral fissures,* inner epicanthal folds, and a short, turned-up nose. Children with the syndrome are at risk for *attention-deficit/hyperactivity disorder and learning disorders*.

Persons with *fragile X syndrome* typically have *long heads and ears, short stature, hyperextensible joints, postpubertal macro-orchidism, and a risk for pervasive developmental disorders,* including autistic disorder.

Down's syndrome is characterized by *a marked deterioration in language, memory, self-care, and problem-solving abilities in the patient's 30s*.

35.15–35.19

35.15. The answer is E (*Synopsis VII*, page 1034).

35.16. The answer is C (*Synopsis VII*, page 1034).

35.17. The answer is B (*Synopsis VII*, page 1028).

35.18. The answer is A (*Synopsis VII*, page 1028).

35.19. The answer is D (*Synopsis VII*, page 1034).

Infants who are exposed to *cytomegalic inclusion disease* in utero may be stillbirths; when they are born alive, they may have *mental retardation with intracerebral calcifications, jaundice, microcephaly, and hepatosplenomegaly*.

Fetuses whose mothers have *acquired immune deficiency syndrome (AIDS)* often die in spontaneous abortions. Children born with AIDS often die within a few years, and up to half of them have *progressive encephalopathy, mental retardation, and seizures within the first year of life*.

Rett's disorder is believed to be *an X-linked* dominant *mental retardation syndrome that is degenerative and affects only females*.

Phenylketonuria (PKU) is a recessive autosomal disease in which the patient is unable to metabolize phenylalanine. Children with PKU often present with *mental retardation, eczema, vomiting, and seizures*.

Rubella in a pregnant woman is a serious risk factor for the fetus. The risk of fetal impairment is greatest when the exposure is early in the first trimester. *Mental retardation, microcephaly, microphthalmia, congenital heart disease, deafness, and cataracts* can result.

35.20–35.24

35.20. The answer is D (*Synopsis VII*, page 1030).

35.21. The answer is A (*Synopsis VII*, pages 1025–1033).

35.22. The answer is B (*Synopsis VII*, pages 1025–1033).

35.23. The answer is E (*Synopsis VII*, pages 1025–1033).

35.24. The answer is C (*Synopsis VII*, page 1033).

Hyperglycinemia, a nonketotic hyperglycinemia, is an autosomal recessive inborn error of metabolism in which large amounts of glycine are found in body fluids. The clinical picture includes severe mental retardation, seizures, spasticity, and failure to thrive. Ketotic hyperglycinemia is characterized by *severe ketosis*. The hyperglycinemia is secondary to blood elevation of several amino acids. The clinical picture includes seizures, mental retardation, vomiting, dehydration, ketosis, and coma.

Histidinemia, which is characterized by a defect in the histidine metabolism, is transmitted by a single autosomal recessive gene and involves a block in the conversion of histidine to urocanic acid. The urine gives a *positive ferric chloride test result* (green). Mild mental retardation and sometimes speech defects are part of the clinical picture.

Homocystinuria is a disorder that comprises a group of inborn errors of metabolism, each of which may lead to the accumulation of homocysteine. The *patients* are mentally retarded and *resemble those with Marfan's syndrome* in outward appearance.

Oculocerebrorenal dystrophy, (Lowe's syndrome), a sex-linked disorder, presents a varied clinical picture that includes buphthalmos, microphthalmos,

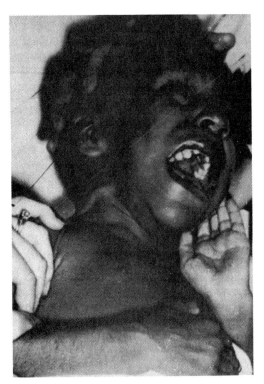

Figure 35.1. A child with oculocerebrorenal dystrophy. (Figure courtesy Michael Malone, M.D., Children's Hospital, Washington, D.C.)

cataracts, and corneal opacities. Renal ammonia production is decreased, and a generalized aminoaciduria is found. Figure 35.1 shows a child with oculocerebrorenal dystrophy.

Cystathioninuria is marked by a metabolic defect that consists of a block at the site of cleavage of cystathionine to cysteine and homoserine. Patients with the disease are mentally retarded. Prolonged *treatment with pyridoxine* may improve the patient's intellectual performance.

Learning Disorders

Learning disorders—called academic skills disorders in the revised third edition of *Diagnostic and Statistical Manual of Mental Disorders* (DSM-III-R)—consist of below-expected abilities in specific academic areas, such as reading, arithmetic, and written expression. Learning disorders are important to diagnose so that the appropriate remediation and educational setting can be put into place as early as possible.

Reading disorder includes impaired ability to recognize words, poor comprehension, and low and inaccurate reading in the presence of normal intelligence. Prevalence studies have identified from 2 to 8 percent of children with the disorder, leading to an estimate of 4 percent of school-age children. Three to four times as many boys as girls have reading disorder. The disorder is diagnosed only when no sensory deficits or neurological condition account for the reading disability. In the past the term "dyslexia" was used for a syndrome including reading disability and speech and language deficits. When it became known that reading disorder often occurs along with other academic skills disorders, the term "learning disorders" began to be used.

No unitary cause of reading disorder is known, although it tends to be found in family members of probands, suggesting a genetic contribution. Reading disorder has been reported to occur with greater than usual frequency in children born in May, June, and July, leading to a possible link between maternal winter infectious disease and the development of reading disorder. Children with reading disorder are also at high risk for other learning disorders and attention-deficit/hyperactivity disorder. A high frequency of reading disorder has been observed in children with cerebral palsy who are of normal intelligence and in children with seizure disorders. Reading disorder is usually apparent by age 7 years. It may coexist with attention-deficit disorders, conduct disorder, and depressive disorders.

Mathematics disorder is characterized by a disability in performing arithmetic skills that are expected for the child's age, given normal intelligence. According to the fourth edition of *Diagnostic and Statistical Manual of Mental Disorders* (DSM-IV), mathematics disorder interferes with school performance, and the impairment is in excess of any sensory deficit present. The prevalence of the disorder is not known, but it is estimated to occur in 6 percent of school-age children with normal intelligence. Mathematics disorder often occurs in conjunction with other learning disorders, such as reading disorder and disorder of written expression, and with developmental coordination disorder.

The cause of mathematics disorder is not known. Currently, cognitive, maturational, emotional, and socioeconomic factors are believed to influence the development of the disorder. The sex ratio of the disorder is not known.

Mathematics disorder includes impairment in a variety of related skills, including linguistic skills (converting written problems into mathematical symbols), perceptual skills (understanding mathematical symbols and ordering clusters of numbers), arithmetic skills (addition, subtraction, multiplication, and division), and attentional skills (copying figures and observing operational symbols correctly). The disorder is usually apparent by age 8 years, and remediation is most useful when offered immediately after diagnosis. Individual attention given to the child to strengthen the specific weaknesses is most useful. For some children with mathematics disorder, computer programs are helpful and increase compliance with remediation efforts. Few data indicate the long-term outcome in children with the disorder. However, children whose mathematics disabilities go untreated may become frustrated, demoralized, and depressed.

Disorder of written expression, also known as developmental expressive writing disorder, is characterized by writing skills significantly below that expected for the person's age and intellectual capacity. The skills can be measured by a standardized test. The disorder includes poor spelling, errors in grammar and punctuation, and poor handwriting. In the past it was assumed that writing disabilities did not occur in the absence of a reading disorder, but it is now known that disorder of written expression can develop on its own. The prevalence of the disorder is not known, but it is estimated to affect from 3 to 10 percent of school-age children with normal intelligence. The disorder often occurs in conjunction with other learning disorders, such as reading disorder, and with communication disorders. Disorder of written expression may be diagnosed later than those disorders, since writing skills are acquired later than language and reading skills. The cause of disorder of written expression is not known, but children with the disorder often have relatives with the same disorder. In addition, children with attention-deficit/hyperactivity disorder are at greater than usual risk for disorder of written expression.

Children with the disorder have difficulty in writing simple sentences. They make grammatical errors and spelling errors. They may even forget to start a new sentence with a capital letter. The prognosis for children with the disorder depends on the severity of the disability, when remediation is started, and the duration of the remediation. Remediation, including individual instruction in creative writing, seems to have a favorable outcome.

Learning disorder not otherwise specified (NOS) is for learning disorders that do not meet the diagnostic criteria for any of the above specific disorders but that cause impairment in academic performance. For example, the diagnosis is made when spelling skills are markedly below the expected performance in a child of normal intelligence.

Students should study Chapter 36 in *Kaplan and Sadock's Synopsis VII* for additional information on learning disorders and then turn to the questions and answers below.

HELPFUL HINTS

The student should define the terms below related to learning disorders.

academic skills disorders	word omissions	visual-perceptual deficits
dyslexia	word additions	hearing and vision screening
right-left confusion	word distortions	

QUESTIONS

DIRECTIONS: Each of the incomplete statements below is followed by five suggested completions. Select the *one* that is *best* in each case.

36.1. Reading disorder is characterized by all the following *except*
A. impairment in recognizing words
B. poor reading comprehension
C. increased prevalence among family members
D. occurrence in three to four times as many girls as boys
E. omissions, additions, and distortions of words in oral reading

36.2. All the following statements are true *except*
A. mathematics disorder is more common in boys than in girls
B. the prevalence of mathematics disorder is estimated to be about 6 percent in school-age children with normal intelligence
C. mathematics disorder includes impairment in addition, subtraction, multiplication, and division
D. mathematics disorder is usually apparent by the time a child is 8 years old
E. mathematics disorder is often found in children with reading disorder

36.3. Disorder of written expression
A. presents earlier than do reading disorder and communication disorders
B. occurs only in children with reading disorder
C. is not diagnosed until the teenage years
D. includes disability in spelling, grammar, and punctuation
E. is always self-limited

36.4. Janet, thirteen years old, had a long history of school problems. She failed first grade, supposedly because her teacher was mean, and was removed from a special classroom after she kept getting into fights with the other children. Currently in a normal sixth-grade classroom, she was failing reading and barely passing English and spelling but doing satisfactory work in art and sports. Her teacher described Janet as a "slow learner with a poor memory" and stated that Janet did not learn in a group setting and required a great deal of individual attention.

Janet's medical history was unremarkable except for a tonsillectomy at age 5 years and an early history of chronic otitis. She sat up at 6 months, walked at 12 months, and began talking at 18 months. An examination revealed an open and friendly girl who was touchy about her academic problems. She stated that she was "bossed around" at school but had good friends in the neighborhood. Intelligence testing revealed a full-scale intelligence quotient of 97. Wide-range achievement testing produced grade-level scores of 4.8 for reading, 5.3 for spelling, and 6.3 for arithmetic. The most likely diagnosis is
A. disorder of written expression
B. expressive language disorder
C. phonological disorder
D. reading disorder
E. none of the above

36.5. Disorder of written expression is often associated with
A. reading disorder
B. mixed expressive/receptive language disorder
C. developmental coordination disorder
D. mathematics disorder
E. all of the above

DIRECTIONS: The questions below consist of five lettered headings followed by a list of numbered statements. For each numbered statement, select the *one* lettered heading that is most closely associated with it. Each lettered heading may be selected once, more than once, or not at all.

Questions 36.6–36.9
A. Reading disorder
B. Mathematics disorder
C. Disorder of written expression
D. Learning disorder not otherwise specified

36.6. Used to be known as dyslexia

36.7. Spelling skills deficit is an example

36.8. Usually diagnosed later than the other learning disorders

36.9. Reported to occur frequently in children born in May, June, and July

ANSWERS

Learning Disorders

36.1. The answer is D (*Synopsis VII*, page 1042).

Reading disorder is reported to *occur in three to four times as many boys as girls.* The rate of reading disorder in boys may be inflated, since boys with reading disorder are more likely than are girls to have behavioral problems, and the boys may be identified initially for their behavioral problems. Reading disorder is characterized by *impairment in recognizing words,* slow and inaccurate reading, and *poor reading comprehension.* Reading achievement is below that expected for the person's age, as measured by standardized tests (Table 36.1). Although no unitary cause of reading disorder is known, it appears to have *increased prevalence among family members,* leading to the speculation that it has a genetic origin. Children with reading disorder make *omissions, additions, and distortions of words in oral reading.* The children may have difficulty in distinguishing printed letter characters and sizes, especially those letters that differ only in spatial orientation and length of line.

36.2. The answer is A (*Synopsis VII*, page 1045).

Unlike reading disorder, in which the rate in boys is reported to be three to four times greater than the rate in girls, the sex ratio for mathematics disorder

has yet to be determined. In fact, *mathematics disorder may be more common in girls than in boys. The prevalence of mathematics disorder is estimated to be about 6 percent in school-age children with normal intelligence. Mathematics disorder includes impairment in addition, subtraction, multiplication, and division. Mathematics disorder is usually apparent by the time a child is 8 years old,* although in some children it may present as early as 6 years of age or as late as 10 years of age. *Mathematics disorder is often found in children with reading disorder.* Table 36.2 lists the diagnostic criteria for mathematics disorder.

36.3. The answer is D (*Synopsis VII*, page 1047).

Disorder of written expression *includes disability in spelling, grammar, and punctuation marks.* The disorder is characterized by writing skills that are significantly below the expected level for the child's age and intelligence, as measured by a standardized test (Table 36.3). Because a child normally speaks well before learning to read and reads well before learning to write, *disorder of written expression presents later than do reading disorder and communication disorders.* Disorder of written expression *can occur in children without reading disorder.* The

---

Table 36.1
Diagnostic Criteria for Reading Disorder

A. Reading achievement, as measured by individually administered standardized tests of reading accuracy or comprehension, is substantially below that expected given the person's chronological age, measured intelligence, and age-appropriate education.

B. The disturbance in criterion A significantly interferes with academic achievement or activities of daily living that require reading skills.

C. If a sensory deficit is present, the reading difficulties are in excess of those usually associated with it.

Coding note: If a general medical (e.g., neurological) condition or sensory deficit is present, code the condition on Axis III.

Table from DSM-IV, *Diagnostic and Statistical Manual of Mental Disorders,* ed 4. Copyright American Psychiatric Association, Washington, 1994. Used with permission.

Table 36.2
Diagnostic Criteria for Mathematics Disorder

A. Mathematical ability, as measured by individually administered standardized tests, is substantially below that expected given the person's chronological age, measured intelligence, and age-appropriate education.

B. The disturbance in criterion A significantly interferes with academic achievement or activities of daily living that require mathematical ability.

C. If a sensory deficit is present, the difficulties in mathematical ability are in excess of those usually associated with it.

Coding note: If a general medical (e.g., neurological) condition or sensory deficit is present, code the condition on Axis III.

Table from DSM-IV, *Diagnostic and Statistical Manual of Mental Disorders,* ed 4. Copyright American Psychiatric Association, Washington, 1994. Used with permission.

Table 36.3
Diagnostic Criteria for Disorder of Written Expression

A. Writing skills, as measured by individually administered standardized tests (or functional assessments of writing skills), are substantially below those expected given the person's chronological age, measured intelligence, and age-appropriate education.

B. The disturbance in criterion A significantly interferes with academic achievement or activities of daily living that require the composition of written texts (e.g., writing grammatically correct sentences and organized paragraphs).

C. If a sensory deficit is present, the difficulties in writing skills are in excess of those usually associated with it.

Coding note: If a general medical (e.g., neurological) condition or sensory deficit is present, code the condition on Axis III.

disorder *is diagnosed in the early school years, not the teenage years,* and it *is not self-limited.*

36.4. The answer is D (*Synopsis VII,* pages 1043–1044).

The most likely diagnosis for Janet is *reading disorder.* Reading disorder is characterized by marked impairment in the development of word-recognition skills and reading comprehension that cannot be explained by mental retardation, inadequate schooling, visual or hearing defect, or a neurological disorder. Reading-disordered children make many errors in their oral reading, including omissions, additions, and distortions of words. Janet's difficulties were apparently limited to reading and spelling. She had average intelligence and normal scores on achievement tests of arithmetic but markedly low scores for spelling and reading.

Disorder of written expression is characterized by poor performance in writing and composition. *Expressive language disorder* is characterized by marked impairment in age-appropriate expressive language. *Phonological disorder* is characterized by frequent and recurrent misarticulations of speech sounds, resulting in abnormal speech. The case described does not meet the criteria for any of these disorders.

36.5. The answer is E (all) (*Synopsis VII,* page 1048).

Reading disorder, mixed expressive-receptive language disorder, developmental coordination disorder, mathematics disorder, and disruptive behavior disorders are often associated with disorder of written expression. The ability to transfer one's thoughts into written words and sentences requires multimodal sensory-motor coordination and information processing. Disorder of written expression is an academic skills disorder that first occurs during childhood and is characterized by poor performance in writing and composition (spelling words and expressing thoughts).

36.6–36.9

36.6. The answer is A (*Synopsis VII,* page 1042).

36.7. The answer is D (*Synopsis VII,* page 1048).

36.8. The answer is C (*Synopsis VII,* page 1045).

36.9. The answer is A (*Synopsis VII,* page 1042).

Reading disorder used to be known as dyslexia. The disorder is *reported to occur frequently in children born in May, June, and July,* suggesting that reading disorder is linked to maternal winter infectious disease.

Disorder of written expression is usually diagnosed later than the other learning disorders, since writing skills are acquired at a later age than are language reading skills.

Learning disorder not otherwise specified is a category of learning disorders that covers disorders in learning that do not meet the criteria for any specific learning disorder. *Spelling skills deficit is an example.*

Mathematics disorder includes deficits in linguistic skills (those related to understanding mathematical terms and converting written problems into mathematical symbols), and perceptual skills (the ability to recognize and understand symbols and to order clusters of numbers).

Developmental Coordination Disorder

Developmental coordination disorder is the only disorder categorized as a motor skills disorder in the fourth edition of *Diagnostic and Statistical Manual of Mental Disorders* (DSM-IV). Children with the disorder may be slow in crawling or walking, and they are often clumsy in gross and fine motor activities, but they are not intellectually impaired. Developmental coordination disorder includes deficits in handwriting. Children with the disorder may resemble younger children. Their poor coordination, according to DSM-IV, must cause significant interference with academic achievement or daily functioning and cannot be explained solely on the basis of a general medical condition such as cerebral palsy or muscular dystrophy. Poor coordination and clumsiness have also been associated with learning disorders, communication disorders, conduct disorder, and attention-deficit/hyperactivity disorder.

The prevalence of developmental coordination disorder has not been well-studied but has been estimated to affect 6 percent of school-age children of normal intelligence. Reports of the male-to-female ratio have ranged from 2 to 1 to as much as 4 to 1.

The causes of developmental coordination disorder are unknown, but its risk factors include prematurity, hypoxia, perinatal malnutrition, and low birth weight. Neurochemical abnormalities and parietal lobe lesions may contribute to the disorder. Developmental coordination disorder and communication disorders are associated; both seem to be prevalent in children with short attention spans and impulsive behavior.

The diagnosis of developmental coordination disorder can be made by getting a history of the child's impairment in early motor skills and by direct observation of the child's motor skills. Informal screening can be done by asking the child to perform some gross and fine motor tasks. Gross motor skills can be assessed by asking the child to hop, jump, and stand on one foot. Fine motor coordination can be screened with such tasks as finger tapping, shoelace tying, and writing. Eye-hand coordination is often impaired in developmental coordination disorder; children with the disorder may have trouble catching a ball or copying figures. Standardized tests of motor coordination include the Bender Visual Motor Gestalt Test and the Frostig Movement Skills Test Battery.

Developmental coordination disorder may be evident in infancy when a child is impaired or delayed in resulting motor milestones, but generally the disorder is first noticed after age 2 years. Affected children seem to drop objects frequently, trip over their own feet, and bump into things. In older children, impaired motor coordination may interfere with their ability to do puzzles, use building blocks, and play ball. Since physical skills, especially those used in sports, are important in everyday life among school-age children, those children with poor coordination may become socially ostracized and demoralized.

No reliable data are available regarding the prognosis of children with developmental coordination disorder. Some children with above-average intelligence are able to compensate for their disability by pursuing other activities that do not require good motor coordination. Treatment for developmental coordination disorder includes perceptual motor training, neurophysiological techniques of exercise for motor dysfunctioning, and modified physical education. Since peer relationship problems may lead to low self-esteem, unhappiness, and withdrawal, counseling is needed.

Students should study Chapter 37 in *Kaplan and Sadock's Synopsis VII* and then turn to the questions and answers below.

HELPFUL HINTS

The student should know the terms listed below.

clumsiness	eye-hand coordination	delayed motor milestones
deficits in handwriting	Bender Visual Motor Gestalt Test	perceptual motor training
finger tapping	Frostig Movement Skills Test	social ostracism
shoelace tying	Battery	learning disorders
catching a ball	Bruininks-Oseretsky Test of Motor	expressive language disorder
informal motor skills screening	Development	attention-deficit/hyperactivity
gross motor skills	cerebral palsy	disorder
fine motor skills	unsteady gait	conduct disorder

QUESTIONS

DIRECTIONS: Each of the questions with incomplete statements below is followed by five suggested responses or completions. Select the *one* that is *best* in each case.

37.1. Children with developmental coordination disorder generally have impairment in all the following *except*
A. jumping
B. hopping on one foot
C. tying shoelaces
D. reading
E. catching a ball

37.2. Developmental coordination disorder is commonly associated with
A. expressive language disorder
B. attention-deficit/hyperactivity disorder
C. conduct disorder
D. social ostracism
E. all the above

37.3. Which of the following is a risk factor for developmental coordination disorder?
A. Birth in May, June, or July
B. Borderline intellectual functioning
C. Female gender
D. Prematurity
E. Dysfunctional family

37.4. Each of the following statements is true *except*
A. children with developmental coordination disorder may motorically resemble children of younger ages
B. developmental coordination disorder is frequently seen in conjunction with a communication disorder
C. the male-to-female ratio in developmental coordination disorder is estimated to be 2 to 1
D. prematurity, low birth weight, perinatal malnutrition, and hypoxia are all risk factors for developmental coordination disorder
E. developmental coordination disorder is usually due to a lesion in the parietal lobe of the brain

ANSWERS

Developmental Coordination Disorder

37.1.   The answer is D (*Synopsis VII,* page 1050).

Developmental coordination disorder is not particularly associated with *reading* impairment. Children with developmental coordination disorder have disability in gross motor tasks, fine motor tasks, and tasks requiring eye-hand coordination. Among the gross motor tasks that may be impaired are *jumping* and *hopping on one foot*. Fine motor tasks that may be impaired include *tying shoelaces*. Tasks involving eye-hand coordination that may be impaired include *catching a ball*.

The diagnostic criteria for developmental coordination disorder are listed in Table 37.1.

37.2.   The answer is E (all) (*Synopsis VII,* pages 1050–1051).

Developmental coordination disorder and communication disorders, such as *expressive language*

Table 37.1
Diagnostic Criteria for Developmental Coordination Disorder

A. Performance in daily activities that require motor coordination is substantially below that expected given the person's chronological age and measured intelligence. This may be manifested by marked delays in achieving motor milestones (e.g., walking, crawling, sitting), dropping things, "clumsiness," poor performance in sports, or poor handwriting.

B. The disturbance in criterion A significantly interferes with academic achievement or activities of daily living.

C. The disturbance is not due to a general medical condition (e.g., cerebral palsy, hemiplegia, or muscular dystrophy) and does not meet criteria for a pervasive developmental disorder.

D. If mental retardation is present, the motor difficulties are in excess of those usually associated with it.

Coding note: If a general medical (e.g., neurological) condition or sensory deficit is present, code the condition on Axis III.

Table from DSM-IV, *Diagnostic and Statistical Manual of Mental Disorders,* ed 4. Copyright American Psychiatric Association, Washington, 1994. Used with permission.

disorder, are often associated, although the specific causative agents for both disorders are not known. Developmental coordination disorder also seems to be frequent in children with *attention-deficit/hyperactivity disorder* and *conduct disorder*. Children with developmental coordination disorder who are clumsy and inept in a variety of sports often experience *social ostracism*, which can lead to demoralization, social withdrawal, and ultimately dysphoria or depression.

37.3.   The answer is D (*Synopsis VII,* page 1050).

Risk factors for developmental coordination disorder include *prematurity*. Reading disorder, not developmental coordination disorder, has been reported to be frequent in children *born in May, June, or July,* suggesting a link between winter maternal infectious illness and the development of reading disorder. *Borderline intellectual functioning,* an intelligence quotient (I.Q.) between 70 and 90, is not identified specifically as a risk factor for developmental coordination disorder. *Female gender* is not a risk factor for developmental coordination disorder; the disorder is reported to occur in at least twice as many males as females. A *dysfunctional family* is not known to be a risk factor for developmental coordination disorder.

37.4.   The answer is E (*Synopsis VII,* page 1050).

Developmental coordination disorder is not usually due to a lesion in the parietal lobe of the brain, although parietal lobe lesions have been suggested as causes of the disorder. *Children with developmental coordination disorder may motorically resemble children of younger ages. Developmental coordination disorder is frequently seen in conjunction with a communication disorder. The male-to-female ratio in developmental coordination disorder is estimated to be 2 to 1* and is estimated to occur in approximately 6 percent of school aged children of normal intelligence. Prematurity, low birth weight, perinatal malnutrition, and hypoxia are all *risk factors for developmental coordination disorder.*

Pervasive Developmental Disorders

The pervasive developmental disorders are a group of conditions in which the core features are deficits in reciprocal social interactions, delayed and aberrant language development and usage, and a severely limited behavioral repertoire for the patient's age. In most cases of pervasive developmental disorders, the appropriate skills do not develop; however, in rare cases, skills do develop and are then lost. Pervasive developmental disorders are manifested early in life, affect multiple areas of functioning, and generally cause persistent impairment.

The fourth edition of *Diagnostic and Statistical Manual of Mental Disorders* (DSM-IV) includes the following disorders within the category of pervasive developmental disorders: autistic disorder, Rett's disorder, childhood disintegrative disorder, Asperger's disorder, and pervasive developmental disorder not otherwise specified (NOS).

Autistic disorder is the best-known of the pervasive developmental disorders. It is characterized by significant impairments in social interaction, marked qualitative impairments in communication, and restricted, repetitive, and stereotyped patterns of behavior. According to DSM-IV, delays or abnormal functioning in social interaction, communication, or symbolic play must begin before the child is 3 years old. Autistic disorder was described by Leo Kanner in 1943, but not until 1980 was it recognized as a distinct clinical entity. Before 1980, children with any pervasive developmental disorder were classified as schizophrenic. Autistic disorder occurs in 2 to 5 per 10,000 children. It is reported to be at least three times more common in boys than in girls.

All children with autistic disorder show impaired social relatedness. About 70 percent of children with autistic disorder are mentally retarded. Autistic infants may lack a social smile and may not show the anticipatory posture when an adult approaches to pick them up. The social development of autistic children is characterized by a lack of apparent attachment to their parents and a lack of comfort-seeking behavior. They may not exhibit the appropriate separation anxiety when left in a new setting. School-age children with autistic disorder are typically unable to engage in the reciprocal social nuances needed to form peer relationships. Although they may interact with peers, their emotional inappropriateness and lack of empathy discourage friendships. Autistic adolescents with good intellectual functioning who desire relationships are usually more successful than mentally retarded autistic adolescents, but they are not able to overcome their inability to relate spontaneously. Gross deviance in language development and usage is another major impairment in autistic disorders.

About half of all children with autistic disorder do not develop useful language skills, although they may acquire occasional words. Unlike normal young children, who have good receptive language skills and understand much before they speak, autistic children who do develop language say more than they understand. Their speech contains immediate and delayed echolalic words and phrases, and stereotyped phrases are often repeated out of context. Children with autistic disorder often reverse pronouns, saying "you" when they mean "I." In addition to peculiar phrasing and idiosyncratic meanings attached to words, children with autistic disorder do not use the normal prosody (intonation).

Stereotyped behavior and restricted repertoire is the third major area of dysfunction in autistic disorder. Children with autistic disorder show a markedly diminished ability to use imagination in play and to play symbolically. Children with autistic disorder may show a fascination with repetitive stereotyped behavior, such as spinning, banging, watching water flow, or lining up objects. They may exhibit bodily movements that are repetitive, such as flapping their hands or fingers or twisting their bodies. They may become attached to an inanimate object, such as a metal pipe or a table.

The cause of autistic disorder is not known, although it is generally believed to be a neurological or biological disorder. Reports comparing the parents of autistic children and the parents of normal children have not shown significant differences in child rearing. A biological cause of autism is supported by evidence that autistic disorder is frequent in conditions with known neurological lesions, such as congenital rubella, phenylketonuria (PKU), and tuberous sclerosis. Children with autistic disorder have significantly more minor physical anomalies than do normal children, suggesting that first-trimester insults may contribute to the disorder. Up to a third of all children with autistic disorder experience seizure disorders, supporting the idea that neurological factors are involved in autistic disorder. Genetic factors are implicated in autistic disorder by family studies that indicate that between 2 and 4 percent of the siblings of children with autistic disorder are also afflicted with the disorder, a rate 50 times that found in the general population.

Autistic disorder has no specific treatment, although various medications have been used to control self-injurious and stereotyped motor behaviors. The prognosis is best in those autistic children with intelligence quotients (I.Q.s) above 70 who have communicative language skills by age 5 to 7 years.

Rett's disorder appears to occur only in girls; it is estimated to have a prevalence of 6 to 7 cases per 100,000 girls. Rett's disorder is characterized by normal development for at least five months after birth, as manifested by normal social and motor milestones and normal head circumference at birth. The onset of the disorder occurs between 5 and 48 months after birth and consists of a deceleration of head growth, the loss of previously acquired purposeful hand movements, and the presentation of stereotyped hand motions, such as handwringing. In addition, the patient shows a loss of social engagement early in the course of the disorder, the appearance of poorly coordinated gait or trunk movements, and marked delay and impairment of expressive and receptive language and motor skills. Rett's disorder then proceeds as a progressive encephalopathy. Associated features include seizures in 75 percent of all affected patients and irregular respiration with episodes of hyperventilation, apnea, and breath holding. As the disorder progresses, the patient's muscle tone seems to increase from initial hypotonia to spasticity to rigidity. Long-term receptive and expressive communication skills remain at a developmental level of less than 1 year.

Rett's disorder probably has a genetic basis, since it appears to occur only in girls, but the initial normal developmental period followed by a rapidly deteriorating course, is also consistent with a metabolic disorder. Treatment is aimed at symptomatic intervention. Behavior therapy has been used to control self-injurious behaviors and to regulate the patient's breathing.

Childhood disintegrative disorder, also known as Heller's syndrome, is a devastating deterioration of intellectual, social, and language functioning in 3-to-4-year-olds with previously normal functioning. After the deterioration, the patients resemble children with autistic disorder. Childhood disintegrative disorder is estimated to be at least one tenth as common as autistic disorder, occurring in one case in 100,000 boys. It appears to be four to eight times as common in boys as in girls. The cause is unknown, but the disorder has been reported to occur with other neurological conditions, including seizure disorders, tuberous sclerosis, and metabolic disorders.

Asperger's disorder has some similarities to autistic disorder and the other pervasive developmental disorders but is distinctive in that there is a lack of clinically significant delays in language and such cognitive development as adaptive behavior and self-help skills. However, the patient has a qualitative impairment in social interaction and restricted, repetitive, and stereotyped patterns of behavior. The cause of Asperger's disorder is unknown, but family studies suggest a relation to autistic disorder. The prevalence of Asperger's disorder has not yet been well-studied. The course and the prognosis of patients with Asperger's disorder is not well-known, but factors associated with good prognoses are normal intelligence and a high level of social skills.

Pervasive developmental disorder not otherwise specified (NOS) is diagnosed when a child has a severe impairment in reciprocal social interaction and verbal and nonverbal communication skills but does not meet the diagnostic criteria for a specific pervasive developmental disorder, schizophrenia, schizotypal personality disorder, or avoidant personality disorder. Compared with autistic children, those who have pervasive developmental disorder not otherwise specified generally have better language skills, more self-awareness, and better outcomes.

Students should study Chapter 38 in *Kaplan and Sadock's Synopsis VII* and then address the following questions and answers to test their knowledge of the area.

HELPFUL HINTS

The student should know the following terms related to pervasive developmental disorders.

Leo Kanner
extreme autistic aloneness
echolalia
pronominal reversal
monotonous repetition
rote memory
dread of change
abnormal relationships
pervasive developmental disorder
autistic disorder
childhood disintegrative disorder
Heller's syndrome
Asperger's disorder
Rett's disorder
echolalic speech
congenital rubella
PKU
tuberous sclerosis
haloperidol (Haldol)
mental retardation
prevalence
sex distribution
social class

psychodynamic and family
  causation
parental rage and rejection
perinatal complications
organic abnormalities
congenital physical anomalies
CT scans
grand mal seizures
EEG abnormalities
failed cerebral lateralization
concordance rates
physical characteristics
dermatoglyphics
eye contact
attachment behavior
separation anxiety
language deviance and delay
voice quality and rhythm
play
rituals
stereotypies
vestibular stimulation

hyperkinesis
self-injurious behavior
enuresis
encopresis
splinter functions
islets of precocity
idiot savant
childhood schizophrenia
communication disorders
acquired aphasia
congenital deafness
disintegrative (regressive)
  psychoses
insight-oriented psychotherapy
educational and behavioral
  treatments
tardive and withdrawal
  dyskinesias
fenfluramine (Pondimin)
ego-educative approach
low purine diet
hyperuricosuria

QUESTIONS

DIRECTIONS: Each of the incomplete statements below is followed by five suggested completions. Select the *one* that is *best* in each case.

38.1. All the following are characteristic of children with autistic disorder *except*
A. delayed functioning in social interaction, language, or symbolic or imaginative play
B. qualitative impairment in social interaction
C. impaired communication
D. stereotyped patterns of behavior
E. normal development during the first two to three years

38.2. Rett's disorder is hypothesized to have a genetic cause because
A. the onset of a deteriorating encephalopathy occurs between the ages of 5 and 48 months
B. some patients with the disorder have hyperammonemia
C. poor muscle coordination and ataxia occur in addition to irregular respiration
D. autistic disorder and Rett's disorder are similar
E. it appears to occur only in girls

38.3. All the following are true of childhood disintegrative disorder *except*
A. it is also known as Heller's syndrome
B. in most cases there is normal development for three to four years
C. the onset may be gradual over several months or occur within days
D. the disorder occurs only with another neurological condition
E. most children with the disorder are left with at least moderate mental retardation

38.4. Asperger's disorder differs from autistic disorder in that Asperger's disorder does not include
A. impaired peer relationships
B. any clinically significant delay in language or impairment in cognitive development
C. impaired nonverbal communication
D. impaired social interaction
E. restricted, repetitive, and stereotyped patterns of behavior

38.5. Treatment of autistic disorder includes
A. insight-oriented individual psychotherapy
B. loosely structured training programs
C. phenobarbital (Luminal)
D. haloperidol (Haldol)
E. all the above

38.6. Unusual or precocious abilities in some autistic children are referred to as
A. Rett's syndrome
B. echolalia
C. splinter functions
D. stereotypies
E. hyperkinesis

38.7. Neurological-biochemical abnormalities associated with autistic disorder include
A. grand mal seizures
B. ventricular enlargement on computed tomography (CT) scans
C. electroencephalogram (EEC) abnormalities
D. elevated serum serotonin levels
E. all the above

38.8. Characteristics thought to be associated with autistic children include all the following *except*
A. intelligent and attractive appearance
B. increased sensitivity to pain
C. ambidextrousness
D. abnormal dermatoglyphics
E. high incidence of upper respiratory infections

DIRECTIONS: The questions below consist of five lettered headings followed by a list of numbered statements. For each numbered word or statement, select the *one* lettered heading that is most closely associated with it. Each lettered heading may be selected once, more than once, or not at all.

Questions 38.9–38.13
A. Autistic disorder
B. Childhood disintegrative disorder
C. Pervasive developmental disorder not otherwise specified
D. Asperger's disorder
E. Rett's disorder

38.9. Normal development for the first five months, followed by a progressive encephalopathy

38.10. A better prognosis than other pervasive developmental disorders because of the lack of delay in language and cognitive development

38.11. Some but not all the features of autistic disorder

38.12. Several years of normal development followed by a loss of communication skills, a loss of reciprocal social interaction, and a restricted pattern of behavior

38.13. Occurs at a rate of 2 to 5 cases per 10,000 and is characterized by impairment in social interaction, communicative language, or symbolic play before age 3.

ANSWERS

Pervasive Developmental Disorders

38.1.   The answer is E (*Synopsis VII, pages 1053–1057*).

Autistic disorder is believed to be a neurological disorder in which aberrant development is usually manifested in infancy; thus, *development during the first two to three years is not normal*. The diagnostic criteria for autistic disorder include abnormal or *delayed functioning in social interaction, language, or symbolic or imaginative play* (Table 38.1). Autistic disorder is also characterized by *qualitative impairment in social interaction, impaired communication,* and *stereotyped patterns of behavior.*

38.2.   The answer is E (*Synopsis VII, page 1058*).

Rett's disorder is hypothesized to have a genetic cause because *it appears to occur only in girls.* Although it is true that *the onset of a progressive encephalopathy occurs between the ages of 5 and 48 months some patients with the disorder have hyperammonemia, poor muscle coordination and ataxia occur in addition to irregular respiration,* and *autistic disorder and Rett's disorder, are similar,* those factors do not indicate a genetic cause of Rett's disorder. The diagnostic criteria for Rett's disorder are listed in Table 38.2.

38.3.   The answer is D (*Synopsis VII, page 1059*).

Childhood disintegrative disorder *sometimes occurs in the absence of another neurological condition* and it has been reported to occur in children with metabolic disorders. Childhood disintegrative disorder *is also known as Heller's syndrome. In most cases there is normal development for three to four years. The onset may be gradual over several months or occur within days. Most children with the disorder are left with at least moderate mental retardation.* The diagnostic criteria for childhood disintegrative disorder appear in Table 38.3.

38.4.   The answer is B (*Synopsis VII, page 1060*).

Asperger's disorder, unlike autistic disorder, lacks *any clinically significant delay in language or impairment in cognitive development,* as manifested by adaptive behaviors. Patients with Asperger's disorder, like patients with autistic disorder, have *impaired peer relationships, impaired nonverbal communication, impaired social interaction,* and *restricted, repetitive, and stereotyped patterns of behavior.* The diagnostic criteria for Asperger's disorder are listed in Table 38.4.

Table 38.1
Diagnostic Criteria for Autistic Disorder

A. A total of six (or more) items from (1), (2), and (3), with at least two from (1), and one each from (2) and (3):

  (1) qualitative impairment in social interaction, as manifested by at least two of the following:

   (a) marked impairment in the use of multiple nonverbal behaviors such as eye-to-eye gaze, facial expression, body postures, and gestures to regulate social interaction
   (b) failure to develop peer relationships appropriate to developmental level
   (c) a lack of spontaneous seeking to share enjoyment, interests, or achievements with other people (e.g., by a lack of showing, bringing, or pointing out objects of interest)
   (d) lack of social or emotional reciprocity

  (2) qualitative impairments in communication as manifested by at least one of the following:

   (a) delay in, or total lack of, the development of spoken language (not accompanied by an attempt to compensate through alternative modes of communication such as gesture or mime)
   (b) in individuals with adequate speech, marked impairment in the ability to initiate or sustain a conversation with others
   (c) stereotyped and repetitive use of language or idiosyncratic language
   (d) lack of varied, spontaneous make-believe play or social imitative play appropriate to developmental level

  (3) restricted repetitive and stereotyped patterns of behavior, interests, and activities, as manifested by at least one of the following:

   (a) encompassing preoccupation with one or more stereotyped and restricted patterns of interest that is abnormal either in intensity or focus
   (b) apparently inflexible adherence to specific, nonfunctional routines or rituals
   (c) stereotyped and repetitive motor mannerisms (e.g., hand or finger flapping or twisting, or complex whole-body movements)
   (d) persistent preoccupation with parts of objects

B. Delays or abnormal functioning in at least one of the following areas, with onset prior to age 3 years: (1) social interaction, (2) language as used in social communication, or (3) symbolic or imaginative play.

C. The disturbance is not better accounted for by Rett's disorder or childhood disintegrative disorder.

Table from DSM-IV, *Diagnostic and Statistical Manual of Mental Disorders,* ed 4. Copyright American Psychiatric Association, Washington, 1994. Used with permission.

Table 38.2
Diagnostic Criteria for Rett's Disorder

A. All of the following:

   (1) apparently normal prenatal and perinatal development

   (2) apparently normal psychomotor development through the first 5 months after birth

   (3) normal head circumference at birth

B. Onset of all of the following after the period of normal development:

   (1) deceleration of head growth between ages 5 and 48 months

   (2) loss of previously acquired purposeful hand skills between ages 5 and 30 months with the subsequent development of stereotyped hand movements (e.g., hand-wringing or hand washing)

   (3) loss of social engagement early in the course (although often social interaction develops later)

   (4) appearance of poorly coordinated gait or trunk movements

   (5) severely impaired expressive and receptive language development with severe psychomotor retardation

Table from DSM-IV, *Diagnostic and Statistical Manual of Mental Disorders,* ed 4. Copyright American Psychiatric Association, Washington, 1994. Used with permission.

Table 38.3
Diagnostic Criteria for Childhood Disintegrative Disorder

A. Apparently normal development for at least the first 2 years after birth as manifested by the presence of age-appropriate verbal and nonverbal communication, social relationships, play, and adaptive behavior.

B. Clinically significant loss of previously acquired skills (before age 10 years) in at least two of the following areas:

   (1) expressive or receptive language

   (2) social skills or adaptive behavior

   (3) bowel or bladder control

   (4) play

   (5) motor skills

C. Abnormalities of functioning in at least two of the following areas:

   (1) qualitative impairment in social interaction (e.g., impairment in nonverbal behaviors, failure to develop peer relationships, lack of social or emotional reciprocity)

   (2) qualitative impairments in communication (e.g., delay or lack of spoken language, inability to initiate or sustain a conversation, stereotyped and repetitive use of language, lack of varied make-believe play)

   (3) restricted, repetitive, and stereotyped patterns of behavior, interests, and activities, including motor stereotypies and mannerisms

D. The disturbance is not better accounted for by another specific pervasive developmental disorder or by schizophrenia.

Table from DSM-IV, *Diagnostic and Statistical Manual of Mental Disorders,* ed 4. Copyright American Psychiatric Association, Washington, 1994. Used with permission.

Table 38.4
Diagnostic Criteria for Asperger's Disorder

A. Qualitative impairment in social interaction, as manifested by at least two of the following:

   (1) marked impairment in the use of multiple nonverbal behaviors such as eye-to-eye gaze, facial expression, body postures, and gestures to regulate social interaction

   (2) failure to develop peer relationships appropriate to developmental level

   (3) a lack of spontaneous seeking to share enjoyment, interests, or achievements with other people (e.g., by a lack of showing, bringing, or pointing out objects of interest to other people)

   (4) lack of social or emotional reciprocity

B. Restricted repetitive and stereotyped patterns of behavior, interests, and activities, as manifested by at least one of the following:

   (1) encompassing preoccupation with one or more stereotyped and restricted patterns of interest that is abnormal either in intensity or focus

   (2) apparently inflexible adherence to specific, nonfunctional routines or rituals

   (3) stereotyped and repetitive motor mannerisms (e.g., hand or finger flapping or twisting, or complex whole-body movements)

   (4) persistent preoccupation with parts of objects

C. The disturbance causes clinically significant impairment in social, occupational, or other important areas of functioning.

D. There is no clinically significant general delay in language (e.g., single words used by age 2 years, communicative phrases used by age 3 years).

E. There is no clinically significant delay in cognitive development or in the development of age-appropriate self-help skills, adaptive behavior (other than in social interaction), and curiosity about the environment in childhood.

F. Criteria are not met for another specific pervasive developmental disorder or schizophrenia.

Table from DSM-IV, *Diagnostic and Statistical Manual of Mental Disorders,* ed 4. Copyright American Psychiatric Association, Washington, 1994. Used with permission.

38.5. **The answer is D** (*Synopsis VII,* page 1058).

Pharmacological treatment of autistic disorder includes *haloperidol (Haldol)*. The administration of haloperidol both reduces the behavioral symptoms of the disorder and accelerates learning. The drug decreases hyperactivity, stereotypies, withdrawal, fidgetiness, abnormal object relations, irritability, and labile affect. *Insight-oriented individual psychotherapy* has proved ineffective as a treatment of autistic disorder. Educational and behavioral methods are currently considered the treatments of choice. Careful training and individual tutoring of parents in the concepts and the skills of behavior modification, within a problem-solving format, may yield considerable gains in the child's language, cognitive, and social areas of behavior. However, the *training pro-*

grams are rigorous (not loosely structured) and require a great deal of the parent's time. The autistic child requires as much structure as possible, and a daily program for as many hours as feasible is desirable. *Phenobarbital (Luminal)* is not an effective treatment of autistic disorder.

38.6. The answer is C (*Synopsis VII,* page 1056).

Unusual or precocious cognitive or vasomotor abilities are present in some autistic children. Those abilities may exist even within the overall retarded functioning and are referred to as *splinter functions* or islets of precocity. Perhaps the most striking examples are the idiot savants who have prodigious rote memories or calculating abilities. Their specific abilities are usually beyond the capabilities of normal peers. Other precocious abilities in young autistic children include hyperlexia, early ability to read well (although they are not able to understand what they read), memorizing and reciting, and musical abilities (singing tunes or recognizing musical pieces).

Rett's syndrome is a disorder of progressive mental retardation, accompanied by autisticlike and neurological symptoms, that occurs only in girls. *Echolalia* is the immediate or delayed repetition of words or phrases said to the person. Often, the speaker's tone and inflection are preserved. *Stereotypies* are repetitive behaviors, often performed rhythmically, that are not goal-directed. *Hyperkinesis,* overactivity, is a common behavior problem among young autistic children, as are aggressiveness and temper tantrums.

38.7. The answer is E (all) (*Synopsis VII,* page 1053).

Current evidence indicates that significant neurological and biochemical abnormalities are usually associated with autistic disorder. *Grand mal seizures* develop at some time in 4 to 32 percent of autistic persons, and about 20 to 25 percent of autistic persons show *ventricular enlargement on computed tomography scans.* Various *electroencephalogram (EEG) abnormalities* are found in 10 to 83 percent of autistic children; although no EEG finding is specific in autistic disorder there is some indication of failed cerebral lateralization. *Elevated serum serotonin levels* are found in about one third of autistic children; however, the levels are also raised in about one third of nonautistic children with severe mental retardation.

38.8. The answer is B (*Synopsis VII,* page 1055).

Many autistic children have a *decreased (not increased) sensitivity to pain.* The children may injure themselves severely and not cry. They may not complain of pain either verbally or by gesture and may not show the malaise of an ill child. Leo Kanner was impressed by autistic children's *intelligent and attractive appearance.* Cerebral lateralization is not found in most autistic children; that is, they remain *ambidextrous* at an age when cerebral dominance is established in normal children. Autistic children also show a greater incidence of *abnormal dermatoglyphics* (for example, fingerprints) than do the general population. *A high incidence of upper respiratory infections* is found in young autistic children. Autistic children may not have elevated temperatures with infectious illness, and their behavior or relatedness may improve to a noticeable degree when they are ill.

38.9–38.13

38.9. The answer is E (*Synopsis VII,* page 1058).

38.10. The answer is D (*Synopsis VII,* pages 1060–1061).

38.11. The answer is C (*Synopsis VII,* page 1061).

38.12. The answer is B (*Synopsis VII,* pages 1059–1060).

38.13. The answer is A (*Synopsis VII,* pages 1052–1054).

Rett's disorder is characterized by *normal development for the first five months followed by a progressive deterioration. Asperger's disorder* may have *a better prognosis than other pervasive developmental disorders because of the lack of delay in language and cognitive development. Pervasive developmental disorder not otherwise specified* (Table 38.5) includes atypical autism—presentations that include *some but not all the features of autistic disorder. Childhood disintegrative disorder* is characterized by *several years of normal development followed by a loss of communication skills, a loss of reciprocal social interaction, and a restricted pattern of behavior. Autistic disorder occurs at a rate of 2 to 5 cases per 10,000 and is characterized by impairment in social interaction, communicative language, or symbolic play before age 3.*

Table 38.5
Diagnostic Criteria for Pervasive Developmental Disorder Not Otherwise Specified

This category should be used when there is a severe and pervasive impairment in the development of reciprocal social interaction or verbal and nonverbal communication skills, or when stereotyped behavior, interests, and activities are present, but the criteria are not met for a specific pervasive developmental disorder, schizophrenia, schizotypal personality disorder, or avoidant personality disorder. For example, this category includes "atypical autism"—presentations that do not meet the criteria for autistic disorder because of late age at onset, atypical symptomatology, or subthreshold symptomatology, or all of these.

Table from DSM-IV, *Diagnostic and Statistical Manual of Mental Disorders,* ed 4. Copyright American Psychiatric Association, Washington, 1994. Used with permission.

Attention-Deficit Disorders

Attention-deficit/hyperactivity disorder is characterized by a developmentally inappropriately short attention span or age-inappropriate levels of impulsivity and hyperactivity. Some children with attention-deficit/hyperactivity disorder (ADHD) have all those symptoms. ADHD affects about 3 to 5 percent of all prepubertal school-age children. It is at least three times more common in boys than in girls. In many cases the symptoms of ADHD are evident when the child is 3 years of age, but often the diagnosis is not made until the child enters school. Then, compared with other children of the same age, the child is seen to be unable to pay attention, sit still, or focus on assigned tasks.

According to the fourth edition of *Diagnostic and Statistical Manual of Mental Disorders* (DSM-IV), ADHD may be diagnosed if a child has multiple symptoms of inattention or hyperactivity-impulsivity compared with other children of the same age for at least six months. Symptoms of inattention include making frequent careless mistakes, failing to follow instructions or complete school tasks or chores at home, seeming to be unable to listen to what is being said, and high levels of distractibility. Symptoms of hyperactivity-impulsivity include fidgeting with hands or feet or squirming, inability to remain seated for the duration of a structured activity, running or climbing inappropriately, blurting out answers to questions before the questions are completed, and difficulty in waiting for a turn in a game or a group. DSM-IV requires that symptoms be present by 7 years of age and that the symptoms be exhibited in at least two settings, such as in school and at home. The three types of attention-deficit/hyperactivity disorder are ADHD, predominantly inattentive type; ADHD, predominantly hyperactive-impulsive type; and ADHD, combined type.

The cause of ADHD is unknown, but genetic factors, neurochemical factors, and maturational factors have all been hypothesized to play a role in its development. Evidence that supports a genetic contribution to ADHD includes the greater concordance of monozygotic twins than of dizygotic twins for the disorder and the fact that siblings of children with ADHD have about twice the risk for the disorder than does the general population. Neurochemical hypotheses for ADHD come in part from the knowledge that drugs that improve ADHD symptoms, such as stimulant medications (for example, methylphenidate [Ritalin]), have effects on both the dopamine system and the norepinephrine system. Therefore, ADHD may be the result of dysfunctions in those systems.

The most obvious sign of ADHD is hyperactivity. Children who have hyperactivity as the predominant feature are more likely to be referred for treatment than are children with inattention but without hyperactivity. Children with predominantly hyperactive-impulsive symptoms are likely to have an enduring disorder and may be the ones who are most vulnerable to concurrent conduct disorder. Children with ADHD are also at high risk for learning disorders including mathematics disorder and reading disorder, communication disorders, and developmental coordination disorder. Since children with ADHD are often intrusive and impulsive, their peer relationships are often poor; over time, children with ADHD are often rejected by their peer group. Children with ADHD generally have normal intelligence and are aware of their social difficulties. Sometimes the children become frustrated, demoralized, or depressed in response to continually being in trouble at school and having difficulties with their schoolwork. Their frustration may take the form of irritability or aggressive outbursts.

A neurological examination of a typical child with ADHD may reveal poor motor coordination, compromised ability to perform rapid alternating movements, and difficulty in copying age-appropriate figures. Many children with ADHD have oppositional defiant disorder and have difficulty in responding to appropriate limit setting by adults.

The majority of children who have ADHD benefit from sympathomimetics. Methylphenidate, dextroamphetamine (Dexedrine), and pemoline (Cylert) are the stimulants used most often for children. Methylphenidate is effective in up to 75 percent of all children with ADHD, and it has relatively few side effects. Methylphenidate is a short-acting drug that has its onset of action within an hour of ingesting it, and the effects last for several hours. The most common side effects associated with methylphenidate are headaches, stomachaches, nausea, and insomnia. During periods of use, methylphenidate is associated with some growth suppression, but that effect is generally compensated for with a growth spurt when the children are taken off medication in the summer and on weekends. Some children experience a rebound effect when the medication wears off; then they become mildly irritable and transiently exhibit increased hyperactivity. Dextroamphetamine is approved by the Food and Drug Administration (FDA) for children over the age of 3 years, whereas methylphenidate is approved only for children over the age of 6 years. Dextroamphetamine has an effect similar to methylphenidate, although dextroamphetamine is a slightly longer-acting drug. Other medications used in the treatment of ADHD include tricyclic drugs, such as imipramine (Tofranil) and desipramine (Norpramin), and clonidine (Catapres).

The course of ADHD is variable; about half of the children with the disorder are still symptomatic in early adolescence, and about one third are still symptomatic in adulthood. The hyperactivity symptoms are often the first ones to remit, and distractibility is the last to remit. Remission is not likely to occur before the age of 12 years. The outcome for patients with ADHD into young adulthood is more guarded than it is for children who are virtually asymptomatic by age 18. Adolescents with persistent ADHD are vulnerable to a number of other disorders, especially conduct disorder, substance abuse, and depressive disorders. Patients with ADHD and conduct disorder in adolescence have a 50 percent chance of having antisocial personality disorder as adults.

Few data prove that the overall outcome is directly correlated to treatment. However, because of the importance of concentration and of being maintained in the classroom, it is worthwhile to treat children with ADHD. Although individual psychotherapy has not been shown to be effective for ADHD, highly structured settings and family education and therapy can help control the symptoms.

Attention-deficit/hyperactivity disorder not otherwise specified (NOS) is a residual category used for disturbances with prominent symptoms of inattention or hyperactivity that cause impairment but do not meet the criteria for ADHD.

Students should study Chapter 39 of *Kaplan and Sadock's Synopsis VII* and then study the questions and answers below to enhance their knowledge of the area.

HELPFUL HINTS

The student should know the terms below.

inattention	learning disorders	matching familiar faces
sympathomimetic	nonfocal (soft) signs	visual-perceptual problems
hyperactivity-impulsivity	antidepressants	rebound effect
PET scan	disinhibition	poor motor coordination
developmentally inappropriate attention	clonidine (Catapres)	right-left discrimination
	disorganized EEG pattern	ambidexterity
secondary depression	growth suppression	emotional lability
hyperkinesis	distractibility	impaired cognitive performance

QUESTIONS

DIRECTIONS: Each of the questions or incomplete statements below is followed by five suggested responses or completions. Select the *one* that is *best* in each case.

39.1. The following statements about attention-deficit/hyperactivity disorder (ADHD) are true *except*
A. children with ADHD can have inattention with no hyperactivity or impulsivity
B. children with ADHD may have symptoms of hyperactivity but no inattention
C. the disturbance must be present in at least two settings
D. children can meet the criteria for ADHD with impulsive symptoms only
E. many children with ADHD have many symptoms of inattention, hyperactivity, and impulsivity

39.2. Which of the following medications used in the treatment of ADHD has been approved by the Food and Drug Administration (FDA) for children 3 years of age and older?
A. Dextroamphetamine (Dexedrine)
B. Methylphenidate (Ritalin)
C. Pemoline (Cylert)
D. Imipramine (Tofranil)
E. None of the above

39.3. All the following disorders are associated with ADHD *except*
A. reading disorder
B. developmental coordination disorder
C. psychotic disorder not otherwise specified
D. oppositional defiant disorder
E. conduct disorder

39.4. All the following statements about ADHD are true *except*
A. many children with ADHD have disorganized EEG patterns that are characteristic of younger children
B. some children with ADHD do not exhibit any signs of hyperactivity
C. borderline intellectual functioning is an associated feature of ADHD
D. children with ADHD into adolescence are at high risk for conduct disorder, substance-related disorders, and mood disorders
E. growth suppression associated with methylphenidate (Ritalin) is compensated for during drug holidays

39.5. The most frequently cited characteristic among children with ADHD is
A. perceptual-motor impairment
B. emotional lability
C. disorders of memory and thinking
D. hyperactivity
E. disorders of speech and hearing

39.6. The first symptom of ADHD to remit is usually
A. overactivity
B. distractibility
C. decreased attention span
D. impulse-control problems
E. learning problems

39.7. The hyperactive child is
A. accident prone
B. explosively irritable
C. fascinated by spinning objects
D. preoccupied with water play
E. all the above

ANSWERS

Attention-Deficit Disorders

39.1. **The answer is D** (*Synopsis VII*, pages 1063–1065).

Children cannot meet the criteria for attention-deficit/hyperactivity disorder (ADHD) with impulsive symptoms only; hyperactivity or inattention symptoms are also needed. *Children with ADHD can have inattention with no hyperactivity or impulsivity if they have at least six symptoms of inattention. Children with ADHD may have symptoms of hyperactivity but no inattention,* but they must then have four symptoms of hyperactivity or at least four symptoms of a combination of hyperactivity and impulsivity. *The disturbance must be present in at least two settings. Many children with ADHD have many symptoms of inattention, hyperactivity, and impulsivity.*

Table 39.1 lists the diagnostic criteria for attention-deficit/hyperactivity disorder, and Table 39.2 lists the diagnostic criteria for attention-deficit/hyperactivity disorder not otherwise specified.

39.2. **The answer is A** (*Synopsis VII*, page 1067).

The Food and Drug Administration (FDA) has approved the use of *dextroamphetamine (Dexedrine)* for children of 3 years of age and older and the use of *methylphenidate (Ritalin)* and *pemoline (Cylert)* for children 6 years of age and older. *Imipramine (Tofranil)* has been approved by the FDA only for the treatment of nocturnal enuresis in children above the age of 6 years.

39.3. **The answer is C** (*Synopsis VII*, pages 1065–1067).

Children with ADHD are often described as concrete thinkers and may exhibit perseveration, but thought disorder consistent with *psychotic disorder not otherwise specified* is not a common associated disorder. Children with ADHD are at higher risk than are the general population for a number of other psychiatric disorders. Learning disorders, including *reading disorder,* are common in children with ADHD. Children with ADHD are also often found to have neurological soft signs and *developmental coordination disorder.* Children with ADHD are likely to have difficulties with aggressive impulse control and are commonly found to have *oppositional defiant disorder.* Those children with ADHD into adolescence are the ones at highest risk for *conduct disorder,* which is found in up to 50 percent of adolescents with ADHD.

39.4. **The answer is C** (*Synopsis VII*, pages 1064–1067).

Borderline intellectual functioning is not an associated feature of ADHD. Children with ADHD have a higher incidence of EEG abnormalities than do the general population. *Many children with ADHD have disorganized EEG patterns that are characteristic of younger children.* In some cases the EEG findings normalize over time. *Some children with ADHD do not exhibit any signs of hyperactivity* but do have multiple symptoms of inattention. *Children with ADHD into adolescence are at high risk for conduct disorder, substance-related disorders, and mood disorders.* Growth suppression is a recognized side effect of methylphenidate (Ritalin) treatment, but evidence indicates that *growth suppression associated with methylphenidate is compensated for during drug holidays*—the times when children are not taking the medication, such as weekends and summers.

39.5. **The answer is D** (*Synopsis VII*, page 1066).

The most frequently cited characteristic among children with ADHD is *hyperactivity,* followed by *perceptual motor impairment, emotional lability,* general coordination deficit, disorders of attention, impulsivity, *disorders of memory and thinking,* specific learning disabilities, *disorders of speech and hearing,* and equivocal neurological signs and electroencephalographic irregularities.

39.6. **The answer is A** (*Synopsis VII*, page 1067).

Overactivity is usually the first symptom of ADHD to remit, and *distractibility* is the last. The course of the condition is highly variable: Symptoms may persist into adolescence or adult life, they may remit at puberty, or the hyperactivity may disappear but the *decreased attention span* and *impulse-control problems* persist. Remission is not likely before the age of 12. If remission does occur, it is usually between the ages of 12 and 20. Remission may be accompanied by a productive adolescence and adult life, satisfying interpersonal relationships, and few significant sequelae. The majority of patients with ADHD, however, undergo only partial remission and are vulnerable to antisocial and other personality disorders and mood disorders. *Learning problems* often continue.

39.7. **The answer is E (all)** (*Synopsis VII*, pages 1065–1066).

The hyperactive child is often *accident-prone, explosively irritable, fascinated by spinning objects,* and

Table 39.1
Diagnostic Criteria for Attention-Deficit/Hyperactivity Disorder

A. Either (1) or (2):

  (1) six (or more) of the following symptoms of **inattention** have persisted for at least 6 months to a degree that is maladaptive and inconsistent with developmental level:

  Inattention:
  (a) often fails to give close attention to details or makes careless mistakes in schoolwork, work, or other activities
  (b) often has difficulty sustaining attention in tasks or play activities
  (c) often does not seem to listen when spoken to directly
  (d) often does not follow through on instructions and fails to finish schoolwork, chores, or duties in the workplace (not due to oppositional behavior or failure to understand instructions)
  (e) often has difficulty organizing tasks and activities
  (f) often avoids, dislikes, or is reluctant to engage in tasks that require sustained mental effort (such as schoolwork or homework)
  (g) often loses things necessary for tasks or activities (e.g., toys, school assignments, pencils, books, or tools)
  (h) is often easily distracted by extraneous stimuli
  (i) is often forgetful in daily activities

  (2) six (or more) of the following symptoms of **hyperactivity-impulsivity** have persisted for at least 6 months to a degree that is maladaptive and inconsistent with developmental level:

  Hyperactivity
  (a) often fidgets with hands or feet or squirms in seat
  (b) often leaves seat in classroom or in other situations in which remaining seated is expected
  (c) often runs about or climbs excessively in situations in which it is inappropriate (in adolescents or adults, may be limited to subjective feelings of restlessness)
  (d) often has difficulty playing or engaging in leisure activities quietly
  (e) is often "on the go" or often acts as if "driven by a motor"
  (f) often talks excessively

  Impulsivity
  (g) often blurts out answers before questions have been completed
  (h) often has difficulty awaiting turn
  (i) often interrupts or intrudes on others (e.g., butts into conversations or games)

B. Some hyperactive-impulsive or inattentive symptoms that caused impairment were present before age 7 years.

C. Some impairment from the symptoms is present in two or more settings (e.g., at school [or work] and at home).

D. There must be clear evidence of clinically significant impairment in social, academic, or occupational functioning.

E. The symptoms do not occur exclusively during the course of a pervasive developmental disorder, schizophrenia, or other psychotic disorder and are not better accounted for by another mental disorder (e.g., mood disorder, anxiety disorder, Dissociative Disorder, or a personality disorder).

Code based on type:
  Attention-deficit/hyperactivity disorder, combined type: if both criteria A1 and A2 are met for the past 6 months
  Attention-deficit/hyperactivity disorder, predominantly inattentive type: if criterion A1 is met but criterion A2 is not met for the past 6 months
  Attention-deficit/hyperactivity disorder, predominantly hyperactive-impulsive type: if criterion A2 is met but criterion A1 is not met for the past 6 months

Coding note: For individuals (especially adolescents and adults) who currently have symptoms that no longer meet full criteria, "in partial remission" should be specified.

Table from DSM-IV, *Diagnostic and Statistical Manual of Mental Disorders,* ed 4. Copyright American Psychiatric Association, Washington, 1994. Used with permission.

Table 39.2
Diagnostic Criteria for Attention-Deficit/Hyperactivity Disorder Not Otherwise Specified

This category is for disorders with prominent symptoms of inattention or hyperactivity-impulsivity that do not meet criteria for attention-deficit/hyperactivity disorder.

Table from DSM-IV, *Diagnostic and Statistical Manual of Mental Disorders,* ed 4. Copyright American Psychiatric Association, Washington, 1994. Used with permission.

preoccupied with water play. In school, hyperactive children may rapidly attack a test but answer only the first two questions, or they may be unable to wait to be called on. At home, they cannot be put off for even a minute. Irritability may be set off by relatively minor stimuli, and they may seem puzzled and dismayed over that phenomenon. The children are frequently emotionally labile and easily inspired to laughter and to tears, and their moods and performances are apt to be variable and unpredictable.

Disruptive Behavior Disorders

Disruptive behavior disorders include oppositional defiant disorder, conduct disorder, and disruptive behavior disorder not otherwise specified (NOS). Oppositional defiant disorder consists of a pattern of negativistic, hostile, and defiant behaviors lasting at least six months. According to the fourth edition of *Diagnostic and Statistical Manual of Mental Disorders* (DSM-IV), at least four of the following symptoms are present in patients with oppositional defiant disorder: often loses temper, often argues with adults, often defies adults' requests or rules, often deliberately does things that annoy other people, often blames others for the patient's own mistakes or misbehavior, is easily annoyed by others, is often angry and resentful, and is often spiteful or vindictive. Some degree of oppositional behavior and negative attitude is developmentally normal in young children. Normative oppositional behaviors seem to peak in children between 18 and 24 months of age, when the children are striving toward greater autonomy; the period is characterized as the terrible 2s. Epidemiological surveys estimate that about one fifth of all school-age children have negativistic traits. The disorder can be diagnosed when the oppositional and defiant behaviors are enduring and cause significant impairment at home or in school. Oppositional defiant disorder is more prevalent in boys than in girls and may begin as early as 3 years of age, but it typically manifests itself by the age of 8 years.

No single cause of oppositional defiant disorder is accepted. A temperamental predisposition to a strong will or stubborn behavior may interact with family and environmental forces to result in a nonadaptive pattern of control and defiance.

Children with the disorder often have difficulty in school because of their lack of cooperation with their teachers' requests. In addition, children with the disorder are often rejected by their peer group and perceive friendships as unsatisfactory. Some children exhibit oppositional defiant behavior in their homes but do not manifest the same behaviors in school or in a clinical setting. Children with oppositional defiant disorder may be especially resistant to receiving help from adults; therefore, any problems they encounter may remain unsolved. Some children with oppositional defiant disorder recognize their difficulties and become demoralized or depressed.

Oppositional defiant disorder is often seen in conjunction with attention-deficit/hyperactivity disorder and learning disorders. Some children who start out with a diagnosis of oppositional defiant disorder eventually meet the diagnostic criteria for conduct disorder. When conduct disorder is present, oppositional defiant disorder can no longer be diagnosed.

The course and the prognosis of children with oppositional defiant disorder depend on the severity of the disorder, the associated disorders, and the ability of the family to work on diminishing the behaviors. Treatment includes individual psychotherapy for the child and family therapy to help the family understand the child's defiance and use behavioral techniques to manage it. About 25 percent of all children who receive a diagnosis of oppositional defiant disorder no longer qualify for the diagnosis several years later.

Conduct disorder consists of an enduring pattern for at least six months of behaviors in which the basic rights of others or age-appropriate societal rules are violated. A pattern of only 3 of 15 symptoms is required for the diagnosis of conduct disorder. The symptoms of conduct disorder include the following: often bullies, threatens, or intimidates; often initiates physical fights; has used a weapon; has stolen with confrontation with a victim; has been physically cruel to people; has been physically cruel to animals; has forced someone into sexual activity; often lies or cons others; often stays out at night against parental rules; has set fires; has destroyed property; and is often truant from school. DSM-IV specifies a childhood-onset type (one conduct problem before age 10) and an adolescent-onset type (no conduct problems before age 10). The severity of the conduct disorder is also specified by DSM-IV as mild, moderate, or severe.

Conduct disorder occurs in about 6 to 16 percent of all boys and 2 to 9 percent of all girls. It is four to twelve times as common in boys as in girls.

No single factor can account for the development of conduct disorder; a combination of parental, biological, and sociocultural factors contribute to its development. Harsh, punitive child-rearing styles and physical or sexual abuse can contribute to aggressive, cruel behaviors in children. Children raised in such harsh environments often have difficulty in verbalizing their feelings and may overreact to situations with anger and violence.

Conduct disorder does not develop overnight; instead, symptoms evolve over time until a consistent pattern is present. Very young children are unlikely to meet the diagnostic criteria for the disorder, since they are developmentally unable to exhibit many conduct disorder features, such as breaking into a home, stealing with confrontation, and forcing someone into sexual activity. The average age of onset of conduct disorder is 10 to 12 years for boys and 14 to 16 years for girls.

Some disturbance of conduct is often seen in many mental disorders, such as mood disorders, attention-deficit/hyperactivity disorder, and sometimes psychotic disorders. In some cases conduct disorder occurs only in the context of major depressive disorder, and it resolves when the depressive disorder remits.

In general, children who meet the diagnostic criteria for conduct disorder at a young age and exhibit the greatest number of symptoms have the worst prognoses. A good prognosis is predicted when the symptoms are few and mild, additional mental disorders are absent, and the child has normal intellectual functioning. Multimodality treatment programs—including family education, community resources, and structured environments—are likely to bring about the best results. Medications such as lithium (Eskalith), haloperidol (Haldol), and propranolol (Inderal) help control the explosive, aggressive outbursts that may accompany conduct disorder.

Disruptive behavior disorder not otherwise specified (NOS) can be diagnosed for disorders characterized by conduct or oppositional-defiant behaviors that do not meet the diagnostic criteria for conduct disorder or oppositional defiant disorder but in which there is clinically significant impairment.

Students should study Chapter 40 in *Kaplan and Sadock's Synopsis VII* and questions and answers below to enhance their knowledge of the area.

HELPFUL HINTS

The student should be able to define the following terms.

violation of rights	negativistic relationships	terrible 2s
harsh child-rearing structure	issues of control	poor peer relationships
socioeconomic deprivation	CNS dysfunction	poor self-esteem
child abuse	ADHD	

QUESTIONS

DIRECTIONS: Each of the incomplete statements below is followed by five suggested completions. Select the *one* that is *best* in each case.

40.1. All the following statements about oppositional defiant disorder are true *except*
A. the most common symptoms include often losing one's temper, arguing with adults, and refusing to comply with adults' requests or rules
B. it is characterized by a pattern of behavior that violates the rights of others
C. oppositional defiant disorder cannot be diagnosed if conduct disorder is present
D. about 25 percent of children with the disorder no longer meet the diagnostic criteria after several years
E. oppositional defiant disorder is not diagnosed if symptoms occur exclusively during a mood disorder

40.2. Conduct disorder
A. has the best prognosis when it has its onset at a young age
B. cannot be diagnosed in a child who has received a diagnosis of oppositional defiant disorder
C. usually includes cruelty to animals, enuresis, and fire setting
D. cannot occur concurrently with major depressive disorder
E. generally has its onset earlier in boys than in girls

40.3. All the following may contribute to the development of conduct disorder *except*
A. harsh and punitive child rearing
B. parental sociopathy, alcohol dependence, and substance abuse
C. physical and sexual abuse
D. single-parent family
E. attention-deficit/hyperactivity disorder

DIRECTIONS: The lettered headings below are followed by a list of numbered statements. For each numbered statement, select the lettered heading most closely associated with it. Each lettered heading may be used once, more than once, or not at all.

Questions 40.4–40.8
A. Oppositional defiant disorder
B. Conduct disorder

40.4. May be diagnosed when symptoms occur exclusively with attention-deficit/hyperactivity disorder, learning disorders, and mood disorders

40.5. May be equally prevalent in adolescent boys and adolescent girls

40.6. Patient often bullies, threatens, or intimidates others

40.7. Patient often actively defies or refuses to comply with adults' requests or rules

40.8. Beginning before 13 years of age, the patient often stays out at night despite parental prohibitions

ANSWERS

Disruptive Behavior Disorders

40.1. The answer is B (*Synopsis VII*, page 1071).

Conduct disorder, not oppositional defiant disorder, *is characterized by a pattern of behavior that violates the rights of others. The most common symptoms of oppositional defiant disorder include often losing one's temper, often arguing with adults, and refusing to comply with adults' requests or rules. Oppositional defiant disorder cannot be diagnosed if conduct disorder is present.* Oppositional defiant disorder is not a stable disorder, since *about 25 percent of children with the disorder no longer meet the diagnostic criteria after several years.* Unlike conduct disorder, *oppositional defiant disorder is not diagnosed if symptoms occur exclusively during a mood disorder.*

Table 40.1 lists the diagnostic criteria for oppositional defiant disorder.

40.2. The answer is E (*Synopsis VII*, page 1072–1073).

Conduct disorder *generally has its onset earlier in boys* (10 to 12 years) *than in girls* (14 to 16 years). The disorder *has the worst prognosis when it has its onset at a young age* and when the child exhibits the greatest number and frequency of symptoms. A good prognosis is predicted by mild conduct disorder, onset at a late age, the absence of coexisting psychopathology, and normal intellectual functioning. Conduct disorder *can be diagnosed in a child who has received diagnosis of oppositional defiant disorder;* however, when conduct disorder is diagnosed, the oppositional defiant disorder diagnosis is preempted. Conduct disorder *does not usually include cruelty to animals, enuresis, and fire setting,* although in the past that triad was believed to be typical of children with conduct disorder. Enuresis is not a diagnostic criterion for conduct disorder, but cruelty to animals and fire setting are diagnostic criteria. Conduct disorder *can occur concurrently with major depressive disorder.* Conduct disorder can be diagnosed even when the conduct symptoms occur only during depressive episodes and resolve when the depression remits.

The diagnostic criteria for conduct disorder are listed in Table 40.2.

40.3. The answer is D (*Synopsis VII*, page 1072).

A *single-parent family* does not necessarily contribute to the development of conduct disorder; instead, the strife between parents is believed to promote conduct disorder. *Harsh and punitive child*

Table 40.1
Diagnostic Criteria for Oppositional Defiant Disorder

A. A pattern of negativistic, hostile, and defiant behavior lasting at least 6 months, during which four (or more) of the following are present:

  (1) often loses temper
  (2) often argues with adults
  (3) often actively defies or refuses to comply with adults' requests or rules
  (4) often deliberately annoys people
  (5) often blames others for his or her mistakes or misbehavior
  (6) is often touchy or easily annoyed by others
  (7) is often angry and resentful
  (8) is often spiteful or vindictive

Note: Consider a criterion met only if the behavior occurs more frequently than is typically observed in individuals of comparable age and developmental level.

B. The disturbance in behavior causes significant impairment in social, academic or occupational functioning.

C. Does not occur exclusively during the course of a psychotic or mood disorder.

D. Does not meet criteria for conduct disorder, and, if the individual is age 18 or older, criteria are not met for antisocial personality disorder.

Table from DSM-IV, *Diagnostic and Statistical Manual of Mental Disorders,* ed 4. Copyright American Psychiatric Association, Washington, 1994. Used with permission.

rearing is thought to promote aggressive and violent behaviors in children. *Parental sociopathy, alcohol dependence, and substance abuse* are associated with conduct disorder in children. *Physical and sexual abuse,* especially when it is long-term abuse, contributes to violent and aggressive behaviors in children. Abused children are likely to violate the rights of others because of their life experiences of being terrorized and brutally treated. Persistent *attention-deficit/hyperactivity disorder* seems to be associated with a high risk for conduct disorder.

40.4–40.8.

40.4. The answer is B (*Synopsis VII*, page 1074).

40.5. The answer is A (*Synopsis VII*, page 1069).

40.6. The answer is B (*Synopsis VII*, page 1071).

40.7. The answer is A (*Synopsis VII*, page 1069).

Table 40.2
Diagnostic Criteria for Conduct Disorder

A. A repetitive and persistent pattern of behavior in which the basic rights of others or major age-appropriate societal norms or rules are violated, as manifested by the presence of three (or more) of the following criteria in the past 12 months, with at least one criterion present in the past 6 months:

Aggression to people and animals

(1) often bullies, threatens, or intimidates others
(2) often initiates physical fights
(3) has used a weapon that can cause serious physical harm to others (e.g., a bat, brick, broken bottle, knife, gun)
(4) has been physically cruel to people
(5) has been physically cruel to animals
(6) has stolen while confronting a victim (e.g., mugging, purse snatching, extortion, armed robbery)
(7) has forced someone into sexual activity

Destruction of property

(8) has deliberately engaged in fire setting with the intention of causing serious damage
(9) has deliberately destroyed others' property (other than by fire setting)

Deceitfulness or theft

(10) has broken into someone else's house, building, or car
(11) often lies to obtain goods or favors or to avoid obligations (i.e., "cons" others)
(12) has stolen items of nontrivial value without confronting a victim (e.g., shoplifting, but without breaking and entering; forgery)

Serious violations of rules

(13) often stays out at night despite parental prohibitions, beginning before age 13 years
(14) has run away from home overnight at least twice while living in parental or parental surrogate home (or once without returning for a lengthy period)
(15) often truant from school, beginning before age 13 years

B. The disturbance in behavior causes clinically significant impairment in social, academic, or occupational functioning.

C. If the individual is age 18 years or older, criteria are not met for antisocial personality disorder.

Specify type based on age at onset:
   Childhood-onset type: onset of at least one criterion characteristic of conduct disorder prior to age 10 years
   Adolescent-onset type: absence of any criteria characteristic of conduct disorder prior to age 10 years

Specify severity:
   Mild: few if any conduct problems in excess of those required to make the diagnosis **and** conduct problems cause only minor harm to others
   Moderate: number of conduct problems **and** effect on others intermediate between "mild" and "severe"
   Severe: many conduct problems in excess of those required to make the diagnosis **or** conduct problems cause considerable harm to others

Table from DSM-IV, *Diagnostic and Statistical Manual of Mental Disorders,* ed 4. Copyright American Psychiatric Association, Washington, 1994. Used with permission.

40.8.   The answer is B (*Synopsis VII,* page 1071).

Conduct disorder may be diagnosed when symptoms occur exclusively with attention-deficit/hyperactivity disorder, learning disorders, and mood disorders, whereas oppositional defiant disorder cannot be diagnosed when symptoms occur exclusively during a mood disorder. *Oppositional defiant disorder may be equally prevalent in adolescent boys and adolescent girls,* but conduct disorder is present more often in adolescent boys than adolescent girls. In conduct disorder the *patient often bullies, threatens, or intimidates others.* A typical core symptom of oppositional defiant disorder is that the *patient often actively defies or refuses to comply with adults' requests or rules.* And, *beginning before 13 years of age, the patient often stays out at night despite parental prohibitions* in conduct disorder.

41 ||||||

Feeding and Eating Disorders of Infancy or Early Childhood

Feeding and eating disorders of infancy or early childhood that are included in the fourth edition of *Diagnostic and Statistical Manual of Mental Disorders* (DSM-IV) are pica, rumination disorder, and feeding disorder of infancy or early childhood. Pica is a pattern of eating nonnutritive substances over a period of at least one month. Pica is more common in young children than in adults. To meet the diagnostic criteria, it must be developmentally inappropriate. Eating nonnutritive substances is usually considered developmentally inappropriate in children older than 18 months. Certain forms of pica, such as geophagia (clay eating) and amylophagia (starch eating), are frequent in certain cultures, especially among pregnant women. When the eating behavior is part of a culturally sanctioned practice, pica is not diagnosed.

Pica has been estimated to occur in 10 to 32 percent of children between 1 and 6 years of age. In children more than 10 years old, the prevalence of pica is about 10 percent. Pica is seen with increased frequency among mentally retarded children and adolescents in institutional settings.

Pica has no single causal explanation, although it seems to run in families. Nutritional deficiencies may play a role in the development of pica in certain situations, such as cravings for ice and dirt associated with iron and zinc deficiencies. Pica is common in children with failure to thrive; thus, parental neglect and deprivation have also been associated with pica.

Pica often has its onset in children less than 2 years old. It may consist of ingesting such substances as paint, plaster, string, hair, and cloth. Pica can result in morbidity or mortality, depending on what is ingested. Among the most

serious complications are lead poisoning from lead-based paint, intestinal parasites from soil, anemia, zinc deficiency after eating clay, and iron deficiency after eating starch. In some cases, zinc and iron deficiencies may induce pica.

No definitive treatment of pica is available. The disorder often resolves with increasing age, and interventions are educational, behavioral, and family-oriented. For patients whose pica is associated with psychosocial deprivation, environmental change must occur. Behavioral methods—such as positive reinforcement, modeling, behavioral shaping, and overcorrection—have been used.

Rumination disorder is the repeated regurgitation and rechewing of food, usually in infants. Its onset typically occurs when the infant is 3 months of age, and the disorder is diagnosed only when the pattern continues for at least one month after a period of normal functioning. Rumination disorder is not diagnosed when the regurgitation occurs in association with a gastrointestinal illness or a medical condition, such as hiatal hernia, pyloric stenosis, or esophageal reflux. Rumination disorder is rare, is found equally in boys and girls, and is seen in up to 10 percent of adults with bulimia nervosa. Rumination disorder is also more common in mentally retarded children and adults than in the general population. Adults with the disorder maintain their normal weight.

The cause is not known, but several factors may contribute to the development of rumination disorder. In some babies the disorder may begin as self-stimulatory behavior and become reinforced by the sensation and by the attention it attracts from adults. In other babies, their dysfunctional autonomic nervous systems may contribute to the disorder. Some infants with rumination disorder are eventually found to have esophageal reflux or hiatal hernia. Overstimulation, tension, and a lack of proper nurturance and stimulation have been suggested as contributing factors in rumination disorder.

The course of rumination disorder is variable. It ranges from spontaneous remission in many babies who have remained healthy and well-nourished to failure to thrive in other babies. When failure to thrive, growth retardation, and developmental delays occur, the prognosis is significantly worsened. Demoralization and discouragement on the part of the mother may further impede feeding the infant.

Treatment includes improving the psychosocial environment and increasing the nurturant feeding by the infant's caregivers. In some cases, behavioral techniques—such as aversive conditioning, using a squirt of lemon juice each time the child ruminates—may be a rapid and effective way to diminish rumination disorder. Feeding disorder of infancy or early childhood is characterized by persistent failure to eat adequately and a failure to gain weight or a significant loss of weight over a period of at least one month. The onset must occur before the child is 6 years old, and the disorder is not accounted for by a lack of appropriate food or by another mental disorder.

Students should study Chapter 41 in *Kaplan and Sadock's Synopsis VII* and then test their knowledge with the questions and answers below.

HELPFUL HINTS

The student should know the following terms.

geophagia	lead poisoning	self-stimulation
amylophagia	psychosocial dwarfism	hiatal hernia
nutritional deficiencies	positive reinforcement	esophageal reflux
anemia	regurgitation	failure to thrive
zinc deficiency	overstimulation	spontaneous remission
iron deficiency		

QUESTIONS

DIRECTIONS: Each of the incomplete statements below is followed by five suggested completions. Select the *one* that is *best* in each case.

41.1. Pica has been associated with all the following *except*
A. pregnancy
B. lead poisoning
C. mercury poisoning
D. failure to thrive
E. zinc and iron deficiencies

41.2. Iron deficiency has been associated with a repeated pattern of ingesting
A. paint chips
B. clay
C. string
D. ice and dirt
E. paper

41.3. In children with pica, serum hemoglobin readings should be obtained because the children may have
A. zinc deficiency
B. lead poisoning
C. intestinal parasites
D. failure to thrive
E. iron deficiency

41.4. All the following statements about rumination disorder are true *except*
A. it is most commonly seen in infants between 3 months and 1 year of age
B. adults with rumination disorder are usually emaciated
C. it occurs equally in boys and girls
D. it is more prevalent in adults with bulimia nervosa than in the general population
E. it is associated with overstimulation and understimulation

41.5 Feeding disorder of infancy or early childhood
A. typically has its onset after the child is 6 years old
B. is diagnosed along with esophageal reflux
C. must be accompanied by a significant failure to gain weight or by significant weight loss
D. must be present for a minimum of three months
E. is diagnosed when food is not available

DIRECTIONS: The questions below consist of lettered headings followed by a list of numbered phrases. For each numbered phrase, select

A. if the item is associated with *A only*
B. if the item is associated with *B only*
C. if the item is associated with *both A and B*
D. if the item is associated with *neither A nor B*

Questions 41.6–41.10
A. Pica
B. Rumination disorder
C. Both
D. Neither

41.6. High rate of spontaneous remission

41.7. Reinforced by pleasurable self-stimulation

41.8. Associated with failure to thrive

41.9. Associated with adult eating disorders

41.10. Associated with pregnant women

ANSWERS

Feeding and Eating Disorders of Infancy or Early Childhood

41.1. The answer is C (*Synopsis VII,* pages 1076–1077).

Mercury poisoning has not been associated with pica. Pica is associated with *pregnancy,* particularly in certain cultures in which the ingestion of substances such as clay and starch is reported to be common. Pica is also associated with *lead poisoning,* since in some instances children with pica ingest paint chips that contain lead-based paint. Pica is one of the symptoms seen in children with *failure to thrive* syndromes, particularly psychosocial dwarfism. *Zinc and iron deficiencies* may cause pica; in some children, when zinc and iron are replaced, pica resolves. The diagnostic criteria for pica are listed in Table 41.1.

41.2. The answer is D (*Synopsis VII,* page 1076).

Iron deficiency has been associated with cravings for *ice and dirt.* The ingestion of *paint chips* has been associated with lead poisoning, since some paint used to be lead-based. The ingestion of *clay* has been linked to anemia and zinc deficiency. The ingestion of *string* and *paper* has not been linked to any nutritional deficiency.

41.3. The answer is E (*Synopsis VII,* pages 1076–1077).

Children with pica should be tested for their hemoglobin count, since many such children may have *iron deficiency* and may be anemic. Children who have ingested large amounts of clay may also end up

with *zinc deficiency* and anemia. Lead levels should also be obtained for children with pica, since they may have ingested paint chips that contain lead, resulting in *lead poisoning. Intestinal parasites* are sometimes found in children with pica who have ingested dirt. Children with pica should be screened for overall nutritional status, since in some cases pica is seen in conjunction with *failure to thrive* syndromes.

41.4. The answer is B (*Synopsis VII,* page 1078).

Adults who have rumination disorder are not usually emaciated. Rumination disorder *is most commonly seen in infants between 3 months and 1 year of age* and in mentally retarded children and adults. It *occurs equally in boys and girls* and *is prevalent in adults with bulimia nervosa than in the general population.* Rumination disorder *is associated with overstimulation and understimulation.* The diagnostic criteria for rumination disorder are listed in Table 41.2.

41.5. The answer is C (*Synopsis VII,* page 1079).

Feeding disorder of infancy or early childhood is characterized by a feeding disturbance that *must be accompanied by a significant failure to gain weight or by significant weight loss* (Table 41.3). The onset of the disorder must occur *before the child is 6 years old,* and it *is not diagnosed along with esophageal reflux* or when another medical condition accounts for it. Feeding disorder of infancy or early childhood *must be present for a minimum of one month, not*

Table 41.1
Diagnostic Criteria for Pica

A. Persistent eating of nonnutritive substances for at least 1 month.

B. The eating of nonnutritive substances is inappropriate to the developmental level.

C. The eating behavior is not part of a culturally sanctioned practice.

D. If the eating behavior occurs exclusively during the course of another mental disorder (e.g., mental retardation, pervasive developmental disorder, schizophrenia), it is sufficiently severe to warrant independent clinical attention.

Table from DSM-IV, *Diagnostic and Statistical Manual of Mental Disorders,* ed 4. Copyright American Psychiatric Association, Washington, 1994. Used with permission.

Table 41.2
Diagnostic Criteria for Rumination Disorder

A. Repeated regurgitation and rechewing of food for a period of at least 1 month following a period of normal functioning.

B. The behavior is not due to an associated gastrointestinal or other general medical condition (e.g., esophageal reflux).

C. The behavior does not occur exclusively during the course of anorexia nervosa or bulimia nervosa. If the symptoms occur exclusively during the course of mental retardation or a pervasive developmental disorder, they are sufficiently severe to warrant independent clinical attention.

Table from DSM-IV, *Diagnostic and Statistical Manual of Mental Disorders,* ed 4. Copyright American Psychiatric Association, Washington, 1994. Used with permission.

three months, and it *is not diagnosed when food is not available.*

41.6–41.10

41.6. The answer is C (*Synopsis VII,* pages 1077 and 1079).

41.7. The answer is B (*Synopsis VII,* page 1078).

41.8. The answer is C (*Synopsis VII,* pages 1077–1078).

41.9. The answer is C (*Synopsis VII,* pages 1077–1078).

41.10. The answer is A (*Synopsis VII,* pages 1076).

Both rumination disorder and pica seem to have *high rates of spontaneous remission. Rumination disorder* seems to be *reinforced by pleasurable self-stimulation. Pica* is sometimes *associated with failure to thrive,* notably psychosocial dwarfism, in which children have been reported to eat garbage and to drink out of the toilet. *Rumination disorder* also has been *associated with failure to thrive,* and in some cases life-threatening malnutrition may accompany rumi-

Table 41.3
Diagnostic Criteria for Feeding Disorder of Infancy or Early Childhood

---

A. Feeding disturbance as manifested by persistent failure to eat adequately with significant failure to gain weight or significant loss of weight over at least 1 month.

B. The disturbance is not due to an associated gastrointestinal or other general medical condition (e.g., esophageal reflux).

C. Not better accounted for by another mental disorder (e.g., rumination disorder) or by lack of available food.

D. The onset is before age 6.

Table from DSM-IV, *Diagnostic and Statistical Manual of Mental Disorders,* ed 4. Copyright American Psychiatric Association, Washington, 1994. Used with permission.

nation disorder in infants. *Both* rumination disorder and pica are *associated with adult eating disorders. Pica* is *associated with pregnant women* and is reported to be especially prevalent in certain cultures, such as the Australian aborigines.

Tic Disorders

Tics are involuntary, sudden, recurrent stereotyped motor movements or vocalizations. Simple motor tics are composed of rapid contractions of similar muscle groups such as eye blinking, neck jerking, shoulder shrugging, or facial grimacing. Simple vocal tics include coughing, throat clearing, grunting, snorting, and barking. Complex tics appear to be more purposeful and ritualistic than simple tics. Complex motor tics include grooming gestures, jumping, smelling of objects, echopraxia (imitating observed behavior), and copropraxia (obscene gestures). Complex vocal tics include verbalization of words without a context, palilalia (repeating one's own last words), echolalia (repetition of others' words) and coprolalia (blurting out obscene words or phrases).

The fourth edition of *Diagnostic and Statistical Manual of Mental Disorders* (DSM-IV) includes four tic disorders: Tourette's disorder, chronic motor or vocal tic disorder, transient tic disorder, and tic disorder not otherwise specified (NOS). In all tic disorders, some patients are able to voluntarily suppress tics for minutes or hours; however, children often do not anticipate their tics or are unable to control them. Stress and anxiety commonly exacerbate tics. They often disappear during sleep, but not always. It is important to differentiate tics from other motor movement abnormalities such as those that occur in Sydenham's chorea, Huntington's disease, Wilson's disease, and Parkinson's disease.

In 1885, George Gilles de la Tourette first described what is now known as Tourette's disorder. Tourette's disorder is characterized by both multiple motor tics and at least one vocal tic that has been present at some time during the illness. The tics may occur many times during the day nearly every day or intermittently for at least a year. In Tourette's disorder, tics are never absent for more than two months at a time. Tourette's disorder is estimated to occur in 4 to 5 persons per 10,000. It is at least three times more common in male patients than in female patients. Motor tics usually emerge by 7 years of age, and vocal tics usually emerge by 11 years of age.

Increasing evidence suggests that genetic factors play a role in the development of Tourette's disorder, as well as in chronic motor or vocal tic disorder since both disorders occur with greater frequency in the same families. A relation exists between Tourette's disorder, obsessive-compulsive disorder, and attention-deficit/hyperactivity disorder. First-degree relatives of people with Tourette's disorder are at risk for developing chronic motor or vocal tic disorder and obsessive-compulsive disorder. Up to 50 percent of children with Tourette's disorder also have attention-deficit/hyperactivity disorder.

Dopamine system involvement is believed to contribute to Tourette's disorder, based upon the observation that dopamine receptor antagonists may exacerbate tics. Haloperidol and pimozide have been effective in over 75 percent of people with the disorder. Tourette's disorder is a chronic illness that naturally waxes and wanes, but it is not a degenerative disorder. Some children with Tourette's disorder are able to function well and lead normal lives without treatment.

Chronic motor or vocal tic disorder consists of either motor or vocal tics, but not both, that have been present intermittently or nearly every day for more than one year. The onset is before 18 years, and the diagnosis cannot be made if Tourette's disorder has previously been diagnosed. The prevalence of chronic motor or vocal tic disorder is estimated to be from 100 to 1000 times greater than Tourette's disorder (approximately 1 to 2 percent). School-age boys are at highest risk for the disorder. Vocal tics are usually not loud or intense and may be caused by thoracic, abdominal, or diaphragmatic contractions. Both Tourette's disorder and chronic motor or vocal tic disorder aggregate within the same families. Twin studies have found a high concordance for either Tourette's disorder or chronic motor tics in monozygotic twins.

Transient tic disorder consists of a single or multiple motor or vocal tics that occur many times a day for at least four weeks but for no longer than 12 consecutive months. It is not diagnosed if either Tourette's disorder or chronic motor or vocal tic disorder has previously been diagnosed. Transient tic-like habits and muscular twitches are common in children with the

disorder. From 5 to 24 percent of all school-age children have a history of tics, but the prevalence of transient tic disorder is unknown. It is unclear during the first year whether a tic will spontaneously remit or become chronic. Pharmacological intervention is generally not recommended for transient tic disorder unless the tics are very intrusive and distressing.

The DSM-IV category of tic disorder not otherwise specified is used for tic disorders that do not meet the criteria for any other tic disorder.

Students are referred to Chapter 42 of *Kaplan and Sadock's Synopsis VII* for a more detailed discussion. Studying the questions and answers below will enhance their understanding of those problems.

HELPFUL HINTS

The terms below relate to tic disorders and should be known by the student.

Tourette's disorder	palilalia	Pelizaeus-Merzbacher disease
motor tic	echolalia	status dysmyelinisatus
vocal tic	echokinesis	Sydenham's chorea
transient tic disorder	dystonia	Wilson's disease
simple or complex tics	hemiballism	Lesch-Nyhan syndrome
eye blinking	stereotypy	Gilles de la Tourette
neck jerking	compulsions	Jean Charcot
shoulder shrugging	hyperdopaminergia	benztropine (Cogentin)
facial grimacing	encephalitis lethargica	tardive dyskinesia
grunting	tremor	pimozide (Orap)
barking	Hallervorden-Spatz disease	clonidine (Catapres)
coprolalia	Huntington's chorea	torsion dystonia

QUESTIONS

DIRECTIONS: Each of the questions or incomplete statements below is followed by five suggested responses or completions. Select the *one* that is *best* in each case.

Questions 42.1–42.2

Alan, a 10-year-old boy, was brought for a consultation by his mother because of "severe compulsions." The mother reported that the child at various times had to run and clear his throat, touch the doorknob twice before entering any door tilt his head from side to side, rapidly blink his eyes, and touch the ground with his hands suddenly by flexing his whole body. These "compulsions" began two years ago. The first was the eye blinking, and then the others followed, with a waxing and waning course. The movements occurred most frequently when the patient was

anxious or under stress. The last symptom to appear was the repetitive touching of doorknobs. The consultation was scheduled after the child began to make the middle-finger sign while saying profanities.

When examined, Alan reported that he did not know most of the time when the movements were going to occur except for the touching of doorknobs. On questioning, he said that, before he felt he had to touch a doorknob, he got the thought of doing it and tried to push it out of his head, but he couldn't because it kept coming back until he touched the doorknob several times; then he felt better. When asked what would happen if someone would not let him touch the doorknob, he said that he would just get mad; when his father tried to stop him, the boy had had a temper tantrum.

During the interview the child grunted, cleared his throat, turned his head, and rapidly blinked his eyes several times. At other times he tried to make it appear that he had voluntarily been performing these movements.

Past history and physical and neurological examinations were totally unremarkable except for the abnormal movements and sounds. The mother reported that her youngest uncle had had similar symptoms when he was an adolescent, but she could not elaborate any further.

42.1. In the case example, the diagnosis is made on the basis of
A. vocal tics
B. coprolalia
C. onset before age 21
D. no known central nervous system disease
E. all the above

42.2. If the onset is after age 18, which of the following tic disorders may be diagnosed?
A. Transient tic disorder
B. Chronic motor or vocal tic disorder
C. Tourette's disorder
D. Tic disorder not otherwise specified
E. All the above

Questions 42.3–42.6

42.3. The dopamine system has been hypothesized to be involved in the development of tic disorders because
A. haloperidol (Haldol) suppresses tics
B. pimozide (Orap) suppresses tics
C. methylphenidate (Ritalin) exacerbates tics
D. pemoline (Cylert) exacerbates tics
E. all the above

42.4. Evidence that genetic factors are likely to play a role in the development of Tourette's disorder is supported by all of the following *except*
A. concordance for Tourette's disorder is significantly higher in monozygotic than dizygotic twins
B. Tourette's disorder and chronic tic disorder are likely to occur in the same family
C. first degree relatives of probands with Tourette's disorder are at higher than average risk for developing Tourette's disorder, chronic tic disorder, and obsessive-compulsive disorder
D. sons of fathers with Tourette's disorder are at highest risk for developing the disorder
E. concordance is high for Tourette's disorder or chronic tic disorder in monozygotic twins

42.5. Which one of the following distinguishes transient tic disorder from chronic motor or vocal tic disorder and Tourette's disorder?
A. Age of onset
B. The presence of motor tics only
C. The presence of vocal tics only
D. The presence of both motor and vocal tics
E. Progression of the tic symptoms over time

DIRECTIONS: The lettered headings below are followed by a list of numbered phrases. For each numbered phrase, select the lettered heading most associated with it. Each heading may be used once, more than once, or not at all.

Questions 42.6–42.9
A. Coprolalia
B. Palilalia
C. Echolalia
D. Echokinesis

42.6 Repetition of the last word, phrase, or sound

42.7. Repetition of socially unacceptable, frequently obscene words

42.8. Repetition of one's own words

42.9. Imitation of observed movements

ANSWERS

Tic Disorders

42.1. The answer is E (all) (*Synopsis VII*, page 1081).

In the case of this 10-year-old boy, the correct diagnosis is Tourette's disorder. He has both chronic motor tics and *vocal tics,* including *coprolalia.* The tics have occurred for more than one year. The disorder started well under *age 18.* He also has *no known central nervous system disease.*

Obsessions and compulsions are often seen, as in Alan's case, in persons with Tourette's disorder. His obsessions and compulsions are not persistent and disruptive enough, however, to meet the diagnosis of obsessive-compulsive disorder. See Table 42.1 for the diagnostic criteria for Tourette's disorder.

42.2. The answer is D (*Synopsis VII*, page 1087).

All tic disorders with onset after age 18 must be diagnosed as *tic disorder not otherwise specified* (NOS), a residual category for tics that do not meet the criteria for a specific tic disorder. *Transient tic disorder, chronic motor or vocal tic disorder,* and *Tourette's disorder* all specify onset before age 18.

Table 42.2 lists the DSM-IV diagnostic criteria for tic disorder NOS.

42.3. The answer is E (all) (*Synopsis VII*, page 1080).

Supportive evidence of dopamine system involvement in tic disorders includes the observations that pharmacologic agents that antagonize the dopamine system, such as *haloperidol (Haldol) and pimozide (Orap), suppress tics,* and observations that agents that increase central dopaminergic activity, such as cocaine, dextroamphetamine (Dexedrine), *methylphenidate (Ritalin), and pemoline (Cylert), exacerbate tics.*

42.4. The answer is D (*Synopsis VII*, page 1080).

Evidence that genetic factors are likely to play a role in the development of Tourette's disorder include the findings that *sons of mothers, not sons of fathers, with Tourette's disorder are at highest risk for developing the disorder.* Twin studies reveal that *concordance for Tourette's disorder is significantly higher in monozygotic twins than in dizygotic twins.* In addition, the findings that *Tourette's disorder and chronic tic disorder are likely to occur in the same family* also supports the view that the disorders are part of a genetically determined spectrum. *First degree relatives of probands with Tourette's disorder are at higher than average risk for developing Tourette's disorder, chronic tic disorder, and obsessive-compulsive disorder,* implying a genetic relation between the three disorders. A genetic relation between Tourette's disorder and chronic tic disorder is also supported by findings that *concordance is high for Tourette's disorder or chronic tic disorder in monozygotic twins.*

42.5. The answer is E (*Synopsis VII*, pages 1085–1086).

Transient tic disorder (Table 42.3) can be distinguished from chronic motor or vocal tic disorder (Ta-

---

Table 42.1
Diagnostic Criteria for Tourette's Disorder

A. Both multiple motor and one or more vocal tics have been present at some time during the illness, although not necessarily concurrently. (A *tic* is a sudden, rapid, recurrent, nonrhythmic, stereotyped motor movement or vocalization.)

B. The tics occur many times a day (usually in bouts) nearly every day or intermittently throughout a period of more than 1 year, and during this period there was never a tic-free period of more than 3 consecutive months.

C. The disturbance causes marked distress or significant impairment in social, occupational, or other important areas of functioning.

D. The onset is before age 18 years.

E. The disturbance is not due to the direct physiological effects of a substance (e.g., stimulants) or a general medical condition (e.g., Huntington's disease or postviral encephalitis).

Table from DSM-IV, *Diagnostic and Statistical Manual of Mental Disorders,* ed 4. Copyright American Psychiatric Association, Washington, 1994. Used with permission.

Table 42.2
Diagnostic Criteria for Tic Disorder Not Otherwise Specified

This category is for disorders characterized by tics that do not meet criteria for a specific tic disorder. Examples include tics lasting less than 4 weeks or tics with an onset after age 18 years.

Table from DSM-IV, *Diagnostic and Statistical Manual of Mental Disorders,* ed 4. Copyright American Psychiatric Association, Washington, 1994. Used with permission.

Table 42.3
Diagnostic Criteria for Transient Tic Disorder

A. Single or multiple motor and/or vocal tics (i.e., sudden, rapid, recurrent, nonrhythmic, stereotyped motor movements or vocalizations)

B. The tics occur many times a day, nearly every day for at least 4 weeks, but for no longer than 12 consecutive months.

C. The disturbance causes marked distress or significant impairment in social, occupational, or other important areas of functioning.

D. The onset is before age 18 years.

E. The disturbance is not due to the direct physiological effects of a substance (e.g., stimulants) or a general medical condition (e.g., Huntington's disease or postviral encephalitis).

F. Criteria have never been met for Tourette's disorder or chronic motor or vocal tic disorder.

Specify if:
Single episode or **recurrent**

Table from DSM-IV, *Diagnostic and Statistical Manual of Mental Disorders,* ed 4. Copyright American Psychiatric Association, Washington, 1994. Used with permission.

Table 42.4
Diagnostic Criteria for Chronic Motor or Vocal Tic Disorder

A. Single or multiple motor or vocal tics (i.e., sudden, rapid, recurrent, nonrhythmic, stereotyped motor movements or vocalizations), but not both, have been present at some time during the illness.

B. The tics occur many times a day nearly every day or intermittently throughout a period of more than 1 year, and during this period there was never a tic-free period of more than 3 consecutive months.

C. The disturbance causes marked distress or significant impairment in social, occupational, or other important areas of functioning.

D. The onset is before age 18 years.

E. The disturbance is not due to the direct physiological effects of a substance (e.g., stimulants) or a general medical condition (e.g., Huntington's disease or postviral encephalitis).

F. Criteria have never been met for Tourette's disorder.

Table from DSM-IV, *Diagnostic and Statistical Manual of Mental Disorders,* ed 4. Copyright American Psychiatric Association, Washington, 1994. Used with permission.

ble 42.4) and Tourette's disorder (Table 42.1) only by following the *progression of the tic symptoms over time.* DSM-IV emphasizes precise and specific symptom patterns, time framework, and age of onset in classifying the tic disorders. Transient tic disorder cannot be distinguished from chronic motor or vocal tic disorder and Tourette's disorder by *the age of onset, the presence of motor tics only, the presence of vocal tics only,* or *the presence of both motor and vocal tics.*

42.6–42.9

42.6   The answer is C (*Synopsis VII,* page 1080).

42.7.   The answer is A (*Synopsis VII,* page 1080.

42.8.   The answer is B (*Synopsis VII,* page 1080).

42.9.   The answer is D (*Synopsis VII,* page 1080).

Vocal tics may be simple. For example, coughing and barking are simple vocal tics. Complex vocal tics consist of repeating words or phrases out of context. *Coprolalia* is the *repetition of socially unacceptable, frequently obscene words.* Palilalia is the *repetition of one's own words.* Echolalia is the *repetition of the last heard word, phrase, or sound* of another person. Echokinesis is a complex motor tic consisting of the *imitation of observed movements.*

Communication Disorders

Communication disorders included in the fourth edition of *Diagnostic and Statistical Manual of Mental Disorders* (DSM-IV) are expressive language disorder, mixed receptive-expressive language disorder, phonological disorder, and stuttering.

Expressive language disorder in a child consists of below-expected ability in vocabulary, the use of correct tenses, the production of complete sentences, and the recall of words. The deficits are confirmed by scores obtained from standardized measures of expressive language and are below the child's nonverbal intellectual capacity, as well as the child's receptive language abilities. The prevalence of expressive language disorder ranges from 3 to 10 percent of all school-age children and is at least twice as common in boys as in girls.

Language disabilities can be acquired secondary to neurologic trauma, but in most cases it occurs developmentally, without a known etiology. It is suspected that expressive language disorder has genetic contributions, since relatives of children with a variety of learning disorders have a higher likelihood of expressive language disability.

Children with the disorder are eager to communicate, and use gestures appropriately to increase their success in meaningful communication. Vocabulary is usually below what is expected for the child's age, and articulation is often immature. Sounds such as r, s, z, y, and l are often mispronounced. By the age of 4 years, most children with expressive language disorder can speak in short phrases, but they acquire new words more slowly than other children and lag in their development of grammatical usage. Children with expressive language disorder are at risk for emotional complications such as chronic frustration, poor self-image, and depressive disorders. Additional disorders such as reading disorder, developmental coordination

disorder, and other communication disorders are also more prevalent in children with expressive language disorder. Delayed motor milestones and enuresis are common in children with expressive language disorder.

As many as 50 percent of children with mild expressive language disorder appear to recover spontaneously without lasting impairment. In moderate and severe cases, language therapy including practicing verbal expression of phonemes is useful. Vocabulary remediation and exercises involving sentence construction are also important. The goals are to increase the number of age-appropriate phrases that the child can use in everyday speech.

Mixed receptive-expressive language disorder consists of functional impairment in the expression and the comprehension of language. Mixed receptive-expressive language disorder is confirmed through lower than expected scores from standardized tests of both receptive (comprehension) and expressive language development for a child's age. Estimates of the prevalence of either expressive language disorder or mixed receptive-expressive language disorder range from 1 to 13 percent. Expressive language is believed to be much more common than mixed receptive-expressive language disorder. The disorder is more common in boys than in girls. The etiology of mixed receptive-expressive language disorder is not known, but some studies suggest that impairment of auditory discrimination may contribute to the disorder. As with expressive language disorder, there is a higher risk of left handedness and ambilaterality among people with mixed receptive-expressive language disorder.

Children with mixed receptive-expressive language disorder have difficulty understanding verbal language and many also have trouble processing (encoding) visual symbols. A young child with mixed receptive-expressive language disorder is unable to point to familiar household objects or follow simple commands. While the children sometimes appear to be deaf, they are not as evidenced by their ability to respond to nonlanguage sounds from the environment. Children with communication disorders should always be given an audiogram to rule out a contributing hearing loss. Children with mixed receptive-expressive are at risk for a number of additional psychiatric disorders, including learning disorders, attention-deficit/hyperactivity disorder, and depressive disorders.

Phonological disorder is characterized by frequent misarticulations, sound substitutions, and omissions of speech sounds for a child's age and intelligence, often giving the impression of baby talk. It is more common in boys and seems to run in families. The speech sounds that are most frequently misarticulated are those acquired late in the developmental sequence. These include misarticulation of r, sh, th, f, z, l, and ch. Sometimes other sounds including b, m, t, d, n, and h, are troublesome. Omission of sounds are thought to be the most serious type of misarticulation, substitutions the next serious, and distortion of sounds the least serious. Most children outgrow phonological disorder by the third grade, but children who persist in misarticulation into the fourth grade are in need of remediation. Other communication disorders are common in children with phonological disorder.

Stuttering is a disturbance in normal fluency and time patterning of speech that is inappropriate for the child's age. Stuttering includes sound repetitions, prolongations, interjections, pauses within words, word substitutions to avoid blocking, and audible or silent blocking. Stuttering is four times more common in boys than in girls, and is more common in family members of affected children.

Stuttering does not suddenly occur, but tends to be episodic with intervals of normal speech for weeks or months. Chronic stuttering does not usually set in until the middle elementary school years. Stutterers may have associated avoidance of particular words or sounds in which stuttering is anticipated. Eye blinks or tremors of the lips and jaw may occur. Frustration, anxiety, and depression often accompany chronic stuttering. Stress and fear, may exacerbate bouts of stuttering in children with the disorder. Most treatments for stuttering are based on the belief that stuttering is a learned behavior.

Communication disorder not otherwise specified is for disorders that do not meet the criteria for any specific communication disorder.

Students should review Chapter 43 of *Kaplan and Sadock's Synopsis VII* and then study the questions and answers below to test their knowledge of the subject.

HELPFUL HINTS

The terms below relate to communication disorders and should be known by the student.

expressive language disorder	audiogram	substitutions
mixed receptive-expressive	baby talk	omissions
language disorder	articulation problems	misarticulation
phonological disorder	comprehension	sound distortion
stuttering	encoding	dysarthria
maturational lag	ambilaterality	fluency of speech
standardized language test	language acquisition	semantogenic theory of stuttering
decoding	phonemes	spastic dysphonia

QUESTIONS

DIRECTIONS: Each of the incomplete statements below is followed by five suggested completions. Select the *one* that is *best* in each case.

43.1. In expressive language disorder
A. scores from standardized measures of expressive and receptive development are usually below intellectual capacity
B. the disorder is often diagnosed with a pervasive developmental disorder
C. the diagnosis can not be made when mentally retardation is present
D. there is limited vocabulary, poor word recall, confusion of tenses, and poor sentence construction for the child's age and intelligence
E. the disorder does not interfere with academic or occupational achievement

43.2. All of the following statements about mixed receptive-expressive language disorder are true *except*
A. scores from standardized measures of both receptive and expressive language disorder are substantially below measures of nonverbal intellectual capacity
B. the diagnosis can not be made if a pervasive developmental disorder is present
C. children with the disorder may initially appear deaf
D. the disorder includes receptive disability in the absence of expressive deficits
E. children with the disorder have difficulty processing visual symbols and pictures

43.3. Phonological disorder
A. is more common in children over 8 years old than in children under 8 years old
B. has a low rate of spontaneous remission in children over 8 years old
C. is two to three times more common in girls than in boys
D. does not occur with other communication disorders
E. includes errors in sound production, substitutions of sounds, and sound omissions

43.4. Stuttering
A. is probably caused by conflicts, fears, or neurosis
B. has two peaks of onset: two to three years and five to seven years
C. is associated with more psychiatric disorders than other communication disorders
D. usually presents as a chronic disorder
E. does not cause impairment in academic or occupational achievement

43.5. Phonological disorder is related to
A. maturational delay
B. genetic factors
C. twins
D. low socioeconomic status
E. all the above

43.6. A phoneme is
A. a constellation of sounds
B. a genetic marker on a chromosome
C. a chemical mediator
D. the smallest sound unit
E. an artificial language device

DIRECTIONS: The lettered headings below are followed by a list of numbered phrases. For each numbered phrase, select the *best* lettered heading. Each lettered heading may be used once, more than once, or not at all.

Questions 43.7–43.8
A. Expressive language disorder
B. Phonological disorder

43.7 May give the impression of "baby talk"

43.8 May forget old words as new words are learned, but comprehension is not affected.

ANSWERS

Communication Disorders

43.1.   The answer is D (*Synopsis VII*, pages 1088–1089).

In expressive language disorder *there are limited vocabulary, poor word recall, confusion of tenses, and poor sentence construction for the child's age and intelligence.* The diagnosis is confirmed using scores of expressive language obtained from standardized measures that are shown to be below nonverbal intellectual capacity as well as receptive language development. The disorder does not include receptive language disability; *scores from standardized measures of expressive, but not receptive, language development are usually below intellectual capacity. The disorder cannot be diagnosed with a pervasive developmental disorder.* However, *the diagnosis can be made if when mental retardation is present,* if the language difficulties are in excess of those usually associated with mental retardation. *The disorder does interfere with academic or occupational achievement* and social communication.

The diagnostic criteria for expressive language disorder appears in Table 43.1.

43.2.   The answer is D (*Synopsis VII*, pages 1090–1091).

Mixed receptive-expressive language disorder is characterized by the child's impairment in both the understanding and expression of language. According to the fourth edition of *Diagnostic and Statistical Manual of Mental Disorders* (DSM-IV), *the disorder cannot include receptive language disability in the absence of expressive deficits* (Table 43.2). In mixed receptive-expressive language disorder *scores from standardized measures of both receptive and expressive language development are substantially below measures of nonverbal intellectual capacity. The diagnosis cannot be made if a pervasive developmental disorder is present. Children with the disorder may initially may appear deaf* because they do not respond appropriately to simple commands, yet they are able to respond to nonlanguage sounds in the environment. In the disorder *children have difficulty processing visual symbols and pictures.*

43.3.   The answer is E (*Synopsis VII*, pages 1093–1094).

Phonological disorder consists of failure to use developmentally expected speech sounds appropriate

Table 43.1
Diagnostic Criteria for Expressive Language Disorder

A. The scores obtained from standardized individually administered measures of expressive language development are substantially below those obtained from standardized measures of both nonverbal intellectual capacity and receptive language development. The disturbance may be manifest clinically by symptoms that include having a markedly limited vocabulary, making errors in tense, or having difficulty recalling words or producing sentences with developmentally appropriate length or complexity.

B. The difficulties with expressive language interfere with academic or occupational achievement or with social communication.

C. Criteria are not met for mixed receptive-expressive language disorder or a pervasive developmental disorder.

D. If mental retardation, a speech-motor or sensory deficit, or environmental deprivation is present, the language difficulties are in excess of those usually associated with these problems.

Coding note: If a speech-motor or sensory deficit or a neurological condition is present, code the condition on Axis III.

Table from DSM-IV, *Diagnostic and Statistical Manual of Mental Disorders,* ed 4. Copyright American Psychiatric Association, Washington,1994. Used with permission.

Table 43.2
Diagnostic Criteria for Mixed Receptive-Expressive Language Disorder

A. The scores obtained from a battery of standardized individually administered measures of both receptive and expressive language development are substantially below those obtained from standardized measures of nonverbal intellectual capacity. Symptoms include those for expressive language disorder as well as difficulty understanding words, sentences, or specific types of words, such as spatial terms.

B. The difficulties with receptive and expressive language significantly interfere with academic or occupational achievement or with social communication.

C. Criteria are not met for a pervasive developmental disorder.

D. If mental retardation, a speech-motor or sensory deficit, or environmental deprivation is present, the language difficulties are in excess of those usually associated with these problems.

Coding note: if a speech-motor or sensory deficit or a neurological condition is present, code the condition on Axis III.

Table from DSM-IV, *Diagnostic and Statistical Manual of Mental Disorders,* ed 4. Copyright American Psychiatric Association, Washington, 1994. Used with permission.

for age. The disability *includes errors in sound production, substitutions of sounds, and sound omissions.* Phonological disorder *is more common in children under 8 years old than in children over 8 years old.* The disorder *has a high rate of spontaneous remission in children over 8 years old;* most children outgrow the disorder by the third grade. Phonological disorder *is two to three times more common in boys than in girls.* Phonological disorder *commonly occurs with other communication disorders,* such as expressive language disorder, reading disorder, and developmental coordination disorder.

Table 43.3 presents the diagnostic criteria for phonological disorder.

43.4. The answer is B (*Synopsis VII,* pages 1096–1097).

Stuttering consists of sound repetitions, word prolongations, interjections, pauses within words and word blocking. It *has two peaks of onset: two to three years and five to seven years.* The precise cause of stuttering is not known, but the current consensus is that it *is not caused by conflicts, fears, or neurosis.* Children who do stutter, however, may have episodic exacerbations when they are under stress. Although children with any type of communication disorder is at higher risk than the general population for a variety of concurrent psychiatric disorders, there is no evidence that stuttering *is associated with more psychiatric disorders than other communication disorders.* Stuttering *usually presents as an episodic disorder, rather than a chronic disorder,* but it can become chronic within several years. Stuttering *causes impairment in academic or occupational achievement* and impairment in social communication.

Table 43.4 lists the DSM-IV diagnostic criteria for stuttering.

43.5. The answer is E (all) (*Synopsis VII,* page 1093).

The cause of phonological order is unknown. It is commonly believed that a *maturational delay* in the neurological processes underlying speech may be at fault.

A disproportionately high number of children with phonological disorder are found to be second-borns, *twins,* or of *low socioeconomic* status. It is now believed that the children, rather than being at risk for the disorder, are the recipients of inadequate speech stimulation and reinforcement.

Constitutional factors, rather than environmental factors, seem to be of major importance in determining whether a child has phonological disorder. The high proportion of children with developmental articulation disorder who have relatives with a similar disorder suggests that there is a *genetic component* to the disorder.

43.6. The answer is D (*Synopsis VII,* page 1094).

Phonological disorder cannot be accounted for by structural, physiological, or neurological abnormalities. Language is within normal limits. The term actually refers to a number of different articulation problems that range in severity from mild to severe. Only one speech sound or phoneme (*the smallest sound unit*), may be affected, or many phonemes may be involved. The child may be completely intelligible, partially intelligible, or unintelligible.

Table 43.3
Diagnostic Criteria for Phonological Disorder

A. Failure to use developmentally expected speech sounds that are appropriate for age and dialect (e.g., errors in sound production, use, representation, or organization such as, but not limited to, substitutions of one should for another [use of /t/ for target /k/ sound] or omissions of sounds such as final consonants).

B. The difficulties in speech sound production interfere with academic or occupational achievement or with social communication.

C. If mental retardation, a speech-motor or sensory deficit, or environmental deprivation is present, the speech difficulties are in excess of those usually associated with these problems.

Coding note: If a speech-motor or sensory deficit or a neurological condition is present, code the condition on Axis III.

Table 43.4
Diagnostic Criteria for Stuttering

A. Disturbance in the normal fluency and time patterning of speech (inappropriate for the individual's age), characterized by frequent occurrences of one or more of the following:

   (1) sound and syllable repetitions
   (2) sound prolongations
   (3) interjections
   (4) broken words (e.g., pauses within a word)
   (5) audible or silent blocking (filled or unfilled pauses in speech)
   (6) circumlocutions (word substitutions to avoid problematic words)
   (7) words produced with an excess of physical tension
   (8) monosyllabic whole-word repetitions (e.g., "I-I-I-I see him")

B. The disturbance in fluency interferes with academic or occupational achievement or with social communication.

C. If a speech-motor or sensory deficit is present, the speech difficulties are in excess of those usually associated with these problems.

Coding note: If a speech-motor or sensory deficit or a neurological condition is present, code the condition on Axis III.

A phoneme in linguistics is a speech sound that serves to distinguish words from one another (for example, the vowels in *tan, ten, tin, ton, tun*). There is a rigid sequence in the process of acquisition of new phonemes by a child learning to speak, and accordingly, this process is reversed in various types of aphasic speech disorders.

A phoneme is not *a constellation of sounds, genetic marker on a chromosome, a chemical mediator,* or *an artificial language device.*

43.7–43.8

43.7. **The answer is B** (*Synopsis VII,* pages 1093).

43.8. **The answer is A** (*Synopsis VII,* pages 1088–1089).

Phonological disorder is characterized by errors in sound production, substitutions of one sound for another, and omissions of sounds such as final consonants. The frequent misarticulations, word substitutions, and word omissions *may give the impression of "baby talk".*

In expressive language disorder, the child is below expected ability in vocabulary, use of correct tenses, and production of complex sentences. In *expressive language disorder* children *may forget old words as new words are learned, but comprehension is not affected.*

Elimination Disorders

Bowel and bladder control develop gradually over a period of time and are affected by a child's intelligence, social maturity, and relationship with his or her parents. The fourth edition of *Diagnostic and Statistical Manual of Mental Disorders* (DSM-IV) includes two elimination disorders, encopresis and enuresis.

Encopresis consists of a pattern of passing feces by a child with a developmental level of at least 4 years into inappropriate places either voluntarily or unintentionally.

In Western culture, bowel control is established in more than 95 percent of children by their fourth birthday. After the age of 4 years, encopresis occurs three or four times more often in boys than in girls. The cause of encopresis is usually a combination of factors. In some cases, children may be vulnerable based on physiologically ineffective sphincter control. Inadequate toilet training or lack of appropriate supervision can also contribute to the development of the disorder. In other instances, children refuse to control their sphincter muscles because of an ongoing power struggle with parents. Sometimes encopresis occurs around the time of the birth of a sibling or a move to a new home. Children who are sexually abused, especially boys who are abused rectally, may be more vulnerable to the disorder.

Once the disorder is established, secondary behavioral and emotional problems are likely to develop since the behavior is socially unacceptable. Children with encopresis often retain feces and become constipated, with resulting bowel distention. The chronic rectal distention may become a megacolon and the hard fecal mass may cause loss of tone in the rectal wall. In that case, the child may not feel the fecal pressure and may not be aware of the need to defecate, and small amounts of soft stool leak out.

In DSM-IV encopresis is divided into two types: (1) with constipation and overflow incontinence and (2) without constipation and overflow incontinence. In order to make the diagnosis of encopresis, medical conditions that cause megacolons, such as Hirschsprung's disease, must be ruled out. Treatment includes an assessment of constipation and a reasonable routine for trying to defecate. Behavioral interventions have also been helpful.

According to DSM-IV, the diagnosis of enuresis is not made until the child is chronologically or developmentally 5 years of age. Enuresis consists of repeated urination into clothes or bed, twice weekly, for at least three consecutive months, or the presence of clinically significant distress or functional impairment. According to DSM-IV, enuresis can be divided into nocturnal only, diurnal only, and nocturnal and diurnal. Additional psychiatric disorders occur in approximately 20 percent of children with enuresis. Enuretic children at highest risk for concurrent psychiatric disorders include girls, day and night enuretics, and children who continue to have symptoms, in later childhood. Children with enuresis are at higher risk of having developmental delays. Enuresis is not diagnosed, according to DSM-IV, if the urination is due to a medical condition.

Genetic and psychosocial factors are involved in the etiology of the disorder. Enuresis does not appear to be related to a specific stage of sleep (since it can occur any time) or to deeper than normal sleep. Some studies have indicated that enuretic children have bladders that are anatomically normal, but functionally feel full when there is a small amount of urine, so that there is an increased urge to void. Other studies have suggested that children with nighttime enuresis have a lower than expected level of antidiuretic hormone so that the bladder becomes full.

Over time, enuresis resolves spontaneously.

Treatment is useful for children whose enuresis interferes with daily activity, causes poor self-esteem and embarrassment, or compromises peer relationships. Treatment for enuresis consists of toilet training with praise and reinforcement. For some children, restricting fluids in the evening and waking the child during the night to urinate are helpful. The bell and pad apparatus which activates a bell to wake the child when the pad becomes wet is very effective for many children. Medications—such as imipramine (Tofranil) and intranasal desmopressin (DDAVP), an antidiuretic compound—have been useful, but relapse is likely when the medications are discontinued.

Students should study Chapter 44 in *Kaplan and Sadock's Synopsis VII,* and then test their knowledge with the questions and answers that follow.

HELPFUL HINTS

The student should know the following terms.

nocturnal bowel control	poor gastric mobility	bell (or buzzer) and pad
diurnal bowel control	behavioral reinforcement	fluid restriction
abnormal sphincter contractions	functionally small bladder	intranasal desmopressin (DDAVP)
rectal distention	low nocturnal antidiuretic hormone	thioridazine
overflow incontinence	obstructive urinary abnormality	Hirschsprung's disease
aganglionic megacolon	ego-dystonic enuresis	toilet training

QUESTIONS

DIRECTIONS: Each of the incomplete statements below is followed by five suggested completions. Select the *one* that is *best* in each case.

44.1. Encopresis
A. always occurs voluntarily
B. must occur at least once per week for at least three months
C. always occurs with constipation and overflow incontinence
D. is diagnosed only in a child who is chronologically or developmentally at least 6 years old
E. may be due to decreased rectal tone and desensitization of rectal pressure

44.2. Children with encopresis
A. may engage in the behavior when they are angry with their parents
B. have high rates of abnormal sphincter contractions
C. may have a fear of using the toilet
D. are at risk for short attention span, poor frustration tolerance, and hyperactivity
E. all the above

44.3. Enuresis
A. is more common in females than in males
B. according to DSM-IV, must occur once a month for at least three consecutive months
C. resolves spontaneously in most cases
D. is always intentional when it is diurnal
E. is not diagnosed until the child is chronologically or developmentally 3 years old

44.4. Risk factors for additional psychiatric disorders that coexist with enuresis include
A. being male
B. having symptoms both diurnally and nocturnally
C. children who have the symptoms in early childhood
D. patients with a family history of enuresis
E. having only nocturnal symptoms

44.5. All the following statements about enuresis (not due to a general medical condition) are true *except*
A. psychiatric problems are present in about 20 percent of enuretic children
B. males are more frequently enuretic than females
C. diurnal enuresis is much less common than nocturnal enuresis
D. enuresis is usually self-limited
E. psychotherapy alone is an effective treatment of enuresis

44.6. Enuresis can be defined as repeated voiding of urine into bed or cloth in children over the age of
A. 2 years
B. 3 years
C. 4 years
D. 5 years
E. 6 years

44.7. Encopretic children are frequently found to have
A. excessive emphasis placed on bowel habits
B. depressed mothers
C. critical fathers
D. gastrointestinal lesions
E. all the above

44.8. Organic causes of enuresis include
A. obstructive uropathy
B. urinary infection
C. diabetes mellitus
D. epilepsy
E. all the above

44.9. The treatment of enuresis includes
A. desmopressin
B. imipramine (Tofranil)
C. a star chart
D. restricting fluids
E. all the above

ANSWERS

Elimination Disorders

44.1.   The answer is E (*Synopsis VII*, page 1100).

Encopresis is the repeated passage of feces into inappropriate places. Many encopretic children retain feces and become constipated either voluntarily or secondary to painful defecation. Encopresis *may be due to decreased rectal tone and desensitization to rectal pressure.* Encopresis *occurs either involuntarily or voluntarily.* Encopresis must occur at least *once a month, not once a week, for at least three months* (Table 44.1). Encopresis *occurs with constipation and overflow incontinence* and without constipation and overflow incontinence. It *is diagnosed only in a child who is chronologically or developmentally at least 4 years old, not 6 years old.*

44.2.   The answer is E (all) (*Synopsis VII*, page 1100).

Encopresis may occur due to the contribution of a variety of physiologic and emotional factors. In some cases, children with encopresis have control over their bowel function and may *engage in the behavior when they are angry at their parents* or as a means of asserting control. Studies have also shown that children with encopresis who do not have gastrointestinal disorders *have high rates of abnormal sphincter contractions.* Abnormal sphincter contractions are especially prevalent in children with constipation and overflow incontinence. Those children have difficulty in relaxing their anal sphincters when trying to defecate, and are not likely to respond well to laxative treatment. Although not common, some children with encopresis may have a specific phobia or *may have a fear of using the toilet.* Children with encopresis are at risk for *short attention span, poor frustration tolerance, and hyperactivity.*

44.3.   The answer is C (*Synopsis VII*, page 1103).

Enuresis is the repeated voiding of urine into bed or clothes whether involuntarily or intentionally. Enuresis *resolves spontaneously in most cases* over time. It is *more common in males than in females.* Enuresis, *according to DSM-IV, must occur twice weekly, not once a month, for at least three consecutive months,* or manifest clear functional impairment due to enuresis (Table 44.2). Enuresis *is not always intentional when it is diurnal,* or nocturnal, although most children find their symptoms ego-dystonic and have enhanced self-esteem and improved social confidence when they become continent. According to DSM-IV enuresis is not diagnosed until the child is *chronologically or developmentally 5 years old, not 3 years old.*

44.4.   The answer is B (*Synopsis VII*, pages 1102–1103).

Psychiatric disorders are reported to occur in at least 20 percent of children with enuresis. Risk factors for additional psychiatric disorders include *hav-*

Table 44.1
Diagnostic Criteria for Encopresis

A. Repeated passage of feces into inappropriate places (e.g., clothing or floor) whether involuntary or intentional.

B. At least one such event a month for at least 3 months.

C. Chronological age is at least 4 years (or equivalent developmental level).

D. The behavior is not due exclusively to the direct physiological effects of a substance (e.g., laxatives) or a general medical condition except through a mechanism involving constipation.

Code as follows:
   With constipation and overflow incontinence
   Without constipation and overflow incontinence

Table from *DSM-IV, Diagnostic and Statistical Manual of Mental Disorders,* ed 4. Copyright American Psychiatric Association, Washington, 1994. Used with permission.

Table 44.2
Diagnostic Criteria for Enuresis

A. Repeated voiding of urine into bed or clothes (whether involuntary or intentional).

B. The behavior is clinically significant as manifested by either a frequency of twice a week for at least 3 consecutive months or the presence of clinically significant distress or impairment in social, academic (occupational), or other important areas of functioning.

C. Chronological age is at least 5 years (or equivalent developmental level).

D. The behavior is not due exclusively to the direct physiological effect of a substance (e.g., a diuretic) or a general medical condition (e.g., diabetes, spina bifida, a seizure disorder).

Specify type:
   Nocturnal only
   Diurnal only
   Nocturnal and diurnal

Table from DSM-IV, *Diagnostic and Statistical Manual of Mental Disorders,* ed 4. Copyright American Psychiatric Association, Washington, 1994. Used with permission.

ing symptoms both diurnally and nocturnally and *being female, not male. Children who have symptoms in late childhood* are also at higher risk for additional psychiatric disorders.

About 75 percent of children with enuresis have a first-degree relative with enuresis or who was enuretic, but there is no data to suggest that *patients with a family history of enuresis* are at risk for additional psychiatric disorders. *Having only nocturnal symptoms* puts a child at less risk for additional psychiatric disorders than children who have it both at night and during the day.

44.5.   The answer is E (*Synopsis VII,* page 1103).

Controlled studies have found that *psychotherapy alone is not an effective treatment of enuresis.* However, psychotherapy is useful in dealing with emotional and family difficulties that arise because of enuresis or with coexisting psychiatric problems.

Psychiatric problems are present in about 20 percent of enuretic children, and they are most common in enuretic girls and in children who wet both day and night.

Classical conditioning with the bell (or buzzer) and pad apparatus is the most effective and generally safe treatment for enuresis. Dryness results in more than 50 percent of cases. *Males are more frequently enuretic than females.*

Diurnal enuresis is much less common than nocturnal enuresis. Only about 2 percent of 5-year-olds have diurnal enuresis at least weekly. Unlike nocturnal enuresis, diurnal enuresis is more common in girls than in boys. Enuresis (not due to a general medical condition) *is usually self-limited.* The child can eventually remain dry with virtually no psychiatric sequelae. Although a medical cause precludes a diagnosis of enuresis (not due to a general medical condition) the correction of an anatomical defect or the cure of an infection does not always cure the enuresis, which suggests that the cause may still be at least partially psychological in some cases.

44.6.   The answer is D (*Synopsis VII,* page 1102).

Enuresis is manifested as a repetitive, inappropriate, involuntary passage of urine. Operationally, enuresis can be defined as repeated voiding of urine into bed or clothes in children over the age of *5 years* (or equivalent developmental level) who fail to inhibit the reflex to pass urine when the impulse is felt during waking hours, and in those who do not rouse from sleep of their own accord when the process is occurring during the sleeping state.

44.7.   The answer is E (all) (*Synopsis VII,* page 1100).

The child who fails to attain bowel control may soon suffer from hostile behavior by one or more family members. As the child associates with others outside the home, there is ridicule by peers and alienation from teachers.

There appears to be *excessive emphasis placed on*

bowel habits, and many encopretics seem to lack the sensory cues as to when they need to defecate. Psychologically, the patient remains blunted to the effect the disorder has on other people. Nevertheless, the child comes to feel unwanted and to have a low self-concept. Dynamically, encopretic children frequently have *depress mothers,* often dissatisfied with her marriage and maternal roles, compulsive, and emotionally unavailable. Such households have *critical fathers* who are emotionally distant, and often absent physically or psychologically or both.

A rash of mechanical problems may result in *gastrointestinal lesions* as the condition continues. The sufferer may require treatment for fissures, rectal prolapse, rectal excoriations, or impaction.

44.8.   The answer is E (all) (*Synopsis VII,* pages 1102–1103).

The combination of nocturnal and diurnal enuresis, especially in the patient with frequency and urgency, should signal the high possibility of an organic basis for the complaint.

Bed wetting may be the presenting symptom in children with *obstructive uropathy,* which is a physical blockage of the urinary tract. *Urinary infections* are often associated with enuresis.

Many enuretics are sleepwalkers, and they attempt to urinate during somnambulism. Therefore, sleepwalking must be differentiated from both enuresis and epilepsy.

In young children, the sudden development of enuresis is a common presentation of *diabetes mellitus,* which is characterized by polyuria (excessive output of urine), polydipsia (excessive intake of fluid), and polyphagia (excessive food intake). Diabetes mellitus is caused by insulin deficiency.

Another possibility to be ruled out is *epilepsy,* a neurological disorder resulting from a sudden, excessive, disorderly discharge of neurons in either a structurally normal or a diseased cerebral cortex. It is characterized by the paroxysmal recurrence of short-lived disturbances of consciousness, involuntary convulsive muscle movements, psychic or sensory disturbances, or some combination thereof. It is termed idiopathic epilepsy when there is no identifiable organic cause. The loss of urine or feces during the seizure is common.

Diagnoses to be considered when a child presents with enuresis include diabetes insipidus, spina bifida, lumbosacral myelodysplasia, sickle-cell anemia, foreign body, calculus, paraphimosis, vaginitis, mental retardation, the presence of intestinal parasites, and spinal tumors. Spinal tumors have a low incidence in childhood, but the loss of sphincter control in a child with progressive weakness, clumsiness, pain, and gait disturbance should alert the doctor to the possibility.

44.9.   The answer is E (all) (*Synopsis VII,* pages 1103).

Desmopressin (DDAVP), an antidiuretic administered intranasally, has been shown in initial studies to be effective in reducing enuresis in some cases. Drugs should rarely be used in treating enuresis and then only as a last resort in intractable cases that cause serious socioemotional difficulties for the sufferer. *Imipramine (Tofranil)* is efficacious and has been approved for use, primarily on a short-term basis, in treating childhood enuresis. Initially, up to 30 percent of enuretics may stay dry, and up to 85 percent may wet less frequently than before taking the medication. This effect, however, does not often last.

Tolerance often develops after six weeks of therapy; once the drug is discontinued, relapses and enuresis at former frequencies usually occur within a few months. A more serious problem is the drug's adverse effects, which include cardiotoxicity; therefore, the drug should not be used on a long-term basis. A *star chart,* a record-keeping device that rewards the child, is helpful in many cases. Other useful techniques include *restricting fluids* before bed and night lifting to toilet train the child.

Other Disorders of Infancy, Childhood, or Adolescence

In the fourth edition of *Diagnostic and Statistical Manual of Mental Disorders* (DSM-IV) the category of other disorders of infancy, childhood, or adolescence includes separation anxiety disorder, selective mutism, reactive attachment disorder of infancy or early childhood, stereotypic movement disorder, and disorder of infancy, childhood, or adolescence not otherwise specified (NOS).

In DSM-IV, separation anxiety disorder is the only anxiety disorder with specific criteria for onset in childhood included with disorders usually first diagnosed in infancy, childhood, or adolescence. It consists of developmentally inappropriate and excessive anxiety in a child, separating from a major attachment figure, usually the mother, and sometimes the father. The child often has a persistent worry that something will happen to the major attachment figure resulting in permanent separation. The child may refuse to go to school, in order to avoid being separated from family members. Fears of catastrophic events and fears of going to sleep without being near a major attachment figure are common features. Anxiety may take the form of multiple somatic complaints such as headaches and stomach pains when separations are anticipated.

Some degree of anxiety on separation is developmentally normal. It does not reach pathologic proportions until it causes impairment in usual activities for the child. Separation anxiety disorder is more common in young children than in adolescents and occurs equally in boys and girls. It occurs in 3 to 4 percent of school age children and in up to 1 percent of adolescents. Children with separation anxiety disorder often have parents with anxiety disorders such as panic disorder or agoraphobia. Anxious parents often communicate their fear to the child who learns that new situations or separations are to be feared. Separation anxiety disorder in adolescents is often more incapacitating than in a young child. A treatment approach that includes family education, family therapy, and individual cognitive-behavioral psychotherapy is helpful. In some cases, imipramine (Tofranil) may be used to reduce fear and panic related to separation.

Children with generalized anxiety symptoms not specifically related to separation who would have met the revised third edition of *Diagnostic and Statistical Manual of Mental Disorders* (DSM-III-R) criteria for overanxious disorder are now covered under the adult category of generalized anxiety disorder in DSM-IV. Children who manifest avoidant symptoms in relation to unfamiliar people but who have warm and satisfying relationships with their families are diagnosed with social phobia in DSM-IV. Additional anxiety disorders that also emerge in children and adolescents include specific phobias, panic disorder, obsessive-compulsive disorder, and posttraumatic stress disorder.

Selective mutism is an uncommon childhood disorder in which a child who is fluent with language consistently refuses to speak in a specific situation, usually in the school setting, or outside the home. Most children are silent in the mute situations, but they use communicative eye contact, head nods, and other nonverbal communication. Some children will whisper but not speak out loud. Children with selective mutism usually continue to speak fluently at home and in some familiar settings. The prevalence of selective mutism is rare and is found in fewer than 1 percent of individuals seen in mental health settings. It is more common in young children than in older children. The etiology of selective mutism is not clear. Some children with this disorder have histories of delayed onset of speech and are usually shy. Selective mutism may be a manifestation of social phobia since it is usually accompanied by social anxiety.

At least half of young children with selective mutism are significantly improved by age 10. Those who continue to be symptomatic after age 10 have a poorer prognosis. Individual psychotherapy and family therapy are used to treat selective mutism in conjunction with a school environment that is sensitive to the disability. Medications such as phenelzine (Nardil) are used in the treatment of selective mutism based on the observation that children with selective mutism have symptoms resembling social phobia.

Reactive attachment disorder consists of markedly disturbed and developmentally inappropriate social behaviors characterized either as a failure to respond to social situations or indiscriminate sociability and excessive familiarity with relative strangers. The behavior is not accounted for by developmental delay and is associated in all cases with pathogenic child rearing. Parental behavior characterized by chronic neglect or disregard of the child's emotional needs or physical needs is presumed to contribute to the child's inappropriate behavior. It is possible that the same social environment meets the social needs of one child satisfactorily, but is markedly inappropriate and insensitive for another.

Reactive attachment disorder is divided into two types: inhibited type, if a failure to respond to social interactions is a predominant symptom, and disinhibited type, if indiscriminate sociability is a predominant symptom. Infants with reactive attachment disorder show little spontaneous activity and decreased initiative of social behaviors toward others. Outcomes of children with reactive attachment disorder range from normal development to persistent abnormal social relatedness and in cases of severe deprivation, failure to thrive. Interventions are based on the recognition that the child's home life is damaging to the child's social development. The disorder often resolves partially or completely when the child is removed from the deprived environment and given nurturance.

Stereotypic movement disorder is characterized by repetitive, nonfunctional behaviors such as rocking, head banging, self-biting, picking, or waving that occur over a period of at least four weeks. The movements interfere with normal activities and in some cases result in injury if preventive measures are not used. Some repetitive behaviors such as nail biting are very common, affecting up to half of all school-age children. Other stereotypic movements such as thumb sucking and rocking are normal in young children but may cause functional impairment if they continue repeatedly in older children. Mentally retarded children and adolescents have an increased rate of stereotypic behaviors including self-injurious behaviors. Stereotypic movement disorder must be differentiated from obsessive-compulsive disorder and tic disorders. Treatment of stereotypic movement disorder must be specific to the symptom being treated and the child's developmental level. Behavioral techniques are sometimes useful. For cases in which the stereotypic behavior is injurious or causes severe impairment, antipsychotic medications, particularly haloperidol (Haldol), are helpful.

Disorder of infancy, childhood or adolescence not otherwise specified is a residual category for disorders that do not meet criteria for any other disorder but cause distress and impairment.

After completing Chapter 45 of *Kaplan and Sadock's Synopsis VII,* students should answer the questions below. A review of the answers and the explanations will help them assess their knowledge in the area.

HELPFUL HINTS

The student should know the following terms.

stress anxiety	selective mutism	indiscriminate familiarity
school refusal	inhibition to speak	lack of stable attachment
generalized anxiety	nonverbal gestures	failure to thrive
specific phobia	delayed language acquisition	"psychosocial dwarfism"
school phobia	social anxiety	stereotypic movements
major attachment figure	social phobia	driven, nonfunctional behavior
anticipatory anxiety	shy	self-injurious stereotypic acts
panic disorder	pathogenic caregiving	Lesch-Nyhan syndrome
desensitization	emotional physical neglect	sensory impairments
separation anxiety	failure to respond socially	dyskinetic movements

---

QUESTIONS

DIRECTIONS: Each of the incomplete statements below is followed by five suggested completions. Select the *one* that is *best* in each case.

45.1. A 16-year-old high school junior was referred by a teacher to the mental health clinic with the complaint that she was unable to make any verbal contributions in her classes. Her inability to speak had begun one year previously, after the death of her mother. It took school personnel some time to realize that she did not speak in any of her classes. She had kept up with her assignments, handing in all her written work and receiving better than average grades on tests.

The patient's father was a janitor in a large apartment building. Because of his work, he usually came home late and was rather passive and indifferent toward the patient and her six younger siblings. He had never responded to school requests for visits to discuss his daughter's problems. Since her mother's death, the patient had assumed the mothering of the siblings: cooking the meals, cleaning, and listening to their requests and complaints.

When seen, the patient was a thin, neatly dressed girl who was alert but responded only with brief nods of her head at first. With reassurance, she began to whisper monosyllabic answers to questions. Her responses were rational and logical, but she denied that her failure to speak was much of a problem. A younger sibling reported that the patient had no difficulty in speaking at home.

As described, the patient's symptoms characteristic of selective mutism include all the following *except*

A. no difficulty in speaking at home
B. difficulty speaking at school
C. communicates by nodding
D. her school performance
E. the onset followed an emotional trauma

45.2. Ten-month-old Molly was brought by her mother, at the suggestion of her pediatrician, for a consultation with a specialist in infant development. Her mother was most concerned because "Molly is not responding to me. She often won't look at me. She looks in the opposite direction. She won't smile, won't play, and bangs her hand on the table, looking angry. She throws toys on the floor. When I talk to her, she closes her eyes." Her mother also reported that her little girl was waking up three or four times each night and refusing to go back to sleep unless she stayed with her in the room, either holding her or stroking her back.

The current problems seemed to begin two months earlier, when Molly's mother, a busy attorney, went back to work full-time. The father, also an attorney, was quite angry at her for returning to work. He had wanted her to give up her career and stay at home. For the first month after she returned to work, Molly was cared for by a baby-sitter, who eventually was fired after a neighbor reported that the baby-sitter was frequently drunk and left Molly in her crib, with a bottle of formula, ignoring her cries. Although Molly's mother had suspected that the baby-sitter was far from ideal, she did not realize how bad she was until she heard about it from the neighbor. For the past month, Molly's care had been arranged on a day-to-day basis, and she had had six different baby-sitters.

During the last two months, because of sleepless nights and feeling overwhelmingly guilty about Molly's distress, yet at the same time feeling compelled to return to work or else "lose my status in my firm," Molly's mother had been "a nervous wreck." Now she blamed herself for all Molly's difficulties, saying, "I've done a terrible thing. Now, not only my husband doesn't love me, but Molly doesn't love me either."

Molly weighed eight pounds at birth and was in good health. The pregnancy had been unremarkable. The pediatrician's report revealed that Molly had slightly increased motor tone bilaterally, with no asymmetries, and tended to be overly sensitive to touch. For example, her mother reported that, when she tried to bathe Molly, the child would often scream and that she had to hold her with soft cotton blankets in order for her to feel comfortable. Molly was also very sensitive to loud noises, turning red and becoming rigid. She often cried if lights were too bright.

Molly had displayed social responsiveness by the fourth month but only if her parents worked hard and found just the right rhythm of sound and "funny faces." By age 6 months she was able to reach for objects, but her parents reported that, if they handed her something, she would often try to knock it out of their hands, rather than grab it.

Molly had always been a fussy eater but nonetheless was gaining adequate weight and was in the 80th percentile for size and weight. Her pediatrician said that her overall physical health was good and that, in terms of motor milestones, she was doing fine.

During the evaluation, the impression of Molly as physically healthy was confirmed. Her gross and fine motor functioning were age-appropriate. Observation of parent-infant interaction revealed an infant who held her body stiffly, looked away from her parents' eyes, and reacted to their vocalization by arching her back. When offered interesting objects, she would usually grab another object or knock the offered object away. Her facial expression was angry and tense. Her mother appeared depressed, and her interaction with Molly had a mechanical quality. Molly's father was impatient and abrupt with her.

The features of Molly's disorder include
A. excessive response to social stimulation
B. stranger anxiety
C. grossly pathogenic care
D. extreme interest in the environment
E. mental retardation

45.3. Separation anxiety disorder
A. is a developmental phase
B. accounts for the most anxiety in childhood
C. has its most common onset at 1 to 2 years of age
D. is less serious when it occurs in adolescence
E. always involves refusal to go to school

45.4. Selective mutism
A. is a disorder in which a child who is not fluent in language consistently fails to speak in certain situations
B. is not associated with an increased risk for separation anxiety disorder
C. often occurs in children who are shy and show anxiety in social situations
D. is more common in boys than in girls
E. usually resolves by 5 years of age

45.5. All of the following may be characteristic of reactive attachment disorder of infancy or early childhood *except*
A. inhibited, withdrawn, and socially unresponsive behavior
B. excessive familiarity with relative strangers
C. chronically emotionally neglectful home environment
D. lack of stable attachment to primary caregiver
E. a pervasive developmental disorder

45.6. In stereotypic movement disorder
A. the behaviors are always specified as intentional
B. the diagnosis can be made with mental retardation or a pervasive developmental disorder
C. hair pulling (trichotillomania) is the sole symptom
D. the diagnosis is made only if the symptoms are not better accounted for by a compulsion (as in obsessive-compulsive disorder) or a tic (as in tic disorder)
E. the age at onset is 7 years

45.7. Separation anxiety in children is characterized by
A. fears that a loved one will be hurt
B. fears about getting lost
C. irritability
D. animal and monster phobias
E. all the above

45.8. Reactive attachment disorder of infancy or early childhood
A. may be reversed shortly after institution of adequate caregiving
B. includes a normal head circumference and a failure to gain weight disproportionately greater than the failure to gain length
C. is usually associated with gross emotional neglect or imposed social isolation in an institution
D. is indicated by a lack of developmentally appropriate signs of social responsivity
E. all the above

DIRECTIONS: The lettered headings below are followed by a list of numbered phrases. For each numbered phrase, select the *best* lettered heading. Each heading may be used once, more than once or not at all.

Questions 45.9–45.12
A. Separation anxiety disorder
B. Selective mutism
C. Reactive attachment disorder
D. Stereotypic movement disorder

45.9. Associated with grossly pathogenic caregiving

45.10. Becomes difficult to treat when the major attachment figure also has the disorder

45.11. Often manifests only outside the home

45.12. Some symptoms—such as rocking or thumb sucking—are considered developmentally normal, self-comforting behaviors when they occur in very young children

ANSWERS

Other Disorders of Infancy, Childhood, or Adolescence

45.1. The answer is D (*Synopsis VII,* page 1108–1109).

As described, the one symptom of the 16-year-old high school junior not typically characteristic of selective mutism is *her school performance.* She kept up with her assignments, handed in all her written work, and received better than average grades. Children with selective mutism generally have *no difficulty in speaking at home,* but they do have difficulty elsewhere, especially *difficulty speaking at school.* Consequently, they often have significant academic difficulties and even failure. Some children with selective mutism *communicate by nodding* or saying "umm-hum," which may be their initial responses to a therapist. In some children *the onset follows an emotional trauma* or a physical trauma. As in this case, the inability to speak can begin after the death of a parent. Table 45.1 lists the diagnostic criteria for selective mutism.

45.2. The answer is C (*Synopsis VII,* page 1100).

Molly's disorder is reactive attachment disorder of infancy or early childhood. The disorder is characterized by *grossly pathogenic care,* persistent failure to initiate or respond to most social interactions, not *excessive response to social stimulation; and* in-

Table 45.1
Diagnostic Criteria for Selective Mutism

A. Consistent failure to speak in specific social situations (in which there is an expectation for speaking, e.g., at school) despite speaking in other situations.

B. The disturbance interferes with educational or occupational achievement or with social communication.

C. The duration of the disturbance is at least 1 month (not limited to the first month of school).

D. The failure to speak is not due to a lack of knowledge of, or comfort with, the spoken language required in the social situation.

E. The disturbance is not better accounted for by a communication disorder (e.g., stuttering) and does not occur exclusively during the course of a pervasive developmental disorder, schizophrenia, or other psychotic disorder.

Table from DSM-IV, *Diagnostic and Statistical Manual of Mental Disorders,* ed 4. Copyright American Psychiatric Association, Washington, 1994. Used with permission.

discriminate sociability, not *stranger anxiety.* Children with this disorder often demonstrate listlessness and disinterest in the environment, not *extreme interest in the environment.*

The disturbance in relatedness in reactive attachment disorder of infancy or early childhood is not a symptom of *mental retardation* or a pervasive developmental disorder. Table 45.2 presents the diagnostic criteria for the disorder.

45.3. The answer is B (*Synopsis VII,* page 1104).

Separation anxiety disorder *accounts for the most anxiety in children,* affecting up to 4 percent of school-age boys and girls. Unlike many other childhood psychiatric disorders, it has been reported to occur in boys and girls equally. While separation anxiety is a developmentally appropriate response to various situations especially in young children, separation anxiety disorder *is not a developmental stage.* The disorder is characterized by impaired function and *has its most common onset at 7 to 8 years of age.* Separation anxiety disorder *is usually more serious when it is seen in adolescence* than when it is seen in childhood. Separation anxiety disorder consists of persistent worry about losing a parent or harm befalling a child's major attachment figure. Separation anxiety disorder *sometimes, but not always, involves refusal to go to school* in order to avoid separating from the parent, but not in all cases. The diagnostic criteria for separation anxiety disorder are presented in Table 45.3.

45.4. The answer is C (*Synopsis VII,* page 1108).

Selective mutism *often occurs in children who are shy and show anxiety in social situations.* Some clinicians believe that selective mutism is a form of social phobia. Selective mutism *is a disorder in which a child who is fluent with language consistently fails to speak in certain situations* in which it is expected, such as in school. Selective mutism *is associated with an increased risk for separation anxiety disorder* and other anxiety symptoms. The prevalence of selective mutism is rare and is found in fewer than 1 percent of individuals seen in mental health settings. Young children are more vulnerable and the disorder *is more common in girls than boys.* Selective mutism has an onset usually before 5 years of age, but *does not usually resolve by 5 years of age.* Half of children with this disorder show improvement by age 10.

Table 45.2
Diagnostic Criteria for Reactive Attachment Disorder of Infancy or Early Childhood

A. Markedly disturbed and developmentally inappropriate social relatedness in most contexts, beginning before age 5 years, as evidenced by either (1) or (2):

(1) persistent failure to initiate or respond in a developmentally appropriate fashion to most social interactions, as manifest by excessively inhibited, hypervigilant, or highly ambivalent and contradictory responses (e.g., the child may respond to caregivers with a mixture of approach, avoidance, and resistance to comforting, or may exhibit frozen watchfulness)

(2) diffuse attachments as manifest by indiscriminate sociability with marked inability to exhibit appropriate selective attachments (e.g., excessive familiarity with relative strangers or lack of selectivity in choice of attachment figures)

B. The disturbance in criterion A is not accounted for solely by developmental delay (as in mental retardation) and does not meet criteria for a pervasive developmental disorder.

C. Pathogenic care as evidenced by at least one of the following:

(1) persistent disregard of the child's basic emotional needs for comfort, stimulation, and affection

(2) persistent disregard of the child's basic physical needs

(3) repeated changes of primary caregiver that prevent formation of stable attachments (e.g., frequent changes in foster care)

D. There is a presumption that the care in criterion C is responsible for the disturbed behavior in criterion A (e.g., the disturbances in criterion A began following the pathogenic care in criterion C).

Specify type:
Inhibited Type: if criterion A1 predominates in the clinical presentation
Disinhibited Type: if criterion A2 predominates in the clinical presentation

Table from DSM-IV, *Diagnostic and Statistical Manual of Mental Disorders,* ed 4. Copyright American Psychiatric Association, Washington, 1994. Used with permission.

45.5. **The answer is E** (*Synopsis VII,* pages 1111–1112).

Reactive attachment disorder of infancy or early childhood is a disturbance of social interaction and relatedness, based largely on grossly inappropriate caregiving such as neglect of a child's basic physical or emotional needs. Reactive attachment disorder of infancy or early childhood cannot be accounted for by *a pervasive developmental disorder* (Table 45.2). Characteristic of reactive attachment disorder of infancy or early childhood include *inhibited, withdrawn, and socially unresponsive behavior, excessive familiarity with relative strangers, chronically emotionally neglectful home environment,* and *lack of stable attachment to primary caregiver.*

45.6. **The answer is D** (*Synopsis VII,* page 1113).

In stereotypic movement disorder (Table 45.4) *the diagnosis is made only if the symptoms are not better*

Table 45.3
Diagnostic Criteria for Separation Anxiety Disorder

A. Developmentally inappropriate and excessive anxiety concerning separation from home or from those to whom the individual is attached, as evidenced by three (or more) of the following:

(1) recurrent excessive distress when separation from home or major attachment figures occurs or is anticipated

(2) persistent and excessive worry about losing, or about possible harm befalling, major attachment figures

(3) persistent and excessive worry that an untoward event will lead to separation from a major attachment figure (e.g., getting lost or being kidnapped)

(4) persistent reluctance or refusal to go to school or elsewhere because of fear of separation

(5) persistently and excessively fearful or reluctant to be alone or without major attachment figures at home or without significant adults in other settings

(6) persistent reluctance or refusal to go to sleep without being near a major attachment figure or to sleep away from home

(7) repeated nightmares involving the theme of separation

(8) repeated complaints of physical symptoms (such as headaches, stomachaches, nausea, or vomiting) when separation from major attachment figures occurs or is anticipated

B. The duration of the disturbance is at least 4 weeks.

C. The onset is before age 18 years.

D. The disturbance causes clinically significant distress or impairment in social, academic (occupational), or other important areas of functioning.

E. The disturbance does not occur exclusively during the course of a pervasive developmental disorder, schizophrenia, or other psychotic disorder and, in adolescents and adults, is not better accounted for by panic disorder with agoraphobia.

Specify if:
Early onset: if onset occurs before age 6 years

Table from DSM-IV, *Diagnostic and Statistical Manual of Mental Disorders,* ed 4. Copyright American Psychiatric Association, Washington, 1994. Used with permission.

accounted for by a compulsion (as in obsessive-compulsive disorder), or a tic (as in tic disorder). Stereotypic movement disorder is defined by repetitive seemingly driven and non-functional motor behavior such as rocking, head banging, self-biting, picking and waving. Although the revised third edition of *Diagnostic and Statistical Manual of Mental Disorders* (DSM-III-R) had specified the behaviors as being intentional, *the behaviors are not specified as intentional in in the fourth edition (DSM-IV).* In stereotypic movement disorder, *the diagnosis can be made with mental retardation or a pervasive developmental disorder* as long as the stereotypic behavior is of sufficient severity to become a focus of treatment. Stereotypic movement disorder is not diagnosed when *hair pulling (trichotillomania) is the sole symptom.* Stereotypic movement disorder often contains self-injurious behaviors, and when self-injurious behav-

Table 45.4
Diagnostic Criteria for Stereotypic Movement Disorder

A. Repetitive, seemingly driven, and nonfunctional motor behavior (e.g., hand shaking or waving, body rocking, head banging, mouthing of objects, self-biting, picking at skin or bodily orifices, hitting own body).

B. The behavior markedly interferes with normal activities or results in self-inflicted bodily injury that requires medical treatment (or would result in an injury if preventive measures were not used).

C. If mental retardation is present, the stereotypic or self-injurious behavior is of sufficient severity to become a focus of treatment.

D. The behavior is not better accounted for by a compulsion (as in obsessive-compulsive disorder), a tic (as in tic disorder), a stereotypy that is part of a pervasive developmental disorder, or hair pulling (as in trichotillomania).

E. The behavior is not due to the direct physiological effects of a substance or a general medical condition.

F. The behavior persists for 4 weeks or longer.

Specify if:
   With self-injurious behavior: if the behavior results in bodily damage that requires specific treatment (or that would result in bodily damage if protective measures were not used)

Table from DSM-IV, *Diagnostic and Statistical Manual of Mental Disorders,* ed 4. Copyright American Psychiatric Association, Washington, 1994. Used with permission.

ior is present it must be specified, according to DSM-IV whether the behavior would result in bodily damage if protective measures were not used. There is *no typical age of onset.* The onset may follow a stressful environmental event.

45.7.   The answer is E (all) (*Synopsis VII,* pages 1105–1106).

Morbid fears, preoccupations, and ruminations are characteristic of separation anxiety in children. Children have *fears that a loved one will be hurt* or that something terrible will happen to them when they are away from important caring figures. Many children worry that accidents or illness will befall their parents or themselves. *Fears about getting lost* and about being kidnapped and never again finding their parents are common. Young children express less specific, more generalized concerns because their immature cognitive development precludes the formation of well-defined fears. In older children, fears of getting lost may include elaborate fantasies around kidnappings, being harmed, being raped, or being made slaves.

When separation from an important figure is imminent, children show many premonitory signs, such as *irritability,* difficulty in eating, and complaining and whining behavior. Physical complaints, such as vomiting or headaches, are common when separation

is anticipated or actually happens. These difficulties increase in intensity and organization with age because the older child is able to anticipate anxiety in a more structured fashion. Thus, there is a continuum between mild anticipatory anxiety before a threatened separation and pervasive anxiety after the separation has occurred.

Animal and monster phobias are common, as are concerns about dying. The child, when threatened with separation, may become fearful that events related to muggers, burglars, car accidents, or kidnapping may occur.

45.8.   The answer is E (all) (*Synopsis VII,* pages 1109–1111).

The essential features of reactive attachment disorder of infancy are signs of poor emotional and physical development, with onset before 8 months of age, and are due to a lack of adequate caretaking. Reactive attachment disorder of infancy or early childhood *may be reversed shortly after institution of adequate caregiving.* The disturbance is not due to a physical disorder, mental retardation, or autistic disorder. The disorder *includes a normal head circumference and a failure to gain weight disproportionately greater than the failure to gain length, is usually associated with gross emotional neglect or imposed social isolation in an institution,* and *is indicated by a lack of developmentally appropriate signs of social responsivity.*

45.9–45.12

45.9.   The answer is C (*Synopsis VII,* page 1110).

45.10.   The answer is A (*Synopsis VII,* pages 1105–1107).

45.11.   The answer is B (*Synopsis VII,* page 1109).

45.12.   The answer is D (*Synopsis VII,* pages 1113–1114).

Reactive attachment disorder is a disorder of social relatedness that is *associated with grossly pathogenic caregiving,* in the form of emotional or physical neglect or multiple caretakers precluding the development of attachments. *Separation anxiety disorder* in children *becomes difficult to treat when the major attachment figure also has separation anxiety disorder.* In such a case the attachment figure (usually the mother) exposes the child to her own anxiety thereby reinforcing the child's discomfort. Treatment for separation anxiety includes the major attachment figure encouraging the child to separate and reinforcing a positive reunion after the separation. *Selective mutism* is a disorder *that often manifests only outside the home* so that at home it is not apparent. In separation anxiety disorder, sometimes symptoms are also not evident at home when the major attachment figure is home, but symptoms would emerge in the home if the mother left and the separation occurred there. In *stereotypic movement disorder some symptoms—such as rocking or thumb sucking—are considered developmentally normal,* *self-comforting behaviors when they occur in very young children.* However, the symptoms can cause functional impairment if they continue into middle childhood and are manifested in socially unacceptable situations.

Mood Disorders and Suicide

Mood disorders in children and adolescents have received increasing attention over the last few decades. The diagnostic criteria in the fourth edition of *Diagnostic and Statistical Manual of Mental Disorders* (DSM-IV) for major depressive disorder, dysthymic disorder, and bipolar I disorder are the same for children and adolescents as for adults, with some minor modifications. Major depressive disorder consists of depressed mood or a loss of interest or pleasure, along with other features such as weight changes, sleep disturbances, feelings of worthlessness, guilt, psychomotor agitation or retardation, diminished ability to concentrate, and recurrent thoughts of death or suicide. There are several modifications in the DSM-IV diagnostic criteria for major depressive disorder in children and adolescents. In children and adolescents, irritable mood may take the place of depressed mood, and a failure to make expected weight gain may take the place of significant weight loss or weight gain. In dysthymic disorder, symptoms such as poor self-esteem, hopelessness, social withdrawal, anger, or guilt may accompany the depressed or irritable mood. The disturbance should last for at least one year to make the diagnosis. The criteria for bipolar I disorder are identical for children, adolescents, and adults.

Although the core features of mood disorders are the same regardless of age, some symptoms are more prevalent in very young children and other symptoms predominate in adolescents or adults. For example, somatic complaints, mood-congruent hallucinations, and sad appearance are more commonly seen in young children than in adults, whereas the frequency of pervasive anhedonia, psychomotor retardation, delusions, and a sense of hopelessness increase with age. Depressed children often complain of a lack of friends and of being picked on by peers. Their complaints may continue even after the episode of depression resolves. Some features such as suicidal ideation, depressed or irritable mood, insomnia, and diminished ability to concentrate present with equal frequency at all ages.

Children's moods are particularly vulnerable to the influence of severe social stressors such as family discord, abuse, neglect, and failure in school. Many young children with severe depression have endured harmful family and environmental conditions. Mood disorders increase in frequency with age. The rate of major depressive disorder in preschool children has been estimated to be about 0.3 percent. In school-age children, major depressive disorder is estimated to occur in up to 2 percent and predominates more in boys than in girls. In adolescents, major depressive disorder is estimated to occur in up to 5 percent and is more common in girls than in boys. School-age children with dysthymic disorder have a very high rate of developing a major depressive episode after the one year required to make the dysthymic disorder diagnosis. In adolescents and adults, major depressive disorder is more common than dysthymic disorder. The rate of bipolar I disorder is extremely low in prepubertal children, and the diagnosis may not be made for years because the onset of a manic episode usually does not occur until adolescence. The lifetime prevalence rate of bipolar I disorder in adolescents is estimated to be about 0.6 percent.

Suicidal ideation and attempts are frequently but not necessarily associated with mood disorders. Suicide attempts occur three times more often in female adolescents than in male adolescents, but completed suicide occurs four to five times more often in male adolescents than in female adolescents. The suicide rate is estimated to be less than 1 in 100,000 in children under 14 years of age. In adolescents from 15 to 19 years, the suicide rate is estimated to be about 14 per 100,000 for males, and 3 per 100,000 females. The actual risk of suicide is low in children under 12 years of age since their plans are often unrealistic. In the United States, the most common method of suicide among children and adolescents is the use of a gun, which accounts for about 66 percent of suicides in adolescent boys, and about 50 percent of suicides in girls. The second most common method of suicide in male adolescents is hanging, whereas the second most common method in female adolescents is the ingestion of toxic substances. Universal features of suicidal adolescents include an inability to solve problems and a lack of coping strategies. Risk factors for suicide in adolescents include a previous suicide attempt, being male, a history of violent or aggressive behavior, a history of substance abuse, a depressive disorder, and access to a gun. In girls, risk factors include a previous suicide attempt, pregnancy, a history of running away, and a mood disorder. Any child or adolescent must be hospitalized if there is persistent suicidal ideation, or a family that is incapable of cooperating with outpatient treatment.

Students should read Chapter 46 of *Kaplan and Sadock's Synopsis VII* and then test their knowledge of the area by studying the questions and answers below.

HELPFUL HINTS

The student should study the terms below.

irritable mood	REM latency	social withdrawal
environmental stressors	insidious onset	sad appearance
developmental symptoms	somatic complaints	double depression
poor concentration	boredom	precipitants of suicide
family history	temper tantrums	poor problem solving
psychosocial deficits	academic failure	lethal methods
cortisol hypersecretion	hallucinations	

QUESTIONS

DIRECTIONS: Each of the questions or incomplete statements below is followed by five suggested responses or completions. Select the *one* that is *best* in each case.

46.1. Major depressive disorder in school-age children
A. may present with irritable mood rather than depressed mood
B. usually includes pervasive anhedonia
C. is more common than dysthymic disorder
D. includes mood-congruent auditory hallucinations less often than in adults with the disorder
E. occurs more often in girls than in boys

46.2. Which of the following symptoms of major depressive disorder are equally common in all age groups?
A. Suicidal ideation
B. Somatic complaints
C. Mood-congruent auditory hallucinations
D. Pervasive anhedonia
E. all the above

46.3. Suicide in adolescents
A. decreases in frequency with increasing age
B. occurs more often in teenagers that are 12 to 14 years of age than in teenagers that are 14 to 16 years of age
C. is more common in girls than in boys
D. is almost always associated with a mood disorder
E. is often precipitated by arguments with family members, girlfriends, or boyfriends

46.4. Risk factors for adolescent suicide include all of the following *except*
A. being female
B. previous suicide attempts
C. a history of substance abuse
D. a history of aggressive behavior
E. being male

DIRECTIONS: Each set of lettered headings below is followed by a list of numbered words or phrases. For each numbered word or phrase, select

    A. if the item is associated with *A only*
    B. if the item is associated with *B only*
    C. if the item is associated with *both A and B*
    D. if the item is associated with *neither A nor B*

Questions 46.5–46.8
    A. Major depressive disorder
    B. Dysthymic disorder
    C. Both
    D. Neither

46.5. Occurs first in double depression

46.6. Mood-congruent auditory hallucinations are not uncommon

46.7. The prevalence increases with age

ANSWERS

Mood Disorders and Suicide

46.1.   The answer is A (*Synopsis VII*, page 1116).

Major depression in school-age children is essentially the same disorder that occurs in adolescents and adults. One modification in the fourth edition of *Diagnostic and Statistical Manual of Mental Disorders* (DSM-IV) criteria for major depressive disorder in children and adolescents is that it *may present with irritable mood rather than depressed mood.* Major depressive disorder in children *rarely includes pervasive anhedonia.* It is *less common than dysthymic disorder* in school-age children, but it is more common than dysthymic disorder in adolescence. The disorder in children includes *mood-congruent auditory hallucinations more often than in adults with this disorder.* It *occurs more often in boys than in girls* in this age group.

46.2.   The answer is A (*Synopsis VII*, page 1116).

Suicidal ideation occurs equally in patients with major depressive disorder in all age groups. Although the core features of major depressive disorder are essentially the same in children, adolescents, and adults, specific symptoms are predominant at different ages. In depressed school age children, *somatic complaints* and *mood-congruent auditory hallucinations* present more often than in depressed adolescents or adults. Mood congruent delusions and *pervasive anhedonia* increase with age, and are more common in adolescents and adults than in young children.

46.3.   The answer is E (*Synopsis VII*, page 1122).

Suicide in adolescents *is often precipitated by arguments with family members, girlfriends, or boyfriends.* Completed suicide is almost non-existent in children under 12 years of age and *increases in frequency with increasing age.* Thus, suicide *occurs more often in teenagers that are 14 to 16 years of age than in teenagers that are 12 to 14 years of age.* Suicide attempts are about three times more common in adolescent girls than in boys, but completed suicide

is more common in boys than in girls. That is primarily due to the increased lethality of the methods that male adolescents use. The most common method of suicide in male adolescents is the use of guns, accounting for $2/3$ of male suicides. Guns account for $1/2$ of completed suicides among female adolescents. The second most common method of suicide in male adolescents is hanging. *Ingestions are a very uncommon method of completed suicides in males,* although they are common nonlethal methods used in suicide attempts by adolescent females. Suicide *is not always associated with a mood disorder,* although the risk of suicide increases when existing mood disorders are severe.

46.4.   The answer is A (*Synopsis VII*, page 1120).

Being female is not a risk factor for adolescent suicide. Female adolescents are more likely to attempt suicide by ingesting pills or a toxic substance, but the results are often non-lethal. Risk factors for suicide in adolescents include *previous suicide attempts, a history of substance abuse,* and *a history of aggressive behavior.*

46.5–46.8

46.5.   The answer is B (*Synopsis VII*, page 1118).

46.6.   The answer is A (*Synopsis VII*, page 1118).

46.7.   The answer is C (*Synopsis VII*, pages 1116–1117).

Double-depression is when dysthymic disorder and major depressive disorder are both present. Usually *dysthymic disorder occurs first in double-depression,* and then major depressive disorders presents some time after the first year of dysthymia. *Mood-congruent auditory hallucinations are not uncommon* in school-age children with *major depressive disorder.* In *both* dysthymic disorder and major depressive disorder, *the prevalence increases with age.*

Schizophrenia With Childhood Onset

Schizophrenia with childhood onset is essentially the same disorder as seen in adolescence and adults. In prepubertal children, schizophrenia includes at least two of the following symptoms over a period of one month: hallucinations, delusions, grossly disorganized speech or behavior, or severe withdrawal. According to the fourth edition of *Diagnostic and Statistical Manual of Mental Disorders* (DSM-IV), social or academic dysfunction must be present, and continuous signs of disturbance must persist for a period of at least six months. The only modification of the diagnostic criteria for schizophrenia when onset occurs in childhood is that children may fail to achieve expected levels of social or academic functioning rather than show deterioration from their previous level of functioning. In the past, the term "childhood psychosis" was used to identify a heterogeneous group of children with symptoms that covered pervasive developmental disorders and psychotic disorders. Currently, the diagnostic criteria for pervasive developmental disorders do not include psychotic symptoms, but schizophrenia may be diagnosed in autistic children if hallucinations or delusions emerge as prominent features.

Schizophrenia in prepubertal children is rare; it occurs less frequently than autistic disorder. In adolescents, the prevalence of schizophrenia is estimated to be 1 to 2 per 1,000 (50 times greater than the rate in prepubertal children). Boys seem to become symptomatic at an earlier age than girls, and schizophrenia appears to be slightly more common in boys than in girls. The prevalence of schizophrenia in a parent of a schizophrenic child is about 8 percent, almost double the rate of schizophrenia in a parent of an adult-onset schizophrenic.

Family and genetic studies provide substantial evidence of a biological contribution to the development of schizophrenia, although no specific biological markers have been identified. The genetic transmission pattern in schizophrenia remains unknown, but it appears that there is more genetic loading for schizophrenia in relatives of probands who present with schizophrenia in childhood. There is no way, however, to identify vulnerable children at highest risk for the development of schizophrenia within a given family.

However, environmental factors also influence the onset of schizophrenia in children and in adults. Children and adolescents who develop schizophrenia are more likely to have premorbid histories of social rejection, poor peer relationships, clingy withdrawn behavior, and academic difficulties than patients with adult-onset schizophrenia. Some childhood schizophrenics have early histories of delayed motor milestones as well as delayed language acquisition.

Auditory hallucinations are commonly manifested by children with schizophrenia. They may hear several voices making an ongoing critical commentary about the child, or command hallucinations may tell the children to kill themselves or others. The voices may be of a bizarre nature, identified as a "computer in my head" or Martians or the voice of someone familiar, such as a relative.

Visual hallucinations are experienced by a significant number of children with schizophrenia and are often frightening; the children may see the devil, skeletons, scary faces, or space creatures. Transient phobic visual hallucinations also occur in traumatized children who do not go on to have a major psychotic disorder.

Delusions are present in at least half of schizophrenic children and may take various forms (for example, persecutory, religious, grandiose). Delusions increase in frequency with increasing age. Blunted or inappropriate affect, loosening of associations, thought blocking, illogical thinking, and poverty of thought are part of the clinical presentation of schizophrenia in children. Core features are similar in schizophrenics of different ages, but age and developmental level influence the ways symptoms present. For example, delusions are less complex in young children than in adolescents and often reflect animal imagery (such as "scary monsters").

The course and prognosis of childhood-onset schizophrenia depends on the child's premorbid level of functioning, the age of onset of the disorder, the degree of recompensation after the initial episode, the child's intellectual functioning, and the degree of support available from the family. Children with compromised premorbid functioning, including developmental delays and premorbid behavior disorders seem to be at risk for poor medication response and guarded outcome.

In general, schizophrenia with childhood on-

set appears to be less responsive to medication than late adolescent-onset or adult-onset schizophrenia. The treatment of schizophrenia with childhood onset includes family education, family support, psychopharmacologic intervention, and appropriate educational placement for the child.

Dopamine receptor antagonists and other antipsychotic medications are used to treat schizophrenia with childhood onset. The high potency drugs (for example, haloperidol [Haldol]) are favored because of the decreased sedative effects. Several case studies have shown treatment-resistant adolescents tolerating and being treated successfully with clozapine (Clozaril).

Readers are referred to Chapter 47 of *Kaplan and Sadock's Synopsis VII* and should then study the questions and answers below to assess their knowledge of the subject.

HELPFUL HINTS

The student should understand the terms below.

childhood psychosis	transient phobic hallucinations	haloperidol (Haldol)
autistic disorder	persecutory delusions	clozapine (Clozaril)
schizotypal personality	premorbid disorders	agranulocytosis
disturbed communication	family support	hypersalivation
expressed emotion	visual hallucinations	sedation
delayed motor development	premorbid functioning	tardive dyskinesia
social rejection		

QUESTIONS

DIRECTIONS: Each of the incomplete statements below is followed by five suggested completions. Select the *one* that is *best* in each case.

47.1. Predictors of poor prognosis in schizophrenia with childhood onset include all the following *except*
A. misdiagnosed schizophrenia in a child with bipolar I disorder
B. onset before 10 years of age
C. premorbid diagnoses of attention-deficit/hyperactivity disorder and learning disorders
D. lack of family support
E. delayed motor milestones and delayed language acquisition

47.2. All the following statements about the difficulties of diagnosing schizophrenia in adolescents are true *except*
A. patients may initially appear depressed
B. psychotic symptoms may be a normal feature of adolescence
C. substance abuse may cloud the clinical picture
D. adolescents tend to act-out defenses
E. all the above

47.3. Schizophrenia with childhood onset differs from schizophrenia with adult onset in that
A. schizophrenic children do not manifest command auditory hallucinations
B. parents of childhood-onset schizophrenia patients are less likely than parents of adult-onset schizophrenia patients to also be schizophrenic
C. in children with schizophrenia there is often a premorbid history of behavior disorders, delayed motor milestones, and delayed language acquisition
D. childhood schizophrenics respond more to medication than do adult schizophrenics
E. Childhood-onset schizophrenics are usually mildly mentally retarded

DIRECTIONS: The lettered headings below are followed by a list of numbered words or phrases. For each numbered word or phrase, select:

    A. if the item is associated with *A only*
    B. if the item is associated with *B only*
    C. if the item is associated with *both A and B*
    D. if the item is associated with *neither A nor B*

Questions 47.4–47.5
    A. Haloperidol (Haldol)
    B. Clozapine (Clozaril)
    C. Both
    D. Neither

47.4. Effective in diminishing positive symptoms in schizophrenia such as auditory hallucinations

47.5. Generally does not induce extrapyramidal side effects

47.6. Associated with agranulocytosis

ANSWERS

Schizophrenia With Childhood Onset

47.1. The answer is A (*Synopsis VII,* page 1127).

Misdiagnosed schizophrenia in a child with bipolar I disorder is a factor in a good prognosis, not a poor prognosis. Although prospective studies are needed, factors that seem to predict poor prognosis in schizophrenia with childhood onset are *onset before the age of 10 years, premorbid diagnoses of attention-deficit/hyperactivity disorder and learning disorders, lack of family support,* and an early history of *delayed motor milestones and delayed language acquisition.*

47.2. The answer is B (*Synopsis VII,* pages 1125–1126).

Psychotic symptoms are never a normal feature of adolescence; there is no developmentally normal psychosis of adolescence.

Diagnosing schizophrenia in adolescents may be difficult because *patients may initially appear depressed* and *substance abuse may cloud the clinical picture.* Schizophrenia is not fundamentally different when it occurs in adolescence, compared with other age groups. However, there are some variations. Patients who are actually schizophrenic may look depressed; and they become withdrawn and isolated, and have impaired eating and sleeping habits. In addition, *adolescents tend to act-out defenses,* that is, they externalize conflicts onto the environment to avoid the pain of loss or the feeling of being helpless and hopeless. This acting out may take the form of drug abuse, promiscuity, and delinquency.

47.3. The answer is C (*Synopsis VII,* pages 1124–1125).

Schizophrenia with childhood onset is recognized as the same disorder as is seen in adolescents and adults. But *in children with schizophrenia there is often a premorbid history of behavior disorders, de-* *layed motor milestones, and delayed language acquisition. Schizophrenic children manifest command auditory hallucinations* similar to adult schizophrenia patients. Yet, there have been reports of increased genetic loading in childhood-onset schizophrenics. *Parents of childhood-onset schizophrenia patients are more likely, not less likely, than parents of adult-onset schizophrenia patients to also be schizophrenic;* about 8 percent of first degree relatives of childhood schizophrenics as opposed to 4 percent of adult onset schizophrenics are affected. Although there have not been well controlled studies, it appears that *childhood schizophrenics respond to medications less, not more, than do adult schizophrenics.* Epidemiologic data indicate that *childhood-onset schizophrenics are usually not mildly mentally retarded,* but rather function in the low average to average range of intelligence.

47.4–47.5

47.4. The answer is C (*Synopsis VII,* page 1127).

47.5. The answer is B (*Synopsis VII,* page 1127).

47.6. The answer is B (*Synopsis VII,* page 1127).

Both haloperidol (Haldol) and clozapine (Clozaril) are *effective in diminishing positive symptoms of schizophrenia such as auditory hallucinations.* Clozapine has been used with some success in schizophrenic adults who are resistant to treatment with multiple conventional antipsychotics. Clozapine has the advantage that it *generally does not induce extrapyramidal side effects* and is not likely to cause tardive dyskinesia. However, *clozapine has been associated with agranulocytosis,* a potentially fatal side effect, so close monitoring is required when clozapine is used.

Child Psychiatry: Additional Conditions That May Be a Focus of Clinical Attention

Additional conditions that may be a focus of clinical attention that present in children and adolescents include borderline intellectual functioning, academic problem, childhood or adolescent antisocial behavior, and identity problem.

Borderline intellectual functioning is defined by the presence of a full scale intelligence quotient within the 71 to 84 range, along with a consistent level of adaptive functioning. In cases where the current level of adaptive functioning has deteriorated into the borderline range in conjunction with the onset of a major mental disorders, the diagnosis is more difficult to make. In that case the clinician must evaluate the patient's history in order to determine whether the compromised intellectual and adaptive functioning was present prior to the mental disorder. Borderline intellectual functioning is present in about 6 to 7 percent of the population. Chronic frustrations, failures, and embarrassment related to borderline intellectual functioning may contribute to the circumstances warranting psychiatric intervention. The etiology of borderline intellectual functioning is probably a combination of genetic factors and environmental conditions. Family studies suggest that multiple genes may be involved in the development of a particular intelligence quotient.

Persons with borderline intellectual functioning may be able to function well in some areas while being markedly deficient in others. Therapeutic interventions include helping patients to become more socially skilled and to accept their limitations while promoting autonomy and accepting challenges.

According to the fourth edition of *Diagnostic and Statistical Manual of Mental Disorders* (DSM-IV) academic problem is a condition that is not due to a mental disorder, such as a learning disorder or a communication disorder, or, if it is due to a mental disorder, it is severe enough to warrant independent clinical attention. Thus, a child or an adolescent who is of normal intelligence and is free of a learning disorder or a communication disorder but is failing in school or doing poorly falls into this category. Numerous factors may contribute to academic problem in children without related psychiatric disorders. Children who have problems with separation from parents, have anxieties, or are troubled by family problems or mood disturbances sometimes fail in school. Some children receive mixed messages from their parents about trusting teachers and may have difficulties accepting appropriate criticism of their work, which can lead to poor performance. Some children have unrealistic expectations of the amount of studying necessary to succeed and become discouraged when they do not do as well as they had expected. Others are so preoccupied with interpersonal relationships or peer problems that they perform poorly.

Sometimes academic failure can be diminished with psychological interventions. Motivation, self-esteem, frustration, and shame can often be dealt with in a therapeutic setting and influence academic success. Once academic failure has started, anger, embarrassment, and a sense of helplessness about school often ensue. Tutoring as well as emotional support may help reverse the process.

Childhood or adolescent antisocial behavior covers a variety of acts that violate the rights of others. Acts of aggression, stealing, truancy, and running away from home fall into that category. The term "juvenile delinquent" is defined by the legal system as a youth who has violated the law, but it does not mean that the youth meets the criteria for a mental disorder. Estimates of antisocial behavior range from 5 to 15 percent of the general population, and somewhat less among children and adolescents. Risk factors in children and adolescents for antisocial behavior include a harsh and physically abusive home environment, parental criminality, a past of impulsive and hyperactive behavior, low intellectual functioning, academic failure, minimal adult supervision, and a history of substance use.

A major task in evaluating a child or adolescent with antisocial behavior is to determine whether there is an underlying psychiatric disorder such as a mood disorder. If present, that disorder requires appropriate therapy. The management of antisocial behavior usually involves behavioral techniques. The family must be willing and able to participate in the program which involves rewards for positive social behavior and positive reinforcement for refraining from antisocial behavior. In cases of aggressive or violent behaviors, medications, such as lithium (Eskalith) and haloperidol (Haldol) may be beneficial.

Identity problem is related to distress about one's goals, friendships, moral values, career aspirations, sexual orientation, and group loyalties. In the revised third edition of the *Diagnostic and Statistical Manual of Mental Disorders* (DSM-III-R) such a disturbance constituted a mental disorder. In DSM-IV, identity problem may cause severe distress, and may become a focus of clinical intervention, but it is not classified as a mental disorder. The etiology of identity problem is multifactorial, and may reflect, in part, the pressures of a chaotic and unsupportive family life. Children with chronic difficulties in mastering the expected developmental tasks in synchrony with peers are likely to struggle with forming a well-defined identity in adolescence. Erik Erikson used the term "identity versus role diffusion" to describe the challenging task of establishing a coherent sense of self as an adolescent. Adolescents with identity problem are often consumed with doubts, lack confidence, and are preoccupied with a sense of alienation. Identity problem must be differentiated from early sign of a psychiatric disorder (such as borderline personality disorder, schizophreniform disorder, or a mood disorder). Identity problem usually resolves by the mid-twenties. Psychotherapeutic intervention may be helpful for some adolescents who benefit from acknowledgment of their struggle, recognition of their conflicts, and support.

Students should review Chapter 48 of *Kaplan and Sadock's Synopsis VII* and then study the questions and answers provided below.

HELPFUL HINTS

The student should be able to define the following terms.

mental retardation	achievement tests	sense of self
adaptive function	violation of rights	sexual orientation
"V" code	juvenile delinquent	abulia
underachievement	superego	irreconcilable conflicts
learning disorder	substance use	physical abuse
academic failure	comorbid disorders	dysfunctional family
performance anxiety	role diffusion	

QUESTIONS

DIRECTIONS: Each of the incomplete statements below is followed by five suggested completions. Select the *one* that is *best* in each case.

48.1. Identity problem
A. often includes doubts related to career choice and friendships
B. does not include uncertainty about sexual orientation
C. occurs when there is minor distress
D. is classified as a mental disorder
E. rarely occurs with a concurrent mood disorder

48.2. The differential diagnosis of identity problem includes
A. borderline personality disorder
B. schizophreniform disorder
C. schizophrenia
D. mood disorders
E. all the above

48.3. All of the following are associated with childhood or adolescent antisocial behavior *except*
A. academic failure
B. substance use
C. physical abuse
D. neglectful home life
E. anticipatory anxiety

DIRECTIONS: Each set of lettered headings below is followed by a list of numbered statements. For each numbered statement, select the *best* lettered heading. Each heading can be used once, more than once, or not at all.

Questions 48.4–48.7
A. Academic problem
B. Childhood or adolescent antisocial behavior
C. Borderline intellectual functioning

48.4. Intelligence quotient (I.Q.) within the range of 71 to 84.

48.5. Normal intelligence and free of a learning disorder or a communication disorder but is failing in school

48.6. Covers many acts that violate the rights of others

48.7. Must be differentiated from conduct disorder

ANSWERS

Child Psychiatry: Additional Conditions That May Be a Focus of Clinical Attention

48.1. The answer is D (*Synopsis VII*, pages 1131–1132).

Identity problem *occurs when there is severe distress, not minor distress*, regarding uncertainty about issues relating to identity. Identity problem *often includes doubts related to career choice and friendship*, and *does include uncertainty about sexual orientation*. Unlike identity disorder in the revised third edition of *Diagnostic and Statistical Manual of Mental Disorders* (DSM-III-R), in the fourth edition (DSM-IV) *identity problem is not classified as a mental disorder*. Identity problem *often occurs with a concurrent mood disorder* or psychotic disorder.

48.2. The answer is E (all) (*Synopsis VII*, page 1132).

Identity problem must be differentiated from a mental disorder (such as *borderline personality disorder, schizophreniform disorder, schizophrenia*, or a *mood disorder*). At times, what initially appears to be identity problem may be the prodromal manifestations of one of those disorders.

Intense but normal conflicts associated with maturing, such as adolescent turmoil and mid-life crisis, may be confusing, but they are usually not associated with marked deterioration in school, vocational, or social functioning or with severe subjective distress. However, considerable evidence indicates that adolescent turmoil is often not a phase that is outgrown but indicates true psychopathology.

48.3. The answer is E (*Synopsis VII*, page 1131).

Anticipatory anxiety is not a common associated feature of childhood and adolescent antisocial behavior. Associated features of childhood and adolescent antisocial behavior include theft, *academic failure*, impulsivity, oppositional behavior, lying, suicide attempts, *substance use*, truancy, *physical abuse*, sexual abuse, and *neglectful home life*.

48.4–48.7

48.4. The answer is C (*Synopsis VII*, page 1129).

48.5. The answer is A (*Synopsis VII*, page 1129).

48.6. The answer is B (*Synopsis VII*, page 1130).

48.7. The answer is B (*Synopsis VII*, page 1130).

Borderline intellectual functioning is defined by the presence of an *intelligence quotient (I.Q.) within the range of 71 to 84*. According to the fourth edition of *Diagnostic and Statistical Manual of Mental Disorders* (DSM-IV), a diagnosis of borderline intellectual functioning is made when issues pertaining to that level of cognition become the focus of clinical attention.

In DSM-IV, *academic problem* is a condition that is not due to a mental disorder, such as a learning disorder or a communication disorder, or, if it is due to a mental disorder, it is severe enough to warrant independent clinical attention. Thus, a child or an adolescent who is of *normal intelligence and is free of a learning disorder or a communication disorder but is failing in school* or doing poorly falls into this category.

Childhood and adolescent antisocial behavior covers many acts that violate the rights of others, including overt acts of aggression and violence and such covert acts as lying, stealing, truancy, and running away from home. However, the *condition must be differentiated from conduct disorder*. The DSM-IV criteria for conduct disorder require a repetitive pattern of at least three antisocial behaviors for at least six months. Childhood or adolescent antisocial behavior consists of isolated events that do not constitute a mental disorder but do become the focus of clinical attention.

Psychiatric Treatments of Children and Adolescents

Psychiatric treatments of children are as varied and multifaceted as the problems that children and their families bring to clinical attention. Consequently, matching a child's psychiatric disturbance, not to mention the individual child, with a specific psychiatric treatment is an important task that is difficult to achieve. The difficulty is a consequence of limited precision in diagnosis and uncertainty about the curative factors in psychotherapy and psychopharmacology. There is no single effective therapeutic element in treatment. Unfortunately, many therapists have been handicapped by a tradition of mutual exclusivity of different therapeutic modalities so that they see value in combining only some modes of treatment, while excluding others.

There are many types of psychotherapy for children: intensive individual psychotherapy, brief psychotherapy, family therapy, behavior therapy, play therapy, and symptom-focused remediation, such as tutoring and speech therapy. The use of those approaches by themselves or in combination should stem not from the therapist's preferences, but from the assessment of the patient and from a broad-based background of knowledge about available treatments.

In child psychiatry, clinicians function as advocates for their patients and are often called upon to make recommendations to schools, legal agencies, and community organizations. Unlike adults, children rarely seek treatment on their own. Thus, one of the first tasks of the clinician is to stimulate the child's motivation for treatment.

Children sometimes have a limited capacity for self-observation, but they are likely to reenact their past experiences in play and verbal conversations. Children should be encouraged to express feelings verbally and in play as long as they understand that the ground rules include not hurting anyone or destroying property. In order to maintain a therapeutic alliance with the child, the clinician has to educate the child and be positive and supportive.

Psychotherapy with children usually includes parental involvement, with confidentiality maintained in a way that is appropriate to the child's age and developmental level. The child may be encouraged to disclose certain information in sessions with the parents if it appears that this is in the best interest of the child. Issues of danger, suicide, and homicide obviously take precedence over confidentiality.

Certain elements in psychotherapy produce complications that militate against a particular type of psychotherapy for a given child. For instance, for many children, a form of exploratory-interpretive psychotherapy aimed at uncovering intrapsychic conflicts is indicated. But if the youngster's ego functioning, particularly in the area of reality testing, is borderline, such an approach calls for considerable caution. To treat a young patient effectively, a clinician should be firmly aware of the indications and contraindications for the various psychotherapies. Students need to be familiar with the differences between psychiatric treatment of children and the treatment of adults.

Pharmacotherapy for psychiatric disorders in children and adolescents is aimed at increasing a child's functioning in school and in the home. Specific issues that are pertinent in children are those related to cognitive function—that is, the clinician must always consider a medication's effect on memory, effect on alertness, sedative effect, and any other adverse effect that might interfere with a child's education and learning. However, sometimes those cautions become secondary to the safety of the child or the safety of others.

Pharmacokinetics must also be considered. Children have greater hepatic capacity, more glomerular filtration, and less fatty tissue than adults. Thus, some medications, such as sympathomimetics, dopamine receptor antagonists, and tricyclic drugs, may be eliminated more rapidly in children than in adults. Medications that have been well studied for effectiveness include methylphenidate (Ritalin) for attention-deficit/hyperactivity disorder, antipsychotics for psychotic disorders and for aggressive behavior, and lithium for bipolar I disorder in adolescents and for aggressive behavior. Tricyclic drugs have been tried to treat a variety of psychiatric syndromes, including enuresis, major depressive disorder, panic disorders, separation anxiety disorder, and attention-deficit/hyperactivity disorder. However, tricyclic drugs have not been shown to be superior to a placebo in double-blind, placebo-controlled studies of children and adolescents with major depressive disorder. In children, developmental differences in neurotransmitters and neuroendocrine systems may be associated with responses to antidepressants. The potentially serious cardiovascular side effects of tricyclic drugs and the recent reports of a number of sudden deaths occurring in children treated with desipramine (Norpramin) for attention-deficit/hyperactivity disorder have increased the caution with which clinicians use tricyclic medications in children. Serotonin-specific reuptake inhibitors, such as fluoxetine (Prozac) and sertraline (Zoloft), are being used to treat depressive disorders, anxiety disorders, and obsessive-compulsive symptoms.

After reading Chapter 49 of *Kaplan and Sadock's Synopsis VII,* students should study the questions and answers below to test their knowledge in that area.

HELPFUL HINTS

The terms below should be known and defined by the student.

psychoanalytic theories	ADHD	acting out
developmental orientation	tardive dyskinesia	self-observation
sequential psychosocial capacities	Tourette's disorder	regression
learning-behavioral theories	haloperidol (Haldol)	therapeutic playroom
classical and operant conditioning	autistic disorder	therapeutic interventions
family systems theory	fenfluramine (Pondimin)	child guidance clinics
relationship therapy	sympathomimetics	confidentiality
remedial and educational	sleep terror disorder	group therapy
psychotherapy	obsessive-compulsive disorder	play group therapy
supportive therapy	communication disorders	group selection criteria
release therapy	cardiovascular effects	activity group therapy
filial therapy	growth suppression	same-sex groups
psychoanalytically oriented	dietary manipulation	combined therapy
therapy	puberty and adolescence	parent groups
child psychoanalysis	(differentiation)	residential and day treatment
cognitive therapy	interview techniques	schizophrenia
modeling theory	atypical puberty	mood disorders
behavioral contracting	substance abuse	tricyclic drugs
group living	suicide	MAOIs
milieu therapy	action-oriented defenses	ECT
biological therapies	masked depression	lithium
parental attitudes	depressive equivalents	conduct disorder
pharmacokinetics	violence	anticonvulsants
renal clearance	compliance	enuresis
liver-to-body-weight ratio	externalization	bell-and-pad conditioning

QUESTIONS

DIRECTIONS: Each of the questions or incomplete statements below is followed by five suggested responses or completions. Select the *one* that is *best* in each case.

49.1. Traditional items in a therapeutic playroom include all the following *except*
A. multigenerational doll families
B. blocks
C. crayons
D. a television set
E. rubber hammers

49.2. Group therapy is useful for all the following childhood problems *except*
A. phobias
B. male effeminate behavior
C. withdrawal and social isolation
D. extreme aggression
E. primary behavior disturbances

49.3. The use of diazepam (Valium) in children has been well established for the treatment of
A. sleep terrors
B. enuresis
C. obsessive-compulsive disorder
D. attention-deficit/hyperactivity disorder
E. all the above

49.4. Group therapy is
A. not useful for mentally ill children
B. generally unfocused with young children
C. useful in the treatment of substance-related disorders
D. more viable with adolescents when the group is composed of mixed-sex, rather than same-sex, members
E. most effective when parents oppose it

49.5. Childhood disorders in which medication is the mainstay of treatment include all the following *except*
A. conduct disorder
B. attention-deficit/hyperactivity disorder
C. Tourette's disorder
D. schizophrenia
E. all the above

49.6. Which one of the following statements about children referred for residential treatment is *not* true?
A. Most children referred are between 5 and 15 years of age
B. Boys are referred more frequently than girls
C. Most children referred have severe learning disabilities
D. Outpatient treatment often precedes residential treatment
E. Suicidal behavior is among the most common referral diagnoses

49.7. The side effects of tricyclic medications in children include
A. dry mouth
B. blurry vision
C. tachycardia
D. palpitations
E. all the above

49.8. "Symptom bearer," "distracter," "scapegoat," and "rescuer" are terms used in
A. behavioral theories
B. supportive therapy
C. psychoanalytic psychotherapy
D. family systems therapy
E. relationship therapy

49.9. Pharmacological treatment of conduct disorder may include
A. haloperidol (Haldol)
B. lithium (Eskalith)
C. carbamazepine (Tegretol)
D. propranolol (Inderal)
E. all the above

49.10. Which of the following statements about the treatment of mental retardation with antipsychotic medication are true?
A. 12 percent of mentally retarded patients living in institutions are receiving antipsychotics
B. The intelligence quotient deficits that define mental retardation respond dramatically to phenothiazines
C. There is no risk of tardive dyskinesia
D. Hyperactivity and stereotypies associated with mental retardation have been found to respond to antipsychotic medications
E. All the above

49.11. Residential treatment centers for children and adolescents
A. are permanent out-of-home placements
B. generally have a psychoanalytically-oriented program
C. accept patients with usually acute psychiatric decompensations
D. are only for children and adolescents who have been psychiatrically hospitalized
E. provide a highly structured and supervised behaviorally-based program

ANSWERS

Psychiatric Treatments of
Children and Adolescents

49.1.   The answer is D (*Synopsis VII*, pages 1017 and 1137).

Traditional items in a therapeutic playroom do not include *a television set*. The goal is not for the child to be entertained. Television puts the child in a passive, noninteractive mode and so is generally not considered useful therapeutically.

The purpose of the therapeutic playroom is to create an environment in which the child feels comfortable enough to play freely and to express a wide range of feelings. The goal is for the child to engage in symbolic play—that is, play that expresses the child's unconscious feelings.

Multigenerational doll families are dolls from three generations and include young children, parents, and grandparents. That concept allows the child to use the dolls to express intrafamilial interactions. *Blocks* are therapeutically useful because they allow the child room to create and to project fantasies onto the creations. The use of blocks may also allow for the ventilation of aggressive impulses, as when a child builds a stack of blocks and then crashes it to the floor. Drawings with *crayons* allow the expression of creative impulses and provide access to the child's fantasy life when the child explains or tells a story about what is drawn. Play tools, such as *rubber hammers,* are also useful, enabling the child to demonstrate identification with a parental figure, to build, and to destroy.

49.2.   The answer is D (*Synopsis VII,* page 1141).

Group therapy is not useful for *extreme aggression.* In children, extreme aggression may indicate a diminished need or ability to be accepted by peers, and peer acceptance is felt by many therapists to be a prerequisite for group membership and treatment. Extremely aggressive children are also potentially disruptive to group functioning and intimidating to other group members, two features that severely impair their capacity for group involvement. Extremely aggressive children may engender such negative reactions from a group that group membership serves only to reinforce an already lowered self-esteem. Finally, extreme aggression in children may at least initially require the primary use of medication and limit setting as the essential therapeutic interventions.

Indications for group therapy that have been investigated include *phobias, male effeminate behavior, withdrawal and social isolation,* and *primary behavior disturbances.*

49.3.   The answer is A (*Synopsis VII*, pages 1146–1150).

The use of diazepam (Valium) in children has been well established for the treatment of *sleep terror disorder*. It is not of use in the treatment of *enuresis, obsessive-compulsive disorder,* or *attention-deficit/ hyperactivity disorder.* Diazepam is an anxiolytic from the general class of drugs called benzodiazepines. There are few indications for the drugs in the treatment of children, and they are frequently overprescribed. Sleep terror disorder consists of repeated episodes of abrupt awakening with intense anxiety marked by autonomic arousal. It occurs during stage IV sleep. Because diazepam interferes with stage IV sleep, the drug prevents the sleep terrors from occurring. Enuresis, nocturnal bed wetting, is treated either behaviorally with bell-and-pad conditioning or with imipramine (Tofranil), a tricyclic antidepressant. Obsessive-compulsive disorder is rare in children and is marked by recurrent thoughts (obsessions) and ritualistic behaviors (compulsions) that if interfered with cause the patient tremendous anxiety. Clomipramine (Anafranil) has been found to be successful in several studies. Attention-deficit/hyperactivity disorder is generally treated with a sympathomimetic, such as methylphenidate (Ritalin). If sympathomimetics are not effective or if the adverse effects are severe, a second line of treatment is the tricyclic drugs. Dopamine receptor antagonists, such as haloperidol (Haldol), have also been tried, but the risk of tardive dyskinesia must be considered.

49.4.   The answer is C (*Synopsis VII,* pages 1139–1141).

Group therapy has been found to be *useful in the treatment of substance-related disorders,* which are more commonly encountered in latency and pubertal-age children than in younger children. Group therapy is *useful for mentally ill children,* as well as healthier children. Group therapy is *generally focused with young children* (preschool and early school age), as they cannot provide that for themselves. Work with the group is usually structured by the therapist through the use of a particular technique, such as puppets or art. Play group therapy emphasizes the interactional qualities among the children and with the therapist in the permissive playroom setting. Group therapy is *more viable with adolescents if the group is composed of same-sex members, as opposed to mixed-sex members*—presumably because the upsurge of sexual energy and interest at this stage interferes, in a group setting, with the psychotherapeutic exploration necessary for psychotherapy. Group therapy is *not effective when parents oppose it;* no treatment is enhanced by opposition from significant family members, especially any therapy involving children.

49.5.   The answer is A (*Synopsis VII,* pages 1146–1150).

There is no specific or consistently effective medication for the treatment of *conduct disorder,* although lithium, carbamazepine (Tegretol), and propranolol (Inderal) have all been studied and have apparently yielded some benefits. Behavioral and verbal therapies have been the mainstay of treatment for conduct disorder, although in severe cases, when behavioral and verbal treatments fail, antipsychotic agents may be used to decrease the severity of aggression.

Childhood disorders in which medication is the mainstay of treatment include *attention-deficit / hyperactivity disorder (ADHD), Tourette's disorder,* and *schizophrenia.*

ADHD provides the clearest indication for psychopharmacological treatment. The symptoms usually prompting therapy are developmentally inappropriate inattention and impulsivity that do not respond to social contact. The first choice among pharmacotherapies is a sympathomimetic. The sympathomimetics include methylphenidate (Ritalin), dextroamphetamine (Dexedrine), or pemoline (Cylert). Tourette's disorder, characterized by multiple motor and vocal tics, is also a clear indication for pharmacotherapy. Haloperidol (Haldol) is the standard treatment against which all proposed treatments are now measured. Schizophrenia in childhood is rare, but when symptoms such as hallucinations and delusions are present, antipsychotic medications are indicated. The same toxic side effects that adults experience—in particular, tardive dyskinesia—can also occur in children, so caution must be exercised.

Table 49.1 covers psychiatric drugs in use with children.

49.6.   The answer is E (*Synopsis VII,* pages 1141–1142).

Suicidal behavior is not among the most common referral diagnoses; in fact, among the reasons to exclude children are behaviors that are likely to be destructive to the children themselves or to others under the treatment conditions. Thus, some children who threaten to run away, set fires, hurt others, or attempt suicide may not be suitable for residential treatment.

Although the age range of children referred for residential treatment varies from institution to institution, *most children are between 5 and 15 years of age. Boys are referred more frequently than girls. Most children referred for residential treatment have severe learning disabilities* and have been seen previously by one or more professional persons, such as a school psychologist or a pediatrician, or by members of a child guidance clinic, juvenile court, or state welfare agency. Unsuccessful attempts at less drastic *outpatient treatment often precede residential treatment.*

49.7.   The answer is E (all) (*Synopsis VII,* page 1150).

The potential adverse effects of tricylic medications in children are usually similar to the adverse effects in adults. They include *dry mouth, blurry vision* (loss of accommodation), *tachycardia* (rapid heart rate), *palpitations* (sensation of the heart's pounding in the chest), constipation, and sweating. The adverse effects result primarily from the anticholinergic properties of the tricyclic drugs.

49.8.   The answer is D (*Synopsis VII,* page 1135)

"Symptom bearer," "distracter," "scapegoat," and "rescuer" are terms used for roles that family members play in *family systems therapy.* In the therapy, the family system is viewed as a constantly evolving, self-regulating structure. The dynamic interactions between the family members are examined by family therapists to identify the roles the family members are assigned and to assess the boundaries and the subsystems within the family. Appreciation of the family system sometimes explains why a minute therapeutic input at a critical junction results in far-reaching changes, whereas in other situations huge quantities of therapeutic effort are absorbed with minimal evidence of change.

Behavioral theories, based on the concepts of classical (Pavlovian) conditioning or operant (Skinnerian) conditioning, hold that abnormal behavior is due to a failure to learn or is due to learning maladaptive behavior through conditioning. Appropriate behaviors are highlighted and rewarded in behaviorally oriented therapy.

Supportive therapy offers support by an authority figure. Supportive psychotherapy is particularly helpful in enabling a well-adjusted youngster to cope with the emotional turmoil engendered in a crisis. It is also used with those disturbed youngsters whose less-than-adequate ego functioning is seriously disrupted by an expressive-exploratory mode or by other forms of therapeutic intervention. At the beginning of most psychotherapy, regardless of the patient's age or the nature of the therapeutic interventions, the principal therapeutic elements perceived by the patient tend to be supportive ones, a consequence of therapists' universal efforts to be reliably

Table 49.1
Common Psychoactive Druge in Childhood and Adolescence

Drugs	Indications	Dosage	Adverse Reactions and Monitoring
Antipsychotics—also known as major tranquilizers, neuroleptics. Divided into (1) a high-potency, low-dosage, e.g. haloperidol (Haldol), trifluoperazine (Stelazine), thiothixene (Navane); (2) low-potency, high-dosage (more sedating), e.g., chlorpromazine (Thorazine), thioridazine (Mellaril); and (3) clozapine (Clozaril)	In general, for agitated, aggressive, self-injurious behaviors in mental retardation (MR), pervasive developmental disorders (PDD), conduct disorder (CD), and schizophrenia Studies support following specific indications: haloperidol—PDD, CD with severe aggression, Tourette's disorder	All can be given in two to four divided doses or combined into one dose after gradual buildup Haloperidol—child 0.5–6 mg a day, adolescent 0.5–16 mg a day Thiothixene—5–42 mg a day Chlorpromazine and thioridazine—child 10–200 mg a day, adolescent 50–600 mg a day, over 16 years of age 100–700 mg a day	Sedation, weight gain, hypotension, lowered seizure threshold, constipation, extrapyramidal symptoms, jaundice, agranulocytosis, dystonic reaction, tardive dyskinesia; with clozapine, no extrapyramidal adverse effects Monitor: blood pressure, complete blood count (CBC), liver function tests (LFTs), electroencephalogram, if indicated; with thioridazine, pigmentary retinopathy is rare but dictates ceiling of 800 mg in adults and proportionately lower in children; with clozapine, weekly white blood counts (WBCs) for development of agranulocytosis
Stimulants Dextroamphetamine (Dexedrine) FDA-approved for children 3 years and older Methylphenidate (Ritalin) and pemoline (Cylert) FDA-approved for children 6 years and older	In attention-deficit/hyperactivity disorder (ADHD) for hyperactivity, impulsivity, and inattentiveness	Dextroamphetamine and methylphenidate are generally given at 8 A.M. and noon (the usefulness of sustained-release preparations is not proved) Dextroamphetamine—2.5–40 mg a day up to 0.5 mg per kg a day Methylphenidate—10–60 mg a day or up to 1.0 mg per kg a day Pemoline—37.5–112.5 mg given at 8 A.M.	Insomnia, anorexia, weight loss (and possibly growth delay), headache, tachycardia, precipitation or exacerbation of tic disorders With pemoline, monitor LFTs, as hepatoxicity is possible
Lithium—considered an antipsychotic drug, also has antiaggression properties	Studies support use in MR and CD for aggressive and self-injurious behaviors; can be used for same in PDD; also indicated for early-onset bipolar I disorder	600–2,100 mg in two or three divided doses; keep blood levels to 0.4–1.2 mEq per L	Nausea, vomiting, enuresis, headache, tremor, weight gain, hypothyroidism Experience with adults suggests renal function monitoring
Tricyclic drugs Imipramine (Tofranil) has been used in most child studies Nortriptyline (Pamelor) has been studied in children Clomipramine (Anafranil) is effective in child obsessive-compulsive disorder (OCD)	Major depressive disorder, separation anxiety disorder, bulimia nervosa, enuresis; sometimes used in ADHD, anorexia nervosa, sleepwalking disorder, and sleep terror disorder	Imipramine—start with dosage of about 1.5 mg per kg a day; can build up to not more than 5 mg per kg a day Start with two or three divided doses; eventually combine in one dose Not FDA-approved for children except for enuresis; dosage is usually 50–100 mg before sleep; clomipramine—start at 50 mg a day; can raise to not more than 3 mg per kg a day or 200 mg a day	Dry mouth, constipation, tachycardia, drowsiness, postural hypotension, hypertension, mania Electrocardiogram (ECG) monitoring is needed because of risk for cardiac conduction slowing; consider lowering dosage if PR interval >0.20 seconds or ORS interval >0.12 seconds; baseline EEG is advised, as it can lower seizure threshold; blood levels of drug are sometimes useful

Continued

Table 49.1
Continued

Drugs	Indications	Dosage	Adverse Reactions and Monitoring
Fluoxetine (Prozac)—a serotonin-specific reuptake inhibitor	OCD, major depressive disorder; may be useful in anorexia nervosa, bulimia nervosa	Fluoxetine dosage not established in children	Nausea, headache, nervousness, insomnia, dry mouth, diarrhea, anorexia nervosa, drowsiness
Carbamazepine (Tegretol)—an anticonvulsant	Aggression or dyscontrol in MR or CD	Start with 10 mg per kg a day; can build to 20–30 mg per kg a day; therapeutic blood level range appears to be 4–12 mg per L	Drowsiness, nausea, rash, vertigo, irritability Monitor: CBC and LFTs for possible blood dyscrasias and hepatotoxicity; blood levels are necessary
Benzodiazepines—have been insufficiently studied in childhood and adolescence	Sometimes effective in parasomnias; sleepwalking disorder or sleep terror disorder; can be tried in generalized anxiety disorder Clonazepam (Klonapin) can be tried in separation anxiety disorder Alprazolam (Xanax) can be tried in separation anxiety disorder	Parasomnias: diazepam (Valium) 2–10 mg before bedtime	Can cause drowsiness, ataxia, tremor, dyscontrol; can be abused
Fenfluramine (Pondimin)—an amphetamine congener	Well-studied in autistic disorder; generally ineffective, but some patients show improvement	Gradually increase to 1.0–1.5 mg per kg a day in divided doses	Weight loss, drowsiness, irritability, loose bowel movements
Propranolol (Inderal)—a β-adrenergic blocker	Aggression in MR, PDD, and cognitive disorder; awaits controlled studies	Effective dosage in children and adolescents is not yet established; range is probably 40–320 mg a day	Bradycardia, hypotension, nausea, hypoglycemia, depression; avoid in asthma
Clonidine (Catapres)—a presynaptic α-adrenergic blocking agent	Tourette's disorder; some success in ADHD	0.1–0.3 mg a day; 3–5.5 µg per kg a day	Orthostatic hypotension, nausea, vomiting, sedation, elevated blood glucose
Cyproheptadine (Penactin)	Anorexia nervosa	Dosages up to 8 mg four times a day	Antihistaminic side effects, including sedation and dryness of the mouth
Naltrexone (Trexan)	Self-injurious behaviors in MR and PDD; currently being studied in PDD	0.5–2.0 mg per kg a day	Sleepiness, aggressivity Monitor LFTs, as hepatotoxicity has been reported in adults at high dosages

Table by Richard Perry, M.D.

and sensitively responsive. In fact, some therapy may never proceed beyond this supportive level, whereas other therapies develop an expressive-exploratory or behavioral modification flavor on top of the supportive foundation.

Psychoanalytic psychotherapy is a modified form of psychotherapy that is expressive and exploratory and that endeavors to reverse the evolution of the emotional disturbance through a reenactment and a desensitization of the traumatic events by the free expression of thoughts and feelings in an interview-play situation. Ultimately, the therapist helps the patient understand the warded-off feelings, fears, and wishes that have beset him or her.

In *relationship therapy* a positive, friendly, helpful relationship is viewed as the primary, if not the sole, therapeutic ingredient. One of the best examples of pure relationship therapy is found outside the clinical setting in the work of the Big Brother Organization.

Table 49.2
Effects of Psychotropic Drugs on Cognitive Tests of Learning Functions*

| Drug Class | Continuous Performance Test (Attention) | Matching Familiar Figures (Impulsivity) | Test Function | | Short-Term Memory* | WISC (Intelligence) |
			Paired Associates (Verbal Learning)	Porteus Maze (Planning Capacity)		
Stimulant	↑	↑	↑	↑	↑	↑
Antidepressants	↑	0		0	0	0
Antipsychotics	↑↓		↓	↓	↓	0

↑ Improved, ↑↓ inconsistent, ↓ worse, and 0 no effect
*Various tests: digit span, word recall, etc.
Adapted from M G Aman: Drugs, learning, and the psychotherapies. In Pediatric Psychopharmacology: The Use of Behavior Modifying Drugs in Children, J S Werry, editor, Brunner/Mazel, New York, 1978.

49.9. The answer is E (all) (*Synopsis VII,* page 1149).

Behavioral and verbal therapies are the mainstays of treatment of conduct disorder. In severe cases, when these treatments have failed, medication may be used to decrease the severity of the aggression. For those children *haloperidol (Haldol)* and *lithium (Eskalith)* are the drugs of choice. Both have been effective in treating hospitalized assaultive conduct disorder children. Recently, some researchers have claimed that *carbamazepine (Tegretol)* and *propranolol (Inderal)* are effective in decreasing the aggressivity of conduct disorder children. The use of those medications needs further study, but they may be helpful in the treatment of some children with conduct disorder.

49.10. The answer is D (*Synopsis VII,* page 1146).

Mental retardation in itself is not an indication for the use of psychiatric drugs, although some associated behaviors may respond to medication. *Hyperactivity and stereotypies associated with mental retardation have been found to respond to antipsychotic medications* and sympathomimetics. Approximately *50 percent of mentally retarded patients living in institutions are receiving antipsychotics,* despite the lack of any clear indications. *The intelligence quotient deficits that define mental retardation do not respond to phenothiazines* or to any pharmacological agent yet tested. *There is risk of tardive dyskinesia* in this population, and some studies show an increased risk compared to the general population, perhaps as a result of the underlying central nervous system impairment.

Some psychotropic drugs may improve cognitive tests of learning functions. For example, amphetamine improves performance on a variety of tasks (Table 49.2).

49.11. The answer is E (*Synopsis VII,* page 1141).

Residential treatment centers *provide a highly structured and supervised behaviorally-based program.* Residential treatment centers are *temporary, not permanent, out-of-home placements* for children or adolescents with serious emotional and behavioral disorders who can not be managed at home. They *do not usually accept patients with acute psychiatric decompensations* for whom psychiatric hospitalization is usually necessary. *Residential treatment centers are not only for children and adolescents who have been psychiatrically hospitalized.* While a variety of individual psychotherapies may be employed for residents, residential treatment centers *do not generally have a psychoanalytically-oriented program.*

50 ||||||

Geriatric Psychiatry

Geriatric psychiatry is one of the fastest growing fields in psychiatry. It is the field concerned with diagnosing, managing, and treating the mental disorders of old age. As with mental disorders at any age, those affecting older people result from a complex interplay of biological, psychological, and sociocultural factors. What distinguishes the mental disorders associated with the elderly from those observed in younger people are the specific biological, psychological, and sociocultural influences unique to the developmental phase of old age. For instance, dementing disorders such as Alzheimer's disease or vascular dementia are essentially mental disorders seen almost entirely among the elderly.

Elderly individuals are more likely to have experienced loss and to feel isolated than younger individuals. One of the most common mental disorders of old age is major depressive disorder. Suicide risk increases with age. Almost 20 percent of all suicides are committed by people over 65 years of age. Other common mental disorders among the elderly include alcohol-related disorders, cognitive disorders, and phobias.

Delusional disorder and some somatoform disorders commonly have an age of onset later in life. Bipolar disorder I, anxiety disorders, sleep disorders, and substance-related disorders may have their onset or may worsen elderly patients. In most instances, the onset of any mental disorder in a patient over the age of 40 years should alert the clinician to rule out an associated medical cause, such as a space-occupying lesion or side effects of a medication.

The psychopharmacological treatment of geriatric disorders is a major component of geriatric psychiatry. The basic tenet of treating elderly patients with medications is the individualization of dosage. Many physiological changes occur as a person ages, including decreased renal clearance, decreased hepatic metabolism, decreased cardiac output, and decreased gastric acid secretion, all of which affect the rate of clearance of drugs from the body. Changes in the lean-to-fat body mass ratio affect drug distribution in the elderly. In general, the lowest possible drug dose should be used to achieve therapeutic response.

Psychotherapy is another major component of geriatric psychiatry. Age-related issues specific to the developmental phase of old age include the need to adapt to recurrent loss, the need to assume new roles, and the need to confront one's own mortality. The institutionalization of elderly patients no longer able to live independently is a difficult and challenging issue.

The student should carefully read Chapter 50 in *Kaplan and Sadock's Synopsis VII*. Once familiar with the material the student will be able to address the questions and answers below.

HELPFUL HINTS

Each of the following terms relating to geriatric issues should be defined.

toxins	dementia	hypomanic disorder
uremia	late-onset schizophrenia	lithium
diabetes	paraphrenia	neurosis
hepatic failure	loss of mastery	hypochondriasis
cerebral anoxia	role of anxiety	anxiety disorder
emphysema	ritualistic behavior	norepinephrine
anoxic confusion	adaptational capacity	serotonin
overt behavior	social capacity	obsessive-compulsive disorder
mood disorder	drug-blood level	conversion disorder
Alzheimer's disease	toxic confusional state	sleep disturbances
transdermal scopolamine	paradoxical reaction	insomnia
developmental phases	agedness	remotivation techniques
nutritional deficiencies	theory of aging	psychotropic danger
ideational paucity	disorders of awareness	akathisia
cognitive functioning	L-dopa (Larodopa)	presbyopia
organic mental disorder	trazodone (Desyrel)	FSH
orientation	rantidine	LH
sensorium	depression	dementing disorder
delirium	manic disorder	fluoxetine (Prozac)

QUESTIONS

DIRECTIONS: Each of the questions or incomplete statements below is followed by five suggested responses or completions. Select the *one* that is *best* in each case.

50.1. Of all patients with dementia, 50 to 60 percent have
A. vascular dementia
B. dementia of the Alzheimer's type
C. dementia due to Pick's disease
D. dementia due to Parkinson's disease
E. dementia due to Huntington's disease

50.2. All of the following are reasons not to use of MAOIs in elderly patients *except*
A. monoamine oxidase (MAO) decreases in the aging brain
B. orthostatic hypotension is common and severe with MAOIs
C. patients need to adhere to a tyramine-free diet
D. the potential for serious drug interactions involving certain analgesics
E. any kind of cognitive impairment

50.3. One of the advantages in the use of serotonin-specific reuptake inhibitors (SSRIs) by the elderly is the absence of
A. nausea and other gastrointestinal symptoms
B. orthostatic hypotension
C. nervousness
D. headache
E. all of the above

50.4. Which of the following drugs have been implicated in producing psychiatric symptoms in the elderly?
A. Ibuprofen (Motrin, Advil)
B. Trazodone (Desyrel)
C. Cimetidine (Tagamet)
D. L-dopa (Larodopa)
E. All the above

50.5. Which of the following statements about the treatment of geriatric patients with psychotherapeutic drugs are true?
A. Elderly persons may be more susceptible than younger adults to adverse effects
B. Elderly patients may metabolize drugs more slowly than do other adult patients
C. Most psychotropic drugs should be given in equally divided doses
D. The most reasonable practice is to begin with a small dose
E. All the above

50.6. Elderly persons taking antipsychotics are especially susceptible to the following side effects, *except*
A. tardive dyskinesia
B. akathisia
C. a toxic confusional state
D. paresthesias
E. all the above

50.7. Abnormalities of cognitive functioning in the aged are most often due to
A. depressive disturbances
B. schizophrenia
C. medication
D. cerebral dysfunctioning or deterioration
E. hypochondriasis

50.8. All the following statements about the biology of aging are true *except*
A. each cell of the body has a genetically determined life span
B. the optic lens thins
C. T-cell response to antigens is altered
D. decrease in melanin occurs
E. brain weight decreases

50.9. All the following statements about sleep disturbances in the elderly are true *except*
A. complaints about sleeplessness are common
B. catnaps may interfere with a good night's sleep
C. frequent visits to the bathroom may lead to problems in resuming sleep
D. tricyclic drugs often induce sleep when insomnia is accompanied by a depressive reaction
E. the elderly do not need as much sleep as they did in their earlier mature years

50.10. Changes in the ratio of lean to fat body mass affect the distribution of all the following *except*
A. imipramine
B. diazepam
C. chlorpromazine
D. lithium
E. fluoxetine

50.11. All the following statements about learning and memory in the elderly are true *except*
A. complete learning of new material still occurs
B. on multiple choice tests, recognition of correct answers persists
C. simple recall remains intact
D. I.Q. remains stable until age 80
E. memory-encoding ability diminishes

50.12. In the physical assessment of the aged, all the following statements are true *except*
A. toxins of bacterial origin are common
B. is the most common metabolic intoxication causing mental symptoms is uremia
C. cerebral anoxia often precipitates mental syndromes
D. vitamin deficiencies are common
E. nutritional deficiencies may cause mental symptoms

50.13. All the following statements about the pharmacological treatment of the elderly are true *except*
A. the elderly use more medications than any other age group
B. 25 percent of all prescriptions are for those over age 65
C. in the United States, 250,000 people a year are hospitalized because of adverse medication reactions
D. 25 percent of all hypnotics dispensed in the United States each year are to those over age 65
E. 70 percent of the elderly use over-the-counter medications

50.14. Sexual activity in persons over age 60
A. occurs in less than 10 percent of women
B. occurs in less than 15.0 percent of men
C. is often accompanied by feelings of guilt
D. may increase, compared with earlier levels of functioning
E. all the above

50.15. Elderly abuse by some caregiving children
A. is most likely to occur when the parent is bedridden
B. occurs most often when the elderly parent has a chronic medical illness
C. is likely to occur if the child was a victim of sexual or physical abuse
D. occurs more often toward women than toward men
E. is characterized by all the above

ANSWERS

Geriatric Psychiatry

50.1. The answer is B (*Synopsis VII*, page 1159).

Of all the patients with dementia, 50 to 60 percent have *dementia of the Alzheimer's type,* the most common type of dementia. About 5 percent of all persons who reach age 65 have dementia of the Alzheimer's type, compared with 15 to 25 percent of all persons 85 or older.

Vascular dementia is the second most common type of dementia. Vascular dementia accounts for 10 to 20 percent of all cases of dementia. *Dementia due to Pick's disease, dementia due to Parkinson's disease,* and dementia due to Huntington's disease each account for 1 to 5 percent of all dementia cases.

50.2. The answer is A (*Synopsis VII*, page 1165).

Monoamine oxidase inhibitors (MAOIs) are useful in treating depression because *monoamine oxidase (MAO) decreases in the aging brain* and may account for diminished catecholamines and a resultant depression. MAOIs may be used with caution in elderly patients. *Orthostatic hypotension is common and severe with MAOIs. Patients need to adhere to a tyramine-free diet* to avoid hypertensive crises. *The potential for serious drug interactions* involving certain analgesics, such as meperidine (Demerol) and *sympathomimetics,* also requires that patients understand what food and drugs they may use. Tranylcypromine (Parnate) and phenelzine (Nardil) are representative drugs that should be used cautiously in patients prone to hypertension. *Any kind of cognitive impairment* precludes MAOI therapy. Table 50.1 lists the geriatric dosages of the MAOIs.

50.3. The answer is B (*Synopsis VII*, page 1166).

The serotonin-specific reuptake inhibitors (SSRIs) do not cause the characteristic side effects of the tricyclic agents. The absence of *orthostatic hy-*

potension is a clinically significant factor in the use of SSRIs by the elderly.

In general, the SSRIs—such as fluoxetine (Prozac), sertraline (Zoloft), and paroxetine (Paxil)—are safe and well-tolerated by elderly patients. As a group, those drugs may cause *nausea and other gastrointestinal symptoms, nervousness,* agitation, *headache,* and insomnia, most often to mild degrees. Fluoxetine is the drug most likely to cause nervousness, insomnia, and loss of appetite, particularly early in treatment. Sertraline is the drug most likely to produce nausea and diarrhea. Paroxetine causes some anticholinergic effects.

50.4. The answer is E (all) (*Synopsis VII*, page 1159).

Ibuprofen (Motrin, Advil), trazodone (Desyrel), cimetidine (Tagamet), and L-dopa (Larodopa) have been implicated in the production in the elderly of psychiatric symptoms, such as depression, confusion, disorientation, and delirium. The symptoms usually cease after the drug is withdrawn, but the clinician must be alert to withdrawal reactions to a drug, especially if it is stopped abruptly.

Various drugs used in medicine can cause psychiatric symptoms in all classes of patients, especially among old patients. The symptoms may result if the drug is prescribed in too large a dose, if the patient is particularly sensitive to the medication, or if the patient does not follow instructions for its use.

50.5. The answer is E (all) (*Synopsis VII*, pages 1164–1165).

Elderly persons may be more susceptible than younger adults to the adverse effects of psychotherapeutic drugs (particularly adverse cardiac effects) and *elderly patients may metabolize drugs more slowly than do other adults. Most psychotropic drugs should be given in equally divided doses* three or four times over a 24-hour period, because geriatric patients may not be able to tolerate the sudden rise in drug-blood level that results from one large dose. *The most reasonable practice is to begin with a small dose,* increase it slowly, and watch for possible side effects. A common concern is that geriatric patients are often taking other medications, and thus psychiatrists must carefully consider the possible drug interactions.

50.6. The answer is D (*Synopsis VII*, pages 1165–1166).

Paresthesias, which are spontaneous tingling sensations, are not a side effect of antipsychotics.

Table 50.1
Geriatric Dosages of Monoamine Oxidase Inhibitors (MAOIs)*

Generic Name	Trade Name	Geriatric Dosage Range (mg a day)
Isocarboxid	Marplan	10–30
Phenelzine	Nardil	15–45
Tranylcypromine†	Parnate	10–20

*Persons taking MAOIs should be on a tyramine-free diet.
†Not recommended in persons over 60 because of pressor effects.

Elderly persons, particularly if they have an organic brain disease, are especially susceptible to the side effects of antipsychotics, including *tardive dyskinesia, akathisia,* and a *toxic confusional state.* Tardive dyskinesia is characterized by disfiguring and involuntary buccal and lingual masticatory movements; akathisia is a restlessness marked by a compelling need for constant motion. Choreiform body movements, which are spasmodic and involuntary movements of the limbs and the face, and rhythmic extension and flexion movements of the fingers may also be noticeable. Examination of the patient's protruded tongue for fine tremors and vermicular (wormlike) movements is a useful diagnostic procedure. A toxic confusional state, also referred to as a central anticholinergic syndrome, is characterized by a marked disturbance in short-term memory, impaired attention, disorientation, anxiety, visual and auditory hallucinations, increased psychotic thinking, and peripheral anticholinergic side effects.

50.7.   The answer is D (*Synopsis VII,* pages 1159–1160).

Abnormalities of cognitive functioning in the elderly are most often due to some *cerebral dysfunctioning or deterioration,* although they may also be the result of *depressive disturbances, schizophrenia,* or the effects of *medication..* In many instances, intellectual difficulties are not obvious, and a searching evaluation is necessary to detect them. The elderly are sensitive to the effects of medication; in some instances, cognitive impairment may occur as a result of overmedication. *Hypochondriasis,* the fear that one has a disease or preoccupation with one's health, is not the cause of an abnormality of cognitive functioning.

50.8.   The answer is B (*Synopsis VII,* page 65).

As a person ages *the optic lens thickens (not thins)* in association with an inability to accommodate (presbyopia), and hearing loss is progressive, particularly at the high frequencies.

The process of aging is known as senescence, and it results from a complex interaction of genetic, metabolic, hormonal, immunological, and structural factors acting on molecular, cellular, histological, and organ levels. The most commonly held theory is that *each cell of the body has a genetically determined life span* during which replication occurs a limited number of times before the cell dies. Structural changes in cells take place with age. In the central nervous system, for example, age-related cell changes occur in neurons, which show signs of degeneration.

Changes in the structure of deoxyribonucleic acid (DNA) and ribonucleic acid (RNA) are also found in aging cells; the cause has been attributed to genotypic programming, x-rays, chemicals, and food products, among others. Aging probably has no single cause. All areas of the body are affected to some degree, and changes vary from person to person.

A progressive decline in many bodily functions includes a *decrease in melanin* and decreases in cardiac output and stroke volume, glomerular filtration rate, oxygen consumption, cerebral blood flow, and vital capacity.

Many immune mechanisms are altered, with impaired *T-cell response to antigens* and an increase in the formation of autoimmune antibodies. These altered immune responses probably play a role in aged persons' susceptibility to infection and possibly even to neoplastic disease. Some neoplasms show a steadily increasing incidence with age, most notably cancers of the colon, prostate, stomach, and skin.

Variable changes are seen in endocrine function. For example, postmenopausal estrogen levels decrease, producing breast tissue evolution and vaginal epithelial atrophy. Testosterone levels begin to decline in the sixth decade; however, follicle-stimulating hormone and luteinizing hormone increase.

In the central nervous system, there is a decrease in *brain weight,* ventricular enlargement, and neuronal loss of approximately 50,000 a day, with some reduction in cerebral blood flow and oxygenation.

50.9.   The answer is E (*Synopsis VII,* page 1163).

Contrary to the popular myth, *most elderly persons need as much sleep as they did in their earlier mature years.* However, *complaints about sleeplessness are common.* To some extent these complaints can be traced to sleep disturbances, rather than to sleeplessness. *Frequent visits to the bathroom* may lead to problems in resuming sleep. with resulting problems in again falling asleep. Furthermore, many of the elderly—retired, unemployed, inactive, and noninvolved—succumb to the practice of taking *catnaps that may interfere with a good night's sleep.*

When insomnia does occur and is unaccompanied by delirium or a psychotic disorder, it usually responds to standard hypnotics. Phenothiazines or *tricyclic drugs often induce sleep when insomnia is accompanied by a depressive reaction.*

50.10.   The answer is D (*Synopsis VII,* page 1166).

Lithium, a hydrophilic drug, is excreted by the kidneys. The elderly person's decrease in renal clearance may cause an accumulation of lithium.

As a person ages, the ratio of lean to fat body mass changes. With normal aging, lean body mass decreases, and body fat increases. Because of that and because of decreases in plasma volume, total body water, and total plasma, the volume of distribution (Vd) for lipophilic drugs is increased. Increases in the Vd of the lipophilic drugs *imipramine, diazepam, chlorpromazine,* and *fluoxetine* may reduce their efficacy if the drugs are given in single or as-needed doses. The increased Vd also contributes to drug accumulation.

50.11.   The answer is C (*Synopsis VII,* pages 1156–1157).

In the elderly, *simple recall becomes difficult* and *memory-encoding ability diminishes.* Those functions decline with age. However, many cognitive abilities are retained in old age. Although the elderly take longer than young persons to learn new material, *complete learning of new material still occurs.* Old adults maintain their verbal abilities, and their *I.Q.s remain stable until age 80. On multiple-choice tests, recognition of correct answers persists.*

50.12. The answer is D (*Synopsis VII,* pages 1155–1156).

Vitamin deficiencies in the aged are uncommon. However, a number of conditions and deficiencies are typical and should be considered in the physical assessment of the aged. *Toxins of bacterial origin* and metabolic origins are common in old age. Bacterial toxins usually originate in occult or inconspicuous foci of infection, such as suspected pneumonic conditions and urinary infections. In the aged, *the most common metabolic intoxication causing mental symptoms is uremia,* which is an excess of urea and other nitrogenous waste products in the blood. Mild diabetes, hepatic failure, and gout are also known to cause mental symptoms in the aged and may easily be missed unless they are actively investigated. Alcohol and drug misuse may cause many mental disturbances in late life, but these abuses, with their characteristic effects, are usually easily determined by taking a history.

Cerebral anoxia often precipitates mental symptoms as a result of cardiac insufficiency or emphysema. Anoxic confusion may follow surgery, a cardiac infarct, gastrointestinal bleeding, or occlusion or stenosis of the carotid arteries. *Nutritional deficiencies may cause mental symptoms* or may be a symptom of a mental disorder.

50.13. The answer is D (*Synopsis VII,* pages 1164–1165).

Psychotropic drugs are among those most commonly prescribed for the elderly; *40 (not 25) percent of all hypnotics dispensed in the United States each year are to those over age 65. The elderly use more medications than any other age group.* Indeed, *25 percent of all prescriptions are written for those over age 65.* Many old persons have adverse drug reactions, as evidenced by the fact that, *in the United States, 250,000 people a year are hospitalized because of adverse medication reactions.* The physician must remember that *70 percent of the elderly use over-the-counter* (OTC) *medications.* These preparations can interact with prescribed drugs and lead to dangerous side effects. The physician should include the use of OTC medications when taking a patient's drug history.

50.14. The answer is D (*Synopsis VII,* page 73).

Sexual activity (e.g., masturbation, coitus) *may increase, as compared with earlier levels of functioning* because as some persons get older, they *resolve feelings of guilt* about sex that may have existed when they were younger.

Sexual activity continues well into old age, with William Masters and Virginia Johnson reporting sexual functioning of people in their 80s. Sexual activity in persons over age 60 *occurs in at least 20 percent (not less than 10 percent) of women* and *occurs in more than 70 percent (not less than 50 percent) of men.*

50.15. The answer is E (all) (*Synopsis VII,* page 1164).

Abuse of the elderly by some caregiving children *is most likely to occur when the parent is bedridden* or *has a chronic medical illness* that requires constant nursing attention or when the abusing children have substance-related disorders, are under economic stress, and have no relief from their caretaking duties. Elderly abuse *is likely to occur if the child was a victim of sexual or physical abuse. Elderly abuse occurs more often toward women than toward men,* and most abuse occurs in the elderly over age 75.

51

Forensic Psychiatry

At various stages in their historical development, psychiatry and law have converged. Both psychiatry and law are concerned with social deviants, persons who have violated the rules of society and whose behavior presents a problem, not only because their deviance has diminished their ability to function effectively, but because it affects the functioning of the community adversely. Traditionally, the psychiatrist's efforts are directed toward elucidation of the causes and, through prevention and treatment, reduction of the self-destructive elements of harmful behavior. The lawyer, as the agent of society, is concerned with the fact that the social deviant presents a potential threat to the safety and security of other people in the environment. Both psychiatry and law seek to implement their respective goals through the application of pragmatic techniques, based on empirical observations.

Forensic psychiatry is the branch of medicine that deals with disorders of the mind and their relation to legal principles. The word "forensic" means belonging to the courts of law.

One of the most confusing aspects of forensic psychiatry is understanding the role of the psychiatrist as expert witness in criminal and other proceedings. Psychiatrists retained as experts for the defense in a criminal trial may declare a person not responsible, while opposing experts testify on behalf of the prosecution with equal conviction that the defendant was responsible for the acts.

There are several explanations to explain the phenomenon: (1) Honest differences of opinion are inevitable in any effort to formulate complex judgments. (2) Knowledge of the human personality in its normal and abnormal manifestations is imperfect, at best. (3) The fact that complex problems must be resolved with imperfect tools and incomplete knowledge tends to enhance the unconscious bias and partisanship that are likely to arise. (4) Frequently, medical experts are not fully conversant with the language, practices, and objectives of the legal procedure in which they are participating. (5) There is common misapprehension among medical experts that in offering testimony they must use legal language as their own. (6) Finally, although it happens only very infrequently, the venality of a medical expert may induce the expert to present testimony favorable to the individual or group that has retained the expert.

Honest differences of opinion may be minimized, but they can never be eliminated entirely. Research in the behavioral sciences is on the threshold of major breakthroughs, which, within the next generation or two, will bring the understanding of psychopathology up to a level comparable to that achieved by most other medical specialists within the last several generations. With regard to the possibility that unconscious bias and partisanship may influence the expert's testimony inasmuch as, for the most part, it occurs when the available data are ambiguous, it follows that the lessened ignorance and confusion that can be expected as a result of scientific advance will be accompanied by a concomitant decrease in bias. Many workers in forensic psychiatry believe that the battle of the experts could be eliminated entirely if the psychiatrists would be appointed by and report only to the court.

Students should read Chapter 51 of *Kaplan and Sadock's Synopsis VII* and then answer the questions following to test their knowledge in this area.

HELPFUL HINTS

The student should be able to define each of the terms and know each of the cases listed below.

habeas corpus	Gault decision	culpability
abandonment	emancipated minor	competency
alliance threat	consent form	probationary status
documentation	custody	rules of evidence
going the extra mile	task-specific competence	leading questions
emergency exception	testamentary capacity	medical expert
Tarasoff v. Regents of University	testator	pretrial conference
of California (I and II)	judgment	hearsay
Judge David Bazelon	competence to inform	plea bargaining
civil commitment	conservator	court-mandated evaluations
right to treatment	*actus reus*	testimonial privilege
Wyatt v. Stickney	*mens rea*	confidentiality
state training school standards	M'Naghten rule	discriminate disclosure
peonage	right-wrong test	disclose to safeguard
O'Connor v. Donaldson	irresistible impulse	duty to warn
Thomas Szasz	Durham rule	civil commitment
forced confinement	model penal code	informal admission
seclusion and restraint	antisocial behavior	voluntary admission
informed consent	insanity defense	temporary admission
classical tort	malpractice	involuntary admission
battery	the four Ds	*parens patriae*
mature minor rule	credibility of witnesses	mental-health information service

---

QUESTIONS

DIRECTIONS: Each of the questions or incomplete statements below is followed by five suggested responses or completions. Select the *one* that is *best* in each case.

51.1. Confidential communications can be shared with which of the following without the patient's consent?
A. A consultant
B. The patient's family
C. The patient's attorney
D. The patient's previous therapist
E. An insurer of the patient

51.2. Product rule is concerned with
A. testimonial privilege
B. involuntary admission
C. criminal responsibility
D. competency to stand trial
E. all the above

51.3. The Gault decision applies to
A. minors
B. *habeas corpus*
C. informed consent
D. battery
E. none of the above

51.4. Situations in which there is an obligation on the part of the physician to report to authorities information which may be confidential include
A. suspected child abuse
B. when the patient will probably commit murder and the act can only be stopped by notification of police
C. when the patient will probably commit suicide and the act can only be stopped by notification of police
D. when a patient who has potentially life-threatening responsibilities (for example, airline pilot) shows marked impairment of judgment
E. all the above

51.5. Of the following, which is the least common cause of malpractice claims against psychiatrists by patients?
A. Suicide attempts
B. Improper use of restraints
C. Failure to treat psychosis
D. Sexual involvement
E. Substance dependence

51.6. To reduce the risk of malpractice, preventive approaches include
A. documenting good care
B. providing only the kind of care the psychiatrist is qualified to deliver
C. utilizing informed consent
D. obtaining a second opinion
E. all the above

DIRECTIONS: Each group of questions below consists of lettered headings followed by a list of numbered phrases or statements. For each numbered phrases or statement, select the *one* lettered heading that is most closely associated with it. Each lettered heading may be selected once, more than once, or not at all.

Questions 51.7–51.8
A. *Tarasoff v. Regents of University of California* (Tarasoff I)
B. *Tarasoff v. Regents of University of California* (Tarasoff II)

51.7. Duty to protect

51.8. Duty to warn

Questions 51.9–51.10
A. One-physician certificate
B. Two-physician certificate

51.9. Temporary admission for 15 days

51.10. Involuntary admission for 60 days

Questions 51.11–51.15
A. *Rouse v. Cameron*
B. *Wyatt v. Stickney*
C. *O'Connor v. Donaldson*
D. *The Myth of Mental Illness*

51.11. Harmless mental patients cannot be confined against their will

51.12. Standards were established for staffing, nutrition, physical facilities, and treatment

51.13. The purpose of involuntary hospitalization is treatment

51.14. A patient who is not receiving treatment has a constitutional right to be discharged

51.15. All forced confinements because of mental illness are unjust

Questions 51.16–51.24
A. Witness of fact
B. Expert witness
C. Direct examination
D. Cross-examination
E. Court-mandated evaluation
F. Privilege
G. Confidentiality

51.16. May draw conclusions from data and thereby render an opinion.

51.17. The psychiatrist functions no differently from laypersons generally.

51.18. Most common role of a psychiatrist in a court proceeding.

51.19. Loss of the confidential relationship between doctor and patient.

51.20. Open-ended questions that require narrative-type answers.

51.21. Right to maintain secrecy or confidentiality in the face of a subpoena.

51.22. Does not exist in military courts.

51.23. Right can be waived by the patient.

51.24. Binds the physician to hold secret all information given by a patient.

Questions 51.25–51.31
A. Informal admission
B. Voluntary admission
C. Temporary admission
D. Involuntary admission
E. Habeas corpus
F. *Parens patriae*

51.25. Patient free to stay or leave at will

51.26. Patients apply in writing for admission

51.27. Need for admission must be confirmed by a psychiatrist on the hospital staff

51.28. Application for admission to a hospital may be made by relative or friend

51.29. Allows the patient to be hospitalized for 60 days

51.30. Casts the state as protector of patients from their own inability to survive unaided

51.31. Proclaimed by those who believe they have been illegally deprived of liberty

Questions 51.32–51.36
A. Irresistible impulse
B. M'Naghton rule
C. Model Penal Code
D. Durham rule
E. Diminished Capacity

51.32. Known commonly as the right-wrong test

51.33. A person charged with a criminal offense is not responsible for an act if the act was committed under circumstances that the person was unable to resist because of mental disease

51.34. An accused is not criminally responsible if his or her unlawful act was the product of mental disease or mental defect

51.35. As a result of mental disease or defect, the defendant lacked substantial capacity either to appreciate the criminality of his or her conduct or to conform their conduct to the requirement of the law

51.36. The defendant suffered some impairment (usually but not always because of mental illness) sufficient to interfere with the ability to formulate a specific element of the particular crime charged

ANSWERS

Forensic Psychiatry

51.1. The answer is A (*Synopsis VII,* page 1173).

Confidentiality pertains to the premise that all information imparted to the physician by the patient be held secret. However, sharing information with other staff members treating the patient, clinical supervisors, and *a consultant* does not require the patient's permission. Sharing patient information with *the patient's family, the patient's attorney, the patient's previous therapist,* or *an insurer of the patient* does require the patient's permission. Courts may compel disclosure of confidential material (*subpoena duces tecum*). In emergencies, limited information may be released, but after the emergency, the clinician should debrief the patient.

51.2. The answer is C (*Synopsis VII,* page 1182).

In 1954, in the case of *Durham v. United States,* a decision was made by Judge David Bazelon, a pioneering jurist in forensic psychiatry in the District of Columbia Court of Appeals, that resulted in the product rule of *criminal responsibility.* An accused is not criminally responsible if his or her unlawful act was the product of mental disease or defect.

Judge Bazelon stated that the purpose of the rule was to get good and complete psychiatric testimony. He sought to break the criminal law out of the theoretical straightjacket of the M'Naghten test.

Testimonial privilege is the right to maintain secrecy or confidentiality in the face of a subpoena. The privilege belongs to the patient, not to the physician, and it is waivable by the patient. *Involuntary admission* involves the question of whether or not the patient is a danger to self, such as in the suicidal or homicidal patient. Because those individuals do not recognize their need for hospital care, application for admission to a hospital may be made by a relative or friend and is involuntary. *Competency to stand trial* refers to defendants being able to understand the nature and the object of the proceedings against them, to consult with counsel, and to assist in preparing the defense.

51.3. The answer is A (*Synopsis VII,* page 1178).

The Gault decision applies to *minors,* those under the care of a parent or guardian and usually under the age of 18. In the case of minors, the parent or guardian is the person legally empowered to give consent to medical treatment. However, most states by statute list specific diseases or conditions that a minor can consent to have treated, such as venereal diseases, pregnancy, substance-related disorders, and contagious diseases. In an emergency, a physician can treat a minor without parental consent. The trend is to adopt what is referred to as the mature minor rule, allowing minors to consent to treatment under ordinary circumstances. As a result of the Gault decision, the juvenile must now be represented by counsel, be able to confront witnesses, and be given proper notice of any charges. Emancipated minors have the rights of adults when it can be demonstrated that they are living as adults with control over their own lives.

A writ of *habeas corpus* may be proclaimed on behalf of anyone who claims he or she is being deprived of liberty illegally. The legal procedure asks a court to decide whether hospitalization has been accomplished without due process of the law, and the petition must be heard by a court at once, regardless of the manner or form in which it is filed. Hospitals are obligated to submit those petitions to the court immediately.

Informed consent is a knowledge of the risks and alternatives of a treatment method.

Under classical tort (a tort is a wrongful act) theory, an intentional touching to which one has given no consent is a *battery.* Thus, the administration of electroconvulsive therapy or chemotherapy, although it may be therapeutic, is a battery when done without consent. Indeed, any unauthorized touching outside of conventional social intercourse constitutes a battery. It is an offense to the dignity of the person, an invasion of the right of self-determination, for which punitive and actual damages may be imposed.

51.4. The answer is E (all) (*Synopsis VII,* pages 1173–1174).

In some situations—such as *suspected child abuse*—the physician must report to the authorities, as specifically required by law. According to the American Psychiatric Association, confidentiality may be broken *when the patient will probably commit murder and the act can only be stopped by notification of police, when the patient will probably commit suicide and the act can only be stopped by notification of police,* or *when a patient who has potentially life-threatening responsibilities (for example, airline pilot) shows marked impairment of judgment.*

51.5. The answer is D (*Synopsis VII,* pages 1183–1185).

Sexual involvement with patients accounts for 6 percent of all malpractice claims against psychiatrists and is the least common cause of malpractice litigation. This fact does not, however, minimize its importance as a significant problem. Sexual intimacy with patients is both illegal and unethical. There are also serious legal and ethical questions about a psychotherapist's dating or marrying a patient even after discharging the patient from therapy. Some psychiatrists believe in the adage "Once a patient, always a patient." Other psychiatrists hold the view that a period of two years after discharge is sufficient time to terminate prohibitions against personal involvement.

For other malpractice claims, the following figures are given: failure to manage *suicide attempts,* 21 percent; *improper use of restraints,* 7 percent; and *failure to treat psychosis,* 14 percent. *Substance dependence* accounts for about 10 percent of claims and refers to the patient's having developed a substance-related disorder as a result of a psychiatrist's not monitoring carefully the prescribing of potentially addicting drugs.

51.6. The answer is E (all) *(Synopsis VII,* pages 1183–1184).

Although it is impossible to eliminate malpractice completely, some preventive approaches have been invaluable in clinical practice. The *documentation of good care* is a strong deterrent to liability. Such documentation should include the decision-making process, the clinician's rationale for treatment, and an evaluation of costs and benefits. Psychiatrists should *provide only the kind of care that they are qualified to deliver.* They should never overload their practices or overstretch their abilities, and they should take reasonable care of themselves. The *informed consent* process refers to a discussion between doctor and patient of the treatment proposed, the side effects of drugs, and the uncertainty of psychiatric practice. Such a dialogue helps prevent a liability suit. A consultation affords protection against liability because it allows the clinician to obtain information about his or her peer group's standard of practice. It also provides *a second opinion,* enabling the clinician to submit his or her judgment to the scrutiny of the peer. The clinician who takes the trouble to obtain a consultation in a difficult and complex case is unlikely to be viewed by a jury as careless and negligent.

51.7–51.8

51.7. The answer is B *(Synopsis VII,* page 1174).

51.8. The answer is A *(Synopsis VII,* page 1174).

In the case of *Tarasoff v. Regents of University of California (Tarasoff I),* in 1974, it was ruled that a physician or psychotherapist who has reason to believe that a patient may injure or kill someone must notify the potential victim, the patient's relatives or friends, or the authorities. The Tarasoff I ruling does not require therapists to report fantasies; rather, it means that, when they are convinced that a homicide is likely, they have a *duty to warn.* The Tarasoff I

decision has not drastically affected psychiatrists, as it has long been their practice to warn the appropriate persons or law enforcement authorities when a patient presents a distinct and immediate threat to someone.

In 1976 the California Supreme Court issued a second ruling in the case of *Tarasoff v. Regents of University of California (Tarasoff II).* It broadened its earlier ruling, the duty to warn, to include the *duty to protect.* The Tarasoff II ruling has stimulated perhaps the most intense debates in the medicolegal field. Lawyers, judges, and expert witnesses argue the definition of prevention, the nature of the relationship between therapist and patient, and the balance between public safety and individual privacy. Clinicians argue that the duty to protect may hinder treatment because the patient may not trust the doctor if confidentiality is not maintained. Furthermore, it is not always easy to determine if a patient is dangerous enough to justify long-term incarceration because of defensive practices. As a result of such debates in the medicolegal field since 1976, state courts have not come up with a uniform interpretation of the Tarasoff II ruling, the concept of the duty to protect.

51.9–51.10

51.9. The answer is A *(Synopsis VII,* page 1175).

51.10. The answer is B *(Synopsis VII,* page 1176).

A *one-physician certificate,* also known as emergency or *temporary admission for 15 days,* is used for patients who are unable to make a decision on their own because they have a mental illness that impairs their judgment (e.g., Alzheimer's disease). Such patients may be admitted on an emergency basis to a psychiatric hospital on the written recommendation of one physician, provided the need for hospitalization is confirmed by a psychiatrist on the hospital staff.

A *two-physician certificate* is used for *involuntary admission for 60 days* when patients are a danger to themselves (suicidal patients) or to others (homicidal patients). Two physicians must make independent examinations of the patient, and the next of kin must be notified if a decision is made to hospitalize the patient. The patient may be hospitalized for up to 60 days; however, during that time the patient has a right to see a judge, who determines whether such involuntary hospitalization may continue. After 60 days, if the patient is to remain hospitalized, the case must be reviewed by a board consisting of psychiatrists, other physicians, lawyers, and other citizens not connected with the institution.

51.1–51.15

51.11. The answer is C *(Synopsis VII,* page 1177).

51.12. The answer is B *(Synopsis VII,* page 1176).

51.13. The answer is A *(Synopsis VII,* page 1176).

51.14. The answer is A (*Synopsis VII,* page 1176).

51.15. The answer is D (*Synopsis VII,* page 1177).

Various landmark legal cases have affected psychiatry and the law over the years. In the 1976 case of *O'Connor v. Donaldson,* the United States Supreme Court ruled that *harmless mental patients cannot be confined against their will* without treatment if they can survive outside. According to the Court, a finding of mental illness alone cannot justify a state's confining persons in a hospital against their will; patients must be considered dangerous to themselves or others before they are confined against their will.

In 1971, in *Wyatt v. Stickney* in Alabama Federal District Court, it was decided that persons civilly committed to a mental institution have a constitutional right to receive adequate treatment, and *standards were established for staffing, nutrition, physical facilities, and treatment.*

In 1966, the District of Columbia, Court of Appeals in *Rouse v. Cameron* ruled that *the purpose of involuntary hospitalization is treatment* and that *a patient who is not receiving treatment has a constitutional right to be discharged* from the hospital.

In *The Myth of Mental Illness,* Thomas Szasz argued that the various psychiatric diagnoses are totally devoid of significance and, therefore, *all forced confinements because of mental illness are unjust.* Szasz contended that psychiatrists have no place in the courts of law.

51.16–51.24

51.16. The answer is B (*Synopsis VII,* page 1172).

51.17. The answer is A (*Synopsis VII,* page 1171).

51.18. The answer is B (*Synopsis VII,* page 1172).

51.19. The answer is E (*Synopsis VII,* page 1172).

51.20. The answer is C (*Synopsis VII,* page 1172).

51.21. The answer is F (*Synopsis VII,* page 1172).

51.22. The answer is F (*Synopsis VII,* page 1173).

51.23. The answer is F (*Synopsis VII,* page 1173).

51.24. The answer is G (*Synopsis VII,* page 1173).

One type of witness is the *witness of fact.* As a witness of fact, *the psychiatrist functions no differently from laypersons generally*—for example, as observers of an accident on the street. The witness's input—the facts—are direct observations and material from direct scrutiny. A witness of fact may be a psychiatrist who reads portions of the medical record aloud to bring it into the legal record and thus make it available for testimony. In theory, any psychiatrist at any level of training can fulfill that role.

In contrast, a psychiatrist under certain circumstances may be qualified as an expert. The qualifying process, however, consists not of popular recognition in one's clinical field but of being accepted by the court and both sides of the case as suitable to perform expert functions. Thus, the term "expert" has particular legal meaning and is independent of any actual or presumed expertise the clinician may have in a given area. The clinician's expertise is elucidated during direct examination and cross-examination of the clinician's education, publications, and certifications. In the context of the courtroom, an *expert witness* is one who *may draw conclusions from data and thereby render an opinion*—for example, that a patient meets the required criteria for commitment or for an insanity defense under the standards of a jurisdiction. Expert witnesses play a role in determining the standard of care and what constitutes the average practice of psychiatry.

The most common role of a psychiatrist in court proceedings is as an expert witness. When psychiatrists are asked to serve as experts, they are usually asked to do so for one of the sides in the case; rarely are clinicians independent examiners reporting directly to the court.

Direct examination is the first questioning of a witness by the attorney for the party on whose behalf the witness is called. Direct examination generally consists of *open-ended questions that require narrative-type answers.* It is a friendly interrogation that is routinely rehearsed with one's attorney before the trial.

Cross-examination is the questioning of a witness by the attorney for the opposing party. Cross-examination usually involves long, possibly leading questions that demand a yes or no answer. Few experiences can be as demoralizing for the clinician as cross-examination by an eager, aggressive, and sarcastic attorney for the opposing side. That segment of the total experience, more than any other, makes many clinicians leery of appearing in the courtroom in any role.

In several legal situations the judge asks clinicians to be consultants to the court, which raises the issue of for whom the clinicians work. In a *court-mandated evaluation* there is a *loss of the confidential relationship between doctor and patient* because clinical information may have to be revealed to the court. Clinicians who make such court-ordered evaluations are under an ethical obligation and, in some states, a legal obligation to so inform the patients at the outset of the examinations and to make sure that the patients understand that condition.

Privilege is the *right to maintain secrecy or confidentiality in the face of a subpoena.* Privileged communications are those statements made by certain persons within a relationship—such as husband-wife, priest-penitent, or doctor-patient—that the law protects from forced disclosure on the witness stand. Privilege is a right that belongs to the patient, not to the physician, and so the right can be waived by the patient. Psychiatrists, who are licensed to practice medicine, may claim medical privilege, but they have found that the privilege is so riddled with qualifications that it is practically meaningless. Purely federal cases have no psychotherapist-patient privilege. Moreover, the privilege *does not exist in military courts,* regardless of whether the physician is military or civilian and whether the privilege is recognized in the state where the court-martial takes place. The privilege has numerous exceptions, which are often viewed as implied waivers. In the most common exception, patients are said to waive the privilege by injecting their condition into the litigation, thereby making their condition an element of their claim or defense. In a number of contexts, clinicians may be ordered to give the court information that is ordinarily considered privileged.

A long-held premise of medical ethics *binds the physician to hold secret all information given by a patient.* That professional obligation is what is meant by *confidentiality.* Understanding confidentiality requires an awareness that it applies to certain populations and not to others. That is, one can identify a group that is within the circle of confidentiality, meaning that sharing information with the members of that group does not require specific permission from the patient. As a rule, clinical information may be shared with the patient's permission—preferably written permission, although verbal permission suffices with proper documentation. Each release is good for only one bolus of information, and permission should be reobtained for each subsequent release, even to the same party. Permission overcomes only the legal barrier, not the clinical one; the release is permission, not obligation. If the clinician believes that the information may be destructive, the matter should be discussed, and the release may be refused with some exceptions.

51.25–51.31

51.25. The answer is A (*Synopsis VII,* page 1175).

51.26. The answer is B (*Synopsis VII,* page 1175).

51.27. The answer is C (*Synopsis VII,* pages 1175–1176).

51.28. The answer is D (*Synopsis VII,* page 1176).

51.29. The answer is D (*Synopsis VII,* page 1176).

51.30. The answer is F (*Synopsis VII,* pages 1174–1175).

51.31. The answer is E (*Synopsis VII,* page 1176).

Informal admission operates on the general hospital model, in which the patient is admitted to a psychiatric unit of a general hospital in the same way that a medical or surgical patient is admitted. Under such circumstances the ordinary doctor-patient relationship applies, with the *patient free to stay or leave at will,* even against medical advice.

In cases of *voluntary admission, patients apply in writing for admission* to a psychiatric hospital. They may come to the hospital on the advice of their personal physician, or they may seek help on their own. In either case the patients are examined by a psychiatrist on the hospital staff and are admitted if that examination reveals the need for hospital treatment.

Temporary admission is used for patients who are so senile or so confused that they require hospitalization and are not able to make decisions of their own and for patients who are so acutely disturbed that they must be immediately admitted to a psychiatric hospital on an emergency basis. Under the procedure a person is admitted to the hospital on the written recommendation of one physician. Once the patient has been admitted, the *need for hospitalization must be confirmed by a psychiatrist on the hospital staff.* The procedure is temporary because patients cannot be hospitalized against their will for more than 15 days.

Involuntary admission involves the question of whether the patients are a danger to themselves, such as suicidal patients, or a danger to others, such as homicidal patients. Because those persons do not recognize their need for hospital care, the *application for admission to a hospital may be made by a relative or a friend.* Once the application is made, the patients must be examined by two physicians, and, if both physicians confirm the need for hospitalization, the patients can then be admitted.

Involuntary admission *allows the patient to be hospitalized for 60 days.* After that time, if the patient is to remain hospitalized, the case must be reviewed periodically by a board consisting of psychiatrists, nonpsychiatric physicians, lawyers, and other citizens not connected with the institution.

The powers of the state to commit mentally ill persons in need of care are known as *parens patriae* and the police power. The *parens patriae* principle *casts the state as the protector of patients from their own inability to survive unaided.* The police power casts the state as the protector of other citizens from patients.

Persons who have been hospitalized involuntarily and who believe that they should be released have the right to file a petition for a writ of *habeas corpus.* Under law, a writ of habeas corpus may be *proclaimed by those who believe that they have been illegally deprived of liberty.* The legal procedure asks a court to decide whether a patient has been hospitalized without due process of law. The case must be heard by a court at once. Hospitals are obligated to submit the petitions to the court immediately.

51.32–51.36

51.32. The answer is B (*Synopsis VII,* page 1181).

51.33. The answer is A (*Synopsis VII,* page 1181).

51.34. The answer is D (*Synopsis VII,* page 1182).

51.35. The answer is E (*Synopsis VII,* page 1182).

51.36.   The answer is C (*Synopsis VII,* page 1182).

The precedent for determining legal responsibility was established in the British courts in 1843. The *M'Naghten rule* is *known commonly as the right-wrong test.* In 1922 jurists in England reexamined the M'Naghten rule and suggested broadening the concept of insanity in criminal cases to include the concept of the *irresistible impulse*—that is *a person charged with a criminal offense is not responsible for an act if the act was committed under circumstances that the person was unable to resist because of mental disease.* To most psychiatrists the law is unsatisfactory because it covers only a small group of those who are mentally ill. However, it was used successfully in Virginia in the 1994 case of *Virginia v. Bobbitt,* where the defendant was acquitted of malicious wounding. She had cut off her husband's penis after enduring years of apparent sexual, physical, and emotional abuse.

In 1954 in the case of *Durham v. United States,* a decision was handed that resulted in the product rule of criminal responsibility or the *Durham rule* which states *that an accused is not criminally responsible if his or her unlawful act was the product of mental disease or mental defect.* Bazelon stated that the purpose of the rule was to get good and complete psychiatric testimony. In 1972, the Court of Appeals for the District of Columbia in *United States v. Brawner* discarded the rule in favor of the American Law Institute's 1962 model penal code test of criminal responsibility.

In its *model penal code* the American Law Institute recommended the following test of criminal responsibility: (1) *Persons are not responsible* for *criminal conduct* if *at the time of such conduct, as the result of mental disease or defect, they lacked substantial capacity either to appreciate the criminality of their conduct or to conform their conduct to the requirement of the law.* (2) The terms "mental disease or defect" in this test does not include an abnormality manifested only by repeated criminal or otherwise antisocial conduct.

Other attempts at reform have included the defense of *diminished capacity,* which is based on the claim that *the defendant suffered some impairment (usually but not always because of mental illness) sufficient to interfere with the ability to formulate a specific element of the particular crime charged.* Hence, the defense finds its most common use with so-called specific-intent crimes, such as first-degree murder.

52 ||||||

Ethics In Psychiatry

The field of ethics is central to the entire practice of medicine; however, it is uniquely and particularly relevant to the practice of psychiatry. Psychiatric patients often suffer from disorders which interfere with their capacity to make informed decisions about their own care. Impairment of insight, judgment, and reality-testing are often hallmarks of psychiatric disorders, making it extremely difficult for patients to know when they are either gravely disabled or dangerous to others. Psychiatric practice has had a long, and not always illustrious, history of treating patients against their will, with the underlying precept that it is for their own good. The evolution of ethical thinking in psychiatry associated with the increasingly intimate relationship between the psychiatric and legal systems is a fascinating and essential component of current psychiatric practice.

The student needs to be aware of the major ethical theories underlying most ethical questions in psychiatry—in particular, utilitarian and autonomy theory—and how those theories view such fundamental concepts as paternalism and beneficence. Such issues as informed consent, the right to die, surrogate decision making, involuntary treatment and hospitalization, and sexual contact with patients, need to be conceptualized from the perspective of ethical theory. The benefits and limitations of professional codes of ethics, especially those specific to the practice of psychiatry, need to be studied and understood.

The student should read Chapter 52 in *Kaplan and Sadock's Synopsis VII* and then study the questions and answers below.

HELPFUL HINTS

The student should be able to define each of the terms and know each of the cases listed below.

utilitarian theory	surrogate decision-making	right to health care
autonomy theory	substituted-judgment principle	*Roe v. Wade*
individual paternalism	best-interests principle	*Cruzan v. Missouri*
state paternalism	decisional capacity	*Planned Parenthood v. Casey*
duty of beneficence	confidentiality	*Principles of Medical Ethics* with
informed consent	duty to protect	annotations especially applicable
right to die	professional standards	to psychiatry

QUESTIONS

DIRECTIONS: Each of the questions or incomplete statements below is followed by five suggested responses or completions. Select the *one* that is *best* in each case.

52.1. Surrogate decision-making
A. is for patients who have lost decisional capabilities
B. may require that a surrogate be designated by a court
C. is usually performed by the next of kin
D. often involves decisions about the costs of medical treatment
E. all the above

52.2. A physician's obligations concerning an impaired physician-colleague is to
A. inform patients
B. refer the impaired physician to a psychiatrist
C. report them to the appropriate local medical authority
D. advise the spouse or next of kin about the problem
E. treat and monitor the impaired physician

52.3. The physician's obligation to refrain from sexual contact with a patient is based on which of the following principles?
A. A patient in the physician-patient relationship is generally too vulnerable to make fully voluntary choices
B. The focus should be on the treatment of the patient
C. Transference issues make voluntary choices about sexual contact almost impossible
D. The physician has an obligation to uphold the standards and the reputation of the profession
E. All the above

DIRECTIONS: The lettered headings below are followed by a list of numbered phrases. For each numbered phrase, select the lettered heading most associated with it. Each lettered heading may be used once, more than once, or not at all.

Questions 52.4–52.7
A. Utilitarian theory
B. Paternalism
C. Autonomy theory

52.4. The basis for making decisions about the allocation of society's resources for treatment and medical research

52.5. The traditional model of the physician-patient relationship

52.6. The physician's duty of beneficence

52.7. The right to informed consent

Ethics in Psychiatry

52.1. **The answer is E (all)** (*Synopsis VII,* pages 1192–1193).

Surrogate decision-making *is for patients who have lost decisional capabilities.* The surrogate may be designated by the patient before losing capacity. Sometimes surrogate decision-making *may require that a surrogate be chosen by a court* if the patient has not designated someone. In some cases, states allow surrogates to be designated by the hospital. Surrogate decision-making *is usually performed by the next of kin,* although next of kin may not always be the appropriate decision makers. Relatives may have psychological and other agendas that interfere with their ability to make just decisions. In the past, surrogates made decisions for patients on a best-interests principle. The surrogate is supposed to decide which treatments could be reasonably expected to be in the patient's best interests; therefore, surrogate decision-making *often involves decision about the costs of medical treatment.* Present autonomy-based legal approaches require surrogates to decide on the basis of what the patient would have wished, known as substituted judgment. The surrogate should be familiar with the patient's values and attitudes. Substituted judgments present problems because it may be difficult to determine whether a surrogate is really able to determine what the patient would have wished. If a substituted judgment cannot be made, the surrogate is to use the best interests approach.

52.2. **The answer is C** (*Synopsis VII,* pages 1193–1194).

The first ethical obligation concerning an impaired physician is to *report them to an appropriate local medical authority.* That authority may be the county or state medical society. It is best to start with the immediate authority (the hospital ethics committee). It is not the physician's responsibility to *inform patients* or to *refer the impaired physician to a psychiatrist,* although that may be done by the appropriate authority after all the facts are determined. *Advising the spouse or next of kin about the problem* is also best left to the local authority to decide.

Impairment in a physician may occur as the result of psychiatric or medical disorders or the use of a substances (for example, alcohol). A number of organic illnesses may interfere with the cognitive and motor skills required to provide medical care competently.

Although the legal responsibility to report an impaired physician varies depending on the state, the ethical responsibility remains universal. A physician should not *treat and monitor the impaired physician.* The physician who treats the impaired physician should not be required to also monitor the physician's progress or fitness to return to work. The monitoring should be done by an independent physician or group of physicians who have no conflicts of interest.

52.3. **The answer is E (all)** (*Synopsis VII,* page 1191).

Physicians have an obligation to refrain from sexual contact with their patients. A number of principles underlie this obligation. *A patient in the physician-patient relationship is generally too vulnerable to make fully voluntary choices* about sexual contact. The physician's *focus should be on the treatment of the patient.* A change in that focus to include sexual contact will compromise the physician's ability to treat the patient appropriately. In the psychiatrist-patient relationship *transference issues make voluntary choices about sexual contact almost impossible* for the patient. In addition, *the physician has an obligation to uphold the standards and the reputation of the profession.*

52.4–52.7

52.4. **The answer is A** (*Synopsis VII,* page 1189).

52.5. **The answer is B** (*Synopsis VII,* pages 1189–1190).

52.6. **The answer is B** (*Synopsis VII,* page 1190).

52.7. **The answer is C** (*Synopsis VII,* page 1190).

Utilitarian theory holds that our fundamental obligation when making decisions is to try to produce the greatest possible happiness for the greatest number of people. Sometimes the choices available are dismal. In that case one should act in ways that produce the least pain. Utilitarian theory is still used as *the basis for making decisions about the allocation of society's resources for treatment and medical research.*

Paternalism may be defined as a system in which someone acts for another's benefit without that person's consent. The requirement that health care practitioners be licensed is an example of state paternalism. Individual paternalism was *the traditional model of the physician-patient relationship.* In this model the physician is supposed to treat the patient as a caring parent would treat a child. The parent is assumed to know what is best for the child and has no obligation to ask the child for permission to perform actions that may benefit the child. *The physician's duty of beneficence,* the principle of doing good and avoiding harm, is a paternalistic principle. The physician is presumed to have knowledge that the patient may not understand or, in certain instances, is better off not knowing.

Autonomy theory presumes that the normal adult patient has the ability and the right to make rational and responsible decisions. The patient is self-governing (autonomous) and has rights to self-determination. The relationship between physician and patient is perceived as a relationship between two responsible adults. The patient's right to refuse treatment, *the right to informed consent,* and the assumption of competence are examples of the person's right to self-determination.

Objective Examinations in Psychiatry

There are a wide variety of objective multiple-choice question formats. Those range from case histories followed by a series of questions relating to diagnosis, laboratory findings, treatment complications, and prognosis to the most widely used form, known as the one-best-response type, wherein a question or incomplete statement is followed by four or five suggested answers or completions, with the examinee being directed to select the one best answer. When psychiatrists from various medical school faculties and hospitals and in private practice were requested to write test questions, it was found that it was best to omit certain complex types of multiple-choice questions and to rely on those item types that are less ambiguous. Too many different types of multiple-choice questions may confuse the examinee and place a premium on his or her test-taking ability, rather than on knowledge of the subject. Consequently, the item types in common usage have been reduced. The multiple-choice questions are described as objective because the correct response is predetermined by a group of experts who compose the items, thus eliminating the observer bias seen in ratings of essay questions. The responses are usually entered on an answer sheet, which is then scored by machine, giving a high degree of reliability.

Two basic item types are used with the greatest frequency—one-best-response type (type A) and matching type (type B), which are detailed in Table 53.1.

The case history or situation type of item consists of an introductory statement that is usually an abbreviated history, with or without the results of the physical examination or laboratory tests, followed by a series of questions, usually of the A type. In similar fashion, charts, electroencephalograms, pictures of gross or microscopic slides, or graphs may be presented, again followed by the one-best-response type or matching type.

Present testing procedures using objective, multiple-choice items are highly effective in regard to reliability and validity in measuring the examinee's knowledge and its application. Experienced test constructors are able to develop items based on a given content and are able to word the answers in a neutral fashion. Thus, both correct and incorrect responses are similar in style, length, and phrasing.

No matter how well constructed a test is, with a high degree of reliability and validity for a large group of examinees, it is subject to inaccuracies about individual testees. Some examinees underscore, and others overscore, depending on their experience and test-taking skills, known as testmanship.

In the final analysis, there is no substitute for knowledge, understanding, and clinical competence when a physician is being evaluated. However, some suggestions and clues inevitably appear in the most carefully composed and edited multiple-choice test. To improve one's testmanship, one should consider the following:

(1) There is no penalty for a wrong response in the objective-type multiple-choice question. The testee has a 20 percent chance of guessing correctly when there are five options. Therefore, no question should be left unanswered.

(2) In medicine it is rare for anything to be universally correct or wrong. Thus, options that imply "always" or "never" are more likely to be incorrect than otherwise.

(3) Especially in psychiatry, many words are often needed to include the exceptions or qualifications in a correct statement. Thus, the longest option is more likely to be the correct response. Test constructors who are also aware of this fact often try to lengthen the shorter incorrect responses by adding unneces-

Table 53.1
Types of Items Used in Multiple-choice Questions

Type A: One-best-response type	Each item consists of an introductory statement or question, known as the stem, followed by four or five suggested responses. The incorrect options are known as distracters, as differentiated from the correct response. Some of the distracters may be true in part, but the one *best* response of those offered must be selected to receive full credit.

DIRECTIONS: Each of the statements or questions below is followed by five suggested responses or completions. Select the *one* that is *best* in each case.

1. A 2-year-old boy occasionally plays with his older sister's doll, imitating her activities. This implies — Stem
A. pathological problems with sibling rivalry
B. undue identification with his mother
C. future problems with heterosexual orientation — Distracters
D. development of problems with gender identity
E. natural exploration of his environment — Correct Response

Choices or Options

2. Children in the fourth grade in urban area schools who cannot read are most commonly — Stem
A. isolated from peers
B. mentally retarded — Distracters
C. culturally disadvantaged — Correct Response
D. brain damaged
E. handicapped by a major perceptual deficiency — Distracters

Choices or Options

Type B: Matching type	**DIRECTIONS:** Each group of questions consists of five lettered headings, followed by a list of numbered words or phrases. For each numbered word or statement, select the one lettered heading or component that is most closely associated with it.

Questions 3–8
A. Mood disorder
B. Psychotic disorder
C. Chromosomal abnormality
D. Cognitive disorder
E. None of the above

Correct responses

3.	Delusional disorder	B
4.	Conversion disorder	E
5.	Down's syndrome	C
6.	Bipolar I disorder	A
7.	Obsessive-compulsive disorder	E
8.	Wernicke's syndrome	D

The use of "None of the above" in a type A or type B question often makes the item more difficult and tends to lower the percentage of candidates giving correct responses. It should also be noted that the same response may be used more than once.

Continued

sary phrases. But that tactic can readily be detected by experienced test takers.

(4) The use of a word like "possibly," or "may," or "sometimes" in an option often suggests a true statement, whereas choices with universal negative or positive statements tend to be false.

(5) Each distracter that can be ruled out increases the percentage chance of guessing correctly. In a five-choice situation, being able to discard three options increases the percentage from 20 percent to 50 percent and enables the examinee to focus on only the two remaining choices.

(6) With questions in which one cannot rule out any of the distracters and the suggestions above do not apply, the testee should select the same lettered option on all questions. The examination constructors try to distribute the correct answers among the five options. In some tests the middle or C response appears to be correct more often than the others.

Examinations are constructed for the most part by persons from the same cultural background in which the test originates. Thus, those who have been trained abroad and whose native languages are not English are often slower in reading the items and have less time to reflect on the options.

Table 53.1
Continued

Type C: A modified form of the matching type (type C) is also used. It necessitates the ability to compare and contrast two entities, such as diagnostic procedures, treatment modalities, or causes. The association is on an all-or-none basis. For instance, even if a treatment is only occasionally used or associated with a given disorder, it is to be included as a correct response.

DIRECTIONS: Each set of lettered headings below is followed by a list of numbered words or phrases. For each of the numbered words or phrases select

  A. if the item is associated with A *only*
  B. if the item is associated with B *only*
  C. if the item is associated with *both* A and B
  D. if the item is associated with *neither* A nor B

Questions 9–13
  A. Down's syndrome (mongolism)
  B. Tuberous sclerosis (epiloia)
  C. Both
  D. Neither

		Correct responses
9.	Mental deficiency	C
10.	Nodular type of skin rash	B
11.	Higher than chance association with leukemia	A
12.	Chromosomal nondisjunction	A
13.	Specific disorder of amino acid metabolism	D

Table adapted from S M Small: Role of Objective Examinations in Psychiatry, *Comprehensive Textbook of Psychiatry,* 3rd edition, H I Kaplan, B J Sadock, editors, p 2976, Williams & Wilkins, Baltimore, 1980.

A significant contribution toward the evaluation of clinical competence is the development of patient-management problem tests. Those tests try to simulate an actual clinical situation, with emphasis on a functional, problem-solving, patient-oriented approach. From thousands of reported examples of outstandingly good or poor clinical performance, test designers defined the major areas of performance, such as history taking, physical examination, use of diagnostic procedures, laboratory tests, treatment, judgment, and continuing care. Armed with that information, the test designers evolved a type of test known as programmed testing. The test provides feedback of information to the examinee, who can use this data in the solution of additional problems about the same patient.

The format starts with general patient information, which gives historical data. The section may be followed by a summary of the physical examination and positive elements in the psychiatric status. Then the testees are presented with a series of problems, each with a variable number of options. If the examinees select an option, they receive the results of the laboratory test they requested, the patients' reaction to the medication they ordered, or just a confirmation of the order. The examinees may select as few or as many options as befits good clinical judgment. The testees lose both credit and informational feedback if they do not select an important and necessary option. They may also lose credit by selecting unnecessary or dangerous options.

Having completed problem 1 about a patient, the testee is usually given some additional follow-up information, and the procedure is repeated for problems 2, 3, and so on.

An oversimplified and much abbreviated example is as follows:

A young college student has been hyperactive, has slept poorly, and has lost weight during the past month. He has been known to use cannabis and possibly other substances on many occasions. Last night he became excited, thought he was going insane, and complained of a rapid pounding sensation over his heart. He was brought to the emergency room by his roommate. No history of prior psychiatric difficulty was obtained. Physical examination reveals a temperature of 99.5° F, pulse rate of 108 per minute, respiration rate of 22 per minute, and a blood pressure of 142/80 mm Hg. His pupils are dilated but react to light, his mouth is dry, and the rest of the examination is noncontributory except for a generalized hyperreflexia.

On psychiatric examination he is irritable, restless, and very suspicious. He states that people are after him and wish to harm him. He is well oriented.

1. At this time you would
A. order morphine sulfate, 30 mg intramuscularly
B. inquire about drug usage
C. order an electrocardiogram
D. tell the patient that no one wants to harm him and that it is all his imagination.
E. arrange for hospitalization plus many additional options

Of the choices given, the feedback on B could be "Roommate states patient was taking amphetamines." D feedback: "Patient becomes excited and refuses to answer questions." E feedback: "Arrangements made."

2. The following morning, after a restless sleep, the patient continues to express fears of being harmed. You would now order
F. chlorpromazine, 100 mg three times daily
G. urine screen for drugs
H. projective psychological tests
I. imipramine, 50 mg four times daily and other options

The feedback on F might be "Patient quieter after a few hours." G feedback: "Ordered." H feedback: "Patient uncooperative." And I feedback: "Order noted."

Although programmed testing differs from the real-life situation—in which the physician has to originate his orders or recommendations, rather than select them from a given set of options—it does simulate the clinical situation to a great extent. Examinees like this type of test and readily appreciate its clinical significance and relevance.

Various modifications of patient-management problems have been introduced. It seems that the format, coupled with other forms of testing, is a favorable development in approaching the goal of a standardized reliable and valid means of evaluating some major components of clinical competence.

New methods of testing using computer-based systems for objective evaluation of clinical competence are being developed and tested. They are useful in patient-management problems because they provide extensive and instantaneous feedback. They also provide contemporaneous scoring so the testee knows the result of the test upon completion.

The National Board of Medical Examiners (NBME) has been exploring the use of interactive, computerized clinical simulations (CBX) in the evaluation of clinical competence. Each CBX case is an interactive, dynamic patient simulation. The student or physician interacting with CBX is presented with a brief description of the condition, circumstances and chief complaints of the simulated patient. The CBX physician is then expected to diagnose, treat, and monitor the patient's condition as it changes over time and in response to treatment. As the case unfolds, patient information is provided only through uncued requests by the CBX physician for tests, therapies, procedures or physical examination.

The material in this section was adapted from S. Mouchly Small, *"Role of Objective Examinations in Psychiatry,"* in the *Comprehensive Textbook of Psychiatry,* third edition, Harold I. Kaplan and Benjamin J. Sadock, editors, Williams & Wilkins, Baltimore, 1980.

Index

Page numbers followed by *t* and *f* indicate tables and figures, respectively.